Contents

The Complete Guide to Finding the

Mammals of Australia

David Andrew

CSIRO
PUBLISHING

National Library of Australia Cataloguing-in-Publication entry

Andrew, David, 1960– author.

The complete guide to finding the mammals of Australia/
David Andrew.

9780643098145 (pbk)

Includes index.

Mammals – Geographical distribution.
Mammals – Australia – Geographical distribution.
Mammals – Australia – Handbooks, manuals, etc.
Mammals – Australia – Identification.

599.0994

Published by
CSIRO Publishing
36 Gardiner Road, Clayton VIC 3168
Private Bag 10, Clayton South VIC 3169
Australia

Telephone: [+613] 9545 8555
Email: csiropublishing@csiro.au
Website: www.publishing.csiro.au

Front cover: Sea lion (ymgerman, istockphoto.com)
Back cover (left to right): Eastern Barred Bandicoot (Rohan Clarke), Grey-headed Flying Fox
(Leo Berzins), Koala (Rohan Clarke)

Set in 9/12 ITC Garamond
Edited by Joy Window
Cover design by Andrew Weatherill
Typeset by Thomson Digital
Printed by Ingram Lightning Source

CSIRO Publishing publishes and distributes scientific, technical and health science books
and journals from Australia to a worldwide audience and conducts these activities autonomously
from the research activities of the Commonwealth Scientific and Industrial Research
Organisation (CSIRO). The views expressed in this publication are those of the author(s) and do
not necessarily represent those of, and should not be attributed to, the publisher or CSIRO. The
copyright owner shall not be liable for technical or other errors or omissions contained herein. The
reader/user accepts all risks and responsibility for losses, damages, costs and other consequences
resulting directly or indirectly from using this information.

Acknowledgements

While researching this book I read many books, dozens of scientific papers and hundreds of magazine and newspaper articles, drove and flew thousands of kilometres, attended numerous scientific conferences, visited many national parks and private reserves, and volunteered on many field surveys. Despite all of this effort, it was amazing how often a chance comment from someone provided some of the best information on where to see Australian mammals – and not just the rare ones. This book would not have been possible without the help of these people – researchers, naturalists, wildlife enthusiasts, tour operators and travellers – who willingly shared information and their enthusiasm, or otherwise contributed advice. They include (in alphabetical order) Eric Andrew, Paul Barden, Darryel Binns, Linda Broome, Ray Chatto, Rohan Clarke, Tania Cochrane, Laurie Conole, Brian Cooke, John Cox, Helen Crisp, Geoffrey Dabb, Meg Doeppel, Tim Dolby, Sean Dooley, Keith and Lindsay Fisher, Greg Ford, Ian Fraser, Tony Friend, Janet Gardner, Alan Gillanders, Denise Goodfellow, Ian Gynther, Jon Hall, Anthony Ham, Dion Hobcroft, Rod Hobson, Alan Horsup, David Jackson, David James, Doug Laing, Peter Lansley, Peter Marsack, Alison Matthews, Alan McBride, Anna McConville, Peter Milburn, Doug Mills, Damian Milne, Barry Nolan, Tony Palliser, Mark Parsons, Sean Pywell, Terry Reardon, Mike Reed, Terry Reis, Charlie Roberts, Greg Roberts, Danny Rogers, Jonathan Rossouw, Klaus Uhlenhut, Steve van Dyck, Simon Ward, Kirsty Wilkes, John Woinarski and John Young. Thanks also to members and campout organisers of the Australasian Bat Society and Australian Mammal Society; and to several unnamed park staff who helped with directions. Apologies if I've left anyone out. Thanks also to those who contributed photos, including John Augusteyn, Leo Berzins, Adrian Boyle, Rohan Clarke, Tim Dolby, John French, David Rhind, 'Shorty' and Roger Williams. And to everyone at CSIRO Publishing for their patience and support for this project: John Manger, Briana Melideo, Lauren Webb, Tracey Millen, Melinda Chandler, Helena Clements, Deepa Travers, Joy Window and everyone else in the editorial and production team.

About the author

David Andrew has an extensive background in ecotourism, publishing, government and science. He created Australia's first ornithological magazine, the Whitley Award–winning *Wingspan*, for the Royal Australasian Ornithologists Union (now BirdLife Australia), and *Australian Birding* – the country's first magazine for birders. After a spell as Editor of *Wildlife Australia* magazine, he became an author then Publishing Manager at Lonely Planet, the global travel guidebook publisher, where he wrote or co-wrote 12 travel guides, including all five *Watching Wildlife* titles (which drew high praise in *New Scientist* among other journals). He has also written dozens of magazine and newspaper articles about wildlife, ecotourism and conservation. While completing an Honours degree in Conservation Biology he was lucky enough to study the Giant Panda in south-west China, and he spent a summer expeditioning season aboard the RV *Aurora Australis* censusing seabirds and cetaceans in Antarctic waters for the Australian Antarctic Division. He has travelled all over the world to search for and write about wildlife, including the Galápagos Islands and Central America, Madagascar, West Papua and, most recently, Ladakh in northern India to track the elusive Snow Leopard. David has also acted as a guide for birding luminaries Bill Oddie and Phoebe Snetsinger on their respective visits to Australia. He has presented TV information pieces for Channel 10's *Totally Wild*, web-delivered travel clips, and countless local, national and international radio interviews on wildlife conservation-related topics. He was co-author of *The Complete Guide to Finding the Birds of Australia* with Richard and Sarah Thomas and Alan McBride; some of his other publications have included *Bird Australia* and the *Birds of Australia Nature Guide*.

How to use this guide

The Complete Guide to Finding the Mammals of Australia is intended to help both resident and visiting wildlife enthusiasts to find as wide a range of native mammals as possible in Australia and its territories. The book is divided into three main parts: the first contains site information organised by locality; the second is a mammal-finding guide, in which all Australian mammals are listed in taxonomic order with hints on where and how to find them; finally there are appendices containing information on introduced species, glossaries of plant names and other terms, information on travelling in and around Australia, and useful contacts and reference material.

Please note that this book is not designed as a site guide: numerous such publications are already available in book, pamphlet and digital formats. Instead, I have made judgements as to where to find as many of Australia's mammals as possible, no matter which state you are based in.

ORGANISATION

Most of Australia's mammal species occur in the tropics and along the eastern seaboard. Whether your aim is to see as many as possible in a short time, or just to see a good variety, it makes sense to start in Queensland. Therefore, mammal-watching sites are arranged state by state, starting with Queensland and running clockwise around the country. However, as many common species have a wide distribution they are also included in more than one state chapter, so a visitor with limited time in, say, Canberra would not have to travel to Brisbane to see a Red-necked Wallaby just because there is no information on where to see it elsewhere. Any apparent geographic bias is unintentional and, obviously, a mammal-watching trip around Australia could start from any base or point of arrival.

GEOGRAPHIC COVERAGE

Each chapter begins with a brief introduction and a list of endemic species or subspecies found in that state. Endemics are those species found only in that state; for example, the Eastern Quoll can now be seen in the wild only in Tasmania (although in the Australian context many have become locally endemic only recently, owing to their extinction in other areas). Highlights are those species for which a key site (though not necessarily the only key site) is in that state; for example, several of Queensland's specialty species are otherwise found only in New Guinea, so the only chance of finding them in Australia would be in Queensland. By referring to the highlights in each section it should become obvious where you should concentrate your efforts to find the mammals that interest you. One strategy for seeing a good selection would be to concentrate on finding each state's endemic and specialty species, watching out for common species as you do so. Each state chapter also includes a short list of highlights.

Some states are divided into sections, which may reflect distinct habitat types, such as the arid zone, or discrete geographic areas where you might be going for a holiday (for example, south-east Queensland). These subregions are given a brief introduction and sometimes a map showing the relative position of each site covered within it. These maps help plan your route when travelling through a subregion. Each site is then treated separately, beginning with a list of key species most likely to be seen, or outstanding and unusual species that make a site important.

There is a separate chapter for Australia's external territories, including Australian Antarctic Territory, areas that hitherto have not been covered by a mammal-finding guide such as this one. Finally, there is a chapter on water-based mammal-watching – Australia is surrounded by oceans and boats are an ideal way to look for and observe cetaceans (whales and dolphins), Dugongs and pinnipeds (seals, fur seals and sea lions).

SPECIAL SECTIONS AND BOXED TEXTS

Because it is often difficult to nominate specific sites to see microbats, each chapter contains boxed text summarising bat occurrences in that state or territory. Similarly, cetacean-watching opportunities vary between regions, and these are summarised in a separate section in each chapter. Other issues or species of interest are described in shorter boxed texts, scattered throughout the locality chapters. 'Big Five' boxes point those readers with limited time to sites where they can see some of the iconic Australian species, such as Koala.

TAXONOMIC COVERAGE

The Mammal Finding Guide that follows the state and territory chapters lists all extant Australian mammals that occur here naturally (introduced species are covered in Appendix A), as well as those known (or believed) to have become extinct since white settlement. For each species, Australian and world distributions are given, followed by notes on preferred habitats and sites in which you are most likely to find it. For many there is also information on behaviour, calls or other clues that may help you to track them down. Where possible, information on distinct subspecies or interesting variations is included. Scientific names in this section are organised as per *The Action Plan for Australian Mammals 2012* by J. Woinarski *et al.*

(CSIRO Publishing, 2014). Taxonomies for some mammal groups are under review (taxonomy of some bats in particular is in a state of flux) and while this taxonomy was the most up-to-date at the time of writing, things will inevitably change. Readers are encouraged to keep abreast of taxonomic revisions in the scientific literature.

APPENDICES

The last main section contains appendices on introduced mammals, followed by useful information on travel and practical hints on finding mammals, plus lists of websites and references such as field guides and CDs, useful organisations and reputable tour operators; and then glossaries of special terms used in this book and of vegetation and landscape terms. Lastly, there are both common and scientific name indexes.

ABBREVIATIONS
States and territories

AAT – Australian Antarctic Territory, ACT – Australian Capital Territory, NSW – New South Wales, NT – Northern Territory, Qld – Queensland, SA – South Australia, Tas – Tasmania, Vic – Victoria, WA – Western Australia

Other

2WD – two-wheel drive vehicle, 4WD – four-wheel drive vehicle, AWC – Australian Wildlife Conservancy, CA – Conservation Area, CBD – Central Business District, CP – Conservation Park, CR – Conservation Reserve, croc – crocodile, EP – Environmental Park, FFR – Flora and Fauna Reserve, FFS – Flora and Fauna Sanctuary, Hwy – Highway, I. – Island, Is. – Islands, IPA – Indigenous Protected Area, MP – Marine Park, Mt – Mount, NP – National Park, NR – Nature Reserve, PNG – Papua New Guinea, Ra. – Range or Ranges, Rd – Road, RP – Regional Park, RR – Recreation Reserve, SF – State Forest, SP – State Park, SR – State Reserve, WR – Wildlife Reserve.

Note: The abbreviations sp. and ssp. are used throughout and refer to species and subspecies, respectively.

Introduction to mammal-watching

Australia has more endemic mammal species than any other country on Earth, including a stellar selection of unusual species such as the Platypus and Tasmanian Devil, as well as the internationally recognised Koala and kangaroos. Seeing some of these species is high on the 'must do' lists of most visitors; and while some are commonplace to many Australians, there is a growing interest in wildlife-watching in general in this country. Apart from the iconic species, more than 30 species of whale and dolphin (cetaceans) inhabit seas reaching from the cool Southern Ocean to tropical shallows; several species of seal and sea lion (pinnipeds) grace southern shores and a large percentage of the world's Dugongs graze in sheltered tropical bays. The night skies are filled with the world's highest diversity of flying foxes – the largest flying mammals – and dozens of microbats, including the unique Ghost Bat, which preys on rodents and small birds, a fishing bat and one specialised for navigating in misty rainforests. A host of rodents has evolved to fill unusual ecological niches, from the otter-like Water Rat to inhabitants of tropical boulder piles, a giant rainforest species and tree-climbing specialists. With such an array, should anyone need convincing to watch mammals?

Mammal-watching doesn't generate the same level of interest that birds do (obvious exceptions being many African countries, plus a few choice locations such as India, Madagascar and Alaska). And, it has to be said, mammal-watching presents its own challenges. In Australia mammals are generally more difficult to see and identify than birds; there's no established 'safari circuit' and few professional guides are adept at winkling out mammals the way birding guides find sought-after species for paying customers. Comparatively few mammals can be seen casually while, say, hiking or at popular tourist sites. And there is less information on finding mammals than birds (a gap that this book attempts to fill).

Nonetheless, many large species such as kangaroos, wallabies, whales and seals can be readily observed during the day. Some possums and gliders are common even in urban environments. And some tourist sites and ecolodges offer excellent mammal-watching opportunities of unusual or less common species.

GETTING STARTED

The basic field kit for a mammal-watcher is much the same as for bushwalking or birdwatching: loose, comfortable clothing in subdued, earthy tones (preferably greens or browns); suitable headwear to provide protection from the sun during the day and also to keep you warm at night; sturdy footwear, such as hiking boots; drinking water to suit conditions (carry extra drinking water in the arid zone); plus a GPS or compass if you will be going off-trail. As you will probably be active mainly at night, carry adequate warm and/or waterproof clothing, depending on conditions.

Nothing beats good research: read books, articles, websites, blogs and scientific papers as much as possible. When you're in the field you may only glimpse an animal, sometimes after a long trudge or when you're tired and about to give up for the night. If all you get is a brief look then you want to be able to tell the rare Northern Bettong from the much more common Rufous Bettong, a Squirrel Glider from a Sugar Glider, and so on. Talk to local naturalists and birdwatchers, many of whom keep notes on mammals they see in the field; birders on pelagic trips in particular usually have a good knowledge of local cetaceans. Make a list of species you'd like to see and read up on those that are rare, unusual or difficult-to-find to maximise your chances of finding (and recognising) them in the field. Luck sometimes plays a big role in wildlife-watching and the more prepared you are the more you can maximise opportunities.

BINOCULARS 101

The one essential piece of equipment for any wildlife-watcher is a pair of binoculars (don't expect other people to share). Any working pair is better than none at all, although you should avoid buying cheap compacts or zoom binoculars (which will have poor light-gathering capabilities). As this will probably be your most expensive wildlife-watching tool, it is worth taking the time to research and select a brand that suits your needs – if you look after them a good pair will last a lifetime. Binoculars come in two basic varieties, roof prism or porro-prism, and there is a bewildering variety to choose from. Roof-prism binoculars look like two cylinders joined together; porro-prisms are the traditional, 'zig-zag' style seen in old movies. The technical differences are too many to go into here; suffice to say, manufacturers these days tend to concentrate on roof-prism designs and the best models offer quality far superior to most of the few porro-prism binoculars still available. Traditionally the leading brands of roof-prism binoculars included Zeiss, Leica, Swarovski and some top-end Nikon models; a former leading brand Bausch & Lomb has been subsumed by Bushnell and Alpen. All of these are dustproof, waterproof and ergonomically designed, and feature lifetime warranties, (usually) excellent after-sales service and unsurpassed optical quality. Some good websites that explain the ins and outs of binoculars will help you choose a pair that suits you (see, for example, www.bestbinocularsreviews.com or www.allbinos.com). Factors to consider include weight (you'll be wearing them around your neck for hours on end), size and 'feel' (to suit your hands) and focusing. Retractable eyecups will let spectacle wearers keep their glasses on while using the binoculars, and are generally recommended, but you will need binoculars with a long *eyepoint* to do this. A good pair will allow you to adjust them to suit the distance between your eyes; and have a *diopter* adjustment to compensate for differences between your left and right eye. Most binoculars will be labelled with a numerical configuration, such as 8 × 32 or 10 × 50. The first number refers to the magnification ('power'); for wildlife-watching 7×, 8× or 10× are usually the preferred options. The second number refers to the diameter (in millimetres) of the glass at the broad (objective) end of the binoculars – for example, 32, 42 or 50 mm. As a rule of thumb, dividing the second number by the first will give you a figure that is a rough guide to the light-gathering ability (brightness) of the optics. Anything over 4 should be suitable for wildlife-watching – for example, 8 × 32, 8 × 42, 10 × 50 – remembering that higher numbers mean a brighter image but also usually greater size and weight. Top brands cost thousands of dollars, so don't rush out and buy an expensive pair until you have handled them. Nowadays there are many other good models that will deliver, say, 80 per cent of the quality at very competitive prices; you can get perfectly serviceable roof prism binoculars for under $500, for example, and a huge array of new and rebadged models with similar specifications are appearing. An increasing number of cheaper binoculars now have ED, LD or HD glass in their specifications – for example, 8 × 42 ED. These tend to be noticeably brighter and sharper than equivalent non-ED. Top-end binoculars really come into their own in critical light conditions; on the other hand, mid-priced binoculars are cheaper to insure or replace if they get damaged or stolen. The important thing is: try before you buy! Talk to people in the field about their choices; when wildlife-watchers get together it's a common topic of conversation and people often pass theirs around to compare. You will quickly notice how the same few styles, brands and configurations crop up. Specialist shops such as The Binocular and Telescope Shop (www.bintel.com.au) have knowledgeable staff, stock a wide range of brands and styles, and will help you make a selection (airport duty-free shops hold limited stock and camera retailers usually don't have the depth of knowledge to help you make a purchase).

Spotting scopes are lightweight telescopes used by birdwatchers. They have the advantage of greater magnification, usually starting at 20×, and large objective lenses that give them amazing brightness. However, they have a couple of disadvantages; for example, they must be mounted on a tripod for stability and in hot conditions the extra magnification amplifies the heat shimmer so often encountered in Australia. For mammal-watchers, a spotting scope would probably be most useful to scan for whales from a headland or other stable vantage point. Locating animals in a spotting scope takes practice, but if you're prepared to lug one around they can bring a distant creature into spectacular close-up. Good spotting scopes cost more than binoculars but with care they will last a lifetime; leading brands are Kowa, Swarovksi, Leica, Zeiss and Bushnell. Again, talk to people, read reviews and compare them under field conditions before you outlay all that hard-earned money.

SPOTLIGHTS AND SPOTLIGHTING

Most Australian mammals are at least partly nocturnal (active at night). This means you will need to be out and about at night at some point to maximise your chances of locating and watching mammals such as possums, gliders and bats. A nocturnal mammal-watching foray could mean simply walking through a city park to see possums or a trek of several kilometres up Thornton Peak to look for the elusive Masked White-tailed Rat. Either way, a reliable torch (flashlight) is going to be essential. Most mammals have a layer at the back of the eye, called the *tapetum lucidum*, which reflects light at night, sometimes in distinctive tones (usually yellow or reddish) and degrees of brightness. The simplest technique for spotting them is to look for their eyeshine while scanning the canopy or understorey. If you align your eyes with the torchlight – for example, by holding it next to your temple and watching along the line of the beam – you will find eyeshine is more easily seen. Large possums and macropods are easily detected this way and will often freeze in the light. However, don't shine a naked light directly into their eyes for extended periods as it may cause undue stress and interrupt their routine, which could make them vulnerable to predation. Once you have located an animal, you will stress it less by just shining the edge of the beam on it. Animals will usually go about their normal behaviour if you cover the torch with red cellophane, which apparently doesn't dazzle them. Some species are notoriously light-shy and will quickly take evasive action once they have been spotlighted.

Countless varieties of torch and spotlight are available. The most useful style is probably a head torch, which will keep both hands free so you can use binoculars while looking at an animal. Many head torches are now of sufficient strength and quality that they can double as spotlights under some conditions (for example, where the canopy isn't too high or in medium-density vegetation); some even have a red filter which can be slipped over the beam for extended observations once you've located the animal. Researchers found that a 50–60 W bulb was more successful at detecting possums and tree kangaroos in Queensland rainforests than a 100 W bulb because animals were less likely to turn away from the light. This may be so but you'll need all the candle power you can get when sweeping across open plains – a light with interchangeable bulbs would be a good idea. Power is another issue. A separate power pack (preferably rechargeable) is also a good idea. Motorcycle batteries give about 2 hours' worth of charge. If you're based in a vehicle the light can be connected directly to the vehicle's battery with alligator clips. The traditional tool of serious wildlife-watchers and researchers was a spotlight with a pistol grip attached to a 9-volt battery pack. These units are powerful and effective but tend to be heavy, especially when held at eye level for long periods. However, they come into their own where the canopy is high or trees are widely spaced, and over long distances on open, flat ground. Lightforce is an Australian brand with a good reputation; Clubman is another recommended brand. Spotlighting on foot works well in forests and woodlands; walk quietly and listen for rustling, scratching and the patter of falling vegetation, dropped by feeding animals from the canopy. You won't be able to hear as much from a moving vehicle, but it will enable you to cover more ground, especially where animals are widely dispersed, such as arid-zone macropods. Interestingly, in dense vegetation it is probably easier to pick up eyeshine at night than it is to see an animal during the day in the same vegetation. If weight is an issue even some of the conventional, hand-held style torches are now of amazing quality and come with rechargeable batteries. Tiablo is one recommended lightweight brand with a strong beam. However, it takes practice to hold an animal in a torch beam while trying to watch it through binoculars.

TRACKS AND SIGNS

Many mammals leave signs and traces of their presence, even if you can't immediately locate the animals themselves. Classic examples include footprints, chewed fruit or seeds, droppings (scats), burrows or tunnels and nests or dens. Looking for the signs and learning to identify them is a great way of finding out what mammals are in an area. Footprints in dust, mud and sand are left by most species (the obvious exceptions being microbats and cetaceans) and with practice they can be identified to species level for some groups (for example, large predators and macropods). Some animals are abroad even in snow.

Many land mammals also have characteristic droppings. Scats of large species such as kangaroos and wombats are easily recognisable and often abundant; others have a distinctive shape (for example, Echidnas); small droppings in a crevice or cave could be a sign that bats or rodents have been using it. The more you look, the more you will see and know where to look – other tell-tale traces of an animal's presence could be fur caught on twigs, thorns, fence posts or barbed wire; and burrows in earth, sand or among leaf litter (some rodents create distinctive burrows, whereas others tunnel through dense vegetation – for example, Broad-toothed Rats make runways through dense tussocks and may be active under the snow in winter). The tell-tale mounds of pebble-mice are fascinating works of engineering. Smooth rocks or bark can indicate where an animal has been rubbing (for example, where wombats enter or leave their burrows). Flattened grass may show where a macropod has been lying up during the day. Common Ringtail Possums construct a nest or drey of dried grasses and leaves, in which they sleep during the day.

Sooner or later all animals must leave shelter to seek food, and signs of feeding can be a great way to see what's in an area and even help to locate the animal when you return at night with a light. Chewed nuts or fruit under a tree can indicate what animals have been eating overhead; scope these sites out during the day and then return after dark to see what's feeding there (birds, such as pigeons, also drop fruit when they're feeding, but fruit-eating birds are never active after dark). Rock-rats use regular sites, such as crevices, in which to cache food. Middens are piles of bones, scraps of flesh and inedible parts such as claws and teeth left behind after a carnivorous (meat-eating) animal has had its meal. Interesting examples include those used by Water Rats, which bring their prey to a waterside platform, such as a log or stone, and leave behind inedible parts of fish and crustaceans. Ghost Bats and Diadem Sheath-tailed Bats are unusual because they habitually use roosts or perches where they consume their prey, leaving behind piles of bones and insect parts that can accumulate over several years. Yellow-bellied Gliders make distinctive V-shaped incisions in the bark of food trees to allow access to sap. Look for fresh ones in likely sites and return after dark – sometimes Sugar and Feathertail Gliders also join the feast. Bandicoots make tell-tale conical holes when digging for invertebrates and other food.

Bear in mind that tracks, scats and other signs break down and disappear over time, although some middens may be in use for years. It takes years of practice to become adept at reading animal signs; the classic guide to tracks and signs of Australian mammals, Barbara Triggs's *Tracks, Scats and Other Traces*, is highly recommended. Even more ephemeral are the calls of animals. In fact as a general rule, Australian terrestrial mammals don't vocalise (bats and cetaceans are very vocal – see the following sections), so calls are not a very useful means of locating most species. However, there are some outstanding exceptions: Sugar and Squirrel Gliders can be quite vocal and the champion is the Yellow-bellied Glider. Male Koalas are extremely vocal when searching for mates. Other species make audible alarm sounds, such as Rufous Bettongs.

WATCHING BATS

In most of eastern and northern Australia flying foxes are a familiar sight, even in the middle of large cities. And small, insect-eating bats (microbats) can be seen silhouetted against the evening sky nearly everywhere, especially in warmer conditions (although less so in winter in southern states). As a rule of thumb, the bigger the bat, the easier it will be to observe. Flying foxes form large camps where they can be observed interacting during the day. There are hundreds of these on the eastern seaboard and across northern Australia, and all you'll need to watch them comfortably is a pair of binoculars.

Microbats, however, are another issue. Apart from a few well-known cave roosts, for example Naracoorte Caves and Mount Etna Bat Cleft, they are very difficult to observe satisfactorily. Some, such as Ghost Bats, Yellow-bellied Sheath-tailed Bats, White-striped Freetail Bats and a few others, can be identified in flight with practice. However, this is rarely a satisfying experience and the best solution is to join a research team or survey where live trapping is involved. The most common technique for catching bats is a harp trap – a lightweight upright frame with fishing wire strung between it; the bats can't detect the strings with their echolocation gear and bounce harmlessly off the strings into a bag, where they are collected for examination. Live trapping provides an opportunity to see many species in the hand. Various electronic devices are available that decode bats' ultrasonic calls; these are a great way to find out what species are in your area and, with practice, can sometimes be used in conjunction with a torch to identify bats in flight.

Regrettably, some bats, especially flying foxes, get caught on wire fences. Eastern Tube-nosed Bats in particular seem to be prone to getting their wings hooked up on barbed wire, where they can overheat after sunrise. If you find an injured or sick live bat, on no account should you handle it unless you have been inoculated against lyssavirus and are wearing gloves. But if you find one alive on a fence and do have the requisite inoculation and gloves, try to cover it with a damp cloth to keep it cool, before gently releasing its wings (which should quickly heal if they are not too badly damaged). Contact a wildlife carer or veterinarian.

WATCHING MARINE MAMMALS

The big exception to the nocturnal rule is of course marine mammals – whales, dolphins, seals and the Dugong; whale-watching in particular is big business at select localities. As marine mammals can be observed both from shore and while aboard boats, it's hard to generalise about apparel and equipment. Boats can be wet and uncomfortable, even in hot climates, and conditions can change quickly at sea. In warm conditions it is important to cover up properly against the sun – wear a broad-brimmed hat and plenty of sunblock, because sunlight is reflected off the water as well as beaming down from above. In the southern states, it can get very cold in winter, and warm, waterproof clothing and footwear is essential, even gloves at times. Similar apparel guidelines would apply during land-based watching. When conditions are good, the opportunities for close observations and photography from a boat can be superb. Indeed, cameras (and video) are excellent tools for recording what may just be a fleeting view, which can later be examined for identification purposes. Binoculars are extremely useful on land and on the water; a spotting scope mounted on a tripod would be useful for land-based cetacean watching.

Migrating Humpback and Southern Right Whales can offer spectacular close-up viewing opportunities between May and October, from both land and boats. There are numerous dolphin-watching and swim-with-dolphin type tours at various points around the country; these provide sometimes exceptional views. Watching and identifying most other species requires patience and good observational skills. The first indication of a whale's presence is usually a cloud of vapour ('blow') as it surfaces to breathe. Most species have a distinctive blow pattern which is described in good whale guidebooks. These blow patterns take practice to recognise and are most easily spotted in calm conditions, but what happens next can be critical: the animal usually briefly shows its back ('dorsum') and fin, and sometimes its tail as well. Such views are often fleeting, however, which is why it is vital do as much research as possible before going into the field: fin shape and size, surfacing pattern and blow pattern often add up to diagnostic views. In general, being on a boat will offer the best opportunity for seeing species other than the common inshore whales and dolphins, and the more you get out to sea, the better your chances of encountering 'rarities' (the distribution and movements of many cetaceans, such as beaked whales, are still poorly known).

Several whale species are known only from specimens washed up on the shoreline, often after storms. Many other species, such as pilot whales, Sperm Whale and some dolphins, become accidentally stranded, sometimes in large groups, and perish after prolonged periods out of water. Depending on its state of decomposition, examining a beach-cast specimen is a great way to see these sometimes rare animals close-up. Remember to report any finds to a local whale database; contact details are given in the whale-watching section in relevant chapters. Participating in a whale rescue team can also be a rewarding experience, although there are some inherent dangers in trying to refloat these large animals, such as becoming trapped under one as it rolls in the surf. It is therefore vitally important to notify the relevant authorities so trained personnel can coordinate rescue attempts.

TRAPPING SMALL MAMMALS

Some species are too small to be detected easily by eyeshine and can almost never be identified in the field. Among them are many small rodents, dasyurids (marsupial carnivores) and pygmy possums. Attempting to identify most small dasyurids, some bats and many rodents is impossible by casual observation: many will not be seen at all unless they are trapped, and some can be identified only in the hand by experts. There are two basic types of trap (although only a basic description is possible here): box and pitfall traps.

Box traps come in a variety of shapes and sizes. The most commonly used version in Australia is the Elliott trap: a rectangular box with a spring-operated door at one end. Bait (usually an aromatic ball of oats and peanut butter, with a dash of truffle oil or vanilla to make it irresistible to small mammals) is placed at the opposite end and the desired target animal activates the trap door when it passes over a treadle to get to the bait. Several traps are usually laid in a line or grid, facing downhill so they don't fill with water during rain, and sometimes a wad of cotton wool or shredded paper is put inside to keep animals warm overnight before the traps are checked in the morning. These traps work well for rodents and small dasyurids, with sometimes interesting by-catch such as large lizards and snakes. Larger traps (cage traps), built on similar principles, are used for trapping bandicoots, possums, bettongs and potoroos.

Pitfall traps are large, cylindrical drums sunk into the soil until the lip is level with the ground, usually in a line of 6–10 traps. A low fence is run down the middle of the line and over each trap, so that any animals running into the fence line will follow it along until they fall into a trap. This technique works well for rodents, dasyurids and a host of small animals such as snakes, lizards, scorpions and spiders! Many students, researchers and conservation organisations welcome volunteers to help with their work. This may involve setting trap lines, digging pits for pitfall traps, and cleaning, baiting and setting cage traps, among myriad novel survey methods tailored to different animals' needs. It can be hard, wet, hot and/or cold work, but the dividends can be enormous. Many small species are encountered only after extensive trapping effort, but this can be a very rewarding way of enjoying several unique species. Check university websites and ask around at scientific conferences to find out who's working on what.

WHERE TO WATCH AUSTRALIAN MAMMALS

Apart from kangaroos and some wallabies, it is unusual to find a mammal by accident in its natural habitat during the day. The problem is compounded because many species are cryptic or extremely rare – some all but vanish from the landscape for years on end only to reappear in great number when conditions are favourable; others are deemed extinct but are rediscovered decades later. In short, watching Australian mammals can present some challenges to the casual observer and researcher alike. But in recent years a growing interest in natural history and 'ecotourism' has meant that for the first time ever some previously little-known species can be watched in the field under natural conditions.

Owing to Australia's unique circumstances and environment, it is difficult to generalise about the whereabouts of native mammals. As a general rule, the more natural the habitat, the more native mammals it will support. However, this varies greatly according to region and taxonomic group, between islands and the mainland, and between the tropics and the south. Understanding an animal's ecology and behaviour will help you to locate it in the wild. Read up on animals' habitat preferences, feeding behaviour and daily or seasonal movements, for example. Many species appear to thrive, or at least survive, in mosaics of natural habitat, farmland and urban areas. Thus, it is often not necessary to go to national parks to see kangaroos, wallabies, possums and wombats (although it may be a more aesthetically pleasing experience to do so). Native mammal abundance may also depend on whether introduced predators, such as European Foxes and feral Cats are present. Some flying foxes and many microbats have become adapted to urban environments; their presence may not be constrained by the presence of feral animals, but as already explained microbats present their own observation challenges.

Many arboreal species use naturally occurring hollows in living or dead trees as dens for sleeping or breeding. These can be a variety of sizes and in many locations, such as 'spouts' (hollow, pipe-shaped branches, often broken off) and 'stags' as well as fallen logs, stumps and even fence posts. Smaller species, such as some possums, pygmy possums and gliders, may use artificial nest boxes. Nest boxes set up at various locations for species such as phascogales (for example, at Chiltern and Perup) and Leadbeater's Possum are checked regularly and volunteers are usually welcomed. Some bats will also occupy specially constructed boxes; at, for example, the Organ Pipes NP (4.03) near Melbourne. Some ecolodges provide feeding stations and these can be excellent places for seeing mammals close-up.

Spotlighting will greatly enhance your chances of seeing wildlife at night but there are no guarantees. A patch of forest can be jumping one night and dead quiet the next, depending on variables such as weather, wind, humidity, cloud cover and phases of the moon – or maybe none of these factors, nobody really knows. In general, rain and spotlighting don't mix very well: raindrops on foliage can look like eyeshine in the spotlight beam and animals usually take cover during downpours. Similarly, windy nights can make spotlighting difficult. And strong moonshine can inhibit mammal activity – small mammals are more vulnerable to predation in bright moonlight. Opinions differ, but in theory an optimum time to start looking for mammals is just after dusk, when they are hungriest.

To see a good selection of the more unusual, unique or rare species, develop a network of researchers. Find out who's working on what and be prepared to volunteer some time on a few projects. This may involve lugging equipment, digging pitfalls and setting up traps, but the payoff can be great and you're usually in good company. By attending scientific conferences you'll find out who's working on what and be able to speak to people directly about their work. The annual Australian Mammal Society scientific congress and the Biennial Australasian Bat Society conference are good places to start. Another approach is to join Australian Wildlife Conservancy as a volunteer (or donor) and take part in one of their surveys – you'll see some amazing parts of the country.

MAKING A LIST

Birdwatching and its corollary, listing species seen in a day/year/life/whatever, is well established in Australia and elsewhere. So why not make a list of mammals seen in the field? There are no established guidelines for 'ticking' Australian mammals. 'Rules' for ticking birds, such as those laid down by British and American birding clubs, obviously don't apply perfectly to some groups of mammals. For example, a large percentage of Australian mammals can be identified only in the hand and must be trapped to do so; ticking a bird in such circumstances would be anathema to serious birders. Most people would agree that any species you count on your list should be a wild animal seen in its natural environment within its natural range. But even this can get complicated – with numerous translocations to sanctuaries where the animals formerly occurred, what constitutes a 'free-living, wild animal in its natural habitat'? The lister's dilemma is therefore whether to count, say, a Bilby where it had been reintroduced to Scotia Sanctuary, or try to see a 'genuine' wild one in the remote Outback. Birders generally assume that if an introduced species is part of a population that has been self-sustaining in an area for 10 years or more, it counts as a genuine wild animal. It seems sensible, therefore, to apply a similar rule to Australian mammals that form part of rehabilitation projects.

Many birdwatchers set goals, such as seeing 700 species on their Australian list. Naturally the higher the goal, the greater the challenge and with mammals the benchmarks are even harder to attain. For example, to see 100 mammal species would be a worthy achievement; but while seeing 100 bird species would be a feasible total for a day's birding in many parts of Australia, it would take weeks of searching to see 100 mammal species. And from there it only gets harder: very few people, including professional mammalogists, have seen even 150 Australian mammal species. Even fewer have seen more than 200. Yet these goals are attainable with determination, planning and effort.

So how many mammals could you hope to see and how long would it take to see them? Using the latest available taxonomy, extant native mammals in Australia currently number 359 species. There are no guarantees, but in one week in Tasmania (Chapter 5) it should be possible to see 20 native species; a week in the Wet Tropics (Chapter 1) could add another 20 to this list; by joining the Wildlife Week at O'Reilly's another 20–30 could be added. From there it gets harder: a trip to Iron Range NP on Cape York Peninsula could bag another 10 species; add another five at Kakadu NP and another 5–10 in south-west Western Australia. Any trip to the Kimberley requires time and planning; with luck you could see a good cross-section of mammals, say 5–10 species. This is still well short of the total and by now you've already travelled round the continent. To fill in the gaps would require years of participation in small mammal- and bat-trapping, and numerous pelagic trips to look for cetaceans. (Unfortunately, introduced species, such as European Foxes, feral Cats and European Rabbits, are among the easiest mammals to see in Australia; whether you add them to your list is up to you, of course, but they will add another half-dozen species to your list.)

One approach when visiting a new location is to concentrate on the hardest species first, such as endemics (because they won't be seen anywhere else) and rarities. In Australia you are spoilt for choice if these are your goal; seeing them is another matter. Go to it and good luck!

STATES AND TERRITORIES

1. Queensland

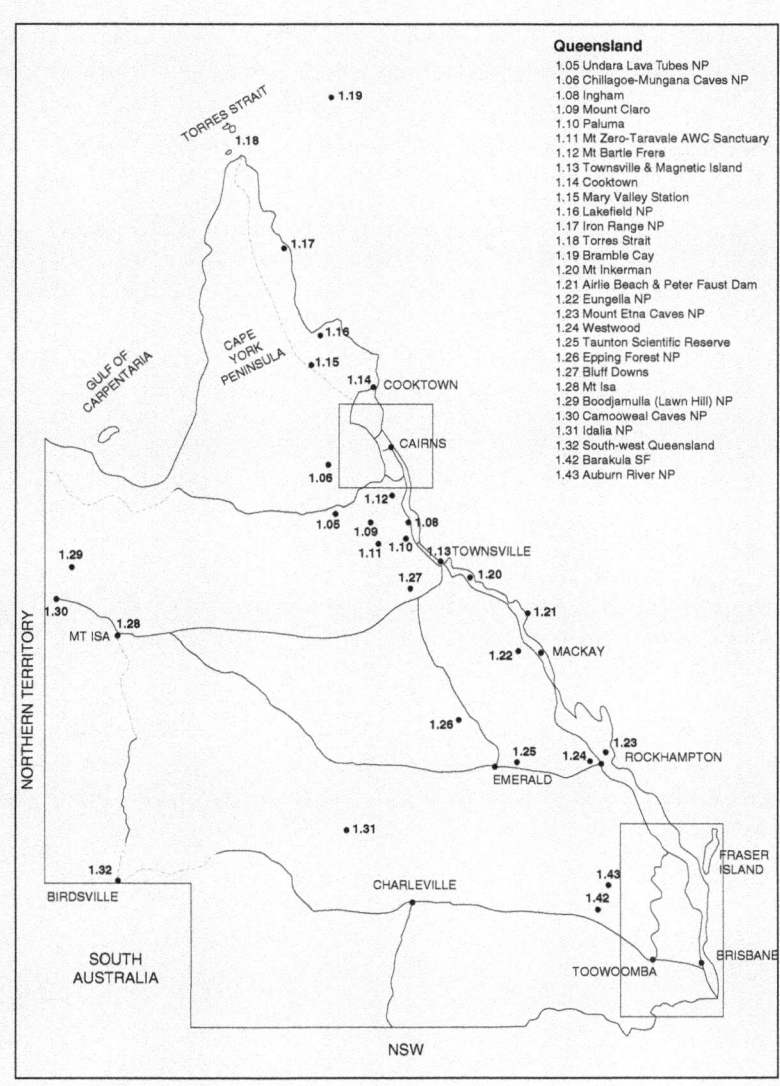

Queensland
1.05 Undara Lava Tubes NP
1.06 Chillagoe-Mungana Caves NP
1.08 Ingham
1.09 Mount Claro
1.10 Paluma
1.11 Mt Zero-Taravale AWC Sanctuary
1.12 Mt Bartle Frere
1.13 Townsville & Magnetic Island
1.14 Cooktown
1.15 Mary Valley Station
1.16 Lakefield NP
1.17 Iron Range NP
1.18 Torres Strait
1.19 Bramble Cay
1.20 Mt Inkerman
1.21 Airlie Beach & Peter Faust Dam
1.22 Eungella NP
1.23 Mount Etna Caves NP
1.24 Westwood
1.25 Taunton Scientific Reserve
1.26 Epping Forest NP
1.27 Bluff Downs
1.28 Mt Isa
1.29 Boodjamulla (Lawn Hill) NP
1.30 Camooweal Caves NP
1.31 Idalia NP
1.32 South-west Queensland
1.42 Barakula SF
1.43 Auburn River NP

Endemics: **Atherton Antechinus, Cinnamon Antechinus, Chestnut Dunnart, Julia Creek Dunnart, Northern Hairy-nosed Wombat, Mahogany Glider, Green Ringtail Possum, Daintree River Ringtail Possum, Herbert River Ringtail Possum, Lemuroid Ringtail Possum, Northern Bettong, Musky Rat-kangaroo, Bennett's Tree Kangaroo, Lumholtz's Tree Kangaroo, Bridled Nailtail Wallaby, Cape York Rock Wallaby, Godman's Rock Wallaby, Mareeba Rock Wallaby, Mount Claro Rock Wallaby, Allied Rock Wallaby, Unadorned Rock Wallaby, Herbert's Rock Wallaby, Proserpine Rock Wallaby, Purple-necked Rock Wallaby, Spectacled Flying Fox, Large-eared Horseshoe Bat, Fawn Leaf-nosed Bat, Semon's Leaf-nosed Bat, Coastal Sheath-tailed Bat, Flute-nosed Bat, Cape York Melomys, Bramble Cay Melomys, Eastern Pebble-mound Mouse, Prehensile-tailed Rat**

The vast state of Queensland occupies the north-eastern quarter of the continent, stretching from the subtropics almost to the great island of New Guinea. It encompasses an incredible range of habitats, including rainforested mountain ranges and hills, true deserts and grasslands, semi-arid mulga woodlands and tropical savannah woodlands, cave complexes and huge floodplains. Fringing almost the entire east coast is the Great Barrier Reef, 2000 km of ribbon reefs, coral atolls, sand cays and continental islands that act as a buffer against the Pacific Ocean. Not surprisingly, Queensland features an amazing biodiversity, the greatest in the country, with many endemic species and subspecies. The main centres of diversity are (from north to south) the rainforests of Cape York Peninsula, the Wet Tropics (between Cairns and Townsville) and the south-east corner, surrounding the urban sprawl of Greater Brisbane. These three centres are all hundreds of kilometres apart, and if time is limited good planning is required to get the most out of them. Weather is also a factor – the tropics (north of about Rockhampton) experience a pronounced wet season from December to March (though it varies from year to year), with high rainfall and sometimes dangerous cyclones that can cause widespread property damage and even loss of life. Travel in these conditions is difficult and wildlife-viewing can be severely curtailed; rising rivers can cause flooding hundreds of kilometres from the storm centre. Similar conditions (without the cyclones) can occur anywhere along the entire coast, much of which used to be covered in rainforest.

Travel to any or all of the three main centres will allow you to see a very good selection of native wildlife. The Wet Tropics are probably the most accessible place to see a range of macropods, bandicoots, bats and rodents, as well as a suite of endemic rainforest possums and the unique **Platypus**. Getting to the Cape York rainforests will entail a well-organised expedition by road; the payoff will be wildlife, such as cuscuses, that shares affinities with New Guinea (the two areas were once connected by a land bridge). Many sites in the south-east are easily accessible from

Brisbane, the state capital, including World Heritage–listed Fraser I. (1.41) and subtropical rainforest at Lamington NP (1.37).

For cetacean enthusiasts, **Humpback Whales** are a star attraction in the winter months (May–October), and three dolphin species are common: **Bottlenose**, **Indo-Pacific Humpback** and **Snubfin**. Queensland has no resident pinnipeds or seal breeding colonies, although up to a dozen **New Zealand Fur Seals** are spotted most years between the Sunshine Coast and the NSW border, with more in exceptional years (up to 50 in 2012), mainly in winter. Queensland has also hosted the most northerly record of the **Leopard Seal** – on Heron I. at the southern end of the Great Barrier Reef! The other marine attraction is **Dugongs**, which occur in good numbers in suitable sites along the coast north of Moreton Bay (1.34).

Bats are extremely well represented, with 54 species of microbat and no fewer than six flying fox species. Flying fox camps occur along almost the entire coastline and a good way inland, especially in wet years. Important cave systems with bat-viewing include Mount Etna Caves NP (1.23), which supports the largest maternity colony of **Little Bentwing Bats** in Australia, as well as **Ghost Bats**; Undara Lava Tubes (1.05) and Chillagoe-Mungana Caves NP (1.06). And of course Queensland has the greatest rodent diversity in Australia, with 33 species, of which two-thirds remain common. Strongholds for rodents include the far west of the state, the south-east corner and the north-east.

SOME STATE HIGHLIGHTS

- Amazing and easily seen mammal diversity at **Lamington National Park**.
- **Musky Rat-kangaroos**, diurnal relics from Gondwanan rainforests.
- The only place in the world where it's possible to see four species of **flying fox** in one camp.
- Getting up close and personal with **Humpback Whales** in Hervey Bay.
- The unique suite of endemic **rainforest possums** on the Atherton Tableland.

A THE WET TROPICS

The well-populated coast between Townsville and Cairns is often referred to as 'Far North Queensland', although the mainland actually stretches another 1000 km or so further north. The entire region is known as the Wet Tropics and is a hotspot for endemic mammals, birds, reptiles and amphibians. Rainforests here are thought to be relics of ancient Gondwanan forests and many primitive species persist in the area. Cairns is a logical starting point for mammal-watching in Australia, particularly for international visitors or those with limited time, and indeed for any wildlife-watching: the Great Barrier Reef on its doorstep offers myriad snorkelling and diving opportunities, and the area offers some of the country's best birdwatching. Endemic

Wet Tropics mammals include a suite of rainforest possums (**Green**, **Daintree River**, **Herbert River** and **Lemuroid Ringtail Possums**), the **Long-tailed Pygmy Possum**, **Mahogany Glider**, a number of macropods (**Northern Bettong**, **Musky Rat-kangaroo**, **Lumholtz's Tree Kangaroo**, and **Mareeba**, **Mount Claro** and **Allied Rock Wallabies**), **Atherton Antechinus** and **Masked White-tailed Rat**. The region also shares affinities with rainforests of Cape York Peninsula and New Guinea (**Striped Possum**, **Prehensile-tailed Rat**, **Giant White-tailed Rat** and **Cape York Rat**) and supports outlying populations of species elsewhere found only much further south (for example, **Yellow-footed** and **Brown Antechinuses** and, strangely, the **White-footed Dunnart**, which is otherwise an inhabitant of southern heaths and woodlands), as well as species more typical of subtropical rainforests (**Long-nosed Bandicoot**, **Red-legged Pademelon**, **Fawn-footed Melomys** and **Bush Rat**). And a few that occur here are becoming rare elsewhere, such as the **Northern Quoll** and **Black-footed Tree-rat**. Many of these are quite easy to see at the sites mentioned in the following pages.

A fair bit of 'ecotourism' traffic heads north to the Daintree–Cape Tribulation area; however, Wet Tropics mammal diversity is higher south of the Daintree River and reaches its peak on the Atherton Tableland (1.03 and 1.04). Most roads are sealed and a conventional vehicle is fine for exploring nearly every site; exceptions are the coast road north of Daintree to Cooktown, and some less-travelled parts of the Atherton Tableland. In the wet season it would be a good idea to check conditions before venturing off sealed roads in a conventional vehicle (www.racq.com.au). The whole area has many campgrounds and guesthouses, several of which are also good for wildlife and/or have knowledgeable staff. There is any number of tour companies touting for business but, as anywhere, check the credentials of any bearing the prefix 'eco' – a few salient questions will soon tell you how much they know about local wildlife. A list of recommended operators is included in Appendix B.

1.01 CAIRNS AREA

Highlights: **Northern Brown Bandicoot, Striped Possum, Spectacled Flying Fox, Coastal Sheath-tailed Bat**

Other possibilities: **Eastern Tube-nosed Bat, Little Red Flying Fox, Bare-rumped Sheath-tailed Bat**

Cairns is a pleasant place to base your exploration of the region. Much of the tourist action takes place along the foreshore ('The Esplanade'), where there are good accommodations and restaurants. There's a camp of some 2000–3000 **Spectacled Flying Foxes** (peaking at about 10 000 and occasionally joined by **Little Red Flying Foxes**) in the large fig and mango trees near the City Library and hotel on the corner of Abbott and Aplin Sts, just one block inland from the Esplanade. At dusk they can also be readily seen flying to blossom and fruiting trees on the Esplanade. With the recent anti-bat hysteria in parts of Queensland there have been efforts to move this colony; regardless of whether the move takes place, some flying foxes are usually camped in the central swampy part of Centennial Lakes park and could turn up anywhere in the city's parks and gardens. Cairns Botanic Gardens and adjacent Centenary Lakes park are pleasant places to while away a morning, and at night a walk along the boardwalk between Collins Ave and the Centenary Lakes is a good place to look for **Striped Possums** by spotlighting into the dense canopy. **Northern Brown Bandicoots** can also be seen at forest edges. Recently roosts of the little-known **Bare-rumped Sheath-tailed Bat** were discovered in the botanic gardens – contact a local bat expert before your visit for an update, as the roosts change periodically. Other microbats recorded around Cairns include the **Little Northern Freetail**, **Northern Freetail**, **Dusky Leaf-nosed** and **Eastern** and **Large-eared Horseshoe Bats**, **Large-footed Myotis**, **Northern Broad-nosed**, **Eastern and Little Bentwing Bats**, **Hoary Wattled Bat** and **Cape York Freetail Bat**.

Mount Whitfield on the northern edge of the city is a patch of rainforest that would be worth exploring for **Common Brushtail Possums**, **Swamp Wallabies** and **Fawn-footed Melomys**. **Dugongs** were once common inshore south of Cairns and at Yarrabah, and may still occur in small numbers. Extensive mangroves and grasslands formerly surrounded the airport, and could still hold species such as the **Agile Wallaby**, **Echidna** and **Grassland Melomys**; **Black Flying Foxes** continue to roost in the mangroves here. The mangroves at the northern end of the Esplanade would be worth checking for **Water Rats**, but beware that mosquitoes can be bad here at dusk (and there may be Saltwater Crocodiles).

At Wangetti Beach about 40 km north of the city, **Coastal Sheath-tailed Bats** roost in a fissure under Rex Lookout on the Captain Cook Hwy. Access is safest at low tide: take the highway towards Port Douglas; just after Hartley Crocodile Farm (on the left), you'll cross a creek, then come to the short unsealed beach access road on the right (it's well signposted but there's a lot of traffic on this stretch and if you miss the turn-off it's hard to turn around). Park here and walk north about 1 km along the beach to an obvious rocky promontory; you'll have to wade or wait for low tide, but a few metres further round there's a large cleft in the rocks where the bats roost. Please keep disturbance to a minimum. This species also roosts at the bulk sugar terminal in Cairns. There's a permanent maternity camp of about 40 000 **Spectacled Flying Foxes** at Gordonvale, on the southern outskirts of Cairns along the Bruce Hwy.

Port Douglas is another popular tourist destination but has little to offer otherwise except a camp of about 35 000 **Spectacled Flying Foxes**. Watch for them along the entrance road and at Dickson Inlet near the Rainforest Habitat (which is a commercial aviary). Port Douglas is 67 km north of Cairns on the narrow, winding Captain Cook Hwy (44) – allow at least an hour for the trip.

Just north of Port Douglas, Mossman Gorge NP is a popular destination for day hikes and protects a good slice of lowland rainforest. **Eastern Tube-nosed Bats** frequent the area and can sometimes be seen at roosts in the gorge itself; ask around for a good local wildlife guide who may be able to find one. From Mossman it's about 40 km to the Daintree River crossing. Daintree Village, several kilometres upstream, is the starting point for good wildlife cruises (see Appendix B for recommended operators). **Spectacled Flying Foxes** often roost in mangroves, especially on the south bank. The Bat House (www.austrop.org.au) at Cape Tribulation always has a few flying foxes for close-up examination and may run harp-trapping some nights. There is no shortage of microbat activity in this part of the coast: **Eastern Tube-nosed Bats** (and potentially both species of blossom bat) feed in orchards near the Bat House, especially at Soursop and Carambola trees when they are in fruit; otherwise stake out fruiting cluster figs, to which the bats are also attracted. **Bare-rumped Sheath-tailed Bats** are also found in the Daintree area, such as between Donovan's Beach and the Daintree River, along the river itself and at the Canopy Tower; they feed up and down Myall Beach south of Cape Tribulation – take a bat detector and with luck you may be able to pin down one of these fast-flying animals.

The Esplanade at Cairns is dotted with restaurants, accommodations and all manner of tours and vehicle hire outlets; it is near bus terminals and an international airport, and walking distance to the marina where boats leave for the Reef daily.

1.02 GREAT BARRIER REEF (NORTHERN SECTION)

Highlights: **Short-flippered Pilot Whale, Dwarf Minke Whale, Humpback Whale**

Other possibilities: **Spectacled Flying Fox, Spinner Dolphin, Dugong**

Boat trips to Great Barrier Reef islands and cays near Cairns, such as Green I. and Michaelmas Cay, are popular tourist activities and run daily year-round (weather permitting). En route there is a chance of seeing dolphins, **Humpback Whales**, **Short-flippered Pilot Whales** (other blackfish may also occur) and, rarely, **Dugongs**. Green I. is closest to Cairns and **Spectacled Flying Foxes** usually roost here; **Humpback Whales** have been sighted near the island, including a rare white individual that has been migrating up the east coast annually for several consecutive years. The snorkelling here is indifferent and far better at Michaelmas Cay, where **Spinner Dolphins** are seen on occasion. Boats also run to Michaelmas Cay from Port Douglas, 67 km to the north; **Humpback Whales** are sometimes seen from these trips. The further out on the reef you go and longer you spend at sea, the greater likelihood of results. Note that early morning departures sail into the sun and glare will affect viewing conditions, although it is pleasantly cool and wildlife-viewing opportunities are usually better.

Recently an annual aggregation of hundreds of **Dwarf Minke Whales** was discovered near Lizard I. north of Cairns. Ribbon Reef 10 is a known hotspot and the window for sightings is usually a 6-week period in June and July, when 90 per cent of sightings occur. Commercial operators run live-aboard tours, leaving from Lizard I., where participants not only get the opportunity to swim and observe the whales underwater, but can also be involved in citizen science (www.minkewhaleproject.org), observing and photographing them in their natural environment. Other species sometimes seen on these cruises include **Humpbacks** and **Spinner Dolphins**. Lizard I. is accessible by light plane from Cairns.

1.03 KINGFISHER PARK AND MOUNT LEWIS

Highlights: **Platypus, Northern Brown Bandicoot, Long-nosed Bandicoot, Green Ringtail Possum, Herbert River Ringtail, Daintree River Ringtail, Lemuroid Ringtail Possum, Striped Possum, Red-legged Pademelon, Canefield Rat, Fawn-footed Melomys, Giant White-tailed Rat, Prehensile-tailed Rat**

Other possibilities: **Echidna, Agile Wallaby, Spectacled Flying Fox, Feathertail Glider, Eastern Blossom Bat**

Long established on the birding circuit, Kingfisher Park Birdwatchers' Lodge (www.birdwatchers.com.au) at Julatten is a great place to stay at the northern end of the Atherton Tableland and, together with neighbouring Mt Lewis, boasts an excellent mammal list – 35 species have been recorded on the property, with several others on Mt Lewis. **Platypuses** are sighted almost daily in the creek behind the lodge and **Echidnas** occasionally trundle through the grounds; **Musky Rat-kangaroo** is the other mainly diurnal species likely to be seen. **Agile Wallabies** come out to feed at dusk on the grassy verges and both **Northern Brown** and **Long-nosed Bandicoots**, **Green Ringtail** and **Striped Possums** (occasionally), **Giant White-tailed Rat** and **Spectacled Flying Fox** are seen regularly in the orchard between the lodge and the creek. Bird feeders outside the cabins are well patronised during the day, but the night shift includes an excellent array of small and medium-sized mammal species: among the list are the **Bush Rat**, **Canefield Rat** and **Fawn-footed Melomys**, and **Northern Brown** and **Long-nosed Bandicoots**. Other small mammals recorded on the grounds have included **Yellow-footed Antechinus**, **Common Planigale**, **Long-tailed Pygmy Possum**, **Feathertail Glider**, **Grassland Melomys**, **Prehensile-tailed Rat** and **Cape York Rat**.

Black and **Little Red Flying Foxes** also visit the orchard, and Kingfisher Park's a respectable microbat list includes **Northern** and **Eastern Blossom Bats**, **Eastern Tube-nosed Bat**, **Dusky** and **Diadem Leaf-nosed Bats**, **Little Bentwing Bat**, **Large-footed Myotis**, **Eastern Long-eared Bat** and **Northern Broad-nosed Bat**.

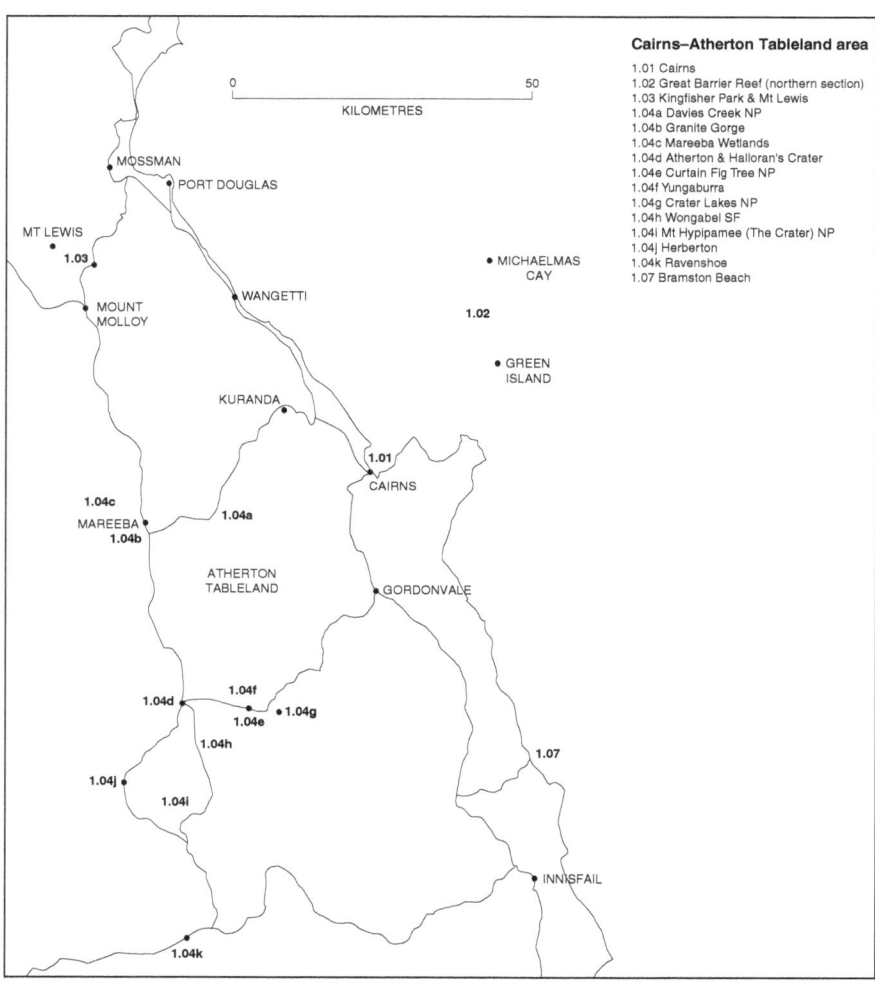

Cairns–Atherton Tableland area

1.01 Cairns
1.02 Great Barrier Reef (northern section)
1.03 Kingfisher Park & Mt Lewis
1.04a Davies Creek NP
1.04b Granite Gorge
1.04c Mareeba Wetlands
1.04d Atherton & Halloran's Crater
1.04e Curtain Fig Tree NP
1.04f Yungaburra
1.04g Crater Lakes NP
1.04h Wongabel SF
1.04i Mt Hypipamee (The Crater) NP
1.04j Herberton
1.04k Ravenshoe
1.07 Bramston Beach

Two more placental mammals – **Water Rat** and the **Dingo** – are also sporadically encountered.

Mt Lewis, reached by taking the King's Hwy through Julatten, is an outpost of upland rainforest at the northern end of the Atherton Tableland and an important centre for biodiversity. Spotlighting along the mountain's 22-km summit road can be a treat, with **Green**, **Herbert River** and **Daintree River Ringtail Possums**, **Red-legged Pademelon**, **Long-nosed** and **Northern Brown Bandicoots**, and **Lemuroid Ringtail Possum** (including the all-white phase of the latter, although it is getting rare); **Northern** and **Spot-tailed Quolls**, and **Long-tailed Pygmy Possums** have been seen. The Queensland subspecies of **Diadem Leaf-nosed Bat** (*Hipposideros diadema reginae*) has been recorded from near the top of Mt Lewis. **Platypuses** are sometimes seen from the bridge over the creek at the base of the mountain.

Kingfisher Park is at the northern end of Julatten, a small sugar town 90 km north-west of Cairns on the Rex Hwy. It has comfortable self-contained cabins, as well as budget accommodation and a campground.

1.04 ATHERTON TABLELAND

Highlights: **Northern Quoll, Yellow-footed Antechinus (ssp.** *rubeculus***), 'Coppery' Brushtail Possum (ssp.** *johnstonei***), Striped Possum, Green Ringtail Possum, Herbert River Ringtail Possum, Daintree River Ringtail Possum, Lemuroid Ringtail Possum, Yellow-bellied Glider (ssp.** *reginae***), Musky Rat-kangaroo, Northern Bettong, Lumholtz's Tree Kangaroo, Mareeba Rock Wallaby, Black-footed Tree-rat, Giant White-tailed Rat, Prehensile-tailed Rat**

Other possibilities: **Platypus, Spot-tailed Quoll, Rufous Bettong, Northern Long-eared Bat, Water Rat**

This superb area of upland rainforest is a must for any serious mammal-watcher, with many endemic species and subspecies, and its generally excellent wildlife-viewing, day and night. Sites are presented here running roughly north to south. Although the distances covered aren't so great by Queensland standards, try not to squeeze too much in – more driving means less wildlife-viewing. It's better to do two or three sites well than try to race across the entire Tableland in a single day – there is a lot of tourist traffic and roads are often narrow and winding. There are many 'ecolodges', some of which are the real thing and can show you wildlife or point you in the right direction. Apart from Kingfisher Park (1.03), other recommended places are listed in Appendix B.

The Tableland is something of a microbat hotspot. The **Large-footed Myotis** hunts over the many creeks, rivers and dams; however, there are crocs up here in some waterways, so exercise extreme caution next to large creeks, rivers and wetlands. Other attractions include the amazing **Tube-nosed Bat**, which appears to be a specialist of cloud forests and is a near-endemic to this area. Several mineshafts have been gated in the Goldsborough Valley to protect roosts of **Dusky Leaf-nosed Bats**, **Eastern Horseshoe Bats**, **Common Bentwings** and **Large-eared Horseshoe Bats**. Ask at Tolga Bat Hospital (www.tolgabathospital.org) for contacts who may be harp-trapping while you're in the area.

1.04a Davies Creek National Park

A significant population of the rare **Northern Bettong** inhabits the grassy woodland on the slopes of the Lamb Range here. Access is via Davies Creek road, off the Kennedy Hwy. The bettongs can also sometimes be spotlighted along Tinaroo Creek Rd, which passes through adjacent suitable habitat to the south; access is less straightforward – spotlight in the state forest just past the gate (a permit may be required).

1.04b Granite Gorge

This minor tourist site west of Mareeba is of little interest apart from resident **Mareeba Rock Wallabies**, which are well habituated to people and simply cannot be missed once you walk into the gorge proper. This is probably the closest you'll ever get to a wild rock wallaby and there are great photo possibilities. Granite Gorge is a few kilometres west of Mareeba; take Paglietta Rd, signposted off Rankin St in Mareeba. There are **Agile Wallabies** along the entrance road, where spotlighting may yield a **Northern Quoll**.

1.04c Mareeba Wetlands

Mareeba Wetlands (www.mareebawetlands.org) is a commercial operation based on a semi-artificial wetland with abundant waterbirds and a respectable mammal list. You'll probably have to stay here to spotlight on the grounds, but this could be worthwhile as some sought-after species, such as the **Northern Quoll**, **Brush-tailed Phascogale** and **Black-footed Tree-rat**, have been recorded. More commonly encountered are **Common Ringtail** and **Brushtail Possums**, **Greater**, **Sugar** and **Squirrel Gliders**, **Spectacled Flying Fox** and a swag of macropods, including the **Antilopine** and **Common Wallaroos**, **Eastern Grey Kangaroo**, **Rufous Bettong**, and **Whiptail** and **Agile Wallabies**. **Dingoes** also occur here. If you aren't planning to stay, seek permission from the owners to spotlight along the park entrance road: the **Common Brushtail**, **Greater Glider**, **Rufous Bettong**, **Spectacled Flying Fox**, **Agile Wallaby** and **Eastern Grey Kangaroo** have all been seen. Ask the staff about **Northern Quoll** sightings – one used to hang around the accommodation complex – and **Black-footed Tree-rats**, which are now becoming rare in their Top End stronghold. If there have been no recent sightings, ask around about macadamia plantations, where the rats sometimes become a nuisance – there may be a cooperative farmer nearby who will let you spotlight on their property. **Water Rats** are resident in the many wetlands on site and the **Canefield Rat** is common in adjacent fields. Turn west off the Kennedy Hwy at Biboohra, just north of Mareeba, to reach the Wetlands. **Whiptail Wallabies** graze on the golf course just outside Mareeba township itself.

1.04d Atherton and Halloran's Crater

The township of Atherton hosts Tolga Bat Hospital (www.tolgabathospital.org), where you can usually see flying foxes up close and often interesting microbats being rehabilitated. Tolga Scrub and Lakeside are two flying fox camps being monitored by Tolga Bat Hospital. The former hosts a permanent camp of 10 000–25 000 **Little Red Flying Foxes** (sometimes as many as 100 000) and **Black Flying Foxes** also occur here. Halloran's Crater on the edge of Atherton is one of the best places on the

Tableland to look for the **Long-tailed Pygmy Possum**, a rarely seen Wet Tropics endemic. They seem to be most common when the Satinash trees are in flower (peaking in August). The crater is a short drive up Robert St opposite the Atherton Tourist Information Centre; turn left at 12th Ave, right at Baxter Ave and left at Wadley Close; it is well signposted.

1.04e Curtain Fig Tree National Park

The Tableland has many remnant pockets of rainforest preserved as national parks and Curtain Fig Tree NP is one of the best sites for **Lumholtz's Tree Kangaroo**. By day this giant spreading fig is a popular tourist attraction, but spotlighting around the trails at night can often bag a tree kangaroo, as well as the **'Coppery' Brushtail Possum** and potentially other species as well.

1.04f Yungaburra

Spotlighting around this little town, especially along the forest-lined Peterson Creek, is very good for the beautiful copper-coloured form of the **Common Brusthtail Possum**. **Lumholtz's Tree Kangaroos** are also seen here on occasion. During the day – especially early morning – the creek is excellent for spotting **Platypuses**. There are two viewing platforms, joined by a walking trail – one by the bridge on the Gillies Hwy and the other at Allumbah Pocket; **Platypuses** could be seen at either end of the track or just about anywhere in between. **Lumholtz's Tree Kangaroos** are sometimes seen on the bank opposite Allumbah Pocket, resting during the day or feeding at night. **Northern Long-eared Bats** sometimes roost in the various picnic shelters along the creek walk. There's sometimes a camp of **Spectacled** and **Little Red Flying Foxes** on Oleander Drive in Yungaburra itself.

Alan's Wildlife Tours (www.alanswildlifetours.com.au) runs nightly spotlighting trips with small groups. These offer a very good chance of seeing **Lumholtz's Tree Kangaroo**, **Lemuroid Ringtail** and **Striped Possums**, as well as virtually guaranteed sightings of **Coppery Brushtail** and **Green Ringtail Possums**, and other interesting and endemic wildlife.

1.04g Crater Lakes National Park

A pair of flooded volcanic craters – Lake Eacham and Lake Barrine – surrounded by rainforest make up Crater Lakes NP and are worth visiting for wildlife, especially if you get there early or walk away from the crowds. The chief attraction at both is the **Musky Rat-kangaroo**, a small, diurnal macropod that is thought to resemble an ancestral form dating back to Gondwanan times. They are quite common along the trails, among undergrowth and piles of rotting logs. **Yellow-footed Antechinuses** are also sometimes seen by day here, especially in July when they are most diurnal; this is the isolated Atherton Tableland form *Antechinus flavipes rubeculus*. Watch also for **Red-legged Pademelons**, especially away from people. Spotlighting around here can be productive, with both **Northern Brown** and **Long-nosed Bandicoots** and **Giant White-tailed Rats** (all of which often cross roads at night – the rats in particular are unmistakable because of their huge size and markings), and the 'Coppery' form of **Brushtail Possum**. The **Large-footed Myotis** hunts at both lakes – watch for them on still evenings – and **Diadem Leaf-nosed Bats** have been recorded here.

The lakes are about 5 km east of Yungaburra on the Gillies Range Rd; turn right at Lake Barrine Rd for Lake Eacham and head north a few kilometres for the entrance to Lake Barrine. Nearby, Chambers Wildlife Lodge (www.rainforest-australia.com) virtually guarantees sightings of **Sugar Gliders** most evenings and is an excellent place to see **Red-legged Pademelons**; **Giant White-tailed Rats** forage around the accommodation units; **Northern Brown** and **Long-nosed Bandicoots**, as well as **Yellow-footed Antechinuses**, occur on the lodge grounds.

1.04h Wongabel State Forest

Just 8 km south of Atherton on the Kennedy Hwy, this is a prime spot for **Lumholtz's Tree Kangaroos**, which may be spotlighted along the easy-gradient trails and are sometimes seen sunning on large boughs in the early morning. Other species that have been seen here include the **Spectacled Flying Fox**, **Dingo**, **Green Ringtail Possum**, 'Coppery' **Brushtail Possum**, **Red-legged Pademelon** and **Striped Possum**.

1.04i The Crater (Mount Hypipamee) National Park

The entrance road to this popular little park used to be very good for rainforest possums, but overuse means that spotlighting is no longer allowed inside the park. There's nothing to stop you spotlighting along the highway outside the park's southern perimeter and this could also be productive for the commoner rainforest possums – **Green** and **Herbert River Ringtails** especially, as well as **Lemuroid Ringtail Possums** and potentially **Lumholtz's Tree Kangaroo**. The **Long-tailed Pygmy Possum** has been seen here. The Crater is 25 km south of Atherton township on the Kennedy Hwy.

1.04j Herberton

There is a large camp of **Little Red Flying Foxes** – up to several hundred thousand – along the Wild River, in the middle of town. Abandoned gold mines in the area provide roosts for **Large-eared** and **Eastern Horseshoe Bats** and **Little Bentwing Bats**.

1.04k Ravenshoe

The southern end of the Tableland increases in elevation, culminating at Mt Bartle Frere (1.12). The historic timber town of Ravenshoe is worth visiting for a chance to see the isolated, northern population of **Yellow-bellied Glider**, which is regarded as an endangered subspecies (ssp. *reginae*) and known locally as the 'Fluffy Glider'. It can be seen by spotlighting in the state forest near town – listen for its loud vocalisations. The road to Tully Falls is good for **Herbert River** and **Lemuroid Ringtail Possums** (including the all-white phase, which is rather scarce and tends to occur at only the highest elevations. An organised tour may be the best way of seeing this species here), **Long-nosed Bandicoots**, **Fawn-footed Melomys**, **Bush Rat** and, apparently, **Atherton Antechinus**.

1.05 UNDARA LAVA TUBES

Highlights: **Rufous Bettong, Unadorned Rock Wallaby, Eastern Horseshoe Bat, Eastern Cave Bat, Troughton's Sheath-tailed Bat, Eastern Bentwing Bat**

Other possibilities: **Antilopine Wallaroo, Euro, Whiptail Wallaby, Mareeba Rock Wallaby, Agile Wallaby**

Although it's technically not part of the Wet Tropics, this and Chillagoe-Mungana Caves NP (1.06) are most easily accessed from Ravenshoe and Mareeba, respectively. Undara Volcanic NP protects a series of volcanic lava tubes, about the same dimensions as railway tunnels, on the western edge of the Great Dividing Range. Collapsed tubes form deep gullies which are moist and green, while those which retain the roofs are home to an estimated 250 000 microbats, including the **Eastern Horseshoe Bat** (which is probably the easiest to positively identify here), **Eastern Cave Bat**, **Troughton's Sheath-tailed Bat** and **Eastern Bentwing Bat**. Between December and March you can witness a fly-out from Barker's Cave, the main maternity cave for **Eastern Horseshoe**, **Eastern Cave** and **Eastern Bentwing Bats**, which are thought to number 40 000 during the breeding season; you'll have to go with a tour guide (March–October) and pay for the privilege. This area marks the overlap in distribution of no fewer than seven macropod species, including the **Rufous Bettong** (easy to see at night around the visitors' centre), **Mareeba Rock Wallaby**, **Eastern Grey Kangaroo**, **Euro**, **Antilopine Wallaroo** (here at the southern limit of its range and common in the Fifteen Mile Spring area of the park) and **Agile Wallaby**. The **Black-striped Wallaby** (at its northern limit) and **Red-legged Pademelon** (at the western edge of its range) are probably better looked for at Forty Mile Scrub NP, about 10 km back up the Kennedy Hwy towards Ravenshoe. **Echidnas** are also generally common and occasionally a **Koala** is sighted.

Undara is 154 km south-west of Ravenshoe via the Kennedy Hwy; the caves are about 14 km south of the highway on a sealed road. Accommodation is available.

WATCHING BATS IN QUEENSLAND

Queensland has the highest bat diversity in Australia and there are many exciting opportunities for viewing some of these fascinating animals. Of the state's six flying fox species, four (**Grey-headed**, **Black**, **Little Red** and **Spectacled Flying Foxes**) can be seen readily. There are hundreds of permanent and temporary camps along the eastern seaboard, between the Gold Coast and the Daintree River, comprised of both single and mixed species. In the south-east, many camps are a mix of **Grey-headed** and **Black Flying Foxes** with **Little Red Flying Foxes** joining both species seasonally or sporadically. It would be worth looking carefully through colonies to see which species are present (each has slightly different roosting behaviour – see pp. 336–339 for details). Well-known and easily visited colonies include Bicentennial Park at Boonah (where all three often occur); Queen's Park, Woodend (three species), where there's an observation platform; Gatton; Cascades Gardens in Broadbeach; and Loder's Creek in Southport. Further north there are sizeable colonies on the Sunshine Coast and an observation platform near a colony at Hervey Bay.

Mobile camps of **Little Reds** appear inland in response to food supplies and in the Wet Tropics **Spectacled Flying Foxes** are the most abundant species. There are readily accessible **Spectacled Flying Fox** camps at Cairns, Kuranda, Mareeba, Tolga Scrub, Gordonvale, Port Douglas and Daintree Crossing. **Little Red Flying Foxes** join **Spectacled** camps periodically, for example at Cairns and Daintree; and at two sites all four species have occurred together recently: Finch Hatton (1.22) and Ingham (1.08). Inland, up to 50 000 **Black** and **Little Red Flying Foxes** camp in Lissner Park at Charters Towers, although there are plans to relocate them to Gladstone Creek, 3 km from the CBD.

Two other flying fox species, the **Bare-backed** and **Large-eared Flying Foxes**, are restricted to Cape York rainforests and islands of Torres Strait, respectively. **Least** and **Eastern Blossom Bats**, and **Eastern Tube-nosed Bat** all co-occur on Queensland's eastern seaboard; all occur in the Daintree region and **Eastern Tube-nosed Bats** roost in Mossman Gorge (1.01).

Queensland has 56 microbat species, four of which are endemic and found on the tropical seaboard: **Large-eared Horseshoe Bat**, **Semon's Leaf-nosed Bat**, **Coastal Sheath-tailed Bat** and the extraordinary **Flute-nosed Bat**. The state's bat fauna has complex affinities, overlapping with the bat faunas of New Guinea as well as tropical northern Australia, the inland and southern Australia.

Widespread species that could be encountered in many parts of the state include the **Yellow-bellied Sheath-tailed Bat**, **White-striped Freetail Bat**, **Gould's Wattled** and **Lesser Long-eared Bats**. Those showing southern affinities (**Large**, **Southern** and **Little Forest Bats**, **Chocolate Wattled Bat**, **Eastern False**

Pipistrelle, **Eastern Broad-nosed Bat**, **Gould's** and **Greater Long-eared Bats**) occur mainly in south-east Queensland outside the tropics.

Tropical Queensland has the richest bat assemblage on the continent, with 44 species. Several species are restricted to Cape York Peninsula: the **Fawn Leaf-nosed Bat**, **Papuan Sheath-tailed Bat** and **Cape York Pipistrelle**; the **Papuan Sheath-tailed Bat** and the pipistrelle are still comparatively little known. Several others occur both on Cape York Peninsula and in the Wet Tropics: the **Large-eared Horseshoe Bat**, **Semon's Leaf-nosed Bat**, **Diadem Leaf-nosed Bat**, **Bare-rumped Sheath-tailed Bat**, and the endemic **Coastal Sheath-tailed Bat** (which can be seen roosting around Cairns (1.01)). The mix is further made up of species that occur along most of the eastern seaboard (the **Eastern Horseshoe Bat**, **Eastern Freetail Bat**, **Golden-tipped Bat**, **Eastern Cave Bat**, **Eastern Forest Bat**, **Little Bentwing Bat**, **Large-footed Myotis**, **Greater Broad-nosed Bat** and **Gould's Long-eared Bat**); others whose distributions just creep into Queensland's Gulf region (the **Orange Leaf-nosed Bat**, **Northern Leaf-nosed Bat**, **Troughton's Sheath-tailed Bat**, **Mangrove Pipistrelle** and **Pygmy Long-eared Bat**); and another suite typically found across much of northern Australia: the **Dusky Leaf-nosed Bat**, **Common Sheath-tailed Bat**, **Northern Freetail Bat**, **Little Northern Freetail Bat** (which roosts in large colonies in several coastal towns), **Hoary Wattled Bat** and **Little Broad-nosed Bat**.

Getting to grips with some of this variety will mean joining bat surveys or setting up your own project. However, two cave systems at the western edge of the Wet Tropics, Undarra Lava Tubes NP (1.05) and Chillagoe-Mungana NP (1.06), offer opportunities to see a spectacular flyout and cave-roosting bats, respectively. Further south, **Ghost Bats** hunt at the famous Mt Etna Bat Cleft (1.23); there are also colonies at Cape Hillsborough and in the Mareeba area. **Ghost Bats** formerly occurred inland but these populations have disappeared. Other bats typical of the arid zone include the **Hill's Sheath-tailed Bat**, **Inland Freetail Bat**, **Bristle-faced Freetail Bat**, **Little Pied Bat**, **Inland Cave Bat**, **Inland Forest Bat** and **Inland Broad-nosed Bat**. In the vast flatness of western Queensland any vertical structure might be attractive to microbats as a roost; check abandoned buildings. The old standby of checking under bridges and culverts often pays dividends (although it really slows up those long drives). And don't write off chance observations: **Ghost Bats** have been seen foraging over dams in central Queensland and **Diadem Leaf-nosed Bats** have been observed using telegraph wires as hunting perches along roads behind Ingham.

The Bat House at Cape Tribulation (www.austrop.org.au) can advise good sites to set up a bat detector. The **Eastern Tube-nosed Bat**, **Least** and **Eastern Blossom Bat**, **Little Bentwing Bat** and the rare **Flute-nosed Bat** have been recorded nearby;

> **Spectacled Flying Foxes** fly along the Daintree River at dusk from their camp near Daintree Village. Tolga Bat Hospital on the Atherton Tableland may have some live microbats in care for you to look at and can advise about local flying fox camps.

1.06 CHILLAGOE-MUNGANA CAVES NATIONAL PARK

Highlights: **Eastern Horseshoe Bat, Large Horseshoe Bat, Diadem Leaf-nosed Bat, Common Sheath-tailed Bat, Little Bentwing Bat, Eastern Bentwing Bat, Eastern Cave Bat**

Other possibilities: **Agile Wallaby, Common Wallaroo, Mareeba Rock Wallaby**

The historic mining town of Chillagoe, west of Cairns, and nearby Mungana have several cave systems where there is a chance of seeing several species of microbat. **Little** and **Eastern Bentwing Bats** and the **Common Sheath-tailed Bat** have all been recorded using the caves as roosts; and **Eastern Horseshoe Bats**, **Diadem Leaf-nosed Bats** and **Eastern Cave Bats** also breed here. Rangers sometimes know of 'tame' bats that you could look at relatively closely without disturbing them. Six caves can be visited, although three (Donna, Trezkinn and Royal Arch caves) are by a ranger-guided tour only (tours run daily). The main complex (Donna, Pompeii, Bauhinia and Trezkinn caves) are about 1.8 km south of Chillagoe; Royal Arch Caves is about 6 km south of town. **Little Red**, **Spectacled** and **Black Flying Foxes** visit the area when figs are in fruit, and other species seen in the vicinity include the **Dingo**, **Agile Wallaby**, **Wallaroo**, **Mareeba Rock Wallaby**, **Red-necked Pademelon**, **Bandicoots**, **Northern Quoll** and **Sugar Glider**.

Chillagoe is 215 km (about 3 hours' drive) west of Cairns via Mareeba and Dimbulah. The road is sealed as far as Almaden, after where there are unsealed and sealed sections which may be impassable during the Wet (December–March). Camping is not permitted in the national park; accommodation and meals are available in Chillagoe.

1.07 BRAMSTON BEACH

Highlights: **Dusky Leaf-nosed Bat**

Back on the coast, a small cave on the premises of a rather run-down holiday park supports a small colony of about 150 **Dusky Leaf-nosed Bats**, of both colour phases. Ask for directions to the cave when you seek permission from the park owners to visit it. Bramston Beach is 16.5 km east of the Bruce Hwy (A1); turn off at Mirriwinni 65 km south of Cairns.

As you head south, **Dugongs** and **Australian Snubfin Dolphins** can sometimes be seen from the boat ramp at Cardwell. **Lumholtz's Tree Kangaroo** reaches the southern limit of its distribution in the Cardwell Range, about 12 km north of Ingham. There is likely habitat inside Girringun NP, just west of the Bruce Hwy, but it can be elusive. **Platypuses** occur in Stony Creek below Wallaman Falls and there are also **Musky Rat Kangaroos** here.

1.08 INGHAM AREA

Highlights: **Mahogany Glider**

Other possibilities: **Spectacled Flying Fox, Black Flying Fox, Little Red Flying Fox, Grey-headed Flying Fox**

Australia's rarest gliding marsupial is the **Mahogany Glider**, originally described in 1883 and thought extinct until its serendipitous rediscovery in 1989. It has an extremely restricted range between Ingham and Cardwell at the southern end of the Wet Tropics, and even there is rather elusive. Some private properties put up nest boxes for the gliders, so ask around. Otherwise they may be found on the road to Wallaman Falls in suitable habitat – mixed eucalypt forest, especially where there are flowering eucalypts, such as Bloodwood, Mahogany and Poplar Gum. Barratt's Lagoon about 5 km south of Tully is also supposed to be a good spot. The nearest site for **Squirrel Gliders** appears to be the Princes Hills west of Ingham.

Late in 2012 it was discovered that four species of flying fox – **Spectacled**, **Black**, **Little Red** and **Grey-headed Flying Foxes** – were roosting in scrub behind the botanic gardens in the middle of Ingham. This was the northernmost record for **Grey-headed Flying Fox** and all species except **Little Red** bred in the 2012–13 wet season. The colony has a core of about 4000 **Black Flying Foxes**, with a few **Grey-headed** and **Spectacled**; **Little Red Flying Fox** numbers have spiked at up to 30 000. This site offers an ideal chance to see them all together and compare identification pointers. Check the Australasian Bat Society email discussion list (www.ausbats.org.au) for updates.

1.09 MOUNT CLARO

Highlights: **Mount Claro (Sharman's) Rock Wallaby**

Other possibilities: **Northern Quoll, Rufous Bettong, Euro, Whiptail Wallaby, Red-legged Pademelon**

The 'plain' rock wallaby with the smallest distribution is **Mount Claro Rock Wallaby** (also known as Sharman's Rock Wallaby), which is restricted to a few ranges west of Ingham. It is relatively easy to find at Mt Claro, an obvious rocky hilltop just south of the Lava Plains–Mt Fox Rd west of Ingham. Mt Claro is part of Kilcloonie Station, about 10 km further along this road – ask permission at the station before striking out across the countryside. The wallabies are around the top of the hill, an easy climb from the roadside (you could probably drive to the foot of Mt Claro with a 4WD but it's only a short walk from the roadside). **Mount Claro Rock Wallaby** also occurs at Mt Fox, an extinct crater that forms an outlier of Girringun NP. However, here they mainly inhabit dense scrub in gullies on the crater sides, and would only be seen after dark as there is little cover for them otherwise. **Euros** and **Whiptail Wallabies** also occur here. The turn-off to Mt Fox is 8 km west of the village of Mt Fox.

A rough, unsealed road (4WD advisable) leads south to Hidden Valley and is a short cut to Paluma (1.10). Spotlighting along the Hidden Valley road or even along the road to Ingham, which sees comparatively little traffic, could be good for **Northern Quolls**, **Common Brushtail Possums**, **Red-legged Pademelons**, **Whiptail Wallabies**, **Euros** and **Rufous Bettongs**, **Giant White-tailed Rats** and **Long-nosed** and **Northern Brown Bandicoots**; there are good stands of timber that would be worth spotlighting in for gliders.

1.10 PALUMA

Highlights: **Platypus, Rusty Antechinus**

Other possibilities: **Long-nosed Bandicoot, Swamp Wallaby, Red-necked Pademelon, Giant White-tailed Rat**

The village of Paluma sits at the top of the range, accessed from the coast up a winding road through rainforest. It is a cool, pleasant place with good wildlife and worth an overnight stay. **Rusty Antechinuses** used sometimes to visit bird feeders at guesthouses – ask around to see if there have been any recent sightings. The village is right in the middle of rainforest and there are numerous walking trails. **Green Ringtail Possums**, **Sugar Gliders**, **Rufous Bettongs**, **Agile Wallabies** and **Spectacled Flying Foxes** are all seen around the village. **Platypuses** also occur in mountain streams, such as Birthday Creek, but also at Lake Paluma. To get to both, take the Mount Spec Forestry Rd; the turn-off is 1 km west of the Star Valley Lookout on the road to Hidden Valley; Birthday Creek is 6.8 km along and Lake Paluma a few kilometres further.

Paluma makes a good base for Jourama Falls in Paluma Range NP, where **Mahogany Gliders** occur. To get there drive to the foot of the range and head north on the Bruce Hwy to the Jourama Falls turn-off and the campground 6 km to the west. **Mahogany Gliders** pass through the campground some nights. Be careful with identification – **Sugar Gliders** also occur here.

A few kilometres west of Paluma the rainforest suddenly gives way to tall, drier and more open forest. This forest is particularly good for gliders, with **Feathertail**, **Sugar**, **Squirrel** and **Greater Gliders** all being seen, as well as **Rufous Bettongs**. Hidden

Valley (www.hiddenvalleycabins.com.au) is an eco-lodge with good environmental credentials that runs spotlighting tours, where some or all of these could be located. **Mount Claro Rock Wallabies** occur on the grounds (even around the swimming pool on occasion!) and in nearby gullies. **Platypuses** occur in the Running River; staff should be able to provide directions. The **Eastern Pebble-mound Mouse** and **Eastern Chestnut Mouse** apparently live in suitable habitat in the vicinity.

1.11 MOUNT ZERO-TARAVALE AWC SANCTUARY

Highlights: **Yellow-footed Antechinus, Northern Bettong, Mount Claro Rock Wallaby, Ghost Bat, Flute-nosed Bat, Golden-tipped Bat**

Other possibilities: **Brush-tailed Phascogale, Spot-tailed Quoll, Greater Glider, Sugar Glider, Squirrel Glider, Rufous Bettong, Northern Bettong, Eastern Grey Kangaroo, Eastern Wallaroo, Swamp Wallaby, Agile Wallaby, Whiptail Wallaby, Red-legged Pademelon, White-striped Freetail Bat, Northern Freetail Bat, Gould's Wattled Bat, Hoary Wattled Bat, Dingo**

This amazing sanctuary owned and managed by Australian Wildlife Conservancy (AWC), stretches 30 km west from the edge of the Wet Tropics, straddling the rainforest ecotone and drier savannah on the edge of the Great Dividing Range as far as the Coane Range. A full inventory has yet to be completed, but the sanctuary is thought to protect up to 70 mammal species, including the **Northern Bettong** and **Mount Claro (Sharman's) Rock Wallaby** (both in drier habitats), **Brush-tailed Phascogale** and **Spot-tailed Quoll**. It is known to have one of the highest densities of **Greater Gliders** in Queensland, as well as **Squirrel, Sugar** and **Feathertail Gliders**, and possibly **Yellow-bellied Glider**. Non-gliding arboreal species include **Green** and **Common Ringtail, Common Brushtail** and **Striped Possums**, and an occasional **Koala**. Other macropods include the **Rufous Bettong, Eastern Grey Kangaroo, Eastern Wallaroo, Swamp Wallaby, Agile Wallaby, Whiptail Wallaby** and **Red-legged Pademelon**. The bat fauna is also interesting: this is a known site for the **Flute-nosed Bat**, a little-studied microbat specialised for hunting in misty upland forests. **Ghost Bats** occur here and the list also includes the **Golden-tipped Bat, Northern Long-eared Bat, Yellow-bellied Sheath-tailed Bat, Eastern Cave Bat** (roosting in old tin adits), **White-striped Freetail Bat, Greater Broad-nosed Bat, Little and Eastern Bentwings**, plus **Black, Little Red** and **Spectacled Flying Foxes**, and **Common Blossom Bats**. There are several creek-lined gorges, where **Platypuses** and **Water Rats** live; **Large-footed Myotises** fish still reaches of the streams. Small ground fauna is represented by **Northern Brown** and **Long-nosed Bandicoots**, the isolated northern race of **Yellow-footed Antechinus** and a host of rodents from the rainforest-dwelling **Fawn-footed Melomys** and **Giant White-tailed Rat** to **Common Rock-rats**. Contact AWC for directions and camping arrangements, and also to see if there are any surveys planned.

1.12 MOUNT BARTLE FRERE

Highlights: **Masked White-tailed Rat, Spot-tailed Quoll**

Other possibilities: **Atherton Antechinus, Bush Rat, Giant White-tailed Rat**

One of Queensland's most elusive endemic mammals is the **Masked White-tailed Rat**, which is found only in the Mt Bartle Frere region at the southern end of the Wet Tropics. It is at times reported to be common near the summit, but as this is Queensland's highest mountain it would require a bit of effort to see it. The best access route is from the end of the Gourka road – follow Lake Eacham Rd to Topaz Rd to reach the start of the trail. **Giant White-tailed Rats** and **Bush Rats** should be easily spotlighted before the summit climb, and the rare **Atherton Antechinus** has been reported. **Spot-tailed Quolls** are reputed to hang around the campsite at the summit. A lookout called Lammins Hill is another locality reputed to have a high density of **Masked White-tailed Rats**.

1.13 TOWNSVILLE AND MAGNETIC ISLAND

Highlights: **Koala, Allied Rock Wallaby, Black Flying Fox**

Other possibilities: **Agile Wallaby, Red-necked Wallaby, Rufous Bettong**

The city of Townsville marks more or less the southern limit of the Wet Tropics. It attracts fewer tourists than Cairns and is not as close to rainforest, although it has some worthwhile attractions in its own right. There's a camp of **Black Flying Foxes** at the Palmetum, on the south bank of the Ross River next to the Bruce Hwy, and they can be seen flying around town at dusk. Microbats that flutter around town include the **Bare-rumped Sheath-tailed Bat**, **Hoary Wattled Bat** and **Eastern Bentwing Bat**. At the northern extremity of the city, Cape Pallarenda CP has **Allied Rock Wallabies** and **Agile Wallabies**. However, this park is open only from 6.30 am to 6.30 pm daily; there are more of these macropods, and they are easier to see, in the Mt Elliot section of Bowling Green Bay NP, south of the CBD. Here, at Alligator Creek Campground, the rock wallabies emerge from cover in the late afternoon and evening, or early morning (vanishing into the undergrowth during the heat of the day). **Agile Wallabies** are also common here but you'll have no trouble separating the two when you see them side by side. **Rufous Bettongs** and **Common Brushtail Possums** also occur in the campground.

Magnetic I. is a popular holiday island near Townsville with a healthy population of **Allied Rock Wallabies**, which used to be fed by locals and tourists, although this practice has largely stopped. One of the best places to see them is the old ferry landing at Geoffroy Bay (not the big new terminal at Nelly Bay). To get there head right as you leave the ferry terminal and walk about 2 km along Arcadia Road. Turn right at the road opposite Arcadia Resort and walk another 200 m to the old ferry site; the rock wallabies hang around here. If you take the first morning ferry you can easily see the rock wallabies, have a leisurely breakfast and return to Townsville the same morning. Alternatively, Magnetic I. is a lovely, tranquil spot with good snorkelling and diving that would repay a longer visit. It also has a good population of **Koalas** (introduced in the 1930s and now numbering about 800); the Forts Walk is good for both **Koalas** and **Allied Rock Wallabies**; **Koalas** are also often seen around the old schoolhouse in Horseshoe Bay and it would be worth poking around in the old WWII gun emplacements for roosting microbats. The trail starts from the junction of Radical and Horseshoe Bay roads, about 2 km north of Alma Bay. Watch for cetaceans such as **Indo-Pacific Humpback Dolphins** in Townsville Harbour and during the crossing.

Northern Quolls are reputed to survive at the tip of Cape Cleveland in the coastal section of Bowling Green Bay NP (south of Townsville), especially in the rocks around the AIMS complex. **Humpback Whales** have been seen from Cape Cleveland and **Dugongs** live in Bowling Green Bay. West of Townsville, the Hervey's Range Developmental Rd leads to the Gregory Developmental Rd on the western side of the Divide. By spotlighting along Pandanus Rd there's a chance of seeing the **Spectacled Hare-wallaby**, as well as more common macropods such as **Red Kangaroos**, **Euros** and **Eastern Grey Kangaroos**.

THE BIG FIVE

Some of Queensland's Big Five can readily be seen in the south-east, although Common Wombats are scarce and Platypus-watching is probably easier in the north.

Kangaroo Eastern Grey Kangaroos are common at many sites between the Atherton Tableland and Brisbane; they can be seen at Karawatha FR near Brisbane (1.33).

Koala Parts of Queensland still support good numbers of Koalas and they can readily be seen at Noosa NP (1.39), near Brisbane (1.33) and at Magnetic I. (1.13).

Wombat Why not volunteer some time to help the conservation of the rare and endemic Northern Hairy-nosed Wombat at Epping NP (1.26)?

Platypus Queensland is also a great destination for Platypus sightings; prime spots include Eungella NP (1.22), Yungaburra (1.04f) and Kingfisher Park (1.03) on the Atherton Tableland.

Whale Hervey Bay (1.40) is the home of the state's Humpback Whale–watching industry and there is great land-based viewing from Point Lookout (1.35).

B CAPE YORK PENINSULA AND TORRES STRAIT

There is a lot more of Queensland north of 'Far North Queensland' – including about 1000 km of Cape York Peninsula (CYP) and a chain of islands in Torres Strait, the body of water between Cape York itself and mainland New Guinea. This region has strong biological links with New Guinea and some species common to both areas do not occur further south, including several microbats, two species of flying fox and two of cuscus. The Great Barrier Reef stretches as far as Torres Strait, and inshore, between Cape York and Cooktown, is important for **Dugongs**, especially the Princess Charlotte Bay area. The highest concentration of Dugongs in the world is in Torres Strait itself. The highest terrestrial mammal diversity is in the rainforests on the east coast at, for example, Iron Range NP (1.17); several other tropical savannah species occur over most of the peninsula. No fewer than 32 microbat species have been recorded from the Cape York region. Of these, three are more or less restricted to the peninsula (some also occur in New Guinea): **Large-eared Horseshoe Bat, Fawn Leaf-nosed Bat** and **Papuan Sheath-tailed Bat**.

The trip to Cape York is an adventure, especially by road. Those with limited time can fly to Lockhart River and hire a vehicle to get to Iron Range, and there are several good accommodation options as well as camping. Much of CYP is inaccessible during the Wet, especially by road – check conditions before you set out. Apart from a few short sections, most of the Peninsula Developmental Rd is unsealed and a high-clearance 4WD is essential.

1.14 COOKTOWN AREA

Highlights: **Bennett's Tree Kangaroo, Northern Nailtail Wallaby, Cape York Rock Wallaby, Godman's Rock Wallaby**

Other possibilities: **Northern Quoll, Long-tailed Pygmy Possum, Eastern Horseshoe Bat, Prehensile-tailed Rat**

Black Mountain is a massive pile of volcanic boulders next to the highway south of Cooktown. It is a strange sight, caused by the fracturing and weathering of an ancient granite mass as it cooled (the black coloration is caused by a coating of lichen on the boulders). This is probably the most accessible place for the **Godman's Rock Wallaby**. They can be seen by scanning from the lookout at dusk or spotlighting at night, but be prepared to put in some time – the rock wallabies are small and the boulders are big. The crevices and caves provide innumerable shelters for other species: **Northern Quolls** are resident here and can occasionally be spotlighted near the lookout; **Spectacled Flying Foxes** and **Ghost Bats** also roost among the boulders.

Mungumby Lodge (www.mungumby.com) is a comfortable setup that makes an ideal base to look for **Bennett's Tree Kangaroos**. They occur sporadically on the lodge grounds and it would be worth asking management if any have been seen recently; spotlighting in the lodge grounds should also yield **Agile Wallabies**, **Antilopine Wallaroos** and with luck a **Striped Possum** or **Sugar Glider**. Ask the owners to put you in touch with a local naturalist who may be able to help you to locate a **Bennett's Tree Kangaroo** or **Long-tailed Pygmy Possum** , which are known to occur in the nearby Shipton's Flat area, as well as the **Prehensile-tailed Rat**. Other species that occur in the area include the **Long-nosed Bandicoot**, **Fawn-footed Melomys**, **Spectacled Flying Fox**, **Northern Quoll** and **Feathertail Glider**. **Eastern Horseshoe Bats** have been known to feed around the lights at the Lion's Den Hotel in Shipton's Flat.

1.15 MARY VALLEY STATION

Highlights: **Little Red Flying Fox**

Other possibilities: **Black Flying Fox, Spectacled Flying Fox**

This popular dry-season campground hosts a vast colony of mainly **Little Red Flying Foxes** – up to five million of them at times – but also **Black** and some **Spectacled Flying Foxes**. Mary Valley makes a convenient place to camp for the night on your way up the Peninsula.

1.16 LAKEFIELD NATIONAL PARK

Highlights: **Northern Nailtail Wallaby, Antilopine Wallaroo, Cape York Rock Wallaby**

Other possibilities: **Echidna, Agile Wallaby, Little Red Flying Fox**

Lakefield (also known as Rinyirru) NP is Queensland's second-largest national park, a wilderness of savannah woodland and flooding plains at the butt of Princess Charlotte Bay. Marina Plains in the north-west of the park is the place to look for the **Northern Nailtail Wallaby**, and **Agile Wallabies** also occur here; spotlight along Marina Plains Rd. Try also Nifold Plain beyond Saltwater Creek. **Echidnas** and **Little Red Flying Foxes** are common in the park. Access to the park from the south is via Laura; if you exit the park west along Marina Plains Rd you can save a large detour and end up at Musgrave (see below). Staff at Lotusbird Lodge (www.lotusbird.com.au) are very helpful with guiding and advice.

Northern Nailtail Wallabies are also common by the airstrip near Musgrave River Roadhouse. Nearby Artemis Station has **Cape York Rock Wallabies**, the least known of all the rock wallabies (it has apparently never been photographed alive). Artemis Station is accessible only with permission, but as birdwatchers often visit permission is usually granted. Take the Edward River road west out of Musgrave and head for a sandstone escarpment, about 10 km away. After about 9 km the road gets closer to the hills; park and walk in to look for **Cape York Rock Wallabies**. They can be elusive and shy, and there is plenty of vine scrub for them to hide in – be prepared to put in some work and time. Watch for **Antilopine Wallaroos** on the drive in.

The next major settlement on the way north is Coen. **Antilopine Wallaroos** and **Agile Wallabies** should be seen roadside at dawn and dusk; **Northern Nailtails** are apparently common on the road past the town rubbish dump.

1.17 IRON RANGE NATIONAL PARK

Highlights: **Cinnamon Antechinus, Rufous Spiny Bandicoot, Southern Common Cuscus, Common Spotted Cuscus, Striped Possum, Bare-backed Fruit Bat, Cape York Melomys, Cape York Rat, Giant White-tailed Rat**

Other possibilities: **Southern Brown Bandicoot, Spectacled Flying Fox, Prehensile-tailed Rat**

The largest surviving tract of lowland rainforest in Australia is protected in Iron Range NP north of Coen. This is a must for any serious naturalist, with many endemic species and subspecies, and it is the easiest place to see several mammals found elsewhere only in New Guinea. There is much to see during the day – this is a prime birding site – but spotlighting for extended periods, preferably over several nights, is the way to see a good selection of mammals. Rainforest around Gordon Creek campsite and the Claudie River crossing are good places to start (beware of crocs). The **Common Spotted Cuscus** is more abundant than the **Southern Common Cuscus** (so-called because it is the commoner of the two in New Guinea, but they are easier to see here, where they don't get hunted); the former should be seen fairly easily. Other readily seen species include the **Giant White-tailed Rat**, **Cape York Melomys**, **Spectacled Flying Fox** (a few hundred occur at Iron Range – beware of mistaking them for **Bare-backed Flying Foxes**) and **Dingo**. The **Rufous Spiny Bandicoot** is one of the target species here; at times it is common, at others elusive, and be aware that **Long-nosed**, **Northern Brown** *and* **Southern Brown Bandicoots** also occur in the area (the latter is an outlying population, living several thousand kilometres away from its nearest congeners).

Listen for the high-pitched 'peep' sound of **Eastern Tube-nosed Bats** around fruiting cauliferous figs, which you should stake out during the day. **Bare-backed Fruit Bats** are another Iron Range specialty and probably best detected by the 'whop-whop-whop' sound they make in flight, caused by pockets of air trapped by their distinctive wing morphology. They often feed in gardens at Portland Roads – ask locals, who usually have an idea of what's around. **Eastern** and **Large-eared Horseshoe Bats** and **Fawn** and **Diadem Leaf-nosed Bats** roost in a gated mine near Gordon Creek campsite. The **Cinnamon Antechinus** is common in rainforest.

Great rainforest can be reached from Portland Roads, where there are guesthouses, a store and cafés. Hire car is available if you've flown in but do book ahead. It is possible to walk from Portland Roads to the campground but after a long day and evening in the field a vehicle makes sense. There are campgrounds in the national park itself.

Much of Cape York's vastness is covered in tropical savannah, dissected by waterways lined with rainforest and floristically rich heathlands. Some rainforest species, such as bandicoots and the **Common Spotted Cuscus**, can be found a long way from rainforests. Another CYP endemic, the **Chestnut Dunnart**, lives in tropical heath – you'll need to be part of a survey team in the right habitat for this one.

1.18 TORRES STRAIT

Highlights: **Grassland Melomys**

Other possibilities: **Black Flying Fox, Large-eared Flying Fox, Dugong, Timor Deer (ssp.** *moluccensis* **)**

In prehistoric times rising sea levels created the Torres Strait between what is now Cape York Peninsula and the island of New Guinea, as well as hundreds of islands ranging in size from inhabited Muralag and Mua to rocks barely large enough to support a lighthouse. No mammals are endemic to this area and terrestrial mammals are quite scarce on all islands, although the area is surprisingly little-known biogeographically. The greatest diversity is found on the larger, western islands. A long history of human habitation has doubtless taken its toll of edible mammals: the **Agile Wallaby** formerly occurred on larger islands, such as Muralug and has most probably been hunted out – if it ever occurred naturally (islanders have moved potential food animals all over the south-west Pacific). Thus records of **Echidna** and **Northern Brown Bandicoot** on Mua could be of translocated food species. The **Grassland Melomys** is the most widespread terrestrial mammal and known from Dauan, Boigu and Saibai. A small herd of the **Moluccan** subspecies of **Timor (Rusa) Deer** *Cervus timorensis moluccensis* occurs on Saibai, self-introduced by swimming across from New Guinea, 3–4 kilometres distant (Rusa that occur elsewhere in Australia, such as Sydney's Royal NP, are of the Javan subspecies *C. t. russa*). **Water Rats** have been recorded on Badu and may well occur on other islands.

The bat fauna is better known. **Black Flying Foxes** island-hop across Torres Strait, and are common on Boigu and Saibai, just off the southern coast of PNG. The **Little Red Flying Fox** has been recorded on some islands and the **Spectacled Flying Fox** has occurred. The **Large-eared Flying Fox**, a species from lowland PNG and Indonesia, apparently crosses from New Guinea to Boigu and Saibai and a small camp has been reported near the airstrip on Saibai. Torresian Tube-nosed Bat was formerly thought to occur on Mua, but this now seems unlikely and the **Eastern Tube-nosed**

Bat is the only member of this genus that has been confirmed here. It and the **Least Blossom Bat** have been recorded near St Paul's village on Mua. Microbats recorded in Torres Strait include **Dusky** and **Fawn Leaf-nosed Bats**, **Large-footed Myotis**, **Little** and **Eastern Bentwing Bats** (which use bunkers and stormwater drains under the airport at Horn I.), **Little Broad-nosed Bat**, **Northern Long-eared Bat**, **Forest Pipistrelle** and **Northern Pipistrelle**. **Coastal Sheath-tailed Bats** roost in abandoned WWII bunkers on Mua I. and in mines on Possession I., as well as cave roosts in the Albany Passage. Unidentified sheath-tailed and blossom bats have been spotlighted on Boigu – hitherto unrecorded species could cross from New Guinea.

Torres Strait supports the largest **Dugong** population in the world (estimated at 15 000), especially in seagrass beds around Badu, Buru and Gabba islands. These animals are hunted by Indigenous people here and although there is no evidence of decline, watching Dugongs elsewhere might be a more aesthetic experience.

The Torres Strait area is seldom visited by naturalists, mainly owing to the distance and expense involved. Waiben (formerly known as Thursday I.) is the main hub, serviced daily by flights from Cairns. A cargo ship also plies this route and takes passengers for whom time is not an issue. Otherwise, Birding Tours Australia (see Appendix B) runs boat-based trips to Boigu and Saibai Is.; obviously these have a bird focus but mammals are often sighted. If you are travelling independently, note that permission is needed to visit some islands.

1.19 BRAMBLE CAY

Highlights: **Bramble Cay Melomys**

A visit to this remote island will put you in an exclusive club – it sits at the top end of the Great Barrier Reef, east of PNG's great Fly River, and supports the world's only known population of **Bramble Cay Melomys**. Until recently, at least: an expedition to assess its status failed to find any trace of it in 2012 and it was last seen by scientists in 2004. It was the only terrestrial mammal known from the island, which is about 350 m long and about 140 m wide, so if you get there identification should be assured. It was thought to burrow among beach jetsam, emerging at night to forage. However, low-lying Bramble Cay (also known as Maizab Kaur) is subject to storm surge and recently has been almost entirely denuded of vegetation by nesting seabirds and sea turtles; there is a good chance the melomys may already be extinct. A private yacht charter is the only likely method of visiting Bramble Cay.

C CENTRAL QUEENSLAND COAST

Between the Wet Tropics and south-east Queensland, the main southern centre for biodiversity, is another vast distance. If you have the time to drive south along the coast, there are many worthwhile diversions. Much of the coast was formerly covered in lowland rainforest, all but a few pockets now cleared for agriculture. The Great Barrier Reef accompanies the highway offshore for most of the way and there are several excellent areas to visit. The central part of the reef has important concentrations of **Dugongs**, especially near Gladstone (where **Indo-Pacific Humpback Dolphins** can be seen in the harbor early mornings); **Humpback Whales** could be seen offshore almost anywhere in season; what is believed to be the southernmost population of **Snubfin Dolphins**, which numbers about 100, inhabits the Fitzroy River mouth near Rockhampton. Blackdown Tableland is an isolated massif that is little-visited by naturalists and supports outlying populations of **Sugar** and **Yellow-bellied Gliders**.

1.20 MOUNT INKERMAN

Highlights: **Unadorned Rock Wallaby**

About 11 km south of Home Hill, the massive outcrop of Mt Inkerman looms on the seaward side of the Bruce Hwy. **Unadorned Rock Wallabies** can be seen at the picnic area near the summit in the late evening and early morning. It's about a 20-minute detour but only worthwhile at the right time of day (early morning or evening) – rock wallabies can make themselves scarce during hot weather!

Unadorned Rock Wallabies can also be seen at one of the caravan parks at Horseshoe Bay in Bowen, another coastal town you'll pass through on the way south; ask at the tourist office if they know which one. They sit on roofs and car bonnets, providing interesting photo opportunities. **Humpback Whales** can sometimes be seen from Flagstaff Hill in Bowen.

1.21 AIRLIE BEACH AND PETER FAUST DAM

Highlights: **Unadorned Rock Wallaby, Proserpine Rock Wallaby**

Other possibilities: **Echidna, Common Brushtail, Greater Glider, Squirrel Glider, Agile Wallaby**

The **Unadorned Rock Wallaby** is part of the complex of seven closely related Queensland rock wallaby species and is sympatric in this part of the Queensland coast with the distinctive **Proserpine Rock Wallaby**. Both can be seen in close proximity at the Peter Faust Dam, 25 km west of Proserpine. **Unadorned Rock Wallabies** loiter on the dam wall and should be easy to see, especially in the evening. **Proserpine Rock Wallabies** are specialists of rainforest vine thickets; they are very shy and rarely stray far from cover. They could be spotlighted here but be aware that the Unadorned Rock Wallabies also leave the safety of the dam wall and forage in roadside undergrowth. Seeing a rock wallaby away from the dam wall does not guarantee it's a

Proserpine Rock Wallaby! **Echidnas**, **Whiptail** and **Agile Wallabies** and **Common Brushtail Possums** also occur.

For another crack at the **Proserpine Rock Wallaby**, the popular tourist town of Airlie Beach is a good bet. The wallabies sometimes feed on verges and lawns in the higher parts of town on the slopes of Mt Lucas. Unfortunately they too frequently become roadkill. Ask around for good sites – you are more likely to see them late in the evening, especially once traffic has died down a bit.

Proserpine Rock Wallabies also occur naturally on a few islands, including Gloucester I., in the Whitsunday group, one of the main tourist draws in this part of the Queensland coast. And a number were introduced to Hayman I. as an insurance population and this is a good bet for seeing it, although you would probably have to overnight so you can hit the trails early in the morning and that would mean staying in the island's expensive resort. Hayman I. is served by daily ferries.

1.22 EUNGELLA NATIONAL PARK

Highlights: **Platypus**

Other possibilities: **Common Brushtail Possum, Greater Glider, Sugar Glider, Black Flying Fox, Little Red Flying Fox, Spectacled Flying Fox, Grey-headed Flying Fox**

This beautiful remnant patch of upland rainforest is one of the best places in the country to see **Platypuses**. One of the best areas is near Broken River Mountain Resort, 6 km south of Eungella township. Park on the south side of the bridge over Broken River and walk the short distance to the bank, where upstream there is a Platypus viewing platform and downstream a rock pool. **Platypuses** can be seen along the entire stretch in between – a path follows the river under the bridge. Sometimes several are seen in close proximity and they may come almost within arm's reach at the viewing platform. Early morning in winter is the best time to look; obviously, fewer people will improve the experience, but the animals seem unconcerned. They can also be seen from the pedestrian walkway on the bridge itself. Broken River Mountain Resort (www.brokenrivermr.com.au) runs nocturnal spotlighting tours to look at mammals and other wildlife, which includes two colour phases of the **Common Brushtail Possum**, plus **Rufous Bettongs**, **Red-necked Pademelons** and **Greater**, **Sugar** and sometimes **Feathertail Gliders**. The **Swamp Rat** also occurs here.

Eungella township is 80 km inland from Mackay on the Mackay-Eungella Rd. If coming from the north it's worth missing Mackay – turn west off the Bruce Hwy 91 km south of Proserpine and drive 9 km to Marian to join the Mackay-Eungella Rd (more at www.eungella.com.au).

En route to Eungella, Finch Hatton Gorge is another scenic attraction and a popular outdoor activities centre nearby – Forest Flying (www.forestflying.com) features a flying fox camp where four species have roosted together. In fact, you can ride a flying fox (zipline) to watch the flying foxes at eye level! Until they were detected at the Ingham camp (1.08), this was the most northerly location known for the **Grey-headed Flying Fox**.

1.23 MOUNT ETNA CAVES NATIONAL PARK

Highlights: **Ghost Bat, Little Bentwing Bat**

Other possibilities: **Common Brushtail Possum, Unadorned Rock Wallaby**

This unique area of limestone outcrops and caves nearly ended up as the main ingredient for cement manufacture. Never mind that it sheltered 80 per cent of Australia's breeding **Little Bentwing Bats** and a significant **Ghost Bat** colony. After a prolonged dispute, what was left of the site was preserved as a national park that supports a large maternity colony of **Little Bentwing Bats** and a significant remnant population of **Ghost Bats**. The bentwings are present in the summer months (December–February), when they give birth. **Ghost Bats** are present year-round but are hard to see; they wait near the Bat Cleft, where the bentwings emerge, to hunt at dusk. You can visit the Bat Cleft independently only between March and October; otherwise it is closed while the bats are breeding (1 November until the end of February), but you can take a ranger-guided tour to see the fly-out between early December and mid-February. **Unadorned Rock Wallabies** and **Common Brushtail Possums** hang around the car park and visitors' centre at night.

Mount Etna is 26 km north of Rockhampton. Turn off the Bruce Hwy 24 km from Rocky to The Caves township. The park entrance and information centre is 2 km further along the Barmpoya Rd, then Cammoo Caves Rd. It is a popular tourist site, with motel-style accommodation (booking is essential in bat season). Access to the Bat Cleft is via Rossmoya Rd.

1.24 WESTWOOD

Highlights: **Herbert's Rock Wallaby**

The south bank of the Fitzroy River, near the city of Rockhampton, marks the northward distribution of **Herbert's Rock Wallabies**, the last of the 'plain' rock wallaby group you'll encounter as you head south. One of the best sites to see it is on a rocky bluff 3 km west of Westwood. You can't miss the hill, but you'll need binoculars and preferably a spotting scope to pick up the rock wallabies at a distance. The hill is on private property, but if you ask the owners they will probably let you wander over their land for a closer look. Westwood is 50 km south-west of 'Rocky' on the Capricorn Hwy (A4); the hill is between the town and the junction of the Leichhardt Hwy (A5) to the south. This species also occurs at Mt Jim Crow NP east of Rockhampton on the road to Yeppoon.

D WESTERN QUEENSLAND AND GULF COUNTRY

Much of Outback Queensland is baking hot, featureless cattle country with little of interest to the naturalist; luckily many of the best sites are preserved in national parks where some interesting species can be seen. The Outback is way too big to wander around randomly (unless you have lots of time to spare) so plan ahead to get the most out of it. The chief areas to concentrate on are the region south of the Gulf of Carpentaria (most easily reached from Townsville), a few choice national parks in the central-west and the Channel Country in the extreme south-west. Note that mobile camps of **Little Red Flying Foxes** could appear in many Outback towns, especially during 'good' years. They follow eucalyptus flowering events for hundreds of kilometres along watercourses and have camped at, for example, Barcaldine, Alpha and Pittsworth in central Queensland. There's also a well-known camp in Lissner Park, Charters Towers, where **Black Flying Foxes** have roosted since the 1930s and **Little Reds** have appeared since 2000. This site has been subject to some vigorous, controversial and, so far, unsuccessful dispersal efforts.

Allow at least a day's drive between each of these sites, then as much time as possible at the sites themselves, as you will only be able to look for wildlife comfortably in the cooler parts of the day and at night. Sites are placed here in rough order from north to south. There are plenty of Outback towns to restock in but it's a long way between stops. At all times carry adequate water, emergency supplies and vehicle spares, such as tyres; people die out here from dehydration and lack of experience driving on Outback roads.

1.25 TAUNTON SCIENTIFIC RESERVE

Highlights: **Bridled Nailtail Wallaby, Black-striped Wallaby**

Other possibilities: **Echidna, Rufous Bettong, Eastern Grey Kangaroo**

One of the most startling mammal discoveries of the 20th century was the reappearance of the **Bridled Nailtail Wallaby** after it was thought extinct for 35 years. Formerly widespread, it was hunted extensively for its attractive pelt and was presumed extinct by the 1930s … until the 1970s, when a fencing contractor read an article about it and realised he had seen them at a property where he had been working. That population is now protected at Taunton SR, where about 150 survive thanks to feral animal control. Recently cattle have been reintroduced to the park in an effort to control buffel grass, an introduced weed that chokes vast areas of Queensland. Access to Taunton is strictly controlled, although you may be able to accompany a parks official or researcher on a visit. **Echidnas**, **Rufous Bettongs**, **Black-striped Wallabies** and **Eastern Grey Kangaroos** also occur here. There is another population of **Bridled Nailtails** at Avocet Station, a working cattle station about 270 km west of Rocky. This species has also been reintroduced to several sites where it formerly occurred, including Scotia Sanctuary (2.29) and Idalia NP (1.31). Taunton is about 150 km west of Rockhampton (about 2 hours' drive) north of the town of Dingo on the Capricorn Hwy. That a comparatively large mammal such as Bridled Nailtail Wallaby should survive unnoticed for so long testifies to the vastness of the Queensland Outback, but also gives hope that other long-lost inland species may 'reappear' one day.

1.26 EPPING FOREST NATIONAL PARK

Highlights: **Northern Hairy-nosed Wombat, Spectacled Hare-wallaby**

Other possibilities: **Echidna, Sugar Glider, Rufous Bettong, Eastern Grey Kangaroo, Swamp Wallaby**

A tiny dot on the map of Queensland marks Epping Forest NP, the last stronghold of the **Northern Hairy-nosed Wombat**. Access to the park is restricted and by permit only, but if you did a stint as a volunteer warden you would have a very good chance of seeing the world's rarest wombat. The reserve is fenced to keep out predators and the wombats seem to be doing well; recently several were translocated to other reserves, where they have bred. All known active burrows are monitored and the animals can sometimes be seen near the park headquarters. **Eastern Grey Kangaroos** and **Swamp Wallabies** are common at Epping, and there is a very good chance of seeing **Rufous Bettongs** and **Spectacled Hare-wallabies** on a night drive. **Sugar Gliders** occur near park HQ and **Echidnas** are sometimes seen. Inquiries about volunteering can be made at the Rockhampton office of the Queensland national parks service.

1.27 BLUFF DOWNS

Highlights: **Rufous Bettong, Black-striped Wallaby, Allied Rock Wallaby**

Other possibilities: **Eastern Grey Kangaroo, Black Flying Fox, [Chital]**

This working cattle station is a pleasant place to stay, with a variety of accommodation options including camping. There is a feral herd of **Chital** deer and spotlighting could yield **Black-striped Wallabies** and **Rufous Bettongs**. Bluff Downs is 170 km west of Townsville (about 2.5 hour's drive).

1.28 MT ISA

Highlights: **Purple-necked Rock Wallaby, Black Flying Fox, Little Red Flying Fox**

Other possibilities: **Euro, Troughton's Sheath-tailed Bat**

Mt Isa is a mining town in far western Queensland nearly 1000 km from the east coast. It makes a good departure point for expeditions into remote parts of the Gulf, and the endemic **Purple-necked Rock Wallaby** is found on the city outskirts. The closest site to Mt Isa for it is a rocky ridge about 200 m south of the Pamela St reservoir, on the eastern edge of town. Park at the water tank, walk east about 50 m and then follow a well-defined track southwards up a steep valley. Scan the ridges and ledges from a high point; the rock wallabies are usually sunning late in the afternoon. Another accessible site for the **Purple-necked Rock Wallaby** is at Mica Creek, 13 km south of town on the Diamantina Developmental Rd. Park about 100 m before the Mica Creek causeway and head west into the low, rocky hills. They can also be seen at Lake Moondarra, an artificial lake 20 km north of town; turn off the Barkly Hwy 5 km north of Mt Isa and follow the lake access road approximately 14 km to the turn-off to the water ski club. Follow this to some low cliffs near the end of the track; the rock wallabies should be visible along these cliffs. Other sites include West Leichhardt Station and the rocks around Spider Bore. **Euros** also inhabit these slopes and you shouldn't have any trouble seeing them.

The area is the core distribution for **Troughton's Sheath-tailed Bat**. At the eastern edge of town you'll pass a rocky hill with a telecoms tower on top; **Troughton's** and **Common Sheath-tailed Bats** have been seen in caves on the northern side of the hill. **Little Red Flying Foxes** form seasonal camps near Mt Isa, typically at the town cemetery and the Tony White Oval; ask around for updates or to see if the camps are active. **Spectacled Hare-wallabies** could possibly be seen by spotlighting along roads north of Mt Isa. Coming from the east, there are **Allied Rock Wallabies** at Chinaman Creek dam, off the Barkly Hwy just west of Cloncurry, where they feed around the picnic ground.

Note that it gets intensely hot out here, and searching will always be more fruitful and more comfortable in the (very) early morning and late evening. Always carry adequate water with you. There are plenty of campgrounds, hotels, motels and eateries in Mt Isa.

1.29 BOODJAMULLA (LAWN HILL) NATIONAL PARK

Highlights: **Rock Ringtail Possum, Northern Nailtail Wallaby, Purple-necked Rock Wallaby, Common Rock-rat, Dingo**

Other possibilities: **Echidna, Red Kangaroo, Agile Wallaby, Antilopine Wallaroo, Euro, Little Red Flying Fox**

The effort of reaching Boodjamulla will be amply repaid by the stunning scenery, tranquil gorges and Aboriginal rock art, but mainly because it is the best place in Queensland to see the **Rock Ringtail Possum**, a species that is more widespread and common in the Top End. There are plenty of rocky sites to search for it in, including an outcrop a few kilometres back from the campground along the access road. Other rock-loving species recorded here include the **Common Rock-rat**, and any rock wallabies you see will be of the **Purple-necked** variety. Other macropods include

Agile Wallabies, **Antilopine Wallaroos** and **Euros**; **Red Kangaroos** occur on the plains outside the park. The park has an impressive bat list, with 15 species including the **Ghost Bat**, and some more typical of further west, such as **Orange Leaf-nosed**, and **Arnhem** and **Pygmy Long-eared Bats**, or the arid zone (**Inland Forest** and **Inland Cave Bats**). Boodjamulla is 340 km north-west of Mt Isa (about 4–5 hours' driving); the last 215 km is on unsealed roads which can be potholed and corrugated in places. A 4WD is recommended and essential after rain – check road conditions before you set out. There is a campground but book ahead (www.qld.gov.au/camping) for the dry months (generally Easter to October). There is a store with petrol and a tented camp if you're not self-sufficient.

1.30 CAMOOWEAL CAVES NATIONAL PARK

Highlights: **Ghost Bat**

This cave system south of Camooweal is still a stronghold for **Ghost Bats** in western Queensland, although they are apparently getting rarer. They roost in 4-mile East Cave, but do not disturb the bats at their roost – wait near the cave entrance at dusk to see if any emerge to hunt. Camooweal is the last town before the NT border as you head west.

1.31 IDALIA NATIONAL PARK

Highlights: **Bridled Nailtail Wallaby, Black-striped Wallaby, Yellow-footed Rock Wallaby**

Other possibilities: **Echidna, Red Kangaroo, Eastern Grey Kangaroo, Western Grey Kangaroo, Euro**

Idalia is one of the best sites for macropods in western Queensland and is being intensively managed for feral predators. A section has been fenced to encourage the establishment of **Bridled Nailtail Wallabies**, which were introduced here as an insurance population.

1.32 SOUTH-WEST QUEENSLAND AND CHANNEL COUNTRY

Highlights: **Kowari, Brush-tailed Mulgara, Crest-tailed Mulgara, Greater Bilby, Red Kangaroo, Western Grey Kangaroo, Euro, Long-haired Rat**

Other possibilities: **Long-tailed Planigale, Lesser Hairy-footed Dunnart, Hairy-footed Dunnart, Fat-tailed Dunnart, Sandy Inland Mouse, Spinifex Hopping-mouse**

Rutted and bone dry most of the time, the remote, almost uninhabited south-west corner is an arid wilderness that shimmers under hundreds of square kilometres of floodwater after periodic rains. It is a challenging place to visit but as floodwaters recede the desert bursts into life. This is the best time to visit for any chance of seeing the myriad small mammals adapted to survive one of the most challenging environments in the country. **Red Kangaroos, Western Grey Kangaroos** and **Euros** are common in suitable areas – the former on open plains, **Western Greys** in more wooded habitat and **Euros** on rocky hills and breakaways. **Echidnas** of course could be encountered nearly anywhere, although they may be nocturnal in hot conditions. Most famous of the smaller inhabitants is probably the **Long-haired Rat**, which appears in plague proportions when conditions are good, then virtually vanishes from the landscape in dry times. During dry times the biggest concentrations of these will be along better-vegetated channels. For example, it was abundant at Lochern NP in March 2011 after good rains, making a nuisance of itself to campers. This is probably the small mammal you are most likely to see and identify in the field; there is no substitute for joining a survey or research team for a chance of seeing a few of the others.

Bush Heritage (www.bushheritage.org.au) manages two adjoining sanctuaries on the north-eastern edge of the Simpson Desert: Ethabuka and Craven's Peak. Ethabuka protects a network of floodplains and dunes while to the north Craven's Peak protects some arid-zone peaks and has populations of the **Mulgara** and **Ampurta**. A good selection of other dasyurids and rodents has also been recorded, including the **Wongai Ningaui, Narrow-nosed Planigale, Lesser Hairy-footed, Hairy-footed** and **Stripe-faced Dunnarts, Long-haired Rat** (in season), **Sandy Inland Mouse, Desert Mouse** and **Spinifex Hopping-mouse**.

Some 20 species of bat have been recorded in the Channel Country, ranging from the nomadic **Little Red Flying Fox** and fast-flying **Yellow-bellied Sheath-tailed Bat** to the cave-dwelling **Hill's Sheath-tailed Bat**. Bat diversity is highest along waterways. **Troughton's Sheath-tailed Bat** has been recorded roosting at Stonehenge on Westerton Station.

Bilbies occur in Diamantina and Astrebla Downs NP; search for suitable habitat and traces such as tracks, scats and burrows, then stake out a likely looking area. Beware though that they are exclusively nocturnal in this part of their range. You simply won't see them until after dark, sometimes not till after midnight and possibly not at all on moonlit nights. Contact the Save the Bilby Fund (www.savethebilbyfund.com) about volunteering at its predator exclosure near Currawinya, about 180 km south-west of Cunnamulla.

E SOUTH-EAST QUEENSLAND

Queensland's south-east is another biodiversity hotspot, with many endemic species (some shared with adjoining parts of northern NSW – see Chapter 2). Superb reserves such as Lamington NP (1.37) and near-natural areas such as Moreton Bay (1.34) and

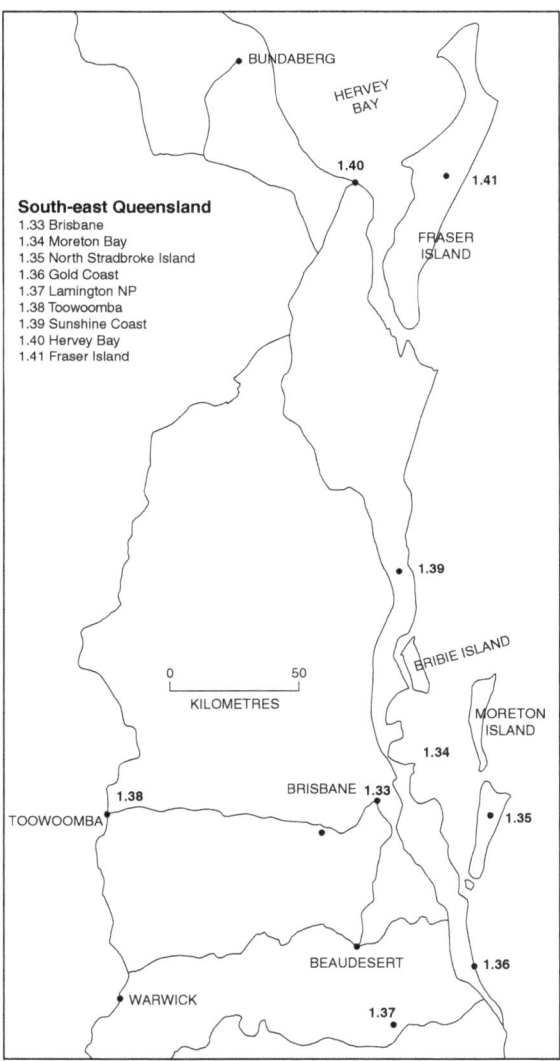

South-east Queensland
1.33 Brisbane
1.34 Moreton Bay
1.35 North Stradbroke Island
1.36 Gold Coast
1.37 Lamington NP
1.38 Toowoomba
1.39 Sunshine Coast
1.40 Hervey Bay
1.41 Fraser Island

North Stradbroke I. (1.35) are within easy reach of the capital Brisbane. Brisbane itself has many pockets suitable for wildlife, despite a fast-growing population and a rather desperate urban sprawl stretching from the NSW border to the Sunshine Coast (1.39). Fraser I., the world's largest sand island, marks the northern limits of this section – a distance of about 350 km from the Tweed River in the south. Adjoining Fraser I. is Hervey Bay, the original home of whale-watching in Australia and still one of the best places in the world to watch **Humpback Whales**.

Brisbane is a logical starting point for this part of Queensland and has an international airport, and freeway and rail links to other parts of the state and northern NSW. The CBD has plenty of eating and sleeping options, but there are many more pleasant places to stay a short drive away. This section is arranged with Brisbane as the starting point, working roughly clockwise to the Sunshine and Fraser Coasts.

1.33 GREATER BRISBANE

Highlights: **Squirrel Glider, Koala, Black Flying Fox, Grey-headed Flying Fox, Little Red Flying Fox**

Other possibilities: **Sugar Glider, Indo-Pacific Humpback Dolphin**

Brisbane sits on the western shore of Moreton Bay, a vast, shallow bay sheltered by Moreton and North Stradbroke Is. Wildlife is generally abundant in Queensland's largest city, and well documented by an army of enthusiasts and a dedicated research community. Numerous urban parks in near-natural condition support a good variety of wildlife, and the rainforested hills to the south and west offer excellent wildlife-watching just an hour or so from the city centre. Flying foxes will probably be the first native mammals you encounter and three species are abundant in the Greater Brisbane area: **Grey-headed** (resident and most abundant May–December), **Black** (resident, with numbers peaking September–November) and **Little Red** (usually present only September–February). There were formerly five permanent camps in the Brisbane area, at Indooroopilly I., Coorparoo, Hemmant, Stafford and Sandgate. Indooroopilly I., 4 km upstream on the Brisbane River from the CBD, was Brisbane's most accessible wildlife highlight, and supported a mix of **Black** and **Grey-headed Flying Foxes**, with a seasonal influx of **Little Reds**. Unfortunately, the camp has been abandoned for reasons unknown. However, there are still plenty of flying foxes in Brisbane and they will be seen flying along the river at dusk in the CBD, botanic gardens and Southbank area. A colony at Woodend (Ipswich) is populated by **Grey-headed** and **Black Flying Foxes** and, at times, half a million **Little Red Flying Foxes**. There are other permanent camps at Norman Creek (mainly **Grey-headed**, **Black** with occasional **Reds**), Sparkes Hill (usually equal numbers of **Grey-headed** and **Black Flying Foxes**), Hemmant along Doughboy Creek (mostly **Blacks**, with a few **Grey-headed** and occasionally **Little Red Flying Foxes**) and at Curlew Park, Sandgate, which is dominated by **Black Flying Foxes**, with a few **Grey-headed** and seasonal **Little Red Flying Foxes**. **Indo-Pacific Humpback Dolphins** are often seen in the Brisbane River, especially downstream of the CBD; keep a lookout from any of the city ferries that ply the waters with commuter and tourist traffic.

Greater Brisbane is something of a hotspot for **Koalas**, with a so-called 'Koala Coast', though with encroaching development and high mortality from motor vehicles and domestic dogs this claim is becoming a bit hollow. Good sites are Point Halloran CA at Victoria Point (access off Orana St), where they may be seen in street trees occasionally;

The Gravel Reserve on the north-east side of Redland Bay Rd; Alexandra Hills between Windermere and Vienna Roads; and Daisy Hill CP, just east of the Pacific Motorway (accessible from Daisy Hill Rd), where staff at the information desk can advise of recent sightings or local hotspots. One of the city's other great claims is **Squirrel Gliders**, which occur in many nature parks, including Minnippi Parklands (Cannon Hill), Toohey Forest, Karawatha Forest, Boondall Wetlands, Tingalpa Wetlands and Bulimba Creek. Three other glider species are present: the rarely seen **Feathertail Glider**; **Greater Gliders**, seen mainly in the south and west, especially in stands of Spotted Gum and Forest Red Gum, for example at Mt Coot-tha and Toohey Forest; and **Sugar Gliders**, again at Mt Coot-tha and reserves such as Boondall Wetlands and Toohey Forest. On the outskirts of town, Mt Glorious has a population of **Long-nosed Potoroo**, but it would take many hours of spotlighting to see one; other species here that *are* readily spotlighted include the **Red-necked Pademelon**, **Short-eared Brushtail Possum**, **Common Ringtail Possum** and **Fawn-footed Melomys**.

Both **Northern Brown** and **Long-nosed Bandicoots** are common in several city reserves, although **Long-nosed Bandicoots** are probably easier to find further afield in the d'Aigular Range or Lamington NP (1.37), for example. There are many smaller species also in the greater metropolitan area, including the **Brush-tailed Phascogale**, **Yellow-footed Antechinus**, **Common Dunnart** and **Common Planigale**; all of these are probably better sought elsewhere with the exception of the localised **Subtropical Antechinus**, which occurs at Mt Glorious and Mt Nebo.

Macropods are not terribly well represented in Greater Brisbane. The closest site to the CBD for **Eastern Grey Kangaroos** would probably be Karawatha FR (where **Platypus** still live – check Scrubby Creek and Illaweena Lagoons). Nerang SF probably has the best diversity, with **Red-necked**, **Agile** and **Swamp Wallabies**, including the 'golden' colour morph of the last. **Swamp Wallabies** and **Red-necked Wallabies** also occur at Daisy Hill CP and at Venman's Bushland NP. The nearest site for **Brush-tailed Rock Wallabies** is White Rock CP, south of Redbank; the sometimes elusive **Black-striped Wallaby** also occurs here.

Brisbane has a healthy microbat population; **White-striped Freetail Bats**, for example, are common and roost in city parks. Other common species include **Gould's Wattled** and **Long-eared Bats**, **Northern Long-eared Bat** (here near the southern limit of its range) and **Greater Broad-nosed Bats**.

Brisbane is an international hub and well connected by air, rail and road to other parts of Australia. There are plenty of eating and sleeping options.

1.34 MORETON BAY

Highlights: **Dugong, Indo-Pacific Humpback Dolphin, Bottlenose Dolphin**

Other possibilities: **Humpback Whale**

Moreton Bay stretches 125 km from north to south, about 25 km across at its widest, and is protected from Pacific swells by two massive sand islands – Moreton and North Stradbroke. To the south it is linked by a chain of smaller islands and a maze of mangrove channels to the Gold Coast; Bribie I. forms its northern limit. It is a warm, rather shallow sanctuary for about 700 resident **Dugongs** and hundreds of **Bottlenose** and **Indo-Pacific Humpback Dolphins**. Herds of up to 400 Dugongs graze in shallow seagrass meadows at the eastern side of the bay, with the main concentration on the Amity Banks adjacent to the South Passage, which separates Moreton and North Stradbroke Is. They are easiest to spot from the air; boats leave from North Stradbroke I. (1.35). Other concentrations of **Dugongs** occur at the southern end of Pumicestone Passage, between Bribie I. and the mainland. **Bottlenose Dolphins** are the most common cetacean species near Brisbane and an estimated 350 live in Moreton Bay. Tangalooma Wild Dolphin Resort (www. tangalooma.com) on the western shore of Moreton I. feeds **Bottlenose Dolphins** each evening. The ferry from Brisbane skirts good **Dugong** feeding areas – keep an eye out for them and dolphins on the way over. The second most common cetacean is the **Indo-Pacific Humpback**, of which there are probably more than 100 in Moreton Bay. They usually frequent shallow waters close to shore; they are seen regularly at the mouth of the Brisbane River, off Amity Point (1.35), in Pumicestone Passage to the north and behind trawlers in Moreton Bay. **Humpback Whales** also sometimes enter the bay and females with calves have been seen near Tangalooma. There has been one record of **Australian Snubfin Dolphin** in the bay.

If you get a chance to explore Moreton I. itself, **Swamp Wallabies** are the most conspicuous terrestrial mammal; **Swamp Rats** inhabit the littoral zone and **Sugar Gliders** also occur. Cape Moreton was formerly a lookout for **Humpback Whales** and would still be a good site to watch the sea coast for cetaceans (**Killer Whales** are sometimes seen from here).

There is a **Grey-headed Flying Fox** camp at Black Swamp in Cleveland, near the North Stradbroke ferry terminal. The little-known **Water Mouse** has its stronghold in the mangrove channels north and south of Moreton Bay at, for example, Bribie I., Pumicestone Passage, North and South Stradbroke Is., and along the Pimpana and Coomera rivers.

1.35 NORTH STRADBROKE ISLAND

Highlights: **Koala, Agile Wallaby, Indo-Pacific Humpback Dolphin, Humpback Whale**

Other possibilities: **Squirrel Glider, Red-necked Wallaby, Swamp Wallaby, Grey-headed Flying Fox, Black Flying Fox, Water Mouse**

'North Straddie' (or just 'Straddie') is a popular weekend and holiday destination for Brisbane residents. It is the second-largest sand island in the world, 38 km long and

QUEENSLAND'S OTHER MARINE MAMMALS

Dugongs reach some of their highest densities in Queensland coastal waters. The biggest concentrations occur in Torres Strait and there are other large populations in Moreton Bay, Great Sandy Strait, Shoalwater Bay, south-western Gulf of Carpentaria and in the Hinchinbrook Channel. There is a chance of watching them from a boat in all these places, but for convenience it's hard to beat Moreton Bay near Brisbane. **Dugongs** graze the seagrass beds on the Amity Banks, near the strait between Moreton and North Stradbroke ('Straddie') islands, and commercial operators based on North Straddie run Dugong-spotting trips. Land-based sightings are also possible, for example from Moreton I. Pinnipeds are comparatively rare in Queensland, although a **Leopard Seal** once hauled ashore on Heron I., at the southern end of the Reef. A few juvenile **New Zealand Fur Seals** are reported most years in the south-east, especially in Moreton Bay, on North Stradbroke I. and off Scarborough.

12 km from east to west, and 239 m high at Point Lookout, the north-eastern tip. Most of the action is in the northern third of the island and you'll need a vehicle to get around (the road up to Point Lookout is a long, steep climb for a bike). Dunwich is the main town and ferry terminal; a few thousand **Grey-headed Flying Foxes** sometimes roost near the town and during flowering events thousands more may fly over from the coast adjacent. The island supports a good population of **Koalas**, mostly in the west and north. Concentrations occur around Dunwich, Amity and Point Lookout; check any good-sized timber for sleeping animals, walk some of the trails off the main road or ask locals where they've been seen lately. Both **Squirrel** and **Sugar Gliders** occur on North Stradbroke and could be spotlighted in likely looking areas. Macropods include **Red-necked Wallabies** and a remnant population of the **Agile Wallaby** (elsewhere in south-east Queensland found only on Peel I.). Four kilometres north of Dunwich, Myora Springs is a hotspot for the **Water Mouse**. Several large mounds can be seen here at the high water level among the mangroves, although chances of seeing the mouse itself are slim. **Water Rats** also occur but beware that the introduced **Black Rat** is probably the most common rodent in mangroves fringing Moreton Bay, and the **Grassland Melomys** also occurs on Straddie.

Point Lookout is one of the few large headlands on this stretch of the Queensland coast and one of the best from which to look for cetaceans – and it's free, to boot. **Humpback Whales** are virtually a given on both their northward (June–July) and southward (September–November) migrations, and usually in-between as well. The whales pass quite close to Straddie and can often be seen spouting and/or breaching with the unaided eye, although binoculars or a spotting scope would be useful. The best viewing is from North Gorge Headland – take the North Gorge Walk and watch from Norm's Seat and from above Whale Rock. Elevated viewing platforms overlooking Boat Rock and The Group rocks have been erected at the Frenchman's Bay end of Timbin Rd. Pods of dolphins also occur inshore, including **Spotted** and **Inshore Bottlenose Dolphins**. **Long-beaked Common**, **Pantropical Spotted** and **Spinner Dolphins** have all been recorded in oceanic waters near Brisbane so keep an eye out for these species. A herd of **Blainville's Beaked Whales** has been observed from Point Lookout and **Killer Whales** are also sometimes seen from here. A **Sperm Whale** stranded south of Point Lookout in 2012, so this species should be regarded as occurring offshore in the vicinity also. From Dunwich it's 22 km to Point Lookout; both **Grey-headed** (about 500) and **Black Flying Foxes** (up to 5000) sometimes camp near the peak.

On the Moreton Bay side of the island, the jetty at Amity Point is one of the best places to see the **Indo-Pacific Humpback Dolphin**, sometimes just a stone's throw from shore. The Amity turn-off is 11 km north of Dunwich on the Point Lookout road.

There is a good variety of accommodation on Straddie plus several eating options. However, book ahead for holiday periods and long weekends. North Stradbroke is accessible by a regular vehicle ferry ('water taxi') from Cleveland (www.flyer.com. au). Watch out for **Dugongs** (which frequent Moreton and Maroom Banks, west of Amity) and dolphins during the crossing.

1.36 GOLD COAST

Highlights: **Swamp Wallaby** ('golden' morph), **Black Flying Fox, Humpback Whale**

Other possibilities: **Agile Wallaby, Dugong**

Such is the awesome biodiversity of Queensland that a few mammals can be seen even in the built-up Gold Coast area (it was once mainly wetlands and lowland rainforest). There's a flying fox colony at Cascades Gardens in Broadbeach. A few **Dugongs** are reputed to inhabit the Broadwater, presumably at the quieter northern end. Although not technically the Gold Coast, South Stradbroke I. is one link in the chain of islands between here and Moreton Bay (1.34) to the north. 'South Straddie' is much smaller than its northern neighbour, but supports an interesting golden morph of the **Swamp Wallaby** (which are much rarer on North Stradbroke I.). The best way to see them is to get to Couran Cove Resort and walk towards the ocean along the road. You should see some among the casuarinas growing between the dunes and near the swamp. **Agile Wallabies** also occur on South Stradbroke and there is a remnant population near Coomera (Jacob's Well) and on Peel I. **Large-footed Myotises** feed in the quiet channels around Coomera. The Gold Coast Seaworld operates whale-watching trips during migration and sometimes excellent close-up views can be had of **Humpback Whales**. **Minke Whales** have occurred in recent years also.

1.37 LAMINGTON NATIONAL PARK

Highlights: **Brown Antechinus, Common Planigale, Common Dunnart, Northern Brown Bandicoot, Long-nosed Bandicoot, Koala, Sugar Glider, Squirrel Glider,**

Greater Glider, Common Ringtail Possum, Short-eared Brushtail Possum, Common Brushtail Possum, Eastern Grey Kangaroo, Whiptail Wallaby, Red-necked Wallaby, Red-legged Pademelon, Red-necked Pademelon, Black Flying Fox, Grey-headed Flying Fox, Little Red Flying Fox, Eastern Horseshoe Bat, White-striped Freetail Bat, Gould's Wattled Bat, Chocolate Wattled Bat, Eastern False Pipistrelle, Large-footed Myotis, Gould's Long-eared Bat, Large Forest Bat, Eastern Forest Bat, Little Bentwing Bat, Eastern Bentwing Bat, Water Rat, Fawn-footed Melomys, Bush Rat, Swamp Rat, Dingo

Other possibilities: **Platypus, Echidna, Black-tailed Antechinus, Dusky Antechinus, Brush-tailed Phascogale, Eastern Pygmy Possum, Rufous Bettong, Long-nosed Potoroo, Black-striped Wallaby, Brush-tailed Rock Wallaby, Swamp Wallaby, Eastern Tube-nosed Bat, Eastern Blossom Bat, Yellow-bellied Sheath-tailed Bat, Northern Freetail Bat, East Coast Freetail Bat, Eastern Freetail Bat, Large-eared Pied Bat, Hoary Wattled Bat, Lesser Long-eared Bat, Golden-tipped Bat, Greater Broad-nosed Bat, Eastern Broad-nosed Bat, Central-eastern Broad-nosed Bat, Eastern Chestnut Mouse, Hastings River Mouse, Pale Field-rat**

O'Reilly's Rainforest Retreat is world-famous for its wildlife viewing and peaceful surrounds in the middle of Lamington NP's pristine subtropical rainforest. This awesome site is probably where a short-term visitor can see the highest diversity of mammals in a single visit in the entire country (weather permitting – remember, it's *rain*forest). **Red-necked Pademelons** graze on grassy verges and lawns near the lodge in the early morning and evening. **Red-legged Pademelons** are more retiring and rarely leave the rainforest interior; they can be seen along the Booyong Walk by walking quietly, especially early and late in the day (they are superbly camouflaged and easy to overlook until they move – usually with a warning thump of a hind foot). **Brown Antechinuses** can also be seen here, darting among the leaf litter and fallen logs, and along the Botanic Gardens Trail and Wishing Tree Track (behind the guesthouse). They may be active by day and in some years are very common. Note that the **Subtropical Antechinus** also occurs in the park, although the exact limits of its occurrence are currently unclear – so far all those found around the guesthouse have proven to be **Brown Antechinuses**. The recently described **Black-tailed Antechinus** (little-known and formerly thought to be a form of Yellow-footed Antechinus) appears to have a limited distribution in the Border Ranges, but a specimen was caught at Moran's Falls in Lamington NP; watch for it on the trails. Spotlighting around the guesthouse most nights can be productive on the well-maintained trails with (generally) easy gradients. **Short-eared Brushtail Possums** (including an all-black colour variant), **Sugar Gliders** and **Common Ringtail Possums** occur along the entrance road, around the car park and near the guesthouse. The brushtails and antechinuses visit feeders around the guesthouse. The Wishing Tree and Booyong Walks are good for rainforest rodents, such as **Bush Rat** and **Fawn-footed Melomys**; both can often be spotlighted – the former rarely climbs, the latter is often seen at head height or even higher among vine tangles. **Platypuses** and **Water Rats** both occur in the stream at the bottom of Wishing Tree Track (there is a hide overlooking a nearby dam where **Platypuses** also occur). Both **Long-nosed** and **Northern Brown Bandicoots** occur around the guesthouse at night. **Swamp Rats** are sometimes seen during the day along Red Rd. **Echidnas** are seen most frequently in the drier forest, along Duck Creek Rd and lower down the Canungra road.

It is worth driving along the entrance road between O'Reilly's and Canungra for a few kilometres. During the day **Whiptail Wallabies** occur in the drier forest and may be seen in the early morning along this road; at night, this is where **Common Brushtail Possums**, **Sugar Gliders** and **Squirrel Gliders** can sometimes be spotlighted. The ecotone between rainforest and tall, drier forest can also be productive: Duck Creek Road (4WD recommended and essential after rain) is a good place to begin; the **Greater Glider** is commonly seen here by spotlighting and **Koalas** are occasionally recorded.

A short (say, 2–3 days) visit to O'Reilly's should turn up most of the foregoing, but to get the most out of this amazing place, the annual Wildlife Week, held in January, is highly recommended: this intensive week of spotlighting, trapping and general observation is brilliant for an excellent range of smaller species that are otherwise rarely seen; for the opportunity to pick the brains of experts; and to see a huge variety of other wildlife (of which the region has many specialties), such as frogs, reptiles and birds. Results of pitfall, cage, Elliott- and harp-trapping are displayed daily, allowing close-up viewing of **Bush** and **Swamp Rats**, **Fawn-footed Melomys**, **Brown Antechinus**, **Common Dunnart** and **Common Planigale**; the **Eastern Chestnut Mouse** is recorded irregularly and a long-running study site sometimes yields the rare **Hastings River Mouse** and **Long-nosed Potoroo**. The bat list is also impressive, with a regular haul of *Vespadelus* species (**Eastern**, **Common** and **Large Forest Bats**); the **Eastern Falsistrelle** with occasional broad-nosed species; **Gould's Long-eared** and **Eastern Horseshoe Bats**; both **Eastern** and **Little Bentwing Bats**; and rarities such as the **Large-eared Pied Bat**, **Greater Broad-nosed Bat** and the awesome **Golden-tipped Bat**. In all, 28 bat species have been recorded since Wildlife Week commenced in the 1990s. Sightings depend on weather and time: some 'weeks' are longer than others, which means habitat coverage and therefore species counts can vary. For example, during longer 'weeks' more lowland sites can be visited and species such as **Black**, **Grey-headed** and **Little Red Flying Foxes**, **Eastern Grey Kangaroos** and **Red-necked Wallabies** add to the tally. If Wildlife Week doesn't include these places during your stay, ask the organisers for tips on where to see species you may have missed. **Eastern Pygmy Possum**, **Brush-tailed Phascogale** and **Spot-tailed Quoll** are on the park list, but are rarely encountered, and **Brush-tailed Rock Wallaby** occurs on Mt Misery, on the outskirts of Canungra.

O'Reilly's can be reached from Brisbane via Beaudesert (69 km); from there head for Canungra (33.5 km); O'Reilly's is another 36 km and well signposted. Beware that the road from here is extremely winding and narrow in places. Allow 45 minutes for the trip in dry weather, and more if it's wet. O'Reilly's offers guesthouse accommodation (www.oreillys.com.au) and a good restaurant, and there is a well-appointed campground (campers can also eat in the guesthouse restaurant). It is a very popular spot and advance bookings are advised for both camping and the guesthouse, at virtually any time of year.

1.38 TOOWOOMBA AREA

Highlights: **Brush-tailed Rock Wallaby**

Other possibilities: **Eastern Grey Kangaroo, Swamp Wallaby, [Red Deer]**

Heading west from Brisbane, the city of Toowoomba marks the edge of the Darling Downs. Possibly the easiest place in the country to see the **Brush-tailed Rock Wallaby** is the rock wall on the northern side of Perseverance Dam. Drive about 35 km north of Toowoomba on the New England Hwy to Pechey, then take the Perseverance Dam turn-off (on the right) and drive to the dam wall, about 8 km to the east. In the early morning or late afternoon you should have no trouble seeing the rock wallabies with a scope or binoculars; they also occur in the surrounding vine scrub-covered hills. About 3 km further east on the same road, the Cressbrook Dam access road is a great place to see **Red Deer**. Yes, it's an introduced pest but a magnificent animal and, perversely, appears on the Queensland coat of arms. Back in Toowoomba, there are **Little Red Flying Fox** colonies at various sites, including Kearney's Spring Historical Park, a couple of kilometres south of the intersection of the Warrego and New England Hwys, close to the town centre.

1.39 SUNSHINE COAST

Highlights: **Koala, Short-eared Brushtail Possum, Black-striped Wallaby, Little Red Flying Fox, Black Flying Fox**

Other possibilities: **Large-footed Myotis, Water Mouse**

Koalas used to be something of a specialty at Noosa NP and they are still seen frequently, although numbers have dropped somewhat lately. Noosa NP is near the centre of Noosa township. **Koalas** can also be seen at Peregian, Caloundra and Sunshine Beach.

There's a good spot for the **Black-striped Wallaby** near Imbil in the Sunshine Coast hinterland. Driving through Imbil township from the south, head towards Borumba Dam, ignoring the Kadanga turn-off to the right. A few hundred metres past the last houses, there's a river (Yabba Ck) on your right. Park by the river, cross the road and walk up the dirt road through the rainforest. After 500 m you'll reach a Forestry Department station (usually deserted). **Black-striped Wallabies** hang around the edge of the grassy clearing surrounding the station, especially at dawn and dusk, sheltering inside the forest during the heat of the day. **Short-eared Brushtail Possums** can be spotlighted in these forests after dark. The main flying fox camp on the Sunshine Coast is at Noosaville, where **Black** and **Little Red Flying Foxes** roost. Donnybrook near Caloundra is home to the rare **Water Mouse**. These amazing animals construct elaborate mounds with internal chambers (rather like a beaver lodge), which are easily seen at certain sites, such as Bullock Creek CP. **Rufous Bettongs** are common near Eidsvold and Monto. **Large-footed Myotis** occupy purpose-built bat boxes under the Grigor Bridge where the Maleny-Kenilworth road crosses the Mary River at Conondale. Conondale is about 50 km west of the Bruce Hwy via Maleny. The bats can be seen emerging at dusk and fishing from the river.

WATCHING WHALES AND DOLPHINS IN QUEENSLAND

Humpback Whales migrate from Antarctica annually to calve and mate in the warm waters of the Coral Sea, sheltering inshore of the Great Barrier Reef along the Queensland coast. The northward migration starts with immatures and females with yearling calves, followed by mature females and then pregnant females. The southward migration commences in July–August and follows a similar pattern, with cows and calves travelling last. During migration most remain with 10 km of the coast, allowing great boat- and land-based viewing and, not surprisingly, **Humpbacks** are Queensland's main cetacean attraction. A travel website recently listed Hervey Bay (1.40) as the world's best site for watching them and whale-watching cruises operate at many other sites between the Gold Coast and north Queensland. The whales can also readily be seen opportunistically from boats almost anywhere along the coast. Prime spots for land-based watching include Point Lookout (1.35), Cape Moreton, Fraser I., the Whitsundays, Bowen and Cape Cleveland, as well as many locations in between. Whale-watching flights also operate from Bundaberg at the southern end of the Reef. Hervey Bay certainly offers excellent boat-based viewing opportunities and has some claim to being the home of whale-watching in Australia: commercial whale-watching has been in operation there at least since the 1980s. **Humpbacks** start to arrive from about mid-July and stay till about November before heading south. In 2013 a rare stranding of **Killer Whales** took place in Great Sandy Strait nearby, so keep an eye out for these predators as well. Recently a trial commenced to allow people to swim with the whales in Hervey Bay and on the Sunshine Coast. The Whitsunday Is. off the central Queensland coast are another good area; 80 per cent of pod sightings occur in July–October, although some **Humpbacks** are present all year, and there are usually lots of mothers with calves in these waters. **Humpbacks** are also the most common species sighted off the Gold Coast, where the seas are often bigger, but where there have also been rare sightings of **Southern Right** and **Dwarf Minke Whales**.

Another exciting development in Queensland whale-watching has been the live-aboard cruises that operate from Lizard I. north of Cairns, where **Dwarf Minke Whales** are regular visitors from June to September. These animals have bold, distinctive markings that make individuals recognisable, and you can take part in a citizen science project to record them. Live-aboard cruises depart Cairns in June and July, with a narrow snorkel or dive window of 6 weeks. **Humpbacks** are also seen occasionally on these cruises.

Overall, whale diversity is lower at Queensland's latitudes and the warm, shallow waters inside the Reef are not attractive to deep-water species. Both **Dwarf Minke** and 'typical' **Minke Whales** occur in Queensland; they often approach boats and may enter rivers. **Bryde's Whale** is most commonly sighted off the south-east coast between August and October.

However, there are significant numbers of three species of dolphin: **Bottlenose, Indo-Pacific Humpback** and **Australian Snubfin Dolphins**. Moreton Bay has resident **Bottlenose Dolphins** and the highest density of **Indo-Pacific Humpback Dolphins** in the state, especially in shallow western parts of the bay. Both species occur from the Tweed River at the state's southern border almost to the northern extremity of Cape York Peninsula, and also in the Gulf of Carpentaria. Inside the Reef, highest dolphin densities are recorded near Gladstone, east of Cape Hillsborough, north of Port Newry, east and south of the Whitsunday group and near Palm I. There has been one record of **Australian Snubfin Dolphin** in Moreton Bay, but it is not commonly seen south of Bundaberg. This retiring, inshore species occurs mainly in mangrove-lined bays and channels, for example near Gladstone and in the Hinchinbrook Channel; it can sometimes be seen from the Cardwell boat ramp.

1.40 HERVEY BAY

Highlights: **Humpback Whale, Dugong**

Other possibilities: **Black Flying Fox, Grey-headed Flying Fox, Little Red Flying Fox, Killer Whale**

The quiet coastal town of Hervey Bay has a rightful claim to being the 'home' of whale-watching in Australia: whale-watching tours have been running here for 40 years, and it's one of the best places in the world to see **Humpback Whales** up close from a boat. Owing to its unique location and topography, there are no other similar sites along the entire east coast. **Humpback Whales** use the large, usually tranquil bay west of Fraser I. as a calving area. Approximately 25 per cent of the east coast Humpback population visits the bay on the southward migration, between August and mid-October each year, each animal staying an average of 2 or 3 days. Boat operators have recently been granted permission to run 'swim-with-whales' trips; it would be a fascinating experience to share the waters with these huge animals. Hervey Bay is also important for **Dugongs**, particularly in the southern part of the bay near the mouth of the Burrum River, and in southern Great Sandy Strait. A pod of **Killer Whales** stranded in Great Sandy Strait in July 2013 (they were possibly following calving Humpbacks). There's a camp of flying foxes and an observation platform at Hervey Bay.

1.41 FRASER ISLAND

Highlights: **Echidna, Pale Field-rat, Dingo, Humpback Whale**

Other possibilities: **Eastern Grey Kangaroo, Swamp Wallaby, Squirrel Glider, Sugar Glider, Water Mouse, Water Rat, Dugong**

Fraser I. is the largest sand island in the world, 120 km long and an average of 15 km wide. Like Moreton and North Stradbroke islands to the south, it is aligned north–south at about 45 degrees to the mainland, forming the Great Sandy Strait – a large, wedge-shaped body of shallow water that narrows at the southern end of the island. Fraser I. is a beautiful spot and deservedly a World Heritage site, boasting forests of massive Satinays growing on sand, crystal-clear lakes, huge sand dunes and long beaches. Among the wildlife attractions is one of the last pure populations of **Dingo**. About 200 **Dingoes** live on the island and they can be seen almost anywhere – on ocean beaches, loitering near picnic and camp sites and along forest tracks. They are very used to people and can often be seen at close quarters, allowing great photo opportunities. However, you will see warning signs and it's worth repeating – these animals can be dangerous and have caused the death of at least one child; in 2014 a man was attacked by a pack while walking alone at night and there have been several other attacks. Heed the warning signs! The only other large terrestrial mammals you are likely to see are **Swamp Wallabies**, which are widespread but uncommon throughout the island, **Long-nosed Potoroos**, and **Eastern Grey Kangaroos** which may swim over from the mainland as they are recorded only occasionally. **Echidnas** are relatively common and look for **Northern Brown Bandicoots** at night around campgrounds; **Long-nosed Bandicoots** also occur. Arboreal species include the **Short-eared Brushtail Possum** (try around Central Station); **Squirrel Gliders**, which can be spotlighted around Kingfisher Bay Resort on the western side of the island; and **Sugar** and **Feathertail Gliders**. Eighteen species of bat have been recorded. There are currently no flying fox camps, but **Black**, **Grey-headed** and occasionally **Little Red Flying Foxes** visit the island from camps near Hervey Bay and at the mouth of the Mary River. Interestingly, both **Little** and **Eastern Bentwing Bats** occur, although they also must fly from mainland roosts as there are no suitable caves on the island. **Eastern Tube-nosed** and **Eastern Blossom Bats** could be spotlighted feeding at suitable sites, such as flowering melaleucas or banksias. The mangroves on the western coast are home to the **Water Mouse** and possibly **Water Rat**, although you won't see the former without taking part in a survey. Other rodents include the **Grassland Melomys** (especially in sedge and tea-tree swamps with dense cover), **Fawn-footed Melomys** (in rainforest with dense understorey, among which it climbs), **Delicate Mouse** and **Eastern Chestnut Mouse**. Watch for the **Pale Field-rat** around campgrounds and the **Bush Rat** (probably the most common mammal on Fraser I.; it occurs in most wooded habitats and also forages around buildings at Happy Valley and rubbish tips) and **Swamp Rat**. Fraser is the only one of the great sand islands on which dasyurids occur. Look for the **Yellow-footed Antechinus** in July, when male activity is at its peak and they may be active by day; **Common Dunnarts** have also been recorded.

The island also has an impressive list of cetaceans, including some known only from specimens found derelict on the long oceanic beaches. **Humpback Whales** can be seen in Platypus Bay at the north end of Fraser I., especially in August–October, occasionally reaching as far south as Kingfisher Bay Resort, as well as offshore in Great Sandy Strait between the island and the mainland, and in open water off the island's east coast. Other cetaceans recorded in Great Sandy Strait include the **Dwarf Minke Whale**, **Bottlenose Dolphin** (also commonly seen off Ocean Beach), **Indo-Pacific Humpback Dolphin** and **Common Dolphin**. A cruise in the strait will probably allow good close-up viewing. With so much ocean beach it's not surprising that a long list of species have been stranded, including **Strap-toothed**, **Blainville's** and **Cuvier's Beaked Whales**. Oceanic dolphin species recorded include **Risso's**, **Fraser's**, **Offshore Bottlenose** and **Striped Dolphins**; blackfish such as **Pygmy Killer**, **Short-flippered Pilot** and **Melon-headed Whales**; and there are records of **Southern Right Whale**, **Bryde's Whale**, **Sperm Whale** and **Pygmy Sperm Whales**. There's a population of **Dugongs** at the southern end of Great Sandy Strait. There are even records of **New Zealand Fur Seal** from Fraser I.

Fraser I. is one of Queensland's most popular tourist attractions and gets busy during peak holiday times. Only 4WD vehicles are allowed on the island; access is by barge at Inskip Point at the southern end. There are few roads – the broad sandy beach on the east coast is one of the main thoroughfares. The alternative is to cross from Hervey Bay to Kingfisher Bay Resort by boat. There are several campgrounds, and general stores selling petrol.

Opposite the southern tip of the island at Tin Can Bay, **Indo-Pacific Humpback Dolphins** are fed as a tourist attraction. Feeding is regulated by the Queensland government and is a great way to see these animals up close. The dolphins are generally around between 7 and 10 am daily, with feeding at about 8 am. To get to the site, follow Tin Can Bay Rd north to Norman Point (a dead end).

1.42 BARAKULA STATE FOREST

Highlights: **Black-striped Wallaby**

Other possibilities: **Greater Glider, Red-necked Wallaby, Swamp Wallaby, Eastern Grey Kangaroo**

The sometimes elusive **Black-striped Wallaby** occurs in the Barakula SF area, north of Chinchilla. Try spotlighting along Auburn Rd north of the Barakula turn-off, north of the Dingo Fence. Common macropods that could also be seen include **Eastern Grey Kangaroo**, and **Red-necked** and **Swamp Wallabies**; **Greater Glider** and **Little Red Flying Fox** occur.

1.43 AUBURN RIVER NATIONAL PARK

Highlights: **Herbert's Rock Wallaby**

Other possibilities: **Greater Glider, Whiptail Wallaby, Red-necked Wallaby, Swamp Wallaby**

The lookout area is a back-up for the **Herbert's Rock Wallaby**, especially in the late afternoon; if none are visible from the lookout itself, try walking down the gorge. **Whiptail**, **Red-necked** and **Swamp Wallabies** occur here also, as does the **Greater Glider**.

2. New South Wales

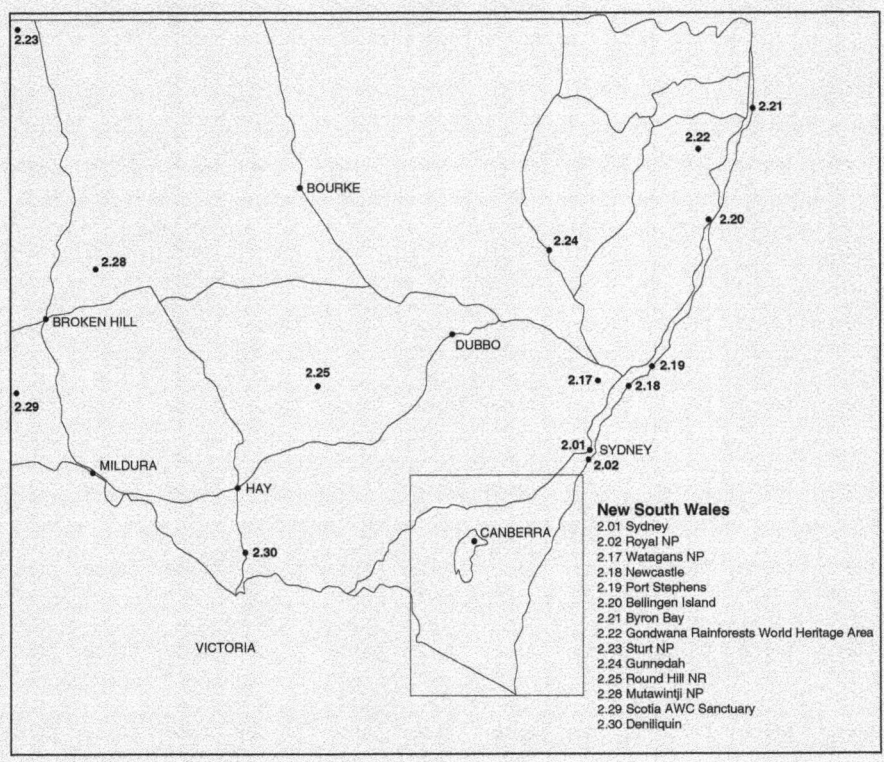

New South Wales
2.01 Sydney
2.02 Royal NP
2.17 Watagans NP
2.18 Newcastle
2.19 Port Stephens
2.20 Bellingen Island
2.21 Byron Bay
2.22 Gondwana Rainforests World Heritage Area
2.23 Sturt NP
2.24 Gunnedah
2.25 Round Hill NR
2.28 Mutawintji NP
2.29 Scotia AWC Sanctuary
2.30 Deniliquin

Endemic species: **Parma Wallaby**

The Great Diving Range stretches the entire length of NSW, separating a well-watered, heavily populated coastal plain from the vast inland. Vegetation and wildlife on the eastern seaboard have much in common with the subtropics, grading to a more temperate climate south of Sydney, where the Great Dividing Range culminates in the Snowy Mountains – Australia's highest – near the Victorian border. Inland a broad swathe of the original woodland has been cleared for agriculture, leaving what is virtually an ecological desert (mallee, for example, has almost completely disappeared from NSW), although some excellent reserves preserve patches of semi-arid and arid habitat. Regardless, NSW's mammal diversity is high and wildlife shares affinities with all these areas. Much of the Divide is still forested, with subtropical rainforests in the far north and a huge variety of wet and dry forest, woodland and heathland protected in numerous national parks, both in the ranges and at sea level. Arboreal species are well represented, with 12 species of possum and glider, including the near-endemic **Mountain Pygmy Possum**. Macropods include the endemic **Parma Wallaby**, thought to be extinct until its rediscovery in 1967.

The entire coast is indented with estuaries and natural harbours, and there are numerous prominent headlands which make prime sites for watching the annual **Humpback Whale** migration. Seabirding trips have been operating for decades from Sydney and Wollongong, and a good cetacean list has been built up over this time. Commercial whale- and dolphin-watching cruises operate from several centres including Eden, Port Stephens and Sydney itself. NSW has few offshore islands, but Montague I., off Narooma, has a healthy **Australian Fur Seal** population. This is the species most frequently reported hauled out on the mainland; there are comparatively few records of **New Zealand Fur Seals** or **Australian Sea Lions**. Southern vagrants, such as the **Antarctic Fur Seal**, **Crabeater Seal** (rare), **Southern Elephant Seal** (rare) and, most commonly, **Leopard Seal** (mainly south of Sydney) turn up on various beaches most years. **Dugong** records are also sparse, with a roughly even spread along the coast.

Bat diversity is high, with 39 species; the northern NSW bat fauna overlaps with that of subtropical Queensland; the southern part of the state has the entire suite of southern species; and the inland bat fauna is well represented west of the Divide. Almost the entire range of the **Grey-headed Flying Fox** is within NSW (with increasing numbers of **Black** as you travel north of Sydney and **Little Reds** in mobile inland encampments). Several caves have significant roosts of **Eastern Bentwing Bats** (for example, Wee Jasper and Bungonia) and **Eastern Horseshoe Bats** (Deua NP). Other interesting species include the distinctive **Golden-tipped Bat** and near-endemic **Eastern Freetail Bat**.

SOME STATE HIGHLIGHTS

- Watching **Humpback Whales** on migration at hotspots such as Eden and Byron Bay.
- The shy and retiring **Parma Wallaby**, the state's only endemic mammal.
- Montague I.'s thriving **Australian Fur Seal** colony.
- The successful reintroduction of arid-zone species at **Scotia AWC Sanctuary**.
- **Common Wombats** sunning themselves in the aptly named Snowy Mountains.

A GREATER SYDNEY REGION

Australia's largest city sits athwart a maze of bays, headlands and peninsulas, every available patch of land crowded with suburbia. It's congested and densely populated, and most of the original forest and heath vegetation has long been cleared, but pockets of native vegetation and a good variety of wildlife survive in Royal NP to the south and Ku-ring-gai Chase NP in the north; to the west the Blue Mountains contain the urban expansion. Sydney boasts some very scenic attractions and chances are that it will be on your itinerary if you're visiting from overseas. These sites are all easily reached from the CBD, traffic notwithstanding, and some native mammals have proven to be urban survivors. Sydney is an international and domestic transport hub, with every possible accommodation, eating, shopping and vehicle hire option.

2.01 GREATER SYDNEY

Highlights: **Long-nosed Bandicoot, Common Brusthtail Possum, Common Ringtail Possum, Koala, Eastern Grey Kangaroo, Swamp Wallaby, Red-necked Wallaby, Grey-headed Flying Fox**

Other possibilities: **Southern Brown Bandicoot, Water Rat, Humpback Whale**

Most people don't go to Sydney for its wildlife, although a few species seem to have survived the urban sprawl. Most accessible of these are several camps of **Grey-headed Flying Foxes**. A long-established camp at the Royal Botanic Gardens held up to 35 000 bats and once provided a spectacular fly-out at dusk, with Sydney Opera House as a backdrop, as these magnificent animals streamed out across the harbour. Sadly, this camp was dispersed and atomised into 15 or 20 colonies within a 30 km radius, although a few try to recolonise the gardens from time to time. The botanic gardens are an easy walk from the city centre; if any bats are there they are easy to find during the day. It's also worth checking Centennial Park, where they sporadically camp at Lachlan Swamp next to Duck Pond. **Common Brushtail** and **Common Ringtail Possums** are common in suburbia – the botanic gardens and numerous parks around the CBD are good places to start looking for them. There's a population of about 100 **Long-nosed Bandicoots** at North Head (part of Sydney Harbour NP), which is partly managed by the Australian Wildlife Conservancy (www.australianwildlife.org). **Echidnas**, **Common Ringtail** and **Common Brushtail Possums** and **Bush Rats** also occur here, but beware of confusing the latter with the introduced **Black Rat**, which also occurs. The bandicoots can also be seen in the bushland between Manly Hospital and Collins Beach, at the northern (landward) end of North Head. **Long-nosed Bandicoots** also occur at Ku-ring-gai Chase, Garrigal and Lane Cove NPs. Strangely, a population seems to persist in the inner suburb of Petersham, particularly in an area near the intersection of West and Thomas Sts, west of Petersham Park.

Sydney's main **Grey-headed Flying Fox** camps (which also frequently include some **Black Flying Foxes**) include about 8000 at Parramatta Park, where there is easy viewing and interpretive signs; watch the fly-out from Rosedale Rd in Gordon at dusk. Flying foxes can generally be seen at dusk in well-treed western suburbs, such as Penrith, Blacktown, Liverpool and Cabramatta.

There's a small population of **Koalas** near Campbelltown on the western edge of the city. The nearest site to central Sydney for **Platypuses** appears to be Blue Gum Swamp at Winmalee, 62 km west of the CBD. **Swamp Wallabies** can be seen in The Basin, Pittwater, late in the afternoon and **Eastern Grey Kangaroos** graze on the grounds of the hospital at Morisset, about 1.5 hour's drive north of Sydney. A more accessible site for **Eastern Greys** would be the Euroka Clearing past the campsite near the Glenbrook entrance to the Blue Mountains, or Royal NP (2.02).

Humpback Whales steam past annually on their migration along the east coast, heading north in June–July and south in October–November. There are many vantage points from which to scan for whales, and they seem to be entering the harbour itself more frequently each year, to attendant media fanfare. Good whale-watching headlands include Sydney Heads, Barrenjoey Head and Cape Solander in Botany Bay NP. These latitudes are about the normal northward limit for **Southern Right Whales**, which also occasionally enter the Harbour and may have even calved there recently; **Dwarf Minkes** have also been recorded inside the Harbour. On a smaller scale, **Water Rats** also inhabit the Harbour, though apparently in low numbers; there have been recent records at Pyrmont foreshore, just west of the CBD, at North Head and near Rodd Point at Iron Cove.

Pelagic birding trips run regularly from Sydney Harbour (for details see Chapter 10) to the Continental Shelf and an excellent cetacean total has accumulated over the years. Apart from regular **Common Dolphins** and **Oceanic Bottlenose Dolphins**, **Risso's Dolphins** are sighted seasonally and a fairly long list has included **Pantropical Spotted Dolphins** and **Sperm Whales**. **Australian** and **New Zealand Fur Seals** are also both seen from Sydney boat trips. These and vagrant seals turn up sporadically on beaches in the region (as well as north and south of Sydney); for example, a **Subantarctic Fur Seal** hauled up at Cronulla Beach in August 2012. Occurrences can't be predicted, however, and there are many beaches to search along this indented coastline.

At least 19 species of microbat occur in the Sydney region, **Gould's Wattled Bat** being the most widespread and the only one known to roost in houses here. **White-striped Freetail Bats** can be heard over Sydney Olympic Park and the flooded Brick Pits; also in the adjacent Newington NR and over the Parramatta River nearby (**Large-footed Myotis** also occurs). **Eastern Bentwing Bats** use artificial structures such as disused railway tunnels, military bunkers and stormwater drains in northern suburbs; there are roosts at Malabar, La Perouse (Henry Head) and Cape Banks, of which Malabar is the most commonly used. Some microbats occur only on the western edge

THE BIG FIVE

Most of NSW's Big Five can be seen within a day's drive of the capital Sydney.

Kangaroo Eastern Grey Kangaroos are common once you leave the metropolis at Royal NP (2.02), along the south coast at Jervis Bay (2.08) and especially in Canberra (see Chapter 3).

Koala The main concentration of Koalas is in the north, especially near Gunnedah (2.24), but there is a population on the western fringe of Sydney near Campbelltown (2.01).

Wombat Southern NSW is a stronghold for the Common Wombat and it is common in Kangaroo Valley (2.07) and Kosciuszko NP (2.16).

Platypus Bombala (2.15) is one of several 'Platypus Capitals of the World' and nearby Delegate is another hotspot; Queanbeyan (2.13) is also excellent.

Whale There are many great headlands for watching Humpback Whales, such as Byron Bay (2.21); there's boat-based whale-watching from Eden (2.12), Sydney itself (2.01) and Port Stephens (2.19).

of the city – for example, the **Large-eared Pied Bat**, **Eastern Horseshoe Bat**, **Eastern False Pipistrelle** and **Eastern Freetail Bat**, and **Lesser Long-eared Bat**.

2.02 ROYAL NATIONAL PARK

Highlights: **Long-nosed Bandicoot, Eastern Pygmy Possum, Common Ringtail Possum, Common Brushtail Possum, Eastern Grey Kangaroo, Swamp Wallaby**

Other possibilities: **Bush Rat, Swamp Rat, [Javan Deer (Rusa)]**

At the southern end of the city, Royal NP is a fine stand of coastal heathland and forested gullies, where some good local wildlife could be located. **Eastern Grey Kangaroos** are common and **Swamp Wallabies** live in densely vegetated gullies. Spotlighting along Lady Carrington Drive can be good for **Common Ringtail** and **Brushtail Possums**, with **Feathertail Gliders** also being reported from time to time. Smaller animals recorded have included the **Bush Rat**, **Swamp Rat**, **Eastern Pygmy Possum** and **New Holland Mouse**. There is a well-established feral population of **Javan Deer** (also known as **Rusa**) in the park; they can be seen around the Era Headland near the Garrawarra car park, among other sites. Royal NP is about 40 km south of the CBD via the Pacific Hwy (M1).

2.03 KU-RING-GAI FLYING FOX RESERVE

Highlights: **Grey-headed Flying Fox, Common Brushtail Possum, Common Ringtail Possum**

Other possibilities: **Echidna, Long-nosed Bandicoot, Southern Brown Bandicoot, Swamp Wallaby**

A small patch of bushland along Stoney Creek in the northern suburb of Gordon has been preserved for its important **Grey-headed Flying Fox** camp. Up to about 70 000 bats have been present; recently the colony has numbered about 25 000. There are bat observation platforms and **Little Red Flying Foxes** are occasionally recorded also. Other species noted in the reserve include the **Brown Antechinus**, **Common Brushtail** and **Common Ringtail Possums**, **Long-nosed Bandicoot**, **Echidna**, **Swamp Wallaby** and **Eastern Pygmy Possum**, as well as a suite of urbanised feral species. Nearby Ku-ring-gai Chase NP is one of the few places where **Southern Brown Bandicoots** survive in the Sydney region (Garingal NP is another).

2.04 CABRAMATTA CREEK, LANSVALE

Highlights: **Grey-headed Flying Fox, Little Red Flying Fox**

Another of Sydney's major **Grey-headed Flying Fox** camps is at Cabramatta Creek. The camp viewing platform and information are accessible from Liverpool St, Lansvale, via a laneway behind the Sunnybrook Hotel. You can view fly-outs from Jacqui Osmond Reserve on the Hume Hwy in Cabramatta.

B THE SOUTH COAST AND SOUTH-EASTERN NEW SOUTH WALES

The south-east corner of NSW is an area of outstanding scenery, much of it preserved in national parks. Superb stands of tall forest support a great variety of possums and gliders, as well as little-known species such as the **Smoky Mouse** (which appears to have a relatively high abundance in a few sites near Eden on the far south coast). Between Sydney and the Murray River **Koalas** become very rare indeed. A few persist in subcoastal forests east of Cooma, including Mt Clifford, Mt Dowling and Numeralla NRs, and have been studied for their unusual bark-chewing behaviour. Montague I. offshore from Narooma has a colony of fur seals, and many **Australian** and **New Zealand Fur Seals** haul out on the adjacent mainland. With dozens of coves and beaches, this coastline is a prime site for vagrant pinnipeds and a few turn up most years, including **Leopard Seals** and, rarely, **Crabeater Seals**. There doesn't seem to be any real pattern to records except that Antarctic and subantarctic species are more likely to occur in winter and spring. This section covers the area south of a line drawn between Wollongong and the far south-western corner, where the state borders of NSW, Victoria and SA intersect. Several sites, including the entire south coast are also easily accessible from Canberra (see Chapter 3).

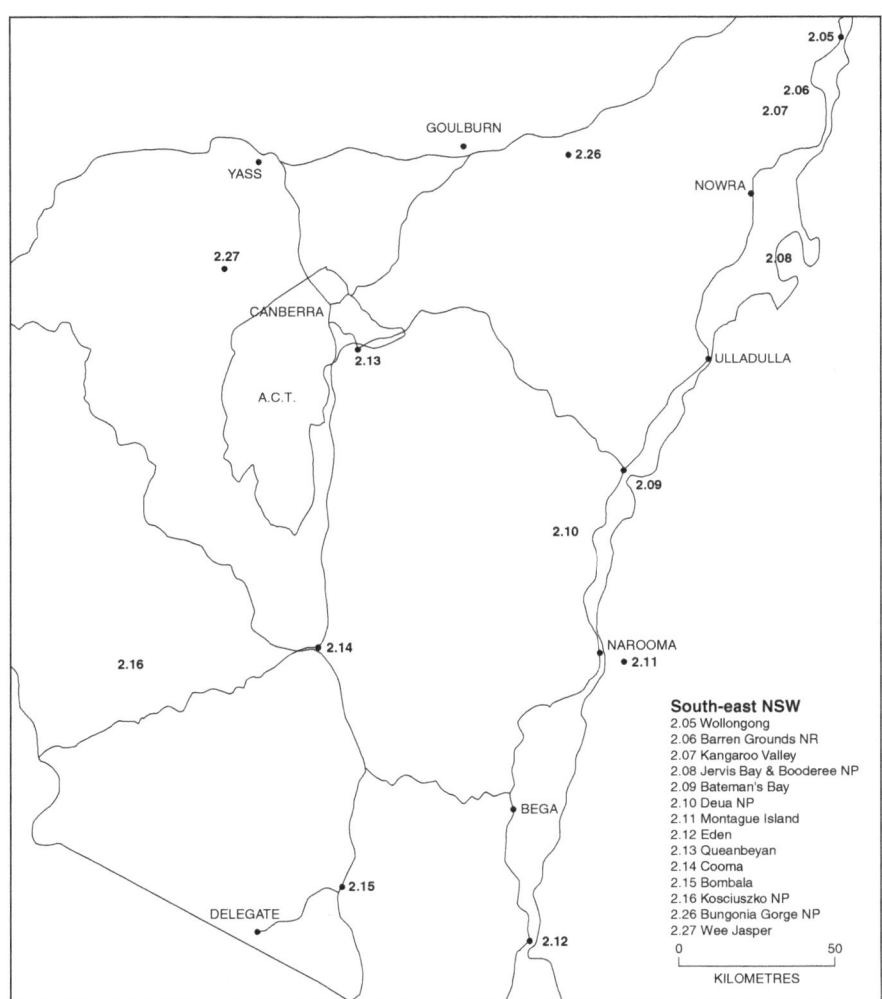

South-east NSW
2.05 Wollongong
2.06 Barren Grounds NR
2.07 Kangaroo Valley
2.08 Jervis Bay & Booderee NP
2.09 Bateman's Bay
2.10 Deua NP
2.11 Montague Island
2.12 Eden
2.13 Queanbeyan
2.14 Cooma
2.15 Bombala
2.16 Kosciuszko NP
2.26 Bungonia Gorge NP
2.27 Wee Jasper

0   50
KILOMETRES

2.05 WOLLONGONG

Highlights: **Humpback Whale, Antarctic Minke Whale, False Killer Whale, Pygmy Killer Whale, Long-snouted Spinner Dolphin, Fraser's Dolphin, Striped Dolphin, Inshore Bottlenose Dolphin, Common Short-beaked Dolphin**

Other possibilities: **Risso's Dolphin, Pygmy Killer Whale, False Killer Whale, [Javan Deer (Rusa)]**

Since the 1970s Wollongong has been the departure point for pelagic birding trips, now run by the Southern Oceans Seabird Study Association (SOSSA) and an impressive list of cetaceans has been accumulated. Regulars include **Inshore Bottlenose** and **Common Short-beaked Dolphins**, and **Humpback Whales** in season. **Southern Right Whales** are not unusual and other regulars include **Risso's Dolphins** and **Pygmy Killer Whales**. See the SOSSA website (www.sossa-international.org) and Chapter 10 for more information. The steep Illawarra Escarpment on the landward side of Wollongong is a haven for the introduced **Rusa Deer**, which roam parts of the suburbs at night and can be a menace to traffic; Mt Ousley, Mt Kembla and Figtree seem to be 'hotspots'. Wollongong is 85 km south of Sydney via the Pacific Hwy (M1).

2.06 BARREN GROUNDS NATURE RESERVE

Highlights: **Brown Antechinus, Common Wombat, Long-nosed Potoroo**

Other possibilities: **Spot-tailed Quoll, Eastern Pygmy Possum, Bush Rat**

Somewhat misnamed, this excellent patch of heathland near the top of the Illawarra Escarpment preserves an area rich in plants and wildlife. The weather can be a bit cold and dismal at times, but it is close enough to Sydney and Canberra for short trips and amply rewards a visit. The main attraction here is the chance to see a wild **Long-nosed Potoroo**, the most common and widespread of the extant potoroos but still generally cryptic and elusive. Barren Grounds offers as good a chance as any to see this animal; they are pretty well nocturnal but are sometimes seen bounding across trails and along the entrance road, especially in the early morning. **Common Wombats** are also regularly encountered along the entrance road, where **Greater Gliders** can often be spotlighted. **Spot-tailed Quolls** have been sighted in this park, near the ranger's residence, and there is a chance they still live here. Smaller species among the dense heath include **Bush Rats**, **Agile Antechinuses** and **Eastern Pygmy Possums**.

2.07 KANGAROO VALLEY

Highlights: **Common Wombat, Eastern Grey Kangaroo**

The 'Southern Highlands' is a geologically uplifted area south of Sydney where **Common Wombats** are indeed common, and Kangaroo Valley is one of the best places to see them. This is also a great area to see **Eastern Grey Kangaroos**. Kangaroo Valley is about 160 km south of Sydney.

2.08 JERVIS BAY AND BOODEREE NATIONAL PARK

Highlights: **Eastern Grey Kangaroo, Swamp Wallaby, Inshore Bottlenose Dolphin, Humpback Whale**

Other possibilities: **Eastern Chestnut Mouse, Swamp Rat, White-footed Dunnart**

This massive, cliff-lined bay has a resident pod of about 80 **Inshore Bottlenose Dolphins** and is big enough for **Humpback Whales** and **Southern Right Whales** to visit in season. Dolphins are often seen inshore at Chinaman's Beach in the early morning. In places the clifftops are 90–120 m above the sea and make ideal vantage points from which to look for cetaceans. Point Perpendicular from Currarong is good for views of migrating whales; seals haul out on rock platforms; and pods of dolphins can be seen off Callala Beach in Callala Bay. Warden Head is another good vantage point and **Killer Whales** have been seen from here. An **Indo-Pacific Humpback Dolphin** turned up near the Shoalhaven River, just north of Jervis Bay, and loitered for some time in 2009–10; this was a very southerly record.

Booderee NP itself is a pleasant area of heathland and forest. It is the most southerly site known for **Eastern Chestnut Mouse**, which shares the swampy lowlands with **Swamp Rats**. **White-footed Dunnarts** have also been trapped in this habitat. The forests are good for possums and **Greater Gliders**, and **Eastern Grey Kangaroos** and **Swamp Wallabies** are common in the park.

Heading south en route to Bateman's Bay, dolphins can often be seen from Dolphins Point at Ulladulla.

2.09 BATEMAN'S BAY AREA

Highlights: **Sugar Glider, Yellow-bellied Glider, Greater Glider, Eastern Grey Kangaroo, Red-necked Wallaby, Grey-headed Flying Fox, Bottlenose Dolphin**

Other possibilities: **Grey-headed Flying Fox, Humpback Whale, Southern Right Whale**

For most of the year Bateman's Bay's is quiet, but its huge popularity during school holidays somehow doesn't detract from its beautiful setting astride the broad, cliff-lined Clyde River estuary. To the north, Muramarang NP has extensive tall forests thick with gliders and possums – **Greater Gliders** and **Yellow-bellied** and **Sugar Gliders** can readily be seen at Kioloa. Camps of **Grey-headed Flying Foxes** can set up almost anywhere along this coast, including the Water Gardens in Bateman's Bay itself. **Bottlenose Dolphins** cruise inshore at several beaches – a small pod visits Surf Beach almost daily and also Long Beach north of the Clyde at Durras. There are numerous headlands from which to look for **Humpbacks** and other cetaceans; a pod of **Southern Right Whales** stayed inshore at Broulee, about 20 km south of Bateman's Bay, in 2009, giving extended stellar views not 50 m from shore. Whale-watching cruises leave from Bateman's Bay in season but the migration is generally a few kilometres offshore from here.

Depot Beach in Murramarang NP, 10 km north of BB, is one of the best places to see **Eastern Grey Kangaroos** in a beach setting – they are abundant around the well-patronised campground. **Swamp** and **Red-necked Wallabies** are also common here and the forests between here and the Pacific Hwy are good for spotlighting, with **Common Ringtail Possums**, and **Greater** and **Yellow-bellied Gliders**. A walking trail by the shores of Lake Durras would be worth exploring for these and other species. There's a large permanent camp of **Grey-headed Flying Foxes** west of the highway about 10 km north of the Clyde. At Potato Point, 60 km south of Bateman's Bay, both **Eastern Greys** and **Red-necked Wallabies** occur side-by-side at the campground and on the beach.

Bateman's Bay can claim to be the capital of the South Coast and its maritime climate makes it a great base for exploring the region; there are many camping grounds and holiday rental cottages, but you'll need to book ahead for peak times.

2.10 DEUA NATIONAL PARK

Highlights: **Eastern Grey Kangaroo, Red-necked Wallaby, Swamp Wallaby, Eastern Horseshoe Bat, Eastern Bentwing Bat**

Other possibilities: **Echidna, Spot-tailed Quoll, Southern Brown Bandicoot**

West from Moruya, a slow route inland through remote forested ranges would repay spotlighting and general exploration. Dendetheda Cave is the largest **Eastern Horseshoe Bat** roost in NSW and Marble Arch is a winter roost for **Eastern Bentwing Bats**. Other species common in these forests include **Swamp** and **Red-necked Wallabies, Eastern Grey Kangaroos, Echidnas**, various possums and **Southern Brown Bandicoot**. **Spot-tailed Quolls** persist in this rugged remote area, and sadly become roadkill occasionally on the King's Hwy between Bateman's Bay and Braidwood; sightings would be purely by chance.

2.11 MONTAGUE ISLAND

Highlights: **Australian Fur Seal, New Zealand Fur Seal**

Other possibilities: **Common Dolphin, Bottlenose Dolphin, Killer Whale, Humpback Whale**

The northern end of this small, rocky island 9 km off Narooma supports the largest colony of **Australian Fur Seals** in NSW. It's mainly a bachelor herd but occasionally pups are born. **New Zealand Fur Seals** are also resident and seem to be increasing in number. A visit to Montague is a good way to compare the two species; **New Zealand Fur Seals** tend to be more solitary and more aggressive. Several operators offer **Humpback Whale**–watching cruises that visit Montague I.; **Common** and **Bottlenose Dolphins**, and sometimes **Killer Whales** are seen. Access is by boat only and commercial trips leave daily in summer from Narooma (see www.montagueisland.com.au). Accommodation is available in the lighthouse (bookings essential). **Australian Fur Seals** also sometimes lob into Narooma Harbour.

2.12 EDEN AREA

Highlights: **Eastern Grey Kangaroo, Red-necked Wallaby, Swamp Wallaby, Killer Whale, Sperm Whale, Humpback Whale, Southern Right Whale, Bottlenose Dolphin, Common Dolphin**

Other possibilities: **Southern Brown Bandicoot, Smoky Mouse**

The extreme south-east of the state is almost equidistant from Sydney and Melbourne, and far enough from both to discourage excessive traffic. It is a tranquil corner with great scenery, tall forest and heathland and a thriving whale-watching industry. **Eastern Grey Kangaroos**, **Swamp Wallabies** and **Red-necked Wallabies** are all common along the highway – take care while driving at night or in the early morning.

Eden was formerly a centre for hunting **Humpback** and **Southern Right Whales** and, in a fascinating twist, a pod of **Killer Whales** used to herd Humpbacks into the bay for the whalers, who rewarded them with choice cuts. In town there's a Killer Whale Museum and various historic sites. One, Ben Boyd's Tower, was used as a lookout for whales and is still a good vantage point from which to scan the offing. There is a Whale Festival in October-November and whale-watching operators ply the waters, especially during peak Humpback viewing time (October–December). **Southern Right Whales** could be seen between May and December, and **Killer Whales**, **Blue** and **Minke Whales** may be seen as well; **Bottlenose Dolphins** and **Common Dolphins** occur inshore and **Australian Fur Seals** are sighted regularly at sea, in the bay and in the harbour itself. A deep trench offshore attracts **Sperm Whales** and possibly supports beaked whales.

The forests in Eden's hinterland are rich in native mammals. Arboreal species include **Greater, Yellow-bellied, Feathertail** and **Sugar Gliders, Common Ringtail Possums,** and **Common** and **Mountain Brushtail Possums**. Smaller species include both **Long-nosed** and **Southern Brown Bandicoots, Bush Rats** and **Agile** and **Dusky Antechinuses, White-footed Dunnarts** and the rare **Smoky Mouse**. Macropods are common, especially **Eastern Grey Kangaroos**, and **Red-necked** and **Swamp Wallabies**. **Long-nosed Potoroos** occur and fox-baiting has probably helped to maintain their population.

Nadgee NR is a wilderness accessible only on foot, and where **Long-nosed Potoroos** and both **Long-nosed** and **Southern Brown Bandicoots** persist. Extensive areas of heath support **Eastern Pygmy Possum** and **White-footed Dunnart**. **Spot-tailed Quolls** survive here but are rarely seen and this is one of the few coastal areas where **Dingoes** still occur. **Eastern Grey Kangaroos**, plus **Red-necked** and **Swamp Wallabies** are also common.

WATCHING WHALES AND DOLPHINS IN NEW SOUTH WALES

The annual **Humpback Whale** migration passes along the entire NSW coast and has spawned many boat-based whale-watching operators; prominent headlands offer some great vantage points for land-based observation. The eastern **Humpback** subpopulation appears to be growing and an estimated 17 000 now pass NSW annually on their way to calve in Queensland waters. The northward migration occurs mainly in June and July and the whales are seen moving southward again mostly in October–November. From the south, good spots for land-based watching include Green Cape, Ben Boyd's Tower near Eden, Tathra, Clifftop Park at Narooma, Moruya Heads and Jervis Bay. In Sydney itself, there's North and South Head, Cape Solander and Barrenjoey Heads. North of Sydney, there are several accessible headlands on the Central Coast, such as Norah Head near Terrigal, and Crackneck Lookout at Bateau Bay, where up to 65 Humpbacks have been seen in a day in good conditions (park rangers hold talks at Crackneck Lookout in peak migration, usually between mid-May and July). Byron Head is also a great whale lookout. Whale-watching cruises operate from many centres, including Eden, Narooma, Sydney, Port Stephens, Port Macquarie and Byron Bay. Albino **Humpbacks** spark much media interest; one in particular, dubbed Migaloo, has been migrating up the east coast for years and is eagerly sought by whale-watchers. It has been seen as far away as Green I. off Cairns, in the Whitsundays and as far south as Port Stephens. Whale-watching can be done by helicopter from Newcastle.

Southern Right Whales are also seen regularly, possibly with increasing frequency, and a female with calf was seen off Coff's Harbour in 2012. A deep trench offshore from Eden in the south-east corner makes this area a hotspot for **Sperm** and **Blue Whales**, and probably beaked whales as well. In fact, Eden was historically a centre for the slaughter of migrating **Humpbacks** and pods of **Killer Whales** used to frequent the area. The old whaling station has been turned over to tourism and whale-watching is now a local attraction, with boat tours in **Humpback** season, the Sapphire Coast Marine Discovery Centre (www.sapphirecoastdiscovery.com.au) and a Whale Festival in October–November each year. Cruises are pretty well guaranteed of seeing **Humpback Whales** during migration, as well as **Common** and **Bottlenose Dolphins**, with a reasonable frequency of **Southern Right Whale** sightings. Less frequent sightings have included **Bryde's Whales**, **Killer Whales** (early October), **False** and **Pygmy Killers**, **Risso's Dolphins**, **Pilot Whales** and **Sperm Whales**. Whales are also sometimes seen on cruises to Montague I. (2.11). The richest area for cetaceans in NSW in terms of species recorded is between Port Stephens and Eden, with a spike between Sydney and Bateman's Bay (probably because of pelagic birding trips). This far southern coastline seems to have good populations of **Pilot** and **False Killer Whales**.

The continental shelf runs close to the coast at many points, a fact not lost on pelagic birders who for decades have run regular trips from Wollongong and Sydney; more recently trips have started from Port Stephens. Impressive cetacean tallies have accumulated over the years: **Humpbacks** are regular in season and **Common** and **Bottlenose Dolphins** are pretty well a fixture; **Southern Right Whales** are reasonably regular and other sightings have included **Dwarf Minke, Sperm, Pygmy Blue, Killer, False Killer, Melon-headed, Long-** and **Short-flippered Pilot Whales, Pygmy Killer Whales, Risso's Dolphin** and the **Pantropical Spotted Dolphin**. See Chapter 10 for details.

Common and **Bottlenose Dolphins** can be seen at many sites along the coast, and Port Stephens has a thriving dolphin-watching industry. Boats operate year round, both in the sheltered Port waters where there are resident herds and offshore, where the sea can be rougher but **Humpback** sightings are possible and other species are sometimes seen.

Pygmy Sperm Whales are among the more commonly stranded species in NSW (for example, near Coff's Harbour in 2013), but strandings are comparatively rare in NSW. Even beaked whales feature poorly, with only the **Southern Bottlenose Whale** and **Blainville's, Andrews', Gray's, Gingko-toothed, Cuvier's** and **Strap-toothed Beaked Whales** having been recorded.

ORRCA (www.orrca.org.au) holds an annual Whale Census day, when up to 1500 **Humpbacks** have been seen at various sites along the coast and there have also been sightings of **Minke, Killer** and **Blue Whales**. ORRCA has a hotline for sightings ((02) 9415 3333) on which seals are also reported.

2.13 QUEANBEYAN

Highlights: **Platypus, Water Rat**

Other possibilities: **Common Wombat, [Fallow Deer]**

The King's Hwy links Bateman's Bay with Canberra (Chapter 3) and is the quickest route inland from the NSW south coast. There are lots of **Common Wombats** along this route, particularly between Braidwood and Queanbeyan. Drive slowly at night and there's a good chance of seeing one alive. Feral **Fallow Deer** are relatively common in bush and farmland near the small town of Bungendore; try the Tarago Rd north towards Lake George (where a wind farm is a useful landmark to head for). Queanbeyan sits just outside Canberra and is included here by dint of the healthy **Platypus** population in the Molongolo River, which cuts through the town centre. Park near the King's Hwy bridge and walk along either bank towards the pedestrian bridge about 200 m upstream. This is a prime **Platypus** haunt and several **Water Rats** have territories here as well. Viewing is best from the footbridge and by walking along the western bank.

Sightings are almost guaranteed in July and August, when males are most active, although early mornings are best (be warned: it can be cold and frosty). When the river flooded recently, **Platypuses** were spotted swimming over the nearby golf course and near the entrance to a city club! The Australian Platypus Conservancy (www.platypus. asn.au) sometimes organises Platypus walks, with good results. **Little Red Flying Foxes** sometimes camp along the Molongolo River between Queanbeyan and Canberra – join the Australasian Bat Society and ask local members about sightings.

Tallaganda SF near Hoskinstown is a mix of dry and wet forest, and is a prime spot for **Greater Gliders**, **Common Wombats**, **Sugar Gliders**, **Swamp Wallabies** and maybe even a **Spot-tailed Quoll**. Tallaganda is about 80 km south-east of Queanbeyan.

C THE HIGH COUNTRY

Inland from Bega, the Great Diving Range reaches its highest peaks in the Snowy Mountains. Much of this region is rugged, remote and forested, with deep river valleys and few roads. The area above about 1600 m in elevation is usually snow-bound from late June to early September, with snow lying in deep valleys and eastern slopes for sometimes months afterwards. However, snow and sleet could occur at any time of year and if you will be hiking or camping out be prepared for all conditions; night-time temperatures can fall well below zero even in summer. Cooma (about an hour's drive south of Canberra) is the main service town in the region but there are plenty of chalets, lodges, ski villages and small towns off the main ski circuit that offer accommodation. Be aware that snow chains may be mandatory in some areas in winter. The Snowy Mountains Hwy connects Cooma with holiday villages in and around Kosciuszko NP (2.16). The quickest route to the coast from here is via Nimmitabel on the B12; beware that this road can be closed because of landslips or flooding at times (check local conditions).

2.14 COOMA

Highlights: **Platypus**

Other possibilities: **Eastern Grey Kangaroo, Swamp Wallaby**

Good **Platypus**-viewing is possible by taking a short detour from Cooma, the main service centre for the High Country. Follow the Mittagang–Shannon's Flat Rd as far as the Murrumbidgee River and park on the right (north) hand side of the road. **Eastern Greys** and **Swamp Wallabies** are also common along these roads. Cooma is 113 km south of Canberra on the Monaro Hwy.

2.15 BOMBALA

Highlights: **Platypus**

The clear, clean waters of the High Country are ideal for **Platypus**-viewing and Bombala is another site that claims to be the 'Platypus Capital of the World'. The area the claim refers to is about 5 km past the town (ask at the information centre for directions) where there's a viewing platform and picnic tables. However, **Platypuses** also occur in town itself: look down into the water from the bridge where the main road crosses the river. The nearby town of Delegate is also reputed to be good for **Platypuses**.

2.16 KOSCIUSZKO NATIONAL PARK

Highlights: **Dusky Antechinus, Mountain Pygmy Possum, Common Wombat, Eastern Grey Kangaroo, Red-necked Wallaby, Swamp Wallaby**

Other possibilities: **Echidna, Agile Antechinus, Bush Rat, Broad-toothed Rat, [Sambar], [Brumby]**

The Snowy Mountains culminate in 2228-m Mt Kosciuszko, which gives its name to a huge national park that protects numerous peaks, alpine lakes and forested river valleys. They are indeed snowy for some of the year, mainly June–September, and weather at higher elevations can change at short notice – be prepared for rain or snow in any month, as well as sunburn in the clear mountain air. In winter check road conditions – a 4WD or chains may be necessary, although most roads are suitable for conventional vehicles in dry conditions. Watch roadsides for **Eastern Grey Kangaroos**, **Red-necked** and **Swamp Wallabies** and **Common Wombats** – all are common along the Snowy Mountains Hwy, especially between Jindabyne and Thredbo.

Very few Australian mammals truly hibernate and some larger species may present unusual photo opportunities in snowy conditions. **Echidnas** occur up to the treeline and have even been recorded on Kosciuszko summit; tracks in the snow are common in spring. **Swamp Wallabies** are the most widely distributed macropod and relatively common above the snowline; **Red-necked Wallabies** are rare at high altitudes, but are not uncommon at snowline in sheltered areas. **Eastern Grey Kangaroos** don't do well in the snow and usually move to frost hollows and grassy forests at lower altitudes in winter (**Common Wallaroos** are rare and generally absent from most of the High Country). **Common Ringtail Possums** occur in mature stands of Snow Gum with hollows; surprisingly, **Mountain Brushtail Possums** do not occur above the snowline and prefer heavily vegetated gullies; **Common Brushtails** are found at lower altitudes. Well-forested valleys at the western edge of the park, especially along the Tumut River valley support a healthy population of **Yellow-bellied Gliders**.

One of the star attractions here is another possum - the **Mountain Pygmy Possum** – and Kosciuszko NP supports about half of its total world population. It hibernates during winter and at other times is active among boulder piles. Some of the best habitat is right under popular ski slopes, such as Charlotte's Pass; it is also found between Dead Horse

WOMBATS IN THE SNOW

Like most marsupials, **Common Wombats** don't hibernate in winter and they continue to forage even while snow covers the ground. Watch for these charismatic animals basking outside their burrows on sunny mornings and at dusk before they venture out to start feeding. You'll probably get your best sightings (and great photos) of wombats in the snow if you go off-piste on Nordic skis. Look for tracks and follow them to a burrow. If you move slowly you can often approach to within a few metres; soft grunting noises may help! Otherwise, campgrounds along the Alpine Way at Thredbo Diggings and Ngarigo have lots of wombats (though not necessarily snow). Island Bend off the Guthega road is also a good spot, but also marginal for snow. Up the Kosciuzsko road there are more wombats around Rennix Gap (try the picnic area turn-off to your right as you head up the road) and near Sponar's Chalet there are burrows on the right and left of the road just before the bridge.

Gap and Cabramurra (north) from Kosciuszko summit down to about 1200 m. The only feasible way to see this species here is to join a survey as a volunteer – inquire through the NSW environment department. **Bush Rats** and **Agile Antechinuses** are the most common small mammals trapped in possum habitat. **Eastern Pygmy Possums** also occur in the park, for example up to about 1360 m on the Guthega Rd.

The walk to the top of Mt Kosciuszko is possibly the easiest climb of any major peak and worthwhile for a good chance of seeing the **Dusky Antechinus**. The easiest access is by taking the Kosciuszko Express chairlift from Thredbo village to the top of Crackenback (which is at about 2000 m), from where a well-maintained boardwalk leads 6.5 km to the summit. It is a straightforward, gentle ascent for which you should allow at least 4 hours return (6 hours is recommended) to enjoy the scenery and fresh air. **Dusky Antechinuses** are partly diurnal and may be seen scurrying about the summit cairn, especially on sunny days during cold spells. In theory they could be seen in any likely looking boulder pile en route (of which there are many, snow cover notwithstanding), but presumably food scraps left by hikers make the summit an attractive spot. Although this species appears to be active year-round, the summit and surrounding area can be under deep snow from June to September, so your best chance of a sighting would be summer or autumn. Only the **Dusky Antechinus** has been recorded at this attitude, so field identification should be accurate: it's a large, distinctive antechinus that is more common than the **Agile Antechinus** above the treeline. **Agile Antechinuses** can occur as high as 2000 m but are most common up to about 1600 m in woodland and rocky habitats; they are sometimes seen in the walkers' huts that dot the park. Note that conditions can change quickly on these exposed alpine plains, even in summer. Under no circumstances should you attempt an extended alpine walk without adequate footwear, sunglasses, hat and a wind- and waterproof jacket, no matter how pleasant conditions are when you start out. There are toilets before the final climb. Take snacks and plenty of water; there's a cozy restaurant waiting at the top of the chairlift on your return! The last chairlift down to Thredbo Village leaves at 4 pm; otherwise it's a very steep downhill walk. Traces of the **Spot-tailed Quoll** have been recorded above Thredbo and there is a small population of this spectacular dasyurid in the Byadbo Wilderness, south of Jindabyne.

'Kosi' is one of the best places to see the secretive **Broad-toothed Rat**, which in NSW is confined to the High Country, mainly above the snowline. They are sometimes seen on the Summit Trail between Charlotte's Pass and Mt Kosciuszko. Otherwise, look for them where you can see their tunnels in the grass, which they use for subniveal activity in winter (these animals do not hibernate). **Water Rats** are also relatively common and have been recorded in Blue Lake. **Platypuses** occur in waterways up to about 1500 m, for example in White's River and Perisher Creek below the Guthega Rd.

Microbat activity in general ceases during winter and bats are most active from about mid-October to early May, unseasonal cold snaps notwithstanding. **Gould's Wattled** and **White-striped Freetail Bats** occur at the highest elevations and have been recorded above 2100 m; it should be easy to detect the latter in particular as it hunts above the treeline on warm evenings. **Lesser Long-eared** and **Southern Forest Bats** occur at Thredbo, **Chocolate Wattled Bats** have been recorded in the park and the **Eastern False Pipistrelle** is known from Rawson's Pass (2010 m). **Eastern Bentwing Bats** roost at Yarongabilly Caves.

Feral hoofed animals are a controversial issue in Kosciuszko NP. **Brumbies** (feral Horses) are abundant in parts of the high plains and cause widespread damage to fragile soils and vegetation. However, many people find them appealing and they are part of the folklore of the region. Introduced **Sambar** are something of a pest near Tumut; again, watch out for large animals while driving at dusk as they can cause serious damage in a collision.

D NORTHERN NEW SOUTH WALES COAST

The Pacific Hwy (M1) north of Sydney follows the coast into progressively more subtropical habitat, although much of the original rainforest has long gone to make way for banana and sugar cane plantations. Much of this coastline is indented with shallow lakes and lagoons, with the Great Diving Range bordering it to the west. The highest mammal diversity is in the far north-east corner, a World Heritage area adjacent to the superb rainforests of south-east Queensland. There is a broad overlap in species between the two states and, in general, many are easier to see on the Queensland side of the border (for example, at Lamington NP (1.37)). The North Coast has several excellent headlands from which to watch the **Humpback Whale** migration and boat-based cruises operate from several locations; see 'Watching Whales and Dolphins in

NSW' on p. 62. **Australian Fur Seals** sometimes haul up north of Sydney, for example at Norah Head, The Entrance, Bateau Bay, Forresters Beach, Terrigal and Winnie Bay; a **Subantarctic Fur Seal** hauled out at Brisbane Water in 2012; and **Leopard Seals** have been recorded at Umina Beach, Avoca, Terrigal and Forresters Beach. Northern NSW is a hotspot for macropod diversity, with the ranges of at least six species overlapping: **Eastern Grey Kangaroo**, **Whiptail Wallaby**, **Red-necked Wallaby**, **Swamp Wallaby**, **Black-striped Wallaby** and **Parma Wallaby**.

2.17 WATAGANS NATIONAL PARK

Highlights: **Parma Wallaby, Red-necked Pademelon**

NSW's only endemic mammal, the **Parma Wallaby**, was thought extinct until its rediscovery in dense coastal forests north of Sydney in 1967. This rare small wallaby tends to be solitary and is best seen by slowly driving the park roads at night – the Basin area is a good place to start looking. These animals tend to freeze when spotlighted, but can be confused with **Red-necked Pademelons**, which are more common in some sections of the park. The Watagans are 140 km north of Sydney in the Newcastle hinterland. This is about the nearest place to Sydney where you can see wild **Parma Wallabies**; they may be more common further north.

2.18 NEWCASTLE AREA

Highlights: **Koala, Grey-headed Flying Fox**

Other possibilities: **Red-necked Wallaby, Black Flying Fox, Little Red Flying Fox**

The Hunter Region Botanic Gardens in Newcastle has a small population of **Koalas**; **Red-necked Wallabies** also occur in the gardens. Mangroves in the Hunter estuary support maternity colonies of **East Coast Freetail Bats** and **Greater Broad-nosed Bats**, as well as eight other species of microbat. The Hunter estuary is great for the **Large-footed Myotis**, which can be seen foraging over the Hunter River and along mangrove creeks, silhouetted at dusk.

The Hunter Valley town of Singleton has a permanent camp of **Grey-headed Flying Foxes** in Burdekin Park, on the south side of the New England Hwy about 1 km past the tourist information centre as you head inland. The camp sometimes spills over into adjoining areas, such as the hospital, church and school; **Little Red** and **Black Flying Foxes** are also recorded here from time to time. There's a smaller camp at Maitland with **Grey-headed** and **Little Red Flying Foxes**.

2.19 PORT STEPHENS

Highlights: **Bottlenose Dolphin, Humpback Whale**

Other possibilities: **Australian Fur Seal, Common Dolphin**

One of Australia's busiest dolphin-watching industries is based in Port Stephens, where there is a resident population of **Bottlenose Dolphins**. Numbers fluctuate seasonally and annually, with an estimated 90–120 resident in the bay, perhaps as many as 150, and others joining them periodically from waters outside the bay. All manner of seacraft run tours, both inside the bay and outside, where conditions may be rougher but there is a chance of seeing **Common Dolphins**, as well as **Humpback Whales** (with peaks in May–July and again in September–November on their southward migration). Pods approach as closely as the Outer Light at Fingal and Shark I. **Australian Fur Seals** haul out at Cabbage Tree I. Port Stephens is 245 km north of Sydney on the Pacific Hwy (Hwy 1); turn off at Raymond Terrace for Nelson Bay, the main settlement.

2.20 BELLINGEN ISLAND

Highlights: **Grey-headed Flying Fox**

Other possibilities: **Black Flying Fox, Little Red Flying Fox**

An island in the small town of Bellingen, just inland from Coff's Harbour, hosts a major permanent camp of **Grey-headed Flying Foxes**. More than 30 000 are generally present, making it one of the five largest known colonies. To get there, turn off the main street at the post office and cross the river; follow this road round to the first street on the left. Leave your vehicle at the site of an old caravan park and walk across it to a pathway that leads down to the island. Cross the dry riverbed at the bottom (don't attempt this if it's in flood) to access the camp. You can watch

WATCHING BATS IN NEW SOUTH WALES

Coastal NSW straddles the interchange between subtropical and temperate bat faunas, with several species restricted to subtropical rainforests in the extreme north-east corner, others found south to about the Sydney region, and some more typical of cool, southern forests that are rarely found north of Sydney. New South Wales also has a good representation of arid-zone species and thus has a very diverse bat fauna, with a total of five megabats and 34 microbats including the near-endemic **East Coast Freetail Bat**.

Almost the entire range of the **Grey-headed Flying Fox** – and approximately 80 per cent of its population – lies in NSW and finding a camp shouldn't be difficult along many parts of the coast. The biggest camps, with more than 30 000 animals, are at Macksville, Bellingen, Fig Tree and Centennial Park. In the Greater Sydney area (2.01), there are permanent camps at Parramatta Park, Cabramatta and Ku-ring-gai, as well as smaller colonies at Kareela and in Cannes Park at Avalon. North of Sydney there are also many camps, for example at Inverell and Bellingen I., and some where

Black and **Grey-headed Flying Foxes** co-occur. Examples include Burdekin Park at Singleton (2.18) and Maclean, where **Little Red Flying Foxes** have occurred with the **Grey-headed** and **Black Flying Foxes**; the camp at Rotary Park, Lismore is a permanent **Grey-headed** camp and a maternity camp for **Black Flying Foxes** from spring to autumn. Temporary **Grey-headed Flying Fox** camps can spring up along the coast, especially in summer, almost anywhere between the Victoria and Queensland borders, and some way inland if conditions are suitable – for example, at Young, Bathurst and Orange; in the high country at Tumut; and along the Murray River at Albury (either in the botanic gardens or along the river itself). **Little Red Flying Foxes** are nomadic and more typically found inland, chiefly occupying southern camps in summer. Concentrations typically occur in the Riverina, between Dubbo and Bourke, near Armidale and on the north coast at Forster–Tuncurry. The interactive map at www.environment.gov.au/node/16393 allows you to click on individual camps and see how many of each species are present after seasonal counts.

Bat diversity in the Sydney area increases as you travel towards the city's western edge. **Gould's Wattled Bat** is the most common urban species and, indeed, the state's most widespread microbat. **White-striped Freetail Bats** formerly roosted in an old warehouse at Olympic Park (2.01) and can still be seen in the area – check the flooded quarry and Newington NR, adjacent to the park, especially in the warmer months; **Gould's Wattled Bat** and **Lesser Long-eared Bats** also occur here and **Large-footed Myotis** use bat boxes under bridges. The Sydney Sandstone is core habitat for the **Large-eared Pied Bat**.

In NSW the stronghold of **Eastern Blossom** (the coast north of about Coff's Harbour) and **Eastern Tube-nosed Bats** (very common) is the far coastal north. Other species restricted to the north-east corner (in NSW, at least) are the **Hoary Wattled Bat** (uncommon), **Eastern Cave Bat**, **Eastern Forest Bat** (in north coast rainforests), **Little Bentwing Bat** (very common north of Sydney) and **Northern Long-eared Bat** (common in rainforest and coastal scrub).

New South Wales has several large cave systems supporting important microbat populations. Microbats recorded near Wombeyan Caves include **Large-eared Pied, Gould's** and **Chocolate Wattled Bats, Eastern False Pipistrelle, Large-footed Myotis, Eastern Bentwing, Gould's** and **Lesser Long-eared Bats, Eastern Horseshoe Bat, Eastern Broad-nosed Bat, White-striped Freetail Bat**, and **Large, Southern** and **Little Forest Bats**. The popular Jenolan Caves area in the Blue Mountains has featured all of these species except the myotis, plus **Western** and **Greater Broad-nosed Bats**, and the **Eastern Freetail Bat**.

Three major maternity caves are known for **Eastern Bentwing Bats (ssp.** *oceanensis*) in NSW: Willi Willi Cave near Kempsey (where **Eastern Horseshoe**

Bats also occur), Drum Cave at Bungonia Gorge NP (2.26) and Church Cave near Wee Jasper (2.27), where spectacular fly-outs take place in summer. Australia's largest colony of **Eastern Horseshoe Bats** – some 9500 of them – roosts in a gated cave in a remote part of Ourimbah SF, in northern NSW. More than 50 roosts for this species are known in NSW, although all but two are small; they can be observed emerging from the entrance to Dendetheda Cave (2.10) in the South Coast hinterland. The **Large-footed Myotis** occurs along the entire east coast and Murray Valley, as well as the Lower Murrumbidgee River. It can be seen feeding along streams at several locations, including Wollombi Brook near the Millfield Bridge (where these bats roost) in the Hunter Valley; near Pottsville on the north coast; and they use artificial roosts beneath a concrete bridge at Koala Beach on the Tweed Coast. The near-endemic **Eastern Freetail Bat** is restricted to the coast between Kioloa and south-east Queensland, its stronghold being the Hunter Valley and Cumberland Plains. It is common in mangroves in the Hunter Estuary, which are also used by **Greater Broad-nosed Bats**.

The Pilliga Scrub in central western NSW features a high microbat diversity and seems to be an important area of interchange between eastern and inland species. It would be worth taking part in a survey here, especially as it is one of the few areas where **Greater Long-eared Bats** occur in the state. The Pilliga list to date includes the **Eastern Broad-nosed Bat** and an as-yet-unnamed broad-nosed bat; **Yellow-bellied Sheath-tailed Bats** are common; and the **Eastern Freetail Bat**, **Chocolate Wattled Bat**, **Little Pied Bat**, **Greater Long-eared Bat**, **Inland** and **Little Broad-nosed Bats**, **Eastern Cave Bat**, **Large-eared Pied** and **Eastern Horseshoe Bats** all occur. Interestingly, nearby Mt Kaputar to the east has a slightly different species composition, more reflective of the east coast bat fauna, that includes the **Grey-headed Flying Fox**, **Southern** and **Large Forest Bats**, **Greater Broad-nosed Bat**, **Eastern False Pipistrelle** and **Eastern Bentwing Bats**, although there is also a high overlap in species, such as the **Little Forest Bat**, **Gould's Wattled Bat**, **Lesser** and **Gould's Long-eared Bats**, **White-striped** and **South-eastern Freetails**, **Yellow-bellied Sheath-tailed Bat** and **Little Red Flying Fox**.

The forests of the southern seaboard are also rich in bat species. The spider-hunting **Golden-tipped Bat** occurs on the South Coast at Kioloa; this species roosts in suspended nests of scrubwrens and conceivably could occur wherever the birds are nesting.

the fly-out without going into the camp (where there are plenty of mosquitoes as well as potentially ticks and leeches) from the bridge over the river. Another good spot is the parking area on the northern side of the river at the western end of the island. **Black Flying Foxes** also occur at Bellingen I., albeit in smaller numbers, and

Little Red Flying Foxes visit occasionally; you'd have to visit the camp proper and look carefully to see if any were present. Flying foxes can be seen at quite close quarters here and there can be good photo opportunities. A fun local activity is to watch them drinking from the river: by sitting in the water or paddling a canoe you could also get some good photos.

2.21 BYRON BAY

Highlights: **Short-eared Brushtail Possum, Common Ringtail Possum, Red-necked Pademelon, Bottlenose Dolphin, Humpback Whale**

Other possibilities: **Koala, Parma Wallaby**

Cape Byron is the easternmost point of mainland Australia and one of the best places to watch for **Humpback Whales** from land as they 'turn' around the headland. Peak numbers are in the last week of June and the first week of July as they head north, and during September and October on the southward migration. There's a well-marked walking trail around the 100-m high headland, with coin-operated telescopes. **Bottlenose Dolphins** are also common inshore here. The few **Koalas** that hang on in the Byron Bay area are under threat from urban development: a few survive at Lilli Pilli Estate, Marshall's Creek between New Brighton and South Golden Beach, the Brunswick River at Mullumbimby and coastal cypress forest at Suffolk Park.

Night Visions (www.visionwalks.com) is a company that runs guided wildlife walks with military-style night-vision goggles in the Nightcap Range NP and Whian Whian State Conservation Area in the Byron Bay hinterland. Species commonly seen include the **Red-necked Pademelon, Common Ringtail Possum, Fawn-footed Melomys, Koala, Short-eared Mountain Possum** and bandicoots. On rare occasions a **Parma Wallaby** is sighted and if you ask the guide they may be able to find you one. Ballina, south of Byron Bay, has an important coastal population of **Koalas**.

Massively popular Byron Bay has all manner of accommodation, catering and travel necessities. It is more easily accessed from Brisbane or the Gold Coast in Queensland, from where it is an easy 2-hour drive; otherwise it is 775 km north of Sydney.

2.22 GONDWANA RAINFORESTS OF AUSTRALIA WORLD HERITAGE AREA

Highlights: **Parma Wallaby, Brush-tailed Rock Wallaby, Red-necked Pademelon**

Other possibilities: **Brown Antechinus, Spot-tailed Quoll, Eastern Grey Kangaroo, Common Wallaroo, Red-necked Wallaby**

The north-eastern corner of the state was once a vast volcano, which erupted 23 million years ago, leaving a massive eroded crater with distinctive Mt Warning at its centre. The northern edge of the crater remnant forms the Lamington Plateau (see 1.37) and the whole area is notable for high rainfall and luxuriant subtropical rainforest. Much of the coastal plain has been cleared for agriculture and settlements, and consequently some of the region's rainforest specialties are better sought at Lamington NP, for example. It is well worth exploring this scenic and interesting area, although campers should be aware that it can be cold and wet at any time of year in highland areas.

2.22a Barrington Tops

Parma Wallabies are sometimes seen on the drive up to Barrington Tops NP. This region also features the Devil Ark, where an insurance population of more than 100 devil facial tumour disease-free Tasmanian Devils is being kept. At present it is not open to the public. Barrington Tops is 267 km north of Sydney via Maitland. **Parma Wallabies** also occur at Gibraltar Range NP.

2.22b Oxley Wild Rivers National Park

Northern NSW is the heartland of the **Brush-tailed Rock Wallaby**, which was formerly found in suitable habitat along the Great Dividing Range from southern Queensland to western Victoria. The rugged forested ranges and rocky cliffs of the Oxley Wild Rivers NP are its stronghold and some 10 000 are thought to survive here. There are several scenic areas where the rock wallabies can be found along Waterfall Way, including Gara Gorge (18 km south-east of Armidale on the Castledoyle Rd); **Brown Antechinuses** are often seen here sheltering in cracks in granite outcrops; and **Spot-tailed Quolls** also occur in the gorge. Other good rock wallaby sites include Dangar's Falls (22 km south-east of Armidale on the Dangarsleigh Rd), Wollombombi Falls Lookout, Misty Creek at Guy Fawkes River NP, and the Green Gully Track. Other macropods in the park include the **Eastern Grey Kangaroo**, **Common Wallaroo**, **Red-necked Wallaby**, **Red-necked Pademelon** and a small population of **Parma Wallabies**.

Various sectors of the park can be visited from different centres, including Armidale, Walcha and Dorrigo. There are various campsites in the park and other accommodation in towns and lodges throughout the area. Highways are sealed but some roads are unsealed, although they should be accessible to 2WDs in all weather conditions.

The Dorrigo Plateau is an elevated area of cool rainforest with an interesting bat diversity; bat-trapping and other research at the Dorrigo Field Studies Centre have recorded the **Large-footed Myotis**, **Eastern** and **Common Bentwings**, **Eastern False Pipistrelle**, **Greater Broad-nosed Bat**, **Golden-tipped Bat**, **Eastern Horseshoe Bat**, **Gould's Long-eared Bat**, **Chocolate Wattled Bat**, and **Large**, **Eastern** and **Southern Forest Bats**.

From the coast, the park is most easily accessed by driving inland from Coff's Harbour towards Armidale on Waterfall Way. It is a good 3 hours' drive between the two towns even if you don't stop on this winding road. As most of the attractions are in-between, consider stopping overnight en route or camping.

A few **Brush-tailed Rock Wallabies** also hang on where they have been reintroduced at Warrumbungle NP, further south.

E INLAND NEW SOUTH WALES

Vast areas of forest and woodland west of the Divide were cleared for agriculture after white settlement, leaving only a few significant patches of intact vegetation. You'll have to pass through hundreds of kilometres of agricultural land to reach the arid zone, with little to break up the monotony. **Eastern Grey** and, further west, **Red Kangaroos** are common by the roadside, especially at dusk and after dark. There is a significant zone of overlap between **Eastern** and **Western Grey Kangaroos** in western NSW. Quanda NR is a patch of mallee isolated in a sea of agriculture where both occur; the **Kultarr** has also been recorded here. **Swamp Wallabies** will also be encountered a long distance inland, often far from water, and **Euros** occur on hillsides and outcrops. **Echidnas** can be seen in areas where there is intact vegetation. There are many species of dasyurid, rodent and microbat once you reach the semi-arid and arid zones, but with few exceptions they won't be readily identified without trapping. One of the best ways to get to grips with some of these species is at the Scotia AWC Sanctuary (2.29).

Sites are listed here running roughly north–south. Remember to take all precautions when travelling in remote areas: spare tyres, adequate water, food and fuel if necessary. Distances between towns can be great and traffic very light on some remote highways.

2.23 STURT NATIONAL PARK

Highlights: **Euro, Red Kangaroo, Western Grey Kangaroo, Eastern Grey Kangaroo, Long-haired Rat**

Other possibilities: **Kultarr, Giles' Planigale, Narrow-nosed Planigale, Fat-tailed Dunnart, Stripe-faced Dunnart**

Sturt NP is the far north-west corner of the state and an area of stony desert, breakaways and Coolibah-lined creeks, which are dry most of the time. **Red Kangaroos** are common here, and both **Eastern Grey** and **Western Grey Kangaroos** also occur. Jump-Up Loop is a good route to follow for kangaroo sightings; watch for **Euros** on rocky hillsides also. **Long-haired Rats** reach plague proportions some years. Wait for news of heavy rains inland and subsequent flooding; animals that rely on the drought–flood cycle start to build up once the floodwaters subside (which may take months) – the rats shouldn't be hard to find under the right conditions. In other years they are very elusive, though they may be more common close to waterways. Sturt NP is just north of the pleasant outback town of Tibooburra, where there are cafés, accommodation and petrol; there are campgrounds in the park itself. Arid-zone dasyurids are well represented in Sturt, and the **Kultarr** possibly occurs here.

2.24 GUNNEDAH

Highlights: **Koala**

Other possibilities: **Eastern Grey Kangaroo, Common Wallaroo**

With some justification, Gunnedah claims to be the 'Koala Capital of the World' and **Koalas** are generally easy to see around the town, occasionally even on the streets when they move from tree to tree. The Visitor Information Centre will be able to tell you where they have been sighted lately. Good sites include the Visitor Centre itself; near St Xavier's School in Henry St; the Tourist Caravan Park; along Stock Rd; Bindea Walking Track on Porcupine Lookout; the TAFE Campus; the western end of the Showground; and Gunnedah Golf Course. **Eastern Grey Kangaroos** and **Common Wallaroos** can be seen from Kangaroo Viewing Point.

Travelling to or from Gunnedah, keep an eye out for **Koalas** along the Kamilaroi Hwy (B51) between Quirindi and Gunnedah; and along the Nea Siding–Spring Ridge Rd. They also inhabit several state forests in the area, such as Vickery SF, and can sometimes be seen along the Tungenbone Rd through Spring Ridge SF. Gunnedah is 410 km north-west of Sydney.

2.25 ROUND HILL

Highlights: **Eastern Grey Kangaroo, Western Grey Kangaroo, Red Kangaroo**

Other possibilities: **Echidna, Kultarr, Yellow-footed Antechinus, Mallee Ningaui, Common Dunnart**

'Round Hill' is actually made up of three nature reserves – Yathong, Nombinnie and Round Hill – that protect the nearest sizeable patch of mallee to Sydney, more or less isolated in a sea of agriculture. This area is close to the eastern edge of the **Western Grey Kangaroo**'s range; **Eastern Grey** and **Red Kangaroos** also occur. Otherwise, the mammals most likely to be seen are **Echidnas** and perhaps **Euros**, although both **Kultarr** and **Mallee Ningaui** are on the park list. Round Hill NR is 650 km west of Sydney.

2.26 BUNGONIA GORGE NATIONAL PARK

Highlights: **Eastern Bentwing Bat**

Other possibilities: **Common Brushtail Possum, Eastern Grey Kangaroo, Eastern Horseshoe Bat**

This is one of only three **Eastern Bentwing Bat** maternity caves known in NSW. Every summer (December–April) some 25 000–35 000 **Eastern Bentwing Bats** use Drum, Grill and Chalk Caves, among others, as maternity roosts; they are empty of bats at other times. **Eastern Horseshoe Bats** have also been recorded using them as maternity caves. There is a spectacular fly-out at dusk but note that entry to the caves is forbidden when the bats are using them. Other common animals in the park include **Eastern Grey Kangaroo** and **Common Brushtail Possum**. Bungonia NP is 30 km east of Goulburn.

2.27 WEE JASPER

Highlights: **Eastern Bentwing Bat**

Other possibilities: **Common Brushtail Possum, Eastern Grey Kangaroo**

Another important **Eastern Bentwing Bat** maternity colony is at Church Cave, Wee Jasper. The cave is easily accessible and the bats can be watched emerging at dusk (about 20 minutes after sunset). It takes about an hour for them to all to emerge, with an amazing rush of wings. **Common Brushtail Possums** sometimes loiter near the cave entrance, and **Eastern Grey Kangaroos** are common in this area. Wee Jasper is 70 km south-west of Yass, which is on the Hume Hwy (M31).

2.28 MUTAWINTJI NATIONAL PARK

Highlights: **Euro, Red Kangaroo**

Other possibilities: **Yellow-footed Rock Wallaby**

The mammal fauna of this national park in the far west of NSW has been well studied and it is a pleasant place to camp a few days. **Red Kangaroos** are common on the surrounding plains (and can be a menace to traffic – try not to drive at night if possible). **Yellow-footed Rock Wallabies** – the only known colony in NSW – were discovered here in 1972.

Many studies of arid-zone mammals have been conducted at Fowler's Gap Research Station (www.fowlersgap.unsw.edu.au), west of Mutawintji NP. There's a high density of **Euros** (ssp. *Macropus robustus erubescens*) and various dasyurids, such as **Giles'** and **Narrow-nosed Planigales**, and **Fat-tailed**, **Stripe-faced** and **Common Dunnarts**. Visit the website to see about volunteering.

2.29 SCOTIA AWC SANCTUARY

Highlights: **Numbat, Mala, Bridled Nailtail Wallaby, Greater Stick-nest Rat**

Other possibilities: **Kultarr, Mallee Ningaui, Bolam's Mouse**

One of the Australian Wildlife Conservancy's most successful reserves is the predator-free Scotia Sanctuary, which protects an extensive area of mallee adjoining the SA border. There have been numerous successful reintroductions of species that formerly occurred in the area, including **Greater Stick-nest Rats**, **Numbats**, **Boodies** (Burrowing Bettongs), **Malas**, **Bilbies** and **Bridled Nailtail Wallabies**. The latter were reintroduced in 2004 and now number about 2000, making it the world's largest population of this species; there are plans to release them into fox-baited areas outside the reserve. Of the 500 **Mala** protected in captivity, 30 are at Scotia. **Numbats** are well established and **Greater Bilbies** are of the subspecies still found wild in western Queensland (Scotia is the only site in NSW where these animals can be seen in a wild state). All are in Stage 1 of the sanctuary; **Bridled Nailtails** and **Numbats** can be seen by day. Volunteers can take part in periodic surveys; contact the Australian Wildlife Conservancy (www.australianwildlife.org.au) for more information. Scotia is about midway between Mildura in Victoria and Broken Hill, west of the B79.

2.30 DENILIQUIN

Highlights: **Platypus, Eastern Grey Kangaroo, Red Kangaroo, Common Brushtail Possum, Common Ringtail Possum, Water Rat**

Other possibilities: **Yellow-footed Antechinus, Fat-tailed Dunnart, Western Grey Kangaroo**

Deniliquin in south-central NSW is well known for its bird attractions and consequently attracts a high number of wildlife-watchers. A few mammals could be seen right in the middle of town at Island Sanctuary, which protects a lagoon near the Edwards River surrounded by River Red Gum woodland. Tourist leaflets claim that a **Platypus** could be seen from Deniliquin's main street; the lagoon runs roughly parallel to the footpath and a footbridge leads over the water into adjoining woodland, and conceivably a **Platypus** could be seen from the road. **Water Rats** have also been recorded. Both **Red** and **Eastern Grey Kangaroos** occur in the woodland (in hot weather they shelter in the cooler, lower area to the right of the entrance). **Echidnas**, **Western Grey Kangaroos** and **Swamp Wallabies** have also been recorded; **Common Brushtail** and **Ringtail Possums** can be spotlighted in the woodland after dark; and smaller species have included **Yellow-footed Antechinus** and **Fat-tailed Dunnart**. Deniliquin is 755 km south-west of Sydney, but note that it is an easy 310 km drive north of Melbourne, Victoria.

3. Australian Capital Territory

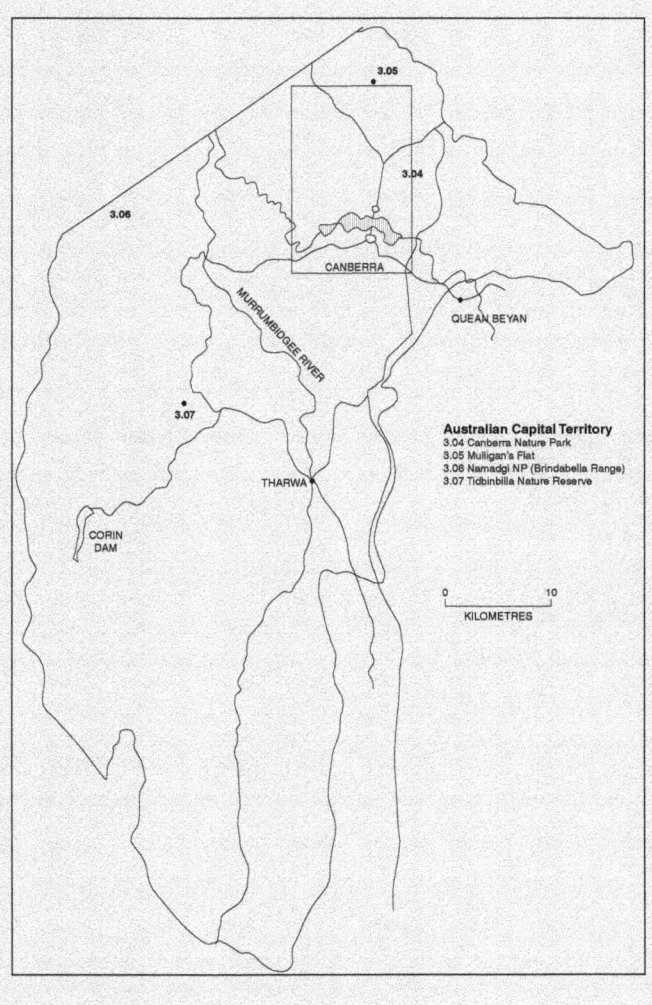

3.05

3.04

3.06

CANBERRA

MURRUMBIDGEE RIVER

QUEANBEYAN

3.07

Australian Capital Territory
3.04 Canberra Nature Park
3.05 Mulligan's Flat
3.06 Namadgi NP (Brindabella Range)
3.07 Tidbinbilla Nature Reserve

THARWA

CORIN
DAM

0   10
KILOMETRES

Highlights: **Platypus, Echidna, Common Wombat, Common Brushtail Possum, Common Ringtail Possum, Sugar Glider, Eastern Grey Kangaroo, Swamp Wallaby, Red-necked Wallaby, Grey-headed Flying Fox, Water Rat**

Other possibilities: **Southern Bettong (reintroduction), Common Wallaroo (Euro), White-striped Freetail Bat, New Holland Mouse (reintroduction)**

The ACT is an administrative enclave whose boundaries were carved out of the southern uplands of NSW. A large part of its area is taken up by Canberra, the national capital, and therefore urbanised, but generous green spaces and a series of artificial lakes have benefited wildlife. Extensive natural habitats, such as grassy woodlands, wet forest and alpine meadows are protected by Namadgi NP, which occupies much of the southern part of the ACT and can be reached within an hour's drive of the city centre. There are no endemic mammals in the Territory, but as Canberra is a hub for government, tourism, education and science many people find themselves here at some point. More than half the ACT is in reserves and 46 per cent is protected by Namadgi NP alone.

Local wildlife is well documented and there are some excellent mammalian attractions. **Eastern Grey Kangaroos** are abundant in urban areas – they can sometimes be seen en route to the airport in the early morning near Duntroon Military Training School, around Campbell Park Defence Offices and grazing on lawns near the Australian War Memorial. Free-ranging populations are also enclosed at Government House in Yarralumla and at the Belconnen Naval Transmitting Station. The city's waterways can provide some of the best **Platypus** and **Water Rat** viewing in the country. Small mammals are scarce, although the **Yellow-footed Antechinus** is seen occasionally and the **Spot-tailed Quoll** turns up sporadically in urban areas adjoining suitable habitat; the quolls possibly follow the Murrumbidgee Corridor from further south in the ACT, and occasionally become roadkill in suburban Canberra. Notable local extinctions have included the **Koala**, which was hunted out in the 1960s, and the **Brush-tailed Rock Wallaby**, which was last seen in the southern ACT at Gibraltar Gap in 1959. Several introduced species are very common, including the European Fox, feral Cat, European Rabbit and Brown Hare. Feral Sambar and Fallow Deer also occur and appear to be getting more common.

Canberra makes an excellent base for trips to the NSW High Country, the forests and coast of southern NSW and further west into the arid zone. Some good nearby mammal sites in NSW include Queanbeyan (2.13), the Bateman's Bay area (2.09), Eden (2.12) and Kosciuszko NP (2.16).

SOME TERRITORY HIGHLIGHTS
- **Eastern Grey Kangaroos** are abundant and commonly visit suburban gardens.
- One of the best places in Australia to see **Platypus** and **Water Rat**.

- The successful reintroduction of **Southern Bettong** to Mulligan's Flat NR.
- **Common Wombats** are easily seen along quiet roads in nearby hills.
- The **Grey-headed Flying Fox** camp at Commonwealth Park.

3.01 LAKE BURLEY GRIFFIN AND MOLONGOLO RIVER

Highlights: **Platypus, Water Rat**

Other possibilities: **Eastern Grey Kangaroo, Swamp Wallaby**

Lake Burley Griffin is an extensive artificial lake that forms the focus for many of Canberra's cultural attractions. Quiet, reed-fringed reaches are excellent habitat for both **Platypuses** and **Water Rats**, and both are quite common. Both could potentially be seen where Sullivan's Creek debouches into the lake; the best access is through the Australian National University grounds. The Molongolo River fills the lake at its eastern end and **Platypuses** occur in the reach between the airport and the lake itself, especially near Duntroon Military College. Jerrabombera Wetlands (the main focus of which is known locally as Kelly's Swamp) is a great wetland at the eastern end of the lake; it is well known to birdwatchers, who occasionally report seeing **Water Rats** from observation hides (such as Bittern Hide) and from the footbridge that crosses the river, and **Platypuses** from the same bridge and Fulica Hide. **Swamp Wallabies** and **Eastern Grey Kangaroos** are also sighted here regularly. On Lake Burley Griffin itself, **Water Rats** are often seen at the little island north of Aspen I. (the island on which the Carillon stands), especially among willow roots on the eastern side; stellar views can be had by hiring a canoe and paddling around this area in the early morning. Norgrove Park is an artificial urban space at the southern edge of the lake where **Water Rats** (and introduced *Rattus* species) occur, especially in the 'Eco Pond'. To get there, head south along Wentworth Ave through the suburb of Kingston and turn left at Dawes St; the park is two blocks along.

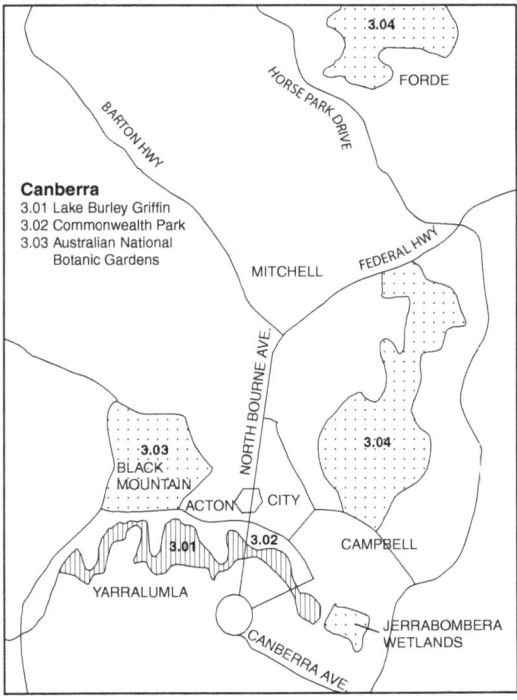

Canberra
3.01 Lake Burley Griffin
3.02 Commonwealth Park
3.03 Australian National
    Botanic Gardens

Platypuses and **Water Rats** have also been recorded at Lake Ginninderra, another of Canberra's artificial lakes. And about 5 km upstream from the Jerrabombera Wetlands, where the Molongolo River runs through the city of Queanbeyan, NSW is one of the finest local sites for both species (see 2.13).

3.02 COMMONWEALTH PARK

Highlights: **Common Brushtail Possum, Common Ringtail Possum, Grey-headed Flying Fox**

Other possibilities: **Water Rat, Little Red Flying Fox**

Just south of the Civic centre and within easy walking distance, Commonwealth Park supports urbanised **Common Brushtail Possums** and **Common Ringtail Possums**. A camp of **Grey-headed Flying Foxes** fluctuates in number from a few hundred to as many as 10 000. The bats usually roost near the outdoor stage (sometimes referred to as Stage 88) in late summer (January–February) and stay till autumn; in late 2010 some 20 females dropped young and a few hundred bats have overwintered in recent years, braving Canberra's sub-zero temperatures. During summer they can often be seen flying over northern suburbs at dusk, around orchards at Pialligo and feeding at the Tasmanian Blue Gums along Anzac Parade if they are in flower. A few **Little Red Flying Foxes** sometimes roost with the Grey-headed camp, though more commonly they are seen along the river in Queanbeyan. A short walk away, Nerang Pool is a quiet inlet from the lake that is also a good spot to see **Water Rats**, especially early on still mornings or at night with a torch (flashlight).

To get to Commonwealth Park drive south along Commonwealth Ave; the turn-off is before you get to the lake. You can also walk there from Civic: a footbridge at the southern end of Allara St goes directly into the park; head left for Stage 88 and Nerang Pool.

3.03 BOTANIC GARDENS AND BLACK MOUNTAIN

Highlights: **Common Brushtail Possum, Common Ringtail Possum, Sugar Glider, Swamp Wallaby, Grey-headed Flying Fox**

Other possibilities: **Yellow-footed Antechinus**

The superb native Australian National Botanic Gardens (ANBG) at the foot of Black Mountain are a good spot for **Swamp Wallabies**, particularly at the far western end (beyond the Glasshouse) and in the Sydney Region botanical section. **Yellow-footed Antechinuses** are sometimes seen foraging in the Rainforest Gully; walk quietly and listen for rustling in the leaf litter, or try squeaking for small birds, a noise which can sometimes attract this species. Strangely, **Sambar** have sometimes strayed into the gardens, presumably from nearby Black Mountain or Aranda Bushland. The gardens' entrance is on Clunies Ross St; opening hours are 8.30 am to 5 pm; see www.anbg. gov.au for more information.

Common Brushtail Possums are common at the adjacent campus of the Australian National University (ANU), and may be seen scavenging around the Union area at night. The university is east of the ANBG, across Clunies Ross St and an easy walk.

Black Mountain itself is a prominent, forested landmark with a telecoms tower on top that can be seen from many points around Canberra. **Eastern Grey Kangaroos** are common here and in the adjacent Aranda Bushland (west) and Bruce Ridge (to the north). You should have no trouble spotlighting **Common Ringtail** and **Brushtail Possums** between the ANBG entrance and the CSIRO complex to the north along Clunies Ross Drive. **Sugar Gliders** are resident and can be seen along trails on the western side of the mountain (access via Caswell Drive). **Swamp Wallabies** also occur on Black Mountain, as well as in adjoining bush areas. (**Common Wallaroos** sometimes become roadkill between the National Zoo (adjacent to Tuggeranong Parkway) and Black Mountain Peninsula; they possibly travel up the Molongolo Valley and feasibly could occur on the western slopes of the mountain.) **Grey-headed Flying Foxes** can be seen flapping into the ANBG to feed at dusk; they are not as common on the western side of the mountain. However, the local area is very good for microbats – see the 'Watching Bats in the ACT' box.

WATCHING BATS IN THE ACT

Grey-headed Flying Foxes now seem to be a guaranteed presence in Commonwealth Park (3.02), at least during summer. The camp varies in size and young have been born some years; recently more animals seem to have stayed on during Canberra's bitter winters, the nearby botanic gardens perhaps guaranteeing them a food supply. **Little Red Flying Foxes** also occur from time to time. The slopes of Black Mountain (3.03) are one of the best sites for microbats in the ACT: natural woodland provides large trees for roosting, and the lake, dams and botanic gardens encourage insect hatchings. Commonly recorded species include the **White-striped Freetail Bat**, **Southern**, **Large** and **Little Forest Bats**, **Gould's** and **Chocolate Wattled Bats**, and **Lesser** and **Gould's Long-eared Bats**. Microbat activity is rather seasonal in Canberra, owing to the cold winters, when some species leave the area or hibernate. **White-striped Freetail Bats**, for example, forage in older, well-treed suburbs during summer; during the annual migration of Bogong Moths they (and other, less distinctive species) can be seen hunting around the spotlights at Parliament House and the beacon on top of Mt Ainslie. However, when temperatures drop in late autumn microbat activity almost ceases until spring. **Eastern Bentwing Bats** pass through Canberra on migration (February and March) between maternity caves at Wee Jasper, NSW (2.27), about

60 km to the north-west, and hibernation sites at the south coast. They have been known to roost under King's Avenue Bridge en route. In all, 14 microbat species have been recorded in the ACT and others known from nearby sites in NSW could be expected to turn up here also.

3.04 CANBERRA NATURE PARK

Highlights: **Echidna, Common Brushtail Possum, Common Ringtail Possum, Sugar Glider, Eastern Grey Kangaroo, Red-necked Wallaby, Swamp Wallaby**

More than 30 separate pockets of natural habitat in the Canberra area have been set aside as the Canberra Nature Park. Many are low, wooded hills and adjoining areas that break up the urban sprawl, although not all are contiguous. There are good walking trails and most are easily accessible by car.

Should it prove scarce elsewhere, many of these reserves are a certainty for **Eastern Grey Kangaroos**. They are abundant throughout the older part of the city and can be seen along suburban streets, especially at dawn and dusk in winter when they can be a traffic hazard. Excellent, more natural, locations include the slopes of Mts Ainslie and Majura, Campbell Park, O'Connor Ridge, The Pinnacle and Mulligan's Flat (3.05). **Sugar Gliders** are not uncommon in Canberra Nature Park, although some areas are better than others; Aranda Ridge is a recommended location and **Swamp Wallabies** are common there also. Mt Ainslie has a population of **Sugar Gliders**, as well as **Common Ringtail** and **Common Brushtail Possums**, **Eastern Grey Kangaroos**, and **Swamp** and **Red-necked Wallabies**. The range of **Sugar Gliders** may mirror that of **Common Ringtail Possums**, in Canberra at least: both seem more common in well-established older suburbs with adjacent native bush, such as Aranda. There is even a record of **Sugar Glider** from the woodlands surrounding Parliament House, which used to be contiguous with other bush areas.

The **Common Dunnart** has been recorded in open woodland on Mt Ainslie, but appears to be rather rare. Several species of microbat feed on insects attracted to the beacon at the top of Mt Ainslie on warm summer nights – most easily identified is the **White-striped Freetail Bat**; it can be recognised by its call and its bold markings distinguished by the light of a good torch (flashlight). **Echidnas** are seen regularly on Mt Taylor and could turn up in any suitable habitat, and **Common Wallaroos** have been reported from Kama NR.

3.05 MULLIGAN'S FLAT NATURE RESERVE

Highlights: **Echidna, Sugar Glider, Eastern Grey Kangaroo, Red-necked Wallaby, Swamp Wallaby**

Other possibilities: **Southern (Tasmanian) Bettong (reintroduction), Common Wallaroo, New Holland Mouse (reintroduction)**

A superb remnant of Yellow Box woodland on the north-eastern boundary of the ACT has been set aside as the Mulligan's Flat NR. This area is one of the best for **Echidnas** near Canberra and **Eastern Grey Kangaroos** are numerous. **Sugar Gliders** are relatively common in tall timber – try around some of the dams. Plans are under way to re-establish some of the local mammal fauna that have been extirpated from the ACT since white settlement. Several species, including **Southern Bettong** are thought to once have been common here (this species is extinct on the mainland and is therefore usually known as Tasmanian Bettong). In 2012 **Southern Bettongs** were introduced into a predator exclosure ('Mulligan's Flat Woodlands Sanctuary'). This was the first attempt at re-establishing this species on the mainland and the animals have already bred. The best site for seeing them seems to be near the old woolshed; very occasionally you might accidentally startle one from its daytime hiding place and rangers conduct guided night walks. A few specimens of the **New Holland Mouse** were introduced recently and Southern Brown Bandicoots may also be allowed to join them eventually. See www.mulligansflat.org.au for updates and more information.

Common Wallaroos are not common in the ACT, but a few seem to be resident at Goorooyaroo NR, to the east of Mulligan's Flat, especially on the north-west slopes of Old Joe Hill. The valley just to the south is called Euro Valley and supports **Eastern Grey Kangaroos, Common Wallaroos, Swamp Wallabies** and **Red-necked Wallabies**. The **Common Dunnart** has been recorded in the Mulligan's–Goorooyaroo area, and the **Fat-tailed Dunnart** formerly occurred in the northern ACT, where it was at the eastern extremity of its range but is probably no longer present.

The easiest access to Mulligan's Flat is through the suburb of Forde; head north along Horse Park Drive, turn right at Jessie St; the Mulligan's Flat car park and entrance is on Amy Ackman St more or less opposite the end of Jessie St.

WATCHING PLATYPUSES IN THE ACT

Platypuses could be encountered in virtually any permanent waterway with large pools, such as the Murrumbidgee, Cotter and Molongolo Rivers, as well as in still, vegetated parts of Canberra's many artificial lakes. Peak **Platypus** sightings are usually in July–August when adult males are active in preparation for breeding. Early morning and late afternoon, particularly in still conditions, are the best times to look for them and also for **Water Rats**, which often occur at the same sites. Try some of the following:

- Along the Murrumbidgee River, for example, at Tharwa Sandwash, Kambah Pool, Point Hut Crossing and any site for about 10 km downstream (north) of Uriarra Crossing, such as below Shepherd's Lookout.
- Along the Gudgenby River in Namadgi NP (3.06).
- The Lower Molongolo River corridor.
- Waterbird enclosures at Tidbinbilla NR (3.07).
- The Murrumbidgee River near Michelago (just outside the ACT, 53 km south of Canberra).

There are other excellent **Platypus** sites further south in NSW near Cooma (2.14) and Bombala (see 2.15) and in Queanbeyan (2.13). Visit www.platypus.asn.au for more information.

3.06 NAMADGI NATIONAL PARK (BRINDABELLA RANGE)

Highlights: **Sugar Glider, Common Wombat, Eastern Grey Kangaroo, Red-necked Wallaby, Swamp Wallaby**

Other possibilities: **Greater Glider, Common Wallaroo, [Sambar]**

The ACT's highest and wildest country is protected by Namadgi NP, which covers nearly half of the Territory. The Brindabella Range, about 40 minutes west of the city centre, features extensive stands of upland wet forest, Snow Gums on the highest ridges and deep, wet gullies in the valleys. The whole area was hit by a major bushfire in 2003 but is recovering well. By taking an early morning drive along the various forest roads you should have no trouble locating **Eastern Grey Kangaroos**, **Swamp Wallabies** and **Red-necked Wallabies**; **Common Wombats** are often seen along these roads at night (they are almost never abroad during the day) – try driving the Uriarra Rd up as far as Piccadilly Circus, or along the road to Corin Dam (where the Square Rock Walking Track is good for **Swamp Wallaby**). There are also sporadic sightings of **Common Wallaroos** at higher elevations (for example, near the junction of Wark's Rd and Pago Break); their stronghold in the ACT is along the Murrumbidgee Corridor, Paddy's River and in southern parts of Namadgi NP. Tall forests support **Greater Glider**; try spotlighting at sites such as Bull's Head Creek and along Wark's Rd. **Sugar Gliders** and **Feathertail Gliders** are also present, although all glider numbers may have been suppressed by the fires. In 2013 an **Eastern Pygmy Possum** was discovered in a campground, and in the past this species has been recorded at 1800 m on Mt Kelly. This habitat is potentially ideal for **Eastern False Pipistrelles**, though bat activity shuts down dramatically in cold weather (the temperature can drop to single figures here even in mid-summer and falls well below zero in winter).

The **Brush-tailed Rock Wallaby** survived into the 1950s in the Orroral Valley, but the last sighting was in 1959. Several other mammal species that were formerly common in the ACT may still persist in remote parts of Namadgi, such as the **Brush-tailed Phascogale**. The Gudgenby Valley further south is reputed to have a relatively high density of **Spot-tailed Quolls**; there is one old record of the rare **Smoky Mouse** from the Brindabellas; and **Mountain Brushtail Possums** and **Yellow-bellied Gliders** may still occur at higher elevations. **Sambar** are occasionally seen near Piccadilly Circus and at the top of Wark's Rd.

To get to the Brindabellas, follow Cotter Rd and turn right towards Uriarra Village after crossing the Murrumbidgee River at Cotter Dam (**Eastern Bentwing Bats** use caves in the Cotter area on their autumn migration to coastal sites). The road is unsealed and may be closed at higher elevations after snow.

3.07 TIDBINBILLA NATURE RESERVE

Highlights: **Platypus, Common Wombat, Eastern Grey Kangaroo, Red-necked Wallaby, Swamp Wallaby**

Other possibilities: **Brown Antechinus, Common Brushtail Possum, Common Ringtail Possum, Water Rat**

After being almost totally destroyed by wildfire in 2003 Tidbinbilla NR is well on the road to recovery. The reserve's wet forests and gullies are contiguous with the Brindabella Range and other parts of Namadgi NP (3.06). **Eastern Grey Kangaroos** and **Red-necked Wallabies** are common in grassy hollows; **Swamp Wallabies** can be seen in dense gullies. The park also supports **Sugar Gliders, Common Brushtail** and **Common Ringtail Possums** and **Common Wombats**, any or all of which you might see on a guided nature walk after dark with rangers. Fishing Gap Track is a pleasant trail along which **Common Wombats** are often seen, even venturing abroad on sunny days during winter. **Echidnas** are not uncommon and there's a healthy population of wild **Platypuses** and **Water Rats** in some of Tidbinbilla's waterbird enclosures; good sites include the 'weir' above Pond 1 (on the far side of pond from the walking trail) and Black Flats Dam, especially in the late afternoon or early morning. Ask volunteer guides for recent sightings. The park organises guided Platypus-viewing walks which generally guarantee results. **Platypuses** are also seen near the bridge at Greens. Rustlings in the undergrowth could prove to be a **Brown Antechinus** – they are sometimes seen from paths in the fenced enclosures. **Bush Rats** also live here, although they are almost never seen during the day. Tidbinbilla is also a conservation and education centre, where several species of native mammal are kept in large enclosures. The reserve has played an important role in captive breeding of, among others, the **Brush-tailed Rock Wallaby**, and many have since been released in parts of its former range where it has been extirpated.

Unfortunately, unless you accompany a ranger on a guided walk after dark (check www.tidbinbilla.com.au to see what activities are on offer), mammal viewing opportunities are rather restricted: opening hours are 7.30 am to 8 pm in summer, closing at 6 pm in winter. However, it would be worth spotlighting in the wet forest on the road to Corin Dam, which starts 4 km south of the park entrance.

4. Victoria

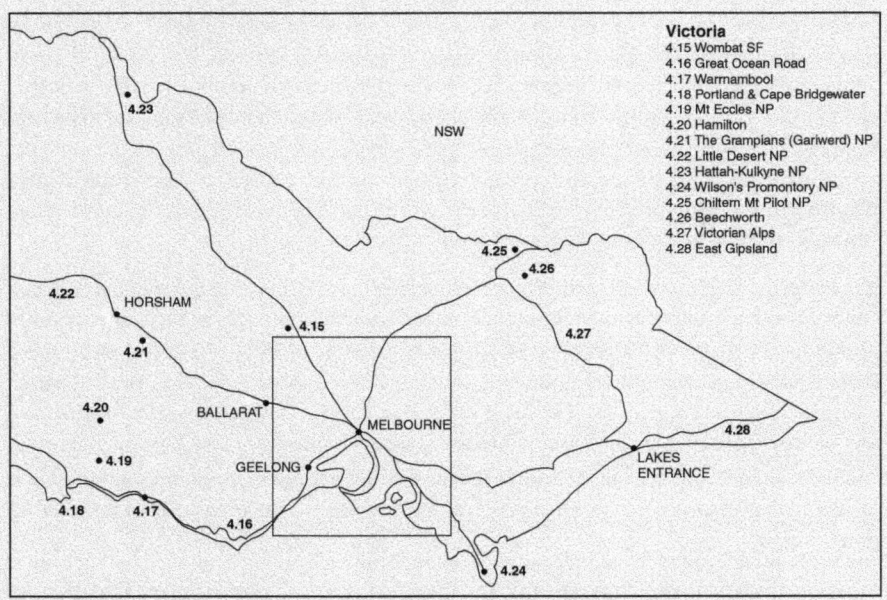

Victoria
4.15 Wombat SF
4.16 Great Ocean Road
4.17 Warrnambool
4.18 Portland & Cape Bridgewater
4.19 Mt Eccles NP
4.20 Hamilton
4.21 The Grampians (Gariwerd) NP
4.22 Little Desert NP
4.23 Hattah-Kulkyne NP
4.24 Wilson's Promontory NP
4.25 Chiltern Mt Pilot NP
4.26 Beechworth
4.27 Victorian Alps
4.28 East Gipsland

NSW

HORSHAM
BALLARAT
MELBOURNE
GEELONG
LAKES ENTRANCE

Endemic: **Leadbeater's Possum**

Australia's smallest mainland state is roughly wedge-shaped, the 'fat' western end stretching some 400 km from the Murray River in the north to the volcanic plains of the south-west, and the 'thin' end tapering off in Gippsland, a mountainous, well-forested region with few roads or towns. In-between is an extraordinary variety of habitats and wildlife: semi-arid mallee and heath, densely forested mountains and a rugged, scenic coastline are all easily accessible within 3–4 hours' drive of Melbourne. The cool, wet ranges east of the state capital support some of the world's tallest hardwood forests, home to various gliders and possums, including Victoria's only endemic mammal – **Leadbeater's Possum** – and a healthy population of **Common Wombats**. These mountains are contiguous with Australia's highest ranges over the border in NSW, and Victoria supports approximately half the world's population of **Mountain Pygmy Possums**. A long, indented coastline features shallow bays and coastal lakes, home to the **Burrunan Bottlenose Dolphin** (which may prove to be a separate species); rocky islets offer numerous haul outs and rookeries for **Australian Fur Seals**; and several prominent headlands make good whale-watching locations. The semi-arid north-west corner has some of the most accessible stands of mallee woodland in the country, with a good representation of small arid-zone dasyurids, pygmy possums and rodents, such as **Mallee Ningaui**, **Western Pygmy Possum** and **Mitchell's Hopping-mouse**. This is the easiest place in Australia to see the three 'great' kangaroos (**Red**, **Eastern Grey** and **Western Grey**) in close proximity. Heathlands in the west support a number of localised small mammals, including the **Heath**, **Silky** and **Smoky Mouse**. The far south-west bears the brunt of winter storms and marks the western limits of many eastern species, such as **Eastern Grey Kangaroo**, **Yellow-bellied Glider** and **Swamp Wallaby**; the south-west also supports a large **Koala** population and Victoria is one of the best states in which to see this popular animal. Offshore, **Southern Right Whales** are a regular sight in winter and the Bonney Upwelling attracts **Blue Whales** in late summer.

It has to be said that, despite Victoria's benevolent climate and civilised human environment, wildlife has sometimes not fared so well. The only surviving mainland population of **Eastern Barred Bandicoot** persisted near the town of Hamilton until 2002. In this state it now exists only where it has been reintroduced into predator-free reserves such as Woodlands (4.02) and Mt Rothwell (4.13). **Leadbeater's Possum** – one of Victoria's faunal emblems – remains critically endangered, and large dasyurids, such as the **Spot-tailed Quoll** and **Brush-tailed Phascogale**, hang on only in small, scattered populations; you could spend a long time in the field and not see either of them.

It would be worth hooking up with the Mammal Survey Group and well-respected Field Naturalists' Club of Victoria (FNCV), which run survey camps at various sites around the state. These can involve small mammal- and bat-trapping, remote camera photography and spotlight surveys, and species encountered have included the **Eastern Pygmy Possum**, **Brush-tailed Phascogale**, **New Holland Mouse**, **Mitchell's Hopping-mouse**, **White-footed Dunnart**, **Common Dunnart** and **Silky Mouse**. Also check out some of the local Friends' groups and Field Naturalists' clubs, whose members may have local knowledge on finding select species.

SOME STATE HIGHLIGHTS
- **Koalas** are easily seen on day trips from the capital Melbourne.
- **Eastern Grey**, **Western Grey** and **Red Kangaroos** all occur in close proximity.
- **Grey-headed Flying Foxes** are common in suburban Melbourne.
- **Southern Brown Bandicoots** are active by day at Cranbourne Botanic Gardens.
- The world's largest **Australian Fur Seal** rookery, at Phillip I.

A SOUTH-CENTRAL VICTORIA

Melbourne is an international hub, with every possible type of accommodation, eating and transport option available. A few mammals are common and easily seen in the city, and several prime sites make easy day trips to see iconic species such as kangaroos, the Koala and wombats.

4.01 GREATER MELBOURNE

Highlights: **Common Brushtail Possum, Common Ringtail Possum, Grey-headed Flying Fox, Water Rat**

Other possibilities: **Platypus, Common Wombat, Koala, Eastern Grey Kangaroo, Swamp Wallaby**

Melbourne is Australia's second-largest city, a vast conurbation that sprawls around Port Phillip Bay from basalt grasslands and salt pans in the west to tall, wet forest on the mountainous eastern edge. Most of the small mammals have disappeared, but numerous green spaces have been preserved, and some species remain surprisingly common even in the inner city. Parks are thick with **Common Brushtail Possums** and they are easily seen after dark a short walk from the city centre at, for example, the Royal Melbourne Botanic Gardens and Domain on the south bank of the Yarra River (opposite the CBD); Fitzroy and Flagstaff Gardens on the northern and eastern edges of the CBD, respectively; Catani Gardens in St Kilda; and, north of the city, at Curtin Square in North Carlton. They are also common in suburban gardens, where the **Common Ringtail Possum** is probably even more abundant. Ringtails are more arboreal than and not as bold as the brushtails. You'll probably need a torch or spotlight to see them; they are generally easier to see in yards of leafy suburbs and are often seen running along fence tops or telegraph wires.

There's a permanent camp of up to 40 000 **Grey-headed Flying Foxes** at Yarra Bend Park, 5 km upstream from the CBD on the southern bank of the Yarra. The best viewing is a short walk from the Bellbird Picnic Area, off Yarra Bend Boulevard, where there's a short trail and lookout points (do not cross the adjacent golf course to view the camp). Watch out for **Black Flying Foxes** here also – they were recorded for the first time in 2010. The best view of the nightly fly-out is from Wills St Picnic Area at the top of a hill nearby: take Molesworth St off Yarra Bend Blvd, turn left (north) at Redmond St and park at the end of the street. There's a grassy area here with a view over the parkland and CBD, from where the emerging bats are silhouetted over the city at sunset. Closer to the CBD the bats can always be seen at dusk, especially where there are mature fig trees; drinking from the river in flight; and in inner suburbs wherever there is good tree cover. You should have no trouble seeing them flying around at dusk anywhere in the Domain and from vantage points such as various bridges over the Yarra.

Melbourne's superb botanic gardens support a small population of **Water Rats**, which can sometimes be seen by sitting quietly by the Nymphaea Lily Lake or the large Ornamental Lake, especially in the early morning or late afternoon before the crowds arrive. They can also be seen at ponds in the Fitzroy Gardens, but the best place to see this species (and one of the best sites in the country) is at St Kilda breakwater. Here they share the groyne with a colony of Little Penguins: follow the St Kilda pier to the café then veer left, where a boardwalk and signs take you to the lee of the stone breakwater. The **Water Rats** are most active at dusk, but could be seen at any time and especially at the seaward end of the boardwalk. They den among the rocks and forage in the sheltered marina waters as well as stormwater drains emptying into the bay. **Water Rats** are the only small native mammal to have survived Melbourne's urbanisation in any numbers; they may also be seen near Elwood canal, a few hundred metres further south. **Water Rats** also frequent the Melbourne Water farm at Werribee, for which you'll need permission to access, and where **Fat-tailed Dunnarts** inhabit open grasslands and shelter among basalt rocks.

Eastern Grey Kangaroos are becoming more common on Melbourne's urban fringes. Reliable sites include Candlebark Park, on the banks of the Yarra some 33 km upstream, where **Eastern Greys** and **Swamp Wallabies** are common along walking tracks, and **Echidnas** also occur. There are **Common Wombats** here, although you would need to go out with a torch (flashlight) after dark to see them. Stake out occupied burrows at dusk; they can be recognised by fresh diggings and the wombats' cube-shaped droppings. **Koalas** have been reported here and in Wonga Park and Warrandyte, among other suburbs, though they are probably more accessible elsewhere (for example, Brisbane Ranges NP (4.11) and You Yangs Regional Park (4.12)). To get to Candlebark Park, take the Eastern Fwy from the city and turn off at Elgar Rd; take a dog-leg right at Doncaster Rd and then follow Williamsons Rd north (past the shopping centre tower). Williamsons Rd eventually becomes Fitzsimon's Lane before crossing the Yarra River. Just before the river bridge, watch for a turn off on the right – take this and park, then walk or cycle the Main Yarra Trail eastwards. Eventually the trail reaches Mullum Mullum Creek near where it debouches into the Yarra – this is a good area for **Platypuses**. They are probably easiest to spot in the creek itself, but also occur upstream of here in the Yarra (in fact, **Platypuses** also inhabit the muddy Yarra above Dight's Falls near the city centre, but sightings here require patience and luck – they are easier to see elsewhere) at Viewbank and Eltham–Warrandyte (visit the Australian Platypus Conservancy www.platypus.asn.au for details of counts and walks). **Platypuses** also occur in the Plenty and Werribee rivers, and Diamond and Gardiner creeks.

Another semi-urban site for **Eastern Grey Kangaroos** and **Swamp Wallabies** is Lysterfield Reservoir-Churchill NP. Both these species, plus **Echidnas**, are common but these are popular places for joggers and day-trippers, and an early start is advised. The Acacia Walk at Lysterfield is recommended. Check park opening hours, but

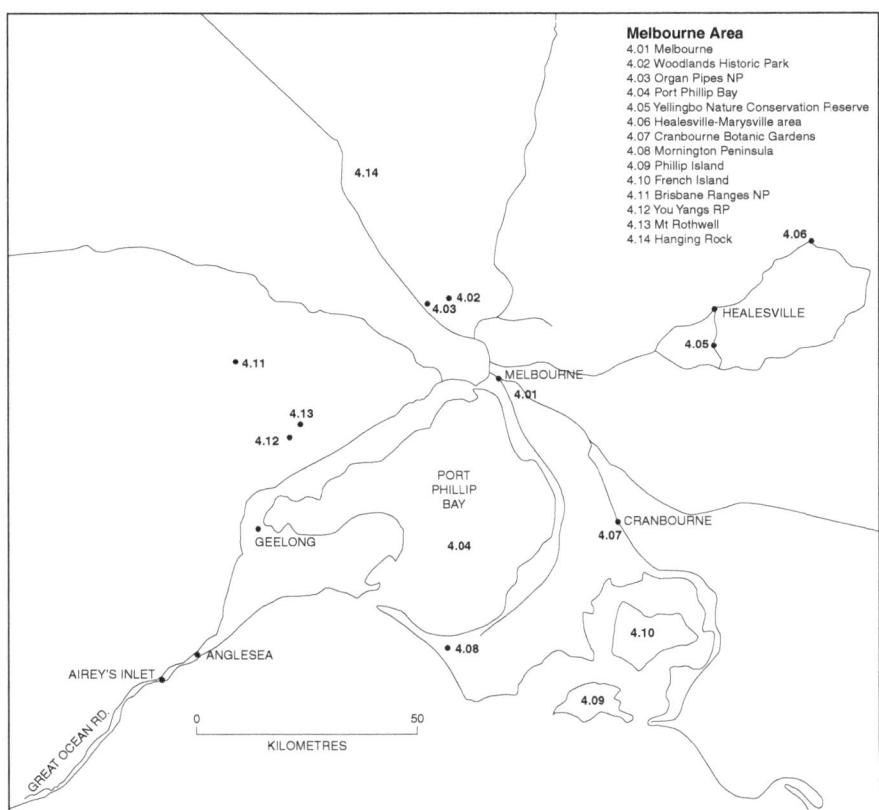

Melbourne Area
4.01 Melbourne
4.02 Woodlands Historic Park
4.03 Organ Pipes NP
4.04 Port Phillip Bay
4.05 Yellingbo Nature Conservation Reserve
4.06 Healesville-Marysville area
4.07 Cranbourne Botanic Gardens
4.08 Mornington Peninsula
4.09 Phillip Island
4.10 French Island
4.11 Brisbane Ranges NP
4.12 You Yangs RP
4.13 Mt Rothwell
4.14 Hanging Rock

Common Brushtail and **Common Ringtail Possums** should be easy to spotlight at either site as well. Rather than battle urban traffic to see **Eastern Greys**, it may be easier to travel to other sites outside Greater Melbourne that are probably more reliable but slightly further, such as You Yangs Regional Park (4.12), Anglesea Golf Course (4.16) and Brisbane Ranges NP (4.11).

Among the microbats, 10 species occur in greater Melbourne. **Gould's Wattled Bat**, **White-striped Freetail Bat** (which can be heard between September and May) and **Southern Broad-nosed Bats** are common suburban species; others include **Chocolate Wattled**, **Large Forest**, **Southern Forest** and **Small Forest Bats**, and **Southern Freetail Bat**.

4.02 WOODLANDS HISTORIC PARK

Highlights: **Eastern Barred Bandicoot**

After some ups and downs the reintroduction of **Eastern Barred Bandicoots** into a Fox-free reserve at Woodlands Historic Park has been deemed successful. This is now one of the best sites to see this species on the mainland (it occurs in the wild only in Tasmania). Visit www.conservationvolunteers.com.au for more information. To get to Woodlands turn north off the Tullamarine Fwy (M2) onto Mickleham Rd then left (west) at Somerton Rd. The park is closed to vehicles after 4.30 pm daily but pedestrian access is possible at all times.

4.03 ORGAN PIPES NATIONAL PARK

Highlights: **Sugar Glider, Gould's Wattled Bat, White-striped Freetail Bat, Large Forest Bat**

Other possibilities: **Platypus, Echidna, Common Brushtail Possum, Common Ringtail Possum, Eastern Grey Kangaroo, Swamp Wallaby, Southern Forest Bat, Chocolate Wattled Bat, Eastern Freetail Bat**

A scenic gorge just north of the city is the site of a long-running bat monitoring project. Both **Gould's Wattled** and **White-striped Freetail Bats** roost in bat boxes at the Organ Pipes NP, where they are monitored bimonthly by volunteers who welcome visitors and participants. **Gould's Wattled Bats** are always present, with numbers peaking in the warmer months, and **White-striped Freetail Bats** nearly so but in smaller numbers that peak in April. The **Large Forest Bat** is the third species that roosts regularly (mostly spring to autumn), and occasional **Little Forest Bats**, **Southern Forest Bats** (Spring-Summer), **Chocolate Wattled Bats** and **Eastern Freetail Bats** also occur. **Sugar Gliders** were reintroduced to the Organ Pipes NP and use nest boxes that have been set up for them. These are regularly inspected during bat surveys, during which **Common Ringtail** and **Common Brushtail Possums** are also encountered. Other mammals seen regularly include **Eastern Grey Kangaroo**, **Swamp Wallaby** and **Echidna**; **Platypuses** have been recorded from Jackson's Creek, which runs through the park.

The Organ Pipes are 26 km north-west of the CBD via the Calder Fwy (you'll need a vehicle to get there). Bat-box surveys are conducted bimonthly (February, April, June, August, October and December). Contact the Australasian Bat Society (www.ausbats.org.au) to find out more.

WATCHING BATS IN VICTORIA

The riverside **Grey-headed Flying Fox** camp at Yarra Bend NP (4.01) is well known but no less spectacular for that. The bats fan out at dusk across well-treed suburbs, many drinking from the river as they fly west towards the parklands surrounding the CBD. This colony formerly roosted in the botanic gardens, but was successfully relocated to Yarra Bend and none have roosted there since 2003. There are also permanent camps at Bairnsdale (4.28), Geelong (where up to 35 000 roost in Eastern Park in summer), in Bendigo's Central Park and in Warrnambool's botanic gardens (4.17), among others. **Grey-headed Flying Foxes** also occur along the Murray River and camp just over the border in Albury, NSW. **Little Red Flying Foxes** make temporary camps regularly in northern Victoria, especially along the Goulburn River valley near orchards. Camps may be opportunistic (usually November–April), for example near Seymour, or annual, as in the main street of Numurkah north of Shepparton, where young have been born. **Black Flying Foxes** also reach Victoria, though there are no permanent camps; they were first recorded in 2010 at the Yarra Bend NP camp.

Some 20 species of microbat have been recorded in Victoria. **White-striped Freetail Bats** are common in urban areas and are often heard overhead from September to May almost anywhere in Melbourne. **Yellow-bellied Sheath-tailed Bat** is a high-flying autumn visitor (mostly March–May) that can sometimes be identified by torchlight. The Organ Pipes NP bat project (4.03) on the outskirts of Melbourne, and another in suburban Heidelberg, 10 km east of the city centre, are great ways to see several widespread species, including the **Gould's** and **Chocolate Wattled Bats**, **White-striped Freetail Bat**, **Eastern Broad-nosed Bat** (mainly December-February), and **Large**, **Southern** and **Little Forest Bats**. It's worth getting involved with both projects for experience in bat identification, handling and survey techniques, as well as great close-up viewing of select species. The **Lesser Long-eared Bat** is probably Victoria's most widespread microbat and is common in dry forests; **Gould's Long-eared Bat** is also common, but mainly in the east of the state (the **Greater Long-eared Bat** is known from only a few records in the north-west).

The extensive forested ranges east of Melbourne are more or less contiguous with eastern seaboard forests, and a night out with an Anabat or harp trap could log a few extra species here, such as the **Eastern False Pipistrelle**. **Eastern Horseshoe Bats** are uncommon and known to breed at only a few locations in Gippsland: near Murrindal, Nowa Nowa and in caves along the Snowy River. As **Golden-tipped** and **Greater Broad-nosed Bats** both occur in southern NSW forests, there is a possibility that either or both could occur in the extreme south-east of Gippsland. Species more typical of the semi-arid zone, such as the **Inland** and **Southern Freetail Bats**, **Inland Forest Bat** and **Inland Broad-nosed Bat** are all found mainly west of Melbourne. The **Large-footed Myotis** occurs in the wetter south-east and along the Murray River corridor; it can sometimes be seen fishing in Badger Creek near Healesville (4.06) and in quiet reaches of the Yarra River.

The state's only maternity colony of the *bassanii* subspecies of **Common Bentwing Bat** is at Starlight Cave, in western Victoria, which is on private land and not open to the public. Winter roosts are known at Grassmer, Panmure, Arch, Yambuk and Byaduk caves, and from Mt Eccles (4.19) and Mt Napier. But please do not disturb these roosts – instead make the trip to Naracoorte Caves in SA (6.06) to see these rare bats under suitably controlled viewing conditions. The eastern subspecies of **Common Bentwing Bat** *Miniopterus schreibersii oceanensis* roosts in a gated adit at Mt Piper Nature CP, 55 km north of Melbourne and at various caves in Gippsland, such as Nowa Nowa Cave north-east of Lakes Entrance, Nargun's Cave and in sea caves on Wilson's Promontory.

The Mammal Survey Group conducts bat-trapping at its regular campouts around the state. Check also local Field Naturalists' clubs to see what activities they may be planning or for local knowledge of bat roosts.

4.04 PORT PHILLIP BAY

Highlights: **Burrunan Bottlenose Dolphin, Short-beaked Common Dolphin, Australian Fur Seal**

Other possibilities: **Common Dolphin, Southern Right Whale, Humpback Whale**

Melbourne almost encircles huge, shallow Port Phillip Bay, where a good variety of marine mammals has been recorded. Most significant of these is possibly the **Burrunan Dolphin**, a distinctive form of Bottlenose Dolphin that may prove to be a new species. It is apparently restricted to the bay and other sheltered waters along the southern coast, such as the Gippsland Lakes (4.28). The population in the bay is estimated at 80–100 individuals. Dolphin-watching tours leave from Sorrento, a good 90 minutes' drive south of the city centre depending on traffic, and promise a good return for your money. You'll be towed on a 'mermaid line' and have to wear a wetsuit in these cool waters, but if the dolphins decide to investigate it's a worthwhile experience. A small number of **Short-beaked Common Dolphins** appear to be resident in the eastern part of the bay (in the cooler months, at least) and are usually sighted offshore between Mt Martha and Mornington. Dolphins of either species could be seen from almost any vantage point on the eastern side of the bay (the western side is much flatter and less accessible); identifying them at a distance is another matter, of course. Sightings of **Humpback Whales** are increasing and they are now almost annual visitors, generally in May–June, although the whales tend not to stay long. **Southern Right Whales** are occasional visitors and sightings of both species are still unusual enough to warrant media attention, so keep an eye on local news services.

Australian Fur Seals, which breed on Seal Rocks at Phillip I. (4.09), are virtually a fixture where they loaf on Chinaman's Hat and Wedge Light, two navigation beacons in the bay's south-west corner. Chinaman's Hat has been refurbished to suit the seals and up to 20 may be seen there at a time. Commercial operators offer 'swim with the seals' tours from Sorrento. **Australian Fur Seals** and **Burrunan Dolphins** are also occasionally seen in the estuary of the Yarra River at the head of the bay, the latter sometimes swimming several kilometres upstream.

Altogether, 19 species of marine mammal have been recorded in Port Phillip Bay. Most records are of single sightings or strandings, and in general vagrant pinnipeds are more frequent than cetaceans. For example, in 2006 two **Leopard Seals** took up residence in the Paterson River near Frankston, 30 km south-east of the CBD (Leopard Seals are most commonly sighted in Victoria between July and October; they could turn up anywhere along the coast). **Southern Elephant Seals** also turn up sporadically – one hauled out at Sorrento in 2006 and another, possible the same one, hauled out near Geelong the same summer. But the most extraordinary record must be of the one which swam up the Maribyrnong River and hauled out in Maribyrnong in the middle of suburbia! **Crabeater** and **Subantarctic Fur Seals** have also been recorded in the bay. **Killer Whales** are sighted on very rare occasions.

4.05 YELLINGBO NATURE CONSERVATION RESERVE

Highlights: **Leadbeater's Possum**

Other possibilities: **[Sambar]**

This small reserve supports the only surviving population of **Leadbeater's Possum** outside of its core distribution in the main ranges (see 4.06). It is likely that fewer than 50 survive at Yellingbo in Mountain Swamp Gum remnant, a habitat that was formerly more widespread and whose disappearance possibly affected the possums historically. Their population is apparently stable and they make use of the nest boxes provided by park managers. Access is strictly controlled, but Friends' groups (such as www.leadbeaters.org.au) hold working bees and educational nights where you may even get a chance to see one of these beautiful possums in the hand. Feral **Sambar** are common in the Yellingbo area and damage Leadbeater's Possum habitat.

The reserve can be reached by heading towards Warburton on the Maroondah Hwy, which becomes the Warburton Hwy (B380); turn south at the Healesville-Koo-wee-rup Rd. The reserve is in several segments straddling various creeks.

4.06 HEALESVILLE–MARYSVILLE AREA

Highlights: **Leadbeater's Possum, Greater Glider, Yellow-bellied Glider, Mountain Brushtail Possum, Common Wombat**

Other possibilities: **Common Brushtail Possum, Common Ringtail Possum, Eastern Grey Kangaroo, Red-necked Wallaby, Swamp Wallaby, Swamp Rat, [Sambar]**

Healesville Zoo has an excellent collection of native animals and is a pleasant place to spend a morning, especially as free-living **Swamp Rats** can sometimes be seen among the enclosures. Badger Creek runs through the heart of the reserve and supports a high concentration of **Platypuses**. There are numerous bridges over the creek within the sanctuary, but with high visitor traffic you'd have to be there early to see one so try elsewhere along the creek outside the reserve. The adjoining Coranderrk Bushland Reserve also supports lots of **Eastern Grey Kangaroos** and **Swamp Wallabies**. The hills around Healesville are full of **Sambar**, for those who are interested; they can usually be spotlighted along the twisting mountain roads – drive slowly to avoid a collision. Healesville is 57 km north-east of Melbourne via the Maroondah Hwy; the zoo is along Badger Creek Rd.

From Healesville take the B360 north-east to Marysville; this passes near Leadbeater's Possum habitat and there are many quiet back roads along which to spotlight. (It would be a good idea to stake out intact vegetation by daylight as much of this area was burnt in 2009). The largest **Leadbeater's Possum** population survives in densely forested mountains 60–80 km east of Melbourne in Mountain Ash forest above 600 m. Unfortunately, catastrophic bushfires that took out swathes of prime habitat in 2009 have added to its endangered status. To see the possums you will have to join a volunteer group, who hold regular surveys in prime habitat (see www.leadbeaters.org.au). This usually involves stag-watching, sometimes in cold, rainy conditions (spotlighting is usually not feasible for this diminutive species as it is very agile, active high in the canopy and isn't readily picked up by eyeshine). The route between Marysville and Cambarville, Steavenson's Falls south of the road, and the Cambarville area itself are very good for arboreal and forest species such as the **Mountain Brushtail Possum, Common Ringtail Possum, Greater Glider, Yellow-bellied Glider, Common Wombat** and **Swamp Wallaby**; all are common and easily spotlighted. **Sambar** are also common in this area. Small terrestrial inhabitants of these forests include **Bush Rats**, and **Agile** and **Dusky Antechinuses**.

4.07 CRANBOURNE BOTANIC GARDENS

Highlights: **Southern Brown Bandicoot, Bush Rat**

Other possibilities: **Echidna, Swamp Wallaby, New Holland Mouse, Swamp Rat**

An annexe of the Melbourne botanic gardens at Cranbourne specialises in native vegetation and is one of the best places in the country to see **Southern Brown Bandicoots**, which here are active by day. The bandicoots can usually be seen around the car park and picnic area, although sightings will be easier in the early morning before too many people arrive (make sure you lock your vehicle and do not leave any valuables on display inside). **Bush Rats** can sometimes be seen darting between bushes. **Swamp Rats** also inhabit this site and the **New Holland Mouse** formerly occurred but now appears to be extinct. **Echidnas** and **Swamp Wallabies** are common. Cranbourne is 52 km south-east of the city centre via the Monash Fwy (M1) and South Gippsland Hwy (M420). The gardens (www.rbg.vic.gov.au/visit-cranbourne) are signposted on the right (west) of the highway as you head south through Cranbourne; turn at Ballarto Rd. Entry is free.

4.08 MORNINGTON PENINSULA

Highlights: **Southern Brown Bandicoot**

Other possibilities: **White-footed Dunnart, Long-nosed Bandicoot, Eastern Grey Kangaroo**

The long, undulating Mornington Peninsula separates Port Phillip Bay from Western Port Bay. It was formerly swampy and largely covered in coastal heath and tea-tree scrub, although much of this has now been cleared for holiday homes. Nonetheless, 'the Peninsula' is one of the state's strongholds for **Southern Brown Bandicoots**, which hang on in some surprising pockets, not all of them reserves. Apart from Quail I., near Warneet, there are still good numbers near Koo-wee-rup and Tooradin, living next to the urban creep. They can sometimes be seen by Boundary Drain Rd in broad daylight. Other local sites for **Southern Brown Bandicoot** include the Pines Nature Conservation Reserve at Frankston North. **Long-nosed Bandicoots** occur in Mornington NP at Point Nepean, and **White-footed Dunnarts** have been recorded at Sandy Point near Balnarring; both of these must be regarded as unlikely for a casual visitor. Dunes and headlands in the Cape Schanck area would be worth checking out for cetaceans. A herd of 36 **Sperm Whales** once stranded at Gunnamatta Beach, although they are not common in Bass Strait.

4.09 PHILLIP ISLAND

Highlights: **Koala, Australian Fur Seal**

Other possibilities: **Echidna, Common Brushtail Possum, Common Ringtail Possum, Swamp Wallaby, Water Rat**

Phillip Island is probably best known for its nightly parade of Little Penguins, which attract half a million visitors annually, but it also supports the world's largest rookery of **Australian Fur Seals**. Seal Rocks, about 2 km offshore from The Nobbies, the headland at the western tip of the island, is home to up to 30 000 fur seals year-round. The colony can be watched through a telescope or coin-operated binoculars from the car park and café, which give an elevated perspective; interactive cameras can zoom in for close-up views. By following the boardwalk down the cliff you'll get closer views (though binoculars or scope are still recommended). As long as the sea is relatively calm, a cruise on the tourist boat that operates out of the main town, Cowes (www.wildlifecoastcruises.com.au), is recommended for the best views of the colony. **New Zealand Fur Seals** have also occurred at Seal Rocks and **Southern Elephant Seal** has been recorded.

Philip Island also supports a substantial population of **Koalas**, which were introduced and now occur all over the island. The Koala Conservation Centre is a sanctuary where you can pay money but be guaranteed sightings; treetop boardwalks allow you to get up close for photos. For a more natural experience, try **Oswin Roberts Koala Reserve**, where there are three well-marked walking trails. To get there, turn right into Rhyll–Newhaven Rd after crossing the bridge from San Remo to the island, then left into Harbison Rd and the car park is 1 km along on your right. Parks and treed areas all over the island support **Common Brushtail** and **Ringtail Possums**, and **Swamp Wallabies** occur in denser habitat. **Water Rats** have been recorded and could occur at Rhyll Swamp. Ocean beaches would be worth checking for vagrant seals – **Leopard Seals** have occurred.

This popular weekend and holiday destination is about 90 minutes' drive south-east of Melbourne, depending on traffic. To get there, take the Monash Fwy (M1) and connect with the South Gippsland (M420) and Bass Hwys. There is plenty of accommodation for overnight stays, and supermarkets, cafés and restaurants in the main town, Cowes.

4.10 FRENCH ISLAND

Highlights: **Echidna, Koala, Long-nosed Potoroo**

Other possibilities: **Common Brushtail Possum, Water Rat, Swamp Rat**

A few kilometres to the north of Philip I., and accessible only by ferry, is French I., a little visited part of the state that supports healthy populations of **Koalas** and **Long-nosed Potoroos**. Some 1500 **Koalas** live here and some can usually be seen by cycling or walking the island's trails. **Echidnas** are also common but the chances of seeing a **Long-nosed Potoroo** would be greatly increased by spotlighting, which would mean staying overnight. The **Common Brushtail Possum**, **Water Rat** and **Swamp Rat** also occur. There are campgrounds and bed and breakfast accommodation. The island is served by ferries (which don't carry motor vehicles) from Ventnor on Phillip I. and, closer to Melbourne, Stony Point. See www.interislandferries.com.au for details. A trial was recently conducted to assess the viability of translocating **Eastern Barred Bandicoots** to French I., so this may be a possibility in future.

THE BIG FIVE

Victoria's compact size makes it possible to see a Big Five within a few hours' drive of the capital Melbourne.

Kangaroo Eastern Grey Kangaroos can be seen at the You Yangs Regional Park (4.12), Brisbane Ranges NP (4.11) and Wilson's Prom (4.24); The Grampians (4.21) are a macropod hotspot.

Koala Victoria has a large Koala population and they are common along parts of the Great Ocean Road (4.16), at Brisbane Ranges NP (4.11) and in the Warrnambool area (4.17).

Wombat Gippsland is very good for Common Wombats at, for example, Wilson's Promontory NP (4.24); closer to Melbourne, try Candlebark Park (4.01) or Wombat SF (4.15).

Platypus Not uncommon in wetter parts of Victoria, but perhaps harder to find than in some other states; try Great Otway NP (4.16), where there's a commercial operation.

Whale Southern Right Whales visit Logan's Beach at Warrnambool (4.17) between June and September, often with calves.

4.11 BRISBANE RANGES NATIONAL PARK

Highlights: **Echidna, Koala, Eastern Grey Kangaroo, Swamp Wallaby**

Other possibilities: **Agile Antechinus, Common Brushtail Possum, Common Ringtail Possum, Sugar Glider**

This is one of the best **Koala** sites close to Melbourne and there's a healthy population that has been periodically supplemented with reintroductions. They can often be seen along the Anakie Gorge Trail; look out also for **Eastern Grey Kangaroos** and **Swamp Wallabies** in denser vegetation. The park also supports good numbers of **Common Brushtail** and **Ringtail Possums**, as well as **Sugar Gliders**, for which you would have to spotlight, naturally. It may be a good idea to contact Friends of the Brisbane Ranges (www.fobr.org.au) to see if they are conducting any surveys or trapping in the park – the **Brush-tailed Phascogale** has been recorded. The park is most directly reached by taking the Western Fwy (M8) to Bacchus Marsh and then turning south off Bacchus Marsh Rd onto Grant St; from there follow the Bacchus Marsh–Balliang Rd to the park.

4.12 YOU YANGS REGIONAL PARK

Highlights: **Koala, Eastern Grey Kangaroo**

Other possibilities: **Echidna, Swamp Wallaby**

The nearest major reserve to Melbourne that isn't (yet) surrounded by suburbia, the You Yangs is a distinctive granite outcrop emerging from a flat basalt plain, and visible for many kilometres around. This forest park is probably the nearest reliable site to Melbourne for **Koalas** and an easy 30 minutes' drive from the CBD. **Eastern Grey Kangaroos** can usually be seen on the approaches to the park in the early morning and at dusk, particularly near the south-eastern corner. The main entrance road takes you near the summit of Flinders Peak along the Turntable Drive loop, from where you can normally also see **Eastern Grey Kangaroos**. Near the summit, the Flinders Peak Walk is good for **Koala** sightings; otherwise scan the canopy for them along Turntable Drive (again, the south-east corner of the park can be good). **Echidnas** are also common in these woodlands. The East-West Walk is a good location for **Swamp Wallabies**. **Common Brushtail Possums** occur in the You Yangs, but note that the park is open only during daylight hours, which will limit any spotlighting activities. To reach the You Yangs, take the Little River turnoff from the Princes Fwy (M1), about 40 km south-west of Melbourne CBD. Follow the signs through Little River, turn left (south) off You Yangs Rd onto Farrars Rd and then turn right (west) after 2 km onto Branch Rd. Start looking for kangaroos by the roadside (especially in the early morning) as you approach the park.

4.13 MT ROTHWELL

Highlights: **Eastern Quoll, Brush-tailed Phascogale, Eastern Barred Bandicoot, Long-nosed Potoroo, Rufous Bettong, Brush-tailed Rock Wallaby, Red-bellied Pademelon**

Other possibilities: **Southern Brown Bandicoot, Red-necked Wallaby, Eastern Grey Kangaroo, Swamp Wallaby, Common Brushtail Possum, Common Ringtail Possum, Sugar Glider, Koala, Fat-tailed Dunnart, Bush Rat**

Victoria's largest predator-free sanctuary is the Mt Rothwell Biodiversity Interpretation Centre, 400 ha of open grassy woodlands and grasslands on the northern slopes of the You Yangs (4.12). It was set up to preserve and re-establish endangered species. **Eastern Barred Bandicoots** were introduced between 2004 and 2009, and now number 40–50 individuals, and there is an interesting range of other species here that used to occur in Victoria, such as **Rufous Bettong** and **Red-bellied ('Tasmanian') Pademelon**. Visitors can take a guided night walk, on which there is a good chance of seeing **Eastern Quolls, Long-nosed Potoroos, Rufous Bettongs** and **Brush-tailed Rock Wallabies**.

Mt Rothwell is 60 km south-west of Melbourne. Directions to get there are as for the You Yangs but turn right (north) at Little River–Ripley Rd; the entrance is about 8 km along here just after the road bends west. Visit www.mtrothwell.com.au for more information and details of guided night walks, which are run on the last Saturday of each month (private walks can also be arranged).

4.14 HANGING ROCK

Highlights: **Eastern Grey Kangaroo, Koala**

An interesting volcanic rock formation north of Melbourne is popular among day-trippers and is a good site for both **Koalas** and **Eastern Grey Kangaroos**. Mobs of kangaroos feed on the playing fields and among paddocks, and are easily seen at dawn and dusk, sometimes with the spectacular rocks as a backdrop. **Koalas** could be seen just about anywhere in the reserve. Hanging Rock is accessible via the Calder Fwy (M79); turn east onto the C324 after the town of Macedon, about 60 km north-west of Melbourne.

B WESTERN VICTORIA

This region stretches from the wet, windy southern coast, which bears the brunt of winter storms, to the semi-arid mallee country in the far north-west, a distance of some 400 km from top to bottom. By Victorian standards this means a bit of travelling, but there is much to see in between. The north-west features huge tracts of mallee woodland, often with a spinifex understorey that supports localised small mammals, such as the **Silky Mouse**, **Western** and **Little Pygmy Possums** and **Common Dunnart**. Most of these will be seen only by trapping, and it is worth joining one of the Mammal Survey Group outings to this area. The one exception might be **Mitchell's Hopping-mouse**, which inhabits sand-dune country in the south of the Murray-Sunset NP, and like some other hopping-mice could possibly be spotlighted in suitable habitat. The Grampians (Gariwerd) NP is roughly in the middle of western Victoria and an important outlier for many species whose main distribution is further east. In the southern part of this region, fertile volcanic plains have largely been cleared but still support abundant **Koalas**, as well as **Southern Brown Bandicoots** and important roosts of **Southern Bentwing Bats**. **Brush-tailed Phascogale** is known from scattered forest patches in central Victoria.

4.15 WOMBAT STATE FOREST

Highlights: **Echidna, Greater Glider, Mountain Brushtail Possum, Common Brushtail Possum, Common Ringtail Possum, Common Wombat, Eastern Grey Kangaroo**

Other possibilities: **Brush-tailed Phascogale**

An excellent mammal diversity – nearly 30 species – has been recorded at this state forest north-west of Melbourne. It marks the western extremity of the ranges of **Greater Glider** and **Mountain Brushtail Possum** (although there is an outlier of the latter at Mt Cole), and supports the largest concentration of its namesake – **Common Wombat** – west of Melbourne. Forestry operations in the 19th century left massive sawdust heaps, which have since become compacted and burrowed into by the wombats at certain sites. Arboreal species include **Greater**, **Sugar** and **Feathertail Gliders**; the forest is particularly good for **Greater Gliders**, especially in the Spargo Creek–Korweinguboora and Spring Hill–Wheatsheaf areas, or wherever tall forest persists. **Common Brushtail** and **Common Ringtail Possums** occur and **Eastern Pygmy Possums** have also been recorded. **Echidnas, Eastern Grey Kangaroos** and **Swamp Wallabies** are all readily seen; and smaller species include **Bush Rat, Swamp Rat, Dusky** and **Agile Antechinuses**. Camera-trapping has shown that **Brush-tailed Phascogales** survive here, and will hopefully also confirm the presence of **Long-nosed Potoroos** and **Spot-tailed Quolls**. Bats recorded in Wombat SF include **Gould's** and **Chocolate Wattled Bats**, **Large** and **Southern Forest Bats**, **Lesser** and **Gould's Long-eared Bats**, the **White-striped Freetail Bat**, **Eastern Falsistrelle** and the **Common Bentwing Bat**.

Wombat SF is accessible via the Western Fwy (M8). There are several roads north of the freeway, such as the C318 and C141, which take you through different parts of the forest. Contact the local Friends' group (www.wombatforestcare.org.au) for tips on good wildlife-viewing areas.

4.16 GREAT OCEAN ROAD

Highlights: **Sugar Glider, Yellow-bellied Glider, Koala, Eastern Grey Kangaroo, Southern Right Whale, Australian Sea Lion**

Other possibilities: **Long-nosed Potoroo, Bush Rat, Blue Whale**

Starting at Geelong, the Great Ocean Road is one of Victoria's most-vaunted tourist attractions: a 243-km coastal drive that conveniently connects a number of good wildlife-watching locations via some rugged coastal scenery. The town of Anglesea is famous locally for its **Eastern Grey Kangaroo** population: the kangaroos congregate on the golf course and can easily be seen from the road. Just after you cross the Anglesea River heading south, take the first right (Noble St), which takes you to the golf course. The dense heath vegetation in Angahook-Lorne SP nearby has been well studied for its small mammals, and formerly supported good populations of the **Agile** and **Swamp Antechinus**, **White-footed Dunnart**, **Bush Rat** and **Swamp Rat** (the most common inhabitant of these heaths). There's a small chance of seeing the partly diurnal **Swamp Rat** and antechinuses, whose populations are highest between December and June.

The next town heading south is Airey's Inlet, about 17 km south of Anglesea; the Great Otway NP adjacent is excellent for **Koalas** and **Sugar** and **Yellow-bellied Gliders**. As you drive south through town turn right into Bambra Rd, which becomes Distillery Creek Rd, and follow it for a few kilometres to a patch of forest on the left. **Koalas** are common here and the gliders can be spotlighted after dark. **Koalas** are also common at many other sites along the Great Ocean Rd, and some caravan parks (for example, Bimbi Park, www.bimbipark.com.au), and other accommodations feature them as attractions.

Great Otway NP skirts the road on the landward side between here and Cape Otway. These forests and heaths support a good variety of small mammals, including **Dusky** and **Swamp Antechinuses**, **Swamp**, **Bush** and **Broad-toothed Rats**, **Eastern Pygmy Possums**, **Southern Brown Bandicoots** and **Long-nosed Potoroos**. However, you are far more likely to see **Common Brushtail Possums**, **Eastern Grey Kangaroos**, **Swamp Wallabies** and especially **Koalas**; a good spot for the latter is where the road to Cape Otway Light Station emerges from the national park. Cape Otway itself is great for scanning the sea for **Southern Right**, **Humpback** and **Blue Whales**. Tantalisingly, a live **Spot-tailed Quoll** was reported from the Otways in 2012 – the first in 10 years – confirming that a population persists in these forests.

Joining a seabirding trip from Portland would be a great way of seeing some marine mammals. Among species periodically encountered are **Southern Right Whales** and **Blue Whales**, as well as **Common Dolphins** and **Australian Fur Seals**. Trips generally leave monthly, subject to sea conditions – see Chapter 10 for more information. **Southern Right Whales** are seen most years in Port Fairy Bay, with several animals at once not unusual. The Cutting near Killarney is also regarded as a good local site from which to see **Southern Right Whales**, and an **Elephant Seal** once hauled up at Killarney Beach near Port Fairy.

The Ralph Illidge Sanctuary near Warrnambool supports 10 native mammal species, including **Bush Rats** and a high concentration of **Long-nosed Potoroos**. Both **Long-nosed** and **Southern Brown Bandicoots** formerly occurred. Note that the sanctuary is normally open only from 11 am to 6 pm, so it would be worth contacting the Friends' group and joining a survey at more mammal-friendly times. Phone (03) 5566 2320 for more information. The sanctuary is at Naringal East, about 15 km east of Warrnambool: take the Allansford turnoff and follow the Cobden road; it is well signposted.

The Great Ocean Road starts on the south side of Geelong and is well signposted. It gets busy at weekends and school holidays – take care on the winding road. Several towns offer plenty of eating and sleeping options; there are various campgrounds and the Cape Otway lighthouse makes a good base (www.lightstation.com).

4.17 WARRNAMBOOL AREA

Highlights: **Koala, Sugar Glider, Eastern Grey Kangaroo, Southern Right Whale**

Other possibilities: **Echidna, Southern Brown Bandicoot, Grey-headed Flying Fox**

The Great Ocean Road ends at the city of Warrnambool, which is arguably Victoria's whale-watching capital. **Southern Right Whales** pass just offshore at Logan's Beach between June and September, sometimes not arriving till August, but females often stay and nurse their calves for several days and even weeks. Usually a few are resident with their calves here or within the 8-km stretch to the east. There are viewing platforms and boardwalks. Females usually take up residence by about mid-June. Viewing depends on conditions – there is no convenient headland from which to view them and sightings are best when the water is calm and clear. **Humpback Whales** are also occasionally seen from here. **Grey-headed Flying Foxes** camp in Warrnambool's botanic gardens some years, usually arriving late summer and leaving in autumn and winter. So far, numbers have peaked at 1800 but they aren't there every year – check the Australasian Bat Society (www.ausbats.org.au) or the local tourist office for an update. Warrnambool is 243 km from Geelong on the Great Ocean Road or 189 km via the more direct Princes Hwy (Hwy 1). Logan's Beach is about 3 km south of the Princes Hwy (Hwy 1).

Tower Hill WR is an extinct volcanic crater about 20 km north-west of Warrnambool. **Koalas**, **Echidnas** and **Eastern Grey Kangaroos** are all common in woodland surrounding the slopes, and there is an introduced population of **Sugar Gliders**. The small towns of Koroit, Kirkstall and Crossley immediately to the north of Tower Hill also support a good population of **Koalas**.

WATCHING WHALES AND DOLPHINS IN VICTORIA

Two phenomena virtually assure sightings of whales in Victoria at the right times of year: the annual migration of **Southern Right** and **Humpback Whales** during the winter months; and the Bonney Upwelling, a seasonal eastward flow of cool, nutrient-rich water that promotes krill blooms in summer. Bass Strait, the broad sea passage between Victoria and Tasmania, is a migratory pathway for **Humpbacks**, **Southern Right**, **Blue** and possibly **Fin Whales** (Sei Whales have yet to be recorded in Victorian waters). **Southern Right Whales** appear annually in western Victoria between June and October, with a peak in July and August, as they move west across the southern coastline to calve. Females with young and small herds often gather in shallow bays at Port Fairy, Portland and Warrnambool. **Humpbacks** travel up the coast of Tasmania on migration before turning to continue up the east coast. They can generally be seen during the northward (May–August) or southward (September–November) migrations. In general, **Humpbacks** are more common in eastern waters and **Southern Right Whales** in western Victoria, but there have been many exceptions and both species periodically enter Port Phillip Bay.

The Bonney Upwelling starts in the east of the Great Australian Bight in November and December and reaches western Victoria by about February. Krill blooms associated with this phenomenon attract baleen whales, most famously **Blue Whales** which are regularly observed in the Discovery Bay and Portland areas, as far east as Cape Otway. Herds of this species (thought mainly to be 'Pygmy' Blue Whales) concentrate off far western Victoria in November, spreading eastwards with a wide distribution across Bass Strait between January and April. **Fin Whales** have also been observed in the Bonney Upwelling in summer and autumn. In June 2007 more than a hundred **Pygmy Right Whales** were spotted off Portland (one stayed in Portland Harbour for more than 2 months in 1986). Other baleen species recorded alive in Victorian waters have included **Minke** and **Bryde's Whales**; most records have been in western Victoria, off Cape Otway and Cape Nelson. Of the blackfish, **Long-flippered Pilot Whales** are the most commonly encountered; large herds have occurred east of Wilson's Prom and in Shallow Inlet; this species often associates with **Common Bottlenoses**. **Killer Whales** could be encountered at any time of year, though mostly they are seen between autumn and spring. They are most likely to be seen near fur seal colonies or along the migration paths of **Humpbacks** and **Southern Right Whales**.

Common and **Bottlenose Dolphins** are the most frequently sighted dolphins in Victoria. **Common Dolphins** are seen more regularly offshore, while **Bottlenose Dolphins** readily enter Port Phillip Bay and the Gippsland Lakes, and even rivers such as the Bass, Brodribb, Yarra and Maribyrnong. The Port Phillip Bay population appears to be resident and has been mooted as a possible new species, the **Burrunan Dolphin**, although its taxonomy is still unresolved.

Much of the Victorian coastline is adjacent to Bass Strait, which is generally not suitable for deep-water species. **Sperm Whales** are therefore not commonly sighted, although there have been several strandings, including a major event at Gunnamatta Beach, on the Mornington Peninsula, involving 36 animals in 1972. Other strandings have occurred at many sites along the coast. **Pygmy Sperm Whales** also seem to be deep water animals; there have been several strandings, mainly on long ocean beaches in Gippsland. The eight species of beaked whale so far recorded – **Southern Bottlenose Whale**, and **Andrews'**, **Blainville's**, **Gingko-toothed**, **Gray's**, **Strap-toothed**, **True's** and **Cuvier's Beaked Whales** – are virtually unknown as live animals in Victoria. Most strandings occur where the Continental Shelf narrows in the south-west and south-east corners of the state, for example near Port Fairy, where **Cuvier's Beaked Whale** has stranded. **False Killer Whales** are also whales of deep, open water. The live animals often associate with **Bottlenose Dolphins** and most strandings take place between May and September, again typically where the shelf is narrow – a mass stranding took place at Croajingolong NP in January 1983. **Risso's** and **Fraser's Dolphins** are known only from strandings, the latter occurring in Corio Bay adjacent to Port Phillip Bay.

There are numerous boat operators offering the chance to get close to whales and dolphins at many sites along the Victorian coast. Other options include sea kayak tours, swimming and scuba diving, mainly with seals and dolphins, and viewing from aircraft. Note that you'll need a wet suit in these waters for most of the year!

4.18 PORTLAND AND CAPE BRIDGEWATER

Highlights: **Blue Whale, Southern Right Whale, Australian Fur Seal, New Zealand Fur Seal**

Other possibilities: **Pygmy Right Whale, Killer Whale**

As you head west, Portland is the last major settlement before the SA border. Marine mammals are a highlight at this part of the coast: the Bonney Upwelling offshore attracts **Blue Whales**, thought to be **'Pygmy' Blue Whales**, in late summer, and **Australian** and **New Zealand Fur Seals** haul out at several sites. Lawrence Rocks, offshore from Portland, are large stacks used by **Australian Fur Seals** as a haul-out. The best vantage point is probably Point Danger: heading south into Portland, follow the Henty Hwy (A200), which eventually becomes Quarry Rd (C194) and ends near Point Danger. From here it's a good 2 km to Lawrence Rocks across the water, so you'll need binoculars or (preferably) a scope. Fur seals also visit the harbour, particularly when fishing boats return from the sea, and when they are about can be seen from the breakwater and near the boat ramp. **Southern Right Whales** also sometimes show up in Portland harbour – the Portland Visitor Information Centre flies a yellow flag outside when whales have been sighted – and in the 1980s a **Pygmy Right Whale** took up residence here for several weeks (in 2007 a herd of more than 100 **Pygmy Right Whales** was observed offshore from Portland during an aerial survey). If whales are in the harbour, the breakwater is a great place to watch them; otherwise, good prominences from which to scan for cetaceans are the lighthouse at Whalers' Bluff and Nun's Beach. The Maritime Discovery Centre near the Visitor Information Centre overlooks the harbour and is a warm place to watch proceedings. **Humpbacks** also occasionally pass by.

Cape Bridgewater, about 15 minutes' drive to the west, features spectacular clifftop walks from which you can look down on colonies of **Australian** and **New Zealand Fur Seals**. Better still, take one of the Zodiac trips from Cape Bridgewater village to get up close for photos. The Blowholes lookout at Cape Bridgewater and cliffs overlooking Cape Bridgewater Bay also make good vantage points to scan for **Southern Right Whales** (March–September), **Blue Whales** and other cetaceans, such as **Killer Whales** (although these are sighted only rarely). Nearby, Cape Nelson lighthouse makes another excellent vantage point, with a viewing platform and a café from where you can watch for cetaceans if the weather is cold. Visit also www.whalemail.com.au and www.bluewhalestudy.org for more information; or call 1800 035 567 for latest sightings. Offshore, Lady Julia Percy I. supports another major breeding colony of **Australian Fur Seals** (about 10 000–12 000 of them), where the **New Zealand Fur Seal**, **Australian Sea Lion** (Victoria's relatively few **Australian Sea Lion** records are mainly from the adjacent coast) and **Southern Elephant Seal** have also occurred.

Portland is 362 km (about 5 hours' drive) south-west of Melbourne and too far for a comfortable day trip. There are cafés and accommodation at Portland.

4.19 MT ECCLES NATIONAL PARK

Highlights: **Echidna, Koala, Yellow-bellied Glider, Sugar Glider**

Other possibilities: **Spot-tailed Quoll, Common Brushtail Possum, Eastern Grey Kangaroo, Eastern Bentwing Bat**

Mount Eccles is a dormant volcanic cone that pokes up above the plains, north of the coastal highway between Warrnambool and Portland. The park's main feature is its crater lake, but it also protects a large stand of Manna Gums and therefore a healthy **Koala** population. There are also **Echidnas**, **Eastern Grey Kangaroos** and **Common Brushtail Possums**; and this is a good location for **Yellow-bellied Gliders**, which here are reaching the western limit of their distribution, as well as **Sugar Gliders**. Smaller species include **Dusky** and **Swamp Antechinuses**, and **Brush-tailed Phascogale** and **Spot-tailed Quoll** are on the park list. There are a number of caves in the park and **Common Bentwing Bats** are known to roost here, although access is prohibited. From Warrnambool it's about 70 km north-west via Port Fairy. There is a campground.

4.20 HAMILTON COMMUNITY PARKLANDS

Highlights: **Eastern Barred Bandicoot**

In an effort to redress the appalling loss of the last mainland population of **Eastern Barred Bandicoots**, which survived along a watercourse on the outskirts of Hamilton until 2002, more than 150 **Eastern Barred Bandicoots** have been released into a predator exclosure at the Hamilton Community Parklands since 1991. After some initial problems, the reserve was declared Fox-free in 2007 and some 50–80 of the bandicoots now occupy the reserve, where they are breeding. The Parklands are behind the Hamilton Institute of Rural Learning on North Boundary Rd, accessible on the northern outskirts of town.

4.21 THE GRAMPIANS (GARIWERD) NATIONAL PARK

Highlights: **Echidna, Squirrel Glider, Sugar Glider, Koala, Eastern Grey Kangaroo, Western Grey Kangaroo, Swamp Wallaby, Red-necked Wallaby**

Other possibilities: **Yellow-footed Antechinus, Agile Antechinus, Dusky Antechinus (ssp. *insularis*), Common Dunnart, Long-nosed Potoroo, Brush-tailed Rock Wallaby, Smoky Mouse, Heath Mouse, [Red Deer]**

This impressive outlier of the Great Dividing Range looms from the surrounding flat countryside from a long way off. Largely isolated by farmland, Gariwerd supports extensive woodlands and stands of heath; it is one of Victoria's mammal hotspots and supports a few specialties as well as outlying populations of **Sugar** and **Squirrel Gliders** and the **Brush-tailed Rock Wallaby**. If you stay at the tourist village at Hall's Gap you should have no difficulty seeing **Eastern Grey Kangaroos** both inside and outside the park, in paddocks and by the roadside at dusk (take care while driving). Both **Red-necked** and **Swamp Wallabies** are common along the less-frequented park roads at dusk or early in the morning. In fact, the Victoria Valley is one of the state's macropod hotspots, with both **Eastern** and **Western Grey Kangaroos** plus **Swamp** *and* **Red-necked Wallabies** occurring; it makes a great place to see all four in close proximity. Studies have shown that **Western Greys** prefer forest such as Brown Stringybark with a heathy understorey, while **Eastern Greys** are more likely to be found in woodland or forest with an understorey of grasses or bracken, such as River Red Gum forest. A reintroduction program has begun to re-establish the park's **Brush-tailed Rock Wallaby** population, which was wiped out late in the 20th century, although their location is not broadcast and you'd be lucky to see one by chance.

Echidnas are common and by spotlighting you should have no trouble locating **Common Brushtail** and **Ringtail Possums** and **Sugar Gliders**. **Squirrel Gliders** occur only at the northern extremity of the park. **Koalas** are also common.

The Grampians support isolated populations of **Smoky Mouse** (it and **Southern Brown Bandicoots** seem most common on Mt William) and **Heath Mouse** (especially in Victoria Valley), as well as the **Agile Antechinus**, **Yellow-footed Antechinus**, **Swamp Rat** and **Eastern Pygmy Possum**. The **Dusky Antechinuses** that occur here are a distinct subspecies, *Antechinus swainsonii insularis*. Late in 2013 a **Spot-tailed Quoll** was recorded by a remote camera – the first record in more than 140 years. Bats present include **Eastern False Pipistrelle**, **Large** and **Southern Forest Bats** and **Chocolate Wattled Bats**. This is the only part of Victoria where **Red Deer** occur; some of their strongholds include the Victoria and Wartook Valleys, and Zumsteins.

The northern section of the park is an easy 4 hours' drive from Melbourne on the Western Hwy (M8); the turn-off for Hall's Gap is just west of Stawell, 235 km north-west of Melbourne. There are plenty of eating and sleeping options in Hall's Gap. The southern end of Gariwerd takes longer to get to, but consequently sees fewer visitors and would repay a visit. There are campgrounds here and B&B style accommodation at Dunkeld, just outside Gariwerd's southern boundary.

4.22 LITTLE DESERT NATIONAL PARK

Highlights: **Western Pygmy Possum, Western Grey Kangaroo, Red-necked Wallaby, Silky Mouse**

Other possibilities: **Echidna, Platypus, Swamp Wallaby, Red Kangaroo, Water Rat**

A magnificent patch of semi-arid heath, rather than true desert, might be a more appropriate way to describe this park. It is well known for birds and wildflowers, and the floristically rich heath is attractive to **Western Pygmy Possums**. Spotlighting for them (and **Feathertail Gliders**, which also occur here) would be feasible, but ask at the Little Desert Lodge (www.littledesertlodge.com.au) if there have been any recent sightings. This is good country for **Echidnas**, and macropods include **Western Grey Kangaroos**, **Red-necked Wallabies** and **Swamp Wallabies**, all of which are generally common, with occasional records of **Red Kangaroos**. Larger arboreal species include **Common Brushtail Possums** and **Sugar Gliders**; the latter occur at Little Desert Lodge. **Fat-tailed Dunnarts** occur in open, grassy areas and can sometimes be spotlighted. The Little Desert is a stronghold for the **Silky Mouse** and it is quite common; look for its distinctive burrow systems among low *Banksia* heath. There have been occasional sightings of **Platypus** (for example, in the Green's Creek area, north-east of Stawell) and **Water Rats** along the Wimmera River. At last count, 11 bat species had been recorded.

4.23 HATTAH-KULKYNE NATIONAL PARK

Highlights: **Eastern Grey Kangaroo, Western Grey Kangaroo, Red Kangaroo**

This popular national park protects a large stand of old growth mallee with a spinifex understorey as well as riverine woodland associated with Murray River floodplains and overflow. Only a few hours' drive north-west of Melbourne, it provides a readily accessible taste of the semi-arid zone and one of the closest sites for **Red Kangaroos** to any capital city. **Eastern Grey Kangaroos** are also common and will be seen around the campground and park roads. **Red Kangaroos** prefer more open areas. Hattah-Kulkyne NP is east of the Calder Hwy north of Ouyen; turn off at Hattah for the main campground.

The semi-arid north-west includes two of Victoria's largest wildernesses, the Big Desert and the Sunset Country (most of which is protected in the Murray-Sunset NP), featuring large swathes of heath, mallee and saltbush. Arboreal mammals are largely absent, but this region does have an interesting diversity of dasyurids as well as some stellar rodents. Among them are the **Mallee Ningaui**, **Giles' Planigale** (restricted to two islands in the Murray River) and **Common Dunnart**; rodents include **Mitchell's Hopping-mouse** and **Silky Mouse**. **Western Pygmy Possums** are common in the Big Desert, and both they and **Little Pigmy Possums** occur in the Sunset Country. **Red Kangaroos** can be seen between the Sturt Hwy (A20) and the Murray River in the extreme north-west of the state. **Western Greys** occur in good numbers on the Birthday Plains in Murray-Sunset NP, where there are no Eastern Greys to confuse them with (the Western Greys favour old stands of *Triodia*, which form large rings in which they rest).

C EASTERN VICTORIA

The Great Dividing Range occupies much of the eastern third of Victoria – a rugged area that includes the state's highest mountains (contiguous with the Snowy Mountains over the border in NSW (2.16)) and extensive tall, wet forests dissected by river valleys. It is a scenic area, known as Gippsland, with few roads and some excellent national parks. Victoria's high country is snow-bound in winter and home to approximately half the world's population of **Mountain Pygmy Possum** (see 4.28). This section also includes areas accessible from the Hume Fwy (M31), the main artery connecting Sydney with Melbourne, which runs north-east through the state. **Brush-tailed Phascogales** hang on in isolated populations in central-eastern Victoria, for example in Rushworth SF (Heathcote-Graytown NP) and in forest corridors and blocks west of the Hume near Euroa. **Yellow-footed Antechinuses** also occur, for example in remnant roadside woodland north of Melbourne near Tallarook and Euroa. The forests of north-eastern Victoria support a lot of **Sambar**, for example in the Bright area; these and other deer species are becoming a serious environmental pest in some areas.

4.24 WILSON'S PROMONTORY NATIONAL PARK

Highlights: **Echidna, Common Ringtail Possum, Common Brushtail Possum, Common Wombat, Koala, Eastern Grey Kangaroo, Swamp Wallaby**

Other possibilities: **Southern Brown Bandicoot, [Hog Deer], Australian Fur Seal, Bottlenose Dolphin**

'The Prom' juts into the stormy waters of Bass Strait and protects the southernmost tip of mainland Australia. Arguably it marks the western edge of Gippsland and offers excellent wildlife viewing: some 30 mammal species have been recorded here. **Echidnas** are often seen roadside en route to Tidal River, the main visitors' area. **Eastern Grey Kangaroos** are the most common large mammal in the park – take care while driving as they feed along the road; another good site for them is the airstrip. **Eastern Greys** plus **Swamp Wallabies** and **Common Wombats** (an unusual blond form occurs here) are easily seen around the campground at Tidal River, seemingly oblivious to people; they can even be seen grazing here late in the afternoon. The Yanakie grasslands and open areas along Five Mile Rd are good for viewing kangaroos and wombats in the evening. **Swamp Wallabies** are common along some of the walking trails (for example, Miller's Landing and Lilly Pilly Gully Walks) and park roads, especially in low-lying areas of dense vegetation. **Red-necked Wallabies** also occur, but in low numbers. **Common Wombats** are another species that may be seen along park roads and also at Cotter's Lake. There are plenty of active wombat burrows around Tidal River and along trails, for example the Squeaky Beach Walk.

Common Brushtail and **Ringtail Possums** are easily spotlighted in the campground area after dark. Ringtails favour stands of large tea-trees (for example, on the Squeaky Beach Walk) and some Brushtails are almost black, showing this area's affinity with Tasmania (**Mountain Brushtail Possum** has also been recorded in the park but appears to be rare). **Koalas** also occur around Tidal River and in virtually any patch of woodland at the Prom: try the Sealers' Cove track and the Lilly Pilly Gully return track, which gives you a view over the trees on the slopes of Mt Bishop. **Eastern Pygmy Possums** are apparently common and there should be plenty of flowering shrubs in season to look for this species; try looking in banksias along Miller's Landing Walk. **Feathertail** and **Sugar Gliders** also occur. The campground area is arguably the best site in the country to see the introduced **Hog Deer** (it has also been recorded at Yanakie, Darby River and Mt Singapore).

Much of the Prom is forested or cloaked in dense heath, where **Long-nosed Potoroos** and both **Southern Brown** and **Long-nosed Bandicoots** are present but uncommon. Smaller and even more cryptic species include the **Swamp Antechinus** in low-lying, damp heath; you won't see them without joining a survey group, but there is a high concentration on Great Glennie I. and they are known from near South Peak. **Agile Antechinus** and **Dusky Antechinus** occur in forested areas; other small mammals include the **White-footed Dunnart** and **New Holland**

Mouse, which lives among sandhills in the northern Prom and on the Yanakie Isthmus (note that the Mammal Survey Group targets this species on some of its outings). **Bush Rats** occur in forested areas and **Swamp Rats** in sandy heath; introduced **Black Rats** also occur. **Broad-toothed Rats** have been recorded near Darby Beach and South Peak.

Scan from lookouts, such as Pillar Point and Norman Point near Tidal River, for **Bottlenose Dolphins**, the most commonly encountered cetacean around the Prom. An estimated 10 000–12 000 **Australian Fur Seals** breed at Kanowna I., and there are regular haul-outs on the Anderson Islets, White Rock, Skull Rock, and Notch, Rag, Cleft and Norman islands. Other marine mammals recorded include **Southern Right**, **Humpback**, **Sperm** and **Killer Whales** and **Common Dolphins**; plus beach-cast **Andrews' Beaked Whales**, **Risso's Dolphins** and **Long-flippered Pilot Whales**.

To get to the Prom, take the South Gippsland Hwy (A440) and turn off at Foster. It is very popular at peak holiday times and bookings months in advance are recommended (see the Victoria government's national parks website, www.parkweb.vic.gov.au).

4.25 CHILTERN-MT PILOT NATIONAL PARK

Highlights: **Echidna, Yellow-footed Antechinus, Eastern Grey Kangaroo, Swamp Wallaby, Sugar Glider**

Other possibilities: **Brush-tailed Phascogale, Squirrel Glider, Southern Freetail Bat**

This excellent national park protects a significant remnant patch of box–ironbark woodland, a habitat that was formerly widespread across eastern Australia and home to numerous species dependent on winter-flowering eucalypts. **Echidnas** and **Eastern Grey Kangaroos** are both common. **Swamp Wallabies** frequent denser vegetation along creeklines but are often seen at roadsides in the evening. Chiltern is a good place to see the **Yellow-footed Antechinus**, which is often active during the day, especially along the White Box Walking track. Other sites worth searching for it include Chiltern Valley No. 2 Dam near the bird hide, and the low hills along Ryan's Rd. This active little dasyurid seems to frequent areas of fallen and half-fallen timber, leaf litter on the ground and even climbs high in trees. It is known locally as the 'Chiltern Golden Mouse' and sometimes responds to squeaking. They also sleep in nest boxes put up for phascogales! The White Box Track is also good for spotlighting possums and, during the day, for **Eastern Grey Kangaroos** and **Swamp Wallabies**. **Brush-tailed Phascogales** survive in low numbers (a few use the nest boxes provided for them) and are occasionally seen by spotlighting. There have been no confirmed records of **Spot-tailed Quoll** since the 1970s.

Sugar Gliders are common (try Frog Hollow) and this is one of the best sites in Victoria for **Squirrel Gliders**, which are more common in the south of the park along roads and watercourses. **Feathertail Gliders** also occur – try looking on heavily flowering eucalypts at night. **Common Brushtail** and **Common Ringtail Possums** can easily be seen near stands of large, hollow-bearing trees and in parks around Chiltern town. **Koalas** sometimes occur around Honeyeater Picnic Area. The **Common Wombat** is not common but occurs in the southern (Mt Pilot) part of the park, near Skeleton Hill and Doma Munji Creek.

Bat species are typically small, forest dwellers such as **White-striped Freetail**, **Gould's** and **Chocolate Wattled**, **Gould's** and **Lesser Long-eared Bats**, **Inland Broad-nosed Bat**, and **Large**, **Southern** and **Little Forest Bats**. **Southern Freetail Bats** roost in the historic Chiltern Town Gaol; however, another freetail species may also share this roost – the best way to determine which is which would be to stand outside at dusk with a bat detector and monitor the calls as they take off. **Grey-headed Flying Foxes** roost on the Murray River nearby and visit Chiltern to feed on blossom.

The park is 275 km north-east of Melbourne (about 3 hours' drive) and about 40 km south of Albury–Wodonga on the NSW border. The little town of Chiltern makes an excellent base, with shops, cafés, petrol station and a wildlife-watcher friendly caravan park. Check out Friends of Chiltern-Mt Pilot NP (www.friendsofchiltern.org.au) for activities such as nest-box checking.

4.26 BEECHWORTH HISTORIC PARK

Highlights: **Common Wombat, Koala, Eastern Grey Kangaroo, Swamp Wallaby**

Tucked away in the forested ranges north-east of the Hume Hwy, Beechworth is a popular weekend retreat where **Common Wombats** are indeed common. The town is a few kilometres south of the southern boundary of Chiltern-Mt Pilot NP (4.25) and the various segments of Beechworth Historic Park are scattered around the town outskirts. **Common Wombats** could be seen in virtually any of these vegetated blocks, as well as along quiet country roads in the area. The Pipeline Walk to Lake Kerferd is recommended for sightings of **Koalas** and **Swamp Wallabies** during the day, and for **Common Wombat** sightings after dark. The most direct route to Beechworth is via the Great Alpine Way (B500), which heads east from Wangaratta; the Beechworth turn-off (C315) is 12 km east of Wangaratta.

4.27 VICTORIAN ALPS

Highlights: **Mountain Pygmy Possum, Common Wombat, Eastern Grey Kangaroo**

Other possibilities: **Agile Antechinus, Dusky Antechinus, Eastern Wallaroo, Dingo**

Victoria's High Country is contiguous with the Snowy Mountains over the border in NSW, a rugged, mainly forested area that is snowbound for several months a year. Roughly half the world's estimated population of 2300 **Mountain Pygmy Possums** inhabit the area around Mt Higginbotham, especially around the Mt Hotham Alpine Resort. They hibernate between May and September, becoming active in summer. An artificial corridor was constructed under the Great Alpine Way to help maintain the integrity of a population fragmented by the road. This may be worth staking out at night to see if any animals are using it. It's a bit of long shot, however – better to join a survey effort or ask around at one of the lodges to see if any have taken up residence (which they sometimes do). Mt Hotham is 132 km south-east of Wangaratta on the Great Alpine Way (B500).

Common Wombats are common in the Alps and often seen at roadsides at dusk. This is also your best chance of seeing a 'real' **Dingo** in Victoria, as many of those in remote areas are regarded as relatively pure stock. The High Country is also where Victoria's only population of the **Eastern Wallaroo** occurs – at Suggan Buggan; it's also Australia's most southerly population. Smaller animals include both **Agile** and **Dusky Antechinuses**: **Agile Antechinus** occurs up to 1800 m on Mt Hotham, whereas **Dusky Antechinuses** occur above 1600 m. As in adjoining NSW, **Broad-toothed Rats** remain active under the snow in winter, at sites such as the Bogong High Plains and Bellell Creek near Lake Mountain. **Eastern Pygmy Possums** also inhabit the subalpine area and this is the only area where the **Smoky Mouse** occurs in snowfields.

4.28 GIPPSLAND LAKES AND EAST GIPPSLAND

Highlights: **Koala, Common Wombat, Eastern Grey Kangaroo, Red-necked Wallaby, Swamp Wallaby, Grey-headed Flying Fox, Australian Fur Seal, Bottlenose Dolphin**

Other possibilities: **Southern Brown Bandicoot, Long-footed Potoroo, [Hog Deer], Humpback Whale**

Heading east on the Princes Hwy (Hwy 1), Bairnsdale has a permanent population of **Grey-headed Flying Foxes**. The highway first reaches the coast at the town of Lakes Entrance, which makes a good base from which to explore the Gippsland Lakes, a series of lakes and lagoons protected from the pounding of Bass Strait by the Ninety Mile Beach. **Bottlenose Dolphins** inhabit the lakes and are chiefly seen between April and December. Boat-based dolphin-watching tours run from Lakes Entrance. Rotamah Island is one of several islands in the lakes and supports **Echidnas, Common Wombats, Koalas, Eastern Pygmy Possums** and **Common**

Ringtail Possums, **Eastern Grey Kangaroos** and **Swamp Wallabies**, **Swamp Rats** and the introduced **Hog Deer**.

The chief mammal prize in East Gippsland is the elusive and little-known **Long-footed Potoroo**, which wasn't described till 1980. It is very rare and won't be seen by a casual visitor; there's nothing to stop you looking, of course, and there are populations in Snowy River, Erinundra, Mt Buffalo and Alpine NPs, as well as Bellbird Creek east of Orbost, Martin's Creek and Goolengook FFRs and Grant Historic Area. They are rumoured to inhabit tracks north of the Princes Hwy (Hwy 1) between Murrungower Rd (Mt Raymond) and the Mackenzie River, but you could spend a long time looking and not see any potoroos; the **Long-nosed Potoroo** also occurs here so identification by sight would probably be difficult.

At the far south-eastern corner of Victoria, the town of Mallacoota is a beautiful spot to spend some time, with great walks, a scenic lake, wild surf beaches and rocky headlands. **Koalas**, **Eastern Grey Kangaroos**, **Red-necked Wallabies** and **Swamp Wallabies** are common along nature trails near the town and in surrounding forests. Spotlighting should reveal **Common Brushtail** and **Ringtail Possums**, and **Sugar**, **Greater** and **Yellow-bellied Gliders**. There's a **Grey-headed Flying Fox** camp in nearby Croajingolong NP and the bats are often seen in Mallacoota itself. The heathlands surrounding Point Hicks lighthouse hold **Common Ringtail** and **Eastern Pygmy Possums**, and other small species such as the **Agile Antechinus** and **Southern Brown Bandicoot**. The lighthouse area is a great place to look for **Humpback Whales** on migration, as well as **Killer Whales**, which occasionally cruise offshore. There is a colony of **Australian Fur Seals** just off Wingan Inlet at The Skerries. The seals also haul out at Gabo I., about 20 minutes away by boat. One of Victoria's biggest cetacean stranding events was in Croajingolong NP, where 87 **False Killer Whales** beached.

5. Tasmania

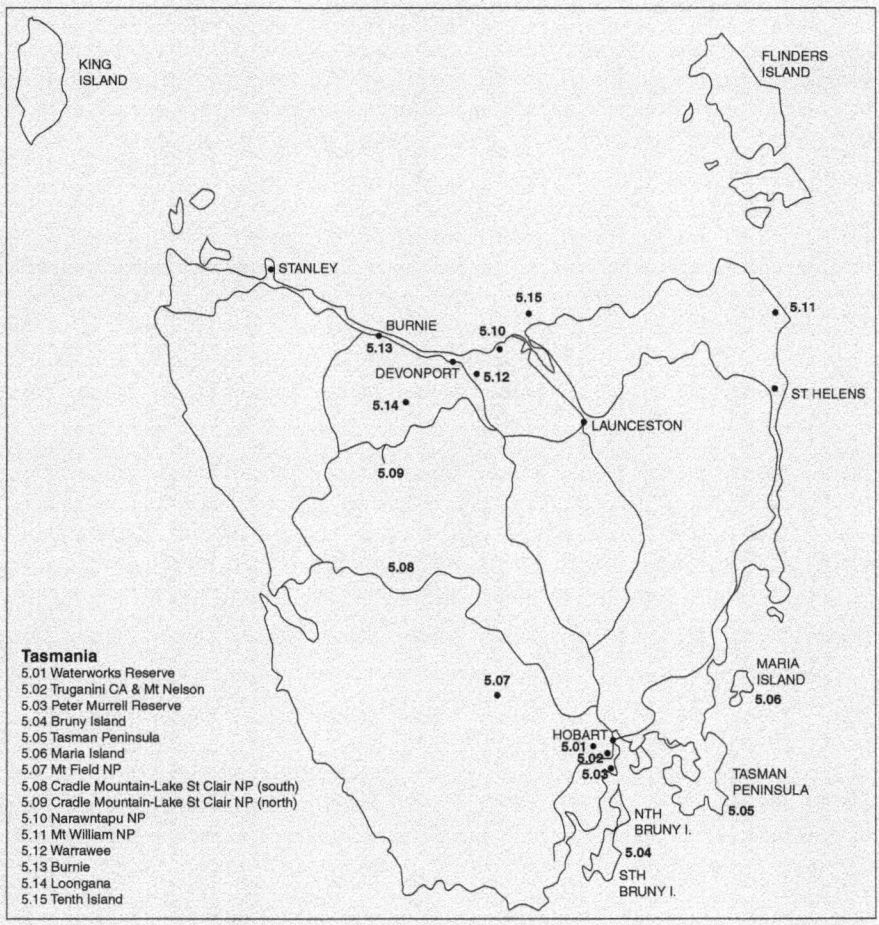

KING
ISLAND

FLINDERS
ISLAND

• STANLEY

5.15

5.11

BURNIE   **5.10**
5.13
DEVONPORT   • **5.12**
             ST HELENS

5.14 •

LAUNCESTON

5.09

5.08

Tasmania
5.01 Waterworks Reserve
5.02 Truganini CA & Mt Nelson
5.03 Peter Murrell Reserve
5.04 Bruny Island
5.05 Tasman Peninsula
5.06 Maria Island
5.07 Mt Field NP
5.08 Cradle Mountain-Lake St Clair NP (south)
5.09 Cradle Mountain-Lake St Clair NP (north)
5.10 Narawntapu NP
5.11 Mt William NP
5.12 Warrawee
5.13 Burnie
5.14 Loongana
5.15 Tenth Island

5.07

MARIA
ISLAND
5.06

HOBART
5.01 •
5.02
5.03

TASMAN
PENINSULA
5.05

NTH
BRUNY I.

5.04

STH
BRUNY I.

**Endemics: Tasmanian Devil, Eastern Quoll, Eastern Barred Bandicoot, Tasmanian
Bettong, Rufous-bellied Pademelon, Long-tailed Mouse**

No wildlife enthusiast can afford to miss the island state of Tasmania. It is Australia's
southernmost state, an area of outstanding natural beauty and one of the few areas left

with a (more or less) intact mammal fauna. Rising sea levels cut the island off from the mainland some 12 000 years ago, stranding both its human and animal inhabitants. Isolation ensured the survival of the **Thylacine**, or Tasmanian Tiger, a large, doglike marsupial carnivore, until modern times. Regrettably, the Thylacine lasted barely 100 years after white settlement, and finally succumbed to bounty hunters in 1936. However, many mammals remain common here; several that have recently become extinct on the mainland are now regarded as Tasmanian endemics; others remain far more common here than on the mainland; and one or two abundant mainland species have evolved into distinct Tasmanian forms. Notably, Tasmania is the last refuge for Australia's largest dasyurid – the **Tasmanian Devil** – and two species of quoll: **Spot-tailed** and **Eastern** (which is also extinct on the mainland). Unfortunately, the fatal devil facial tumour disease or DFTD has afflicted a large number of Tasmanian Devils and they are not as common as formerly. It is also arguably the easiest state in which to see the **Platypus**, with several excellent sites, and several macropod species are abundant: the Southern Bettong, which also recently went extinct on the mainland, remains common and by default is now often known as the **Tasmanian Bettong**. The Tasmanian form of the Eastern Grey Kangaroo is known locally as the **Forester Kangaroo**; it is shaggier and darker than its mainland relative, though not nearly as abundant. The widespread Red-necked Wallaby also differs slightly from the mainland form, and is known locally as **Bennett's Wallaby** (although it is not regarded as a separate subspecies).

Of the small mammals, **Swamp Rats** are probably the most abundant and are sometimes active by day. The **Long-tailed Mouse** is a not uncommon visitor to walkers' huts on the Overland Track and also may be partly diurnal; **Little Pygmy Possums** are sometimes encountered in these huts and the **Eastern Pygmy Possum** also occurs. Strongholds of the **New Holland Mouse** include Flinders I. and Mt William NP (5.11).

It is gratifying to visit a part of Australia where native mammals are still common (abundant in places) and you can glimpse ecosystems as they once were. Tasmania is an exceptional scenic destination that apart from wildlife can boast fascinating historic sites, excellent wineries, seafood and local produce. Not surprisingly, it is a popular destination and flights, hire cars and accommodation can book out well ahead, especially in peak holiday periods. Also, being in the higher latitudes, the weather is notoriously fickle: expect rain, high winds and even snow at any time of year, and carry appropriate clothing, especially in alpine areas. Take particular care while driving at night because of the danger of collision with wallabies, pademelons and devils.

SOME STATE HIGHLIGHTS
- Arguably the best place in Australia to see a **Platypus**.
- The only place where you can see a wild **Tasmanian Devil**.

- **Spot-tailed** and **Eastern Quolls** are still relatively common.
- Excellent commercial boat trips visit **Australian Fur Seal** rookeries.
- **Echidnas** are commonly seen at roadsides during the warmer months.

A HOBART AND THE SOUTH-EAST

Tasmania's capital, Hobart, sits at the foot of towering Mt Wellington on the shores of the Derwent River. It is well served by air routes to the mainland and all major hire car companies have offices at the airport, 19 km from the city centre. Hobart makes a good base for exploring the south and east of the island; it is within an easy drive of several good wildlife-watching sites and there's a wide range of accommodation and eating options. The Derwent used to be a calving area for **Southern Right Whales** until they were wiped out by whaling in the 19th century; they are still sometimes seen here between May and October, and at nearby sites such as Seven Mile Beach. **Humpback Whales** cruise past the Derwent mouth occasionally, pods of **Bottlenose** and **Common Dolphins** enter this broad river also and, in 2010, a pod of **Killer Whales** swam up as far as Sandy Bay. **Leopard Seals** occasionally fetch up on the shores of the Derwent, in the city harbour or on beaches near Hobart (for example, Swansea); records peak from August–September to as late as November. Check local media and keep your ear to the ground for sightings of cetaceans and unusual pinnipeds.

5.01 WATERWORKS RESERVE

Highlights: **Bennett's Wallaby, Tasmanian Pademelon, Tasmanian Bettong, Eastern Barred Bandicoot, Common Brushtail Possum**

On the shoulders of Mt Wellington, Waterworks Reserve is one of the best places to look for the **Eastern Barred Bandicoot** and **Tasmanian Bettong**. The large Tasmanian form of the **Common Brushtail Possum** is indeed common and the **Southern Brown Bandicoot** also occurs here (you will have to spotlight for these species). A network of trails joins this reserve to other parts of the mountain. The track to Fern Tree is good for the **Tasmanian Pademelon** and in dense wet areas there's a chance of seeing a **Dusky Antechinus** or **Long-nosed Potoroo**. The Waterworks Reserve is easily reached from the city centre (though it would be a strenuous walk uphill) and would repay an evening visit if time is limited. Access from the city centre is via Davey St (A6) – stick to the right-hand side and turn left at Lynton Ave, then right into Waterworks Rd. The gates are closed to vehicles at night but you can walk into the reserve to spotlight.

5.02 TRUGANINI CONSERVATION AREA AND MT NELSON

Highlights: **Southern Brown Bandicoot, Eastern Barred Bandicoot, Common Ringtail Possum, Common Brushtail Possum, Tasmanian Bettong**

This small park jostling with suburbs on the slopes of Mt Nelson is worth spotlighting in for the **Southern Brown Bandicoot** and the Tasmanian subspecies of **Common Ringtail** and **Brushtail Possums**. The bandicoots are most often seen at the top of the reserve in open woodland; **Tasmanian Bettongs** occur in flatter ground at the bottom of the slope in the adjoining Cartwright Reserve, near Sandy Bay Rd. Access to the top of Mt Nelson is via the C643 off the Southern Outlet (A6); otherwise it's a steep walk up from the Cartwright Reserve.

5.03 PETER MURRELL RESERVE

Highlights: **Platypus, Tasmanian Bettong**

Other possibilities: **Common Ringtail Possum, Tasmanian Pademelon**

This is probably the closest place to Hobart for seeing a **Platypus**. Near the car park there are two small lakes – Penrhyn and Heron Ponds – where they occur. Early morning or dusk, especially in still conditions, are the best viewing times. You should have no trouble seeing the **Common Ringtail Possum** and **Tasmanian Pademelon** here after dark; the **Tasmanian Bettong** and **Eastern Barred Bandicoot** also occur. To get to the reserve from Hobart take the Southern Outlet (A6) to Kingston; continue towards Kettering to a roundabout after the Australian Antarctic Division headquarters on your left. Take the second exit then the next left onto Huntingfield Ave; after 500 m turn left onto a dirt road after a large building on the left. This will bring you to the reserve car park.

WATCHING BATS IN TASMANIA

Isolation and a cool climate mean that Tasmania's bat fauna is not as rich as that of the mainland opposite. Flying foxes are extremely rare: only the **Grey-headed Flying Fox** has ever strayed across Bass Strait from Victoria (where it is common) and then only in the warmer months. Most records have been from King I. and the Furneaux Group; others were from near Hobart and on the Tasman Peninsula. Microbats are represented by eight resident species: **Gould's Wattled Bat, Chocolate Wattled Bat, Large Forest Bat, Southern Forest Bat, Little Forest Bat, Eastern False Pipistrelle, Lesser Long-eared Bat** and **Tasmanian Long-eared Bat** (recently split from the Greater Long-eared Bat and recognised as a separate species). However, since 2009 **White-striped Freetail Bats** have been recorded on several occasions; previously unrecorded in Tasmania, it is unclear whether they have been overlooked in the past (which seems unlikely) or have strayed across from the mainland during favourable weather conditions. Otherwise, no species are particularly rare or even uncommon, and all have been recorded on the slopes of Mt Wellington near Hobart. Bat activity in Tasmania is seasonal because of the cool winters, and there are no accessible roosts because caves tend to be too cool for maternity sites – all resident Tasmanian bats roost in tree hollows, under bark and in buildings. Your best chance of seeing a few species would be to accompany a research team; join the Australasian Bat Society (www.ausbats.org.au) to make contacts.

5.04 BRUNY ISLAND

Highlights: **Echidna, Eastern Quoll, Long-nosed Potoroo, Australian Fur Seal, Southern Right Whale**

Other possibilities: **Common Brushtail Possum, Common Ringtail Possum, Bennett's Wallaby, Tasmanian Pademelon**

In a state with many highlights, Bruny I. stands out. It is a large island lying off Tasmania's south-east corner, separated from the main island by a narrow strait and serviced by a vehicular ferry from Kettering, about 30 km south of Hobart. Aligned north–south, Bruny is about 50 km long, but has virtually become two islands owing to a narrow isthmus, only a few hundred metres wide, known as The Neck, about 25 km south of the ferry crossing point. The northern half of Bruny I. has largely been cleared and now supports only small forest patches. However, South Bruny supports an excellent variety of mammals; indeed, of the common Tasmanian species, only the Platypus, Tasmanian Devil, Spot-tailed Quoll and Common Wombat are missing. Both 'halves' of Bruny are worth exploring, although most accommodation options are on South Bruny.

Bennett's Wallabies and **Tasmanian Pademelons** are common all over the island, the former sometimes abroad during the day; **Echidnas** are also encountered frequently, especially during the summer months. Back roads on North Bruny are good for spotlighting **Eastern Quolls**, which are also sometimes seen during the day, depending on weather conditions. Adventure Bay east of The Neck is one of the state's best sites for **Southern Right Whales**, which are present between August and November; **Humpbacks** also occur occasionally. Check with locals in Adventure Bay village to see if there have been any recent sightings (the village is reached by turning left off Bruny Island Main Rd (B66) onto Adventure Bay Rd, just south of The Neck). Bruny is home to a white morph of the **Bennett's Wallaby**, known locally as the 'Painted Wallaby'; some are usually seen near the village, along with the regular colour variety, and at the Fluted Cape car park. **Common Brushtail Possums** are abundant and also occur in a golden variety, as well as the more usual coloration; they may be seen around Adventure Bay at night. **Little Pygmy Possums** sometimes take advantage of nest boxes placed around the island – ask one of the local guides if there have been any recent sightings.

South Bruny supports the island's highest diversity of wildlife and has many scenic attractions. Both colour morphs of the **Eastern Quoll** (black and brown) occur and this is one of the best parts of Tasmania in which to see this species. Common also is the **Long-nosed Potoroo** and spotlighting tours usually manage to find this species.

Australian Fur Seals frequent the southern end of the island: some 800 haul out at The Friars, a small group of islets off Tasman Head; **New Zealand Fur Seals** are also seen at The Friars and **Australian Fur Seals** sometimes haul up at Cloudy Beaches. Best sightings will be on a boat tour (www.brunycruises.com.au) from Adventure Bay, weather permitting. This should guarantee close-up views of the fur seals; **Common** and **Bottlenose Dolphins** are seen on most trips, and there is a possibility of **Southern Right** and/or **Humpback Whales** in season, as well as rarer species such as **Killer**, **Pygmy Right** and **Minke Whales**. **Leopard Seals** also occasionally haul up on Bruny beaches.

To get the most out of Bruny I. a visit of several days is recommended. There is accommodation at Adventure Bay and at several lodges, and you can camp at Cloudy Bay near the extreme southern tip. One of the best ways to see Bruny's nocturnal mammals is to take a guided tour with Inala Nature Tours (www.inalabruny.com.au). The proprietor is a long-term Bruny I. resident who is also actively engaged in conservation work on the island.

5.05 TASMAN PENINSULA

Highlights: **Eastern Quoll, Eastern Barred Bandicoot, Southern Brown Bandicoot, Tasmanian Bettong, Australian Fur Seal**

Other possibilities: **Tasmanian Devil, Common Brushtail Possum, Common Ringtail Possum, Tasmanian Pademelon, Bennett's Wallaby**

The rugged Tasman Peninsula south-east of Hobart is one of the state's top tourist attractions, not least for the superb convict ruins at Port Arthur (Tasmania was founded as a British penal colony and has a colourful history). The spectacular dissected coastline features interesting geological formations, towering stacks and massive cliffs. **Tasmanian Devils** here were found to be DFTD-free and there have been efforts to quarantine them by preventing infected 'mainland' devils from crossing the isthmus onto Tasman Peninsula. There are also plans to reintroduce DFTD-free devils here.

Offshore from the settlement of Eaglehawk Neck, at the north end of the peninsula, are the Hippolyte Rocks, used as a haul-out year round by **Australian Fur Seals**. Pelagic birding trips have been running from this tiny harbour for years, and good views are often obtained of the seals; recently a pod of **Shepherd's Beaked Whales** was seen and photographed on one of these trips. **Tasmanian Bettongs** have been seen in the hotel grounds at night and **Eastern Barred Bandicoots** occur in the vicinity. Visit www.tasmancruises.com.au for details on boat trips from Eaglehawk Neck.

Bennett's Wallabies, **Tasmanian Pademelons**, **Common Brushtail** and **Ringtail Possums**, and **Eastern Barred Bandicoots** all occur around the basic but secluded campground at Fortescue Bay. Look out also for **Eastern Quolls** here or foraging on the beach nearby. To get to Fortescue Bay take the Arthur Hwy (A9) south and turn off at the C344. A walking track leads to Cape Hauy (about 3 km), where **Australian Fur Seals** haul out at the base of the cliffs (binoculars or a scope would be useful). Other fur seal haul-outs include Tasman I., visible from Cape Pillar at the end of the Cape Hauy walking track (about 10 km), and Cape Raoul south of Nubeena. As both these sites involve long walks, a boat cruise makes an attractive option; cruises leave from Port Arthur or Eaglehawk Neck, depending on sea conditions, and approach a variety of haul-outs for excellent viewing (see www.tasmancruises.com.au for more information). There is a chance of meeting fur seals in the water en route as well as **Common Dolphins** and other species. These coastal walking tracks are excellent for scanning for cetaceans inshore; pods of **Bottlenose** and **Common Dolphins** are most commonly seen, followed by **Southern Right** and **Humpback Whales**, and (rarely) **Long-flippered Pilot Whales**. **Southern Elephant** and **Leopard Seals** are also seen occasionally along these coasts.

The serenity of Port Arthur today belies its brutal past and it is worth spending a whole day at this fascinating site. **Tasmanian Pademelons** graze on the lawns at dusk, and **Eastern Barred** and **Southern Brown Bandicoots** occur in the grounds. A good variety of small mammals has been recorded on the Tasman Peninsula, including the **Dusky** and **Swamp Antechinus, Swamp Rat, Long-tailed Mouse** and both **Eastern** and **Little Pygmy Possums**.

From Hobart, the Tasman Peninsula is reached along the Arthur Hwy (A9) from Sorell, which is 27 km north-east of Hobart on the Tasman Hwy (A3). Eaglehawk Neck is 56 km south of Sorell. The main settlements are at Port Arthur and Nubeena. Accommodation is also available elsewhere on the peninsula.

If you're heading up the east coast afterwards, it would be worth taking the (unsealed) Wielangta Forest drive between Copping and Orford, which passes through Three Thumbs SR and Cape Bernier NR, for wildlife encounters (especially at dusk and shortly after nightfall). From the Copping end (nearest to Hobart), turn north at Kellevie Rd (a sign says Kellevie and Nugent) just west of the town. From Orford, turn south onto Charles St at the roundabout before the Prosser River bridge; this becomes Rheban Rd and then turns into Wielangta Rd past Spring Beach and Rheban. Check road conditions before you go.

5.06 MARIA ISLAND NATIONAL PARK

Highlights: **Tasmanian Bettong, Forester Kangaroo, Bennett's Wallaby, Tasmanian Pademelon, Bottlenose Dolphin, Common Dolphin**

Other possibilities: **Tasmanian Devil, Long-nosed Potoroo**

Maria Island presents a wildlife watcher's dilemma – although it has abundant and tame mammals, many were introduced here during the 20th century as security against their predicted extinction elsewhere. Most have proliferated and have self-sustaining populations; indeed, the island is now possibly overstocked with some macropods. Nonetheless, Maria is a great place to visit and stay, and offers the nearest **Forester Kangaroo** viewing opportunities to Hobart as well as lots more to see and do. In 2012 the island was the release site for 14 DFTD-free **Tasmanian Devils**, which bred within 6 months and now number more than 50; they will ideally become self-sustaining on Maria. Note that they sometimes steal (and chew) unattended boots from campsites!

Foresters and **Bennett's Wallabies** (both species were introduced) are common near the historical site and mobs of both graze near the airstrip a short walk north of the town. **Long-nosed Potoroos** and **Tasmanian Pademelons** occur naturally on the island, but are more retiring than the two larger species; they are more likely to be seen in wet forest, such as along the Reservoir Track.

Ferries (www.mariaislandferry.com.au) run from Triabunna, 85 km (about 90 minutes' drive) from Hobart on the Tasman Hwy (A3) via Sorrell. Note that this is not a vehicular ferry but bicycles are allowed and a sturdy mountain bike would be a good way to explore the island. Maria can be visited as a day trip, but a longer visit is warranted – there's camping and accommodation in a guest house (book ahead for both). During the crossing watch for **Common** and **Bottlenose Dolphins**, and **Southern Right Whales**, which sometimes use the Mercury Passage between Maria and the mainland.

WATCHING WHALES AND DOLPHINS IN TASMANIA

Common and **Bottlenose Dolphins** are the most commonly encountered cetaceans in Tasmanian waters. Both **Humpback Whales** and **Southern Right Whales** pass the coast on their respective annual migrations to and from Antarctica. **Humpbacks** may be seen heading north in May–July, but generally pass closer to shore on their southward migration in October–December. **Southern Right Whales** move northward between June and September, some staying to calve in Tasmanian waters, before heading south again between September and late October. Most of the migrating whales follow the east coast, although some travel up the west coast, where observations are fewer owing to inaccessibility, rougher weather and fewer people. The coastline between Bicheno and Orford on the east coast offers a few vantage points from which to look for both species; Whaler's Lookout is an easy walk from the Bicheno Tourist Information Centre (check Bicheno Whale Watching on Facebook for recent sightings). Up to 30 whales have been seen in a single day off Bicheno, sometimes only 10–20 m from shore near the rocks below Whaler's Lookout. Numerous headlands and clifftops in the south-east make excellent observation sites; other sites include Frederick Henry Bay and Great Oyster Bay. **Common** and **Bottlenose Dolphins** are often seen from the Maria I. ferry, and whales are seen on various cruises to seal colonies. It would be worth taking a pelagic birding trip from Eaglehawk Neck – a pod of **Shepherd's Beaked Whales** was reported offshore recently by birdwatchers (see 5.05). Other species recorded in Tasmanian waters include **Killer Whales** (a pod of which entered the Derwent River in 2010) and **Blue**, **Fin**, **Sei** and **Bryde's Whales**; rarer small species have included **Dusky** and **Southern Rightwhale Dolphins**, and the **Spectacled Porpoise**.

Tasmania has the highest frequency of cetacean strandings in the country, particularly mass strandings and especially in summer (November–February). **Sperm Whales** and **Long-flippered Pilot Whales** (with a single record also of **Short-flippered Pilot Whale**) and **Common Bottlenose** and **Short-beaked Common Dolphins** are the most commonly reported, followed by **Pygmy Right**, **Minke** and **False Killer Whales**. Altogether, 28 of the 30 cetacean species that occur, or are thought to occur, in Tasmanian waters have stranded here. In fact, some species are known only from records of a single stranded animal. Among these are several of the beaked whales, of which nine species have been recorded. **Strap-toothed**, **Gray's** and **Goose-beaked Whales** have occurred most frequently, followed by **Hector's Beaked Whale**; much rarer occurrences have included **Blainville's**, **Andrews'**, **True's** and **Arnoux's Beaked Whales**, and a **Southern Bottlenose Whale**. Strandings regularly hit the news, particularly on the rugged west and north-west coasts where they seem to be prevalent. Hotspots include the Circular Head and Macquarie Harbour–Ocean Beach (near Strahan) areas. The Nut, a prominent headland near Stanley on the north-west coast, makes a good observation point for migrating whales; **Sperm**, **Long-flippered Pilot** and **Pygmy Right Whales** have all been stranded near here. Adventure and Cloudy bays on Bruny I. have also had many strandings, with a list that includes **Common**, **Bottlenose** and **Southern Rightwhale Dolphins**, blackfish such as **Long-flippered Pilot** and **False Killer Whales**, as well as true **Killer Whales**; baleen species including **Sei** and **Pygmy Right Whales** (a specimen of the latter has been captured alive off Bruny); and beaked species such as **Hector's**, **Gray's**, **Strap-toothed** and **Cuvier's**. The Tasmanian government's 24-hour whale hotline for reporting strandings is 0427 942 537 (0427 WHALES).

B CENTRAL TASMANIA

The highest part of the state is in the rugged central highlands, which are popular among tourists and walkers. Wildlife is common and easily seen in several excellent national parks. The Epping Forest region supports an important population of **Tasmanian Bettongs**, especially around the Tom Gibson NR west of Epping Forest township. Ben Lomond NP is a scenic national park near Launceston that is known for its **Eastern Quolls**, which are regular visitors to walkers' huts. Pepper Bush Adventures (www.pepperbush.com.au) runs a 'Quoll Patrol' tour to the area where they see quolls and other species regularly.

5.07 MOUNT FIELD NATIONAL PARK

Highlights: **Platypus, Echidna, Eastern Quoll, Eastern Barred Bandicoot, Southern Brown Bandicoot**

Other possibilities: **Common Brushtail Possum, Common Wombat, Bennett's Wallaby, Tasmanian Pademelon, Water Rat**

Not far from Hobart, this scenic national park tucked into a fold in the hills features a range of habitats from tall, wet forest to alpine heaths and bogs. The campground and picnic area are good places to start looking for **Bennett's Wallabies** and **Tasmanian Pademelons**, which emerge from cover to graze in the late afternoon. After dark, the day-use area is also a great place to see **Southern Brown** and **Eastern Barred Bandicoots**, **Common Brushtail Possums** and **Common Wombats**. Both colour phases of the **Eastern Quoll** occur around the main car park and campground at night. If you miss the quoll here, then try driving slowly along park roads at night. **Echidnas** are common at Mt Field and there are several sites to look for **Platypuses** – for example, along quiet stretches of the Tyenna River near the park entrance (watch for **Water Rats** here also) and in the alpine tarns, such as Lake Dobson and Seal Lake, which are reached by taking the Dobson Rd. (**Platypuses** stay active in winter and will even cross snowy ground between waterways.)

Other mammals recorded at Mt Field include the **Tasmanian Devil** (now rare), **Spot-tailed Quoll**, **Common Ringtail Possum** and **Long-nosed Potoroo** (in dense vegetation). Small nocturnal species include the **Eastern Pygmy Possum** and **Little Pygmy Possum**, **Swamp Rat** and **Broad-toothed Rat**. The endemic **Long-tailed Mouse** is reputed to occur on scree slopes, but in reality few people encounter it by chance.

Mt Field NP makes an easy day trip from Hobart. The capital is close enough to use as a base if you just want to visit in the evening to maximise mammal viewing, but there is ample accommodation in the area for a less rushed visit. From Hobart take the Brooker Hwy (A10) north-west to New Norfolk, then either continue on the A10 or take the B2 (south of the Derwent River) to Westerway; from there it is another 6.5 km to the village of National Park and the park entrance.

Beyond Mt Field, the Gordon River Rd (B61) to Lake Pedder heads into the south-west wilderness area; **Eastern Quolls**, **Tasmanian Devils** and **Common Brushtail Possums** could be encountered along the way at night.

5.08 CRADLE MOUNTAIN-LAKE ST CLAIR NATIONAL PARK (SOUTHERN ACCESS)

Highlights: **Echidna, Platypus, Tasmanian Devil, Spot-tailed Quoll, Eastern Quoll, Common Wombat**

Other possibilities: **Common Brushtail Possum, Common Ringtail Possum, Eastern Pygmy Possum, Bennett's Wallaby, Tasmanian Pademelon**

There are two main entrances to this popular national park in the central highlands. The southern part (Lake St Clair) is most easily reached from Hobart; the northern section (Cradle Mountain) is about 120 km west of Launceston via Sheffield, and too far from Hobart to be sensibly attempted as a day trip. You cannot drive between the two entrances while inside the park, so they are treated here as two sections; see 5.09 for the northern (Cradle Mountain) section.

One of the first sights that will greet you at the park entrance will be **Bennett's Wallabies** jostling tourists for handouts. **Tasmanian Pademelons** are also here but are more retiring – look for them among vegetation bordering the picnic areas. After dark, the picnic area and campground are frequented by **Common Brushtail** and **Common Ringtail Possums** and (rarely nowadays) **Tasmanian Devils**. You'll increase your chances of seeing devils and both **Eastern** and **Spot-tailed Quolls** by spotlighting along park roads at night: try St Clair Lagoon, Rufus Weir Rd and unsealed roads around Derwent Bridge. **Echidnas** are relatively common and most often seen in sunny dry weather; watch for them in dry eucalypt forest, along the Shadow Lake Track, the Aboriginal Culture Walk and even by the shores of Lake St Clair. There are probably better places to see **Platypuses**, owing to the high visitor numbers here, but the Platypus Bay Track offers vantage points from which to start looking; Shadow Lake also has resident **Platypuses**. **Common Wombats** can be seen along the Mt Rufus Track. **Eastern Pygmy Possums** are sometimes found in accommodation huts along the Overland Track.

To reach the southern part of Cradle Mountain-Lake St Clair NP, take the Lyell Hwy (A10) to Derwent Bridge, 175 km north-west of Hobart. Lake St Clair is another 5 km

FOXES IN TASMANIA

The Red Fox is arguably the most destructive carnivorous pest ever to become established in Australia. Fortunately its onslaught was stopped by Bass Strait and Tasmania was free of its depredations until about 1998, when one escaped from a container ship and was never relocated. On the mainland the Fox is a common, even diurnal, hunter, but in Tasmania it remains elusive and for many years evidence of its presence was equivocal. Interestingly, it took several attempts before the Fox actually became established on the mainland. When it did, however, it cut a trail of devastation through native wildlife. If it were to become established in Tasmania it could spell disaster for many of the small mammals that are still common here. Evidence collected in Tasmania since 2001 indicates the Fox is present; this can only mean that more accidental introductions have taken place or that it has been deliberately introduced. If you see a Fox in Tasmania, please report it immediately to the 24-hour Fox Hotline 1300 369 688. Don't approach a den as vixens will move cubs if they suspect trouble; and if you find a carcass leave it where it is until authorities can examine it in situ before disposing of it. Visit the Tasmanian national parks website (www.parks.tas.gov.au) for more information.

from there and well signposted. Allow plenty of time for the journey as the highway has many winding sections and may be icy in winter.

5.09 CRADLE MOUNTAIN-LAKE ST CLAIR NATIONAL PARK (NORTHERN ACCESS)

Highlights: **Echidna, Platypus, Tasmanian Devil, Spot-tailed Quoll, Eastern Quoll, Common Wombat**

Other possibilities: **Dusky Antechinus, Long-nosed Potoroo, Bennett's Wallaby, Tasmanian Pademelon, Broad-toothed Rat**

The northern part of Cradle Mountain-Lake St Clair NP offers a very different experience from the southern (see 5.08). It is an average of 200 m higher in elevation and consequently cooler, with extensive areas of pristine alpine wilderness. It is very popular with walkers and campers, and advance bookings are advised for campsites and the lodge. The main campground is on the right a couple of kilometres before the park entrance; the park entrance is well signposted and the popular Cradle Mountain Lodge sits opposite its entrance. The main park road heads south from here, finishing at Waldheim and Dove Lake.

The area boasts one of the highest mammal diversities in the state, with 20 species recorded. Some of these are very common; by walking the tracks and boardwalks in the Waldheim and Ronny Creek areas you should have no trouble seeing **Bennett's Wallabies** and **Common Wombats**, even during the day (some of the wallabies in Cradle Mountain NP have blond coloration). **Tasmanian Pademelons** keep more to the forest edge but are also common. All three species can also be seen along the Cradle Valley Boardwalk. Cradle Mountain Lodge (www.cradlemountainlodge.com.au) used to put out food scraps for **Tasmanian Devils** and **Spot-tailed Quolls**; this practice has now stopped, but there is still a chance of seeing both species around the lodge and campground at night (devils are not as common as formerly). Check the

Lodge's website for details of spotlighting walks that may be running. **Common Brushtail** and **Ringtail Possums** and **Eastern Quolls** are typically seen around the campground. By driving slowly along the road from the campground to Dove Lake car park after dark you'll increase your chance of seeing dasyurids; **Tasmanian Pademelons** and **Common Wombats** are also seen along this road. **Platypuses** are relatively common in this section of the park, and occur in pools and streams, even in the lodge grounds, and along The Enchanted Walk, which follows Pencil Pine Creek. **Long-nosed Potoroos**, **Dusky Antechinuses** and **Broad-toothed Rats** occur in the dense undergrowth.

Access to Cradle Mountain is via Sheffield, 92 km west of Launceston on Route 1; from Sheffield take the C136 and turn off at Cradle Mountain Rd (C132). Note that park roads can be covered in snow and get icy in winter (check road conditions before you set out). This part of the park is the start of the Overland Walk, a popular long-distance hike through the rugged south-west; the **Long-tailed Mouse** and **Eastern Quolls** are regular visitors to walkers' huts on the track.

C NORTHERN TASMANIA

Tasmania's second city, Launceston, makes a good alternative base to Hobart or the starting point for exploring the state's north and north-west. A few mammals can be seen at Cataract Gorge, a short walk from the town centre: check the lawns near the restaurant at dusk for **Bennett's Wallabies, Rufous Pademelons, Southern Brown Bandicoots** and **Common Brushtail Possums**.

5.10 NARAWNTAPU NATIONAL PARK

Highlights: **Common Wombat, Forester Kangaroo, Bennett's Wallaby, Tasmanian Pademelon**

Other possibilities: **Spot-tailed Quoll, Tasmanian Devil, Long-nosed Potoroo, White-footed Dunnart**

Formerly known as the Asbestos Range NP, Narawntapu is a small coastal park where wombats and Tasmania's three largest macropod species are abundant. Ignoring the hyperbolic comparisons with Tanzania's Serengeti NP in tourist literature, the visitor is nonetheless virtually guaranteed sightings of **Common Wombats**, **Forester Kangaroos**, **Bennett's Wallabies** and **Tasmanian Pademelons**. Wombats can generally be seen, day or night, on the open grassy plains near the ranger's station. Start looking around the park HQ and camping area at Springlawn (early morning and late afternoon are peak viewing times), or climb the small hill nearby and look over the lawn-like grazed areas below – sometimes dozens of large marsupials are visible at once. **Forester Kangaroos** were extirpated from this area in the 19th century, but were reintroduced in 1975 and are now well established. **Bennett's Wallabies** are common in heath by park roads; the **Tasmanian Pademelon** is more skulking and tends to emerge later in the evening than the park's other macropods. **Common Brushtail Possums** and **Spot-tailed Quolls** occur around the campground (the former more than the latter) and there is still a good chance of locating a **Tasmanian Devil** in Narawntapu – try spotlighting along park roads well after dark. **Long-nosed Potoroos** occur in dense vegetation. **White-footed Dunnarts** are reputed to be common in dense vegetation along Sheepwash Creek; in reality your chances of seeing them are low, although you could try spotlighting in likely habitat.

Narawntapu is about an hour's drive north-west of Launceston, most easily on the B71 west of Devonport. There are designated camping areas with toilets and barbecues, although if time is limited you should be able to see the four main species here easily in a day or evening visit.

5.11 MT WILLIAM NATIONAL PARK

Highlights: **Echidna, Eastern Quoll, Spot-tailed Quoll, Forester Kangaroo, Common Wombat**

Other possibilities: **Common Brushtail Possum, New Holland Mouse, Swamp Rat**

THE BIG FIVE

There are no Koalas in Tasmania, but the world's largest surviving dasyurids make up for it; other iconic species are readily seen at several sites.

Kangaroo Forester Kangaroos, Tasmania's subspecies of Eastern Grey Kangaroo, is readily viewed at Nawrantapu (5.10) and Mt William NPs (5.11) and on Maria I. (5.06).

Tasmanian Devil Still relatively common in the north-west at, for example, Loongana (5.14) and an insurance population is thriving at Maria I. (5.06).

Wombat The Common Wombat is indeed common in Tasmania and can be readily seen at Nawrantapu NP (5.10) and Mt William NP (5.11).

Platypus Tasmania is one of the best states in which to see this amazing animal; prime sites include Warrawee FR (5.12), Burnie (5.13) and Loongana (5.14).

Quoll This is the best state in which to see quolls; Spot-tailed Quolls are often sighted at Loongana (5.14) and Eastern Quolls are common on Bruny I. (5.04).

Mt William NP sees fewer visitors than most Tasmanian parks and was originally declared to protect the **Forester Kangaroo**, which was exterminated over most of the state in the 19th century. **Foresters** are indeed common here and sightings are almost guaranteed along Forester Kangaroo Drive, especially at dawn and dusk; open grassy areas are best. **Common Wombats**, **Bennett's Wallabies** and **Tasmanian Pademelons** also occur along Forester Kangaroo Drive (suitable for 2WD). **Common Brushtail Possums** are common around the campgrounds, where **Spot-tailed Quolls** also forage for titbits. The quolls and **Tasmanian Devils** were formerly common in this part of the state; the devils have been badly affected by DFTD but still occur and even forage along beaches. **Eastern Quolls** are still relatively abundant – try driving the Musselroe Bay–Cape Portland road at night; **Spot-tailed Quolls** are also sometimes seen along this route. Mt William NP is a stronghold for the rare **New Holland Mouse**, of which a healthy population persists in mosaics of burnt and unburnt heath; your only chance of seeing one would be to participate in a survey with a research team. **Swamp Rats** are also common in this habitat.

The southern end of Mt William NP can be reached from Hobart via St Helen's and Gladstone; there's a basic campground at Deep Creek near Eddystone Point. From Gladstone it's 17 km to the northern park entrance via the C843 and C845 (both unsealed). There are also basic camping facilities at Top Camp and Stumpy's Bay.

5.12 WARRAWEE FOREST RESERVE

Highlights: **Platypus, Eastern Barred Bandicoot, Tasmanian Bettong**

Just south of LaTrobe on the north coast, Warrawee Park claims to be the 'Platypus Capital of the World' and indeed offers excellent **Platypus** viewing opportunities, particularly at dawn and dusk. This neat bushland reserve has been restored by a local community group and Platypus walks are conducted on request at certain times of the year. **Tasmanian Bettongs** and **Eastern Barred Bandicoots** also occur and there is a good chance of sightings of both in the grassy woodland bordering the stream. Warrawee is just outside of Latrobe on Shale Rd (turn off Gilbert St); see www.latrobetasmania.com.au for details of tours.

5.13 BURNIE

Highlights: **Platypus, Eastern Barred Bandicoot, Long-nosed Potoroo**

Full points to this otherwise rather unappealing town for the big effort it has made in recent years to cater to wildlife tourism. Apart from good **Platypus** viewing, it offers a chance to see **Long-nosed Potoroos** and **Eastern Barred Bandicoots** within the city limits. There is a 13-km wildlife-watching circuit and the *Burnie Wildlife Guide*, available at the Pioneer Museum, tells you more about the plants and

HOPE FOR THE TASMANIAN DEVIL?

In recent years the Tasmanian Devil population has crashed because of devil facial tumour disease (DFTD), one of only three cancers known that can spread like a contagious disease. The cancer is passed from devil to devil through biting, and is characterised by the appearance of small lesions or lumps in and around the mouth that develop into large, hideous facial cancers. DFTD affects mainly adults – first males, then females, and juveniles as young as 1 year old. Infected devils may become emaciated because the tumours prevent them from feeding properly; it makes females lose their young and infected animals die within months of contracting the disease. So far there is no cure, and isolation and prevention seem the best remedies. Healthy animals have been released onto Maria I. to form an insurance population and have started to breed. There are plans afoot to rid the Tasman Peninsula of diseased devils, put up an exclusion barrier across the isthmus and release DFTD-free devils to restock the area. And DFTD-free insurance populations have been set up on the mainland. More information can be found on the Save the Tassie Devil website (www.tassiedevil.com.au).

animals of the area. Fern Glade Reserve, reached by turning off the Bass Hwy (A2) at Old Surrey Rd, just west of the river crossing, is a quiet reach of the Emu River and a pleasant place to look for **Platypuses**. There are several sites to look for them on a track that follows this part of the river. Note that Fern Glade Reserve is closed between dusk and 7.30 am. Romaine Reserve (reached by following Reeves St off the Bass Hwy, about 1 km west of Old Surrey Rd) has resident **Eastern Barred Bandicoots** and **Long-nosed Potoroos**, which will only be seen by spotlighting, and **Platypuses** have also been seen in the reserve's pond.

Burnie is 48 km west of Devonport on the Bass Hwy (A2), the main road along Tasmania's north coast. There is a choice of accommodation and eateries in town.

5.14 LOONGANA

Highlights: **Platypus, Tasmanian Devil, Spot-tailed Quoll**

Other possibilities: **Common Ringtail Possum, Common Brushtail Possum, Common Wombat, Bennett's Wallaby, Tasmanian Pademelon**

The excellent Mountain Valley ecotourism lodge (www.mountainvalley.com.au) is highly recommended for almost guaranteed sightings of **Tasmanian Devil**, and a better than average chance of seeing **Spot-tailed Quolls** and **Platypuses**. For two decades the owners have been putting out carcasses for the devils and sightings are virtually guaranteed – face-to-face if you watch them through the window of your cabin. **Tasmanian Pademelons** are also common in the grounds, and other species likely to be seen are **Common Ringtail** and **Brushtail Possums**, **Common Wombats** and **Bennett's Wallabies**.

Loongana is tucked away in the hills south of Burnie, a good 2 hours' drive from Launceston. The most direct route would be to head to Ulverstone on the north coast, then take the B15 to Nietta; the Mountain Valley turn-off is on the left 15.9 km from Nietta on the Loongana Rd (C128). It is a popular retreat and bookings are advised; accommodation is in self-contained cabins.

5.15 TENTH ISLAND

Highlights: **Australian Fur Seal, New Zealand Fur Seal**

This small reserve off the north coast is home to between 500 and 600 **Australian Fur Seals**, which use the island both for breeding and hauling out, and about 60 pairs of **New Zealand Fur Seals**. A charter boat company (www.sealandsea. com) based at nearby George Town runs regular tours to Tenth I. George Town is 52 km north of Launceston on the Tamar Hwy (A8), which follows the east bank of the Tamar River. An **Australian Fur Seal** cruise also departs from Stanley, near the north-western tip of Tasmania; visit www.stanleysealcruises.com.au for details.

5.16 OTHER SITES

Tasmania has plenty of lesser known and seldom-visited wildlife-watching sites, as well as lots that are better for observing other wildlife where, nonetheless, a few mammals can also be seen.

Flinders Island

Largest of the Furneaux Group and one of Australia's largest islands, Flinders I. supports a small human population and abundant **Common Wombats**, **Bennett's Wallabies** and **Tasmanian Pademelons**. **Echidnas** are frequently seen and the island is a stronghold for the rare **New Holland Mouse**, especially near East Coast Lagoons; **Common Brushtail** and **Ringtail Possums** can be spotlighted in Strzelecki NP and wherever there are good stands of trees. **Australian Fur Seals** use many of the smaller islands and islets in the Furneaux Group, including Moriarty Rocks and Double I.

Freycinet National Park

This is a popular scenic area that attracts numerous tourists annually. **Bennett's Wallabies** and **Rufous Pademelons** are common around campgrounds, and by spotlighting you should manage to see a few of the following: **Eastern Quoll**, **Common Brushtail** and **Ringtail Possums**, **Sugar Glider** (note that Sugar Gliders were probably introduced to Tasmania – they don't occur on offshore islands) and **Long-nosed Potoroo**. **Common** and **Bottlenose Dolphins** and **Humpback** and

Southern Right Whales occur offshore; **Australian Fur Seals** occur on islands to the south, such as Schouten I. (visit www.freycinetseacruises.com for cruises that visit this area).

King Island

Tasmania's second-largest offshore island sits at the western end of Bass Strait. It was once a rookery for **Southern Elephant Seals**; unfortunately they were killed off long ago although individuals occasionally still haul up. Other casual pinniped visitors include **Australian Fur** and **Leopard Seals**; and **Southern Right Whales** and **Common Dolphins** are sometimes seen inshore (strandings of **Long-flippered Pilot Whales** and **Bottlenose Dolphins** have occurred). **Bennett's Wallabies, Rufous Pademelons, Common Brushtail Possums** and **Common Wombats** are all still common; **Echidnas** are seen often by day, at least in warm weather, and there's a good chance of seeing a **Platypus**. Less frequently recorded species include the **Swamp Antechinus, Common Ringtail Possum, Long-nosed Potoroo** and **Eastern Pygmy Possum**. See www.kingisland.org.au.

Maatsuyker Island

A small island off the rugged southern coastline that once supported a **Southern Elephant Seal** rookery. The seals were wiped out in the 19th century, but these enormous pinnipeds have returned to breed three times in recent decades. Non-breeding animals come ashore most frequently in August and September. It is also a haul-out for **Australian Fur Seals**.

Melaleuca

This remote site in the south-west is accessible only by light plane from Hobart, by boat or on foot. It is well known for its endangered Orange-bellied Parrots and also boasts 21 native mammal species. Both **Eastern** and **Spot-tailed Quolls** are seen here regularly, plus **Bennett's Wallabies, Common Wombats, Tasmanian Pademelons** and **Common Ringtail Possums. Swamp Rats, Swamp Antechinuses, Broad-toothed Rats** and the **Long-tailed Mouse** also occur. The utter seclusion of the area make it a naturalist's delight, but you must bring all supplies including wet-weather gear. Accommodation is in walkers' huts.

6. South Australia

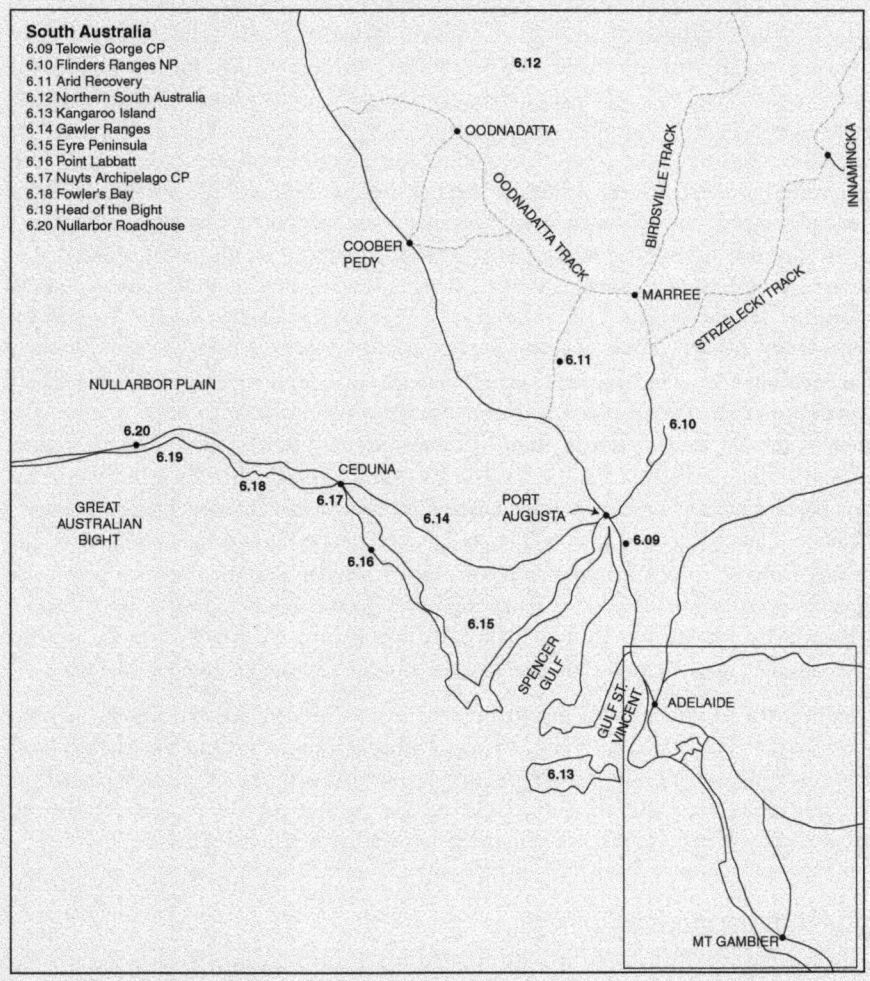

South Australia

6.12

OODNADATTA

INNAMINCKA

OODNADATTA TRACK

BIRDSVILLE TRACK

COOBER PEDY

MARREE

STRZELECKI TRACK

6.11

NULLARBOR PLAIN

6.10

6.20

6.19

CEDUNA

6.18

6.17

6.14

PORT AUGUSTA

6.16

6.09

GREAT AUSTRALIAN BIGHT

6.15

SPENCER GULF

GULF ST. VINCENT

ADELAIDE

6.13

MT GAMBIER

Endemics: **Greater Stick-nest Rat**

Much of SA lies in the arid zone. It is a vast area of deserts, gibber, saltbush plains and shallow, saline lakes, dissected by waterways that may be dry for years and then overflow for hundreds of square kilometres after good rains. Needless to say, this is fascinating but challenging country to explore, with extreme heat in summer and few towns or even roads. South of the arid zone is a broad mallee belt, contiguous with north-western Victoria's mallee and still covering swathes of Kangaroo I. The latter is one of the state's highlights – a predator-free haven where many mammals are still common; another is the privately run Arid Recovery reserve, an outstanding project that focuses on re-establishing a suite of small mammals that have vanished from the arid-zone landscape. The comparatively wet south-east corner is where several species that occur on the eastern seaboard, such as the **Common Wombat**, reach the western extremity of their range. Attractions in the south-east include the World Heritage–listed Naracoorte Caves, which host a large maternity colony of **Common Bentwing Bats**. South Australia has Australia's largest concentration of pinniped breeding colonies, including most of the endemic **Australian Sea Lions** and several colonies of **New Zealand Fur Seal**. **Southern Right Whales** migrate annually to calve in the Great Australian Bight, as well as other sites along the coast. The state's only endemic mammal is the **Greater Stick-nest Rat**, which fortunately survived on an offshore island after becoming extinct on the mainland; the extremely rare and localised **Kangaroo Island Dunnart** is now regarded as a subspecies of the Grey-bellied Dunnart. The **Plains Mouse** and **Greater Stick-nest Rat** are currently known only from SA (except where the latter has been reintroduced to other sites) although both were formerly widespread across the inland. The arid zone features a suite of near-endemic dasyurids and rodents, such as the **Kowari**, **Ampurta**, **Sandhill Dunnart**, and **Fawn** and **Dusky Hopping-mouse**, some of which could be seen by spotlighting, especially when their numbers build up after wet years. Others, such as the **Silky Mouse** and **Heath Mouse**, are mallee–heath specialists that are just as likely to be encountered in other parts of their respective ranges. However, you will have virtually no chance of encountering most of these small species without live-trapping, and the best way to do this is to volunteer to help a research team doing survey work. The Royal Geographical Society of South Australia (www.rgssa.org.au) periodically organises expeditions to remote parts of the state.

Unfortunately, SA has suffered a disproportionate number of mammal extinctions and many beautiful scenic areas that are worth visiting for other reasons are rather devoid of mammals. The attractive **Toolache Wallaby**, formerly endemic to the south-east and adjacent parts of Victoria, hasn't been seen since 1924. On the positive side, SA is well served by learned societies and research institutions, and the state's wildlife is well documented.

SOME STATE HIGHLIGHTS
- The best state in which to see the fabulous **Yellow-footed Rock Wallaby**.
- Abundant wildlife, including sea lions, on Fox-free **Kangaroo I**.

- The maternity cave of **Common Bentwing Bats** at Naracoorte Caves NP.
- Australia's highest concentration of **Australian Sea Lions** and **New Zealand Fur Seals**.
- Outstanding **Southern Right Whale** viewing at Head of the Bight.

A ADELAIDE AND THE SOUTH-EAST

Adelaide, the state capital, is a pleasant enough place with plenty of eating, sleeping and vehicle hire options; stock up here on supplies before venturing further afield. Broadly speaking, the Adelaide area marks the northern and western boundaries for several species found in south-eastern SA, but mammal-viewing opportunities in the immediate vicinity are rather limited. There are several mallee sites and other attractions in the state's south-east quarter, a few hours' drive away. If you're based in Adelaide for any length of time, note that various sites in western Victoria (for example, The Grampians NP (4.21) and Portland (4.18)) are as easily reached from Adelaide as they are from Melbourne.

The far south-east is the only part of the state where you are likely to see **Eastern Grey Kangaroos** or **Common Wombats**, as this is where they reach the western limit of their distribution. Both are uncommon, the former known only from Myora and Caroline Forest Reserves, in grassland around Mt Benson and near Meringa Swamp at Cape Jaffa; and the wombat from Canunda NP, Beachport CP and Comaum FR. It is doubtful whether the **Swamp Wallaby** now persists in SA; it was formerly seen near the Victorian border in the vicinity of Dismal Swamp. The **Red-necked Wallaby** hangs on in small numbers at scattered, undisturbed sites, but is nowhere common. One colony of **Yellow-bellied Gliders** survives among Manna Gums near Caroline; and the **Dusky Antechinus** was recorded in Lower Glenelg CP for the first time in 2013. **Feathertail Glider** taxonomy remains unresolved at the time of writing, but two forms appear to survive in SA: one in the Murray Riverlands, the other in the South-East.

6.01 ADELAIDE AREA

Highlights: **Koala, Western Grey Kangaroo, Water Rat, Indo-Pacific Bottlenose Dolphin**

Other possibilities: **Common Ringtail Possum, Common Brushtail Possum, Grey-headed Flying Fox, Australian Sea Lion**

Adelaide occupies a coastal plain sandwiched between the Gulf St Vincent and the Mt Lofty Ranges (known locally as the Adelaide Hills), which form a steep escarpment to the east. The CBD is surrounded by parklands where you should have no trouble locating **Common Brushtail Possums** after dark, a short walk from city hotels; **Common Ringtail Possums** also occur, but in smaller numbers.

This is probably the best place in the state to see **Water Rats**, which are common in quiet stretches of the Torrens River, on the west side of the CBD, even during the day (**Platypuses** formerly occurred in the Torrens and Onkaparinga rivers, but SA's only stable population is now on Kangaroo I. (6.13)). **Grey-headed Flying Foxes** have taken up residence in the botanic gardens and now number about 1400 (with young born in 2011 and 2012). South Australia's first record of **Black Flying Fox** was here in 2013.

The Mt Lofty Ranges are still partly forested and experience higher rainfall than the coastal plain, with consequently a higher biodiversity. However, the whole area is highly modified by suburbia, and only a few common species can be seen in parks and patches of natural vegetation. These include the two common large possums and **Koalas**, which were introduced here and now number more than 100 000; some can be seen at Deep Lead FFR. The **Western Grey Kangaroo** is the only macropod that survives in the Adelaide region. The **Western Pygmy Possum** occasionally turns up in back gardens, particularly near stands of flowering native vegetation. Other small mammals that cling on include the **Yellow-footed Antechinus**, **Bush Rat** and **Swamp Rat** (in the wetter southern part of the ranges). There is a small population of **Southern Brown Bandicoots** at Belair NP, where they inhabit dense vegetation near water in Melville Gully in the south-east of the park (which is closed at night).

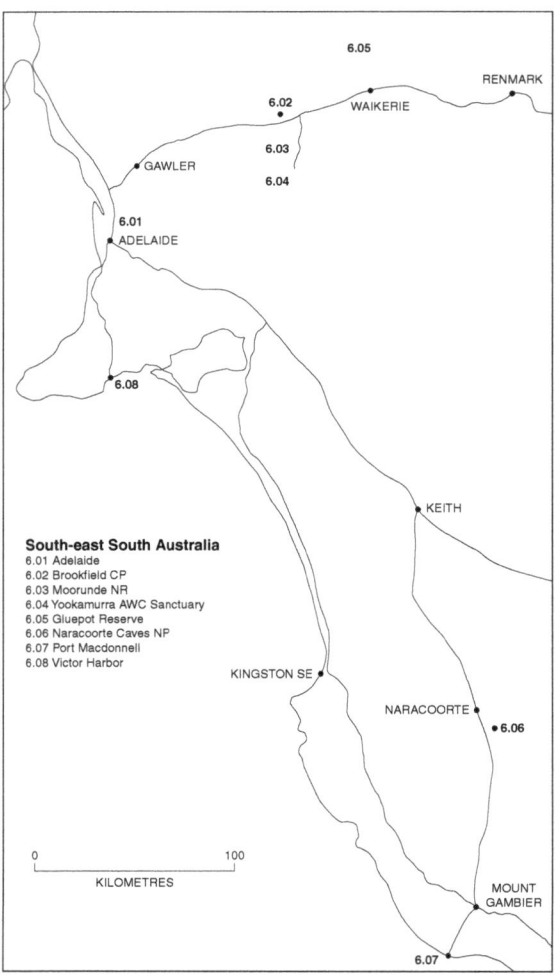

6.05

RENMARK

6.02
WAIKERIE

6.03

GAWLER

6.04

6.01
ADELAIDE

6.08

KEITH

South-east South Australia
6.01 Adelaide
6.02 Brookfield CP
6.03 Moorunde NR
6.04 Yookamurra AWC Sanctuary
6.05 Gluepot Reserve
6.06 Naracoorte Caves NP
6.07 Port Macdonnell
6.08 Victor Harbor

KINGSTON SE

NARACOORTE
● 6.06

0   100
KILOMETRES

MOUNT
GAMBIER

6.07

Check out the Valley of the Bandicoots project for further information on this species (www.communitywebs.org/bandicootvalley/projects.html).

The Port Adelaide River estuary–Barker Inlet has a permanent population of 30 or so **Bottlenose Dolphins**. The whole area has been declared the Adelaide Dolphin Sanctuary and the Port River Dolphin Trail brochure (www.portenf.sa.gov.au/webdata/resources/files/DolphinBrochure.pdf) lists sites where the dolphins may be seen from land, plus contact details of boat operators that run dolphin cruises (on which **Common Dolphins** are also sometimes seen). The Torrens I. bridge makes a good vantage point from which to look for pods; other likely places include Largs Bay and the North Haven Marina. **Australian Sea Lions** are frequently seen on the breakwater of the Outer Harbour and can occur year-round; **New Zealand Fur Seals** also occur, most commonly in winter and spring. Both species also haul out on Adelaide city beaches from time to time, as have stray **Leopard Seals**. **Southern Right Whales** enter Gulf St Vincent most years on migration and are sometimes seen close to the city, usually attracting plenty of media attention. **Fin**, **Bryde's** and **Humpback Whales** are also seen occasionally. Other species that have been recorded in the gulf – with occasional strandings – include **Long-flippered Pilot Whales**, **Killer Whales**, **Pygmy Right Whales** and **Pygmy Sperm Whales**.

Microbats are well-researched in the Adelaide region; by heading into the field with a survey team there's a good chance of spending quality time with **White-striped** and **Southern** and **Western Freetail Bats**, **Gould's** and **Chocolate Wattled Bats**, and **Common Bentwing**, **Large** and **Little Forest** and **Lesser Long-eared Bats**.

6.02 BROOKFIELD CONSERVATION PARK

Highlights: **Southern Hairy-nosed Wombat, Red Kangaroo, Western Grey Kangaroo**

Other possibilities: **Echidna, Common Dunnart, Fat-tailed Dunnart, Western Pygmy Possum, Common Brushtail Possum**

This former sheep station was purchased by the Chicago Zoological Society to protect the **Southern Hairy-nosed Wombat** back when conservation was an alien concept to Australian governments. The wombats tend to favour areas of Sugar Gum and several active burrow complexes are easily seen along access roads. However, the park is closed between sunset and 7 am, and since the removal of livestock much of the original chenopod vegetation has regenerated and wombat viewing is not as easy as formerly. The best strategy is to wait quietly near an active burrow complex (look for fresh scrapes, footprints and droppings near burrow entrances) in the late afternoon and hope one emerges to sun itself or graze. Otherwise, by arriving at dawn you may also see wombats sunning, especially after a cold winter night.

Follow the main entrance road (OK for 2WDs in dry weather) to a large shed and then turn east till you get to the picnic ground (about 3 km along). From here the Three Habitats Walk passes close to some active wombat burrows. There are also active burrows about halfway along the Bluebush Track heading back to the entrance. Both **Western Grey** and **Red Kangaroos** are common in the park – watch for them as you drive along tracks. The **Western Pygmy Possum**, **Common Brushtail Possum**, **Common Dunnart** and **Fat-tailed Dunnart** have also been recorded, although the **Echidna** is the only species you are likely to see during a daytime visit.

Brookfield CP is 130 km north-east of Adelaide on the Sturt Hwy. The main park entrance is well-signposted 11 km west of Blanchetown (where accommodation is available at the roadhouse) on the north side of the highway. The park is managed by Conservation Volunteers (www.conservationvolunteers.com.au), who run weekend surveys for the wombats and other species.

6.03 MOORUNDE WILDLIFE RESERVE

Highlights: **Southern Hairy-nosed Wombat**

If you luck out at Brookfield CP, there are other wombat-watching options south of the Sturt Hwy. Moorunde WR occupies the land opposite Brookfield and has been fenced, destocked and revegetated to encourage proliferation of **Southern Hairy-nosed Wombats**; there is estimated to be 2000 of them here. To see wombats you will probably have to arrange a visit through the Natural History Society of South Australia, which manages the site, as there are currently no visitors' facilities on the reserve. See nhssa.com.au for contact and access details.

If all else fails, head south from Blanchetown to look for the wombats along the west bank of the River Murray to Swan Reach, 26 km away. There are burrow networks either side of the road on the last few kilometres before Swan Reach and on the continuation of this road south of the Sedan road. There is a campground by the river – by staying overnight you would be able to spend some time late evening and early morning spotlighting, but take heed of the signs that mark private property (the wombats are not always popular with farmers).

6.04 YOOKAMURRA AWC SANCTUARY

Highlights: **Echidna, Southern Hairy-nosed Wombat**

Other possibilities: **Numbat, Greater Bilby, Brush-tailed Bettong, Burrowing Bettong, Greater Stick-nest Rat**

This Australian Wildlife Conservancy (AWC) property virtually adjoins Moorunde to the south. There are of course **Southern Hairy-nosed Wombats** here, as well as **Echidnas** and reintroduced populations of **Numbats**, **Greater Bilbies**, **Brush-tailed**

THE BIG FIVE

Platypuses survive in SA only on Kangaroo I., where they were introduced, but that other outstanding monotreme, the Echidna, makes a good substitute.

Kangaroo Not surprisingly, Kangaroo I. (6.13) supports abundant Kangaroo Island Kangaroos; Western Greys and Reds can be seen in the Flinders Ranges NP (6.10).

Koala Most of SA's Koalas are descended from introduced animals, though they are wild and self-sustaining; they are common in Flinders Chase on Kangaroo I. (6.13).

Wombat SA is the stronghold of Southern Hairy-nosed Wombats, which may be seen in the Riverlands at Brookfield CP (6.02).

Echidna Kangaroo Island (6.13) is one of the most reliable places to see Echidnas and they could be encountered almost anywhere on the island.

Whale Southern Right Whales migrate along the coast between May and October, with many females calving at Head of the Bight (6.19); whale-watching cruises operate from Victor Harbor (6.08), among other sites.

and **Burrowing Bettongs**, and **Greater Stick-nest Rats**, although at the time of publication it was unclear what their status was, nor whether general wildlife-watching was possible. Volunteer and educational programs are run by AWC (www. australianwildlife.org) at Yookamurra.

6.05 GLUEPOT RESERVE

Highlights: **Echidna, Common Ringtail Possum, Common Brushtail Possum, Western Grey Kangaroo, Red Kangaroo**

Other possibilities: **Mallee Ningaui, Common Dunnart, Western Pygmy Possum, Koala, Bolam's Mouse**

Gluepot (www.gluepot.org), managed by BirdLife Australia, supports impressive stands of old-growth mallee woodland with spinifex hummocks, where **Echidnas, Western Grey Kangaroos** and the two larger possum species are common. This is good habitat for small arid-zone mammals, including **Western Pygmy Possum, Common Dunnart, Mallee Ningaui** and **Bolam's Mouse**; 11 species of microbat are known from this area. It would be worth seeking out a research team to get closer to some of these smaller mallee specialties.

Gluepot is about 50 km (up to 1.5 hours' drive) on an unsealed road north of Waikerie, which is 175 km north-east of Adelaide. Note that it is so-named for a reason: the black soil in these parts turns to impassable mud after rains – check with the rangers (08) 8892 9600 for an update. Camping is the only accommodation option.

There is a good chance of seeing **Koalas** in Renmark, the main service centre for this part of the state, or nearby Paringa. Koalas were introduced to this area and have become well established – the Renmark Paringa Visitor Information Centre (www.murrayriver.com.au/renmark-paringa-visitor-information-centre-1120) may know where they have been sighted lately.

6.06 NARACOORTE CAVES NATIONAL PARK

Highlights: **Common Bentwing Bat (ssp. *bassanii*), Sugar Glider**

Other possibilities: **Echidna, Common Brushtail Possum, Western Grey Kangaroo**

The famous cave system here is a World Heritage site (because of its amazing fossil deposits) and home to one of only two maternity colonies of the southern subspecies of **Common Bentwing Bat** *Miniopterus schreibersii bassanii* (which some scientists now regard as a separate species *M. bassanii*). South-eastern SA marks the western limit of its distribution. The maternity roost is in Bat Cave and can be watched on CCTV at the Bat Observation Centre. In summer they emerge en masse at dusk. Small numbers of the bats also occur in other caves in winter, including Blanche, Wet, Cathedral and Robertson caves. There are daily tours of Blanche Cave – the guide may be able to point out bats to you if you visit outside of maternity

WATCHING BATS IN SOUTH AUSTRALIA

The standout bat attraction in SA is Naracoorte Caves NP (6.06), where thousands of **Common Bentwing Bats** (of the southern subspecies *M. s. bassanii*) can be observed during summer. Facilities here include CCTV so visitors can watch goings-on in the maternity cave without disturbing the bats, and the nightly fly-out at dusk between October and April; roosting bats and some other species may be seen during cave tours year-round. **Grey-headed Flying Foxes** have recently colonised Adelaide's botanic gardens, where some 1200 appear to be resident; they also occur irregularly in the south-east and along the Murray. **Little Red Flying Foxes** reach SA most years, with scattered records mostly from the north-east of the state, and old records from Kangaroo I. **Black Flying Fox** has occurred in Adelaide but must be regarded as a rarity.

SA's microbat list numbers 17 species (including as yet undescribed freetail species), with two broad areas of occurrence: the semi-arid and arid northern part of the state, and the wetter south-east. The widespread **Yellow-bellied Sheath-tailed** and **White-striped Freetail Bats** could be identified by spotlight or, in the case of the latter, call, nearly anywhere, especially in the warmer months. Others with widespread distributions include **Gould's** and **Chocolate Wattled Bats**, and the **Lesser Long-eared Bat**. Microbats with a typically more inland distribution are the **Hill's Sheath-tailed Bat**, **Bristle-faced** and **Inland Freetail Bats**, **Central Long-eared Bat**, **Inland** and **Little Broad-nosed Bats**, **Inland Forest Bat** and **Inland Cave Bat**. Encountering these will be a matter of chance or by taking part in a trapping survey. However, over much of the arid zone roosting sites such as trees may be at a premium and it would be worth checking artificial structures, such as derelict sheds and ruined houses, as well as rocky outcrops.

The richest microbat diversity is in the south-east where, in addition to more widespread species, several eastern species also reach SA. These include the **Southern** and **Eastern Freetail Bats**, **Little Pied Bat**, **Eastern False Pipistrelle** (in the extreme south-east only), **Corben's Long-eared Bat**, **Large**, **Southern** and **Little Forest Bats** and **Gould's Long-eared Bat** (again, only in the extreme south-east). The **Large-footed Myotis** is specialised for fishing and formerly occurred along the Murray River corridor, but has not been recorded for some years and may be extinct in SA.

It would be worth joining a field research project to see some of these species in the hand or to visit remote areas – check with the Australasian Bat Society (www. ausbats.org.au) or universities to see what's going on. And if you find a dead or injured bat, SA's Fauna Rescue has a 24-hour helpline (08) 8289 0896.

season – and tours to watch the fly-out at dusk until about April. **Echidnas**, **Western Grey Kangaroos** and **Common Brushtail Possums** are common here; **Sugar Gliders** are seen regularly by spotlighting around the campground and the **Yellow-footed Antechinus** has also been recorded. **Grey-headed Flying Foxes** occasionally make it over the border to the south-east as far as Naracoorte and Kingston. Naracoorte is 84 km south of Bordertown, which is on the Dukes Hwy, or 102 km north of Mt Gambier if you're following the coastline. The caves are 10 km south of Naracoorte. The park has a campground, barbecues and toilets; supplies and other accommodation are available in town.

6.07 PORT MACDONNELL

Highlights: **Blue Whale, Southern Right Whale**

Other possibilities: **Fin Whale, Sei Whale, Humpback Whale**

The Bonney Upwelling is a cool water mass that flows east from the Bight to south-eastern SA and western Victoria, bringing with it masses of krill that attract **Blue Whales**, and sometimes **Sei** and **Fin Whales**. The main event is offshore from Portland, Victoria (4.18) in late summer and early autumn, but pelagic birdwatching trips run from Port Macdonnell would be worth joining for a chance of seeing these

SOUTH AUSTRALIA'S SEALS AND SEA LIONS

South Australia has Australia's highest concentration of breeding pinnipeds. Most abundant is the **Australian Sea Lion**, which numbers about 12 500 here (85 per cent of the world population). All of its major breeding sites are in SA, including Dangerous Reef and Lewis, West Waldegrave and Olive Is. off Eyre Peninsula, North and South Page Is. in Backstairs Passage, Seal Bay (6.13) and Purdie I. in Nuyts Archipelago. **New Zealand Fur Seal** colonies at North and South Neptune Is., Kangaroo I. and Liguanea I. account for 80 per cent of breeding in Australia. Smaller numbers of **Australian Fur Seals** also occur (for example, at the Neptune Is.) and have bred at Casuarina Islets near Kangaroo I. South Australia is also one of the best places for vagrant pinnipeds: **Antarctic** (Kangaroo I.) and **Subantarctic Fur Seals** (Kangaroo I., Encounter Bay, Eyre Peninsula), and the full suite of Antarctic 'true' seals have occurred: most commonly **Leopard** (chiefly Kangaroo I. and Encounter Bay), but also **Southern Elephant** (Kangaroo I., Encounter Bay and Fleurieu Peninsula) and, more rarely, **Weddell**, **Crabeater** and **Ross's Seals**.

and other cetaceans. The boat trips run roughly every month, weather permitting (see Chapter 10 for details). **Southern Right Whales** cruise past Port Macdonnell on their annual migration (May–October). Port Macdonnell is about 35 km south of Mt Gambier and 464 km south-east of Adelaide.

6.08 VICTOR HARBOR AND ENCOUNTER BAY

Highlights: **Southern Right Whale**

Other possibilities: **Australian Sea Lion, New Zealand Fur Seal**

The former whaling centre of Victor Harbor at the head of Encounter Bay makes a good base for shore- or boat-based whale-watching during the **Southern Right Whale** migration. Encounter Bay was the site of a historic meeting between Matthew Flinders and Nicolas Baudin in 1802, during their respective voyages of exploration of the Australian coastline. Today it is a great site for **Southern Right Whales**, which sometimes calve here, as well as occasional **Humpback Whales**, and **Oceanic Common** and **Bottlenose Dolphins**. A few kilometres south of town, The Bluff is a 150-m-high headland from which land-based whale-watching can be done; **Southern Right Whales** sometimes approach closely to Rosetta Wharf at the foot of the cliffs here. About 20 km south-west of Victor Harbor, Newland Head is another good observation point and, in-between here and The Bluff, Waitpinga Cliffs. Another good site is Basham's Beach, 10 km north-east of town, where up to 18 whales were visible at once in 2009 and numbers have peaked at 40; the dunes and hills behind the beach make good vantage points. The general store at the small town of Middleton, at the head of the bay, has a whale information centre. **Southern Right Whales** were the main target of whalers in the 19th century, but **Sperm Whales** were also pursued and probably still occur in these waters (though most likely further offshore). **Pygmy Sperm Whales** and **Pygmy Right Whales** have also been seen in Encounter Bay.

A couple of kilometres south of Victor Harbor, Seal Rock has resident **Australian Sea Lions** and **New Zealand Fur Seals**. Encounter Bay has also had its share of vagrant seal sightings, including **Leopard** (at the foot of Waitpinga Cliffs), **Weddell** and **Southern Elephant Seals**.

Victor Harbor is also home to the South Australian Whale Centre (www.sawhalecentre. com), an interpretation centre with a museum and good information on watching marine mammals locally. It also has an information line so you can phone ahead to get updates on latest sightings. The Big Duck (www.thebigduck.com.au) runs a variety of tours to see marine wildlife, including whale-watching (June–September), and dolphin-watching and visits to Seal I. year-round. Victor Harbor is 83 km south of Adelaide, and has plenty of eating and accommodation choices.

B FLINDERS RANGES AND THE ARID ZONE

While SA's arid zone is an area of outstanding interest and beauty, it has suffered more than most of the country in terms of mammal extinctions. Bilbies, bandicoots, rat-kangaroos, various rodents and small wallabies have disappeared over most of the state for reasons that are not entirely clear. Curiously, numerous other species have persisted but, apart from the three large kangaroo species, most of the extant native mammal fauna in SA's north now consists of small dasyurids and rodents. Apart from great scenery and hiking attractions, the main reason to visit the Flinders Ranges is for the **Yellow-footed Rock Wallaby**, arguably the most attractive of all the macropods. The sites given below for this species are all in or near the Flinders Ranges, but note that a significant population also lives in the Vulkathunha-Gammon Ranges NP to the north-east.

6.09 TELOWIE GORGE CONSERVATION PARK

Highlights: **Yellow-footed Rock Wallaby, Euro**

This is probably the nearest site to Adelaide at which to see **Yellow-footed Rock Wallabies**, although it is usually easier to find in the Flinders Ranges (6.10). There's an easy walking track for about 1 km along the gorge; the rock wallabies are most often seen basking when the late afternoon sun hits the cliffs at the end of the trail; **Euros** also occur here. The gorge is 8 km east of the Princes Hwy (A1) and signposted a few kilometres south of Port Germein, which is 247 km north of Adelaide. It's not the most reliable site for the rock wallabies but it's only a short detour from the main north–south road.

6.10 FLINDERS RANGES

Highlights: **Yellow-footed Rock Wallaby**

Other possibilities: **Western Quoll, Common Brushtail Possum, Euro, Western Grey Kangaroo, Red Kangaroo**

One of SA's most popular tourist attractions, especially among campers and bushwalkers, the Flinders Ranges are one of the easiest places to see the fabulous **Yellow-footed Rock Wallaby**. Most of this spectacular area is protected in a national park, but there are sites outside the park boundaries that are also good for the rock wallaby. Three of the state's large macropods – the **Euro**, **Western Grey Kangaroo** and **Red Kangaroo** – can be seen readily early in the early morning or late afternoon in many places; there is a high danger of collision with any of these species if you are travelling after dark. **Red Kangaroos** are most common in the north; **Western Greys** occur mainly on outer slopes of the ranges; and the **Euro** is an animal of rocky outcrops, grazing on lower ground at night. The rock wallabies are most common in the north of the park and the only other native mammal likely to be encountered is the **Echidna**, which is uncommon and possibly mainly nocturnal in hot weather. Four species of dasyurid are known to survive in the region: **Narrow-nosed Planigales**, **Fat-tailed Dunnarts** and **Stripe-faced Dunnarts** are all widespread; the **Kultarr** may persist and **Common Dunnarts** also occur, mainly in the south-eastern Flinders Ranges. **Western Quolls** and **Common Brushtail Possums** have been reintroduced to some areas and could be spotlighted along treed watercourses. Ancient nests of both **Greater** and **Lesser Stick-nest Rats** can still be seen at some sites, such as Chambers Gorge, though the rats themselves are long gone. For decades the Flinders Ranges suffered from infestations of feral Goats and Foxes; it is hoped that the SA government's recovery work in the region will be maintained, as it is a magnificent scenic area made poorer by a paucity of wildlife.

The towns of Quorn and Hawker in the southern Flinders Ranges are the best places to fill up with petrol and last-minute supplies. There are accommodations here and at other sites in the region, but to get the most out of your trip take advantage of the park's many good campgrounds (bookings are essential in holiday season, especially in winter). Remember this is a desert – take adequate precautions against sunburn and dehydration in hot weather.

6.10a Warren Gorge

Warren Gorge is a reliable site for **Yellow-footed Rock Wallabies**. At the southern end of the Flinders Ranges, this small gorge is easily accessible from Quorn: just after the highway bends right into the township turn left on Arden Vale Rd; the gorge (signposted) is 21 km from here on a dirt road that is OK for 2WD vehicles in dry conditions (watch for sudden dips at creek crossings).The road passes through a rocky defile as it enters the main camping area – **Yellow-footed Rock Wallabies** can be seen here, often at close quarters. The Wallabies are usually easy to see on boulder faces around the large campground. Be warned: when standing still they blend perfectly into their surrounds and are almost invisible until they move!

6.10b Brachina Gorge

About 65 km north of Hawker there's a well-signposted turn-off to Brachina Gorge, widely regarded as *the* place for **Yellow-footed Rock Wallabies**. Head east off the highway (B53) to the start of Brachina Gorge Geological Trail, about 9 km away (the trail itself should probably be attempted only in a 4WD vehicle). The best site for the rock wallabies is an obvious jumble of boulder scree on the northern side of the track past the intersection of the Bunyeroo Gorge road. The wallabies are nearly always present and this is a well-known site for photos – note that part of the area has been fenced off to encourage revegetation. The best viewing time is late afternoon, when sunlight streams in from the west. The rock wallabies also occur at Aroona Valley campground – a good population lives in the hills nearby.

6.10c Stokes Hill

Stokes Hill offers panoramic views of the southern Flinders Ranges as well as abundant **Euros**, which graze around the car park and on the spinifex-covered slopes, offering nice photo opportunities.

6.11 ARID RECOVERY

Highlights: **Giles' Planigale, Stripe-faced Dunnart, Fat-tailed Dunnart, Greater Bilby, Western Barred Bandicoot, Burrowing Bettong, Greater Stick-nest Rat, Plains Mouse, Forrest's Mouse, Spinifex Hopping-mouse, Bolam's Mouse, Desert Mouse, Sandy Inland Mouse**

Other possibilities: **Echidna, Red Kangaroo, Dingo**

The largest predator-free exclosure in the arid zone, Arid Recovery is surrounded by a 1.8 m high fence that excludes Rabbits, Foxes and feral Cats. The reserve was created in the 1990s, when a core population of **Burrowing Bettongs**, **Bilbies**, **Western Barred Bandicoots** and **Greater Stick-nest Rats** were released. Since then AR's 'Big Four' have proliferated and now form self-sustaining populations. Most abundant is the **Burrowing Bettong** and there is an excellent chance of seeing them on most visits (they are common around the maintenance shed, underground viewing area and lookout). **Greater Bilbies** number about 500 and are frequently seen on night drives, especially in dune habitat, but sightings of the **Western Barred**

Bandicoot and **Greater Stick-nest Rat** can be hit or miss (some of the latter are generally resident around the maintenance shed, otherwise ask staff for good locations). **Echidnas** have also been recorded but are uncommon and generally nocturnal in the arid zone. There are usually a few **Red Kangaroos** about, both inside and outside the fence; they lick moisture or pooled rainwater from the rubber mats used as footing where fences cross sand dunes. The reserve supports an important population of the **Plains Mouse**, which is elsewhere rather scarce. The **Spinifex Hopping-mouse** is abundant and there are good numbers of **Bolam's Mouse**; other rodents include **Forrest's**, **Desert** and **Sandy Inland Mouse**; the **House Mouse** also occurs. Dasyurids include **Giles' Planigale** and **Stripe-faced** and **Fat-tailed Dunnarts**. The only realistic way to see most of these small species is to join one of Arid Recovery's small vertebrate–trapping weeks, held annually for paying 'volunteers'. Trapping is conducted on dunes and swales in alternating years, with different species compositions in each habitat. Outside the fence, there is a chance of seeing **Dingoes**, as well as **Rabbits**, feral **Cats** and **European Foxes**; there are very good reasons why all these animals are kept out of Arid Recovery. Golden Bandicoot, Common Brushtail Possum and Ampurta also once occurred in the area but so far there are no plans to reintroduce them. (A **Numbat** reintroduction failed for various reasons; a second attempt is planned based on further studies and lessons learnt from the first trial.) Volunteering at Arid Recovery offers a unique opportunity to take part in hands-on conservation work. Otherwise, visitors' nights are held regularly – see www.aridrecovery.org.au for details. Arid Recovery is 16 km north of Roxby Downs.

6.12 NORTHERN SOUTH AUSTRALIA

Highlights: **Dusky Hopping-mouse, Plains Mouse, Long-haired Rat**

Other possibilities: **Red Kangaroo, Euro, Yellow-footed Rock Wallaby (reintroduction), Dingo, [One-humped Camel]**

Northern SA is a remote, arid landscape of sand dunes, chenopod steppe and hard, stony deserts, a sea of wildflowers after goods rains but torrid and windswept in summer. Several desert tracks through this land have become popular on the 4WD circuit: the Strzelecki Track from Leigh Creek to Innamincka is probably the most accessible of them. From Innamincka you can push north to join the Birdsville Track in the Channel Country of south-western Queensland before heading south-west to follow it, more or less parallel with the Strzelecki, to Marree; from there you can take the Oodnadatta Track west to Marla, or turn off at William Creek and head west to Coober Pedy. A reliable 4WD is essential and all the precautions of remote desert travel apply here.

Red Kangaroos are common in open country, such as the gibber plains; they are replaced by **Euros** on rocky hillsides and outcrops. **Yellow-footed Rock Wallabies**

have been successfully reintroduced into the Aroona Dam FFS near Leigh Creek, at the southern end of the Strzelecki Track. **Echidnas** occur, especially in rocky areas, although they may be primarily nocturnal in hot weather, and **Common Brushtail Possums** frequent River Red Gums growing along the Cooper and Diamantina creeks. Otherwise, mammal-watching is rather limited, but time and patience could be rewarded with sightings of some small dry-country mammals, especially in seasons with higher than average rainfall. (Note that several of these species can be seen at Arid Recovery (6.11) during its annual small mammal–trapping week.)

Among the rodents, **Long-haired Rat** and **Plains Mouse** periodically irrupt and can become very common indeed after good rains at, for example, Witjira NP. At other times they virtually disappear from the landscape. Three species of hopping-mouse occur in the far north of SA: **Spinifex**, **Dusky** and **Fawn**. **Spinifex** and **Dusky** are inhabitants of sandhill country – check dunes in the early morning for signs of their presence and then try spotlighting for them after dark. The dunes around Montecollina Bore are a good area for the **Dusky Hopping-mouse**; the **Fawn Hopping-mouse** is an animal of gibber plains. The **Desert Mouse** is apparently rare though it has recently been recorded in the Marqualpie dunes in the north-eastern part of Innamincka Regional Reserve. **Water Rats** live in permanent pools in the Cooper and Diamantina Rivers. **Bolam's Mouse** occurs near Lake Frome and further west, and the **Sandy Inland Mouse** and **Forrest's Mouse** have also been recorded. Watch for Letter-winged Kites – these striking nocturnal birds of prey respond to rodent numbers and their presence can be a good indicator of small mammal abundance (though be aware that the introduced **House Mouse** also occurs out here).

Dasyurids in this vast region include **Ampurtras** and **Kowaris** (in the far north); those more or less restricted to the north-west and Great Victoria Desert include **Fat-tailed False Antechinus**, **Wongai Ningaui**, and **Hairy-footed** and **Ooldea Dunnarts** (the last chiefly around Oodnadatta); and in the north-east **Kultarr** (which has been spotlighted on Moon Plain near Coober Pedy), **Giles'**, **Long-tailed**, and **Narrow-nosed Planigales**, which inhabit cracking clay in creek beds; and **Fat-tailed**, **Lesser Hairy-footed** and **Stripe-faced Dunnarts**.

Twelve bat species have been recorded from SA's arid zone. Of these, the wide-ranging **Little Red Flying Fox** and **Yellow-bellied Sheath-tailed Bat** are visitors, the former during irruptions following fruiting or rainfall events, the latter as a regular migrant during the summer months. **White-striped Freetail Bats** are common and can be heard by the unaided human ear. The region is littered with abandoned buildings that would be worth searching for microbat roosts. About 100 km north along the Strzelecki Track you'll encounter the 'Dog Fence', designed to keep Dingoes out of SA's pastoral lands. **Dingoes** north of here are regarded as being some of the purest in Australia (Dingoes readily interbreed with domestic and feral Dogs, and pure strains are becoming rare). **Dingoes** will also be encountered on the Birdsville and Oodnadatta Tracks, which are largely north of the fence. At times introduced species appear to dominate the mammal fauna: the more interesting ones include **One-humped Camels** in sandy country around Innamincka and Moomba; and feral **Donkeys** near Oodnadatta.

This is all extremely remote but some of the most fascinating Outback travel you'll ever undertake. Travellers should take all necessary precautions and ascertain beforehand where fuel and other supplies are available (generally only at Leigh Creek, Innamincka, Maree, William Creek and Coober Pedy). From Coober Pedy the Stuart Hwy pushes north into the NT; Alice Springs, the next major settlement on this road, is 688 km away.

C THE SOUTH COAST AND FAR WEST

The long road across the Nullarbor and on into WA is an adventure in itself. A series of islands on the south coast and the gulfs – St Vincent and Spencer – would also be worthwhile to visit if you have the time and inclination, for it is here that several species otherwise extinct on the mainland can still be seen with a bit of effort. But for an excellent wildlife-watching experience look no further than predator-free Kangaroo I., Australia's third biggest island and a fabulous place to explore for many reasons – abundant wildlife being high on the list.

6.13 KANGAROO ISLAND

Highlights: **Echidna (ssp.** *multiaculeatus***), Southern Brown Bandicoot, Koala, Kangaroo Island Kangaroo (ssp.** *fuliginosus***), Tammar Wallaby (ssp.** *décres***), New Zealand Fur Seal, Australian Sea Lion**

KOALAS IN SOUTH AUSTRALIA

Australia's favourite marsupial has had a complicated history in SA. **Koalas** probably occurred naturally here only in the south-east corner, from where they were extirpated by 1924 by fur hunters. They were introduced to Kangaroo I. in the 1920s, but proliferated to the point where their browsing put severe pressure on food trees. Sterilisation and translocation programs have had to be conducted as population control measures. From Kangaroo I., **Koalas** were transported to the Riverland, the Port Lincoln area on Eyre Peninsula, the Mount Lofty Ranges and back to the south-east. They are now well established in all these areas, with the highest densities outside Kangaroo I. in the Mount Lofty Ranges (100 000 of them!). The only naturally occurring **Koalas** in SA today are individuals that have become established after crossing the border from south-western Victoria, where their numbers have been supplemented with sterilised animals transported from Kangaroo I.

Other possibilities: **Platypus, Kangaroo Island Dunnart, Common Brushtail Possum, Australian Fur Seal, Bottlenose Dolphin, Common Dolphin, Southern Right Whale**

Known locally as 'KI', Kangaroo I. was named by Matthew Flinders in 1802 after he spotted several large macropods here on his epic voyage of exploration. Fox- and Rabbit-free KI is one of SA's highlights and apart from several endemic subspecies of mammal it boasts several other species in abundance. A number of native mammals were introduced – like Maria I. in Tasmania (5.06), in the early 20th century KI was selected as an 'island ark' for the preservation of certain species it was feared were in danger of extinction.

Much of the island is covered in mallee and significant swathes are protected in national parks, most famously Flinders Chase NP, which protects the western end of the island. Elsewhere, clearing for agriculture has, if anything, benefited the island subspecies of **Western Grey Kangaroo** and **Tammar Wallaby**, which are abundant. Indeed, this is the easiest place in the country to see the **Tammar Wallaby**, as it is rare on most of the mainland. The island subspecies is endemic and common in many places, such as Flinders Chase NP headquarters and Kelly Hill CP, but also in open grassy areas around settlements. **Tammars** tend to shelter under bushes during the heat of the day. The island race of Western Grey Kangaroo, commonly known as the **Kangaroo Island Kangaroo**, is darker, longer-haired and more heavily built than the mainland form. It is common in any suitable habitat, though rather retiring during the day; animals in Flinders Chase NP are used to cars and people, however, and can be readily seen around picnic grounds and the visitors' centre. The **Echidna** is abundant and also regarded as a separate subspecies, distinguished by its long, thin spines and paler coloration than mainland forms. This is one of the best places in the country to see **Echidnas** and while driving around you could expect to see one almost anywhere, although they are often inactive during cooler weather. **Common Brushtail Possums** are abundant and can be seen by spotlighting around campgrounds, such as West Bay in Flinders Chase NP. The KI form is larger than its mainland equivalents and often forages on the ground. Smaller mammals include the **Bush Rat** (common, but be aware that **Black Rats** also occur here) and **Swamp Rat**, which occurs in suitable habitat at many sites, including the North West and North East Rivers and Larrikin Lagoon. The **Heath Mouse** has also recently been recorded on KI. There is a chance of running into the **Western Pygmy Possum** in flowering shrubs – it is widespread – but the **Little Pygmy Possum** is seen only rarely and seems restricted to the western end of the island. Once regarded as a species endemic to KI, the **Kangaroo Island Dunnart**, is a rare and little-known animal of mallee heath; there are no sites where it can readily be seen and even researchers have trouble tracking it down. KI is also the best place in the state to see **Southern Brown Bandicoots**, which occur at many sites in a variety of habitats, for example in Flinders Chase NP, and Pelican Lagoon and Cape Hart CPs. The race that occurs here is the same that occurs in mainland SA, where it is now rare.

Several native mammal species were introduced to KI in the first half of the 20th century when it was thought they were in danger of extinction on the mainland. Most prospered, which has been a mixed blessing. **Platypuses** were introduced in the permanent pools of the Rocky River near the Flinders Chase park headquarters, and can still be seen, especially at dawn or dusk, at the Rocky River Waterhole (this is the only wild **Platypus** population known to persist in SA). The waterhole can be reached by a short walking track north of the park headquarters; there are also some in the Breakneck and South West rivers. From their initial release site at Rocky River in the 1920s, **Koalas** have spread and proliferated, causing widespread damage to their food trees – a sterilisation program has been necessary to reduce their numbers. **Koalas** can easily be seen at Flinders Chase NP, near Cygnet River or indeed nearly anywhere their favourite food plants, such as Manna Gum and Brown Stringybark, grow. **Common Ringtail Possums** do not appear to have done so well, and are now apparently rare; they could be encountered in the western half of the island.

Pinnipeds are another major highlight of Kangaroo I. and thousands of tourists visit the island's seal colonies annually. Most famous are the **Australian Sea Lions** at Seal Bay CP, which contains about one-sixth of the world population of this Australian endemic. Numbers fluctuate seasonally, with a maximum of about 400, peaking when females and pups are present; subadults and bulls are present year round. Most pupping occurs in the rocky coves to the west; as the seals mature they tend to move east to the sandy beaches, where there are always adults and subadults loafing. Rangers run guided tours that allow good close-up views. Sea lions are also periodically seen at Cape Gantheaume and Cape Bouger. There are large breeding colonies of **New Zealand Fur Seals** at Admiral's Arch near Cape du Couedic in Flinders Chase NP, on the Casuarina Islets offshore (binoculars would be useful here) and at Cape Gantheaume. Numbers are at their peak in February and March after pups are born, when up to 500 have been counted, declining to their lowest level in August and September, although immatures and adults are present year-round. Nautilus Rock is another of the island's five **New Zealand Fur Seal** breeding sites. A few **Australian Fur Seals** are sometimes seen at both sites, allowing direct comparisons (New Zealand Fur Seals are generally smaller and have a slightly longer snout). Recently sea lions have started to breed on the North Casuarina islets. Other pinnipeds that have been recorded as vagrants on KI include **Antarctic** and **Subantarctic Fur Seals**, **Leopard Seals** (at Stokes, Emu, D'Estree, Nepean and Vivonne bays), **Southern Elephant Seals** (a male hauled out among New Zealand Fur Seals at Cape Gantheaume in 2001, and one was seen regularly until 2010 at the Seal Slide, 10 km north-east of Cape Gantheaume, among Australian Sea Lions) and **Weddell Seals**. Fur seals and sea lions can be difficult to identify, but KI offers a great opportunity to compare at least two species in close proximity. A useful guide is that fur seals prefer rocky sites with caves and ledges, close to the sea, whereas sea lions are often found on sandy beaches or dunes far from the water's edge.

Southern Right Whales may approach close inshore in winter and spring (May–October); sightings typically occur off Cape du Couedic, Penneshaw, Vivonne Bay, Remarkable Rocks and Cape Borda, among others, but individuals rarely linger for more than a few days. There have also been several sightings of **Killer Whales**, especially near seal colonies, and **Blue Whales**, which are sometimes seen off Cape du Couedic. Of the 18 cetacean species recorded from KI, many are known only from strandings, including **Gray's Beaked Whale** and **Strap-toothed Whale**, which may feed in the Murray Canyons south-east of the island. There have also been strandings of **Sperm Whales** and **Long-flippered Pilot Whales**, especially on the southern coastline, while **Pygmy Right Whales** have stranded mainly on the north coast; **Bryde's Whale** has been recorded live off Island Beach.

Dolphins are chiefly represented by **Inshore** and **Offshore Bottlenose Dolphins**; good areas to look for them include D'Estree Bay, Nepean Bay, Hog Bay, Dashwood Bay and Emu Bay. **Common Dolphins** sometimes occur in large pods off the west coast. The seal-viewing boardwalks at Seal Bay and Cape du Couedic also make good vantage points from which to scan for cetaceans. Kangaroo Island Dolphin Watch (www.kangarooislanddolphinwatch.com.au) should be able to tell you about recent sightings.

There are no regular bat-watching haunts on KI. Apart from old records of the **Little Red Flying Fox** and **White-striped Freetail Bat**, bat fauna is comprised of five species: the **Gould's** and **Chocolate Wattled Bats**, **Large Forest Bat**, **Southern Forest Bat** and **Lesser Long-eared Bat**.

Kangaroo Island is easily accessible by a 45-minute vehicle ferry (www.sealink.com.au) from Cape Jervis, 106 km south of Adelaide. The island's main town, Kingscote, has accommodation and shops, and there are good camping spots and other accommodation on many parts of the island. Flinders Chase NP is about 95 km (about 90 minutes' drive) from Kingscote. Note that visitors require a daily visitor's pass (available from www.environment.sa.gov.au). Allow at least 3 days to explore this amazing island, preferably longer, to get the most out of its wildlife and outstanding photo opportunities. Kangaroo Island Marine Adventures (www.kimarineadventures.com.au) offers dolphin tours.

6.14 GAWLER RANGES

Highlights: **Southern Hairy-nosed Wombat, Yellow-footed Rock Wallaby**

Other possibilities: **Western Grey Kangaroo, Red Kangaroo, Euro**

The Gawler Ranges hove into view as you head west from Iron Knob, breaking up the rather flat landscape north of the Eyre Hwy. The area has an impressive list of small, arid-zone rodents and dasyurids that would be seen only during trapping surveys, including the **Sandy Inland Mouse** and **Bolam's Mouse**; **Fat-tailed,**

Stripe-faced and **Little Long-tailed Dunnarts**; **Mitchell's Hopping-mouse** and **Mallee Ningaui**. You are much more likely to see the three large macropods – **Western Grey** and **Red Kangaroos**, and **Euros** – and the area is another stronghold for the **Southern Hairy-nosed Wombat**. **Western Greys** are common around campgrounds in Gawler Ranges NP; **Euros** are easily seen on rocky hillsides, especially at dusk; and **Red Kangaroos** also emerge at dusk on flatter ground and plains. **Red Kangaroos** are more common in the north of the Eyre Peninsula (see next section), south to about Fowler's Bay and Whyalla, and Cowell in the east. The highest density of wombats occurs on the southern shores of Lake Acraman, north of the park, but they also occur in lesser numbers up to 25 km south and south-west of the lake; watch for them on the roads between Minnipa and Yardea. Hiltaba NR borders the national park to the north-west and is actively managed to protect the westernmost outpost of the **Yellow-footed Rock Wallaby**, although this spectacular macropod is endangered here. Individuals are also sometimes seen in the Scrubby Peak area near Gawler Ranges NP's southern entrance.

6.15 EYRE PENINSULA

Highlights: **Black-footed Rock Wallaby (ssp. *pearsoni*), Greater Stick-nest Rat, Bush Rat (ssp. *greyi*)**

Other possibilities: **Echidna, Sandhill Dunnart, Southern Hairy-nosed Wombat, Koala, Western Grey Kangaroo, Euro**

South of the Gawler Ranges, the semi-arid Eyre Peninsula is a huge wedge that juts into the Southern Ocean. It was once covered mainly in mallee woodland, but much is now degraded agricultural land. Dakalanta AWC Sanctuary (www.australianwildlife.org) is a good place to volunteer your time and get to know the local fauna better. The sanctuary list includes **Echidnas, Common Brushtail Possums, Southern Hairy-nosed Wombats, Western Grey Kangaroos** and **Euros**. The reserve also supports a good population of **Western Pygmy Possums**; plus **Fat-tailed, Grey-bellied** and **Little Long-tailed Dunnarts, Mitchell's Hopping-mouse, Bolam's Mouse** and **Bush Rats** also occur.

Echidnas, Western Grey Kangaroos, Euros and **Southern Hairy-nosed Wombats** are still common in other parts of the peninsula, and there is a well-established population of introduced **Koalas** near Sleaford. **Common Brushtail Possums** can be seen in forest remnants around Port Lincoln and Iron Knob. Other dasyurids recorded on the peninsula include the **Stripe-faced Dunnart** (on saltbush plains near Whyalla) and **Kultarr** (open plains around Kyancutta). A population of the rare and little-known **Sandhill Dunnart** was recently discovered near Cowell and the **Mallee Ningaui** occurs at Lake Gilles CP. There are small, isolated populations of **Bush Rats** in Hincks CP and Lincoln NP, and also on Pearson, Reevesby and Eyre Is. **Tammar Wallabies** were reintroduced to Innes NP on the peninsula's southern tip between 2004 and 2008, and appear to have become established (there have been other successful introductions to Greenly and Wardang Is.).

The Eyre Peninsula coastline is surrounded by numerous islands, where some relict populations persist and reintroduction efforts have had varying degrees of success. For example, a naturally occurring wild population of **Black-footed Rock Wallabies** survives on Pearson I. in the Investigator Group, south of the peninsula. Much of this southern coastline is remote and accessible only by boat, but one place where **Black-footed Rock Wallabies** can be seen is Thistle I., accessible by boat or light plane from Port Lincoln and by plane from Adelaide; the island also has introduced populations of **Bilbies** and **Common Brushtail Possums**, plus two **New Zealand Fur Seal** colonies and one of **Australian Sea Lions**. After its extirpation on the mainland, a colony of **Greater Stick-nest Rats** survived on uninhabited Brothers I. in Coffin Bay; this species has been reintroduced successfully to Reevesby and St Peter Is.

6.16 POINT LABBATT

Highlights: **Australian Sea Lion**

Other possibilities: **Offshore Common Dolphin, Inshore Bottlenose Dolphin**

The so-called Chain of Bays stretches some 60 km from Anxious Bay to Streaky Bay in the western crook of the Eyre Peninsula. **Australian Sea Lions** breed at numerous sites along this coastline, and Point Labbatt features the only permanent mainland breeding colony. They can be viewed from a clifftop boardwalk here, although they are about 50 m away and binoculars would be handy. **Offshore Common** and **Inshore Bottlenose Dolphins** are seen in the various bays (and further east off Eyre Peninsula). Streaky Bay, the nearest town, is 50 km from the colony at Cape Labbatt. Streaky Bay itself is 62 km south of the Eyre Hwy by the most direct route (turn off at Poochera, 33 km west of Minnipa). There is camping and other accommodation at Streaky Bay.

6.17 NUYTS ARCHIPELAGO CONSERVATION PARK

Highlights: **Southern Brown Bandicoot (ssp. *nauticus*), Black-footed Rock Wallaby, Greater Stick-nest Rat**

St Francis is the largest island in the Nuyts Group, about 15 km south of Ceduna, and once supported **Brush-tailed Bettongs** and possibly **Tammar Wallabies**. Neither is extant today and a vigorous reintroduction experiment in the 1980s doesn't seem to have worked. **Southern Brown Bandicoots** and **Greater Stick-nest Rats** are the only surviving native land mammals. Both also live on Franklin I., where an estimated 700 of the rats are outnumbered 10:1 by the bandicoots. Access is possible only as part of a research team.

6.18 FOWLER'S BAY

Highlights: **Southern Right Whale, Southern Hairy-nosed Wombat**

Chances are that if you're heading across the Nullarbor you'll visit Head of the Bight (6.19), but a short detour south of the Eyre Hwy will bring you to Fowler's Bay, which also features **Southern Right Whales** inshore between May and October. Fowler's Bay Eco Park (www.fowlerseco.com) makes a good base and runs daily whale-watching boats from Fowler's Bay jetty during whale season (June–October). Whale numbers vary, but up to 18 have been present at a time. Intriguingly, Fowler's Bay was once recorded as the southern limit of distribution of the **Southern Marsupial Mole**.

WATCHING WHALES AND DOLPHINS IN SOUTH AUSTRALIA

With more than 30 species recorded, SA has a rich cetacean diversity and offers stellar **Southern Right Whale** viewing opportunities – from land, sea and air – during the whales' annual winter migration from Antarctica to southern Australian waters. **Southern Right Whales** start to arrive in May, skirting the coastline as they move westwards to the Great Australian Bight and beyond. Numbers peak in July–September, when females congregate at Head of the Bight (6.19) to calve, and by October most have headed southward again. During this entire time they could be seen from virtually any headland or clifftop along the SA coast. Other good sites include Encounter Bay (6.08), Kangaroo I. (6.13) and Fowler's Bay (6.18).

The other major cetacean event is the Bonney Upwelling, a seasonal mass of cool water that moves eastwards from the Bight to south-eastern SA and adjacent Victoria in late summer to early autumn. Krill blooms associated with the upwelling attract **Blue Whales**, which are seen regularly off the south-east corner; seabirders use Port Macdonnell (6.07) as a base for regular pelagic outings, during which cetaceans are often seen. **Humpback Whales** are also seen along the coast in winter in small numbers.

Smaller cetaceans are also well represented in SA: **Bottlenose Dolphins** and **Common Dolphins** are commonly sighted inshore – again, Encounter Bay and Kangaroo I. are good places to start looking. Rarer sightings include the **Dusky Dolphin**, which has occurred off Kangaroo I. Port Adelaide has a land-based dolphin-watching trail and **Bottlenose Dolphins** are readily seen in the port area. Other species regularly recorded alive in SA waters include **Killer** and **False Killer Whales** (a mass stranding of this species once occurred at Port Prime), **Sperm Whales**, **Long-flippered Pilot Whales**, and baleen whales such as **Fin**, **Sei**, **Minke** and **Pygmy Right Whales**. South Australia also has an extraordinary record of cetacean strandings, indicating the high diversity of whales and dolphins offshore. Among the baleen whales there have been records of **Dwarf** (Eyre Peninsula) and

Antarctic Minke Whales (Eyre Peninsula, Kangaroo I. and Encounter Bay), **Sei**, **Fin**, **Bryde's** and **Blue Whales**, and the little known **Omura's Whale** (on Fleurieu Peninsula); **Pygmy Right Whales** have stranded on Kangaroo I., Eyre Peninsula and in the south-east. By far the most frequently stranded cetacean in the state is the **Short-beaked Common Dolphin**, followed by the **Indo-Pacific Bottlenose Dolphin**; other dolphin records include **Risso's**, **Southern Rightwhale** and **Common Bottlenose Dolphins**. Blackfish have been represented by strandings of **Pygmy Killer Whale**, both **Short-flippered** and **Long- flippered Pilot Whales** (mainly in the south-east), and **False Killer** and **Killer Whales** (the latter is also sometimes sighted in the Bight). There has been one sight record of the **Dusky Dolphin** in Backstairs Passage and a specimen of the **Spectacled Porpoise** in Encounter Bay. **Sperm Whales** were hunted from Victor Harbor and live ones continue to be seen, though usually well offshore in the Bight and south of Kangaroo I.; strandings also occur, mainly in the south-east. Both **Pygmy** and **Dwarf Sperm Whales** occur in SA waters, though the latter is known only from a single specimen; **Pygmy Sperm Whales** are known from numerous strandings and at least one sight record in the south-east. Eight beaked whale species have been recorded, with live sightings of the **Southern Bottlenose Whale** (Eyre Peninsula), and **Arnoux's** (Kangaroo I.), **Hector's** and **Strap-toothed** (both in Streaky Bay), **Shepherd's** (in the extreme south-east) and **Cuvier's** (offshore in the Great Australian Bight) **Beaked Whales**. All have been recorded as strandings, most commonly the **Strap-toothed Whale**, followed by **Gray's Beaked Whale**.

6.19 HEAD OF THE BIGHT

Highlights: **Southern Right Whale**

Other possibilities: **Southern Hairy-nosed Wombat, Dingo, Australian Sea Lion**

Between mid-May and late October each year the northernmost point of the Great Australian Bight hosts Australia's largest **Southern Right Whale** nursery. Despite the vast distance that must be travelled to get there, this site is a must for stellar views of females with calves (weather permitting). Most whales start to arrive in early June, when females begin to calve, and there is a good chance of watching mothers with calves from the viewing platform, perched 90 m above the water on the sheer Bunda (or Nullarbor) Cliffs, which form a spectacular backdrop to the action. **Humpback Whales** also pass by occasionally. It is estimated that one-third of **Southern Right Whales** seen in Australian waters are born in the Great Australian Bight, and sightings are guaranteed between June and September. In recent years numbers at Head of the Bight have hovered around the hundred mark at the peak of the season (August and September), with nearly 150 being seen in 2011. Calving is concentrated on a 15 km stretch of coastline and whale-spotting flights, run out of

Nullarbor Roadhouse (6.20), would be a great way to enjoy the sight and spectacular cliffs. Note that tourism promotions generally show sparkling clear water and sunny skies; this is not always the case and although you'll need a hat and sun block most days you should also be prepared for cold, blustery conditions.

The last **Southern Right Whales** have gone by November, but **Australian Sea Lions** haul out at the base of the cliffs year-round, and the sea would be worth scanning at any time for pods of dolphins. **Southern Hairy-nosed Wombats** and **Dingoes** are common along this stretch of the Nullarbor Plain towards the WA border (Head of the Bight is west of the Dog Fence).

Head of the Bight is 12 km south of the Eyre Hwy on a sealed road; the turn-off is about 300 km west of Ceduna (allow 3.5 to 4 hours' driving) and about 15 km east of Nullarbor Roadhouse; it is well signposted. The land is owned by the Yalata people and permits must be purchased on an honour system (cash only) at the White Well Ranger Station on Head of the Bight Rd, 2 km south of the turn-off on the left-hand side (a permit is essential at any time of year, even when the whales aren't present). The only facilities here are toilets and shaded picnic areas. The nearest accommodation is at Nullarbor Roadhouse or Fowler's Bay (6.18), although bush camping is possible in the Nullarbor NP – ask at the national parks office in Ceduna about permits.

6.20 NULLARBOR ROADHOUSE

Highlights: **Southern Hairy-nosed Wombat**

Other possibilities: **Red Kangaroo, Western Grey Kangaroo, [One-humped Camel]**

Just 296 km west of Ceduna and 186 km east of the WA border, the Nullarbor Roadhouse has long been a reliable site for **Southern Hairy-nosed Wombats**. Their warrens are behind the roadhouse and by driving slowly at night on the tracks through the saltbush you should have no trouble seeing one. Other species in the area include **Western Grey** and **Red Kangaroos** and feral **One-humped Camels**. The roadhouse ((08) 8625 6271) is on the north side of the highway and has a 24-hour restaurant and budget accommodation. Bush camping is possible in the Nullarbor NP but there are no facilities – ask at the national parks office in Ceduna.

7. Western Australia

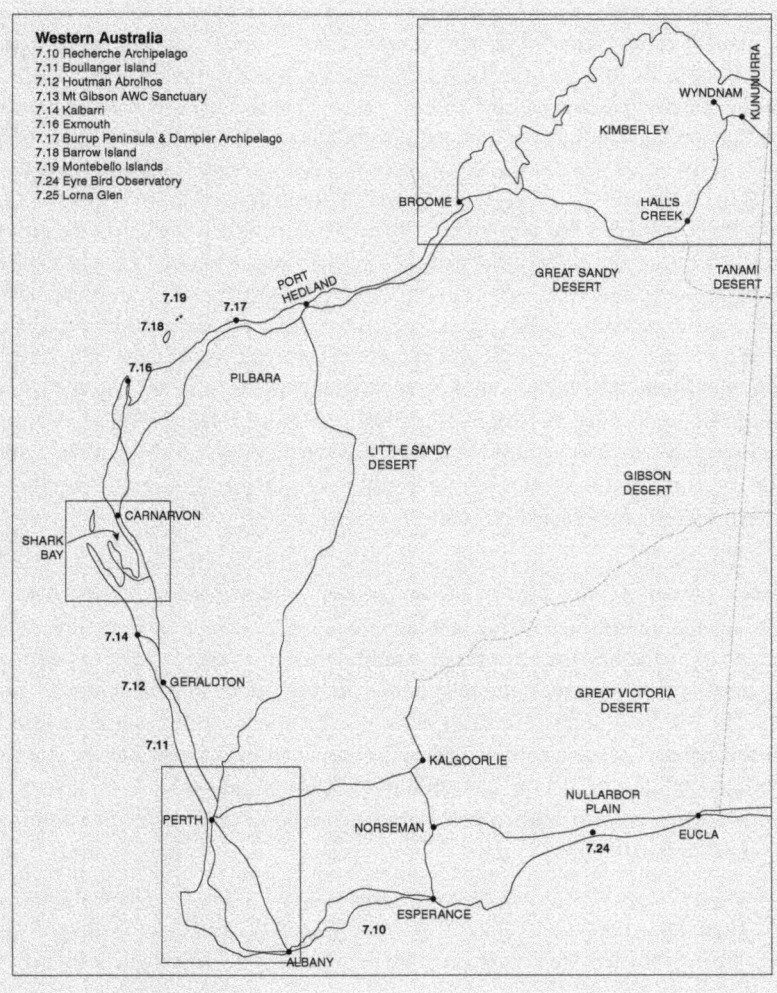

Western Australia
7.10 Recherche Archipelago
7.11 Boullanger Island
7.12 Houtman Abrolhos
7.13 Mt Gibson AWC Sanctuary
7.14 Kalbarri
7.16 Exmouth
7.17 Burrup Peninsula & Dampier Archipelago
7.18 Barrow Island
7.19 Montebello Islands
7.24 Eyre Bird Observatory
7.25 Lorna Glen

KIMBERLEY
WYNDNAM
KUNUNURRA
BROOME
HALL'S CREEK
GREAT SANDY DESERT
TANAMI DESERT

7.19
7.17
7.18
PORT HEDLAND
7.16
PILBARA
LITTLE SANDY DESERT
GIBSON DESERT
CARNARVON
SHARK BAY
7.14
7.12 GERALDTON
7.11
GREAT VICTORIA DESERT
KALGOORLIE
PERTH
NORSEMAN
NULLARBOR PLAIN
EUCLA
7.24
ESPERANCE
7.10
ALBANY

Endemics: Western Quoll (Chuditch), Red-tailed Phascogale, Numbat, Dibbler, Kaluta, Woolley's False Antechinus, Pilbara Ningaui, White-tailed Dunnart, Grey-bellied Dunnart, Western Barred Bandicoot, Scaly-tailed Possum, Honey Possum, Western Ringtail Possum, Burrowing Bettong, Woylie, Gilbert's Potoroo, Western Brush Wallaby, Quokka, Banded Hare-wallaby, Monjon, Rothschild's Rock Wallaby, Yellow-lipped Cave Bat, Western False Pipistrelle, Kimberley Rock-rat, Ash-grey Mouse, Western Mouse, Djoongari (Shark Bay Mouse), Pilbara Pebble-mouse

Australia's largest state occupies nearly a third of the continent but has the population of a medium-sized city. Various climatic zones have created pockets of endemism and, not surprisingly, it has many unique species, including 28 endemic mammals, and good populations of many that are rare elsewhere. Western Australia is an excellent mammal-watching destination, especially if you have some time to travel to several sites. Key areas to visit are the south-west, Shark Bay, the Pilbara and the Kimberley. Travel here is measured in days and what looks like a short distance on some maps can actually be hundreds of kilometres on the ground. Most of the human population is crowded into the south-west corner in and around the capital Perth, which is the only international hub and is serviced by flights from Europe, Asia and South Africa. The south-west is comparatively cool and wet, especially in winter and Perth makes an ideal starting point for your exploration of WA. Even so, be aware that the distance between Perth and Albany on the south coast is 420 km; consider flying to Broome as a base for exploring the Kimberley. The whole state is extremely hot in summer and the tropical north is prone to cyclones between December and March most years. This chapter is arranged roughly south to north, with Perth as a starting point for travelling wildlife-watcher; you could just as easily work your way south, starting in Kununurra with your own transport, but allow plenty of time!

It would be difficult to exaggerate the importance of WA's offshore islands, many of which have provided refuges for a suite of mammals now extinct, or nearly so, on the mainland. Among them are Rottnest and Barrow Is., the Archipelago of the Recherche and islands in Shark Bay. Islands off the Kimberley, in the state's far north, may also prove their worth in time, with the relentless march of the Cane Toad across northern Australia. The WA government is making vigorous attempts to restore some ecosystems to their former state, with captive breeding and reintroduction programs in key areas: the Western Shield Project is attempting to control introduced predators and reintroduce native animals, and Project Eden aims to restore the native fauna of Peron Peninsula at Shark Bay.

Several widespread species are referred to by sometimes obscure local names in Western Australia; these have been used here if they have general currency in the west, or seem likely to attain it, together with more generally accepted names to avoid confusion.

SOME STATE HIGHLIGHTS

- The charming **Numbat** – terrestrial, diurnal and instantly recognisable.
- Rottnest Island, where you can't miss the abundant **Quokkas**.
- **Bottlenose Dolphins**, **Dugongs** and endangered marsupials at Shark Bay.
- The **Kimberley**, home to several marsupials and rodents that are rare elsewhere.
- Watching **Humpback Whales** from land and sea at many sites along the west coast.

A PERTH AND THE SOUTH-WEST

South-western WA has many areas of outstanding biodiversity and natural beauty, for the most part preserved in national parks and other reserves. A broad diagonal band, largely devoid of natural vegetation and known as the 'wheatbelt' stretches from north of Perth to the coast east of Albany, skirting the wetter south-west corner. However, the south-west itself has many wildlife attractions and is great for watching endemic mammals; whale-watching off the coast is also very good during the **Humpback** and **Southern Right Whale** migrations. Some of the local vegetation types (for example, Karri and Jarrah forests) are named after distinctive species of eucalypt and learning to recognise them can give clues when looking for mammals and other wildlife. Wildflowers are a big draw in the south-west and also affect mammal behaviour, for example when various woody shrubs are in blossom.

7.01 PERTH AREA

Highlights: **Quenda (Southern Brown Bandicoot), Common Brushtail Possum, Western Ringtail Possum, Honey Possum, Quokka, Australian Sea Lion**

Other possibilities: **Chuditch, [Five-striped Palm Squirrel], New Zealand Fur Seal, Humpback Whale, Southern Right Whale**

Perth is WA's biggest city and has an international airport plus all the usual accommodations, eating, shopping and vehicle hire options. It is virtually contiguous with the port of Fremantle, the departure point for Rottnest I. (7.02), which can be reached directly by suburban train or road. King's Park near Perth city centre is a pleasant place with resident **Honey Possums**, although to have a chance of seeing them there you'd probably have to stake out a patch of flowering shrubs and return after nightfall with a torch. There's a resident population of **Indo-Pacific Bottlenose Dolphins** in the Swan-Canning Riverpark. The Dolphins could be encountered anywhere along the river system and in the Inner Harbour in Fremantle; and inshore outside the river system. The **Five-striped Palm Squirrel** is an introduced exotic (the only squirrel that has become established in Australia), and can be seen in and around Perth Zoo and nearby suburbs. Perth's whale-watching vessels operate mostly during the south-bound **Humpback** migration, from September to late November (see www.whalewatchingperth.com).

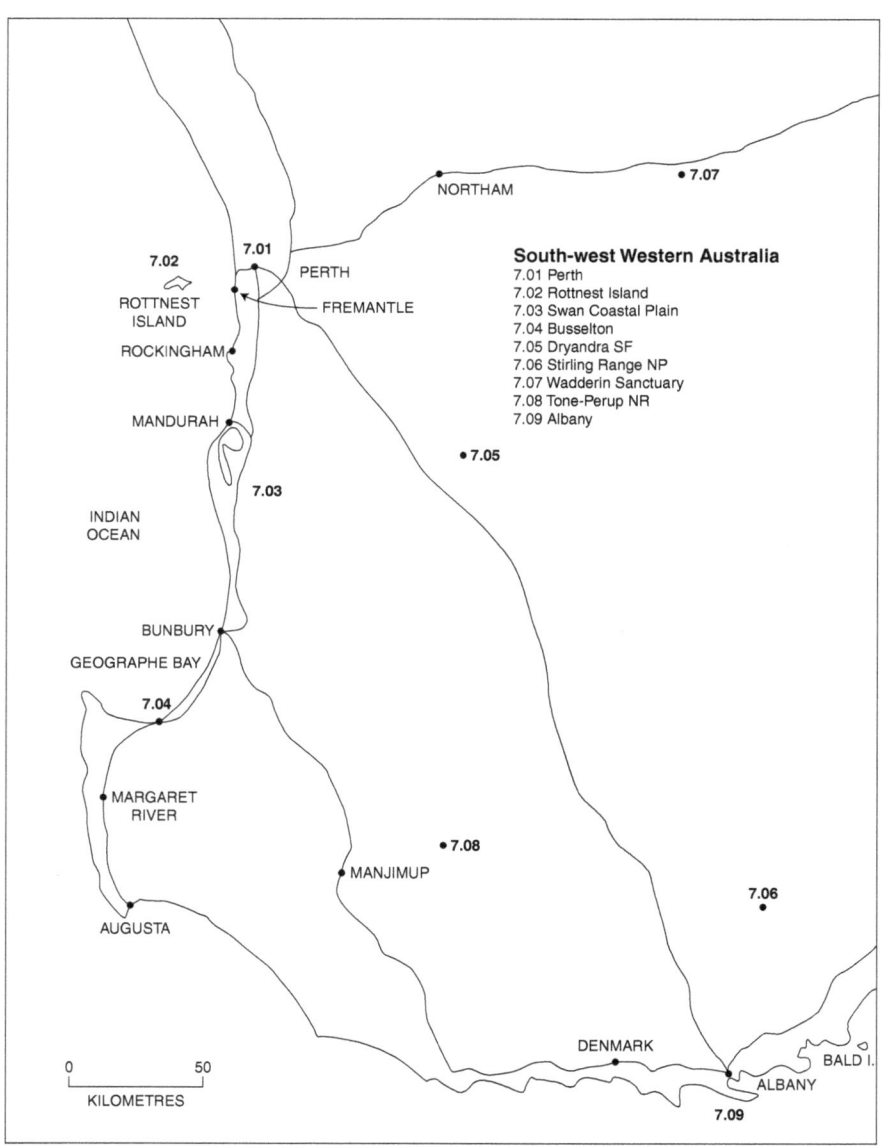

NORTHAM

• 7.07

7.02

7.01

PERTH

South-west Western Australia
7.01 Perth
7.02 Rottnest Island
7.03 Swan Coastal Plain
7.04 Busselton
7.05 Dryandra SF
7.06 Stirling Range NP
7.07 Wadderin Sanctuary
7.08 Tone-Perup NR
7.09 Albany

ROTTNEST
ISLAND

FREMANTLE

ROCKINGHAM

MANDURAH

• 7.05

7.03

INDIAN
OCEAN

BUNBURY

GEOGRAPHE BAY

7.04

MARGARET
RIVER

• 7.08

MANJIMUP

7.06

AUGUSTA

DENMARK

BALD I.

ALBANY

7.09

0   50

KILOMETRES

The Australian Wildlife Conservancy (www.australianwildlife.org) runs two sanctuaries in the hills east of Perth. Karakamia AWC Sanctuary preserves a patch of Jarrah forest where **Woylies**, **Quenda** (ssp. *fusciventer*), **Tammar Wallabies**, **Quokkas** and **Western Ringtail**s have been reintroduced and thrive behind a predator exclusion fence; **Brushtail Possums** are also common here. Evening spotlighting tours operate

Wednesday to Sunday; call (08) 9572 3169. **Chuditch**, **Quenda (Southern Brown Bandicoot)** and **Woylies** have been reintroduced to Paruna AWC Sanctuary. **Echidnas**, **Western Pygmy Possums**, **Western Grey Kangaroos** and **Western Brush Wallabies** occur at both sites, and of the microbats **White-striped Freetail Bats** could probably be detected at dusk with the aid of a torch.

7.02 ROTTNEST ISLAND

Highlights: **Quokka, Australian Sea Lion**

Other possibilities: **New Zealand Fur Seal, Bottlenose Dolphin, Humpback Whale, Southern Right Whale**

Rottnest Island – 'Rotto' to the locals – is a limestone island 18 km west of Fremantle which you should visit to see the endemic **Quokka**. The island supports the world's largest population of this distinctive macropod, which on the mainland occurs only in dense heath in the extreme south-west (at, for example, Kesner's Swamp near Dwellingup and Victor Road near Collie, and at Muddy Lakes, south of Dalyellup). It is far easier to see on Rottnest, where there are an estimated 8000–12 000 of them, and in fact you would be very unlucky *not* to see one (some shops on the island put boards across their doorways to keep Quokkas out!). Quokkas are mainly nocturnal but they can be reliably seen sheltering under tea-tree bushes on the western shore of Garden Lake, 10 minutes' walk west of the ferry pier. Failing that, skirt the golf course to the north and you're bound to see some. They can be ridiculously tame and make great subjects for photos. Females usually have joeys in pouch in autumn and winter (March–August) and youngsters can be seen September–November. If you caught an early ferry over you could visit Rottnest as a day trip to see the Quokkas, but try to spend a night or two just to enjoy the surroundings. The island is about 15 km from east to west and bicycles can be hired to explore areas away from the main settlement. The only other native terrestrial mammal recorded here is **White-striped Freetail Bat**, but there are secluded rocky coves and islets where **Australian Sea Lions** periodically haul out. At West End, about 10 km from the settlement, there's a viewing platform from which **Humpback Whales** can be sighted during migration (usually starting from early July till about November, with a peak September to December, including females with calves); whale-watching tours run from the island (inquire at the Information Centre). **Southern Right Whales** are also occasionally sighted. **New Zealand Fur Seals** have recently begun to haul out at Cathedral Rocks, near the western tip of the island. **Bottlenose Dolphins** are also sometimes seen in Salmon Bay on the north coast.

Rottnest ferries (see www.rottnestexpress.com.au) leave daily from the dock at Fremantle (about 19 km south-west of Perth CBD and serviced by a direct train route). There are free guided walks to see Quokkas and various 'eco' adventures such as whale-watching.

7.03 SWAN COASTAL PLAIN

Highlights: **Chuditch, Western Ringtail Possum, Australian Sea Lion**

Other possibilities: **Tammar Wallaby, Bottlenose Dolphins**

Perth's suburban sprawl stretches south along the Swan Coastal Plain, a sand plain formerly covered in endemic forests which are becoming increasingly fragmented. Garden Island is a naval base on which **Tammar Wallabies** are common; public access is currently restricted and possible only with permission from the relevant authority. **Bottlenose Dolphins** occur in Cockburn Sound, 10 km to the south.

Just offshore from Rockingham, 50 km south of the CBD, Seal I. (part of Shoalwater Islands MP) is a haul-out for **Australian Sea Lions**. Up to 30 bulls haul out here or on nearby Penguin I. (females and juveniles congregate at Jurien Bay north of Perth (7.11)). **Bottlenose Dolphins** are often seen, especially at Crystal Bay, and Capricorn Seakayaking (www.capricornseakayaking.com.au) does day trips on sea kayaks to see the seals up close. Landing is permitted on Penguin I.

Lane-Poole Reserve near Dwellingup is a good area for **Chuditch**, especially in the Nanga Mill area. At Yalgorup NP, south of Mandurah-Peel Inlet, there is a population of **Western Ringtail Possums** in the Lake Clifton area west of Harvey.

7.04 BUSSELTON

Highlights: **Western Ringtail Possum, Common Brushtail Possum, Western Grey Kangaroo, Australian Sea Lion**

Other possibilities: **Brush-tailed Phascogale, Quenda (Southern Brown Bandicoot)**

Busselton, 224 km south of Perth, is a good starting place to look for the endemic **Western Ringtail Possum**. The largest remaining population is protected in Tuart Forest NP west of the Bussel Hwy between Capel and Busselton. The Tuart is a tree unique to the coastal plains of south-western WA and a dense understorey of Peppermint provides ample food for the possums. The area bounded by Tuart Drive, Layman Rd and the Abba River seems to be particularly good for this species; there's a self-guiding trail that starts more or less opposite the Layman picnic area off Layman Rd with reflectors to help you get around at night with a torch. Tuart Forest is also home to the densest known population of **Common Brushtail Possums** in WA. **Western Grey Kangaroos** are common in the area; smaller species recorded include the **Brush-tailed Phascogale**, **Bush Rat** and **Quenda**. The Kookaburra Caravan Park has a small population of **Western Ringtail Possums** – inquire at reception about whether they have been seen recently.

7.05 DRYANDRA STATE FOREST

Highlights: **Chuditch, Brush-tailed Phascogale, Red-tailed Phascogale, Numbat, Common Brushtail Possum, Woylie, Tammar Wallaby, Western Brush Wallaby, Western Grey Kangaroo**

Other possibilities: **Honey Possum, Quenda (Southern Brown Bandicoot)**

This remnant of natural vegetation in the biologically dead wheatbelt is the best site to look for the endearing **Numbat**, WA's state faunal emblem and one of Australia's most appealing mammals. The open, park-like landscape – dominated by attractive Wandoo trees, Mallet and Kwongan as well as stands of Marri and Powderbark – is unusual and features stands of grass trees as well as a suite of endemic birds. Dryandra supports some 30 per cent of the world's **Numbat** population, and they can generally be seen by driving the trails; they are diurnal and in winter emerge from burrows well after sunrise – even mid-morning – to sun themselves. They favour areas with lots of fallen logs and rotting wood, where they forage for termites and ants. The park's list of native mammals totals 26 species. The **Western Brush Wallaby** and **Tammar Wallaby** can be seen by driving the trails, especially at dawn and dusk, although you could flush one or two while walking through suitable bush with a sheltering understorey. The **Echidna** is also commonly encountered, especially in the warmer months. **Western Grey Kangaroos** are common and graze on the lawns around Dryandra Village. Dryandra used to be a great spot for **Woylies (Brush-tailed Bettongs)**, which grazed on the lawns near the cottages at Dryandra Village after dark. They are not as common as formerly but can still be seen if you are prepared to put in some work. The **Tammar Wallaby** can be seen even in daylight on Gura Rd. The **Common Brushtail Possum** is very common and can be seen around the campground and in just about any patch of bush while spotlighting. The **Greater Bilby** and **Boodie (Burrowing Bettong)** have been reintroduced and the **Quenda (Southern Brown Bandicoot)** is being seen again after becoming locally extinct. The **Chuditch (Western Quoll)** also occurs but is rather rare. The park brochure recommends the nocturnal Wandoo Walk for **Woylies**, **Tammar Wallaby** and **Common Brushtail Possum**. Woylie Walk may have **Numbats** during the day and at night also **Woylies**.

Red-tailed Phascogale and **Honey Possum** are the standouts among Dryandra's smaller mammals. The phascogale occurs in stands of she-oak (*Casuarina*), such as that on Kowena Rd about 2 km from the village. It is best seen after breeding, when with luck it could be spotlighted; it is very scarce in winter. Small-mammal-trapping is conducted periodically by the state conservation department; check its website for details. Lol Gray Loop takes you through a variety of heath where **Honey Possums** occur. **Western Pygmy Possum**, **Fat-tailed** and **White-bellied Dunnarts** and **Mardos** (**Yellow-footed Antechinus**) have all been recorded in the park.

THE BIG FIVE

There are no Platypuses or Koalas in WA, but the endemic Numbat makes an excellent substitute and this is the best state in which to see Dugongs.

Kangaroo Western Grey Kangaroos are common at Dryandra SF (7.05), where they can easily be seen around the visitor's centre.

Numbat WA's state mammal emblem is also most easily seen at Dryandra SF (7.05); watch for it among fallen timber and sunning itself in winter.

Wombat Southern Hairy-nosed Wombats just make it into WA on the Nullarbor Plain; you'll need to travel way out east to see one.

Dugong Shark Bay (7.15) supports Australia's largest population of this unusual sea herbivore; they are common here and boat tours can take you to see one.

Whale Good areas to experience the annual Humpback Whale migration include Exmouth Gulf, the Houtman Abrolhos, Kalbarri and Albany; numerous boat operators run cruises at all these locations.

Dryandra's position between the wheatbelt and moist Jarrah forests makes it an important remnant. Barna Mia is a captive breeding facility in the heart of the forest that aims to re-establish a suite of species that formerly occurred here: the **Greater Bilby** (Dalgyte), **Western Barred Bandicoot** (Marl), **Boodie**, **Rufous Hare-wallaby** (Wurrup), **Woylie** and **Banded Hare-wallaby** (Merrnine). Eventually it is hoped that all these species can be released back into Dryandra to form self-sustaining populations. Night tours (there is no visitor access during the day) are currently conducted on Mondays, Wednesdays, Fridays and Saturdays (except public holidays) and are a good way of getting close to some of these species; expect them to be popular during school holidays and at weekends. Check the state Department of Parks and Wildlife website for prices and further details (http://parks.dpaw.wa.gov.au/site/barna-mia); trapping sessions may also be held occasionally.

Dryandra is about 180 km south-east of Perth; the nearest fuel and food supplies are at Narrogin (26 km away) or Cuballing. Accommodation huts are available for hire at Dryandra Village and there is basic camping at Congelin, although you must take your own drinking water.

7.06 STIRLING RANGE NP

Highlights: **Echidna, Honey Possum, Western Grey Kangaroo**

Other possibilities: **Western Pygmy Possum, Yellow-footed Antechinus**

The tree-covered Stirling Range emerges from the flat agricultural plains surrounding it and bursts into a famous wildflower display in springtime. It is among the south-west's most scenic attractions and Bluff Knoll Café on the north side of the Stirling Range attracts **Honey Possums** when *Grevillea* and *Hakea* bushes are in flower. Ask at the café if they're being seen – October is often good; check the flowering shrubs along the path near the door at dawn or late afternoon/dusk. About 20 native mammal species have been recorded from the park, including **Echidnas**, **Western Grey Kangaroos** and smaller species such as the **Western Pygmy Possum**, **Yellow-footed Antechinus**, **Gilbert's Dunnart** and **Ash-grey Mouse**. Efforts are apparently under way to introduce **Dibblers** to the park.

7.07 WADDERIN SANCTUARY

Highlights: **Woylie, Red-tailed Phascogale, Southern Brown Bandicoot, Common Brushtail Possum**

Other possibilities: **Echidna, Western Grey Kangaroo, Euro**

An interesting restocking initiative is being carried out by the local farming community at Wadderin Sanctuary, near Narembeen. The reserve is fenced to protect a series of granite tors in remnant mallee woodland in the central wheatbelt where **Echidnas**, **Western Grey Kangaroos** and **Euros** have survived. So far there have been successful reintroductions of the **Woylie**, **Red-tailed Phascogale**, **Quenda (Southern Brown Bandicoot)**, **Common Brushtail Possum** and **Western Brush Wallaby**. Narembeen is 280 km east of Perth. Inquire locally about access, taking part in surveys or visiting farmers who have put up nest boxes on private property around Wagin. **Red-tailed Phascogales** also occur in suitable habitat along the Arthur River and at Wagin Lakes. The Wagin-Woodanalling Landcare Group keeps a register of sightings.

Nangeen Hill NR, 200 km east of Perth near Kellerberrin, formerly supported the largest colony of **Black-flanked Rock Wallabies** in the wheatbelt. Fox control and reintroduction programs have commenced and breeding has occurred once again.

7.08 TONE-PERUP NATURE RESERVE

Highlights: **Numbat, Common Brushtail Possum (ssp. *hypoleucus*), Western Ringtail Possum, Woylie, Tammar Wallaby, Western Brush Wallaby, Quenda (Southern Brown Bandicoot)**

Other possibilities: **Chuditch, Brush-tailed Phascogale (ssp. *tapoatafa*), Quokka**

The Perup area south of Boyup Brook is an important area for south-western endemics and rarities, with a total mammal list of 30 species. Tone-Perup NR is central to the area and it is linked to several other reserves, such as Lake Muir, especially to the south. There is accommodation at Perup and by walking or driving around at night there's a good chance of seeing **Western Ringtail Possums**; this is the most inland population of this species and the only one that does not appear to be dependent on Peppermint trees; they can sometimes be seen near the guesthouse and Perup Ecology Centre. **Common Brushtail Possums** are indeed common along park roads and **Quendas** are another possibility. The Perup area has a high density of **Numbats**, but check with authorities before you drive around looking for them – parts of the area have restricted access. Driving at dawn or dusk may yield **Tammar Wallabies** or **Western Brush Wallabies**; the latter are more common around Lake Muir and shelter in copses of Mohan during the day. Check with the state environment department about fauna surveys for a chance of seeing **Woylies** (there's a good population in the area), **Chuditches** and **Brush-tailed Phascogales** (you might be able to take part in the annual nest-box checking); there are small numbers of **Quokkas** but they are very cryptic and **Water Rats** also occur here. You may also be lucky enough to visit the 'Perup Sanctuary', a predator exclosure where an emergency stock of up to 500 **Woylies** is held.

To get here turn south off the Boyup Brook–Kojanup Rd 11.5 km south of Boyup Brook; the accommodation area is about 20 km along the Boyup Brook–Cranbrook Rd. Lake Muir can be reached along the Muirs Hwy between Manjimup and Rocky Gully; there are extensive stands of Mohan at the north-east corner of the lake, along the Nabagup Rd and south of the Muirs Hwy for 3–4 km – good places to look for **Western Brush Wallabies**.

7.09 ALBANY AREA

Highlights: **Western Pygmy Possum, Western Ringtail Possum, Gilbert's Potoroo, Western Grey Kangaroo, Humpback Whale**

Other possibilities: **Dibbler, Yellow-footed Antechinus, Quenda (Southern Brown Bandicoot), Quokka**

There's a semi-urban population of **Western Ringtail Possum** in Albany, WA's second-largest city – check patches of Peppermint woodland near the outskirts of town. Two Peoples Bay, so named because ships from opposing sides met peacefully here during the Napoleonic Wars, is a scenic location covered in dense heath 52 km east of Albany. The area was intensively studied from the 1970s onwards after the rediscovery of the endangered Noisy Scrub-bird. Incredibly, another long-lost species, **Gilbert's Potoroo**, turned up in 1994 right under the noses of scientists who had been working at the site for years. There's a small colony of **Gilbert's Potoroos**, numbering about 40, in heathland near Little Beach, but the chances of seeing them are virtually nil. Some have been translocated to Bald I., 25 km to the east, as an insurance population, where they are thriving; **Quokkas** also occur naturally on Bald I. There's another population of **Gilbert's Potoroo** in a predator-free exclosure near Waychinicup NP. Volunteering to help with the conservation of these animals is the only way to see them. There are also **Quokkas** in the dense heath, although again they are rarely seen, and **Southern Brown Bandicoots** are seen near the visitors' centre. The heath is of course excellent habitat for **Honey Possums** and **Western Ringtail Possums** occur in stands of trees in sheltered areas of this windswept coast. **Yellow-footed Antechinuses** are also known to occur in the reserve. **Western Grey Kangaroos** can be seen along the access road and in more open areas of the reserve.

Cheyne's Beach, a former whaling station about 75 km north-east of Albany, was the site of another interesting rediscovery: the **Dibbler**. Nest boxes (lengths of padded pipe) are put out for **Western Pygmy Possums** at the Cheynes Beach Caravan Park ((08) 9846 1247); ask at the reception desk where they may be seen. Other species recorded in these dense heaths include **Bush Rats**, **Honey Possums** and **Quendas**. Cheyne's Beach was once a commercial whaling station, with a focus mainly on **Humpback** and **Sperm Whales**. **Humpbacks** are still seen in the area but the **Sperm Whales** occur much further offshore (usually about 30 km) and are rarely encountered. Other marine mammal records in the area have included **Subantarctic Fur Seal** and **Strap-toothed Beaked Whale**. Whale-watching tours leave from Albany during the migration (www.albanywhaletours.com.au) and have featured many good sightings of both **Humpbacks** and **Southern Right Whales**. There's a **New Zealand Fur Seal** colony on Eclipse I, south of Albany.

WATCHING WHALES AND DOLPHINS IN WESTERN AUSTRALIA

Western Australia has a varied coastline of nearly 13 000 km that changes from the massive Nullarbor Cliffs in the Great Australian Bight through the rocky, indented south-western coast to the shallow seas of the tropical north-west, where the daily tide range covers several metres. It's not surprising, therefore, that all but four of Australia's cetaceans have occurred in WA: 40 species have been recorded in the state, dead or alive. Many of these are rare or little known, of course, but there are some outstanding cetacean attractions and several sites where watching could be well rewarded.

The West Australian **Humpback Whale** migration takes place along the west coast each year, mainly from June (though individuals may appear as early as April) to October, with stragglers as late as November. An estimated 29 000 of them migrate from Antarctic waters annually, making it the largest known **Humpback** subpopulation in the world. 'Bottlenecks', where the majority of the migration passes within 30 km of the coast, include Geraldton and the Houtman Abrolhos Is. and Point Cloates to North-West Cape. **Humpbacks** are also seen regularly off Kalbarri and Broome, and numerous whale-watching operators work out of Albany, Broome, Exmouth, Denham, Kalbarri and Geographe Bay (where 1000 Humpbacks passed through in 2011).

The whales seem to travel faster and further offshore during the northward migration, calving in the warm waters of the Kimberley between Broome and Camden Sound, before returning at a more leisurely pace inshore. First to head south are the newly pregnant females, followed by immature males and females, then mature adults; last come the females with newborn calves, which often linger in bays and inlets. Resting areas used by cow–calf pairs and attendant males during the southward migration include Exmouth Gulf, Shark Bay, Geographe Bay and waters adjacent to the Houtman Abrolhos.

The annual migration of **Southern Right Whales** reaches West Australian waters from May to November, mainly along the southern coast south of Perth, but occasionally as far north of Kalbarri (where a calving occurred at the mouth of the Murchison River in 2012) and North-West Cape. The main calving area for **Southern Rights** in WA is Doubtful Island Bay, east of Israelite Bay; smaller numbers are seen at Twilight Cove, Flinders Bay, the Albany-Cape Riche area and the Yokinup Bay-Cape Arid area.

A migratory 'bottleneck' of **Blue Whales** sometimes aggregates in Geographe Bay north of Cape Leeuwin, mainly in the southern section adjacent to Cape Naturaliste, which is a resting point as they move west through the bay. Most observations are in October–December, sometimes in water as shallow as 10–30 m and as close as 200 m from the Cape. The Perth Canyon, a large, deep sea canyon south-west of Rottnest I., is known for localised upwellings that attract **Blue** and **Pygmy Sperm Whales**. Recent research has shown that the **Blue Whales** travel north from the Perth Canyon to the Banda and Molucca Seas in Indonesia to calve, hugging the coastline as far as North-West Cape and then swimming north to the Sulawesi region.

Killer Whales seem to follow the **Humpback** migration north along the coast and are seen some winters in the Ningaloo Reef area and near North-West Cape; they have also been reported west of Cape Naturaliste. There are many smaller canyons along the south coast, including one south of Fitzgerald River where a population of **Killer Whales** appears to be more or less resident.

Probably the best-known West Australian cetacean attraction is the dolphin-feeding at Monkey Mia in Shark Bay World Heritage Area (7.15a). Every day **Bottlenose Dolphins** are fed by park rangers, providing tourists with great photo opportunities and an educational experience. However, **Bottlenose**

Dolphins occur around the entire WA coastline and can also be seen at, for example, Coral Bay, North-West Cape, Port Hedland, the Dampier Archipelago and near Broome. Closer to Perth, they are resident in the Swan-Canning Estuary and Mandurah Estuary-Peel Inlet. In the Bunbury area they can be seen in Bunbury Harbour, Woodman Point and Koombana Bay; 'swim-with-dolphin' tours are run from Bunbury Dolphin Discovery Centre.

Indo-Pacific Humpback Dolphins reach their most southerly limit at Shark Bay, but further north they occur off several coastal towns, including Exmouth, Onslow, Dampier, Port Hedland and Broome, with North-West Cape a possible hotspot. This species is reputed to be approachable in the Dampier Archipelago. **Australian Snubfin Dolphins** are more likely to be found among mangroves and Roebuck Bay south of Broome is a great spot to see them.

The warm seas of the north-west coast seem to be particularly good for observations of blackfish. **False Killer** and **Melon-headed Whales** are regularly recorded on voyages between Broome and Ashmore Reef. **Spinner Dolphins** (both offshore and inshore forms) are commonly encountered on these trips, and **Fraser's**, **Risso's**, **Rough-toothed** and **Pantropical Spotted Dolphins** have also been seen.

In all 34 cetacean species have stranded on WA coasts. Most commonly these have been **Long-flippered Pilot Whales** (for example, at Dunsborough) and **Bottlenose Dolphins**, which have stranded in mixed herds, for example at Hamelin Bay. Other species involved in mass strandings (that is, of more than 20 animals) have been **False Killer** and **Short-flippered Pilot Whales**, and **Striped Dolphins**. Most strandings occur in the south-west, with 85 per cent occurring south of Geraldton, especially around Busselton, Augusta and South West Cape. Very few occur on the Nullarbor, Pilbara or Kimberley coasts. Nine of Australia's 12 beaked whales have been recorded in WA, either alive or as stranded specimens. Most common has been **Gray's Beaked Whale** (mostly in summer and possibly because the cooler, north-flowing Cape Current brings them inshore from subantarctic waters) and it is therefore probably the most common species occurring in these waters. As with all beaked whales, however, sightings are infrequent and opportunistic; in descending order of stranding frequency, **Strap-toothed**, **True's**, **Cuvier's** and **Shepherd's Beaked Whales** are all known from multiple strandings; while **Arnoux's**, **Hector's**, **Blainville's** and **Andrews' Beaked Whales** are each known from only one or two strandings in WA.

About 250 km east of Albany, Fitzgerald River NP supports more than 22 mammal species, including a number of localised species, such as the **Dibbler**, **White-bellied Dunnart**, **Heath Mouse** and **Bush Rat**. Much of the park is heathland where **Honey Possums** are apparently common.

The region between Esperance, 480 km east of Albany, and Cape Arid NP is very good for **Southern Right Whale**-watching during migration. Prime sites near Esperance include Observatory Point and local beaches such as Castletown Quays, and West and Twilight Beaches. Heading east, other good sites include Cape le Grand NP (where **Western Grey Kangaroos** can be seen on or near Lucky Bay and **Australian Sea Lions** occur); and between Cape le Grand and Wylie Bay. One of the best sites is Yokinup Bay round to Dolphin Bay in Cape Arid NP, where mothers and calves sometimes come close to headlands.

7.10 RECHERCHE ARCHIPELAGO

Highlights: **Black-flanked Rock Wallaby (ssp. *backetti* and *lateralis*), Tammar Wallaby**

Other possibilities: **Southern Brown Bandicoot (ssp. *nauticus*), Australian Sea Lion, New Zealand Fur Seal, Southern Right Whale**

A little-visited chain of islands off the south coast opposite Esperance and Cape Arid NP supports an interesting relictual selection of mammals. Two subspecies of the **Black-flanked Rock Wallaby** were stranded on these islands by rising sea levels, and today *Petrogale lateralis hackettii* is restricted to three islands – Mondrain, Wilson and Westall; while *P. l. lateralis* (the same race that occurs in the NT and northern SA) occurs on Salisbury I., at the eastern extremity of the group. Similarly, the *nauticus* race of **Southern Brown Bandicoot** – the same that lives on islands off southern SA – also lives on one island (Daw I.). **Tammar Wallabies** occur on Middle and North Twin Peak Is. Both **Australian Sea Lions** and **New Zealand Fur Seals** occur in the archipelago. This part of the coast is the stronghold of **New Zealand Fur Seals** in WA; they breed on, for example, Middle I., haul out on Investigator and Red Is., among others, and recently colonised Chatham and Stanley Is. further west near Walpole. Pups occasionally haul up on beaches adjacent, especially in late summer. **Australian Sea Lions** occur on Draper I. and **Subantarctic Fur Seals** also occur occasionally.

B THE MID-NORTH

North of Perth the climate quickly gets hotter and drier, and you don't have to go far before the desert stretches all the way to the coast. **Red Kangaroos** start to get more common by the highway north from the Denham turnoff.

7.11 BOULLANGER ISLAND

Highlights: **Dibbler, Boullanger Island Dunnart (ssp. *boullangerensis*)**

Other possibilities: **Australian Sea Lion, Inshore Bottlenose Dolphin**

Boullanger is a low, scrub-covered limestone island only a few hundred metres long that supports the only known population of **Dibblers** north of Perth. They are common here and on Whitlock I., 300 m to the south-west, and captive-bred **Dibblers** have also been introduced to nearby Escape I. The **Dibblers** are semi-diurnal, mostly active at dawn and dusk, foraging among dense leaf litter and sheltering in seabird burrows. They typically occur in the low, closed heath that grows all over Boullanger I., but are more common in dense heath at the southern end of Whitlock and among *Nitraria billardieri* bushes on the central dune. Male die-off occurs in April and they may be easier to see at this time; strangely though, not all males die and die-off does not seem to occur at other sites. The **Boullanger Island Dunnart**, a subspecies of the more widespread Grey-bellied Dunnart, also occurs here, as does the introduced **House Mouse**. The islands are just a couple of kilometres offshore from Jurien Bay township, 223 km north of Perth; access is possible only by boat. **Australian Sea Lions** haul out on the islands and **Inshore Bottlenose Dolphins** may be seen on the crossing.

7.12 HOUTMAN ABROLHOS

Highlights: **Tammar Wallaby (ssp. *derbianus*), Australian Sea Lion**

Other possibilities: **Bush Rat, Bottlenose Dolphin, Striped Dolphin, Common Dolphin, Humpback Whale, Southern Right Whale**

After several Dutch sailing ships literally ran into this archipelago back in the 17th century, cartographers gave it a name that roughly translates as 'watch out!'. So the story goes, anyway. These islands are the northernmost breeding site for **Australian Sea Lions**; the population numbers about 90 and they could be seen on sandy beaches on just about any of the islands. East and West Wallabi Is. in the north of the chain support an isolated population of **Tammar Wallabies**; a population introduced to North I. is now established. Individuals on West Wallabi grow larger than those on East Wallabi, and they can survive by drinking sea water when fresh water is not available. They are relatively easy to find by walking through the scrub near the airfield. **Bush Rats** have also been recorded on East and West Wallabi, although they may be extinct on East Wallabi. Waters between here and Geraldton see lots of **Humpback Whales** on migration (generally between April and October), and they are often seen among the islands themselves; **Southern Right Whales** also sometimes venture this far north. Dolphins encountered in these waters most commonly include **Bottlenose**, but **Striped** and **Common Dolphins** are also known. The Abrolhos (as they are usually known) are 60 km west of Geraldton. By chartering a plane from Geraldton you could make it a day trip, taking in a couple of islands (which also support huge seabird colonies and historic ruins – the islands were the site of a gruesome mutiny in 1629). Otherwise, various live-aboard cruise ships visit the islands.

7.13 MOUNT GIBSON AWC SANCTUARY

Highlights: **Echidna, Western Grey Kangaroo, Euro, Red Kangaroo, Western Brush Wallaby, Dingo**

Other possibilities: **Chuditch, Red-tailed Phascogale, Numbat, Western Barred Bandicoot, Greater Bilby, Woylie, Banded Hare-wallaby, Greater Stick-nest Rat, Shark Bay Mouse (reintroductions)**

An ambitious project run by the AWC (www.australianwildlife.org) aims to reintroduce 10 native mammal species to a predator-free exclosure at Mount Gibson. It is an important area of remnant woodland in the northern wheatbelt, straddling the boundary between the arid zone, dominated by mulga, and the wheatbelt, which formerly supported stands of eucalypt woodland. It already supports a range of mammals typical of both zones, such as **Western Grey** and **Red Kangaroos**, **Western Brush Wallabies, Euros**, plus the **Mallee Ningaui, Woolley's False Antechinus, Fat-tailed** and **Little Long-tailed Dunnarts**, the WA endemic **White-tailed Dunnart** and near-endemic **Gilbert's Dunnart**. Native rodents include the **Spinifex** and **Mitchell's Hopping-mouse**, and both **Desert** and **Sandy Inland Mouse**. Following on from the success of the Scotia AWC Sanctuary (2.29), Mount Gibson will have 40 km of predator-proof fencing erected then all feral predators removed, which will hopefully help the re-establishment of the **Woylie, Red-tailed Phascogale, Numbat, Greater Stick-nest Rat, Greater Bilby, Banded Hare-wallaby, Shark Bay Mouse** and **Western Barred Bandicoot**. Reintroduction of a 10th species, the **Common Brushtail Possum**, will complement the reduced numbers of this species elsewhere in the south-west. The first reintroductions were scheduled for 2015 and the program is expected to be complete by late 2017. AWC plans to install a campground and run guided night walks in the predator exclusion area eventually. Mt Gibson is about 350 km north-east of Perth via Dalwallinu; access is east of the great Northern Hwy (95) between Wubin and Payne's Find.

7.14 KALBARRI

Highlights: **Humpback Whale**

The last town before Shark Bay heading north is Kalbarri, where accessible cliffs overlooking Gantheaume Bay provide good **Humpback Whale** viewing between June and November. The whales start to pass by on their northward migration in May and June, returning by late September. There are good lookouts on the south side of the Murchison River mouth or from the sandy beach about 100 m north of the river. Females and calves often hang around, and sometimes use the sandy bottom near the river mouth to scrape barnacles off their skin. **Southern Right Whales** also sometimes occur here. Kalbarri is 585 km north of Perth and 64 km west of the West Coastal Hwy (Hwy 1).

7.15 SHARK BAY WORLD HERITAGE AREA

Highlights: **Bilby, Southern Brown Bandicoot, Red Kangaroo, Euro, Dugong, Inshore Bottlenose Dolphin**

Other possibilities: **Little Long-tailed Dunnart, Golden Bandicoot, Western Barred Bandicoot, Burrowing Bettong (ssp. *lesueur*), Banded Hare-wallaby, Rufous Hare-wallaby (spp. *bernieri* and *dorreae*), Djoongari (Shark Bay Mouse), Water Rat, Ash-grey Mouse, Sandy Inland Mouse, Indo-Pacific Humpback Dolphin, Humpback Whale**

This scenic complex of islands and peninsulas frames a huge sheltered bay nearly 100 km across. It was Australia's first World Heritage site and several islands are refuges for mammals that are extinct on the mainland. Thousands of people flock here annually to enjoy the area's outstanding wildlife attractions, including the famous dolphins at Monkey Mia (7.15a). The area formerly had a rich mammal fauna, with some 23 terrestrial species. Several of these have become extinct but the WA government and AWC are making vigorous efforts to return the entire region to its original condition, through reintroduction programs, feral animal control and predator fences.

Shark Bay itself is home to 10 000–12 000 **Dugongs** (some 10 per cent of the world's population). Their location varies according to time of year; during the cooler months, when most visitors come to Shark Bay, they tend to congregate off Dirk Hartog, Bernier and Dorre Is., where waters are warmer; in the hot summer months they head for the eastern part of Shark Bay, especially the seagrass-rich Gladstone Special Purpose Zone and at the southern end of the Henri Freycinet Harbour, Disappointment Reach just north of Gladstone and the Wooramel Seagrass bank. **Indo-Pacific Humpback Dolphins** are at the southern limit of their WA distribution here and are rare although they have been seen off Cape Peron. **Humpback Whales** pass Shark Bay between July and October, generally passing closest to the islands in the west (there are probably easier places to see them in WA). The awesome 200 m-high Zuytdorp Cliffs in the south-west also make a great vantage point from which to scan for cetaceans.

Shark Bay is 10 hours north from Perth and about 100 km west of the Northwest Coastal Hwy. There are numerous camping areas as well as basic supplies and a few eating places in the town of Denham (the only settlement of any size). The whole area gets extremely hot in summer – carry adequate water in your vehicle and while out walking, and always wear a hat. Various tours are available by boat, air and 4WD. Visit www.sharkbay.org, www.sharkbayvisit.com and www.australiascoralcoast.com for more information.

7.15a Monkey Mia and Peron Peninsula

Sooner or later most visitors head to Monkey Mia, where since the 1960s **Inshore Bottlenose Dolphins** have been visiting the shallow waters to be fed. It's a very different scene today, when during school holidays hundreds of tourists may line the

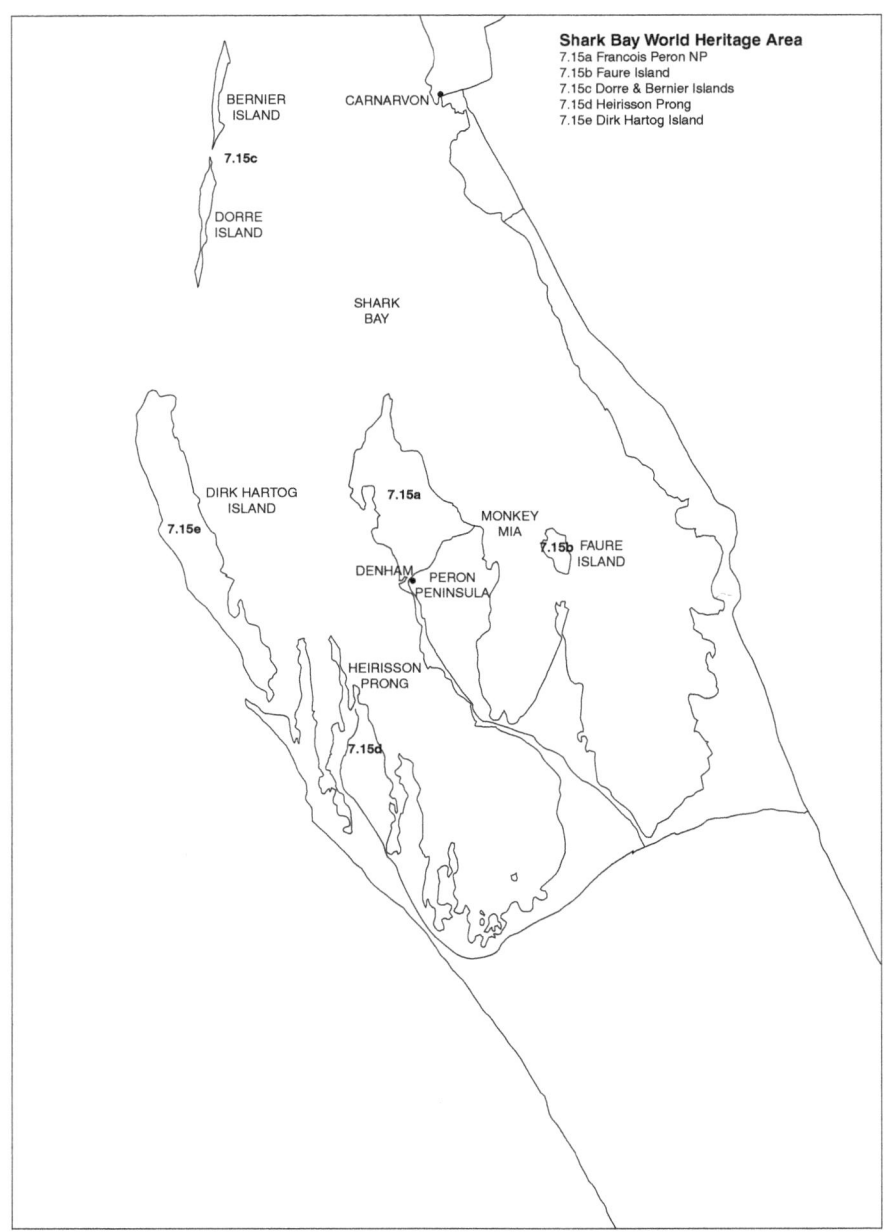

shore, jostling for a view. About 200 dolphins live in the Monkey Mia region, forming subgroups that visit the feeding area, out of a total estimated population of 2000 in Shark Bay. Individuals of this intensively studied population has been known to beach themselves to catch herded fish and to use sea sponges to protect their snouts while rooting about on the sea floor – the only known tool-using dolphin population in the world. Only adult females are fed and there are random feedings between about 7.30 am and 12 pm daily. You could see them at any time of day, but early mornings are generally best. Feedings are strictly managed by rangers. Some visitors find the spectacle crass and touristy, but it can offer great photo opportunities, especially during quiet times. And watch offshore for **Dugongs**.

The entire northern part of the peninsula, north of the Monkey Mia road, is Francois Peron NP. Wanamalu Trail is a 1.5 km clifftop boardwalk between Cape Peron and Skipjack Point, from where you can sometimes see **Inshore Bottlenose Dolphins** and **Dugongs**, as well as sea turtles and sharks. **Euros** and **Echidnas** occur in the area. Eagle Bluff is another lookout from which to scan for cetaceans and **Dugongs** (mainly in summer). Project Eden (www.sharkbay.org/project_eden.aspx) aims to return the Peron Peninsula to some semblance of its original condition before most of the native mammals were wiped out. This involves controlling European Foxes and feral Cats; and a 2-m-high, 3.4-km-long predator fence has been erected at the Taillefer Isthmus just south of Shell Beach. Translocations commenced in 1997 and **Bilbies** and **Southern Brown Bandicoots** have been successfully reintroduced; the Mala and Banded Hare-wallaby reintroductions failed but **Greater Stick-nest Rats** have survived where they were introduced to Salutation I. in 1990 and are used to restock populations elsewhere. **Bilbies** are sometimes seen on roads at night and even around Denham and Monkey Mia. **Southern Brown Bandicoots** are sometimes seen among the dense *Lamarkea* scrub. **Woylies** haven't fared so well and are present now only in very low numbers. The Western Barred Bandicoot, Mala, Bilby and Banded Hare-wallaby continue to be bred at the government-run Peron Captive Breeding Centre, and there are plans to reintroduce the Chuditch, Red-tailed Phascogale, Shark Bay Mouse and Western Barred Bandicoot in the future. Meanwhile, several extant species have also recovered, including **Echidnas** and various small dasyurids, such as the **White-tailed Dunnart** and **Hairy-footed Dunnart**. Note that the national park is accessible by 2WD only as far as Peron Homestead; north of the homestead only high-clearance 4WDs can access the park. There are several camping sites in the national park but no drinking water is available. Camping and other accommodation are available at Denham and Monkey Mia.

7.15b Faure Island AWC Sanctuary

Locals pronounce it *for-ay*, but this 6000-ha island in Shark Bay's Disappointment Reach was named after Pierre Faure, the French geographer who first charted the island, and technically should be pronounced *for*. More importantly, this uninhabited island is a former pastoral station, now run by the AWC, who have eradicated cats and goats, and, appropriately enough, reintroduced the **Djoongari** (**Shark Bay Mouse**), which formerly occurred here. Echidnas, Western Barred Bandicoots, Woylies and Pale Field-rats also once lived here; Echidna tracks have been found and

AWC has restocked the island with **Western Barred Bandicoots**. Insurance populations of **Banded Hare-wallaby**, **Boodie (Burrowing Bettong)** and **Greater Stick-nest Rat** have also been established. The Boodies in particular have prospered and now number at least 400. Day visits are permitted but for a better chance to see some of these species an overnight stay would be essential; for that you'll have to volunteer on an AWC team (visit www.australianwildlife.org). Faure Island is about 18 km east of Monkey Mia and can be reached as a day trip.

7.15c Dorre and Bernier islands

The northernmost 'arm' sheltering Shark Bay is formed by two elongated continental islands – Dorre and Bernier. They lie some 50 km west of Carnarvon, from where they are best accessed, and are notable as the last bastions of several mammals that no longer occur naturally on the mainland: **Shark Bay Mouse**, **Banded Hare-wallaby**, **Western Barred Bandicoot** and **Rufous Hare-wallaby** (**Mala**). The Malas here are apparently comprised of two separate subspecies. Access to Dorre is prohibited and only day visits are permitted to Bernier. No camping is allowed on either and there are no visitor facilities.

Bernier once supported the only surviving population of **Djoongarri**; the mice are still there and luckily have been translocated to other sites. **Banded Hare-wallabies** are the most abundant species on both islands. About 3000 live on Bernier, where the highest density is in the north of the island, particularly among spreading heath vegetation. **Malas** number about 2400 on Bernier and they are most abundant in the south of the island. **Burrowing Bettongs** number about 500–600 on Bernier and they seem to be evenly spread across the island; they are perhaps most abundant near the coastal fringes, as they construct burrow systems under the rock capping of coastal cliffs. **Western Barred Bandicoots** number about 600 on Bernier. The **Shark Bay Mouse** and **Ash-grey Mouse** also occur, the former on coastal sandy fringes and the latter in heaths inland.

7.15d Heirisson Prong

Numerous 'prongs' – narrow isthmuses running north-south – fringe the southern boundary of Shark Bay. One of these, Heirisson Prong, has been fenced off at its narrowest point in an ambitious attempt to eradicate all feral animals and reintroduce native species. To date, the **Western Barred Bandicoot**, **Boodie** and **Greater Stick-nest Rat** have been reintroduced with varying success. The future of this initiative seems uncertain.

7.15e Dirk Hartog Island

This huge island forms the western arm of Shark Bay. Although it is not yet a prime mammal-watching destination, a vigorous feral Cat eradication program is being undertaken and various native species may be reintroduced as part of the state government's 'ecological reconstruction' of the island. Of 13 terrestrial mammal species, only three survive, but the list of casualties gives some idea of how rich the Shark Bay fauna was once: Boodie, Woylie, Western Barred Bandicoot, Chuditch, Crest-tailed Mulgara, Dibbler, Greater Stick-nest Rat, Desert Mouse, Shark Bay Mouse and Heath Mouse. The Banded Hare-wallaby and Rufous Hare-wallaby may also once have occurred as they still survive on Bernier and Dorre Is. (7.15c). **Dugongs** are seen close to the island generally in the cooler months. Access is by barge or boat; eight vehicles (4WD only) are allowed on the island at a time.

C THE PILBARA

The next big centre for endemicity north of Perth is the Pilbara, an arid rugged landscape known for its spectacular scenery and rich mineral deposits. Although it is technically within the tropics, it is really a rocky desert, with annual rainfall more typical of the arid zone but with periodic tropical cyclones that sweep south and inundate the area, creating permanent waterholes in sheltered gorges. This complex climate with numerous refuges has allowed the evolution of many unique plants and animals. The Pilbara is home to four endemic mammals (the **Little Red Kaluta**, **Pilbara Ningaui**, **Rothschild's Rock Wallaby** and **Pilbara Pebble-mouse**), as well as an endemic population of the **Orange Leaf-nosed Bat**, which may prove to be a separate species. It and the **Ghost Bat** have strongholds in mines and adits in the eastern Pilbara near Marble Bar; **Common Sheath-tailed** and **Inland Cave Bats** are also common in this area. The region also shares numerous species with inland Australia, including **Mulgara**, **Woolley's** and **Rory's False Antechinuses**, **Stripe-faced**, **Ooldea** and **Lesser Hairy-footed Dunnarts**, the **Greater Bilby** and rodents such as the **Spinifex Hopping-mouse**, **Desert Mouse** and **Sandy Inland Mouse**. The biological boundaries are indistinct, and isolated Pilbara populations of several species (the **Long-tailed Dunnart**, **Common Sheath-tailed Bat**, **Chocolate Wattled Bat**, **Northern Long-eared Bat**, **Common Rock-rat** and the **Northern Short-tailed Mouse**, **Delicate Mouse** and **Western Chestnut Mouse**) are also found in the Kimberley to the north. Offshore, Barrow I. (7.18) is an important refuge for endangered marsupials that were formerly widespread here and elsewhere on the mainland. Unless you are lucky enough to visit Barrow I., few of the smaller Pilbara mammals will be encountered unless you participate in surveys. However, **Euros** are common in this rocky landscape and **Red Kangaroos** are usually easy to see roadside along the main highways.

Roughly speaking, the Pilbara starts at the Ashburton River as you head north and finishes at the deGrey River, about 500 km to the north-east, stretching inland to the Hamersley Ranges and petering out to the east in the Little Sandy Desert. There are some superb reserves, such as Millstream-Chichester and Karajini NPs, and Meentheena CP; the main towns are Onslow, Karratha and Port Hedland. Note that

WATCHING BATS IN WESTERN AUSTRALIA

Megabat diversity is comprised of only three species in WA, all restricted to the coastal and subcoastal tropics. Neither **Black** nor **Little Red Flying Foxes** will be seen south of about Shark Bay, but both are relatively common along most of the coast northward from the Pilbara. **Black Flying Foxes**, for example, can be seen around Broome township and roost in mangroves nearby; **Little Reds** roost at Tunnel Creek NP (7.21). In WA the **Least Blossom Bat** occurs only in the Kimberley, where it is common on the Mitchell Plateau (7.21) and can be spotlighted at, for example, flowering tea-trees.

Of the state's 34 microbat species, four – the **Mangrove Freetail, South-western Freetail, Yellow-lipped Cave Bat** and **Western False Pipistrelle** – are endemic. A population of **Orange Leaf-nosed Bat** isolated in the Pilbara may prove to be a separate species. Diversity is highest in the tropics, particularly the Kimberley, where 22 species occur. Some of these, such as the **Yellow-bellied Sheath-tailed Bat, Gould's Wattled Bat** and **Lesser Long-eared Bat**, could also be seen almost anywhere in the state. Most, however, are restricted to the Kimberley or have a more general distribution across northern Australia. Among them are the **Ghost Bat**, which in WA occurs only in the Kimberley and Pilbara (a colony in the Gibson Desert is now extinct). **Ghost Bats** and **Orange Leaf-nosed Bats** have similar roosting requirements and both frequent mines south-east of Marble Bar in the Pilbara (**Common Sheath-tailed** and **Inland Cave Bats** also inhabit mines in this area). Other species that roost mainly in caves include the endemic **Yellow-lipped Cave Bat**, plus **Orange, Dusky** and **Northern Leaf-nosed Bats**, the **Common Sheath-tailed Bat**, the **Northern Cave Bat** and **Common Bentwing Bats**. Some of these also roost in crevices and among boulder piles; bats that more commonly roost under bark, for example, may also use overhangs and boulder piles as roosts in the rocky Kimberley landscape. The endemic **North-western Freetail Bat** and **Mangrove Pipistrelle** are confined mainly to mangroves. Others may roost under bark, in old buildings, among boulder piles and in dense vegetation, such as the dried fronds that skirt *Pandanus* palms. These include the **Northern Freetail Bat, Hoary Wattled Bat, Large-footed Myotis, Little** and **Northern Broad-nosed Bats**, and **Arnhem, Northern** and **Pygmy Long-eared Bats**. Note: Be extremely wary among waterside vegetation (that includes mangroves) – Saltwater Crocodiles are common in parts of the Kimberley and are extremely dangerous.

The arid zone occupies two-thirds of WA but even the vast central deserts support a good bat diversity that includes the **Hill's Sheath-tailed Bat, Inland Freetail Bat, Inland Cave, Inland Forest** and **Inland Broad-nosed Bats**. Roosts in these flat, generally treeless landscapes are at a premium; check derelict buildings and other likely sites for signs of bat activity. Murra-el-elevyn Cave on the Nullarbor Plain is a major maternity roost for **Chocolate Wattled Bats**.

The cool, wet south-west corner supports a comparatively poor bat fauna. Indeed, the range of the endemic **Western False Pipistrelle** may have shrunk and its stronghold appears to be dense forests south of Donnybrook and east to Albany. Apart from the other south-western microbat endemic, the **South-western Freetail Bat**, the only species that occur here are the **White-striped Freetail Bat**, **Gould's** and **Chocolate Wattled Bats** (the latter has a roost at Quininup Lake Cave), the **Southern Forest Bat**, and **Lesser**, **Gould's** and **Greater Long-eared Bats**. The northern Jarrah forests are reputed to have the south-west's richest microbat faunas.

this is an intensely hot environment most of the time; always carry adequate water and take safety precautions commensurate with outback travel. A 4WD is recommended for travel anywhere off the main highways, and essential for visiting some national parks.

7.16 EXMOUTH AREA

Highlights: **Indo-Pacific Humpback Dolphin, Bottlenose Dolphin, Humpback Whale**

Other possibilities: **Red Kangaroo, Euro, Killer Whale, Dugong**

Ningaloo MP protects a fringing coral reef west of the Cape Range Peninsula with excellent diving and snorkelling, Whale Sharks and Manta Rays, plus a resident population of about 1000 **Dugongs** and migrating **Humpback Whales** in season. Boat operators take whale-watchers out between September and November. A total of 16 cetacean species have been recorded in these waters, including **Blue Whales**, and **Indo-Pacific Humpback** and **Bottlenose Dolphins**. Winter sightings of **Killer Whales** have become more common in recent years, commensurate with the gradual increase in **Humpback** numbers in the area. Coral Bay is the town nearest the action.

Exmouth Gulf, on the eastern side of the peninsula, is a major resting point for **Humpback Whales** on their southward migration. A high percentage of the whales are cows and this is possibly a calving area; migration peaks in early to mid-September and most have departed by November. **Indo-Pacific Humpback Dolphins** also occur off Exmouth (check from the boat ramps north along the peninsula, such as Bundegi), especially at the tip of North West Cape, and sometimes in mixed herds with **Bottlenose Dolphins**. **Red Kangaroos** and **Euros** are common in Cape Range NP, and **Black-footed Rock Wallabies** can be seen on boat trips on Yardie Gorge near Exmouth. The **Djoongari** (**Shark Bay Mouse**) has been reintroduced to Doole I.

7.17 BURRUP PENINSULA AND DAMPIER ARCHIPELAGO

Highlights: **Northern Quoll, Rothschild's Rock Wallaby**

Other possibilities: **Indo-Pacific Humpback Dolphin, Indo-Pacific Bottlenose Dolphin**

Karratha is a mining service town 645 km north of Carnarvon. Immediately to its north is the rocky Burrup Peninsula (part of which is in the Murujuga NP) and, on its seaward side, the Dampier Archipelago. Both are strongholds for the **Rothschild's Rock Wallaby**, a species restricted to the Pilbara area and which thrives among the piles of boulders. They are harder to find on the peninsula but abundant in the archipelago, especially on East and West Lewis Is., and on Enderby I. To get there you'll obviously need a boat, so bring your own, hire one or find a local who will ferry you out there. A local operator should be able to point you towards some rock wallabies, but they are generally common and approachable, especially in the cooler parts of the day. **Northern Quolls** occur on the islands, and the **Delicate Mouse, Little Red Kaluta, Pilbara Ningaui** and **Rory's False Antechinus** have also been recorded. **Bottlenose** and **Indo-Pacific Humpback Dolphins** occur among the islands, and the **Australian Snubfin Dolphin** has been reported. **Humpback Whales** pass through the archipelago and offshore in July and August as they head north, and again in August and September as they swim south.

South-east of Karratha, Millstream-Chichester NP has some scenic gorges and a chance to see an attractive red form of the **Euro** plus **Echidnas**; **Northern Quolls** are periodically seen at Python Pool, accessible along a scenic walking trail. Among the 36 mammal species recorded in the park are the Pilbara endemics **Little Red Kaluta, Rory's False Antechinus** and **Pilbara Pebble-mouse**. Offshore between Karratha and Port Hedland, **Black-flanked Rock Wallabies** occur at Depuch I. **Inland Cave Bats** roost at Tommy Lee Mine about 35 km along Hamersley Iron road, and also at Hearson's Cove.

7.18 BARROW ISLAND

Highlights: **Golden Bandicoot (ssp. *barrowensis*), Common Brushtail Possum (ssp. *arnhememsis*), Burrowing Bettong (Boodie), Spectacled Hare-wallaby, Barrow Island Euro (ssp. *isabellinus*), Common Rock-rat**

Other possibilities: **Black-flanked Rock Wallaby, Djoongarri (Shark Bay Mouse), Dugong**

Western Australia's second largest island is an unspoilt wildlife haven lying some 70 km offshore from the Pilbara coast. Thanks to isolation and strict visitor control, Barrow I. is completely free of feral animals (even the House Mouse) and the only exotics are some weeds growing near the airport. It supports good populations of

13 non-marine mammals, including several unique subspecies and others which elsewhere survive on only a few islands. Several mammal species are easy to see; most abundant is the **Golden Bandicoot**, which numbers 40 000–60 000, some of which run around the compound and accommodation blocks. **Boodies** (**Burrowing Bettongs**) are also abundant – some 5000 inhabit the island – and can usually be seen by spotlighting along roads. Some of Barrow's 10 000 **Spectacled Hare-wallabies** graze on the sports oval near camp; during the day they remain in the shelter of dense clumps of spinifex that are the dominant vegetation on the island. The northern subspecies *arnhemensis* of **Common Brushtail Possum** is regularly seen around camp, although this is probably the only part of the Pilbara where it is still common. During the day it shelters under termite mounds, and in caves and crevices among limestone outcrops. **Barrow Island Euros** (also known locally as biggadas) are easy to approach, and often lie in shade around work areas and beside vehicles. Interestingly, Euros sometimes dig for moisture at soaks on Barrow's west coast, although apparently most get their requirements from licking dew off plants on this nearly waterless island. **Common Rock-rats** can be seen by spotlighting and also visit buildings. Some 120–160 **Black-flanked Rock Wallabies** live on Barrow I., mainly on cliffs and boulder piles on the western side of the island (where they bask in the late afternoon) but also behind pumping station Q21.

Small mammals include a Barrow race of the **Western Chestnut Mouse**, which is widespread here, the **Shark Bay Mouse** and unnamed species of *Antechinus* and *Pseudantechinus* (probably *roryi*). The **Water Rat** also occurs in the mangroves, and **Common Sheath-tailed** and **Inland Cave Bats** roost in crevices and small caves. **Dugongs** graze in Bandicoot Bay at the southern end of the island and **Bryde's Whale** has been recorded off the south coast. **Spinner Dolphins** are regular in these waters. Appropriately enough, **Boodies** have been reintroduced to Boodie I., a small island off the southern end of Barrow.

Barrow Island is one of Australia's unspoilt gems and will probably stay that way as long as the gas giant running the extraction plant keeps up its excellent environmental record. Unfortunately, access is almost impossible and ironically probably easier for an unskilled labourer than for a bona fide naturalist. If you are lucky enough to visit as part of a research team, savour the experience because you will be part of an exclusive club.

7.19 MONTEBELLO ISLANDS

Highlights: **Golden Bandicoot, Burrowing Bettong (Boodie), Spectacled Hare-wallaby**

Other possibilities: **Mala, Djoongari (Shark Bay Mouse), Australian Snubfin Dolphin**

The arid archipelago 30 km north of Barrow I. was once considered so remote it was used for nuclear tests by the British government. Like Barrow I., the Montebellos are composed of low-lying limestone with a covering of spinifex grassland; there are some mangroves on Hermite I., the largest of the group, and numerous shallow lagoons throughout the islands. **Spectacled Hare-wallabies** and **Golden Bandicoots** occurred naturally on Hermite and possibly Trimouille I. as well. The bombs weren't enough to kill them off but eventually they succumbed to feral Cats; **Water Rats** also formerly occurred. After an intense feral Cat and rat eradication program, the WA conservation department airlifted **Golden Bandicoots**, **Boodies**, **Spectacled Hare-wallabies** and **Common Brushtail Possums** from Barrow I. to repopulate Hermite. **Malas** caught in the Tanami Desert were set free on Trimouille in the 1990s as an insurance population and have become established. The **Shark Bay Mouse** has also been successfully reintroduced to North West I.

Dugongs occur in these waters and **Humpback Whales** are regular visitors during June and July as they head north and in August and September on their way south. Other cetaceans recorded have included **Minke**, **Bryde's**, **Sperm**, **Short-flippered Pilot**, **Killer** and **False Killer Whales**, as well as **Common**, **Striped** and **Bottlenose Dolphins**. **Australian Snubfin Dolphins** have been reported. Unlike Barrow, it is possible to visit the Montebellos by boat and camping is permitted on Hermite and several other islands (note that low-level radiation is still present on parts of Trimouille and some other islands in the north of the group). All visitors must be self-sufficient. The nearest port is Dampier, about 120 km to the east.

D THE KIMBERLEY

Highlights: **Northern Quoll**, **Brush-tailed Phascogale (ssp. *pirata*)**, **Kaluta**, **Kultarr**, **Scaly-tailed Possum**, **Rock Ringtail**, **Common Brushtail Possum (ssp. *arnhemensis*)**, **Monjon**, **Nabarlek**, **Mangrove Freetail Bat**, **Yellow-lipped Cave Bat**, **Golden-backed Tree-rat**, **Common Rock-rat**, **Kimberley Rock-rat**

Other possibilities: **Ningbing False Antechinus**, **Central Pebble-mouse**

The Kimberley is a huge area, twice the size of Victoria, famous for its uplifted plateaus of eroded sandstone, grand scenery and spectacular waterfalls. It is awash in the wet season and intensely hot during the Dry, and features extraordinary biodiversity including several endemic mammals, such as the **Wyulda** (or **Scaly-tailed Possum**), **Monjon**, **Yellow-lipped Cave Bat** and **Kimberley Rock-rat**, and near-endemics (the **Ningbing False Antechinus**, **Butler's Dunnart**, **Nabarlek** and **Central Pebble-mouse**). The mammal fauna is still relatively intact, especially as the Cane Toad has yet to penetrate the whole region, and indeed the North Kimberley has not suffered any mammal extinctions to date. Several species now rare elsewhere are still common in places; these include the **Northern Quoll**, **Brush-tailed Phascogale**, **Golden Bandicoot**, **Golden-backed Tree-rat** and **Brush-tailed Rabbit-rat**, and a visit to this near-pristine region would be your best way of enjoying some of these species.

The entire coastline is heavily eroded and indented, and hundreds of offshore islands are accessible only by boat; some are large enough to hold significant intact populations of mammals such as the **Northern Quoll**, **Common Rock-rat**, **Water Rat**, **Golden-backed Tree-rat**, **Scaly tailed Possum** and **Golden Bandicoot**. A significant percentage of WA's **Humpback Whale** population – an estimated 20 000 – reaches the Kimberley coast on its annual northward migration. They congregate off Dampier Peninsula, at Middle Lagoon and Pender Bay, and further north at Camden Sound, which is an important calving area where about 1000 young are born each year. You would probably require a boat to reach some of these locations. **Blue Whales** pass offshore in deeper reaches as they head to feeding areas in the Timor Sea; **Sperm Whales** and **Cuvier's Beaked Whales** are other deep-water species that occur off the Kimberley Coast. Annual birdwatching trips to Ashmore Reef in the Timor Sea regularly log interesting cetacean species, including the **Rough-toothed Dolphin**, and would be worth joining to visit an area that sees few travellers (see Chapter 10).

Most of the Kimberley is untracked and uninhabited, and unless you join a tour the best way to visit is on a well-equipped expedition in a 4WD. A long-wheel-base, high-clearance vehicle, such as a Toyota LandCruiser or similar, is essential; boutique SUVs are *not* suitable for this trip. Suitable vehicles and equipment can be hired in Broome, the major starting point for most trips. However, buying a good second-hand 4WD may work out just as cheap: vehicle hire costs are enormous, petrol is very expensive along the way and insurance is onerous. You must be properly equipped with adequate water and food, extra tyres and emergency supplies. October to March are the wettest months and parts of the Gibb River Road (7.21) can be impassable after rain. Of all the major mammal-watching destinations in Australia, the Kimberley is the most remote and difficult to get to. But a journey to this amazing landscape will be unforgettable and you will have the privilege of seeing wildlife in a virtually pristine landscape.

Heading east from Derby, Windjana Gorge and Tunnel Creek are worthwhile stops. Most people head north after Gibb River itself for the Mitchell Plateau and its scenic attractions. From there you'll have to retrace your footsteps to Derby or continue east to Kununurra. The small town of Kalumburu on the north Kimberley coast sees few visitors, but **Golden-backed Tree-rats** still apparently live in roofs here and this area was where the Kimberley population of **Butler's Dunnart** was discovered in the 1960s (remember this is Aboriginal land and permission may be necessary to visit). Note that an isolated population of the **Black-footed Rock Wallaby** inhabits sedimentary ranges with low, flat-topped hills and scree slopes in the Edgar, Erskine and possibly Grant Ranges of the West Kimberley.

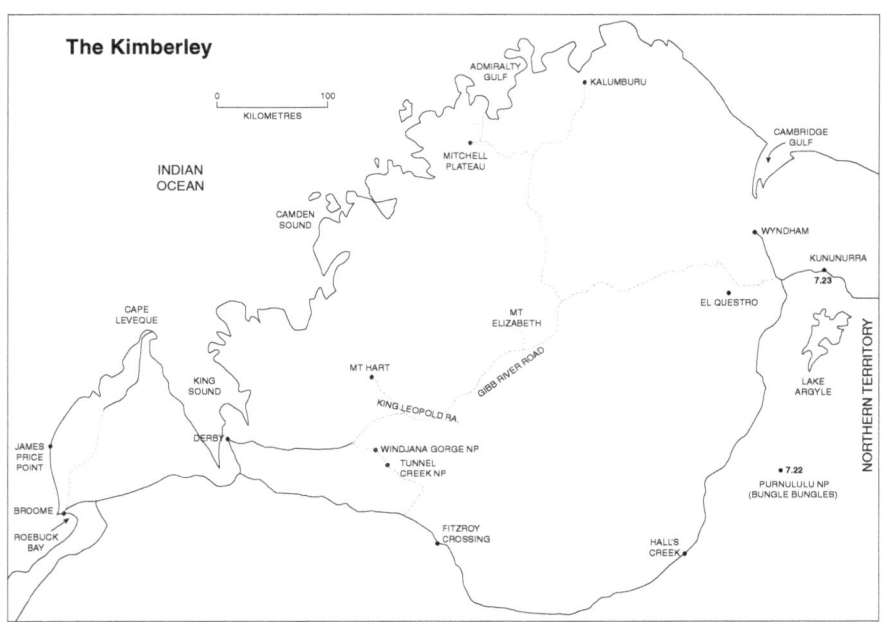

The AWC has taken a big interest in the Kimberley recently. **Mornington Sanctuary** is an outstanding area where domestic livestock have been removed with amazing benefits to small mammals: the **Western Chestnut Mouse**, **Pale Field-rat**, **Delicate Mouse**, **Common Rock-rat**, **Common Planigale**, **Long-tailed Planigale** and **Northern Short-tailed Mouse** have all bounced back within a short period of destocking. The property also supports **Northern Quolls** and **Rock Ringtail Possums**. Mornington is contiguous with two other AWC properties and near another, Artesian Range Wildlife Sanctuary.

7.20 BROOME

Key species: **Greater Bilby, Northern Nailtail Wallaby, Black Flying Fox, Australian Snubfin Dolphin**

Other possibilities: **Agile Wallaby, Long-beaked Bottlenose Dolphin, 'Dwarf' Spinner Dolphin, Humpback Whale, Dugong**

This popular tourist destination is a bit of an oasis after a long, hot drive and makes the ideal base for exploration of the Kimberley proper. **Long-beaked Bottlenose Dolphins** could be seen anywhere near town, including popular Cable Beach and further south at Eco Beach. The '**Dwarf**' subspecies of **Spinner Dolphin** *Stenella* *longirostris roseiventris* has also been reported in the Cable Beach area, although you would probably have to go further offshore by boat to see some. **Australian Snubfin Dolphins** are occasionally reported off Cable Beach, and Roebuck Bay to the south seems to be an important site for this species. Broome Bird Observatory, south of town on the Crab Creek Rd, is a good spot for **Snubfins**. They are normally seen down the bay a little way at the mouth of Crab Creek (when the tide is in), where low cliffs provide vantage points, but could appear near the observatory itself. For best results, take a small boat out into the mangroves at high tide. This would also be the best way to see **Dugongs**, which graze on seagrass beds in Roebuck Bay. **Northern Nailtail Wallabies** graze on the plains near the bird observatory, especially at Lake Eda; observatory staff can probably arrange a visit to the area, which is a popular birding site. **Agile Wallabies** live in the Pindan scrub and **Northern Brushtail Possums** occur around Cable Beach Resort. **Black Flying Foxes** and **Least Blossom Bats** roost in the mangroves close to the town centre; the latter are attracted to Apple Mangrove flowers. Microbats recorded in the Crab Creek area include the **Yellow-bellied Sheath-tailed Bat**, **Northern** and **North-western Freetail Bats**, **Gould's Wattled Bat**, **Little Broad-nosed Bat**, **Mangrove Pipistrelle** and **Arnhem Long-eared Bat**.

The Golden-backed Tree-rat was formerly found in Broome but sadly now appears to have been extirpated. However, the Broome area is good for **Bilbies** and they have been seen along the dirt road to Dampier Downs: turn off the Great Northern Hwy about 25 km south of Roebuck Plains roadhouse; after 65 km bear right at a fork – **Bilbies** have been seen 6–10 km after the fork, but only at night (a 4WD will be necessary for this trip). **Bilbies** also occur at James Price Point, a good headland for watching **Humpback Whales** between June and November, including cow–calf pairs on southward migration (peaking in August and September). James Price Point is about 50 km north of Broome (4WD recommended). Another good spot for **Humpbacks** is Lombadina, 200 km north of Broome on the road to Cape Leveque, but the whole Kimberley coastline north of Broome hosts a major concentration of **Humpbacks** annually, and especially off Pender Bay, the Buccaneer Archipelago and Camden Sound.

7.21 GIBB RIVER ROAD AND MITCHELL PLATEAU

Highlights: **Echidna, Northern Quoll, Sugar Glider, Agile Wallaby, Euro, Antilopine Wallaroo, Short-eared Rock Wallaby, Northern Nailtail Wallaby, Black Flying Fox, Little Red Flying Fox, Dingo, Golden-backed Tree-rat, Grassland Melomys**

Other possibilities: **Brush-tailed Phascogale, Rock Ringtail Possum, Ghost Bat, Orange Horseshoe Bat, Yellow-lipped Cave Bat**

The Gibb River Road provides the main access to the Kimberley proper, connecting Derby with Kununurra about 700 km to the east. 'Doing' the Gibb River Road is almost a rite of passage for 4WD enthusiasts. Widespread species that could be encountered anywhere along the way include the **Echidna**, **Agile Wallaby**, **Northern Nailtail Wallaby** and **Dingo**. Most Kimberley visitors head for the Mitchell Plateau, a spectacular region of gorges and waterfalls, with relict palm forests and patches of rainforest. It is an outstanding area and one of the best mammal-watching sites in Australia, with some 50 species recorded and many sought-after species still common. Although more and more people travel this route every year, it is still an adventure and not to be attempted without adequate preparation, equipment and precautions. No visit will be for less than a week anyway and the longer you can spend here, the greater the wildlife-watching rewards. There are several popular places to stay en route.

Five species of bat live in Tunnel Creek NP, a 750-m-long volcanic tube that makes a worthwhile detour south of the Gibb River Road. **Orange Horseshoe Bats** roost away from other species, **Ghost Bats** roost on higher ledges, the rare **Yellow-lipped Cave Bat** occurs and **Little Red Flying Foxes** roost where the tunnel roof has collapsed. **Rock Ringtail Possums** occur here, attracted to Rock Figs – stake some out during the day and return at night.

While crossing the King Leopold Ranges watch for **Euros** on rocky hillsides and **Antilopine Wallaroos**, which are common in the Kimberley generally; **Short-eared Rock Wallabies** are plentiful in suitable habitat, often grazing away from rocks at dawn or dusk; **Agile Wallabies** are also common and tend to be more diurnal. **Golden-backed Tree-rats** occur at Silent Grove near Bell Gorge; other small animals include the **Stripe-faced Dunnart**, **Long-tailed Planigale** and, on grassy plains, **Delicate Mouse**, **Western Chestnut Mouse** and **Pale Field-rat**. Flying foxes occur at Mt Barnett Gorge in paperbarks.

Mt Hart Homestead has a pleasant campground about 50 km north of the Gibb River Road among the King Leopold Ranges NP. **Northern Quolls** and **Golden-backed Tree-rats** occur in the garden; **Sugar Gliders** and **Black Flying Foxes** can be seen around the orchard, **Northern Nailtail** and **Agile Wallabies** near the airstrip. The **Western Chestnut Mouse** has been seen along the creek.

Bachsten's Creek is a rough 140 km along the Munja Track from Mt Elizabeth Station. Here **Euros**, **Short-eared Rock Wallabies** and **Sugar Gliders** are common around the campground. **Monjons** and **Kimberley Rock-rats** occur on the ridge immediately behind the campsite and across the river. The **Northern Quoll**, **Ningbing False Antechinus** and **Rock Ringtail** also apparently occur here. **Northern Nailtail Wallabies** occur at Drysdale River Station.

The Mitchell Plateau itself has several major attractions and key mammal species, such as the **Scaly-tailed Possum**, **Monjon** and **Golden-backed Tree-rat**, are probably best sought here. Little Mertens' Falls is usually the first stop. **Golden-backed Tree-rats** occur between the campsite and the falls. **Monjons** can usually be seen near the falls themselves and frequent jumbled sandstone blocks where they can dart into cover if startled. **Wyuldas** inhabit vine thickets and rainforest halfway along the trail to the falls; they are secretive, and tend not to emerge until well after dark. They are partial to Sandstone Cocky Apples, so if you can identify one with fruit and flowers near likely-looking habitat it would be worth staking out for this sometimes elusive animal. Note that Wyuldas have a strong odour – look for traces such as droppings and if one is nearby, say in a crevice or tree hollow, you should be able to smell it! **Northern Quolls** occur around the campground and **Kimberley Rock-rats** frequent scree and boulder piles. **Black Flying Foxes** are common, and smaller species that also occur include the **Ningbing False Antechinus**, **Pale Field-rat** and **Grassland Melomys**. Beyond the falls is a region of hummock grassland and *Acacia* woodland on sandstone with pockets of monsoon vine forest: the **Golden Bandicoot, Monjon, Western Chestnut Mouse, Kimberley Rock-rat, Scaly-tailed Possum** and **Least Blossom Bat** have all been reported in this area.

For many, Mitchell Falls marks the end of a long trip and the turning back point. It is an outstanding scenic area, but intense heat makes wildlife secretive during the day. **Euros** occur in the car park and **Northern Quolls** occur around the campground and near the falls themselves. The **Brush-tailed Phascogale** is becoming scarce but has also been seen near the campground in recent years. **Monjons** emerge from shelter in the late afternoon and at dusk, and can be spotlighted after dark. **Golden-backed Tree-rats** are typically found in vine thickets; and have also recently been seen near the rangers' camp. **Brush-tailed Rabbit-rats** are also still relatively

GIANT ECHIDNAS IN AUSTRALIA?

The **Short-beaked Echidna** is a true survivor, found in almost every habitat all over Australia. Its only living relatives are restricted to the great island of New Guinea to the north, although fossil evidence indicates that giant echidnas, weighing up to 10 kg and measuring a metre in length, roamed northern Australia until at least the arrival of humans to the continent. Rock art that clearly depicts these animals has been dated at 5000 years old, but this and many other giant species were wiped out by Aboriginal hunters before white settlement. Or so it was believed until recently: a growing school of thought now says a giant echidna that once inhabited the north-west may still do so. A previously overlooked specimen, collected in 1901 in the Kimberley, has been identified as the **Western Long-beaked Echidna** *Zaglossus bruijnii*, a species that today survives only in the western half of New Guinea. The fact that it was collected so recently and lives in such a remote part of the continent raises the exciting possibility that these animals may still survive on the Australian continent.

common at, for example, Lone Dingo, north of the main Mitchell Plateau, and at Surveyor's Pool. Other species that should be seen include the **Golden Bandicoot** and **Kimberley Rock-rat**. Look for flowering trees, such as Darwin Woollybutts, for **Least Blossom Bats** and **Black Flying Foxes**. **Common Rock-rats** also occur, and **Northern Leaf-nosed Bats** and **Common Sheath-tailed Bats** roost in crevices.

Recently the **Wyulda** was rediscovered in the Eastern Kimberley near the tourist resort at Emma Gorge on El Questro Station, near the Kununurra end of the Gibb River Road. **Northern Quolls**, **Short-eared Rock Wallabies** and **Common Rock-rats** also occur here.

7.22 PURNULULU (BUNGLE BUNGLES) NATIONAL PARK

Highlights: **Central Pebble-mouse, Western Chestnut Mouse**

This extraordinary and picturesque formation of eroded sandstone lies east of the Great Northern Hwy about 55 km south of Turkey Creek. The **Desert Mouse** and **Western Chestnut Mouse** have been studied here. The **Desert Mouse** lives in rocky country with a good spinifex cover, on which they have been recorded feeding during the day. The **Western Chestnut Mouse** burrows in flat, grassy areas and is strictly nocturnal. The **Stripe-faced Dunnart** also occurs and numerous microbats doubtless roost among the myriad crevices and canyons. Watch over permanent pools for the **Large-footed Myotis** fishing.

7.23 KUNUNURRA

Highlights: **Short-eared Rock Wallaby, Black Flying Fox, Little Red Flying Fox, Long-haired Rat**

Other possibilities: **Dingo, Northern Brown Bandicoot, Agile Wallaby**

Heading east, the last town before the NT border is Kununurra, which is the centre of a major irrigation scheme and marks the eastern extremity of the Kimberley. There is a small permanent population of **Long-haired Rats** here, a species otherwise found mainly in Queensland's Channel Country and on the Barkly Tablelands. Look for them in canefields near town: take Ivanhoe Rd, right on to Research Station Rd, bear left at a Y junction at the end and check canefields around there. The mammal fauna is less rich in this part of the Kimberley, but larger species include **Echidnas**, **Euros**, **Short-eared Rock Wallabies** (these can be seen at Rainbow Valley NP just outside the town and on Lake Argyle cruises), **Agile Wallabies**, **Northern Nailtails** (uncommon, but they occur in stony grasslands and among low undulating hills in the Lake Argyle area) and **Dingoes**. **Little Red Flying Foxes** occur in sometimes large camps and **Black Flying Foxes** roost in mangroves.

Kununurra is at the eastern end of the Gibb River Road, some 700 km east of Derby, and also on the Great Northern Hwy, which connects Broome with the NT. There are plenty of accommodation and eating options, vehicle, boat and equipment hire.

E INLAND WESTERN AUSTRALIA

The Pilbara and Kimberley are dwarfed by the true inland of WA, a largely untracked wilderness the size of a central Asian republic but almost uninhabited. The region encompasses several deserts, including the Little Sandy Desert, abutting the south-east Pilbara; Great Sandy and Gibson Deserts, traversed by the Canning Stock Route; the Great Victoria Desert straddling the WA–SA border north of the Nullarbor Plain; and the Nullarbor Plain itself. Borders between these great arid subdivisions are indistinct, and determined by variations in climate, topography, substrate and rainfall.

Large mammals that will most likely be encountered include the **Red Kangaroo** (fairly common on plains), **Euro** (north of the Nullarbor), **Western Grey Kangaroo** (southern Nullarbor and south-western WA only), **Dingo** (common and widespread) and **Echidna** (common and widespread, often in rocky areas). **Southern Hairy-nosed Wombats** occur on the Nullarbor Plain in the far east of the state; look for burrows along the Eyre Hwy. **Bilbies** occur in the Gibson Desert and have been reintroduced to Lorna Glen (7.25). The **Western Pygmy Possum** is the only possum that still occurs naturally and has been recorded in the Great Victoria Desert. **Common Brushtail Possums** formerly occurred further north and have also been reintroduced to Lorna Glen. There's a good chance of seeing feral **One-humped Camels**, for example on the Canning Stock Route.

To see any of the smaller desert mammals you will have to join a survey or expedition. Western Australia's deserts are rich in dasyurids, including a number of rare and little-known species, such as **Mulgara**, **Kultarr**, **Fat-tailed False Antechinus**, **Wongai** and **Mallee Ningauis**, and **Long-tailed**, **Little Long-tailed**, **Gilbert's**, **White-tailed**, **Hairy-footed** and **Lesser Hairy-footed Dunnarts**; as well as more widespread examples such as **Fat-tailed** and **Stripe-faced Dunnarts**. The rare **Sandhill Dunnart** is known from Queen Victoria Springs NR in the Great Victoria Desert (where the **Western Pygmy Possum**, **Desert Mouse** and **Mulgara** have also been recorded). Both **Southern** and **Northern Marsupial Moles** occur in WA deserts; most records are from the Great Sandy Desert. **Southern Marsupial Mole** has been recorded at Queen Victoria Spring in the Great Victoria Desert, and in the Gibson Desert.

Comparatively few rodents inhabit this vast region and, again, most won't be seen without trapping. The exceptions might be two species of hopping-mice: the **Spinifex Hopping-mouse** is widespread north of the Nullarbor and **Mitchell's Hopping-mouse** occurs on the Nullarbor and in arid south-western Australia. Look for tracks during the day on sand dunes and return at night to spotlight in suitable habitat. Other rodents in WA's central deserts include the **Forrest's Mouse** (eastern Gibson Desert), **Desert Mouse** (Great Sandy and Gibson Deserts), **Bolam's Mouse** (Great Victoria Desert) and **Sandy Inland Mouse** (widespread north of the Nullarbor).

Access to this area is by a few overland tracks, the Canning Stock Route probably being the best known of them. There are few settlements so travellers in these parts must be properly prepared for Outback travel.

7.24 EYRE BIRD OBSERVATORY

Highlights: **Western Pygmy Possum**

Possibly one of the most remote inhabited places on Earth is the Eyre Bird Observatory, a converted telegraph station on the edge of the Southern Ocean. **Western Pygmy Possums** are quite common in the mallee here, and use nest boxes put up by the wardens. Getting here requires a 4WD and time, so a stay of a few days is recommended. It's a beautiful, tranquil spot and the possums sometimes sleep or nest in the observatory buildings – ask the wardens for the latest sightings. Contact BirdLife Australia (www.birdlife.org.au) for information about visiting.

7.25 LORNA GLEN CONSERVATION RESERVE

Highlights: **Greater Bilby, Common Brushtail Possum**

Other possibilities: **Mulgara, Long-tailed Dunnart**

An ambitious reintroduction program has begun at Lorna Glen (known as Wiluna by local Aboriginals), a former pastoral lease in the north-east Goldfields acquired by the WA government. This Rangelands Restoration Project aims to reintroduce to Lorna Glen 11 mammal species that once lived in the region by 2020: the **Bilby, Common Brushtail Possum, Mala, Burrowing Bettong (Boodie), Golden Bandicoot, Western Barred Bandicoot, Numbat, Red-tailed Phascogale, Chuditch, Shark Bay Mouse** and **Pale Field-rat**. The **Mulgara** and **Long-tailed Dunnart** are known already from the property. **Common Brushtail Possums** and **Bilbies** have been reintroduced and appear to have bred. To date Mala re-establishment has failed as this species seems to be particularly susceptible to predation by feral Cats. Other than active management, it is unclear what plans the WA government has for this reserve once feral animals are under control and reintroduced species are better established. It may be possible to join a survey or volunteer for other tasks – check with the state government.

8. Northern Territory

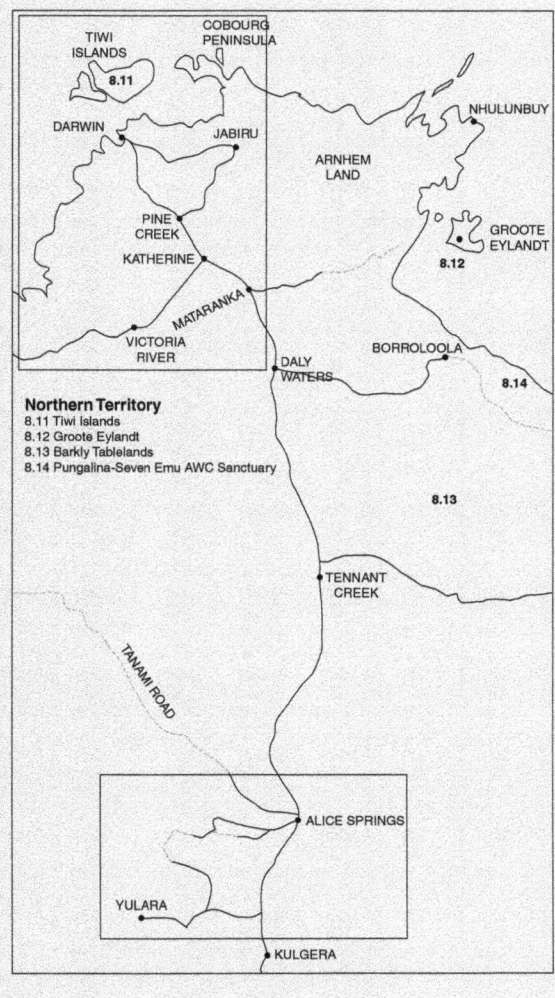

Northern Territory
8.11 Tiwi Islands
8.12 Groote Eylandt
8.13 Barkly Tablelands
8.14 Pungalina-Seven Emu AWC Sanctuary

Endemics: **Fawn Antechinus, Sandstone False Antechinus, Kakadu Dunnart, Black Wallaroo, Arnhem Sheath-tailed Bat, Northern Hopping-mouse, Arnhem Land Rock-rat, Carpentarian Rock-rat, Central Rock-rat, Calaby's Pebble-mound Mouse, Central Pebble-mouse, Dusky Rat**

Australia's Northern Territory can be roughly divided into two zones: a vast, arid inland that includes true deserts that grade into mulga and eucalypt woodlands in the north; and the Top End, the roughly rectangular land mass at the top of the Territory that juts into the Arafura Sea. Naturally there is an area of overlap and the boundaries have shifted over aeons of climatic variation. Not surprisingly, the biodiversity of both areas is impressive and each zone has one of Australia's most famous national parks: Kakadu in the Top End and Uluru–Kata Tjuta (Ayers Rock) near Alice Springs.

The Top End is comprised mainly of savannah woodland, drained by powerful rivers that flood for hundreds of square kilometres in the wet season (roughly December–March). Arnhem Land is a huge, elevated area of weathered sandstone on the eastern side of the Top End, with many distinct species and subspecies. The whole region has a high number of endemic mammals, including four dasyurids, the **Black Wallaroo**, **Arnhem Sheath-tailed Bat** and three rodents; many forms shared with the Kimberley Sandstone, such as the **Nabarlek** and **Short-eared Rock Wallaby**; others localised on the Barkly Tablelands or on islands; as well as many others found in similar habitats across much of tropical Australia. A number of inshore cetaceans can be seen and the **Dugong** is always a possibility around Darwin (no seal has ever been recorded in the Territory). The Top End is also a refuge for **Banteng**, wild cattle from Indonesia originally introduced for food that now make up a fully protected herd on the Cobourg Peninsula (8.04). The Top End offers good mammal-watching opportunities, despite the ravages of the introduced Cane Toad and a precipitous decline in several erstwhile common species for reasons unknown. Strong suits are the fauna associated with Arnhem Land 'stone country' in Kakadu NP and outlying sandstone areas such as Litchfield NP. The Territory also has high bat diversity but, aside from a few well-known roosts, you will need to accompany a researcher to locate most species.

The vast majority of inland mammals are small, nocturnal and difficult to see; many in fact are rare or endangered. Some notable exceptions include macropods such as the **Black-flanked Rock Wallaby**, **Red Kangaroo** and **Euro**; and rodents and dasyurids, such as the **Long-haired Rat**, **Plains Mouse** and **Kultarr**, that attain high populations in good seasons. Some, such as the enigmatic **Central Rock-rat** (the only non-tropical rock-rat), apparently vanish from the landscape in dry periods, only to reappear in times of plenty.

Wildlife-watching in the Territory is very seasonal. Summer temperatures (and flies) in the desert are usually unbearable during the day; winters feature cooler days with sometimes freezing nights. The Top End experiences distinct monsoonal wet and dry seasons, featuring high daytime temperatures but no rainfall in the Dry (roughly April–November), and oppressive humidity, high rainfall and flooding in the Wet, with regular cyclones that can cause widespread damage and loss of life. April to September is by far the best time to visit any part of the Territory, with clear skies, pleasant temperatures and little or no rainfall.

The Territory has two main hubs: Darwin in the Top End and, 1500 km to the south Alice Springs in the Red Centre, joined by a single road, the Stuart Hwy. Long distances are involved wherever you base yourself. Darwin is the point from which to start exploring the Top End and can be a good place to source a vehicle for exploration further afield in the Kimberley (see Chapter 7). Alice Springs is a good spot to begin searching for the arid zone species. Both are serviced by domestic air routes (Darwin is also an international entry point) and have hire cars, camping equipment for hire or sale, accommodation, supermarkets and eating options. The Territory is a popular tourist destination and key attractions can book out quickly, especially during school holidays. Fees apply at major parks; see www. parksandwildlife.nt.gov.au/parks for information on those run by the Territory government; the Kakadu and Uluru-Kata Tjuta fee structures can be found at the Australian government website, www.parksaustralia.gov.au.

SOME TERRITORY HIGHLIGHTS

- **Red Kangaroos** and reintroduced **Malas** against the magnificent backdrop of Uluru.
- **Kakadu National Park**, where many endemic mammals are common and easy to see.
- Umbrawarra Gorge, great for **Rock Ringtail Possums** and **Short-eared Rock Wallabies**.
- The nightly fly-out of **Ghost Bats** at Kohinoor adit near Pine Creek.
- **Black-footed Rock Wallabies** posing for photos at Heavitree Gap, Alice Springs.

A TOP END AND GULF COUNTRY

The Top End is one of Australia's special places for wildlife and 123 species of non-marine mammal occur here. Darwin is the Territory's only international hub, well served by direct flights from Denpasar (Bali), Singapore and Hong Kong, and by all mainland capitals. It is the only feasible base for exploring the Top End (unless you are already self-sufficient with a 4WD); the best (and cheapest) place to stock up on food, petrol and other supplies before venturing further afield. Darwin has a pleasant climate in the Dry (usually April–August), but is unbearably humid in the build-up (October–November) and *very* wet for much of the Wet, with periodic cyclones featuring flooding and dangerously high winds. All sorts of accommodation is available (sometimes at bargain rates during the Wet), but it is popular with holiday-makers and drifters alike, so cheap rooms and campgrounds fill up quickly, especially during school holidays. Vehicle hire options range from regular sedans to 4WDs and campervans. Be aware that there will be a daily mileage limit (usually 100 km per day), after which a fee will apply per kilometre (and travel around the Top End means a *lot* of kilometres); 2WD vehicles generally can't be insured for travel off surfaced roads (which precludes large parts of Kakadu NP). It is advisable to hire a 4WD campervan or other 4WD vehicle (with air-conditioning), as it will allow greater freedom to explore quieter reaches of the Top End. Those with a week or so to spare could do the Darwin–Kakadu NP–Pine Creek–Litchfield NP–Darwin triangle. This will give you a good cross-section of prime wildlife-watching spots. Plan your trip carefully – to see mammals you'll need to be at the best spots in the coolest part of the day, which means travelling when it's hottest. It is not advisable to drive after dark owing to the high risk of collision with large animals, such as cattle, horses, wild buffalos and macropods.

Unfortunately, the entire Top End has recently experienced a near wipeout of small carnivorous mammals, partly owing to the unchecked march of the introduced Cane Toad. Where several species such as Northern Quoll and Brush-tailed Phascogale were once common, they succumbed to toxins when they ate the Toads and are now very rare indeed. Note that you must never enter any waterways in the Top End unless signs specifically say it is safe to do so: Estuarine ('Saltwater') Crocodiles are very common around the entire coastline and for hundreds of kilometres inland. During the Wet they move long distances across floodplains and can end up in areas seemingly safe. These animals can be very large and are extremely dangerous. All warning signs should be heeded as fatalities occur regularly (2014 set something of a record, with four human deaths).

8.01 DARWIN AND ENVIRONS

Highlights: **Common Brushtail Possum (ssp. *arnhemensis*), Agile Wallaby, Black Flying Fox**

Other possibilities: **Least Blossom Bat, Common Bentwing Bat (ssp. *orianae*), Little Red Flying Fox, Black-footed Tree-rat, Indo-Pacific Humpback Dolphin, Bottlenose Dolphin, Australian Snubfin Dolphin, Dugong**

A few mammals can be seen around the city itself: the northern subspecies of **Common Brushtail Possum** is common in the Darwin Botanic Gardens – just walk through the park at night with a torch (flashlight) – and at East Point at the eastern end of the CBD; it would be worth taking the mangrove boardwalk at East Point after dark as these possums are known also to frequent mangroves. This subspecies is smaller, paler and more slender than its southern counterparts, and has been mooted as a potential split. **Agile Wallabies** usually graze at the edges of recreation fields at East Point at dawn and dusk. **Black-footed Tree-rats** used to be common and probably still hang on in remnant woodland; try spotlighting in Berrimah or Holmes Jungle (note that this is a hotspot for petty crime – carry anything of value with you and do not leave your car unlocked). This species is becoming hard to see on the mainland and its habit of turning away from spotlights makes detection even more difficult. **Northern Quolls** also used to occur on the city's outskirts at, for example, Charles Darwin NP, but have not been recorded in the area for some years.

Bats have fared rather better and Darwin has an excellent bat fauna. **Black Flying Foxes** could be encountered flying overhead almost anywhere at dusk. There's a roost of the northern subspecies of **Common Bentwing Bat** *M. s. orianae* (which has been mooted as a separate species) in a culvert on Lakeview Drive near Darwin University. Note that you must not enter this or any other waterways near Darwin unless signs specifically say it is safe to do so: Saltwater Crocodiles are common in Darwin Harbour and are extremely dangerous. **Northern Freetail Bats** have roosted under the main pier; they can sometimes be detected by their contact calls at roost, but it's a long pier – watch for a fly-out and then return the next day to look in the vicinity. **Least Blossom Bats** have been recorded in mangroves at Charles Darwin NP and in the botanic gardens, where they also roost. If you can coax a local bat expert to set up harp traps, other species that may be caught include the **Northern** and **Pygmy Long-eared Bats**, **Mangrove Pipistrelle**, **Gould's Wattled Bat**, **Northern Bentwing** and **Little** or **Northern Broad-nosed Bats**. Good places to go batting include Charles Darwin NP and Holmes Jungle Swamp.

A few **Dugongs** frequent reef flats near Channel I. in Darwin Harbour, and appear to be present in all months except possibly September–December. The best ways to see them would be from a boat or to scan from Channel Island Bridge – a rising tide is usually best. They also occur in Fogg Bay 60 km south-west of Darwin, where a boat would be the most feasible option for looking. Three dolphin species are resident in Darwin Harbour: **Indo-Pacific Humpback**, **Bottlenose** and **Australian Snubfin Dolphins** (see boxed text on p. 213 for more information). Larger species occur offshore (a **Sperm Whale** once washed up at Casuarina) but, owing to the Top End's rather flat coastal profile, it's difficult to find a vantage point for seawatching; try the pier, East Point and Channel Island Bridge.

About 30 km east of Darwin CBD, Howard Springs Nature Park has crocodile-free natural hot springs and good wildlife-viewing. **Agile Wallabies** are common on the lawns near the park entrance and along the trail that circles the pools. **Common Brushtail Possums** and **Northern Brown Bandicoots** could still be spotlighted here, and there are usually a few **Black** or **Little Red Flying Foxes** roosting in the woodlands. The **Northern Quoll** has also occurred here in times past.

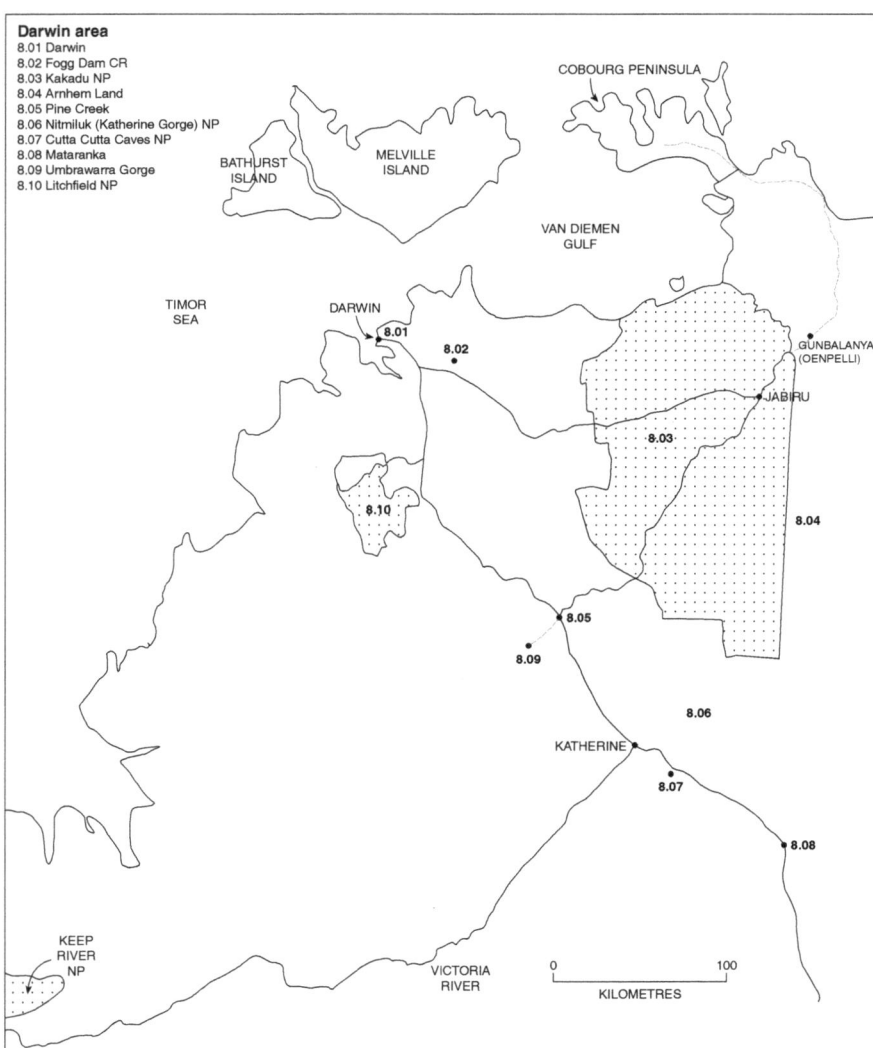

Darwin area
8.01 Darwin
8.02 Fogg Dam CR
8.03 Kakadu NP
8.04 Arnhem Land
8.05 Pine Creek
8.06 Nitmiluk (Katherine Gorge) NP
8.07 Cutta Cutta Caves NP
8.08 Mataranka
8.09 Umbrawarra Gorge
8.10 Litchfield NP

8.02 FOGG DAM CONSERVATION RESERVE

Highlights: **Black Flying Fox, Agile Wallaby, Water Rat, Dusky Rat**

Heading east to Kakadu, Fogg Dam makes a great detour for birdwatching during the day, and for seeing some mammals and reptiles at night. There's a large population of **Dusky Rats** here, although it fluctuates and is generally highest after the wet season. You should have no trouble spotlighting **Agile Wallabies** and **Black Flying Foxes**, and **Water Rats** are often seen crossing the causeway at night. Note that there are crocodiles in this park – you must never enter the water and do not linger by the water's edge. **Least Blossom Bats** feed on the melaleucas lining the causeway (listen for their distinctive calls). The **Red-cheeked Dunnart**, **Common Planigale** and **Northern Quoll** have all been recorded. The Fogg Dam turn-off is 67 km south-east of Darwin on the Arnhem Hwy. It is close enough to Darwin for a day trip and there is accommodation in the general area.

8.03 KAKADU NATIONAL PARK

Highlights: **Northern Brown Bandicoot, Sugar Glider, Rock Ringtail Possum, Short-eared Rock Wallaby, Black Wallaroo, Agile Wallaby, Antilopine Wallaroo, Black Flying Fox, Little Red Flying Fox, Common Rock-rat**

Other possibilities: **Northern Quoll, Brush-tailed Phascogale, Fawn Antechinus, Sandstone False Antechinus, Arnhem Rock-rat, Calaby's Pebble-mouse, Brush-tailed Rabbit-rat, Delicate Mouse, Pale Field-rat**

World Heritage–listed Kakadu NP encompasses near-pristine wilderness areas and several distinct habitats, including huge tracts of savannah woodland and giant weathered sandstone outliers of the Arnhem Land escarpment. It is justifiably famous for its birdlife and the park is also a hotspot for mammals. A few species are commonly seen with a little effort and several others can be seen with a bit of application. Timing is important – this is an intensely hot environment for much of the year, and most wildlife is active only at night or in the cooler parts of the day. For ease of planning, the park is divided here into broad representative habitats – floodplains, the sandstone escarpment and outliers that border the park's eastern boundary; and savannah woodland, which covers vast areas in between. There are many places to stay in the park; the main resorts have shops and petrol; and the various campgrounds range from luxurious to basic.

Some species occur in many habitats or use different habitats in different seasons. **Echidnas** and **Dingoes** could occur anywhere (for example, Dingoes are seen around Jabiru and both occur along the Kakadu Hwy). **Agile Wallabies** are the commonest macropod and are sometimes approachable around campgrounds and resorts; they will also be seen in woodland adjacent to sandstone outcrops, on floodplains and at many sites while driving through the park. Likewise, there is a good chance of seeing **Northern Brown Bandicoots** while driving to and from sites after dark. There are numerous camps of **Red** and **Black Flying Foxes**, and both could be encountered feeding wherever paperbarks and eucalypts are in flower.

Kakadu was invaded by the introduced, toxic Cane Toad in 2001–03. A number of formerly common predators, such as the **Northern Quoll**, **Brush-tailed Phascogale** and **Fawn Antechinus**, are now uncommon, possibly as a direct result of toad poisoning. However, several other species, such as the **Black-footed Tree-rat** and **Brush-tailed Rabbit-rat**, have apparently disappeared from the park, and others such as the **Northern Brown Bandicoot, Common Brushtail Possum** and **Pale Field-rat** are in severe decline for reasons unknown. Several large-scale studies have documented this unfortunate phenomenon and make grim reading. However, with the exception of the quoll, phascogale and tree-rat, individuals of these species are still recorded by good observers. The keys to success are persistence, diligence and good research; as well as putting in the effort of looking and a degree of luck.

Kakadu still has its share of feral animals, including feral **Pigs**, **Horses**, **Water Buffaloes** and **Cats**. Take great care if you must travel after dark, owing to the very real risk of collision with a large animal – help can be a long way off. The park entrance nearest to Darwin is about 150 km to the east. There are several tourist villages with fuel, shops, accommodation and campgrounds. The main town is Jabiru, where **Sugar Gliders** and **Black Flying Foxes** can be seen and **Antilopine Wallaroos** graze on the golf course. Jabiru was also formerly something of a stronghold for **Brush-tailed Phascogales**, and **Black-footed Tree-rats** and **Brush-tailed Rabbit-rats** also used to occur here.

8.03a Floodplains

Several broad rivers that meander north across the park into the Timor Sea burst their banks and flood across vast low-lying areas during the wet season. By the middle of the Dry the floodplains are covered in grass and small animals retreat into cracks in the soil to escape the heat. This habitat sees the most visitors and there are several areas where you can get a good feel for it. Heading east on the Arnhem Hwy you'll cross the South Alligator floodplain first, stretching for several kilometres either side of the South Alligator River. **Dusky Rats** inhabit this black-soil plain during the Dry; try spotlighting for them around Mamukala wetland. As floodwaters rise they abandon their cracked soil sanctuary and seek higher ground; during the height of the Wet they may be seen sheltering in the tops of trees and bushes! **Fawn Antechinus** formerly inhabited the woodlands closer to the river itself, although it now appears to be rare. **Agile Wallabies** are common on these grasslands and **Antilopine Wallaroos** may be seen away from the edge of the floodplains, crossing the highway at sites such as Gimbat. Iligadjarr is a walk where **Agile Wallabies** are common, and there are good populations of **Water Rat**, **Dusky Rat** and **Grassland Melomys**. **Northern Brown Bandicoots** could be seen crossing roads at night and foraging around tourist complexes. The **Water Mouse** is known from the South Alligator River area and a few other sites, but don't go looking for it among mangroves, its main habitat, because of the very real risk from crocodiles. **Dingoes** may be encountered in many areas, and frequently hunt on floodplains. Note that the daily cruises at Yellow Water are worthwhile at any time of year, though few mammals are usually seen; these generally include only **Agile Wallabies** plus feral **Horses** and **Pigs**.

8.03b Sandstone escarpment and outliers

The Arnhem Land Plateau towers above the woodlands and floodplains, and forms a spectacular backdrop to the eastern edge of Kakadu. It is a vast, dissected landscape of sandstone outcrops and gorges, known locally as 'stone country', and features many endemic forms of wildlife. Several sites are high on every visitor's list for their galleries of Indigenous rock art, as well as waterfalls and stunning scenery, which can make them crowded at times.

Nourlangie Rock is one of the best sites to look for **Black Wallaroo**, which is endemic to the stone country. It is at times easily seen in the early morning and late afternoon at, for example Anbangbang, Mirrai and Gunnwardewarde Lookouts, where individuals have become somewhat used to tourists; at other times this animal can be retiring and elusive. Best results are usually to be had in the pre-dawn cool and late in the day; in hot conditions it typically shelters under overhangs and boulders (where it is well camouflaged!). The Barrk Sandstone Walk is also good for **Black Wallaroos**, as well as **Short-eared Rock Wallabies** and **Euros**. Note that this walk is long and strenuous – start early and take adequate water and snacks. And keep an eye out for **Troughton's Sheath-tailed Bats**, which roost in crevices and among boulder piles.

Just south-west of Nourlangie is an outlier, formerly known as Little Nourlangie, where a pioneering study on Kakadu's small mammals recorded 18 terrestrial species. This may be a more productive site than Nourlangie itself, which attracts the vast majority of visitors. **Black Wallaroo, Euro** and **Short-eared Rock Wallaby** occur in the rocky environs, though Black Wallaroo is more common at Nourlangie; **Euros** and **Agile Wallabies** drink at nearby Anbangbang Billabong at sunset (**Orange Horseshoe-bats** and **Ghost Bats** shelter in rocky areas but hunt over the billabong at night). **Rock Ringtails** and **Echidnas** also occur at this site, though neither is commonly seen. Smaller species known from the rock itself include both **Common** and **Arnhem Rock-rats**; in the field they can be distinguished (with practice) by the Common's smaller size, browner coloration and more naked tail. The two also have slightly differing habitat preferences: the Arnhem Rock-rat is restricted to patches with large sandstone boulders, or escarpment with fissures and cracks; especially where they adjoin monsoon forest along gullies and creeks. **Sandstone False Antechinuses** have also been recorded and **Northern Quolls** were formerly common at this site.

Ubirr Rock is a very good site for **Short-eared Rock Wallabies**, which sometimes hang around the Main Gallery (the first art gallery), even during the heat of the day, seemingly oblivious to tourists. They are also sometimes seen at the top of the rock where the guides hold evening talks (at sunset this makes a magical site to take in the adjacent floodplain: the fly-out of **Black Flying Foxes** from distant forest patches to the accompaniment of howling **Dingoes** is an experience not to be missed). **Common Rock-rat**, **Sandstone False Antechinus** and **Ghost Bats** occur here at night, after the crowds have gone, and **Northern Quolls** formerly occurred. Watch for **Northern Brushtail Possums** along the entrance road.

Bardedjilidji is another excellent and easily accessible site for **Short-eared Rock Wallabies** and **Black Wallaroos. Rock Ringtail Possums** feed in trees adjacent to rocky areas. Other exciting species recorded here recently have included **Sandstone False Antechinus**, **Arnhem Rock-rat**, **Pale Field-rat** and **Fawn Antechinus**. **Least Blossom Bats** feed in flowering Darwin Woollybutts and **Black Flying Foxes** commonly wing overhead after sunset.

Gunlom (Waterfall Creek) in the south of the park is another great site with an excellent campground adjacent to the escarpment (bookings essential). A path leads to the top of the escarpment, where **Black Wallaroos** occur. The further you walk away from the crowds, the better your chances of seeing this and other endemic wildlife, but you'll have to start early. **Rock Ringtail Possums** could probably be spotlighted close to the campground without your having to scramble up the cliff in the dark (not advisable). The scree slopes in the vicinity may be your best shot at **Arnhem Rock-rat**. Koolpin is a secluded area deep in the south of Kakadu for which a special permit is needed to visit; this would be as good a place as any to look for the **Sandstone False Antechinus**.

Bats are also common in stone country, with a particularly high diversity in the southern part of the park. Look carefully in fissures, crevices, deep in jumbles of boulders and in overhangs. Kakadu remains the only known stronghold for the **Arnhem Leaf-nosed Bat**, which has been recorded from Deaf Adder Gorge and the upper South Alligator River.

There are many less well-known sites where some of the aforementioned species could also occur. For example, **Short-eared Rock Wallabies** occur at Plum Tree Creek on the way into Gunlom; the other main macropod prize, **Black Wallaroo**, has been recorded at Nourj Rock and on the Kurrundie Falls walk.

Note that the occurrence of the **Nabarlek**, a small rock wallaby of sandstone country, in the park is now doubtful; or it may just have been overlooked owing to its similarity to **Short-eared Rock Wallaby**. It is rumoured to persist at Jim Jim Falls and probably survives at Mt Borradaile (8.04) in Arnhem Land. **Brush-tailed Phascogales** used to be seen at Jim Jim ranger station. **Sugar Gliders** and **Pale Field-rats** occur at the Jim Jim campground (note that Jim Jim is accessible only to 4WD and then only usually near the end of the dry season).

8.03c Savannah woodland

The dominant habitat over most of Kakadu is savannah woodland – open eucalypt forest with a grassy understorey. Many of the campgrounds and visitor facilities are sited in this habitat, making it convenient to spotlight after dark or get up early and be among the wildlife action. In the past, species such as the **Northern Quoll**, **Brush-tailed Phascogale**, **Black-footed Tree-rat** and **Brush-tailed Rabbit-rat** were almost a given at some locations; several formerly good areas that now appear to be rather mammal-deficient could still be worth trying. **Antilopine Wallaroo** could be encountered almost anywhere in this habitat, for example along the Nourlangie entrance road.

Mardugal was formerly a prime site and still has plenty of **Agile Wallabies**, **Sugar Gliders** and possibly **Northern Brushtail Possums**. This was the last refuge in the park for the declining **Brush-tailed Rabbit-rat** and with luck it could still be spotlighted there, although **Black-footed Tree-rats** and **Brush-tailed Phascogales** appear to have vanished. Merl is another good spot, with the usual **Agile Wallabies** plus **Sugar Gliders** and (formerly) the **Northern Quoll**; the sandstone areas adjacent hold **Rock Ringtail Possums**, **Echidnas** and the **Sandstone False Antechinus**. **Ghost Bats** could be spotlighted around the campground. It would also be worth spotlighting even at busy sites, such as South Alligator and Cooinda, for **Northern Brown Bandicoots** and **Common Brushtail Possums**. The **Fawn Antechinus** has been seen along the Gum Tree Walk. **Northern Brown Bandicoots**, **Pale Field-rats**, **Black-footed Tree-rats** and **Northern Quolls** were all formerly common at Gunlom (Waterfall Creek); **Diadem Leaf-nosed Bats** have been spotlighted around the campground. The (unsealed) road into this area passes through an area of high biodiversity and is a known site for the **Calaby's Pebble-mouse**; you are probably best off scoping out pebble mounds during the day and staking them out at night (good luck); try the area round Plum Tree Creek and along the road to Koolpin.

The **Bare-rumped Sheath-tailed Bat** is known only from tall open eucalypt forest and *Pandanus* woodland in southern Kakadu. **Little Red Flying Foxes** are more common in the south of Kakadu and **Black Flying Foxes** are more common in the northern, better-watered parts. Watch for the latter decamping at dusk from Manngarre Monsoon Forest Walk, and there's another large camp at Mary River Roadhouse.

Savannah woodlands also adjoin many sandstone sites; for example, check the woodlands adjacent to Little Nourlangie for the **Fawn Antechinus**, **Northern Brown Bandicoot**, **Agile Wallaby**, **Antilopine Wallaroo**, **Pale Field-rat** and **Western Chestnut Mouse**. Gungurul is an area of woodland with volcanic rock rather than sandstone; the **Kakadu Dunnart** has been recorded here.

8.04 ARNHEM LAND AND COBOURG PENINSULA (GARIG GUNAK BARLU NATIONAL PARK)

Highlights: **Nabarlek, Brush-tailed Rabbit-rat (ssp. *penicillatus*), Banteng**

Other possibilities: **Northern Quoll, Golden Bandicoot (ssp. *auratus*), Short-flippered Pilot Whale, Indo-Pacific Humpback Dolphin, Dugong**

Gunbalanya (formerly called Oenpelli), just over the East Alligator River from Kakadu, is the part of Arnhem Land most people visit, mainly to see Aboriginal artists at work. The guided walk up Mt Injalak is worth doing to see the rock art, hear stories of country, for the view over the floodplain and because bats may sometimes be seen sheltering in crevices.

Mt Borradaile is the last known stronghold of **Nabarleks** in the Top End, although they cling on only in small numbers. Most visitors to this area are high-end fishermen who stay at Mt Borradaile Safari Camp (www.arnhemland-safaris.com); few naturalists go here so make sure the tour operator knows you're interested in wildlife. **Short-eared Rock Wallabies** are common, **Black Wallaroos** occur and by spotlighting there's a chance of seeing **Rock Ringtails** and **Sandstone False Antechinuses**.

Garig Gunak Barlu NP protects the area formerly known as the Cobourg Peninsula at the north-westernmost tip of Arnhem Land. This park is one of the few remaining mainland strongholds for the beautiful **Brush-tailed Rabbit-rat**. As well as tall open woodland, in Garig this species occurs among large *Casuarina equisetifolia* trees on coastal grasslands and even forages on beaches. Another attraction is the protected herd of **Banteng**, which can be seen along the access road, usually in the cooler parts of the day. The peninsula was chosen as the site of the first British settlement in the Top End: Victoria Settlement. The ruins are across Port Essington, accessible only by boat, and these waters are something of a cetacean hotspot. Watch on the way over for **Short-flippered Pilot Whales**, as well as **Indo-Pacific Humpback Dolphins**; **Dugongs** also occur in Port Essington. The **Northern Quoll** and **Delicate Mouse** have been recorded in the park. Garig is remote and accessible only with a permit (visit the NT government's national parks website for details); it gets busy so apply well in advance if you'll be travelling in school holidays.

Off the north-east tip of Arnhem Land, Cane Toad-free (for now) Marchinbar I. supports a natural population of the **Northern Quoll** and the Territory's only natural population of the **Golden Bandicoot**, though it can be seen more easily in WA. The **Brush-tailed Phascogale** has been recorded.

NORTHERN QUOLL RESCUE

The relentless march of the introduced Cane Toad from north Queensland into the NT and its likely effects on native wildlife were predicted decades ago. Unfortunately, little was done to stop it and small predators that tried to eat the toads succumbed to its toxins. Among them was the formerly abundant **Northern**

Quoll, which became vanishingly scarce in the Top End within a few years of the toads' arrival there: a large toad is toxic enough to kill an adult quoll. In an effort to mitigate the population crash, researchers transferred a number of quolls to toad-free islands offshore. Another strategy has involved training quolls to avoid eating toads: captive-bred quolls were offered small dead toads laced with a chemical that made them sick; they subsequently refused to attack Cane Toads. These quolls were then released into Kakadu NP and have since bred successfully. Northern Quolls have survived in pockets elsewhere (for example, in north Queensland) even where the toads occur, so it is hoped that eventually their numbers will recover with the help of quolls that have had 'toad aversion therapy'.

8.05 PINE CREEK (KOHINOOR ADIT)

Highlights: **Ghost Bat, Black Flying Fox**

Other possibilities: **Euro, Dusky Leaf-nosed Bat, Northern Leaf-nosed Bat, Orange Leaf-nosed Bat, Common Sheath-tailed Bat, Northern Cave Bat**

The small town of Pine Creek is just below the point where the Kakadu Hwy meets the Stuart Hwy at the southern end of Kakadu NP, and makes the southern apex of the 'Top End triangle'. Camps of **Black Flying Foxes** periodically set up near the middle of town and **Euros** can be seen on the surrounding rocky hills. Australia's – and therefore the world's – largest known **Ghost Bat** colony occupies the adit of Kohinoor, an abandoned gold mine just south of the township. The colony has ranged in number from lows of 300 to as many as 2000 **Ghost Bats**. On no account should you attempt to enter this site: it is a nursery cave and **Ghost Bats** are extremely sensitive to disturbance. Instead, get into position an hour before dark and sit quietly until just after sundown, when hundreds of bats start to emerge, usually about 20 minutes after sunset. The whole area is riddled with mines, connecting shafts and air vents. At least five other microbat species are known to use the complex, including **Dusky**, **Northern** and **Orange Leaf-nosed Bats**, the **Common Sheath-tailed Bat** and the **Northern Cave Bat**. Kohinoor adit is well known to locals who can readily direct you to the site. To get to the adit, walk or drive about 1 km south from the pub on Chinaman Rd to an obvious pull-in. The adit is on the right (west) and faces directly onto the road about 50 m into the scrub and up a slight rise.

Pine Creek is 225 km south of Darwin (about 3 hours' drive) on the Stuart Hwy (Hwy 1). There is a campground and other accommodation, a general store, café and petrol station.

WATCHING BATS IN THE NORTHERN TERRITORY

You should have no trouble spotting **Black Flying Foxes** winging across the sky at dusk in Darwin; there's a large camp on the Gunn Point Peninsula near the city. Both **Black** and **Little Red Flying Foxes** are also abundant in Kakadu NP (8.03) and easily seen. Further south, both species occur at Katherine and Nitmiluk NP, and famously at Mataranka FFR, where over 1 million have roosted in the past, and **Little Red Flying Foxes** have been recorded as far south as Tennant Creek. The diminutive **Least Blossom Bat** occurs in the Darwin Botanic Gardens and can sometimes be located by its call and eyeshine – stake out flowering trees during the day and return at night with a torch. Look for it also by spotlighting around *Melaleuca* blossom at Fogg Dam (8.02) and Umbrawarra Gorge (8.09). These are the only megabats in the Territory so identification should pose few challenges.

With 25 species out of a total of 33 recorded in the Territory, the Top End is the Territory's microbat hotspot. The sole endemic is the **Arnhem Sheath-tailed Bat**; other species are shared with bat faunas of the Kimberley, northern Queensland or both (that is, the **Northern** and **Diadem Leaf-nosed Bats**, **Bare-rumped Sheath-tailed Bat**, **Cape York Freetail Bat**, **Mangrove** and **Cape York Pipistrelles**, **Northern Cave Bat**, **Northern Broad-nosed Bat**, and **Arnhem** and **Pygmy Long-eared Bats**). Mangroves at East Point, Darwin, or Charles Darwin NP would be good places to pull out a bat detector and start listening for the **Mangrove Pipistrelle** and **Large-footed Myotis**. However, two sites stand out for their microbat diversity: Umbrawarra Gorge (8.09) and the southern part of Kakadu NP (8.03). Fifteen microbat species have been recorded at Umbrawarra and a further six are suspected of occurring there. Southern Kakadu has long been known as a microbat hotspot; most species that occur here will be detected only with the aid of an electronic device or in an official survey, but keep an eye out for bats roosting among crevices and boulder piles at, for example, Gunlom. The world's biggest known roost of **Ghost Bats** is at Kohinoor adit near Pine Creek (8.05), where you can watch a fly-out at dusk. There's a large camp of **Little Red Flying Foxes** at Mary River Ranger Station, where tiny **Northern Cave Bats** roost under buildings.

The bat fauna of the Territory's Gulf region is little known, but recently a high diversity has been recorded at the Pungulina-Seven Emu AWC Sanctuary (8.14), including the **Ghost Bat**; it would be well worth volunteering your time to join a survey in this remote but biologically rich area.

The **Yellow-bellied Sheath-tailed Bat** could be spotlighted in Kakadu, although it can probably be distinguished from the **Arnhem Sheath-tailed Bat** only in the hand. Its identification will be more certain at Uluru-Kata Tjuta NP (8.18), where a good selection of the Territory's 14 inland microbats occurs. Unfortunately, Ghost Bats no longer occur here or elsewhere in NT's arid zone, but other species include **Hill's Sheath-tailed**, **Inland** and **Bristle-faced Freetails**, the widespread

White-striped Freetail Bat, Gould's and Chocolate Wattled Bats, plus a trio of inland specialists: **Inland Cave**, **Inland Forest** and **Inland Broad-nosed Bats**. Check for microbats in quiet parts of the many gorges in the Macdonnell Ranges, in derelict buildings, in culverts and under bridges. There's a roost of **Inland Cave Bats** near Alice Springs that local bat enthusiasts should be able to point you to.

8.06 NITMILUK NATIONAL PARK (KATHERINE GORGE)

Highlights: **Echidna, Northern Brown Bandicoot, Common Brushtail Possum, Agile Wallaby, Euro, Antilopine Wallaroo, Black Flying Fox, Little Red Flying Fox, Dingo**

Other possibilities: **Sandstone False Antechinus, Rock Ringtail Possum, Sugar Glider, Large-footed Myotis**

Ever-popular Katherine Gorge is included here by dint of its position on the Top End tourist circuit. It receives thousands of visitors annually, few of them interested in wildlife, but nonetheless has a high mammalian diversity (44 native species) and a few could be seen on an overnight stay. Most obvious will be the **Agile Wallabies** and possibly **Dingoes** around the campground during the day, and both **Black** and **Little Red Flying Foxes** leaving camps at dusk. By night, **Common Brushtail Possums** and **Sugar Gliders** inhabit the wooded campground. Most visitors spend their day swimming or paddling in the scenic gorge, which is very pleasant indeed, but to see a greater variety of mammals you will have to make an effort and walk in some of the surrounding countryside. **Echidnas** and **Antilopine Wallaroos** may be encountered in forested areas by day; watch also for **Euros** on rocky hillsides. As the park abuts the southern end of Kakadu NP the sandstone supports many species in common, such as the **Black Wallaroo, Short-eared Rock Wallaby, Rock Ringtail Possum** and **Common Rock-rat**. To see some of these and the **Sandstone False Antechinus** you will probably have to spotlight far from the main tourist area and possibly camp overnight. Make sure you obtain all necessary permits and carry adequate water with you. The park has a fine list of microbats – some 19 species including the **Ghost Bat** – and as the **Large-footed Myotis** is on the park list it could conceivably be seen fishing in the gorge at dusk. Rarities have included the **Northern Quoll** and **Kakadu Dunnart**. The **Spectacled Hare-wallaby** and **Northern Nailtail Wallaby** must be regarded as an outside chance, but look in damp areas (away from the gorge) for the **Red-cheeked Dunnart, Water Rat** and **Grassland Melomys**. Nitmiluk is 29 km from Katherine and well signposted.

8.07 CUTTA CUTTA CAVES

Highlights: **Orange Leaf-nosed Bat**

These limestone karst caves are an important roosting site for five species of bat, including **Orange-Leaf-nosed Bats**. The turn-off to Cutta Cutta Caves is 30 km south of Katherine; the caves are about 1 km off the Stuart Hwy on a sealed road. Note that they may be closed in the wet season because of flooding.

8.08 MATARANKA HOT SPRINGS

Highlights: **Black Flying Fox, Little Red Flying Fox**

Other possibilities: **Northern Brushtail Possum, Agile Wallaby**

This refreshing oasis with natural hot pools makes a pleasant stop after a hot, dusty journey. But before it became popular with tourists it was a well-established **Little Red Flying Fox** camp. You could float on your back and watch the bats overhead, or nearly so. Inevitably the camp came into conflict with this major tourist draw and the bats have been moved on. However, there are usually lots of **Little Red Flying Foxes** in the Katherine area, even roosting in town, and **Black Flying Foxes** also occur. **Northern Brushtail Possums** and **Agile Wallabies** can be seen around the Mataranka campground.

8.09 UMBRAWARRA GORGE NATURE PARK

Highlights: **Rock Ringtail Possum, Short-eared Rock Wallaby, Least Blossom Bat, Little Red Flying Fox, Black Flying Fox**

Other possibilities: **Grassland Melomys, Ghost Bat**

This small nature park 25 km south-west of Pine Creek protects a scenic sandstone gorge with secluded dry season swimming holes. More importantly, it is a local hotspot for cave- and tree-roosting bats, with 19 species recorded and more expected to occur. The gorge is about 100 m wide for most of its length, with a well-worn walking trail down one side that connects the main pools (it is safe to swim here but check with rangers anyway). The action starts after dark, when **Ghost Bats** and **Little Red** and **Black Flying Foxes** could cruise along the creekline at any time; watch for them drinking in pools. To date the bat tally includes **Dusky** and **Northern Leaf-nosed Bats, Yellow-bellied** and **Common Sheath-tailed Bats, Northern Freetail Bats, Northern, Eastern** and **Lesser Long-eared Bats,** the **Large-footed Myotis** (watch for it fishing in pools), **Gould's** and **Hoary Wattled Bats, Little Broad-nosed** and **Northern Cave Bats** and the **Forest Pipistrelle.** Six other species are also suspected to occur here.

Umbrawarra also supports populations of the **Rock Ringtail Possum** and **Short-eared Rock Wallaby. Rock Ringtails** are best seen after dark and in the pre-dawn. Walk about 100 m along the gorge walk – the ringtails are generally seen by spotlighting onwards (west) from the first obvious outcrop. **Short-eared Rock Wallabies** are also here but are rather retiring. The **Grassland Melomys** occurs in adjoining habitat and the **Northern Quoll** has been recorded.

The Umbrawarra Gorge turn-off is on the west side of the Stuart Hwy about 3 km south of Pine Creek. The nature park is 22 km along an unsurfaced, rather corrugated road, suitable for 2WDs in the dry (May–September) but 4WDs only from October to April (check www.roadreport.nt.gov.au for conditions). There is a campground with toilet, tables and barbecues, but no fresh water; a fee applies (honesty system).

Further north up the Stuart Hwy, Robyn Falls has been frequently reported as a refuge for the elusive **Nabarlek**. They no longer seem to be there, although it's a pleasant enough place and **Short-eared Rock Wallabies** certainly occur. The turn-off to Robyn Falls is near Adelaide River, 111 km north-west of Pine Creek.

8.10 LITCHFIELD NATIONAL PARK

Highlights: **Echidna, Agile Wallaby, Antilopine Wallaroo, Short-eared Rock Wallaby, Black Flying Fox, Ghost Bat, Arnhem Leaf-nosed Bat, Orange Leaf-nosed Bat, Northern Freetail Bat, Dingo**

Other possibilities: **Sandstone False Antechinus, Northern Brushtail Possum**

Less well-known and regarded by some as 'Kakadu lite', Litchfield NP protects an isolated sandstone massif and is also well worth a visit. It has the advantage over its more famous relative of being less crowded, closer to Darwin and smaller, making travel around the park easier. The park has an excellent mammal list numbering more than 50 species. Several of the Arnhem sandstone endemics are also found here, with the important exception of Black Wallaroo, Rock Ringtail Possum and Arnhem Land Rock-rat.

Litchfield is a very good spot for **Short-eared Rock Wallabies**, which live on the cliffs adjoining Tolmer and Florence Falls, two popular visitors' sites. They usually remain hidden until the day cools off – try spotlighting at dusk. Other macropods that should be encountered include **Agile Wallabies**, **Euros** (on slopes near Tolmer Falls) and **Antilopine Wallaroos**, chiefly in the northern part of the park. **Dingoes** are common and could be encountered during the day in many areas or around campgrounds at night.

The other chief attraction at Tolmer Falls is an **Orange Horseshoe Bat** roost: a few of these rare microbats use the cave near the waterfall year-round and can be seen emerging at dusk. The roost is closed to the public, but the bats can be picked out by spotlight above the plunge pool; **Ghost Bats** hunt in the area and the **Large-footed Myotis** and **Diadem Leaf-nosed Bat** have been recorded here too. Both **Little Red** and **Black Flying Foxes** form camps along waterways and in patches of monsoon forest at, for example, Petherick's Rainforest. The park's microbat fauna also includes **Common Sheath-tailed**, **Northern Long-eared**, **Arnhem Long-eared** and **Pygmy Long-eared Bats**, plus **Common Bentwing** and **Northern Cave Bats**.

Rodents are well represented at Litchfield: **Dusky Rats** are locally common on floodplains, **Pale Field-rats** in open forest and woodland, the **Grassland Melomys** in many habitats and the **Delicate Mouse** in sandy lowland areas. **Common Rock-rat** has been described as 'abundant' in the park and occurs in all types of rocky habitat, such as at Tolmer and Florence Falls, Sandy Creek and the Lost City. The park supports the only populations of the **Arnhem Pebble-mouse** known outside of Kakadu NP; it is said to be locally common in stony woodland. **Black-footed Tree-rats**, **Water Rats**, the **Western Chestnut Mouse** and **Forrest's Mouse** also occur. **Echidnas** seem to be most commonly observed in rocky habitat. **Northern Brown Bandicoots** are common in many habitats, **Common Brushtail Possums** rather uncommon and **Sugar Gliders** have been reported from near Tolmer Falls. The **Northern Quoll** was formerly common in Litchfield and would be worth searching for on the off chance that a few survive. Of the other dasyurids, the **Fawn Antechinus** and **Red-cheeked Dunnart** have been recorded near Tolmer Falls; the **Sandstone False Antechinus** occurs in very rocky areas; and the **Common Planigale** on floodplains (for example, near the famous magnetic termite mounds in the north of the park).

The Litchfield NP turn-off is 90 km south of Darwin on the Stuart Hwy; from here it's another 31 km to the park via the small town of Batchelor, where there is accommodation, a store and petrol. **Northern Brushtail Possums** occur here and **Northern Freetail Bats** roost under the bridge over the Finniss River (watch out for crocs). Camping is permitted at various sites within the park – see the NT government parks website for fees and restrictions.

8.11 TIWI ISLANDS

Highlights: **Northern Brush-tailed Phascogale, Northern Brown Bandicoot, Common Brushtail Possum, Agile Wallaby, Black-footed Tree-rat, Brush-tailed Rabbit-rat (ssp. *melibius*)**

Other possibilities: **Butler's Dunnart, Delicate Mouse, Indo-Pacific Humpback Dolphin, Dugong**

Two major islands – Bathurst and Melville – some 20 km north of the mainland have yet to feel the small mammal declines that have blighted much of the Top End. These huge (Melville is Australia's second-largest island), sparsely populated islands are largely covered in savannah woodland, with pockets of monsoonal rainforest, extensive mangroves and swamps in low-lying areas. Several of the formerly common Top End species survive here (presumably because of the absence of Cane Toads) although the Northern Quoll is naturally absent. **Agile Wallabies** and **Dingoes** are the only large terrestrial mammals, and are readily seen on both islands. An endemic subspecies of **Brush-tailed Rabbit-rat** occurs on both Melville and Bathurst Is., mainly in tall, open eucalypt forest. **Black-footed Tree-rats** are also relatively common, though they are absent from Bathurst I. (where **Common Brushtail**

Possums appear to be more common). The only other arboreal species is the **Sugar Glider**, which occurs on both Bathurst and Melville Is. Most of the smaller terrestrial mammals are found on both islands, and include the **Northern Brown Bandicoot** (more common on Bathurst), **Delicate Mouse**, **Red-cheeked Dunnart** (swampy areas), **Western Chestnut Mouse**, **Tunney's Rat** (shrublands), and **Grassland Melomys** (coastal rainforest and swampy areas). **Butler's Dunnart** is endemic to the Tiwis and is found on both Melville and Bathurst Is. The few records are (it is rarely seen or trapped) mainly associated with open forest and *Melaleuca* woodland, where it apparently shelters under logs and other cover. Fortunately **Brush-tailed Phascogales** have been recorded on Melville (they have apparently almost disappeared from the mainland adjacent) and the aquatic **Water Mouse** also occurs (the usual caveats about crocs apply here also). Marine mammals include **Indo-Pacific Humpback Dolphins** at Cape van Diemen and **Dugongs**. The Tiwis also have a rich bat fauna: **Black** and **Little Red Flying Foxes** are present (though the latter seemingly only on Melville I.); **Least Blossom Bat** is the only other megabat. Sixteen microbats have been recorded. Access to the Tiwi Is. is usually by special arrangement or as part of a tour.

WATCHING WHALES AND DOLPHINS IN THE NORTHERN TERRITORY

The NT has mainland Australia's lowest cetacean diversity, but several previously unrecorded species could be expected to be noticed here with the recent increase in small boat traffic in Top End waters. Indeed, fishermen photographed the Territory's first live **Killer Whales** off north-east Arnhem Land in 2012. Access to suitable vantage points makes land-based searches difficult – much of the coastline is comprised of sand flats, estuaries and mangrove forests, and few headlands are more than 30 m high. The ever-present danger of Saltwater Crocodiles makes a small boat ('tinny') the most desirable way of looking for inshore species, such as the **Indo-Pacific Humpback**, and **Long-nosed Bottlenose** and **Australian Snubfin Dolphins**, all of which are resident in Darwin Harbour and nearby waterways (in descending order of abundance). The Howard River estuary and Hope Inlet, north-east of the city, are important areas for the **Humpbacks**; **Bottlenoses** are more common in the open harbour and the estuary on the west side of the harbour seems to be a prime spot for **Snubfins**. **False Killer Whales** are also recorded regularly. Any or all could be seen on the ferry between Darwin and Cox Peninsula, but there's no substitute for hiring a tinny and tootling about in likely habitat. All these species could be expected in similar environments across the Top End; for example, **Australian Snubfin Dolphins** are common in the Alligator River estuaries where they empty out of Kakadu NP (8.03) and around Cobourg Peninsula (8.04). In fact, Port Essington has a high diversity of cetaceans: **Indo-Pacific Humpback**, **Long-nosed Bottlenose**, **Pantropical Spotted** and

Spinner Dolphins, and **Short-flippered Pilot** and **False Killer Whales** (the latter mainly in the wet season) have all been recorded in this large bay. Other hotspots seem to be the Sir Edward Pellew Group, where **Melon-headed** and **False Killer Whales** have been recorded, and Melville I., from where **Short-flippered Pilot Whales** and **Indo-Pacific Humpback Dolphins** are known. Whales have also been are reported from Fogg Bay, 75 km south-west of Darwin.

Some species are known only from stranded specimens, for example **Cuvier's Beaked Whale** (again, from the Cobourg Peninsula), **Sperm Whale** (several records, including one from Casuarina Beach near Darwin, indicate this species may be present only in summer), **Dwarf Sperm Whale** (initially washed up alive at Darwin's Nightcliff Beach but later found dead) and **Blue Whale**. The largest stranding event known from the Territory was of 40 **Melon-headed Whales** at Elcho I.; the **Sei Whale** has been recorded dead in deeper waters and surprisingly the **Humpback Whale** is known only from stranded specimens, although some are possibly present in northern Australia year-round. Wide-ranging tropical species that could be expected include **Fraser's**, **Rough-toothed**, **Striped**, **Risso's** and **Common Dolphins**, and **Pygmy Killer**, **Bryde's**, **Minke**, **Blainville's Beaked** and **Tropical Bottlenose Whales**. If you see an unusual cetacean please report it to the Marine WildWatch Hotline 1800 453 941.

8.12 GROOTE EYLANDT

Highlights: **Northern Quoll, Northern Hopping-mouse**

Other possibilities: **Common Planigale, Black-footed Tree-rat, Brush-tailed Rabbit-rat**

Australia's third largest island (excluding Tasmania) is about 40 km east of the mainland in the Gulf of Carpentaria. Its isolation has kept it free of Cane Toads and consequently it supports a healthy population of **Northern Quolls**. The **Northern Hopping-mouse**, the only hopping-mouse that occurs outside the arid and semi-arid zones, also occurs here; it appears to be widespread and abundant, and is known from Anindilyakwa (Groote Eylandt) Indigenous Protected Area and Nanydjaka (Cape Arnhem) IPA. The **Common Planigale** is indeed apparently common on sand dunes on Groote Eylandt. **Brush-tailed Rabbit-rats** and **Black-footed Tree-rats** may still occur in this region. There's also a population of the **Northern Hopping-mouse** near the coastal town of Nhulunbuy (formerly called Gove), which may be more accessible.

8.13 BARKLY TABLELANDS AND GULF COUNTRY

Highlights: **Carpentarian False Antechinus, Long-tailed Planigale, Long-haired Rat, Carpentarian Rock-rat**

Other possibilities: **Central Pebble-mouse, Western Chestnut Mouse**

The Gulf of Carpentaria separates the Top End from Queensland's Cape York Peninsula and much of its coast is fringed with extensive stands of mangrove. The Barkly Tablelands is the region east of the Stuart Hwy and south of the Gulf. Most visitors cross the Tablelands on their way to or from Queensland, and try to complete the journey as quickly as possible. Closer to the coast, however, there are rewards for those prepared to take the time and make the effort. The Tablelands are one of the northern strongholds of the **Long-haired Rat**, which exists in low numbers during dry times and then periodically irrupts when rains come. They may be locally common on black soil plains even in non-plague years; check fenced-off bores, which may act as refuges (watch out for concentrations of Letter-winged Kites, which prey on this species). The **Western Chestnut Mouse** occurs along creek lines and on adjacent plains, rises and rocky outcrops. There are reputed to be **Central Pebble-mouse** mounds east of Barkly Homestead; and **Long-tailed Planigales** are common on cracking clay soils. Note that the black soil plains are impassable after rain – don't get caught out!

About 450 km north-east of Tennant Creek, Wollogorang Station is the only known site for the **Carpentarian Rock-rat**; it occurs at only Banyan Gorge, Camel Creek, Moonlight Gorge, McDermott Springs and Redbank Mine, with the biggest densities at Moonlight and Banyan Gorges. The **Rock Ringtail Possum, Short-eared Rock Wallaby, Sandstone False Antechinus, Long-tailed Planigale** and **Long-haired Rat** have also been recorded.

The Sir Edward Pellew Is. in the south-west Gulf were once an important refuge for several species, including **Brush-tailed Rabbit-rat** (Centre I.), **Northern Quoll** (Vanderlin I.), **Brush-tailed Phascogale** (West I.), **Common Brushtail Possum** and **Canefield Rat** (South-West I., the only part of the Territory in which it occurs; it is restricted to grassy open woodland on sandy soils). Sadly this is no longer the case, as their populations appear to have been compromised for reasons not fully understood, but probably including the introduced domestic Cat and Cane Toad. 'The Pellews' also support the Territory's only population of the **Carpentarian False Antechinus**, which has been recorded on North, South-West, Centre and Vanderlin islands, and is otherwise found only near Mt Isa, Queensland (1.28). The **Northern Brown Bandicoot, Grassland Melomys, Western Chestnut Mouse, Delicate Mouse, Common Rock-rat, Pale Field-rat** and **Long-haired Rat** also occur. There is a healthy population of **Dugongs** offshore.

8.14 PUNGALINA-SEVEN EMU AWC SANCTUARY

Highlights: **Echidna, Northern Brown Bandicoot, Sugar Glider, Agile Wallaby, Antilopine Wallaroo, Euro (Common Wallaroo), Short-eared Rock Wallaby, Black Flying Fox, Little Red Flying Fox, Common Rock-rat, Dingo**

Other possibilities: **Rock Ringtail Possum, Northern Nailtail Wallaby, Ghost Bat, Common Rock-rat**

This outstanding AWC sanctuary protects a complete cross-section of the Gulf coast from inland sandstone outcrops, through savannah woodland to coastal lagoons and mangroves. Macropods and bats feature prominently in a total of (so far) 34 mammal species. Among the former are the widespread **Agile Wallaby**, **Antilopine Wallaroo** and **Euro**, as well as more restricted species such as **Northern Nailtail** and **Short-eared Rock Wallabies**. Smaller terrestrial mammals include the **Northern Brown Bandicoot** and **Rock Ringtail Possum**; dasyurids such as **Sandstone** and **Carpentarian False Antechinuses**, and the **Common Planigale**; and among the rodents so far recorded are the **Water Rat**, **Northern Short-tailed Mouse**, **Delicate Mouse**, **Western Chestnut Mouse** and **Long-haired Rat**, here surely at the northern limit of its range in the Territory. But bats are the stand-out group, with a stellar selection that includes the **Ghost Bat**, **Northern** and **Mangrove Freetail Bats**, **Orange** and **Dusky Leaf-nosed Bats**, **Northern Cave Bat**, **Pygmy**, **Arnhem** and **Northern Long-eared Bats**, **Yellow-bellied** and **Common Sheath-tailed Bats**, **Mangrove Pipistrelle** and **Hoary Wattled Bat**. Obviously taking part in a survey would be the only feasible way to see many of these species, but visitors should have little trouble seeing **Black** and/or **Little Red Flying Foxes**, the former roosting in mangroves and the more mobile Little Reds choosing riparian camps inland. Visit www.australianwildlife.org for details of donating to AWC or volunteering.

8.15 VICTORIA RIVER AREA

Highlights: **Short-eared Rock Wallaby, Ghost Bat**

Other possibilities: **Euro**

The sandstone escarpment lining the Victoria River is home to **Short-eared Rock Wallabies**, which can be seen on the Escarpment Walk near Victoria River. They are rather more retiring here than in Kakadu or Litchfield NPs, and observations will be easiest in the very early morning or late evening. **Ghost Bats** also roost in caves along the escarpment and have been known from this walk. Victoria River Roadhouse, about 195 km south-west of Katherine on the Victoria Hwy, is a popular stopover on the way to WA. There is a store, petrol, hotel and campground.

Virtually the last stop before the WA border, Keep River NP is a little-visited national park that is sometimes good for **Short-eared Rock Wallabies**, which occur on the Gurrandalng Walk. This is one of only two sites where the **Ningbing False Antechinus** is known in the Territory (the other being Bradshaw Station further east). Gurrandalng campground is 18 km north of the Victoria Hwy.

B ALICE SPRINGS AND THE CENTRAL DESERTS

'Alice' can be used as a base for travel to the world-famous geological attractions in the Red Centre. Mammal watching here is hard work, with many small, cryptic species and often extreme heat that makes most of them strictly nocturnal. Some are also very rare. Sites are arranged here as if you were using Alice as a base. If you're heading up the Stuart Hwy towards Darwin, **Black-footed Rock Wallabies** occur at the Devil's Marbles, a scenic landmark about 400 km north of Alice on the 1500 km route. However, don't make the journey specially as they are readily seen around Alice itself. Intriguingly, mounds attributed to **Central Pebble-mouse** have been recorded near the Marbles (and near Renner Springs); live animals have been recorded in the Davenport and Murchison Ranges (see 8.21). Ferals in the Red Centre include large numbers of **One-humped Camels**, although a culling program has thinned them out somewhat. The Stuart Hwy north is a well-travelled route and features large road trains. It is inadvisable to travel on this road after dark because of a high risk of collision with anything from a kangaroo to a camel. For a real adventure, the Tanami Desert (8.21) is one of the lesser-known desert treks, but make sure you take all necessary precautions for travel through remote Outback areas.

8.16 ALICE SPRINGS

Highlights: **Common Brushtail Possum (ssp. *vulpecula*), Black-footed Rock Wallaby, Euro**

Other possibilities: **Mulgara, Inland Cave Bat**

For the best possible looks at **Black-footed Rock Wallaby** and nice photo opportunities, head straight to Heavitree Gap, where they hang around day and night waiting for handouts. They occur at many other sites in the region, including the Alice Springs Telegraph Station Historical Reserve and West MacDonnell NP (8.17). They usually emerge in the late afternoon or early evening, and may bask in the early morning after cold nights. **Euros** also occur at Heavitree Gap and on other rocky hills in Alice itself; **Red Kangaroos** occur on the city outskirts. **Common Brushtail Possums** are reputed to survive in the tree-lined creeks and gullies around the city. Although here it belongs to the abundant southern subspecies, it is becoming increasingly rare in this part of the world. Other small mammals that are occasionally spotted include the **Mulgara**, which has been recorded in suburban Alice Springs, though this must be regarded as a long shot nowadays; and the **Kultarr**, **Desert Mouse** and **Long-tailed Dunnart**. The **White-striped Freetail Bat** is one of the more common microbats – listen for it hawking along River Red Gum-lined creeks. The **Little Freetail Bat**, **Lesser Long-eared Bat** and **Gould's Wattled Bat** also commonly hunt around town; ask a local for directions to a cave south of Alice where **Inland Cave Bats** roost.

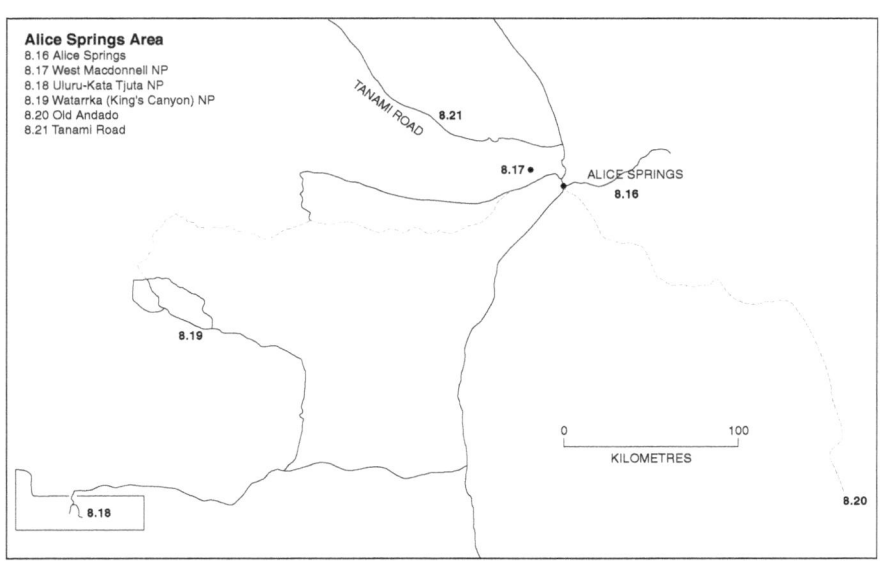

The Alice Springs Desert Park (www.alicespringsdesertpark.com.au) is a tastefully done zoo, and actively involved in research and captive breeding of arid-zone wildlife. It is well worth a visit and will give you some idea of what you're missing out there.

8.17 WEST MACDONNELL NATIONAL PARK

Highlights: **Mulgara, Red Kangaroo, Euro, Black-footed Rock Wallaby, Dingo**

Other possibilities: **Echidna, Long-tailed Dunnart, Common Brushtail Possum, Central Rock-rat**

Heading west from Alice, Simpson's Gap is the first of many gorges you'll encounter on the well-worn tourist circuit. This is another fine site at which to see the **Black-footed Rock Wallaby**, as well as **Red Kangaroos** and **Euros**. Simpson's Gap is 23 km west of Alice on Larapinta Drive. **Black-footed Rock Wallabies** also occur at Trephina Gorge Nature Park.

You won't see a great many species in scenic Ormiston Gorge, another 120 km west of the Simpson's Gap turn-off – **Dingoes**, **Black-footed Rock Wallabies**, **Euros** and **Red Kangaroos** being the most likely. However, the enigmatic **Central Rock-rat**, endemic to the southern NT and the only rock-rat species outside of the tropics, was rediscovered here in 1996 after a mysterious 36-year absence. It remains elusive and since then has made only sporadic reappearances in the West MacDonnell Ranges, such as at Mt Sonder and Haast's Bluff (where the **Mulgara** has also occurred). The **Fat-tailed False Antechinus** occurs at Ormiston Gorge also, and with luck you might spot one basking after a cold night. Look among clefts, crevices and caves for bats such as **Hill's Sheath-tailed Bat**, which is known to occur in the park.

The West Macdonnells are a stronghold in the region for the **Common Brushtail Possum**; riverine habitat and moist gullies at, for example, Ormiston Creek and Roma Gorge, could repay a search, and it has been recorded on rocky slopes among large Coolibah trees. The **Long-tailed Dunnart** is another enigmatic species that vanished for decades only for two specimens to be caught south of Ormiston Gorge in 1993; since then it has also been trapped between Mt Sonder and Serpentine Gorge. There are many other scenic gorges in the area and despite the paucity of mammals there is excellent birdwatching and they are well worth visiting to soak up the arid-zone ambience.

8.18 ULURU-KATA TJUTA NATIONAL PARK (AYERS ROCK AND THE OLGAS)

Highlights: **Red Kangaroo, Mulgara, Spinifex Hopping-mouse, Dingo**

Other possibilities: **Echidna, Mala (reintroduction), Euro, [One-humped Camel]**

The Territory's other internationally famous national park protects the amazing rock formations known in the local Anangu Aboriginal language as Uluru and Kata Tjuta, but to many outsiders still as Ayers Rock and The Olgas. Both formations are incredible in their own right and well worth a visit. The national park still has a reasonable mammal list, although the tally is less than half of what occurred formerly. You are likely to see **Red Kangaroos** along park roads, and indeed anywhere between here and Alice Springs, especially at dawn and dusk. A small population of **Euros** still inhabits Uluru; ask a ranger where they have been seen lately, but the Rock is huge and there's plenty of room for them to hide. The only other macropod here now is a reintroduced population of **Malas**, which are held in a predator exclosure and now number about 220. **Echidnas** are most commonly recorded near the monoliths but may be more or less nocturnal in hot conditions. The **Spinifex Hopping-mouse** is common around campgrounds and the resort, and can be seen at the sunset viewing area, where they forage for scraps. **Mulgaras** are reputed to frequent the dunes at the bus parking area (not the car parking area) at the Sunset Viewing Area; otherwise, you may be lucky enough to see one basking after a cold night (park staff manage habitat for this species; ask around if they know a good site to look for them). **Dingoes** are famously associated with the park and you should have little trouble seeing one. Note that these are wild animals that should not be fed or handled; they can be dangerous.

Other small mammals can be quite abundant, especially after good rains, with the highest diversity in areas of spinifex (note that the **House Mouse** also occurs in the park, particularly around the tourist complex and heavily visited areas such as

Uluru). The **Desert Mouse** occurs in mature spinifex and in dense grass at the foot of Uluru; it can be partly diurnal in winter. The **Sandy Inland Mouse** occurs across the greatest range of habitats. Other dasyurids include **Fat-tailed Antechinus** (often in the vicinity of the monoliths), **Ooldea Dunnart** (mainly in mulga) and, with varying degrees of abundance among spinifex, the **Wongai Ningaui**, **Hairy-footed Dunnart** and **Lesser Hairy-footed Dunnart**. (The **Stripe-faced Dunnart** has occurred and the **Fat-tailed Dunnart** could occur as it has been recorded at Curtin Springs, 100 km to the east). Microbats recorded include wide-ranging species such as **Gould's** and **Chocolate Wattled Bats**, and the **White-striped Freetail Bat**, **Yellow-bellied Sheath-tailed** and **Lesser Long-eared Bats**, as well as inland specialities such as **Hill's Sheath-tailed**, **Inland Forest** and **Inland Cave Bats**, **Little** and **Inland Broad-nosed Bats** and the **Inland Freetail Bat**. The Ghost Bat has been recorded historically. **Gould's Wattled Bats** have been recorded roosting in the roof of the Cultural Centre.

The mammal fauna in the region was formerly much more diverse and **Black-footed Rock Wallabies** and **Common Brushtail Possums** have become locally extinct only recently; there have been proposals to reintroduce both these species and **Burrowing Bettongs** to the park; check the park website for updates. **Southern Marsupial Mole** has been recorded historically and probably occurs here still.

Uluru-Kata Tjuta NP is served by direct flights from Alice Springs as well as several other major cities. However, you'll have more freedom with your own vehicle, which can be hired in Alice. A 2WD is fine for the trip to Uluru, which is 465 km from Alice (about 4.5 hours' drive) on a good surfaced road, but if venturing further afield then a 4WD is a good idea. There is a resort, campground, shops, restaurants and other facilities at Yulara. It is massively popular, especially in the cooler months, and bookings are advised.

8.19 WATARRKA (KING'S CANYON) NATIONAL PARK

Highlights: **Red Kangaroo, Euro, Black-footed Rock Wallaby, Spinifex Hopping-mouse, Dingo**

Other possibilities: **Mala (reintroduction), Sandy Inland Mouse**

This is another spectacular and popular tourist centre, with well-marked walking trails and a resort offering meals, accommodation and a campground. It is also notable as the site of a **Mala** (**Rufous Hare-wallaby**) breeding centre. This is one of only two such sites in the inland (the other being at Uluru (8.18)). The only place it now survives naturally is on an island in Shark Bay, WA, so it is well worth a look. The Mala Paddock is adjacent to the rangers' station about 10 km south-east of the resort on Larapinta Drive. Otherwise, luck will play a big part in what else you see here. These should include **Red Kangaroos** and **Euros** at least, as well as

Black-footed Rock Wallabies in the canyon itself (although early morning is by far the best time to go, before the crowds arrive). **Dingoes** often come close to the resort reception area and campground at night – these animals are dangerous and must not be fed or treated like domestic dogs. The **Sandy Inland Mouse** and **Spinifex Hopping-mouse** can also sometimes be seen around the reception area at night; both live in sand dune country dominated by hummock grassland, and can breed up after good rainfall. **Southern Marsupial Moles** have been recorded in the area, although chances of seeing them are close to zero. Watarrka NP is about 320 km south-west of Alice Springs.

8.20 OLD ANDADO STATION

Highlights: **Kultarr, Plains Mouse, Long-haired Rat, Sandy Inland Mouse, Spinifex Hopping-mouse**

Other possibilities: **Red Kangaroo, Euro, Dingo**

After good rains this historic station on the edge of the Simpson Desert makes a good place to look for irruptive rodents, especially the **Plains Mouse** and **Long-haired Rat** (commonly called Plague Rat when it occurs in large numbers). Along the way, about 40 km west of Old Andado, the Mac Clark Conservation Reserve hosts a colony of **Plains Mouse**. In good years they can be spotlighted anywhere along the track within 20 km of the reserve, as can **Long-haired Rats**. **Kultarrs** occur on gibber plains. The rats are apparently common in a big dune system west of the homestead at Old Andado; this could be worth checking even in poor years. At the station itself, the **Sandy Inland Mouse** mixes it with **Long-haired Rats**, and **Spinifex Hopping-mouse** frequents the dunes behind the homestead. Watch also for the **Lesser Hairy-footed Dunnart** and **Forrest's Mouse**, which could occur in the area. There should be no problem seeing larger species such as **Red Kangaroos**, **Euros** and **Dingoes** while travelling along the main track. **Brumbies** (wild horses) and **One-humped Camels** also occur. Old Andado Station (www.oldandado.com) is 300 km east of Alice; allow about 6 hours for the drive.

8.21 TANAMI DESERT

Highlights: **Mulgara, Greater Bilby, Spectacled Hare-wallaby, Red Kangaroo, Euro, Northern Nailtail Wallaby, Spinifex Hopping-mouse, Dingo**

Other possibilities: **One-humped Camel**

The Tanami Track leaves the Stuart Hwy north of Alice Springs and heads north-west through the Tanami Desert to Hall's Creek in WA, just over 1000 km away. All travellers must be self-sufficient and properly equipped for Outback travel. The first 120 km of road is sealed but thereafter a 4WD is essential. Fuel and limited supplies are available at Rabbit Flat Roadhouse ((08) 8956 8744), after which it is 315 km to Yuendumu. The road starts to deteriorate after Yuendumu, and it's then 550 km to Billiluna ((08) 9168 8988), which marks the start of the Canning Stock Route. Note that some areas adjoining the Track are Aboriginal land to which access is not permitted.

This is a remote, little-travelled region where some choice inland mammals still survive, despite the tragic extinction of the **Mala** in recent decades. The Tanami is still a stronghold for the **Greater Bilby** and this is one of the best places to see it in the wild. It is widespread and abundant except in the eastern Tanami, and occurs in good numbers between Kintore in the south and Newcastle Waters and Wave Hill in the north; Sangster's Bore (Lungkartajarra) is one of the most important sites. It is strictly nocturnal, but can often be spotlighted from a slowly moving vehicle in a wide variety of habitats: these include open shrubby sandplains near stony rises, salt lakes and salty depressions, and drainage systems dominated by large termite mounds. It is never common among dense vegetation. During the day, look for suitable habitat and places where signs are abundant, such as scats, tracks, diggings and burrows, then return at night with a spotlight.

Dingoes are widespread and abundant, and other large species that will probably be encountered include **Echidnas**, **Euros** and **Red Kangaroos**. Two other macropods deserve mention as they can be elusive elsewhere: the **Spectacled Hare-wallaby** and **Northern Nailtail Wallaby**. The former is widespread and occupies many habitats, but it can be difficult to flush from under a spinifex clump unless you are within a metre or so of it. **Northern Nailtail Wallabies** are also widespread and common, especially at the northern end of the Track, in the vicinity of Tanami Downs homestead and near The Granites Goldfields.

The Tanami Desert has an impressive list of dasyurids, many of which still seem to be widespread and common. **Mulgara** is locally abundant and could be spotlighted in suitable habitat near Sangster's Bore and in The Granites area. Others include the **Fat-tailed Antechinus**, **Wongai Ningaui**, and **Stripe-faced** and **Lesser Hairy-footed Dunnarts**. **Fat-tailed Dunnarts** also possibly occur in places, and the black cracking soil plains near Lake Buck support an isolated population of **Long-tailed Planigales**.

Rodents are also well represented: the **Long-haired Rat** has been recorded in the past but possibly occurs only during plagues, spreading along drainage lines such as Sturt Creek or from the Victoria River area. Those that definitely occur, sometimes in large numbers, include the **Sandy Inland Mouse**, **Desert Mouse**, **Western Chestnut Mouse** and **Spinifex Hopping-mouse**, which is in places very abundant (this species can often be spotlighted on suitable dune habitat). Less common species include the **Forrest's Mouse** and **Delicate Mouse**. The **House Mouse** is widespread but uncommon.

Bats include a good range of widespread and arid-zone species, such as the **Common Sheath-tailed**, **Yellow-bellied Sheath-tailed** (commonly spotlighted), **White-striped Freetail Bat**, **Lesser Long-eared Bat**, **Gould's Wattled Bat**, **Inland Broad-nosed Bat** and **Little Cave Bat**. **Little Red Flying Foxes** can occur during good years in the northern Tanami.

Northern Marsupial Moles occur in the south-west Tanami south of the road; they are most commonly found in large, east–west oriented sand dunes. There is a tantalising old record of **Central Rock-rat** (1952) from The Granites area, where **Common Brushtail Possums** may also persist, but as this species has declined over much of central Australia its current status is uncertain. The **Central Pebble-mound Mouse** occurs in the Murchison Range and feral **Donkeys** occur in the Murchison and Davenport Ranges.

9. Oceanic islands and external territories

Australia governs a number of external territories and dependencies, ranging from tropical islands to a large slab of Antarctica itself. Biologically they have disparate affinities and the wildlife of some has little in common with that of continental Australia. For a mammal-watcher, subantarctic Heard and Macquarie Is. and AAT are the most interesting to visit; tropical Christmas I. once supported several endemic species, although all but one are now almost certainly extinct. There are no endemic land mammals on Cocos-Keeling, Lord Howe or Norfolk Is., although all are places of exceptional natural beauty with spectacular birdlife.

9.01 LORD HOWE ISLAND

This beautiful subtropical island 600 km east of the mainland is worth visiting for its abundant birdlife, scenery and coral reefs. The only endemic land mammal was the now-extinct **Lord Howe Long-eared Bat**, known only from a single skull found in Gooseberry Cave in 1972 and which is now held in the Australian Museum, Sydney. The bat was possibly seen alive by naturalists in the 1880s and probably succumbed to predation by introduced Black Rats. The only surviving resident native mammal is the **Large Forest Bat**. Of the cetaceans, **Bottlenose Dolphins** are sighted regularly on fishing charters and **Humpback Whales** occur on migration.

9.02 NORFOLK ISLAND

Even more remote Norfolk I. is 1400 km east of the mainland and 900 km north-east of Lord Howe I. It has been extensively cleared and there are no native land animals. **Gould's Wattled Bats** formerly occurred but haven't been seen since the 1980s and Norfolk I. was assumed to be the type locality for the **East Coast Freetail Bat**, although there is now some doubt about this because the type specimen may have been mislabelled. Recent surveys have failed to record or trap any bats on Norfolk I. There are plenty of introduced rodents and feral Cats, and not surprisingly there have been several bird extinctions here. **Humpback Whales** pass the island on migration.

9.03 CHRISTMAS ISLAND

Highlights: **Christmas Island Flying Fox**

Other possibilities: **Christmas Island Pipistrelle, Christmas Island Shrew, Spinner Dolphin, Humpback Whale**

Australia's Christmas I. (there is another bearing this name in the Pacific Ocean) is an uplifted tropical limestone atoll in the Indian Ocean, about 2600 km north-west of Perth, WA. Although it is administered as an Australian territory, it is only 360 km south of Jakarta, Indonesia, and as a consequence its wildlife shows affinities with both the Australasian and Oriental regions. At the time of settlement in 1888 the island supported two endemic rats (the **Bulldog Rat** and **Maclear's Rat**), plus the **Christmas Island Shrew** – the only native shrew to occur on Australian territory – and two endemic bats: the **Christmas Island Pipistrelle** and **Christmas Island Flying Fox**. Unfortunately, both rats disappeared early in the 20th century, possibly succumbing to disease spread by the introduced Black Rat; the shrew and pipistrelle are now both almost certainly extinct and only the **Christmas Island Flying Fox** remains.

The **Christmas Island Shrew** was formerly common in the vicinity of Flying Fish Cove, but became rare shortly after settlement and had apparently disappeared around the turn of the 20th century. Incredibly, a live specimen was discovered in 1984 and another the following year, but despite intense surveys it has not been recorded since. There is a chance it may still occur in remote, trackless areas at the western end of the island – its last known whereabouts and the least disturbed part of Christmas I. Its habits are poorly known; it was probably nocturnal or nearly so and, like most shrews, highly active. The only terrestrial mammals remaining on the island are the introduced **Black Rat**, **House Mouse** and feral **Cat**; all are most commonly encountered near the Settlement. Recently, an initiative has begun to remove Cats from the island, by sterilising pets and banning the importation of new ones. A feral Cat eradication program was due to begin as this book went to press.

The **Christmas Island Pipistrelle** was the island's only microbat and was common at least until the 1980s, when its precipitous decline commenced for reasons unknown. A number of invasive species have been implicated in the disappearance of both the shrew and the pipistrelle, including the Common Wolf Snake, a species of giant centipede and Yellow Crazy Ants, whose supercolonies overrun swathes of forest. By the time a captive-breeding program was initiated for the microbat only one specimen could be located; it was last seen in August 2009 and conservation efforts were abandoned. This made it Australia's first mammalian extinction for the 21st century. It would certainly be worth looking casually for this species at dusk along roads and tracks; Winnifred Beach Track, for example, was a former haunt. If you see *any* microbat on Christmas I. please report it to the Australasian Bat Society immediately (www.ausbats.org.au).

Recently, the endemic **Christmas Island Flying Fox** has also undergone a dramatic decline, again for reasons that are unclear. It was formerly common and relatively easy to see because of its partly diurnal habits: it appears to play an important role in pollinating rainforest trees that flower during the day. Individuals may be active at any time, with a peak period of activity in the few hours before dusk. The biggest roost, Hosnie's Spring, is difficult to get to and the best place to view them is from Margaret Knoll Lookout as they leave camps (usually between 4 and 6.30 pm). They also sometimes roost around the short walking track to Greta Beach or in the casuarinas above the tractor shed at the Golf Course. To see them up close feeding on fruit (the exotic West Indian Cherry is a favourite food plant), try around the Pink House, Grant's Well and Territory Day Park Lookout late in the afternoon. There is another camp at Dolly Beach/McMicken Point. Otherwise, the flying foxes could be encountered anywhere on the island, although camps can be small and hard to locate, and they also roost alone at times; as with any flying fox species, listen for tell-tale squabbling and loud wingbeats.

Despite its sad losses, Christmas I. remains a superb wildlife destination. Some 75 per cent of the island supports tropical rainforest and there are few roads or tracks. The island is famous for its annual migration of millions of red land crabs, great snorkelling and whale shark sightings, as well as abundant seabirds, including several endemic species. **Spinner Dolphins** are present year-round offshore; there are no other regularly sighted cetaceans although **Humpback Whales** occasionally reach these waters and **Baird's Beaked Whale** has been recorded.

Access to Christmas I. is only by air from Perth or from Jakarta, Java. It may in fact be cheaper to go via Java, even from Australia, although the scheduled flights from Perth stop at Cocos-Keeling Is. (see 9.04). Birding Tours (www.birdingtours.com.au) runs trips every year that take in both islands. Remember this is a tropical island, with distinct wet and dry seasons; heavy rain and strong winds can occur between November and June. Find out more about the island, accommodation and facilities at www.christmas.net.au.

9.04 COCOS-KEELING ISLANDS

This remote group of Indian Ocean atolls is 980 km south-west of Christmas I. and 2750 km north-west of Perth, the nearest hub. The atolls are mainly of interest to birdwatchers as there are no land mammals. **Dugongs** occasionally occur in the large lagoon of the main atoll, but to see cetaceans you would have to go offshore to

North Keeling; this is difficult to organise and big seas are common. **Oceanic Bottlenose** and **Spinner Dolphins** have been recorded regularly and in theory pelagic species such as **Rough-toothed** and **Fraser's Dolphins** should be present. Cocos-Keeling is a scheduled stop on flights between Perth and Christmas I. (9.03). Birding Tours (www.birdingtours.com.au) includes the atoll as part of its itinerary in the region, although these tours have a primarily birding focus.

9.05 MACQUARIE ISLAND

Highlights: **Southern Elephant Seal, Subantarctic Fur Seal, Antarctic Fur Seal, Hooker's Sea Lion, Killer Whale**

Other possibilities: **Long-flippered Pilot Whale, Strap-toothed Beaked Whale**

'Macca' is one of those magic destinations, boasting abundant wildlife and important breeding populations of several species. Like most subantarctic islands it suffered at the hands of sealers, who killed vast numbers of elephant and fur seals for profit, and also introduced to Macquarie I. destructive pests such as Rabbits and rodents. Exploitation of wildlife stopped in 1920 and seal numbers have increased significantly since then. And after a massive clean-up operation it is believed that all pests have been eradicated or nearly so, and vegetation and seabird numbers have already begun to recover. The island is 33 km long, about 5 km across and aligned roughly north–south. There's a permanent research base at the northern tip where all visiting ships anchor.

Southern Elephant Seals and three species of fur seal – **New Zealand, Antarctic** and **Subantarctic Fur Seals** – breed on Macca; two other seal species are regular visitors and two more occur as vagrants, making it one of the most diverse pinniped sites in the world. Up to 1000 **New Zealand Fur Seals**, mainly immature males, haul up annually, peaking in March. **Antarctic** and **Subantarctic Fur Seals** breed in small numbers, but all three species interbreed and there are few pure specimens of Antarctic or Subantarctic Fur Seals. Macca supports about 10 per cent of the world's **Southern Elephant Seal** population – recently estimated at 70 000–80 000 animals. The largest haul-out is near the research station, where visitors land and are virtually guaranteed sightings. Breeding **Subantarctic Fur Seals** use the cobblestone beaches at Secluded Head and North Head peninsula, while non-breeding animals loaf among the tussocks on the slopes above the colonies. **Hooker's Sea Lions** visit in small numbers during winter and spring; **Leopard Seals** are also regular visitors in these seasons while **Weddell** and **Crabeater Seals** are rare vagrants from Antarctica.

Most cetacean sightings around Macquarie I. are of **Killer Whales**, which occur year-round with peak sightings in October–December, when the elephant seals are breeding. The **Long-flippered Pilot Whale** is the only other species recorded regularly, usually in small pods offshore, and the **Southern Right Whale, Minke**

Whale and **Sperm Whale** have also been recorded. Remains of various toothed whales, including **Cuvier's**, **Blainville's**, **Andrews'** and **Strap-toothed Beaked Whales** and **Southern Bottlenose Whale**, have been found beach-cast in years past (**Strap-toothed Beaked Whales** and **Fin Whales** have been seen from cruise ships en route to Macquarie I.).

Macca is 1466 km south-east of Hobart, Tasmania, yet still the most accessible of Australia's subantarctic territories. The climate is cool (summer maximum temperatures are below 10°C) and damp year-round, with some form of precipitation occurring on most days. Unless you are part of the Australian Antarctic Division's revictualling team, the best way to enjoy the island is as a passenger on a cruise ship. A few visit annually in summer, usually as part of a circuit leaving from New Zealand and taking in several other subantarctic islands (see Appendix B for operators). Cruise ships usually anchor in Hasselborough Bay at the north end of the island and ferry tourists ashore by Zodiac.

9.06 HEARD ISLAND

Highlights: **Antarctic Fur Seal, Southern Elephant Seal, Leopard Seal**

There are few remoter – or more pristine – places on Earth than Heard I., which lies in the southern Indian Ocean, 4120 km south-west of Perth, WA. Heard is dominated by 2745-m-high Big Ben, the only active volcano on Australian territory, which constantly issues steam from fissures and is often obscured by cloud. It is an inhospitable region, fog-bound in still weather but usually cold, storm-wracked and beset with big seas. Not surprisingly, the island wasn't discovered till 1853 and few vessels visit even today. There are no land mammals, native or introduced, but Heard I. is an important site for several species of pinniped, which have recovered dramatically since hunting stopped: some 29 000 **Antarctic Fur Seals** were present during a recent summer survey. They are especially common at the base of Elephant Spit and the coastline to the north of there. **Southern Elephant Seal** numbers peak at over 3000 in early summer; there are usually good numbers at Spit Bay and Atlas Cove. **Leopard Seals** occur commonly, especially during winter, when the island supports the largest population (up to 750) of this species north of the pack ice. They tend to frequent South West Bay in summer; should you happen to be there in winter, try Corinthian Bay and Atlas Cove. Pupping has occurred. **Subantarctic Fur Seals** have been recorded breeding in very small numbers. On rare occasions when prevailing wind and temperature conditions bring pack ice to within 500 km of Heard I., **Weddell** and **Crabeater Seals** occur, though none have been reported since the 1950s, and **Ross's Seal** has been recorded even more rarely. Cetaceans are uncommon, with only **Killer Whale** being seen regularly; remains of six other species have been recorded: **Long-flippered Pilot Whale**, **Strap-toothed Beaked Whale**, **Spectacled Porpoise**,

Minke Whale, **Hourglass Dolphin** and **Southern Bottlenose Whale**. The **Commerson's Dolphin** is known to occur in nearby waters.

Access to Heard is extremely difficult; private boat charter is possibly the easiest option, although voyagers should be aware that oceanic conditions can pose a serious risk at times. If you have the right qualifications you may be able to join a scientific expedition. Even if you manage to reach the island, landing can be hazardous: the sea floor is constantly shifting owing to uplift, and dense sea fogs occur. The effort would be amply rewarded.

9.07 AUSTRALIAN ANTARCTIC TERRITORY (AAT)

Highlights: **Crabeater Seal, Weddell Seal, Leopard Seal, Southern Elephant Seal, Hourglass Dolphin, Antarctic Minke Whale, Humpback Whale, Southern Right Whale, Killer Whale, Sperm Whale**

Other possibilities: **Ross's Seal, Southern Bottlenose Whale, Fin Whale**

Access to the vast slab of Antarctica governed by Australia – Australian Antarctic Territory (AAT) – is difficult unless you are on a private vessel or can secure a berth on one of the voyages that regularly revictual the Australian Antarctic Division's three bases in AAT (Casey, Mawson and Davis). For the privileged few who make the trip each year a wildlife cornucopia awaits. Summer is the best time to go as there is almost continuous daylight and wildlife activity is at its peak. Watch for cetaceans the whole way; at least six species can be expected, including **Humpback**, **Sperm**, **Antarctic Minke**, **Southern Right** and **Killer Whales**; the pretty **Hourglass Dolphin** is also spotted frequently. Depending on conditions, luck, weather and hours spent watching, **Blue Whales** and unusual species such as **Southern Bottlenose Whales** could also be encountered. **Subantarctic Fur Seals** investigate ships at sea, especially if the ships are stationary for any length of time; watch for them hauled out where ice floes become prevalent (especially south of the Antarctic Convergence). **Elephant Seals** also haul out on floes. Pack ice is the haunt of **Crabeater** and **Weddell Seal**s; the former is abundant, the latter common. **Leopard Seals** are much rarer and rarer still is **Ross' Seal**. Once among the pack ice watch in laneways for **Antarctic Minke Whales**, which can be common. Check the Antarctic Division's website (www.antarctica.gov.au) for opportunities.

10. Boat-based whale- and dolphin-watching

Cetaceans (whales and dolphins) are very well represented in Australia, with several species easily seen from shore or on organised boat trips and many more seen on specialised pelagic trips or opportunistically at sea. A great way to see a range of cetaceans in Australian waters is to take a whale- or dolphin-watching cruise or to join one of the pelagic birding trips that run from many ports, especially in the south-east. Dedicated whale-watching tours on the east and west coasts usually focus on the annual **Humpback Whale** migration; along the south coast, particularly in SA, they cater to the **Southern Right Whale** migration. In addition, numerous boat operators run dolphin-watching cruises at many sites around the country, chiefly near big population centres and holiday destinations. Pelagic birdwatching trips run year-round (weather permitting) from Southport, Port Stephens, Sydney, Wollongong, Portland (or Port Fairy) and Eaglehawk Neck; and less frequently from the Sunshine Coast, Eden, Port Macdonnell, Perth and Albany; there's also an annual cruise to Ashmore Reef in the Timor Sea. A long list of cetaceans has accumulated over the years on these trips and they are organised by people who have plenty of field experience with identifying whales and dolphins. Seabirding trips are popular and often booked out months ahead; unfortunately cetacean sightings aren't usually quantified the same way bird sightings are, so picking the best times and locations has been an inexact science to date. Many of these trips also record pinnipeds, especially in southern waters.

The following sites are presented clockwise from north Queensland to WA. Note that Dugong- and pinniped-watching trips are also offered at some sites – see individual chapters for more information.

CAIRNS, QUEENSLAND

Big, powerful boats full of day trippers leave daily for Green I. and Michaelmas Cay (weather permitting). **Short-flippered Pilot Whales** are sometimes seen not far off

Cairns and **Spinner Dolphins** have been recorded near Michaelmas Cay. The longer your Reef cruise, the more chance of seeing interesting wildlife – ask around on the Esplanade for alternative tours. Live-aboard cruises (www.marineencounters.com. au) where you can interact with **Dwarf Minke Whales** operate from Lizard I. from June to September; **Humpback Whales** are sometime seen on these trips as well.

THE WHITSUNDAYS, QUEENSLAND

The Whitsunday Is. crowd the central Queensland coast near Airlie Beach (visit www.whitsunday-tourism.com.au). **Humpback Whales** are a fixture in these waters during migration (peaking May–September). Whale-watching cruises operate out of Airlie Beach and other holiday centres. **Short-flippered Pilot Whales** are also seen reasonably frequently.

HERVEY BAY, QUEENSLAND

Regarded by many as the home of whale-watching in Australia, commercial tours have run from Hervey Bay for more than 40 years. **Humpback Whales** are the main attraction here and sightings are guaranteed in the warm, shallow waters of the bay during the peak of the season (generally September–November, when

THE CETACEAN BIG FIVE

With Australia's high cetacean diversity there are naturally some outstanding opportunities to interact with whales and dolphins. Please note that all human interactions with cetaceans are carefully regulated in Australia and there are penalties for infringements.

Humpback Whale Some cruise boat operators now allow people to snorkel with these giants at Hervey Bay; more opportunities are planned.

Southern Right Whale Watching mothers tending their calves from the top of the Nullarbor Cliffs is an awesome experience.

Antarctic Minke Whale Live-aboard dive cruises from Lizard I. guarantee underwater interactions and the chance to be part of a citizen science project between June and September.

Bottlenose Dolphin For a cold-water treat, don a wetsuit and join a mermaid line in Port Phillip Bay, where there's a resident population of Burrunan Bottlenose Dolphins.

Indo-Pacific Humpback Dolphin This tropical and subtropical species has been hand-fed daily for years at Tin Can Bay, near Fraser I.

mothers and calves often linger). There are plenty of operators – visit www.whalewatchingherveybay.com.au or www.herveybaywhalewatch.com.au, for example; some also advertise swim-with-whale trips. Several **Killer Whales** beached here in 2013; they are rare in these waters and presumably this pod was following the Humpback migration.

SUNSHINE COAST, QUEENSLAND

Several operators take advantage of the **Humpback** migration (for example, www.whalewatchingsunshinecoast.com.au). Pelagic birdwatching trips started recently from Mooloolaba (see www.whaleone.com.au and www.sunshinecoastbirds.blogspot.com.au) and have accumulated a modest cetacean list.

MORETON BAY, QUEENSLAND

There are resident **Bottlenose** and **Indo-Pacific Humpback Dolphins** in Moreton Bay, as well as a major herd of **Dugongs**. All can sometimes be seen from passenger ferries that service North Stradbroke and Moreton Is. Dedicated trips run from Brisbane (www.brisbanewhalewatching.com.au) and **Humpback Whales** are also sometimes seen in the bay.

SOUTHPORT, QUEENSLAND

The Gold Coast Seaworld (www.seaworldwhalewatch.com.au) has a large, comfortable vessel, which is just as well as sea conditions in southern Queensland are not always as tranquil as further north. Excellent sightings of **Humpbacks** are common in season, and rarer visitors include **Minke**, **Bryde's** and **Southern Right Whales**. See also www.whalesinparadise.com.au.

BYRON BAY, NEW SOUTH WALES

This popular holiday town is one of the best centres for watching the **Humpback Whale** migration in northern NSW. Dedicated cruises run during migration (visit www.byronbaywhalewatching.com.au) and Cape Byron is an excellent lookout for land-based whale-watching.

PORT STEPHENS, NEW SOUTH WALES

Nelson Bay is the main service town for the natural harbour of Port Stephens, where a year-round dolphin-watching industry centres on a permanent population of about 165 **Bottlenose Dolphins**. Resident pods can be seen inside the port and if you are prepared to brave bigger seas there are more outside, as well as **Humpback Whales** during migration (June–August heading north and September–November as they return southward). Visit www.imaginecruises.com.au, www.moonshadow.com.au and www.cruiseportstephens.com.au for a few choices.

SYDNEY, NEW SOUTH WALES

An excellent range of cetaceans has been seen from both pelagic birding cruises and dedicated whale-watching trips that have run for years out of Sydney. **Humpback Whales** are the mainstay on both northern and southern migrations, and **Common** and **Oceanic Bottlenose Dolphins** are regularly encountered. There is a good chance of seeing **Risso's Dolphins** (mostly spring and summer) and, more rarely, **Pantropical Spotted Dolphins**. The species list is not as long as that of Wollongong to the south (see the next section), but includes **Southern Right**, **Dwarf Minke**, **Sperm** and **Pygmy Blue Whales,** and **Killer Whales** and blackfish such as **False** and **Dwarf Killers**, **Melon-headed** and both **Long-flippered** and **Short-flippered Pilot Whales**. Birding trips currently run six or seven times a year, mostly over the winter months; whale-watching tours are run by various operators during migration (try www.whalewatchingsydney.net or www.sydneywhalewatching.com). And listen for media noise regarding sightings in the harbour itself: both **Humpbacks** and **Southern Right Whales** are entering Sydney Heads more frequently.

WOLLONGONG, NEW SOUTH WALES

South of Sydney, Wollongong hosts the longest-running pelagic birdwatching venture in the country and an unmatched list of cetaceans has built up over some 30 years of operation. Seas and weather can be an issue, and trips are sometimes cancelled, but generally there is one trip a month, sometimes two. Apart from regular **Humpbacks** and a few **Southern Right Whales** in season, **Blue**, **Fin**, **Sei**, **Bryde's**, **Dwarf Minke**, **Antarctic Minke**, **Sperm** and **Pygmy Sperm Whales** have all been recorded. Blackfish also fare well, with **False** and **Pygmy Killer Whales**, **Short-flippered** and **Long-flippered Pilot Whales** and **Melon-headed Whales**. Even beaked whales have been seen over the years: **Southern Bottlenose Whales**, and **Shepherd's**, **Arnoux's**, **Cuvier's**, **True's**, **Strap-toothed** and **Blainville's Beaked Whales**. Dolphins are also well represented; apart from **Indo-Pacific Bottlenose** and **Short-beaked Common Dolphins**, the selection has featured **Killer Whales**, and **Dusky**, **Fraser's**, **Spotted**, **Striped**, **Long-snouted Spinner** and **Risso's Dolphins**. Note that these trips are run by the Southern Oceans Seabird Study Association (SOSSA) and are primarily for studying pelagic seabirds. Check out their website (www.sossa-international.org) for details about participating or joining SOSSA. This impressive list is partly because of the huge number of trips that have run over the years – the more often you go to sea, the more you are likely to see.

NAROOMA, NEW SOUTH WALES

Humpback Whales are often seen on cruises to Montague I. and dedicated whale-watching trips run during the migration: visit www.naroomacharters.com.au. Other species recorded have included **Southern Right**, **Fin**, **Bryde's**, **Sei**, **Blue** and **Killer Whales**, and large pods of **Common** and **Bottlenose Dolphins** are an added bonus. Whales are often sighted only 5 minutes from port. Visit www.wildaboutwhales.com.au for an overview of whale-watching on the NSW south coast.

EDEN, NEW SOUTH WALES

Tucked into the far south-eastern corner of NSW, Eden is a former whaling port and ideally positioned near a deep trench where **Sperm Whales** and beaked whales aggregate at certain times of year. It is ideally placed on the 'Humpback Highway', and at the peak of the migration excellent **Humpback** sightings can often be had in sheltered Twofold Bay within minutes of leaving port. **Humpbacks** normally occur June–August on their northward migration and September–November as they head south. **Common Dolphins** are seen on many cruises, **Bottlenoses** less often and on a good day **Southern Right Whales** are also seen. During the whaling years **Killer Whales** were a feature off Eden; they are now rare but still seen occasionally. Other species periodically recorded include **Bryde's** and **Dwarf Minke Whales** and, exceptionally, a herd of over 100 **False Killer Whales** was recorded in August 2014. Check out the annual whale festival in October or November (www.edenwhalefestival.com.au); excellent whale-watching charters are run by Cat Balou Cruises www.catbalou.com.au and Freedom Charters www.freedomcharters.com.au. From Eden, NSW the **Humpback** migration heads more or less south, so sightings aren't as common 'round the corner' in eastern Victoria.

PORT PHILLIP BAY, VICTORIA

Dolphin-watching tours run from the Mornington Peninsula (www.polperro.com.au) and Queenscliff (www.dolphinswims.com.au) and include the chance to swim with **Bottlenose Dolphins** or be towed behind the boat on a mermaid line. This population could be a distinct form, the **Burrunan Dolphin**. Remember the water can be cold in southern Victoria – you'll probably need a wetsuit.

PORT FAIRY AND PORTLAND, VICTORIA

Pelagic birdwatching trips have run regularly (weather permitting) from either Portland or Port Fairy for many years and often encounter **Southern Right Whales** and **Common** and **Bottlenose Dolphins**; more rarely, **Humpback**, **Blue** and **Fin Whales** are also seen. Birding trips are organised through BirdLife Australia (www.birdlife.org.au); visit www.whalemail.com.au for information on commercial whale-watching trips.

WARRNAMBOOL, VICTORIA

Logan's Beach at Warrnambool is a centre for land-based watching of **Southern Right Whale** mothers and calves in winter. **Humpback** and **Blue Whales** also occur offshore; visit www.warrnamboolcam.com.

EAGLEHAWK NECK, TASMANIA

Seabirders have known about this quiet little spot for years owing to its proximity to the continental shelf. It has delivered some excellent pelagic birding and a few marine mammals including a stellar sighting of **Shepherd's Beaked Whales** in 2012. More commonly encountered are **Common** and **Bottlenose Dolphins**, as well as the occasional **Humpback Whale**. Watch the Birding-Aus chatline (www.birding-aus.org) for news of forthcoming trips.

BRUNY ISLAND, TASMANIA

Bruny Island is one of Tasmania's cetacean hotspots. **Humpbacks**, **Southern Right Whales** and **Common Dolphins** are often seen on cruises to seal colonies at the southern end of the island. Visit www.brunycruises.com.au.

WHALE STRANDINGS

Cetacean strandings (including dead animals and skeletons) have occurred along most of the southern Australian coastlines (though less commonly in waters protected by the Great Barrier Reef and along the northern coastline, where diversity is lower) and in all months. There is no national register of strandings and dissemination of information is generally poor unless a mass stranding happens near a big population centre. Whales are stranded most frequently on Tasmania's west and north-west coasts, usually in spring-summer. Indeed, 80 per cent of Australia's whale strandings are in Tasmania, which is also one of three world hotspots for Sperm Whale strandings. Strandings in all states are possibly skewed to the summer months, because of the high number of beach-goers, but it is worth checking beaches at any time of year. Apart from the mouth of Macquarie Harbour and Ocean Beach in Tasmania, likely sites for strandings include Geographe Bay in WA, Encounter Bay and Kangaroo I. in SA, Croagingolong NP and Nelson Bay in Victoria, and any number of beaches and coves along the NSW coast. If you witness a stranding event, or notice whales moving up and down the coast in your area, contact state wildlife authorities or a local wildlife care organisation.

TASMAN PENINSULA, TASMANIA

Excellent cruises around the shores of the Tasman Peninsula (www. tasmanadventurecruises.com.au) regularly encounter **Humpback Whales**, **Common** and **Bottlenose Dolphins** and other features, as well as spectacular scenery and **Australian Fur Seals**.

VICTOR HARBOR, SOUTH AUSTRALIA

July to August are peak viewing times for **Southern Right Whales**, which often approach close to shore near Victor Harbor and at other sites in Encounter Bay. Visit www.sawhalecentre.com for details about cruises (which look for dolphins at other times of year). Further south, pelagic birding trips run sporadically from Port Macdonnell; check the Birding-Aus chatline for upcoming trips or contact http:// remarkablefishingcharters.com.au.

PORT ADELAIDE, SOUTH AUSTRALIA

There is a resident population of **Bottlenose Dolphins** at Port Adelaide; visit www. dolphinexplorer.com.au for more information.

KANGAROO ISLAND, SOUTH AUSTRALIA

Kangaroo Island is something of a cetacean hotspot, with many interesting records of both live and stranded animals. Visit www.kangarooislanddolphinwatch.com.au for news on the resident pods of **Common** and **Bottlenose Dolphins**; www. kimarineadventures.com.au runs dolphin- and whale-watching cruises.

FOWLER'S BAY, SOUTH AUSTRALIA

Fowler's Bay Ecopark (www.fowlerseco.com) runs boat trips along the coast to see the **Southern Right Whales** during migration. (Note that it is not possible to launch a boat at the Nullarbor Cliffs so whale-watching is land-based there, although a light plane operates out of Nullarbor Roadhouse.)

ESPERANCE, WESTERN AUSTRALIA

July through to October are peak months for watching **Southern Right Whales** and to a lesser extent **Humpback Whales** at Esperance (www.esperancedivingandfishing.com.au).

ALBANY, WESTERN AUSTRALIA

Migrating **Humpback Whales** and **Southern Right Whales** cross paths in the south-west and Albany (www.albanywhaletours.com.au) is a good base to see both species. **Humpbacks** transit Albany's bays from about June onwards heading north, and again until November on their return to Antarctica. **Southern Right Whales** are near the western limit of their migration path here (although some always continue 'round the corner' and up the west coast to about Kalbarri). They shelter in bays near Albany to mate and calve. Pelagic birding trips also run out of Albany, with sporadic sightings of **Humpbacks** and **Southern Right Whales**, as well as **Common Bottlenose Dolphins**.

PERTH, WESTERN AUSTRALIA

The **Humpback** migration is usually at its best off Perth from mid-September through early December. During this time tours run daily (weather permitting) with guaranteed sightings. Visit www.whalewatchingperth.com.

GERALDTON, WESTERN AUSTRALIA

Significant numbers of **Humpbacks** frequent the waters between Geraldton and the Houtman Abrolhos every year. Live-aboard cruises visit the Abrolhos (www.pelsaertchartercompany.com.au) as the islands are too far offshore for day trips.

EXMOUTH, WESTERN AUSTRALIA

Herds of **Humpbacks** gather in Exmouth Gulf on their southern migration, although the major focus for marine wildlife-watching is at Ningaloo Reef on the other side of the Cape Range Peninsula. Visit www.visitningaloo.com.au for more information – there are also lots of **Humpbacks** in the Ningaloo area, and **Killer Whales** have recently become more common, probably in response to the recovery of **Humpback** numbers.

BROOME, WESTERN AUSTRALIA

With **Australian Snubfin Dolphins** in Roebuck Bay, and **Indo-Pacific Humpback Dolphins** and **Bottlenose Dolphins** near Cable Beach there are good reasons to tootle around in a boat near Broome. Local operators join in the whale-watching fun during **Humpback Whale** migration: for more information visit www.kimberleywhales.com.au and www.broomewhalewatching.com.au.

ASHMORE REEF, WESTERN AUSTRALIA

The farthest outpost of WA is Ashmore Reef, a cluster of three sand cays on a larger atoll, north-west of the Kimberley coast and accessible only by charter boat. No land mammals have been recorded here, but an excellent selection of cetaceans has been logged by birdwatchers during their annual visits to the area, with a maximum of 13 species recorded on one voyage. **Spinner Dolphins** are a feature of these trips, and sometimes occur in huge herds. Both the offshore and 'dwarf' inshore forms are seen, the latter in shallow shelf waters close to Broome. **Common**, **Indo-Pacific Bottlenose** and **Pantropical Spotted Dolphins** are also encountered, as are a number of blackfish, including **Short-flippered Pilot**, **False Killer** and **Melon-headed Whales**. Species seen less regularly include **Fraser's**, **Risso's** and **Rough-toothed Dolphins**. **Sperm** and **Humpback Whales** are also seen occasionally. In between, there are tropical seabirds, sea turtles and sea snakes to look at on the way. Tours run annually from Broome, generally in October–November (see www. kimberleybirdwatching.com.au); if you go there under your own steam, make sure you get the correct permits – the islands are administered through the Commonwealth government and there is a constant security presence there. Beware that it is seriously hot, but calm conditions at this time of year mean cetaceans are often observed well and photographed.

The **Platypus** (p. 258) is widespread and relatively common along the eastern seaboard and in Tasmania, where it shares waterways – and can be confused with – the Water Rat.
Photo: Roger Williams

Echidnas (p. 259) could be encountered almost anywhere, especially in open woodland; watch for trains of males following females during the mating season (June–September).
Photo: Rohan Clarke

Tasmanian Devils (p. 266) are not as common as formerly owing to the fatal Devil Facial Tumour Disease, although an insurance population on Maria I. is thriving. **Photo: Adrian Boyle**

The **Northern Quoll** (p. 264) is an attractive, distinctively marked predator that has all but disappeared over much of its range; it remains moderately common in the Kimberley. **Photo: Adrian Boyle**

Known locally as the 'Chiltern Golden Mouse', the **Yellow-footed Antechinus** (p. 267) is partly diurnal and can often be seen hunting among timber or on tree trunks. **Photo: Tim Dolby**

The distinctively marked **Eastern Barred Bandicoot** (p. 280) remains common in parts of Tasmania and is being reintroduced to select locations in its former range in Victoria. **Photo: Rohan Clarke**

Common Wombats (p. 282) can readily be seen in the south-east and Tasmania; they can be partly diurnal in protected areas and bask outside their burrows in cold weather.
Photo: Leo Berzins

The **Koala** (p. 281) is easily recognisable and has a widespread though patchy distribution; southern animals are larger and usually darker that their northern counterparts.
Photo: Rohan Clarke

The **'Coppery' Brushtail Possum** (p. 291) is a spectacular subspecies of the widespread Common Brushtail Possum; it is endemic to Wet Tropics rainforests and easily spotlighted. **Photo: Adrian Boyle**

Mountain Brushtail Possums (p. 291) are generally found in dense, wet forests, and not necessarily at higher elevations; note the shorter ears of this species. **Photo: Rohan Clarke**

Also known as the Scaly-tailed Possum, the **Wyulda** (p. 291) is endemic to the Kimberley, where it inhabits sandstone outcrops and is especially fond of Rock Figs. **Photo: David Rhind**

In general appearance the **Squirrel Glider** (p. 286) is similar to the Sugar Glider, but it is much bigger and has a larger, bushier tail which always lacks a white tip. **Photo: Rohan Clarke**

The **Common Ringtail Possum** (p. 288) is the most widespread and abundant ringtail possum; it shows great colour variation across its range, which includes large cities.
Photo: Rohan Clarke

The **Green Ringtail** (p. 288) is the most common of the Wet Tropics' endemic possums; during the day it curls into a ball and sleeps on a branch. **Photo: Rohan Clarke**

Largest of the Atherton Tableland ringtails, **Herbert River Ringtails** (p. 288) usually have pale or white underparts, although males can be all-dark. **Photo: Rohan Clarke**

Southern Bettongs (p. 293) reintroduced to Mulligan's Flat in the ACT have prospered, and may become a more common sight during the day, as they probably once were. **Photo: RAWShorty**

An unobtrusive inhabitant of dense heaths and undergrowth, the **Long-nosed Potoroo** (p. 295) can be quite common and even abroad by day where foxes are controlled. **Photo: Leo Berzins**

The **Musky Rat-Kangaroo** (p. 292) is a 'primitive', omnivorous species of Wet Tropics rainforests that probably resembles an ancestral form of macropod dating back to Gondwanan times. **Photo: Rohan Clarke**

Unlike the closely related Red-necked Pademelon, the **Red-legged Pademelon** (p. 309) rarely strays far from the forest interior, where it is superbly camouflaged until it moves. **Photo: Adrian Boyle**

The **Monjon** (p. 304) is the smallest macropod and occurs only in the Kimberley, where it is common among sandstone on the Mitchell Plateau and on several offshore islands.
Photo: Adrian Boyle

The **Bridled Nailtail Wallaby** (p. 303) was rediscovered 30 years after it was thought to have become extinct, although it occurs in only a few reserves in western Queensland.
Photo: John Augusteyn/QPWS

Note the **Mala's** (p. 297) 'hairy avocado' appearance – not so obvious perhaps when the animal is bolting from cover, as it usually does when threatened. **Photo: John French**

Winter in the New South Wales High Country can provide great photo opportunities, because large mammals such as **Red-necked Wallabies** (p. 302) are often abroad during daylight. **Photo: Leo Berzins**

The **Ghost Bat** (p. 316) is Australia's largest microbat – almost as large as a flying fox – and a voracious predator of invertebrates, amphibians, small birds and mammals.
Photo: Adrian Boyle

The **Diadem Leaf-nosed Bat** (p. 318) is a tropical, typically cave-roosting, microbat; individuals vary in colour from fawn, sometimes with white markings, to an orange morph. **Photo: Rohan Clarke**

Endemic to eastern Australia, the **Grey-headed Flying Fox** (p. 315) forms large camps in major cities, such as Brisbane, Sydney and Melbourne, as well as in more natural habitat. **Photo: Leo Berzins**

The **Little Red Flying Fox** (p. 315) is probably the most abundant Australian flying fox, and may occur far inland in good years when it feeds at flowering trees along watercourses. **Photo: Adrian Boyle**

North Queensland's **Prehensile-tailed Rat** (p. 353) is an arboreal rainforest species that appears to be distinct from similar forms in New Guinea with which it was formerly classified. **Photo: Rohan Clarke**

The **Water Rat** (p. 350), or Rakali, is one of Australia's largest rodents and occupies an ecological niche similar to that of otters elsewhere in the world. **Photo: Leo Berzins**

Australia's largest pinniped, the **Southern Elephant Seal** (p. 360), formerly bred on islands in Bass Strait and off Tasmania; individuals still periodically haul up on southern shores. **Photo: Rohan Clarke**

Not all **Dingoes** (p. 360) are the characteristic golden colour and they can vary greatly, even where interbreeding with feral and domestic dogs is rare. **Photo: Leo Berzins**

MAMMAL-FINDING GUIDE

ABBREVIATIONS

ACT – Australian Capital Territory
CYP – Cape York Peninsula
I.   – Island
Is.   – Islands
inc. – including
Mt   – Mount
NP   – National Park or Nature Park
NR   – Nature Reserve
NSW – New South Wales
NT   – Northern Territory
PNG – Papua New Guinea
Qld – Queensland
Rd   – Road
RR   – Recreation Reserve
SA   – South Australia
SF   – State Forest
Tas – Tasmania
Vic – Victoria
WA   – Western Australia
WR   – Wildlife Reserve
*   – Australian endemic species

MAMMALS – CLASS MAMMALIA

Mammals make up the smallest vertebrate class and are defined as warm-blooded animals that have hair (fur) and produce milk to nourish their growing young. Similarities aside, they reproduce in three radically different ways: by laying and incubating eggs; by bearing undeveloped young that are then raised in an external pouch; and by giving birth to live young in varying stages of development that are raised outside their mothers' bodies. Taxonomists therefore divide class Mammalia into three separate subclasses and Australasia is the only part of the world where all three occur.

■ EGG-LAYING MAMMALS – SUBCLASS PROTOTHERIA

Unique to Australia and New Guinea, five extant species that make up this subclass lay soft-shelled eggs and suckle their young through ducts on the females' abdomen, rather than teats. They are often described as 'primitive', although this is more a reflection of their ancient ancestry because they are great survivors and superbly adapted for what they do.

Platypus and echidnas – Order Monotremata

All living species in this order lack whiskers, teeth and external ears. None has gone extinct since European settlement, testament perhaps to the robustness of their evolutionary traits. This order is comprised of just two families.

Platypus – Family Ornithorhynchidae (world 1; Australia 1 (endemic))

The Platypus – the fabulous 'water-mole' that so perplexed naturalists in early colonial days – is relatively common, if unobtrusive, on the eastern seaboard and particularly so in Tas. A 'must-see' for anyone interested in natural history.

*Platypus

Ornithorhynchus anatinus   (eastern mainland and Tas)

Found east of the Great Dividing Range between Cooktown, Qld and south-west Vic, plus King I. and Tas; the Platypus also occurs a surprising distance inland and is possibly overlooked in many places. Several sites offer a high chance of sightings; among them are Kingfisher Park (1.03), Yungaburra (1.04f), Eungella NP (1.22), Queanbeyan (2.13), Cooma (2.14), Bombala and Delegate (2.15), Lake Burley Griffin and Molongolo River (3.01), Warrawee (5.12) and Loongana (5.14); the Platypus can also be seen on Kangaroo I. (6.13), where it was introduced. Some sites claim to be the 'best' place to see a Platypus, but all these sites are good and at times excellent (especially in winter, when males are most active). Any quiet stretch of unpolluted river within its range would be worth checking. See the boxed text below for tips on viewing Platypuses.

Other names: Duck-billed Platypus

Echidnas – Family Tachyglossidae (world 4; Australia 2)

All echidna species have their upper surface covered in stout spines; a tubular snout and long, sticky tongue for eating ants or termites; and long, sharp claws with which they dig vertically into the soil, leaving their spines exposed for defence, when threatened.

Short-beaked Echidna

Tachyglossus aculeatus   (continental Australia and Tas; New Guinea)
Common in many habitats throughout the continent, including rainforests, wet and dry forests, woodland, grassland and desert; generally absent from developed areas and farmland. Echidnas have an ambling gait and are often encountered trundling along roadsides or through forest by day, although they are also active on warm nights and more or less nocturnal in arid areas. Several colour forms occur. Good sites include Chiltern-Mt Pilot NP (4.25) and The Grampians (Gariwerd) NP (4.21). The Tas subspecies *T. a. setosus* is distinctively less spiny and common throughout the island; *T. a. multiaculeatus* occurs on Kangaroo I. (6.13) where it is very common.

Other names: Spiny Anteater

Western Long-beaked Echidna

Zaglossus bruijnii   (north-west Australia; New Guinea)
Almost certainly extinct in Australia. 'Giant' echidnas are known to have existed in Australia until about 5000 years ago and are depicted in Aboriginal rock art. However, a recently examined museum specimen appears to have been collected in the early 20th century in the Kimberley, WA and is included here on that basis. There is a faint hope that it survives in some remote corner of the north-west.

PLATYPUS-WATCHING

Australia's two most common aquatic mammals are the extraordinary, egg-laying Platypus and the Water Rat, a large, attractive rodent that occupies a niche filled by otters on other continents. Seeing a wild Platypus is not as difficult as you might expect and Water Rats often occur in close proximity in the same habitats. Both can be surprisingly common; although Platypuses keep a low profile they are not particularly shy, but it is possible to confuse the two while they are swimming or hunting for prey. Here are some tips for seeing both and to help you differentiate between them.

Where to look: Both Platypuses and Water Rats are widespread along nearly the entire eastern seaboard and in Tas, from sea level to about 1500 m. Platypuses no longer occur naturally west of Vic, although there is an introduced population on Kangaroo I., SA; Water Rats also occur further inland, across northern Australia and in the south-west, although nowhere near as commonly as in the east. Both inhabit most types of natural waterway, including lakes, rivers, creeks and billabongs; as well as artificial wetlands such as weir pools, dams, irrigation channels and reservoirs. Water Rats can occur even in built-up urban areas and will also frequent ornamental ponds and urban lakes, as well as coastal environments such as mangroves, estuaries, breakwaters and storm drains. Platypuses can also be seen in clean waterways in urban environments, but are less common in saline coastal wetlands.

Platypuses are almost never seen out of water, although they may occasionally pause on a log or rock to groom, whereas Water Rats are equally at home in water and on land, and may be seen while swimming, feeding or running along a bank. Ripples in the water are often the key to first spotting these animals. Both are easier to spot where the surface is flat and calm, so ripples are more conspicuous when the animals move.

When to look: Platypuses and Water Rats are most active in the early morning or at dusk, although both may be active at any time of day. Platypus activity is generally most obvious is winter, especially July–September, when males are seeking mates and several may be visible on the same stretch of water for extended periods. Water Rats may also be active at night and can be spotlighted.

Identification: From a distance of about 20 m the two species can be difficult to tell apart. Platypuses float low in the water, resembling a pieces of waterlogged driftwood (about 40–50 cm long), with two rounded bumps marking the top of the head and rump (and sometimes a bit of tail visible as they swim on the surface). With closer views, the first thing to look for is the tail – that of the Platypus is broad, short and rather flat; the Water Rat's tail is long and narrow, with a distinctive white tip.

Platypuses and Water Rats could also be confused with aquatic diving birds, such as grebes and cormorants; large fish such as carp and eels; with freshwater tortoises. This is especially so in dim light or when they are glimpsed only briefly. One of the most commonly confused species is the Musk Duck, a diving duck that swims low in the water; displaying males often sit semi-submerged, with only the head and part of their back showing. In general, though, birds sit higher in the water and have a distinctive profile when seen well.

Swimming and diving: While floating, Platypuses may paddle with their front feet to stay in one spot or to avoid drifting downstream. This creates a conspicuous bull's eye pattern of ripples, which is often the first clue that one is active nearby. The brief arching of their back as they dive leaves an expanding ring of ripples on the surface; the ripples become stronger before gradually fading away. Rings are most obvious where the surface is smooth, but even when it is slightly ruffled by wind the bull's eye effect can be apparent. In contrast, the ripples created by a diving Water Rat are weaker. Normally Platypuses dive silently, but if startled by a predator they may make an audible splash. During a normal feeding pattern a Platypus stays under water for less than a minute and will usually resurface within 20 m of where it dived (Water Rats actively pursue prey underwater and can surface some distance away from where they dive). It will then float on the surface for up to 30 seconds, chewing its prey before diving again. Platypuses can remain underwater for up to 10 minutes – sometimes their progress underwater can be watched by a stream of small bubbles, as pockets of air are squeezed from their fur by water pressure.

While swimming on the surface Platypuses use only their front legs to paddle; this creates a strong bow wave but leaves a long, narrow wake, which can appear as a distinctive silver streak in calm water. Water Rats paddle with their hind legs, leaving a wider, more confused wake. Platypus wakes can be obvious when males are looking for a female or warding off a rival. In winter male Platypuses will sometimes swim along the surface for hundreds of metres.

Other behaviour: While swimming at the surface, a Platypus will often groom itself by scratching and combing its fur with its hind feet. While grooming it can appear oblivious to everything else and even ecstatic. Water Rats usually groom on land, although they will sometimes have a quick scratch on the surface. Platypuses return to the surface to chew their food (which is a great time to observe them). Water Rats usually take their prey to a 'midden' – a platform, such as a rock, log or flattened clump of vegetation, where they dismember and chew larger prey items, leaving a characteristic scatter of discarded mussel shells, yabby claws and carapaces, etc. While feeding they can often be easy to watch.

For more information on both of these fascinating animals, to report a sighting or to take part in a survey, visit the Australian Platypus Conservancy's website (www.platypus.asn.au).

◾ MARSUPIALS (POUCHED MAMMALS) – SUBCLASS MARSUPIALIA

Marsupial young are born as undeveloped embryos and cling to their mother's teats after birth until they are old enough to fend for themselves. Adult females of most species have a pouch in which the young shelter until they become independent, although pouches can be almost non-existent, as in dasyurids, or well developed, as in macropods. Australasian marsupials (they also occur in the Americas) fall into four taxonomic orders: carnivorous marsupials; marsupial moles; bandicoots and bilbies; marsupial herbivores such as koalas, kangaroos, and wombats and possums.

Carnivorous marsupials – Order Dasyuromorphia

Australia is the stronghold of carnivorous marsupials, which range from tiny, shrew-like planigales to the Tasmanian Devil and dog-sized Thylacine. All are nocturnal or primarily so and voracious predators of invertebrates – often several times their own body weight – small mammals, birds and, in the case of the Tasmanian Devil, carrion.

Carnivorous marsupials – Family Dasyuridae (world 70; Australia 55 (53 endemic))

This large family includes all of Australia's extant marsupial carnivores. Dasyurids lack a well-defined pouch, their young instead clinging to their mother's teats until they are literally too big for her to carry. Some species feature massive male die-off at the end of the breeding season, when all the males in a population die after mating. At these times the males may be active during the day and consequently easy to observe. Most dasyurids are small, shrew- and rodent-sized species that are very difficult or impossible to identify in the field. Others, such as quolls, are large, attractively marked and sometimes encountered during the day, especially in Tas where they are still relatively common.

*Brush-tailed Mulgara

Dasycercus blythi   (arid WA, NT, western Qld)

The taxonomy of mulgaras is unresolved and the limits of their distribution vague and overlapping in places (for example, the Canning Stock Route and southern NT). Positive identification may be possible only in the hand, but tail morphology is a critical feature – the tail is short, fattened at the base and has a black tip. This species is an inhabitant of spinifex grasslands and constructs burrows in dune swales and lower slopes; they may bask outside burrows during warm winter days. It occurs near Uluru (8.18) and in the Tanami Desert (8.21).

*Crest-tailed Mulgara

Dasycercus cristicauda   (arid NT, SA)

Until recently lumped with Brush-tailed Mulgara, this species is larger and differs in having brighter coloration and a distinct ridge of black hairs along the upper surface of its tail. It has a much smaller distribution, in the southern Simpson Desert and northern Strzelecki and Tirari deserts of SA. Both mulgara species occur in close proximity in the Simpson Desert. The Crest-tailed Mulgara hunts on sand dunes with sparse canegrass and stands of Nitre Bush *Nitraria billardieri* on the edges of salt lakes; burrows are usually located at the base of these plants (where they overlap in range, Brush-tailed Mulgara burrows tend to be on lower dune slopes and on flat ground between dunes).

Other names: Mulgara, Ampurta

*Kaluta

Dasykaluta rosamondae   (Pilbara and Little Sandy Desert, WA)
Fairly common in subtropical arid hummock grassland within its range. Generally easy to recognise by its size, reddish colour, stocky appearance and carrot-shaped tail.

Other names: Little Red Kaluta, Little Red Antechinus, Spinifex Antechinus

*Kowari

Dasyuroides byrnei   (Lake Eyre basin)
A rat-sized, phascogale-like predator that inhabits gibber plains in the Channel Country of arid north-east SA and south-west Qld. Its beautiful tail brush is a diagnostic feature. It is generally found in sparsely vegetated areas between braided river channels and sand dunes, burrowing in islands of sand on gibber plains. It is generally rare but periodic irruptions occur – it preys on Long-haired Rats, among other species, and can be common when suitable conditions occur; such events have occurred around Birdsville, at Sandringham Station and Koonchera Sand Dune. It can be spotlighted in suitable habitat, for example in the Diamantina and Astrebla Downs NPs, Qld.

Other names: Brush-tailed or Bushy-tailed Marsupial Rat

Quolls can be readily identified in the field, owing to their attractive ginger, brown or black coats spotted with white or cream. After the Tasmanian Devil they are the largest living dasyurids, about the size of a small domestic cat, and were formerly known as 'native cats'. On the mainland they tend to be rare and retiring; only Tas offers near-guaranteed sightings. Quolls use rock crevices, tree hollows, disused burrows, hollow logs and woodpiles as dens. They may be partly diurnal, especially during breeding season (after which males die off) and on overcast days.

*Western Quoll

Dasyurus geoffroyi   (south-west WA)
This species formerly occurred across much of inland Australia, but is now endangered and restricted to a few pockets of forest and woodland in the south-west. Chance encounters are not common and it is perhaps most likely to be seen at Dryandra SF (7.05) or Perup (7.08).

Other names: Chuditch, Western Native Cat, Idnya

*Northern Quoll

Dasyurus hallucatus   (tropical northern Australia)

The smallest quoll and likely to be confused only with the Spot-tailed Quoll, with which its range overlaps in northern Qld. It has all but disappeared from the Top End in recent years, possibly as a result of the Cane Toad invasion, even at former strongholds such as Kakadu NP (8.03), but survives in pockets throughout the tropics, even being relatively common in the Kimberley and parts of north Qld. It may be spotlighted on back roads in the Wet Tropics near, for example, Granite Gorge (1.04b), Mareeba Wetlands (1.04c) and Mt Carbine, and is also reputed to survive at Cape Cleveland near Townsville (1.13). This quoll is both terrestrial and arboreal.

Other names: Northern Native Cat

*Spot-tailed Quoll

Dasyurus maculatus   (south-east mainland and Tas)

The largest dasyurid surviving on the mainland, this attractive, domestic cat-sized predator inhabits rugged, hilly country and is more arboreal than other quolls. Adults have a luxuriant pelt and long tail, and come in various shades from ginger to almost black. The subspecies *D. m. maculatus* occurs in south-east Australia, but is common only in Tas, particularly in karst country in the rugged north-west. Some are fed carcasses at Loongana (5.14), although they are shy and sightings are not guaranteed every night. Otherwise, night drives in suitable habitat could pay off; the northern approaches to Cradle Mountain-Lake St Clair NP (5.09) seem to be reliable. This subspecies is still relatively common in the New England Tablelands and individuals turn up sporadically in Canberra. The north Qld subspecies *D. m. gracilis* occurs in many habitats and, like its southern counterpart, often turns up unexpectedly, for example, at Mareeba Wetlands (1.04c), Kingfisher Park (1.03) and in the Mt Molloy area.

Other names: Spotted-tailed Quoll, Tiger Quoll, Tiger Cat

*Eastern Quoll

Dasyurus viverrinus   (Tas)

Now extinct on the mainland, the Eastern Quoll is still relatively common in Tas. It could be confused with the much larger Spot-tailed Quoll, which has a more luxuriant, spotted tail; the two aren't usually found in close proximity. Eastern Quolls vary in colour from fawn to black and inhabit a variety of forest and heath habitats. It is often seen on night drives, for example between Hobart and Mt Field; in the car park and picnic grounds at Mt Field NP (5.07); and on Bruny I. (5.04). Sometimes seen foraging in paddocks, especially near tree cover, and scavenges around mountain huts and lodges, for example at Ben Lomond – where it may sometimes be seen during the day – and Cradle Mountain Lodge (5.09).

Other names: Eastern Native Cat

*The **Dibbler** is an unusual dasyurid endemic to the south-west. It is largely nocturnal but at least partly diurnal on Boullanger I. Male die-off occurs but not necessarily in the whole population.*

*Dibbler

Parantechinus apicalis   (south-west WA)

An anomalous species that occurs in disparate parts of the south-west, including Boullanger I. (7.11) where it is abundant in heath; Whitlock I. and Escape I., to where it has been translocated; Fitzgerald River NP, where it is relatively common in old growth mallee; and the Cheyne's Beach area near Albany where daytime sightings have been claimed. Probably recognisable in the field by its fattened, carrot-shaped tail and whitish eye-ring. There are plans to reintroduce it to Peniup NR and the Stirling Range NP (7.06).

Other names: Southern Dibbler

The six species in the genus Pseudantechinus *were formerly considered part of the genus* Antechinus *and are usually known as **False Antechinuses**, although some texts still use pseudantechinus as a common name. They closely resemble antechinuses, which they replace in the arid zone.*

*Sandstone False Antechinus

Pseudantechinus bilarni   (Top End and south-west Gulf Country)

Relatively common in boulder scree and slabs in rock piles, especially among open forest with a grassy understory. This is the only false antechinus with a thin tail. It is partly diurnal and known from various sites including the Table Top Range, Nourlangie Rock (8.03b), Arnhem Land escarpment and Wollogorang Station (8.13).

Other names: Sandstone Antechinus or Pseudantechinus, Harney's Antechinus

*Fat-tailed False Antechinus

Pseudantechinus macdonnellensis   (central Australia)

Uncommon on sparsely vegetated rocky slopes and nearby plains, for example West MacDonnell NP (8.17); also on red sand plains in the Tanami Desert (8.21), where it may nest in termite mounds. Mainly nocturnal but basks on warm winter days. Its tail is often carrot-shaped and it has a large orange patch behind the ears.

Other names: Fat-tailed Antechinus or Pseudantechinus, Red-eared Antechinus

*Carpentarian False Antechinus

Pseudantechinus mimulus   (sandstone of south-west Gulf country)

Known only from the Sir Edward Pellew Group of islands in the Gulf of Carpentaria and scattered mainland sites, including Mt Isa and Alexandria Station, NT. Found on stony hillsides with shrubs, open woodland and hummock grass.

*Ningbing False Antechinus

Pseudantechinus ningbing   (Kimberley and adjacent NT)

Locally common throughout the Kimberley east to Gregory River NP, NT. Occupies rocky outcrops in sandstone and limestone among a range of vegetation types.

*Rory's False Antechinus

Pseudantechinus roryi   (Pilbara and adjacent deserts)

A reddish-brown species of false antechinus, known from the Cape Range to near the NT border and also Barrow I. (7.18). Apparently most common around granite tors on sand plains (where it may co-occur with Woolley's False Antechinus); also known from woodlands, Spinifex grasslands and boulder piles. Associates with termite mounds.

*Woolley's False Antechinus

Pseudantechinus woolleyae   (Pilbara and adjacent deserts)

Uncommon on rocky hillsides with acacia scrub and hummock grasses. The largest false antechinus, similar to the preceding species, from which it is difficult to tell apart, even in the hand. *P. woolleyae* has a less swollen tail, less prominent red ear patch and a tail shorter than its body length. Its range overlaps with that of Rory's Antechinus.

*The **Tasmanian Devil** is the largest surviving dasyurid; it is unmistakable and now occurs naturally only in Tas, although it lived on the mainland before the arrival of the Dingo.*

*Tasmanian Devil

Sarcophilus harrisi   (Tas)

Australia's largest surviving native terrestrial carnivore is unmistakable and frequents mosaics of farmland and forest. It was formerly common, but the hideous devil facial tumour disease (DFTD) has wiped out large numbers and has so far eluded a cure. Captive breeding programs have been initiated on the mainland and a population has been translocated to Maria I. (5.06). It can still be seen at close quarters at Mountain View Cottages (5.14) and less reliably at Cradle Mountain-Lake St Clair NP (5.09). The traditional method for seeing devils was to drive around at night in suitable habitat; this method would probably still work throughout the hilly and mountainous parts of Tas's north-west. This species is very vocal, uttering loud grunts and screams, and fighting among individuals is common.

Antechinuses and phascogales – Subfamily Phascogalinae

*The 12 species of **antechinus** are mouse-sized predators of coastal forests; some at least are partly diurnal, especially during male die-off, although they are usually seen only with patience and luck. Most can be reliably separated only in the hand, although others can be recognised in the field; for example the Yellow-footed Antechinus by its coloration and Dusky Antechinus by its large size.*

*Rusty Antechinus

Antechinus adustus   (Wet Tropics)

A recently described species from highland tropical forest above about 600 m between Paluma and Mossman, Qld. Mainly diurnal and found at edges of undisturbed rainforest, particularly among rotting logs. Terrestrial and arboreal, nesting in tree hollows. Its range overlaps with the Atherton Antechinus and Yellow-footed Antechinus. Male die-off occurs.

*Agile Antechinus

Antechinus agilis   (south-east mainland)

Almost identical to the Brown Antechinus and common in hilly, forested country in the south-east up to about 2000 m. Often trapped on fauna surveys, otherwise infrequently encountered. It is small, furtive and fast, and climbs readily. Common at Lamington NP (1.37), Barren Grounds NR (2.06) and Nullica SF, NSW. Male die-off occurs.

*Silver-headed Antechinus

Antechinus argentus   (south-east Qld)

Described in 2013 and known only from the eastern escarpment of Kroombit Tops NP in south-east Qld, about 60 km south-west of Gladstone. It is apparently rare but easily distinguished in the field by its silvery-grey appearance, with much paler feet and a deeper grey-olive rump than Yellow-footed Antechinus, which also occurs in the general area.

*Black-tailed Antechinus

Antechinus arktos   (south-east Qld and north-east NSW)

A recently described species known only from the rim of the ancient Tweed Volcano caldera (parts of which are included in Lamington NP and the Gondwanan Rainforests World Heritage Area). A large, distinctively marked antechinus found only at high altitude forest in the region. Rare and little known.

*Fawn Antechinus

Antechinus bellus   (Top End)

The only antechinus that occurs in Top End woodlands, including Kakadu NP (8.03), where it was formerly common, even being seen around campgrounds and preying on geckoes near houses. Rather arboreal, and vocal, uttering a *zit* sound as it hunts, sometimes in close proximity to other individuals. Its pale coloration should be diagnostic.

Other names: Fawn Marsupial Mouse

*Yellow-footed Antechinus

Antechinus flavipes   (south-east and south-west mainland, Wet Tropics)

A large antechinus that can be identified in the field by its pale legs and feet, and the contrast between its grey head and russet body colour. It is found in a wide variety of habitats, from tropical forests to woodland, mulga and heath. It also enters houses and gardens, and may be active on overcast days. It hunts with darting, furtive movements, and climbs well but is hard to observe. This species is a bloodthirsty hunter that eviscerates introduced mice and raids aviaries. Several subspecies are recognised: *A. f. leucogaster* occurs in the south-west; *A. f. flavipes* in the south-east; and *A. f. rubeculus* in north Qld. Northern specimens are larger and redder; those in the south-west palest with white underparts; and paler, yellower feet in southern regions. Chiltern-Mt Pilot NP (4.25) is a good place to see it and it occurs in Red Ironbark-Box Woodland from there north to Back Yamma SF, NSW. It sometimes responds to squeaking and can be very visible during male die-off occurs in July, for example at Lake Eacham (1.04g).

Other names: Yellow-footed Marsupial Mouse, 'Chiltern Golden Mouse', Mardo

*Atherton Antechinus

Antechinus godmani (Wet Tropics)

A rare and little-known species patchily distributed in rainforest above 600 m between Cardwell and the Atherton Tableland. Larger than the two other antechinuses with which it co-occurs; its almost naked tail is a diagnostic feature. Partly diurnal. Male die-off occurs. Absent from forest remnants smaller than about 190 ha.

*Cinnamon Antechinus

Antechinus leo (Cape York Peninsula)

Restricted to semi-deciduous rainforest between the McIlwraith and Iron Ranges on Cape York Peninsula. Very agile and partly arboreal; on the ground it uses logs and tree roots as pathways. Mainly nocturnal but also active at dusk. It is the only antechinus in its range. Male die-off occurs.

Other names: Iron Range Antechinus, Cape York Antechinus

*Swamp Antechinus

Antechinus minimus (coastal south-east SA, Vic, Tas)

A terrestrial inhabitant of dense, swampy vegetation in southern states from Robe, SA to South Gippsland, Tas and islands of Bass Strait. Occurs at Wilson's Promontory (4.24) and Anglesea (4.16). Unlikely to be encountered other than by trapping. Generally found below 200 m on the mainland and below 1000 m in Tas.

Other names: Little Tasmanian Marsupial Mouse

*Buff-footed Antechinus

Antechinus mysticus (southern Qld)

Another recently described species, currently known from north of the NSW border to about Mackay, Qld although it could be expected to occur in north-east NSW as well. Similar to the Yellow-footed Antechinus but distinguishable in the field by its paler feet and tail base, and a greyish head that merges to buff–yellow on the rump and flanks.

*Brown Antechinus

Antechinus stuartii   (eastern mainland)

Almost identical to the Agile Antechinus, with which it overlaps near Kioloa, NSW; and the Subtropical Antechinus, overlapping in the NSW–Qld border region. Common in forests and heaths with thick ground cover and plenty of fallen timber at, for example, Barren Grounds (2.06). Male die-off occurs. Mainly terrestrial, but more arboreal in dry forest and where it co-occurs with the larger Dusky Antechinus. Males are vocal in the lead up to mating, uttering a staccato *chee*. Active during the day in cool weather.

Other names: Macleay's Marsupial Mouse, Stuart's Antechinus

*Subtropical Antechinus

Antechinus subtropicus   (south-east Qld, north-east NSW)

Replaces the Brown Antechinus in south-east Qld, with an area of overlap in the NSW–Qld border region. Common in subtropical forest below 1000 m between Gympie, Qld and Dorrigo, NSW, especially where there is dense undergrowth and rotten logs. It often enters gardens and houses. Male die-off occurs.

*Dusky Antechinus

Antechinus swainsonii   (south-east mainland, Tas)

The largest antechinus and most abundant in montane heath or forest with a dense understorey. Often active by day and largely terrestrial, although young animals climb low branches. Replaces other antechinus species above about 1800 m and sometimes seen basking on boulders in Kosciuszko NP (2.16) at, for example, Charlotte's Pass and Mt Kosciuszko summit. Fast-moving, with jerky movements. Male die-off occurs.

Other names: Swainson's Antechinus, Dusky Marsupial Mouse

*The three species of **phascogale** are smaller than quolls and lack their distinctive coloration, but can be recognised by their bushy 'bottlebrush' tails. Phascogales are reputedly difficult to spotlight. Male die-off occurs in all three species.*

*Red-tailed Phascogale

Phascogale calura   (south-west WA)

Rare and restricted to blocks of remnant vegetation in the WA wheatbelt. Particularly associated with stands of Rock Sheoak *Allocasuarina huegeliana* and Wandoo *Eucalyptus wandoo*, where it is highly arboreal. Mainly nocturnal, sometimes active by day and possible to spotlight, especially in June and July when mating is at its peak. Known strongholds include Dryandra SF (7.05) and Wadderin Sanctuary (7.07).

Other names: Red-tailed Wambenger

*Northern Brush-tailed Phascogale

Phascogale pirata   (Top End)

Restricted to the Top End, potentially overlapping with the Brush-tailed Phascogale at the western and eastern edges of its range; it can be distinguished in the field by its white hind feet. An arboreal inhabitant of savannah woodland dominated by Darwin Woollybutt and Darwin Stringybark. Formerly common, it is now rare and seen mainly in Kakadu NP (8.03), Litchfield NP (8.10), around Batchelor and in remote areas such as the Cobourg Peninsula (8.04) and Melville I. (8.11).

*Brush-tailed Phascogale

Phascogale tapoatafa   (Kimberley, east and south-west Australia)

An active, agile and mainly arboreal predator in forests ranging from mallee to rainforest. Now uncommon everywhere; difficult but not impossible to spotlight in suitable areas. The best chance of seeing one would probably be to take part in a survey at, say, Perup (7.08) or in Vic, where there are isolated populations in reserves such as Rushworth SF. Taps its forefeet against bark when alarmed. Subspecies in the Kimberley and south-west await description.

Other names: Tuan (Vic), Common Wambenger (WA)

Planigales and ningauis – Subfamily Planigalinae

*These tiny predators are among the world's smallest carnivorous mammals and are found mainly in the arid zone. All have more or less flattening of the skull to allow access to tiny crevices in rocks and cracked clay soils. **Planigales** are distinguished by narrow, almost triangular faces, and narrow bodies adapted for squeezing between rocks and into cracks in dried mud. All are active, mainly nocturnal hunters that are mainly terrestrial but will also climb low vegetation. Undescribed planigales occur in WA and may prove to be distinct species.*

*Giles' Planigale

Planigale gilesi   (arid eastern Australia)

An inhabitant of dense lignum and canegrass on clay-soil floodplains and dune swales where deep cracks offer shelter. Often occurs alongside the Narrow-nosed Planigale. Basks on cool days. Moves with hind feet alongside body. Tail can become swollen with stored fat in good seasons. More crepuscular than the Narrow-nosed Planigale and most active after sunset and just before dawn.

Other names: Paucident Planigale

*Long-tailed Planigale

Planigale ingrami   (northern Australia)

The world's smallest marsupial and Australia's smallest mammal, weighing as little as 4 g. Lives and hunts in crevices on black soil plains and riparian habitats including seasonally flooded grasslands. Abundant in suitable habitat and sometimes active in the early morning after cold nights.

Other names: Northern Planigale, Ingram's Planigale, Blacksoil Planigale

*Common Planigale

Planigale maculata   (eastern and northern mainland)

Found in a variety of habitats, including dense vegetation fringing floodplains in the Kimberley and Top End, and forest and rainforest in eastern Australia. Two subspecies are recognised: *P. m. maculata* in Qld and NSW, and *P. m. sinualis* in the NT and adjacent areas; populations on Barrow I. and the Pilbara may be one or two separate species. Common but little known, even though it occurs on urban fringes. Some individuals have small pale spots.

*Narrow-nosed Planigale

Planigale tenuirostris   (inland eastern Australia)

Occurs in open habitats with cracking clay soils, such as dry lake beds, gibber and among Mitchell Grass, saltbush, canegrass and mallee. Mainly terrestrial but climbs low vegetation. Basks on sunny winter days, but spends a great deal of time underground when hunting.

*Wongai Ningaui

Ningaui ridei   (arid Australia)

Inhabits hummock grassland with scattered trees and shrubs on sandy soils over a wide area of central Australia. It occurs at Uluru (8.18), in the Simpson Desert at Ethabuka, and Wanjarri and Gibson Desert NRs, WA.

Other names: Ride's Ningaui

*Pilbara Ningaui

Ningaui timealeyi   (Pilbara)

Found only in the Pilbara, where it inhabits dense hummock grassland along drainage lines with mallee or scrub. Partly arboreal. Common, but retreats to damp refugia during dry conditions.

Other names: Ealey's Ningaui

*Mallee Ningaui

Ningaui yvonneae   (southern mainland)

This ningaui occurs in semi-arid heath and mallee with spinifex in scattered locations across southern Australia. Uses Spinifex hummocks as cover, with forays into adjacent leaf litter. Occurs in Sunset Country and Big Desert (4.23), Round Hill (2.25) and southern WA.

Other names: Southern Ningaui

Kultarr and dunnarts – Subfamily Sminthopsinae

The **Kultarr** *is an extraordinary, hopping-mouse-like carnivore with elongated hind legs.* **Dunnarts,** *formerly known as 'marsupial mice', make up the largest dasyurid genus. Some are relatively common but detected only when they are caught in pitfall traps. In the hand care must be taken to separate some dunnarts from the House Mouse, which has a distinct musky odour, a sparsely furred, flesh-coloured tail and lacks the notched ears of some dunnarts.*

*Kultarr

Antechinomys laniger   (arid inland)

Wide-ranging but irruptive on open treeless plains, gibber and sparsely vegetated sand deserts. Present at Scotia AWC Sanctuary (2.29), where it may best be seen on trapping surveys; very occasionally seen at Arid Recovery (6.11). It is quadrupedal and doesn't actually hop, but is capable of moving very quickly. It is recognisable by its long, tufted tail and dark eye-ring. Two subspecies are recognised: *A. l. laniger* of eastern Australia, which is typically found in claypans among *Acacia* woodland; and *A. l. spenceri*, found on stony plains among *Acacia*, *Eremophila* and *Cassia* scrub in central and western Australia. Uncommon, possibly with seasonal fluctuations.

Other names: Jerboa-marsupial, Jerboa Pouched-mouse, Jerboa Marsupial mouse, Wuhl-wuhl, Pitchi-pitchi

*Kangaroo Island Dunnart

Sminthopsis aitkeni   (Kangaroo I.)

Endemic to Kangaroo I. (6.13), where it is rare and little known. Only a few specimens have ever been trapped and retraps are uncommon. All records are from the western half of the island in mallee heath on laterite soils, for example in Flinders Chase NP.

Other names: Sooty Dunnart

Chestnut Dunnart

Sminthopsis archeri   (PNG; north Qld)

Rare and known only from woodland on red earth soils and tropical heaths. Most records are from Cape York Peninsula, including Iron Range NP (1.17), with outlying populations near Townsville and in the Wet Tropics, indicating it may be more widely distributed.

*Kakadu Dunnart

Sminthopsis bindi   (Top End)

A tiny, delicate dunnart that frequents gravelly hillsides with eucalyptus woodland in the Top End. Little known.

*Butler's Dunnart

Sminthopsis butleri   (Tiwi Is., Kimberley)

Known only from Melville and Bathurst Is. (8.11) and from near Kalumburu in the northern Kimberley (7.21). Rare; encountered only during surveys using pitfall traps. Coastal eucalyptus and melaleuca woodland on sandy soils appear to be its favoured habitat.

Other names: Carpentarian Dunnart, Munjol

*Fat-tailed Dunnart

Sminthopsis crassicaudata   (inland southern Australia)

Widespread and relatively common in grasslands, gibber, saltbush plains and pasture. Its fat, carrot-shaped tail is a good identification feature, although this may vary in girth depending on conditions. Forages in open areas with sparse cover, where it can sometimes be spotlighted.

Other names: Fat-tailed Marsupial Mouse

*Little Long-tailed Dunnart

Sminthopsis dolichura   (south and south-west mainland)

A small dunnart of dry forest, woodland, mallee and heath. Its size and long tail are diagnostic features. This species seems to colonise recently burnt areas, especially three or four years after fire.

*Julia Creek Dunnart

Sminthopsis douglasi   (central Qld)

The largest dunnart within its range. Little known and endangered, it inhabits Mitchell Grass downs and cracking clay soils between Julia Creek and Richmond in central inland Qld.

*Gilbert's Dunnart

Sminthopsis gilberti   (southern SA and WA)

Found mainly in heath and associated forest in southern WA, with an outlying population on the Roe Plain near the SA–WA border. A white patch behind the ear is a useful identification feature. Populations are known from Tutanning, Dragon Rocks and Nuytsland NRs, WA.

*White-tailed Dunnart

Sminthopsis granulipes   (south-west WA)

A little-known species of coastal heath and mallee shrubland. There are two disjunct populations: one north of Perth between Jurien and Kalbarri; the other in the Goldfields region. Its tail is more or less white and a diagnostic feature. Known from Dragon Rocks and Jilbadgi NRs and Kalbarri NP, WA.

Other names: Granular-footed Marsupial Mouse, Ash-grey Dunnart

*Grey-bellied Dunnart

Sminthopsis griseoventor   (south-west WA and Eyre Peninsula)

Relatively common in coastal forest, woodland and heath between Geraldton and Cocklebiddy, WA with populations on Boullanger I. (7.11), which it shares with the Dibbler, and the Eyre Peninsula (6.15). Its pinkish tail is diagnostic. It appears to be most common in sandy heaths that haven't been burnt for at least 10 years. Two forms are recognised: the mainland subspecies *S. g. griseoventer* and the Boullanger I. subspecies *S. g. boullangerensis*.

*(Greater) Hairy-footed Dunnart

Sminthopsis hirtipes (arid mainland)

Found south of the tropics in arid and semi-arid woodland, heath and hummock grassland. Outlying populations occur at Shark Bay, for example at Francois Peron NP (7.15a), as well as Kalbarri NP (7.14) and on the Eyre Peninsula (6.15); it is also known from Wanjarri, Neale Junction and Queen Victoria Spring NRs in WA; and from the Mamungari (formerly known as Unnamed) CP in SA.

Other names: Fringe-footed Sminthopsis, Hairy-footed Pouched Mouse

*White-footed Dunnart

Sminthopsis leucopus (south-east mainland and Tas, Wet Tropics)

Restricted to southern Vic and NSW; Tas, including some islands of Bass Strait, where it is the only dunnart species; with an outlying population in upland rainforest near Paluma, Qld. It is almost indistinguishable from the Common Dunnart although their ranges barely overlap. Found in heaths, woodland and forest. Known from Mumbulla SF, NSW and Great Otway NP (4.16); it appears to be a species of early to mid-successional stages after fire or logging. The subspecies *S. l. leucopus* occurs on the mainland and *S. l. ferruginifrons* in Tas. Outlying populations could be due a taxonomic review.

Other names: White-footed Marsupial Mouse

*Long-tailed Dunnart

Sminthopsis longicaudata (western arid zone)

Tail twice body length. Known only from rocky scree with hummock grassland and shrubs in rocky ranges of the central deserts between the Pilbara and the MacDonnell Ranges near Alice Springs, for example in Gibson Desert NR, the Murchison Ranges and Ormiston Gorge NP (8.17).

Other names: Long-tailed Marsupial Mouse, Large Long-tailed Dunnart

*Stripe-faced Dunnart

Sminthopsis macroura (central and northern mainland)

An attractive dunnart with distinctive face markings that occurs over much of the inland in grassland and shrublands, especially on sandy soils. Where its range overlaps that of the Fat-tailed Dunnart, its striped head and longer tail are diagnostic. The three recognised subspecies may prove to be separate species, although they are almost indistinguishable even in the hand. *S. m. macroura* occurs in central, eastern and western Australia; *S. m. stalkeri* in central northern Australia; and *S. m. froggatti* in the Kimberley.

*Common Dunnart

Sminthopsis murina (south-east mainland and Wet Tropics)

Very similar to the White-footed Dunnart, although it occurs in drier habitats, including woodland and mallee, as well as coastal heath. There is an outlier on the Atherton

Tableland, *S. m. tatei*, that may also be a distinct species. The south-eastern subspecies *S. m. murina* occurs over much of Vic and NSW, as well as south-east SA and south-east Qld, with an outlying population in the Flinders Ranges, SA.

Other names: Mouse Dunnart, Common Marsupial Mouse, Mouse-sminthopsis, Slender Mouse-sminthopsis

*Ooldea Dunnart

Sminthopsis ooldea   (central arid zone)
An inhabitant of arid woodland, mulga, mallee and hummock grassland in extremely remote country between the Tanami Desert (8.21) and Ooldea, SA. Known from Uluru-Kata Tjuta (8.18) and West MacDonnell (8.17) NPs; Gibson Desert and Plumridge Lakes NR, WA; and Mamungari (formerly Unnamed) CP, SA, among other sites.

Other names: Troughton's Dunnart

*Sandhill Dunnart

Sminthopsis psammophila   (southern arid zone)
Rare and endangered. Known only from scattered locations in the deserts of SA (including the Great Victoria Desert), WA and the NT. Its preferred habitat appears to be low parallel dunes with open woodland and an understorey of shrubs and hummock grass. Its tail colour is diagnostic – light grey above and dark below.

Other names: Large Desert Sminthopsis

Red-cheeked Dunnart

Sminthopsis virginiae   (northern Australia; New Guinea)
The largest tropical dunnart. If seen well in the field it can be identified by its distinctive reddish facial coloration. It occurs in savannah woodland, grasslands, wetland edges and forest margins. Two subspecies occur in Australia: *S. v. virginiae* in tropical Qld and *S. v. nitela* from the Top End and scattered locations in the Kimberley. It can be common in Kakadu NP (8.03) after good seasons.

*Lesser Hairy-footed Dunnart

Sminthopsis youngsoni   (northern arid zone)
A tiny dunnart with bold facial markings, found in subtropical hummock grassland on sandy substrate in central Australia. Known from Uluru-Kata Tjuta NP (8.18).

Numbat – Family Myrmecobiidae (world 1; Australia 1 (endemic))

The Numbat is diurnal, distinctively marked and terrestrial – traits that make it unique among Australian marsupials and hence unmistakable. It feeds by digging up termites from under the soil. It was formerly widely distributed across southern Australia, but now

survives in the wild only in south-west Western Australia and where it has been reintroduced to conservation reserves elsewhere.

*Numbat

Myrmecobus fasciatus   (south-west WA)

Numbats are most easily seen in Jarrah and Wandoo forests at Dryandra SF (7.05) and Perup (7.08), although there are also populations at Batalling SF, Boyagin NR, Tutanning NR and Dragon Rocks NR in the south-west. Elsewhere, they have been reintroduced to Scotia (2.29), Karakamia (7.01) and Yookamurra (6.04) AWC Sanctuaries. Numbats frequent fallen timber, where they run squirrel-like along the ground and can be quite approachable but will dart into hollow logs or under bushes if threatened. They are active year-round, retreating to burrows at night. In summer they may take a siesta in the hotter part of the day; in winter they typically bask outside their burrows but may not emerge until after 9 in the morning, retiring at about 4 pm, depending on conditions. Burrows may be under copses of dense shrubs such as *Dryandra* or among fallen timber.

Other names: Banded Anteater

Thylacine – Family Thylacinidae (world 1; Australia 1 (endemic))

The largest marsupial carnivore to survive into historic times, the Thylacine was a doglike animal that is often cited as a textbook case of convergent evolution (dogs did not appear in Australia until the Dingo was introduced by Aboriginal hunters about 3500 years ago). It went extinct on the mainland about 2000 years ago, probably succumbing to competition or even predation from the Dingo. The last extant population hung on in Tas until the early 20th century, when trappers and hunters finally wiped it out.

*Thylacine

Thylacinus cyanocephalus   (Tas)

Extinct. Sorry, folks, it's gone. There's a romantic notion that the Thylacine hangs on somewhere in Tas, but there has been no hard evidence of its continued survival since 1936, when the last known specimen died in Hobart Zoo. There have been plenty of claimed sightings since (even on the mainland!) and some dubious photos, but so far no evidence has withstood independent scrutiny. If you want to mount an expedition, the best place to look would probably be in its last stronghold: the dense, remote scrub of north-west Tas.

Other names: Tasmanian Tiger, Tasmanian Wolf

Marsupial moles – Order Notoryctemorphia

Marsupial moles are a fascinating case of convergent evolution – marsupials that live almost their entire lives underground and consequently resemble 'true' moles, especially the golden moles of southern Africa. This order is unique to Australia and is comprised of a single family and only two species.

Marsupial moles – Family Notoryctidae (world 2; Australia 2 (both endemic))

Although marsupial moles are widespread in arid areas, they are rarely seen by casual observers and several aspects of their life remain a mystery. The two species are probably indistinguishable in the field; if you are lucky enough to encounter one, accurate identification would be safest at the extremities of their respective distributions as there is an area of overlap. Both inhabit sandy desert country, where they burrow through soft sand just below the surface, and are most often detected when they emerge after heavy rain, leaving tracks unique to each species.

*Northern Marsupial Mole

Notoryctes caurinus   (deserts of inland Australia)
Smaller than the Southern Marsupial Mole, with a narrower and shorter snout. Sparsely distributed in the sand-dune deserts of the north-west, including the Great and Little Sandy Deserts, and Eighty Mile Beach.

Other names: Kakarratul

*Southern Marsupial Mole

Notoryctes typhlops   (deserts of inland Australia)
Occurs in sandy deserts over a vast area of central Australia. When moving over the surface it leaves a distinctive, sinuous drag mark caused by pressing its tail into the ground; the surface tracks of the Northern Marsupial Mole resemble those of a sea turtle hauling itself over sand.

Other names: Itjaritjari

Bandicoots and bilbies – Order Peramelemorphia

Bandicoots are terrestrial marsupials, endemic to Australasia, that range from rat- to rabbit-sized. They are mainly or exclusively nocturnal, feeding on arthropods, small vertebrates and plant matter such as fungi and tubers. The name 'bandicoot' probably came from Dutch explorers, who thought them akin to the bandicoot of the Indian subcontinent (which is actually a type of rodent). 'Bilby' refers to the long-legged, large-eared desert species. This marsupial order has suffered a high extinction rate since European settlement as all species fall into the Critical Weight Range category (see boxed text p. 278); some hang on only in isolated areas or on offshore islands. Recent taxonomic changes now recognise three families.

Pig-footed Bandicoot – Family Chaeropodidae (world 1; Australia 1 (endemic))

An extraordinary, long-legged bandicoot whose toenails formed a hooflike claw like a pig's trotter and probably gave it a quadrupedal gait.

*Pig-footed Bandicoot

Chaeropus ecaudatus (arid and semi-arid inland Australia)

Extinct. Formerly widespread in grassy woodland, shrubland, dunes and sandy country with hummock grassland. The last specimen was collected in 1901 although some possibly survived until the 1950s in the Great Sandy and Gibson Deserts.

Bandicoots – Family Peramelidae (world 7; Australia 7 (6 endemic; 1 extinct))

Some of the 'typical' bandicoots are still common on the outskirts of large cities, such as Sydney and Brisbane. Members of this family are usually solitary and mainly nocturnal, digging characteristic funnel-shaped holes in search of invertebrates, larvae and fungi.

Long-nosed Echymipera

Echymipera rufescens (northern Cape York Peninsula; New Guinea)

The so-called spiny bandicoots are restricted to rainforests of New Guinea and Cape York Peninsula (CYP). Formerly classified in their own family, they are now included in the Peramelidae. The Australian subspecies *E. r. australis* occurs in rainforests of CYP north of the McIlwraith Range. It appears to be the most abundant rainforest bandicoot on CYP and is generally common at Iron Range NP (1.17). However, Northern and Southern Brown Bandicoots also occur on the Cape. Diagnostic features when seen well include stout, black spiny hairs; its short, naked, almost black tail (although other species can have missing or shortened tails from fighting); and echymiperans have the most attenuated snouts of all bandicoots.

Other names: Rufous Spiny Bandicoot

CRITICAL WEIGHT RANGE ANIMALS

Australia has lost more species of mammal in the modern era than any other nation, and the process continues. The factors involved are many and varied, but a few common themes emerge: predation by feral animals such as Red Foxes and feral Cats; habitat change and destruction through grazing by hoofed livestock; changed fire regimes; and soil destabilisation by the introduced European Rabbit. Particularly hard hit have been mammals in the so-called Critical Weight Range (CWR) of 35–5500 g. Thus the bandicoots, bilbies, bettongs and small wallabies have borne a disproportionate percentage of extinctions. The pattern seems to be that CWR mammals are most vulnerable to all or some of the major causes of extinction. The CWR model best explains extinctions in the semi-arid and arid zones; arboreal CWR mammals and those from high rainfall areas do not seem to be similarly affected.

*Golden Bandicoot

Isoodon auratus   (north-west and northern Australia)

This species has been extirpated from most of its former range across inland Australia. It is mainly associated with sandy or sandstone country, among spinifex and woodlands. On the mainland the subspecies *I. a. auratus* is restricted to the Kimberley at, for example, Mitchell Plateau (7.21); healthy populations survive on Augustus and Unwins Is., the Yampi Peninsula and Prince Regent River NR. *I. a. arnhemensis* occurs on Marchinbar I. in the NT. Fortunately *I. a. barrowensis* is common on Barrow I. (7.18), where there is estimated to be 20 000 animals. If you are lucky enough to see one, it is generally unmistakable with its small size, golden coloration and stiff guard hairs, giving it a neat appearance. Kimberley and Barrow I. specimens are darker.

Other names: Northern Golden Bandicoot, Northern Golden-backed Bandicoot

*Northern Brown Bandicoot

Isoodon macrourus   (northern and eastern Australia)

A large, common bandicoot of most forest types and even suburban gardens between Sydney and the Kimberley, including Fraser, Moreton and North and South Stradbroke Is. This is the largest 'true' bandicoot, and two subspecies are recognised: *I. m. torosus* is found from Cape York to the Sydney region, easily seen by spotlighting at Mt Lewis (1.03) and common in Sydney at, for example, North Head (2.01); *I. m. macrourus* occurs in the NT and Kimberley, and occurs in Kakadu NP (8.03).

*Southern Brown Bandicoot

Isoodon obesulus   (Vic, WA, Tas, Cape York Peninsula)

The most common bandicoot of southern Australia, where it is found in a variety of forested habitats with sandy soils and a heathy understorey. This species is probably most abundant in Tas and offshore islands; mainland populations appear to be declining in some areas. There are five recognised subspecies: *I. o. obseulus* is easily seen at Cranbourne Botanic Gardens (4.07); *I. o. affinis* occurs in Tas; *I. o. nauticus* is found only in the Nuyts Archipelago, on East and West Franklin, and St Francis Is. in SA; *I. o. fusciventer* is the only bandicoot in the south-west, where it is known as the Quenda. An outlying subspecies, *I. o. peninsulae*, occurs in north Qld and CYP, where Rufous Spiny and Northern Brown Bandicoots also occur. This species is crepuscular and often partly diurnal. It is solitary and leaves tell-tale conical holes where it has been digging for food.

Other names: Quenda (WA)

*Western Barred Bandicoot

Perameles bougainville   (islands of Shark Bay in WA)

The mainland subspecies *P. b. fasciata* of this formerly widespread bandicoot is now extinct and it holds on naturally only at Bernier and Dorre Is. in Shark Bay (7.15), where it is most commonly associated with dune scrub. Populations have been reintroduced to Heirisson Prong (7.15d) and Arid Recovery (6.11).

*Desert Bandicoot

Perameles eremiana (central SA, WA and NT)

Presumed extinct. The last specimen was collected on the Canning Stock Route in 1943 although it may have hung on till the 1960s. Formerly common on grassy sandplains and dune country. There is some doubt that this is a valid species (it is possibly conspecific with Western Barred Bandicoot).

*Eastern Barred Bandicoot

Perameles gunnii (eastern and northern Tas)

Until late last century this distinctive bandicoot could still be seen on the mainland, but the last remaining population eventually succumbed to feral and domestic predators. Fortunately the Tas subspecies *P. g. gunnii* is still relatively common, especially in the south-east and north-west of the island (it is very rare or absent from the Midlands and east coast). It can generally be seen at Waterworks Reserve (5.01). Vigorous attempts to resurrect it are underway at several sites in Vic, including Woodlands (4.02).

*Long-nosed Bandicoot

Perameles nasuta (coastal eastern Australia)

Found along almost the entire eastern seaboard from Cape York Peninsula to SW Vic. Generally common in forest and heath with grassy clearings, and suburban gardens. Where it co-occurs with other species, its longer, more pointed ears are a useful diagnostic feature. Long-nosed Bandicoots also grunt and squeak when foraging. Two subspecies are recognised: *P. n. nasuta* and *P. n. pallescens*, which occur south and north of Townsville, respectively, and which may be separate species.

Bilbies – Family Thylacomyidae (world 2; Australia 2 (endemic))

Bilbies are burrowing, nocturnal bandicoots of the arid zone, characterised by long legs, large ears and furred tails. Only the Greater Bilby survives – it has been proposed as a replacement for the Easter Bunny in Australian popular culture.

*Greater Bilby

Macrotis lagotis (inland Qld and NT to north-west WA)

Most charismatic and spectacular of the bandicoots, the amazing Greater Bilby (often referred to simply as 'the' Bilby) formerly occurred over much of the continent in arid and semi-arid areas. It is now uncommon and occurs mainly in the Tanami and Great Sandy Deserts with an outlying population between Boulia and Birdsville in western Qld, although in the Pilbara it appears to be holding its own. It is exclusively nocturnal, often emerging from burrows after midnight and not at all when there is strong moonlight. Nonetheless, it can be encountered by spotlighting along the Tanami Track (8.21) and near Broome (7.20). This species has been successfully reintroduced to Arid Recovery (6.11) and Scotia AWC Sanctuary (2.29).

Other names: Dalgyte

*Lesser Bilby

Macrotis leucura   (remote deserts of WA, SA and NT)

Extinct. Last reported in 1931 in north-east SA, possibly surviving in some areas till the 1960s. Smaller than the previous species, the Lesser Bilby burrowed into sandhills while the Greater Bilby was more common in swales.

Koala, wombats, possums and macropods – Order Diprotodontia

This order includes most of the marsupials that Australians are familiar with – at first glance an eclectic bunch but all united by features such as having only one pair of functioning incisors in the lower jaw, and the conjunction of the second and third toes on their hind feet (except for the claws). Among them are most of the marsupial all-stars: the Koala, wombats, possums and gliders, pygmy possums and macropods big and small. ('Possum' is almost certainly a corruption of 'opossum', the most common marsupials in the Americas; Australasian possums belong to a different order and look quite different.)

Koala – Family Phascolarctidae (world 1; Australia 1 (endemic))

The Koala – sometimes erroneously called 'koala bear' – is one of Australia's animal icons and should be instantly recognisable. It is the sole member of a unique family, most closely related to the wombats. No subspecies are recognised, although Koalas from Qld tend to be paler in colour and almost half the weight of their southern counterparts, which are often brown across the back and 'shoulders'.

*Koala

Phascolarctos cinereus   (eastern and south-east Australia)

The Koala is relatively common in southern Australia, particularly in parts of Vic, where it can be readily seen at, for example, You Yangs Regional Park (4.12), Brisbane Ranges NP (4.11), Phillip I. (4.09), French I. (4.10) and at sites along the Great Ocean Rd (4.16). In SA it was introduced to Kangaroo I. (6.13), where it is now abundant (see boxed text p. 152 [in SA chapter]). During the 19th century it was extensively hunted for its fur in NSW, where it remains rare except in the north-east of the state. Indeed, Gunnedah (2.24) claims to be the Australia's 'Koala capital', and there are populations close to other towns such as Lismore. South-east Qld is another stronghold, but it is nowhere as common as formerly as urbanisaton takes its toll; it can still readily be seen at, for example, Noosa NP (1.39) and on the so-called 'Koala Coast' (1.33). Koalas are usually inactive during the day, typically sleeping in a vertical fork in the canopy, where they are easily overlooked. They are most active at night – listen for the loud, piglike grunting of males in spring and summer. Unfortunately, these endearing animals often become roadkill or get mauled by dogs when they descend to the ground in search of mates. When spotlighted Koalas have bright yellow eyeshine.

Wombats – Family Vombatidae (world 3; Australia 3 (all endemic))

The three species of these unique, burrowing marsupials are restricted to eastern and southern Australia. Early settlers weren't sure what to make of these stocky, bearlike animals – the world's largest fossorial (burrowing) marsupials – and common names such as 'badger' gained currency in some areas. These endearing herbivores feature a backward-facing pouch so their young don't get a faceful of dirt when mother is digging. Wombats are nocturnal and relatively easy to observe by spotlighting, although they can move surprisingly fast when alarmed.

*Northern Hairy-nosed Wombat

Lasiorhinus krefftii   (central Qld)
Largest of the wombats, this species was formerly found in southern NSW and central Qld. It is now endangered and restricted to Epping Forest NP (1.26) near Clermont in central Qld, where it numbers only about 160 individuals, and a translocated population at St George. Epping is a Strict Scientific Reserve to which public access is not possible. However, it would be worth joining a volunteer program for a chance at seeing this rare animal. Contact the Qld national parks office at Rockhampton.

*Southern Hairy-nosed Wombat

Lasiorhinus latifrons   (semi-arid SA and south-east WA)
Formerly wide-ranging in mallee woodlands from eastern SA to the Nullarbor Plain, this species's range is now fragmented. It can be readily seen at Brookfield CP (6.02) and nearby sites along the Murray River; colonies also occur on the Eyre Peninsula (6.15) and there are burrows near the Nullarbor Roadhouse (6.20).

*Common Wombat

Vombatus ursinus   (south-east Australia and Tas)
Although this species occurs in a fragmented distribution between south-east SA and southern Qld, its strongholds are Tas and montane forests of the south-east mainland. It is frequently encountered on rural highways at night, particularly in hilly, forested country; take care on these roads as wombats run in front of vehicles without warning. The mainland subspecies *V. u. hirsutus* grazes on lawns at the campground at Wilson's

Promontory NP (4.24), where a blond form occurs; it is common in the High Country at, for example, Kosciuszko NP (2.16). Wombats can generally be seen by driving slowly along quiet roads at night near Kangaroo Valley (2.07); in the Brindabella Range near Canberra (3.06); between Canberra and Bateman's Bay, NSW; and in east Gippsland, Vic. The Bass Strait subspecies *V. u. ursinus* is found only on Flinders I. and is slightly smaller than other subspecies. The Tas subspecies *V. u. tasmaniensis* is easily seen at Narawntapu NP (5.10).

Other names: Bare-nosed Wombat

Pygmy possums – Family Burramyidae (world 5; Australia 5 (4 endemic))

These tiny, mouse-sized possums are generally arboreal, feeding on nectar and invertebrates. All are rather similar in appearance and, to the inexperienced eye, may even be difficult to separate from mice; all have strongly prehensile tails. Finding any pygmy possum is often a matter of luck. In the field they are difficult to locate and often move away rapidly when spotlighted. However, some will sleep or even nest in artificial structures such as meter housings and walkers' huts. Your chances of encountering most species would be greatly improved by participating in systematic mammal surveys. During the day all but Mountain Pygmy Possum sleep in spherical nests of leaves and twigs that are well concealed in a tree hollow or crevice.

*Mountain Pygmy Possum

Burramys parvus   (alpine south-east Australia)

A rare pygmy possum of alpine areas above 1400 m in Vic and southern NSW. In Vic it occurs at Mt Buller, and between Mt Higginbotham and Mt Bogong; in NSW it is found only in Kosciuszko NP (2.16). It is the only marsupial known to go into hibernation for long periods, spending winter in torpor deep under boulder scree which itself may be under several metres of snow. At Mt Hotham (4.27) you could get lucky at the so-called 'tunnel of love', built so the possums can cross under a busy road, but the best way to see this species is as a volunteer on one of the annual surveys held in Kosciuszko NP. Depending on latitude and elevation, they enter hibernation between February and May, emerging 5–7 months later.

Other names: Burramys

Long-tailed Pygmy Possum

Cercartetus caudatus   (Wet Tropics; New Guinea)

The only Australian pygmy possum that occurs in the tropics; found between Mt Spec and Cooktown in north Qld. South of the Daintree River it occurs in montane rainforest and adjoining sheoak stands 300 m or more above sea level; north of the Daintree it occurs to sea level in rainforest and eucalypt forest. It is nowhere common and is extremely active, making it difficult to see as it runs along branches. It runs away from a white spotlight and could be confused with a Prehensile-tailed Rat. It is most often seen when feeding on the flowers of the Bumpy Satinash *Syzigium cormiflorum* in August–September. Halloran's Crater, Atherton (1.04d) is a good spot to look for it and it has also been seen in the vicinity of Shipton's Flat near Cooktown.

Other names: Queensland Pygmy Possum

*Western Pygmy Possum

Cercartetus concinnus (semi-arid southern Australia)

Despite its name this species has a wide distribution across the semi-arid zone from western Vic to southern WA; it is the only pygmy possum in south-west WA. It is common and abundant in heaths, woodland and mallee, especially where there is a wide variety of flowering trees and shrubs. Apparently it is most active on windy nights, which may help to disguise its movements. It can often be seen at Cheyne's Beach caravan park (7.09); otherwise the best chance would be to accompany a survey at suitable sites within its range. It is often caught in pitfall traps when it moves between flowering shrubs. In the east its range overlaps that of Little Pygmy Possum, from which it can be separated by coloration and dentition.

Other names: South-western Pygmy Possum, Lesser Dormouse-phalanger, Elegant Dormouse Opossum, Mundarda

*Little Pygmy Possum

Cercartetus lepidus (semi-arid SA and Vic, Tas)

The smallest pygmy possum. Found in a variety of habitats across its rather disjunct distribution, including mallee in Vic, wet and dry forest in Tas and heath in the Murray Valley of SA. The Tas population may be a separate species. In Tas it is sometimes encountered in walkers' huts, such as Lake St Clair (5.08), and in specially provided nest boxes on South Bruny I. (5.04). Where they all co-occur, this species is smaller than the Eastern Pygmy Possum and greyer than the Western Pygmy Possum. The tails of both Little and Eastern Pygmy Possums may be swollen at the base.

Other names: Tasmanian Pygmy Possum

*Eastern Pygmy Possum

Cercartetus nanus (south-east mainland and Tas)

Widespread in a variety of habitats in the south-east, including wet and dry forest, woodland, banksia heaths and subalpine forests. Primarily a nectar feeder and best looked for among flowering shrubs such as banksias. Sometimes seen crossing roads at night; hisses when handled. Only this species and the Little Pygmy Possum occur in Tas.

Other names: Pygmy Possum, Common Dormouse-phalanger, Dormouse Opossum, Possum Mouse

Striped possums and wrist-winged gliders – Family Petauridae (world 28; Australia 6 (4 endemic))

At first glance this family contains a mixed bunch, but external features that all petaurids share include a dark dorsal stripe that extends onto the forehead and a long, furry, prehensile tail. They also share distinctive dentition and some gliders make incisions in tree trunks which they visit repeatedly to feed on oozing sap; staking out an active feed tree is a good way to see aggregations, sometimes of two or three species. Most Australian gliders belong to this family and the term 'wrist-winged gliders' refers to the point of attachment of the gliding membrane (the Greater Glider is not a petaurid). Striped possums are boldly marked tropical possums that occur mainly in New Guinea; one species occurs in Australia.

Common Striped Possum

Dactylopsila trivirgata   (north Qld; New Guinea)

One of the most distinctive of all Australian mammals, this tropical possum has a rather skunk-like appearance and an elongated fourth digit on each forepaw for extracting larvae from soft wood. It can sometimes be detected by tearing sounds as it rips up bark, grunting as it does so. It is restricted to rainforests and adjoining forests between Mt Spec and Cape York Peninsula. It is quite common in places, even a nocturnal visitor to gardens on the Atherton Tableland, although its occurrence is unpredictable. Good sites to try include Kingfisher Park (1.03), Centennial Lakes (1.01) and Iron Range NP (1.17).

*Leadbeater's Possum

Gymnobelideus leadbeateri   (Vic)

This critically endangered possum looks like a miniature Sugar Glider without the gliding membrane. It is endemic to the Mountain Ash forests of central Vic (4.06) and a small population also lives at Yellingbo Reserve (4.05). It is extremely agile and difficult to spot in the foliage of what are some of the tallest hardwood trees in the world, and hides or runs away from spotlights. Cataclysmic bushfires affected much of its habitat in 2009 and the best chance of seeing one would be to join a survey with the Friends of Leadbeater's Possum group – contact details are given in Appendix B.

*Yellow-bellied Glider

Petaurus australis   (eastern Australia)

Primarily a wet forest species and relatively common in suitable habitat between western Vic and the Wet Tropics. It is extremely vocal, uttering loud shrieks that can be heard up to 500 m away, and even calling while airborne. Yellow-bellied Gliders make characteristic V-shaped incisions in bark for feeding; fresh incisions are worth staking out as they may be used over several consecutive nights and sometimes attract other species, including Feathertail Gliders.

Good sites include Bateman's Bay (2.09) and Airey's Inlet (4.16). This species is easily spotlighted and has dull, pale-red eyeshine; in summer it may still be active at dawn.

Sugar Glider

Petaurus breviceps (eastern and northern Australia; New Guinea)

The most widespread glider, ranging from south-east SA right along the eastern seaboard to the Top End and Kimberley; it is the only glider species that occurs in Tas. It occurs in a variety of wet and dry forest types, particularly favouring more open forest with dense patches of acacias, and is more common in southern Australia than in the north. It is sometimes seen at dusk, although it tends to freeze or hide when spotlighted; its eyeshine is medium- or pale-red. Good sites include Naracoorte Caves NP (6.06), Great Otway NP (4.16), Canberra Nature Park (3.04), Lamington NP (1.37), Atherton Tableland (1.04), Kakadu NP (8.03) and the Kimberley (7.21). Note that Sugar Gliders were probably introduced to Tasmania, where they still occur. This is also a vocal species, yapping when alarmed and screaming when fighting.

Other names: Sugar Squirrel, Lesser Flying Squirrel, Short-headed or Lesser Flying Phalanger, Lesser Glider

*Mahogany Glider

Petaurus gracilis (Wet Tropics)

Endemic to the Wet Tropics with a restricted distribution below 200 m from south of Ingham to Tully. A rare and localised species whose identification was not confirmed until 1993, 110 years after its discovery. It is superficially similar to the Squirrel Glider, which occurs in adjacent dry sclerophyll forest, but inhabits swampy lowland forest. It is not easy to see as much of its habitat has been cleared and fragmented. It occurs at the campground at Paluma Range NP (1.10).

*Squirrel Glider

Petaurus norfolcensis (eastern Australia)

Found primarily in drier habitats than the Sugar Glider, which it resembles, including open forests and woodlands. Commoner in the north of its range, for example in Greater Brisbane (1.33) and generally rare in Vic and NSW. It is larger than the Sugar Glider, has paler underparts and never has a white-tipped tail. Squirrel Gliders can make prodigious glides of up to 80 m between trees and are less vocal than either Sugar or Yellow-bellied Gliders. This species has pale red eyeshine.

Ringtail possums and Greater Glider – Family Pseudocheiridae (world 28; Australia 8 (all endemic))

All members of this family are leaf-eaters that can oppose the first two digits of their forepaws for gripping branches. Ringtail possums are small forest possums with short-furred, strongly prehensile tails; four species are endemic to Wet Tropics rainforests

– watch for them crossing rope bridges over roads at night on the Atherton Tableland. Gliding membranes evolved separately in at least three possum families and the Greater Glider is included in the Pseudocheiridae because its gliding membrane is not attached at the wrists as in the Petauridae (see p. 285). The Rock Ringtail Possum is a semi-terrestrial ringtail specialised for life on the rocky escarpments of northern Australia.

*Lemuroid Ringtail Possum

Hemibelideus lemuroides   (Wet Tropics)

Common in upland rainforest above 450 m (most abundant above 900 m), with an isolated population above 1100 m on the Carbine Tableland. Most individuals are charcoal-grey, but an almost-white form also occurs, especially on the Carbine Tableland. It may be seen on Mt Lewis (1.03), depending on access and weather. Lemuroid Ringtails jump heavily between branches, making a tell-tale noise that gives away their position, and can sometimes be detected by their strong, musky odour. They have brilliant, silvery-yellow eyeshine and may occur in feeding aggregations. This species is superficially similar to the Greater Glider, but lacks its elongated, furred ears and the latter is not found in rainforests.

Other names: Brush-tipped Ringtail Possum, Lemur-like Ringtail Possum

*Greater Glider

Petauroides volans   (eastern seaboard)

Australia's largest gliding marsupial, unmistakable if seen well with its shaggy coat, long tail and long, furry ears. It is generally found in tall, open forests, from just west of Melbourne to Mossman in the Wet Tropics, wherever there are large tree hollows for nesting. There are several colour varieties, from almost black to pale grey or whitish, but this species always has white underparts. Good sites include Kioloa (2.09), Wombat SF (4.15), Tallaganda NP (2.13) and the Brown Barrel-Alpine Ash forests of the High Brindabellas near Canberra (3.06). Greater Gliders are capable of covering 100 m in a single glide, big enough to be seen silhouetted against the sky when gliding at dusk and usually freeze in a spotlight beam. The eyeshine of most populations is bright yellow (pale red in rare exceptions).

Other names: Greater Flying Phalanger, Dusky Glider, Great Glider-possum, Squirrel

*Rock Ringtail Possum

Petropseudes dahli   (Kimberley, Top End and Gulf Country)

A distinctive inhabitant of rocky escarpments with adjacent food trees. Highly sociable, resting and foraging in family groups. Easily spotlighted by its bright red eyeshine. Scent posts – rusty-looking patches on rocks, branches or termite mounds with a distinctive musky smell – are a good indication of their presence. Common in Kakadu NP (8.03), Umbrawarra Gorge (8.09), the Kimberley (7.21) and at Lawn Hill NP (1.29).

Other names: Rock-haunting Ringtail, Rock Possum

*Green Ringtail Possum

Pseudochirops archeri   (Wet Tropics)

A common possum of upland rainforests between Paluma and the Mt Windsor Tableland, above about 300 m and most commonly between 800 and 1200 m. Readily spotlighted at popular sites on the Atherton Tableland, such as Mt Hypipamee NP (1.04i), near Yungaburra (1.04f), Kingfisher Park (1.03) and at various tourist lodges. It sleeps by curling up on a branch and is sometimes seen among foliage during the day. The green coloration is actually caused by a combination of silver, yellow and black hairs. It has weak red eyeshine and is usually solitary.

Other names: Striped Ringtail Possum

*Daintree River Ringtail Possum

Pseudochirulus cinereus   (Wet Tropics)

Restricted to upland rainforest above 420 m in three isolated areas: the Carbine and Mt Windsor Tablelands, and the Thornton Peak massif. Generally common in suitable habitat and more abundant above 1000 m. Good sites include Mt Lewis (1.03).

Other names: Cuscus

*Herbert River Ringtail Possum

Pseudochirulus herbertensis   (Wet Tropics)

The Herbert River Ringtail occurs above about 350 m from west of Ingham to the Lamb Range near Mt Molloy. It is generally found in upland rainforest but sometimes also in adjoining tall eucalypt forest. This species is solitary and slow moving, and has bright red eyeshine. All-dark and white-bellied forms exist. Good sites include Mt Lewis (1.03).

*Western Ringtail Possum

Pseudocheirus occidentalis   (south-west Australia)

Endemic to south-west WA, but becoming scarce in places owing to urban development on the coastal plain south of Perth. Commonly associated with Peppermint *Agonis flexuosa* and Tuart *Eucalyptus gomphocephala*, and most abundant in coastal peppermint stands south of Busselton (7.04). Busselton Big 4 Peppermint Eco Park boasts sightings and it is resident at Perup (7.08). This species has weak red eyeshine.

Other names: Ring-tailed Possum

*Common Ringtail Possum

Pseudocheirus peregrinus   (eastern seaboard and Tas)

A rather dainty possum when compared to the Common Brushtail, with which it co-occurs in parks and gardens of many large cities. Common or very common in places, and very variable in coloration. Outside of urban areas it lives in a variety of wooded habitats, including rainforest; it sleeps during the day in a spherical drey of leaves, grass and bark. The brightly marked subspecies *P. p. pulcher* occurs in northern NSW and south-east Qld; *P. p. convolutor* is very common in Melbourne (4.01) and in Tas at Mt Nelson (5.02); *P. p. cookii* occurs in Sydney (2.01); *P. p. peregrinus* occurs west of the Great Dividing Range, in Adelaide (6.01) and in most of coastal Qld. Vocal when alarmed, uttering a high-pitched twittering; weak red eyeshine.

Other names: Grey Queensland Ringtail, Rufous Ringtail, South-eastern Ringtail, Tasmanian Ringtail, Banga

Honey Possum – Family Tarsipedidae (world 1; Australia 1 (endemic))

The extraordinary Honey Possum is the sole member of its family and endemic to south-west WA. These beautiful but tiny possums feed on nectar and pollen, and thrive among the diverse nectar-bearing flora of WA's heaths.

*Honey Possum

Tarsipes rostratus   (south-west Australia)

Distinctively marked and highly active among vegetation or on the ground (it is often caught in pitfall traps); confiding when feeding. During cooler weather it may be crepuscular or even partly diurnal. Common at Dryandra SF (7.05) and sometimes seen feeding in the early morning at the Stirling Ranges (7.06).

Other names: Honey Mouse, Noolbenger

Feathertails – Family Acrobatidae (world 2; Australia 1 (endemic))

*The feathertails include a possum found only in New Guinea and the mouse-sized Feathertail Glider, the world's smallest gliding mammal. As its name suggests, the Feathertail Glider's tail has a row of stiff hairs on either side giving it a featherlike appearance. Recent research indicates there are two species of feathertail glider in Australia (*Acrobates pygmaeus *and* A. frontalis*), apparently with differing habitat preferences; however, their distribution and ecology remain unresolved and field ID would be impossible. All references in this guide are to* A. pygmaeus, *but it must be assumed that some information will become obsolete when these issues are sorted out.*

*Feathertail Glider

Acrobates pygmaeus   (eastern Australia)

Probably common in many places but easily overlooked owing to its small size and unobtrusive nature, and because it often feeds in the canopy. Most abundant in diverse forests that provide nectar sources year-round; more common in wet and old growth forest than in drier habitats (which are possibly occupied mainly by *A. frontalis*). It moves rapidly over branches and trunks, making short, quick glides although it is capable of gliding up to 25 m. It occurs at Kingfisher Park (1.03).

Other names: Pygmy Glider, Pygmy Phalanger, Flying Mouse

Brushtail possums, cuscuses and Wyulda – Family Phalangeridae (world 24; Australia 6 (4 endemic))

This family contains cat-sized, mainly arboreal possums with rather long, prehensile tails. It includes the familiar Common Brushtail Possum, found in many city parks and gardens; the strikingly coloured cuscuses of tropical forests; and the Wyulda, a semi-terrestrial species of Kimberley sandstone country.

Southern Common Cuscus

Phalanger mimicus   (Cape York Peninsula; New Guinea)
Common in rainforest at Iron Range NP (1.17), where it is far more commonly seen than Common Spotted Cuscus. This species lacks the latter's sometimes colourful markings, and has a lighter build, more prominent ears and a dark dorsal stripe. It is not usually encountered away from rainforest and doesn't usually turn away from spotlights, making its red eyeshine easy to detect.

Other names: Grey Cuscus, Grey Phalanger

Common Spotted Cuscus

Spilocuscus maculatus   (Cape York Peninsula; New Guinea)
In Australia this species is much less common than the Southern Common Cuscus and is only so-called because it is the common species in lowland New Guinea. Care is needed to differentiate the two where they both occur (for example, at Iron Range NP (1.17)). Both occur in rainforest, but the Common Spotted Cuscus also occurs in riparian forest, for example in paperbarks and Nipa Palms at the edge of mangroves. It sleeps in the canopy during the day (Southern Common Cuscuses sleep in dens) and may climb to the ground in order to move between trees or patches of vegetation. When spotlighted it tends to look away and is difficult to pick up by its eyeshine (which is red).

Other names: Spotted Phalanger

*Short-eared Brushtail Possum

Trichosurus caninus   (subtropical eastern Australia)
Taxonomists split this species from Mountain Brushtail Possum in 2002 on morphological differences including ear, hindfoot and tail length, features which are probably not very useful in the field. The best guide to identification is location: the 'short-eared' species replaces Mountain Brushtail Possum in upland areas of northern NSW and south-east Qld; the area of demarcation is currently unknown but thought to be somewhere between Sydney

and Newcastle, NSW. Its steely grey colouration is apparently consistent across its range, although jet black individuals also occur in the north. It occurs most commonly in forest gullies and where there are plenty of hollow-bearing trees. Common at Lamington NP (1.37).

Other names: Mountain Brushtail Possum, Bobuck

*Mountain Brushtail Possum

Trichosurus cunninghami   (upland south-east Australia)
This and the preceding species replace the Common Brushtail Possum in dense wet forest between central Vic and south-east Qld. The Mountain Brushtail is the more abundant possum at higher elevations, generally above 300 m, though there is some overlap with the Common Brushtail Possum, from which it can be identified by its less prominent ears and less luxuriantly furred tail. It occurs in the higher reaches of the Great Dividing Range near Marysville (4.06). It is often seen on or near the ground, and in Silver Wattle *Acacia dealbata*, its key food resource; it freezes when spotlighted and has red eyeshine.

Other names: Bobuck

*Common Brushtail Possum

Trichosurus vulpecula   (most of Australia and Tas)

One of the commonest and most easily seen of all Australian marsupials. The eastern mainland form *T. v. vulpecula* is abundant in all large southern cities, including Melbourne (4.01), Canberra (3.02), Adelaide (6.01), Sydney (2.01) and Brisbane (1.33); a visit to any major urban park at night should locate a few. Unfortunately it is getting scarce in central Australia, but it may be seen along River Red Gum–lined creeks near Alice Springs (8.16). The large Tas subspecies *T. v. fuliginosus* is common at many sites, while *T. v. eburacensis* occurs north of Townsville. Several other subspecies may be candidates for elevation to full species: the spectacular 'Coppery Brushtail' of the Wet Tropics, *T. v. johnstonii*, which can be seen near Yungaburra (1.04f); the 'Northern Brushtail' *T. v. arnhemensis* of the Top End and Kimberley, easily spotlighted in Darwin parks and at East Point (8.01); and the south-western form *T. v. hypoleucus*, which often sports a white or black-and-white tail tip (locally called 'columbine') and can be seen at Perup (7.08) and Karakamia AWC Sanctuary (7.01). Common Brushtails have red eyeshine and can be extremely vocal, with loud guttural hisses and screeching.

Other names: Silvery-grey Possum, Brushtail Possum, Northern Brushtail Possum

*Wyulda (Scaly-tailed Possum)

Wyulda squamicaudata   (Kimberley)
Endemic to rugged sandstone country in the Kimberley, where it occurs in Prince Regent NR, on Mitchell Plateau (7.21) and on Bigge and Boongaree Is. It shelters exclusively among rocks near woodland and forest, foraging after dark in trees, and is not uncommon but not easy to find. It closely resembles the Rock Ringtail Possum

which inhabits similar sandstone country; they can be told apart most easily by the Wyulda's completely naked tail.

Musky Rat-kangaroo – Family Hypsiprymnodontidae (world 1; Australia 1 (endemic))

The sole remnant of an ancient group of 'primitive' kangaroo-like animals, the Musky Rat-kangaroo probably resembles an ancestral macropod and has distinctive teeth structure commensurate with its omnivorous diet.

*Musky Rat-kangaroo

Hypsiprymnodon moschatus   (Wet Tropics)
The smallest macropod (about the size of a small rabbit), with a bandicoot-like gait as it forages for fallen fruit, fungi and invertebrates among leaf litter. Common in upland rainforests of the Wet Tropics from west of Ingham (Mt Lee) north to Mt Amos, south of Cooktown; also at sea level at, for example, Mission Beach and Cape Tribulation. Diurnal and easily seen at Lakes Eacham and Barrine NP (1.04g), particularly in the early morning and late afternoon; and around various ecolodges, such as Cassowary House near Kuranda (see Appendix B).

Bettongs and potoroos – Family Potoroidae (world 10; Australia 10 (all endemic))

The bettongs and potoroos are small (about rabbit-sized) nocturnal macropods, collectively known as potoroids and generally placed in their own family. Potoroos are rather skulking animals, restricted to dense coastal heath and forest undergrowth; bettongs are found in drier habitats and formerly occurred across much of the continent. Both move by hopping although their hind feet are short relative to their forelimbs, which are equipped with sharp claws for digging in leaf litter and soil for truffles and invertebrates. They typically shelter during the day in nests made of vegetation and have a semi-prehensile tail which is used to carry nesting material. Like bandicoots, members of this family fall into the Critical Weight Range (CWR) category (see boxed text p. 278) and have suffered drastic range reductions: two species are extinct, some are extremely rare and most are difficult to observe in the wild.

*Rufous Bettong

Aepyprymnus rufescens   (subcoastal eastern Qld, northern NSW)
The largest potoroid and probably the easiest to observe in the wild. It has a wide distribution in tropical and subtropical eastern Australia, from open woodlands to tall forests. Its domed nest is typically placed against a log or tree trunk. This species can sometimes be seen by spotlighting in likely habitat near Brisbane, Townsville and on the Atherton Tableland (1.04). It also occurs at Epping Forest NP (1.26), Mareeba Wetlands (1.04c) and Idalia NP (1.31). This bettong is very vocal, uttering growls and hisses.

Other names: Rufous Rat-kangaroo

*Southern (Tasmanian) Bettong

Bettongia gaimardi   (Tas)

Often referred to as the Tasmanian Bettong because it is extinct on the mainland and now confined to Tas. The mainland subspecies *B. g. gaimardi* had disappeared by about the 1920s. *B. g. cuniculus* is still relatively common in eastern Tas and some offshore islands. It frequents open dry sclerophyll forest (particularly in Peppermint–Silver Wattle associations) and woodland with an open understorey; it is rarely seen in paddocks grazing with other macropods. Tasmanian Bettongs are normally solitary but may frequent similar habitat to Long-nosed Potoroos. They can usually be seen at Waterworks Reserve (5.01), among other sites, including Bruny (5.04) and Maria (5.06) Is. In 2012 this species was successfully reintroduced to the mainland at Mulligan's Flat NR (3.05) near Canberra, where it is thought to have once been common; the experiment has been very successful and the animals are breeding.

Other names: Eastern or Gaimard's Bettong, Eastern or Gaimard's Rat-kangaroo.

*Burrowing Bettong (Boodie)

Bettongia lesueur   (islands off north-west Australia)

Also known as the Boodie, the Burrowing Bettong is now extinct on the mainland, where it was formerly widespread across the arid and semi-arid zones from west of the Great Dividing Range to the Indian Ocean. It survives naturally on only three islands in WA: Bernier (7.15c), Dorre (7.15c) and Barrow (7.18), where it is abundant. Fortunately, where it has been translocated the Burrowing Bettong has been something of a success story: there are now healthy breeding populations at Arid Recovery (6.11), Scotia AWC Sanctuary (2.29), Faure I. (7.15b) and Heirisson Prong (7.15d); with a smaller reintroduced population at Boodie I. (7.18). This is the world's only burrowing macropod and lives in sometimes large warrens whose remains can still be seen in parts of the arid zone. Burrows tend to be in compact sand, such as at dune edges or where there is a cap of limestone rock. Burrows in sandy soils typically have two or three entrances, and more than 100 entrances in other soil types. Other mammals, such as the Common Brushtail Possum, Western Quoll and the introduced Rabbit may also use their burrows. This species is nocturnal, vocal and, unlike many other potoroids, gregarious.

Other names: Lesueur's or Burrowing Rat-kangaroo, Boordi

*Woylie (Brush-tailed Bettong)

Bettongia penicillata   (south-west WA)

Despite its distinctive black brush this species is now commonly known as Woylie. It was formerly widespread across semi-arid southern and north-west Australia, but now survives on the mainland only in south-west WA at Tutanning, Dryandra (7.05) and Perup (7.08), and at several reserves where it has been reintroduced, such as Francois Peron NP

(7.15a), Wadderin Sanctuary (7.07) and Scotia AWC Sanctuary (2.29). It is found in open, dry forest with a dense, clumped understorey, such as Jarrah–Wandoo communities with *Gastrolobium* patches. This species strips bark from stringybark trees for its nests, and signs of its presence include pale, shredded areas to a height of 30–40 cm at the base of Jarrah trees.

Other names: Brush-tailed Rat-kangaroo, Woylyer, Karpitchi

*Northern Bettong

Bettongia tropica (Wet Tropics)

The Northern Bettong is endemic to north-east Qld, where it occurs between 800 and 1200 m above sea level on the western edge of the Lamb Range, the Mt Carbine Tableland and the Coane Range near Paluma. It inhabits open forest with a grassy understorey on granitic soils in a narrow strip between rainforest and drier habitat to the west. The largest and most accessible population is at Davies Creek (1.04a); it also occurs near Hidden Valley and at Mt Zero-Taravale AWC Sanctuary (1.11). It apparently heads for ridgetops shortly after emerging from nests in the early evening. Traces of its presence include chewed pellets of fibre next to diggings.

Other names: Tropical Bettong, 'Brush-tailed' Bettong

*Desert Rat-kangaroo

Caloprymnus campestris (north-east SA and south-west Qld)

Extinct. Last recorded in 1935; formerly inhabited gibber plains and associated flats in the Lake Eyre Basin.

Other names: Plains or Buff-nosed Rat-kangaroo, Oolacunta

*Gilbert's Potoroo

Potorus gilbertii (south-west WA)

This potoroid is Australia's rarest mammal and was rediscovered in 1994 after being thought extinct for 100 years. It numbers only a few dozen individuals, which inhabit dense *Melaleuca* heath with a ground layer of sedge around the Mt Gardner peninsula at Two Peoples Bay NR (7.09). A small population has been successfully introduced to nearby Bald I. Given that this species remained hidden for so long and access to Bald I. is strictly controlled, your best chance of seeing it is to join a volunteer team.

Other names: Ngilgyte

*Long-footed Potoroo

Potorus longipes (south-east Vic, southern NSW)

Cryptic, nocturnal and endangered, this potoroo was only discovered as recently as 1967. It is known from temperate rainforests and wet sclerophyll forests at a few sites 100–1100 m above sea level in eastern Vic and adjacent NSW. The only chance of seeing this species alive would be to join a scientific survey team (it is sometimes found as roadkill on remote logging roads).

*Broad-faced Potoroo

Potorus platyops   (south-west WA)

Extinct. This species was last recorded alive prior to 1875 and virtually nothing is known of its life history. It formerly lived inland of WA's tall subcoastal forest belt.

*Long-nosed Potoroo

Potorus tridactylus   (south-east mainland Australia, Tas)

The commonest and most widespread potoroo, favouring coastal heath and forest with dense ground cover. The subspecies *P. t. apicalis* is reasonably abundant in eastern and northern Tas, for example, at Cradle Mountain-Lake St Clair NP (5.09); it also occurs on King and Flinders Is. A few used to shelter under cabins at Bowen Park Holiday Village at Risdon Cove outside of Hobart, Tas – check with the proprietors to see if they are still there. On the mainland *P. t. tridactylus* occurs in a narrow coastal strip from southern Vic to south-east Qld. Good sites include French I. NP (4.10) and Barren Grounds NR (2.06). This species is sometimes active during the late afternoon. It hops with its tail extended directly backwards, forepaws held close to the body. Tasmanian specimens have the longest 'nose' and 80 per cent have a white tail; animals in the northern part of its range lack white in the tail.

Kangaroos and wallabies – Family Macropodidae (world 62; Australia 45 (42 endemic))

Australia is the stronghold of kangaroos and wallabies; none occurs naturally outside of Australia or New Guinea and most species that occur in Australia are endemic to the continent. They are collectively known as macropodids ('big feet') but more commonly referred to as macropods; as they are the country's dominant mammalian herbivores, many species can be seen easily and a few species are abundant. Despite the extinction of four species since 1789, two have 'returned from the dead': the Parma Wallaby was rediscovered in dense NSW forests in 1967 and the beautiful Bridled Nailtail Wallaby at a remote site in central Qld in 1973.

'Kangaroo' refers to the large, fast-moving members of the genus Macropus*; kangaroos are the largest surviving marsupials and rank among the most abundant large animals on Earth. The term 'wallaby' generally applies to smaller macropods, but to confuse matters many wallabies are also placed in the genus* Macropus*. Adult kangaroos weigh more than 24 kg and have other differences such as dentition. In-between are the wallaroos, which are similar to kangaroos but stockier and tend to inhabit rocky terrain. It sounds confusing but in practice the common species can be told apart fairly readily. Wallabies are further divided into several subgroups: rock wallabies form the biggest genus and are small wallabies typically found in rocky habitats such as boulder fields or escarpment country; pademelons are compact, densely furred wallabies of eastern rainforests; nailtail wallabies have a peculiar outgrowth at the end of their tail; hare-wallabies are cryptic species of inland grasslands and deserts; tree-kangaroos occur in the Wet Tropics and, as their name suggests, are arboreal; the Quokka and Swamp Wallaby are two anomalous*

species in monotypic genera. Large macropods are often crepuscular or even partly diurnal, especially where they are used to humans.

*The two Australian species of **tree kangaroo** are restricted to rainforests of the Wet Tropics in north Qld. Tree kangaroos are specialised for life in the trees, with stocky forearms; short, almost rectangular hind feet; and independently moving back legs. They can climb tree trunks and vines; hop along large boughs; and jump between trees or even to the ground from heights of up to 15 m. Both species are similar in appearance and rather hard to find during the day, when they shelter in vine tangles in the canopy. Despite the difficulty of finding them, you'll have a far better chance of seeing a tree kangaroo in Australia than in New Guinea, where they reach their greatest diversity.*

*Bennett's Tree Kangaroo

Dendrolagus bennettianus   (northern Wet Tropics)

The larger of Australia's tree kangaroos, Bennett's is relatively common between the Daintree River and Mt Amos south of Cooktown. It shelters in dense vine clumps in the canopy during the day, especially in gallery forest, where it is very difficult to detect. It occurs at a relatively high density at Mt Poverty near Shipton's Flat (1.14) and is sometimes seen by spotlighting at Mungumby Lodge ((07) 4060 3972) near Helenvale. Your chances will be greatly improved with the help of a local guide – the lodge should be able to put you in touch with one.

Other names: Dusty Tree Kangaroo, Grey Tree Kangaroo, Tree-climber, Tree Wallaby, Jarabeena, Tcharibeena

*Lumholtz's Tree Kangaroo

Dendrolagus lumholtzi   (Wet Tropics)

Endemic to the Wet Tropics, where it occurs in montane rainforest above 800 m between Mt Spec and Mt Spurgeon. It is a relatively common arboreal species in patches of rainforest on the Atherton Tableland, and probably even more so in adjoining wet sclerophyll forest – searching the ecotone between these two habitats can be a good way to locate it. It is relatively easy to see when spotlighted, but be prepared to put in some hours and possibly more than one night searching; it is sometimes seen sunning on high exposed branches after rain or cold nights. Regular sites include Crater Lakes NP (1.04g), Curtain Fig Tree NP (1.04e) and Mt Baldy. Alan's Wildlife Tours (www.alanswildlifetours. com.au) has a pretty high success rate with finding tree kangaroos. They also occur at The Crater (1.04i), where spotlighting is not allowed, but you could try along the highway nearby. Watch for this species while driving at night on the Tableland – Lumholtz's Tree Kangaroos are often hit by vehicles while they are on the ground, especially in the Yungaburra area.

Other names: Tree-climber, Boongarry, Mabi, Mapee

Hare-wallabies are small, rather cryptic wallabies of woodlands and grasslands. Their small size made them vulnerable to introduced predators: two species are now extinct and only one is still common. They are primarily nocturnal, sheltering by day under dense vegetation, in burrows or among tussocks.

*Central Hare-wallaby

Lagorchestes asomatus   (inland Australia)

Extinct. Known from a single specimen collected in 1932 in desert sandhills of the southwest NT; only the skull survives and no skin remains for study.

Spectacled Hare-wallaby

Lagorchestes conspicillatus   (tropical arid Australia; New Guinea)

A beautifully marked hare-wallaby that is widespread and still relatively common across the northern third of the continent. It is locally common north of Mt Isa (1.28), around Daly Waters, NT and at Epping Forest NP (1.26); a population has recently been discovered in open grazing country south of Broome, WA. A dark subspecies, *L. c. conspicillatus*, is abundant on Barrow I. (7.18), and it has been reintroduced to Dorre I. in Shark Bay (7.15c) and Hermite I. in the Montebello Group (7.19). On the mainland it is patchily distributed in open woodlands with an understorey of tussock grass, shrubland and spinifex country. Confusion with the Rufous Bettong is possible in the eastern part of its range, but Spectacled Hare-wallaby has distinctive orange eye patches and a white 'moustache'.

*Mala

Lagorchestes hirsutus   (islands of Shark Bay in WA)

The last mainland population survived in the Tanami Desert until 1991 and Malas exist now only where they have been reintroduced to sites such as Scotia AWC Sanctuary (2.29). Fortunately it is common on Bernier and Dorre Is. (7.15c); breeding populations are held in predator exclosures at Uluru (8.18), King's Canyon (8.19) and Dryandra (7.05); and there has been a successful re-establishment on Trimouille I. in the Montebello Group (7.19). This species inhabits spinifex and hummock grassland and shrubland in sandy country; when startled it bounds with a distinctive, rapid zig-zag movement, often with an accompanying squeak.

Other names: Rufous Hare-wallaby, Western Hare-wallaby, Brown Hare-wallaby, Spinifex-rat, Whistler, Ormala, Wurrup

*Eastern Hare-wallaby

Lagorchestes leporides   (inland SA, Vic, NSW)

Extinct. Formerly common on semi-arid grassy plains; the last specimen was collected from western NSW in 1890.

*The 14 species of 'typical' **kangaroos** and **wallabies** in the genus* Macropus *show a wide variety of sizes, habitat preferences, abundance and social behaviours. They range from*

the cat-sized Parma Wallaby of dense forests to the plains-dwelling Red Kangaroo, the largest living marsupial. At least one Macropus *species is found in every part of the country – in many places several occur together; regrettably the spectacular Toolache Wallaby has become extinct since white settlement. Superficially some appear rather similar; good identification features to look for include facial markings, flank stripes, relative tail length and overall size.*

*Banded Hare-wallaby

Lagostrophus fasciatus   (islands of Shark Bay in WA)
Unfortunately extinct in the wild on the mainland and now restricted to Bernier and Dorre Is. (7.15c), where it has been reintroduced and is not uncommon; and to Faure Island AWC Sanctuary (7.15b), where a small population has become established. On Bernier and Dorre Is. it often frequents dense *Acacia–Ficus* thickets, where several individuals may shelter together during the day. There is a captive population at Dryandra (7.05). This is a distinctive, boldly marked species whose 'zebra stripes' are diagnostic if seen well.

Other names: Munning

Agile Wallaby

Macropus agilis   (northern Australia; New Guinea)
The common, sometimes abundant, small to medium wallaby of tropical Australia between Rockhampton, Qld and Broome, WA. Easily seen in grassy woodland, especially near water, wooded plains and along roads at dusk. Often tame around campsites in the Top End, including Kakadu (8.03), Litchfield (8.10) and Nitmiluk (8.06) NPs, and even urban parks, for example East Point RR (8.01). In Qld it is readily seen at many sites, including Kingfisher Park (1.03). Outlying populations occur on North and South Stradbroke Is. (1.35), where animals are 20 per cent smaller than on the mainland. This species moves with a distinctive upright posture and has a diagnostic black facial stripe.

Other names: Sandy Wallaby, Kimberley Wallaby, Jungle, Grass or River Wallaby

*Antilopine Wallaroo

Macropus antilopinus   (northern Australia)
A fast-moving wallaroo of northern savannahs from Cape York Peninsula to the Kimberley. It is found in a variety of wooded habitats with a grassy understorey, preferring flat to undulating country (unlike the Common Wallaroo). It is not uncommon at Litchfield (8.10) and Kakadu (8.03) NPs: watch for it along the wooded edges of open areas, usually well away from roads and especially at dawn and dusk. It is gregarious but generally not very approachable. This species is strongly dimorphic: males are rufous and females grey; males have a distinctive head shape, with a 'Roman nose'. Where it coexists with the Common Wallaroo, the latter rests during the day in higher, rocky areas.

Other names: Antilopine or Antelope Kangaroo, Darwin Red Kangaroo

*Black Wallaroo

Macropus bernardus   (Top End)

Endemic to the NT, where it is uncommon, rather elusive and restricted to rocky escarpments of the Arnhem Land sandstone country. A 'chunky', strongly dimorphic macropod with long, shaggy fur: males are black to dark brown; females grey-brown with dark highlights on their paws, feet and tail tip. Nourlangie Rock and Gunlom in Kakadu NP (8.03) are classic sites at which to look for it (it does not occur at Litchfield NP). Black Wallaroos rest during the heat of the day under shady overhangs, where they are well camouflaged and difficult to detect unless accidentally startled. Occasionally, individuals hang around popular lookouts, apparently unfazed by tourist activity. To maximise your chances of seeing one, hit the trails in the early morning or at dusk. It apparently favours areas characterised by large boulders.

Other names: Black Kangaroo, Northern Black Wallaroo, Bernard's Wallaroo or Kangaroo, Barrk (male), Djukerre (female)

*Black-striped Wallaby

Macropus dorsalis   (southern Qld, northern NSW)

Uncommon and patchily distributed in tropical and subtropical eastern Australia between Coonabarabran, NSW and Chillagoe, Qld (1.06). Grazes morning and evening at forest edges, usually in small groups, especially where a dense understorey provides cover. During the day it lies up in semi-permanent camps in dense undergrowth, including lantana. Imbil (1.39) is a reliable site for it. Similar to and largely sympatric with Red-necked Wallaby, the Black-striped has a distinct white face stripe, is more rufous on the forequarters and has a white flank stripe, as well as the eponymous black back stripe; its gait is distinctive.

Other names: Scrub Wallaby

*Tammar Wallaby

Macropus eugenii   (Kangaroo I., south-west WA, islands off WA)

This species is most easily seen on islands including the Houtman Abrolhos (7.12), Garden I. near Perth, the Recherche Archipelago (7.10) and especially Kangaroo I. (6.13), where it can readily be seen at American River township (the only other macropod on Kangaroo I. is the much larger Kangaroo Island Kangaroo, and confusion is highly unlikely). In south-western Australia Tammars occur in Jarrah forest, with dense thickets for cover, near open areas for grazing at sites such as Perup (7.08), where they are more common than Western Brush Wallaby, at Tutanning, Boyagin, and Karakamia and Paruna AWC Sanctuaries (7.01). There have been vigorous reintroduction and Fox control programs in the south-west, with encouraging results. They are reasonably easy to find in denser thickets of casuarina woodland with grass and sedge cover.

Other names: Tammar, Dama Wallaby, Dama Pademelon, Kangaroo Island Wallaby

*Western Grey Kangaroo

Macropus fuliginosus (central and western mainland)

'Southern' Grey Kangaroo would possibly be a more apt name for this species as it is the common woodland kangaroo in the southern part of the continent. It actually reaches its greatest abundance in western NSW, where there is an extensive area of overlap with the Eastern Grey Kangaroo. The two also overlap in north-west Vic at, for example, Hattah-Kulkyne NP (4.23) and The Grampians (Gariwerd) NP (4.21). They are easy to differentiate in the field with practice – Western Grey is more rufous and a close view of the muzzle will clinch ID; it also has a more upright bounding posture. As only Western Grey occurs in WA (where it is common at Dryandra SF (7.05)) it should pose no identification challenge there. In SA it is the only grey kangaroo over most of the state (at, for example, Gawler Ranges NP); Eastern Greys occur in SA only in the extreme south-east and at the eastern edge of the Lake Eyre Basin. There can be no mistaking the Kangaroo I. subspecies *M. f. fuliginosus*, which is abundant (6.13).

Other names: Black-faced Kangaroo, Mallee Kangaroo, Sooty Kangaroo, Stinker

*Eastern Grey Kangaroo

Macropus giganteus (eastern Australia)

Common to very common in open forests, woodlands and adjoining farmland, on golf courses, waterfront reserves adjoining native bush, large urban parks with native tree cover and, yes, even on the streets of rural cities such as Canberra. The Tas subspecies ('Forester Kangaroo') is darker and shaggier, and common in Narawntapu (5.10) and Mt William (5.11) NPs. You will almost certainly see Eastern Greys by visiting any rural area within its range: watch along roadsides at dusk and take care where they are abundant, as collisions with vehicles are frequent. These kangaroos are now more frequently seen in peri-urban areas as the sprawl encroaches on farmland fringes, even entering gardens to feed, although traffic and domestic dogs take a heavy toll. When alarmed they strike the ground with both feet in quick succession to make an audible 'ka-thump'. In some areas Eastern Grey Kangaroos can become quite tame (for example, Canberra Nature Park (3.04)); however, mature males are large animals that have been known to injure dogs and humans when cornered, also where they are hand-fed and food aggressive.

Other names: Forester, Great Grey Kangaroo, Scrub Kangaroo, Scrubber

*Toolache

Macropus greyi (south-east SA, south-west Vic)

Extinct. This species formerly occurred in The Coorong hinterland of SA and adjacent parts of Vic on swampy plains and adjoining woodland. It appears to have died out because of hunting for sport and the total destruction of its habitat; the last specimen died in captivity in 1939.

*Western Brush Wallaby

Macropus irma   (south-west WA)

Restricted to dry forest and woodland, including mallee, with a grassy understorey, where it is uncommon. At least partly diurnal, it occurs at Dryandra SF (7.05), but is probably easier to see at Lake Muir (7.08). Diagnostic features to look for include white inner ears contrasting with black edges and a white facial stripe from the mouth to the base of the ear; as it bolts from cover look for its black tail tip and horizontal bands on the rump of some individuals. The head and tail are held almost horizontally while hopping.

Other names: Black-gloved Wallaby, Kwoora

*Parma Wallaby

Macropus parma   (subtropical central NSW)

A small wallaby, endemic to subcoastal NSW, that was thought to be extinct in the wild until it was rediscovered in 1967. It is a rare inhabitant of dense understorey and difficult to see well, although it is reputed to freeze when spotlighted or caught in vehicle headlights. Probably best found by driving slowly through wetter parts of the Watagans NP (2.17); it also grazes at picnic spots at Allyn River FP in Gloucester Tops NP and occurs at Gibraltar Range NP. Usually solitary, emerging from dense cover at dusk to feed in adjacent open areas. The Red-necked Pademelon is far more common in most of these forests, but is larger and lacks the Parma Wallaby's facial stripe, has more rufous coloration and has a shorter, stiffer tail. The Parma Wallaby has a distinctive, almost horizontal hopping gait with its forearms tucked against the body.

Other names: White-throated Wallaby or Pademelon

*Whiptail Wallaby

Macropus parryi   (south-east Qld, northern NSW)

A common and attractive wallaby of grassy open forest in hilly country along the Great Dividing Range between northern NSW and Cooktown, Qld. Most abundant in the south and largely diurnal – it is easily seen en route to O'Reilly's at Lamington NP (1.37); also at Washpool NP, NSW and on the golf course at Mareeba (1.04c). Its long tail and distinctive rump pattern make this species relatively easy to identify.

Other names: Pretty-face Wallaby, Grey-faced Wallaby, Blue or Grey Flyer

*Common Wallaroo (Euro)

Macropus robustus   (eastern, central and northern mainland Australia)

Built like a stocky kangaroo with shaggy fur, the Common Wallaroo overlaps with all three 'great' kangaroos over much of its range (the alternative name 'Euro' is more commonly used west of the Great Dividing Range). Identification is easier when the different species are seen in close proximity – Common Wallaroos are broader across the chest, have a more elongated 'face' and, with good views, dense guard hairs are visible on their chest and flanks. Wallaroos are also highly variable in coloration (the two grey kangaroos tend to be rather homogenous over their respective ranges): those from the south-east are pale fawn; north-west Euros are dark rusty-red; and animals from the far north-east have a shorter coat and show marked dimorphism, males being dark rufous or rusty-red and females varying between light rufous and blue-grey. All forms have a naked rhinarium, and dark paws and feet; their tail is not normally tipped black as in the greys. Common Wallaroos classically frequent hilly, rocky terrain, lying up during the day in caves, among boulders or under overhangs. However, habitat is not diagnostic – they also feed on slopes and plains, and along drainage lines. This species has a distinctive upright bounding posture. Three rather poorly defined subspecies are recognised: the abundant 'Barrow Island' Euro (formerly known as *M. r. isabellinus*) is now thought to be a stunted form of the widespread Euro *M. r. erubescens*. Elsewhere, *M. r. erubescens* is common in suitable habitat and can be seen readily at Mutawintji NP and Fowler's Gap (2.28). The 'Northern Wallaroo' *M. r. woodwardi* occurs at Litchfield NP (8.10), where the Black Wallaroo *does not* occur (where the two coexist on the Arnhem Land escarpment, Black Wallaroos tend to occur higher up, Euros occupying lower and flatter habitat). The 'Eastern Wallaroo' *M. r. robustus* occurs along the Great Dividing Range and can be seen at Lark Quarry. At Lake Argyle in the Kimberley, Euros have been observed swimming between islands despite the presence of crocodiles.

Other names: Hill Kangaroo, Roan Wallaroo, Red Wallaroo, Biggida, Mandya

*Red-necked Wallaby

Macropus rufogriseus (eastern Australia)

Larger and paler than the Swamp Wallaby, with which it co-occurs over much of its range, this is a common species of forest edges along the eastern seaboard between Gladstone, Qld and western Vic. On the mainland it is most common in north-east NSW and south-east Qld. It can usually be seen in any wooded habitat and along roadsides at dawn and dusk just about anywhere in its large range. Good sites include The Grampians (4.21), coastal southern NSW and near Canberra (3.06). An attractive pale morph – the so-called 'Golden Wallaby' – occurs on South Stradbroke I. (1.36). The Red-necked Wallaby's black paws and feet, and white facial stripe, are helpful identification features, but in reality it shouldn't be hard to separate from Swamp Wallaby. The subspecies *M. r. rufogriseus* – 'Bennett's Wallaby'– is endemic to Tas (where the Swamp Wallaby does not occur); it is abundant over most of the state and easily seen at Narawntapu NP (5.10) and along just about any forested roadside at night. Pale and albino individuals occur at Bruny I. (5.04).

Other names: Bennett's Wallaby (Tas), Brush Wallaby or Kangaroo, Eastern Brush Wallaby, Brusher, Red Wallaby, 'Golden' Wallaby, Painted Wallaby (Bruny I.)

*Red Kangaroo

Macropus rufus (central Australia)

A large, attractively marked kangaroo that is common to abundant in the arid zone, especially in the rangelands of NSW and Qld. This species has a broad, deer-like head with large, pricked ears. Adult males are easily identified by their large size and short, reddish fur; both sexes have a black-and-white muzzle pattern that is absent in grey kangaroos and the Common Wallaroo. In the eastern part of its range, sexes are highly dimorphic, females being a smoky blue colour (they shouldn't be mistaken for a grey kangaroo – the 'blue' is quite distinctive). Blue females are much less prevalent among specimens in true desert. The forepaws, feet and tail tip are normally a contrasting cream to grey colour. Red Kangaroos can readily be seen on outback drives just about anywhere within their vast range, especially in the early morning and at dusk. They lie surprisingly low during the day among sparse vegetation, or under trees or bushes.

Other names: Blue Flyer (female), Plains Kangaroo

The distinctively marked wallabies of the genus Onychogalea *are known as **nailtail wallabies** because of a small, horny outgrowth at the end of their tails. Only the Northern Nailtail Wallaby survives in any numbers; another nailtail species is extinct and the third was thought to be so until its remarkable rediscovery in 1973. When moving quickly nailtail wallabies 'pump' their forelimbs in a distinctive circular motion.*

*Bridled Nailtail Wallaby

Onychogalea fraenata   (central Qld)

This handsome nailtail is endangered and restricted to Taunton Scientific Reserve (1.25) near Dingo in central Qld; populations have become established from reintroductions at Idalia NP (1.31), Scotia AWC Sanctuary (2.29) and at Avocet Nature Refuge. Access to Taunton is strictly controlled, but you could join a volunteer group working there or at Avocet. This species rarely strays far from cover although it may bask in the open on cold winter days. During the day it usually shelters in a scrape under thick vegetation or in a hollow log. Its black 'nail' is usually hidden by a black terminal tail tuft.

Other names: Merrin, Flashjack, 'Pademelon', Organ Grinder, Waistcoat Wallaby

*Crescent Nailtail Wallaby

Onychogalea lunata   (inland Australia)

Extinct. Formerly common in arid and semi-arid shrublands and woodlands; it disappeared for reasons unknown and was last seen in the 1940s.

*Northern Nailtail Wallaby

Onychogalea unguifera   (northern Australia)

A rather elusive species despite its wide distribution in tropical grassland and grassy woodlands. It is common, though hard to observe, on heavily grazed pastoral land, particularly at the edges of blacksoil plains on the Barkly Tableland, in the Gulf Country and the east and west Kimberley (7.21). Mobs graze on the airstrip at dusk at Laura (1.16), and it also occurs at Dunmarra, NT and on Roebuck Plains near Broome (7.20). Where it coexists with other species, such as the Agile Wallaby and Antilopine Kangaroo, it tends to favour grassy valleys. Northern Nailtails usually freeze when danger approaches, then suddenly burst from cover with a startling 'wut-wut' call. The terminal half of its tail may be all-dark or striped.

Other names: Sandy Nailtail Wallaby, Organ Grinder

Rock wallabies are small to medium-sized wallabies specialised for life on rocky escarpments, cliffs, gorges, breakaways and boulder fields, usually with a northerly aspect. Some have colonised the retaining walls of large dams. By day they shelter under overhangs, in crevices and caves, typically sunning themselves in the late afternoon at habitual sites they defend from rivals. They are extremely agile, scaling almost vertical rock faces and even leaning trees. They occur only on the mainland and a few nearby islands; small populations restricted to rocky ranges within a sea of agriculture are vulnerable to extinction. All species are social and may live in large colonies of 100 or more animals. A group of six genetically distinct species endemic to Qld are almost indistinguishable in the field; fortunately their ranges mostly don't overlap and there are good sites at which you can be confident of identification. Otherwise, most rock wallabies have long furry tails, distinctive flank and tail markings and some even have patches of colour that make them among the most attractive of macropods. All of the 16 currently recognised species are well camouflaged, at best unobtrusive but often invisible when standing motionless against a broken background.

*Allied Rock Wallaby

Petrogale assimilis   (central Qld)
This species is common and easily seen close to Townsville (1.13) on Magnetic I. and at Bowling Green Bay NP. Other sites include Cape Pallarenda just north of Townsville, Horseshoe Bay in Bowen and the wall of the Ross River Dam.

Other names: Torrens Creek Rock Wallaby

*Short-eared Rock Wallaby

Petrogale brachyotis   (Top End, Kimberley)
Widespread in the Top End and Kimberley, where it is not uncommon but generally unobtrusive on sandstone bluffs, outcrops and cliffs. Where its range overlaps with that of Nabarlek, for example in Kakadu NP (8.03), this species is far more common. Good Kakadu sites include the lookout and walk to Ubirr Rock, Barrdelidji, Gunlom and Plum Tree Creek; it also may be seen near the Tolmer Falls lookout in Litchfield NP (8.10). Further west, it occurs at Keep River NP (8.15) and at many sites in the Kimberley, including Mt Hart Station. This species is quite variable in size and coloration across its range, and DNA analysis has recently shown the northern and eastern populations to be a distinct species, Wilkins' Rock Wallaby *P. wilkinsi*.

*Monjon

Petrogale burbidgei   (Kimberley)
Australia's smallest macropod and endemic to the King Leopold Sandstone of the Kimberley, between the Mitchell Plateau (7.21) and Prince Regent River NR. Cryptic and

mainly nocturnal in this intensely hot environment. If seen well its size and appearance should help separate it from the Nabarlek and Short-eared Rock Wallabies, with which it co-occurs. The Monjon also occurs on Bigge (where it is partly diurnal and apparently abundant), Katers and Boongaree Is., where Nabarlek does not occur. Monjons are reputed to be inquisitive and may even approach cautiously.

*Cape York Rock Wallaby

Petrogale coenensis   (eastern Cape York Peninsula)

One of the most difficult rock wallabies to see – photos of live animals are rare. It inhabits rocky outcrops, gullies, ridges and dry creeks in open woodland, between Musgrave and the Pascoe River on Cape York Peninsula. It occurs in Lakefield NP and there are populations near Coen.

*Nabarlek

Petrogale concinna   (Top End, Kimberley)

A little-known, infrequently encountered rock wallaby. It occurs in two widely separated locales and the respective populations are regarded as subspecies. *P. c. canescens* occurs in the Top End, where it is rarely encountered although it persists at Mt Borraidale in Arnhem Land (8.04). *P. c. monastria* of the Kimberley also has a patchy distribution; it occurs on Augustus, Borda, Hidden and Long Is. This species is smaller than but similar to the Short-eared Rock Wallaby, with which it co-occurs over part of its range (they may share the same habitat and a young Short-eared Wallaby could be confused with a Nabarlek). It shelters in caves and crevices during the day, feeding mainly at night, although it may be partly diurnal during the wet season and bask on ledges. Nabarleks could be found feeding up to several hundred metres away from shelter, unlike Short-eared Rock wallabies, which tend to stick close to shelter. Nabarleks are fast and agile; when hopping they hold their tail arched over their back, fluffing out the terminal tuft. Monjons are similar but smaller and also have a tufted tail. On many Kimberley islands only one or the other occurs.

Other names: Little Rock Wallaby, Pygmy Rock Wallaby

*Godman's Rock Wallaby

Petrogale godmani   (north Qld)

Known from near Mt Carbine, the Mitchell River, north to Bathurst Head and west to the 'Pinnacles'. Black Mountain (1.14), south of Cooktown, is the best-known site. This mass of jumbled volcanic boulders is an attraction in its own right; the wallabies are best looked for after dark and with luck could be spotlighted from roadside pull-ins (be prepared to put in some time).

*Herbert's Rock Wallaby

Petrogale herberti   (central Qld)

The most southerly in distribution of the 'plain' rock wallaby complex. This species occupies a large range in south-east Qld between the south bank of the Fitzroy River and Nanango, and west to Rubyvale and Clermont. At the southern end of its distribution its pelage is similar to that of the Brush-tailed Rock Wallaby, although the two don't overlap.

*Unadorned Rock Wallaby

Petrogale inornata   (central Qld)
Common at several sites between Home Hill and the north bank of the Fitzroy River; also occurs on Whitsunday I. Obvious on and around Peter Faust Dam (1.21), where it co-occurs with Proserpine Rock Wallaby (which is far less common, more retiring and tends to stay in or near cover). This species also occurs on the wall of the Eungella Dam near Mackay and at Cape Upstart NP.

Other names: Plain Rock Wallaby

*Black-footed Rock Wallaby

Petrogale lateralis   (central and western inland Australia, some islands)
The most widespread rock wallaby, with a disjunct distribution across the arid zone plus the Kimberley, south-west, Recherche Archipelago (WA) and islands off southern SA. There are three subspecies and at least two more distinct forms are recognised. The MacDonnell Ranges subspecies is hard to miss at Heavitree Gap in Alice Springs (8.16) and at several other tourist sites, including Simpson's Gap. *P. l. lateralis* was formerly widespread but now occurs only on Barrow I. (7.18), where it numbers possibly fewer than 100 animals, in scattered locations across the south-west and on Salisbury I. in the Recherche Archipelago. In WA there are translocated populations at Avon Valley, Walyunga and Cape Le Grand NPs, Paruna AWC Sanctuary (7.01) and Querekin Rock. The similar but genetically distinct Hackett's Rock Wallaby *P. l. hacketti* is common on three other Recherche islands: Westall, Mondrain and Wilson. In SA, the Pearson Island Rock Wallaby is morphologically distinct and occurs naturally at Pearson I., with long-established introductions at South and Middle Pearson Is., Thistle I. (6.15) and Wedge I. The as yet undescribed West Kimberley form is still common in the Edgar, Grant and Erskine Ranges, plus Mt Wynne and Mt Anderson.

Other names: Black-flanked Rock Wallaby, Side-striped Rock Wallaby, West Australian Rock Wallaby, Recherche Rock Wallaby, Pearson Island Rock Wallaby, Warru (central Australia)

*Mareeba Rock Wallaby

Petrogale mareeba   (Wet Tropics)
A highly sociable species that you cannot miss at Granite Gorge (1.04b), although a more natural experience could be had at Mt Carbine and on outcrops along the Tinaroo Rd on the Atherton Tableland (1.04). This species is variable in coloration and has a patchy distribution west to Mungana and Undara Lava Tubes (1.05), and between the Mitchell and Burdekin Rivers.

*Brush-tailed Rock Wallaby

Petrogale penicillata   (subcoastal eastern Australia)
Formerly widespread along the southern half of the Great Dividing Range, this species has been hit particularly hard by feral predators, chiefly Foxes, and is now extremely

rare or extinct over much of its former range. Its stronghold is northern NSW, particularly the gorges of the Macleay and Clarence Rivers. Small populations persist at Warrumbungle NP and Mt Kaputar; other populations are being actively managed at the Shoalhaven River, NSW and The Grampians (Gariwerd) NP (4.21). However, the only places it is easy to see are at Perseverance Dam (1.38) and Watagan's Lookout, in Watagans NP (2.17).

Other names: Western Rock Wallaby

*Proserpine Rock Wallaby

Petrogale persephone   (Whitsunday region in Qld)
The largest and rarest rock wallaby, this species was discovered in 1976 and has the most restricted range of any macropod. It is a specialist of boulder piles among rainforest vine thickets. Much of its natural habitat has been subsumed by coastal development, where it often falls victim to traffic and domestic dogs. It can sometimes be seen grazing in suburban gardens adjoining suitable habitat at Airlie Beach; try along Shute Harbour Rd, Mandalay Rd and Staniland Drive. It also occurs on several islands in the Whitsunday Group, including Gloucester I.; and near Proserpine, where it co-occurs with the Unadorned Rock Wallaby at Peter Faust Dam (1.21); Proserpine Rock Wallaby is much less abundant, emerging from cover after dark and never straying far from vine thickets on the slopes near the dam. With good views the two can be told apart fairly easily; the Proserpine Rock Wallaby has a more attenuated snout, rufous rump and an overall mauve tinge to the upperparts. It basks in morning sunshine and is known locally for its tree-climbing ability. There has also been a successful translocation program to Hayman I., where it can be seen along forest trails.

Other names: 'Tree kangaroo'

*Purple-necked Rock Wallaby

Petrogale purpureicollis   (western Qld)
Not uncommon on outcrops near Mt Isa (1.28), at Dajarra and Boodjamulla (Lawn Hill) NP (1.29). The purple coloration is most obvious in males. Basks on sunny ledges after cold nights and late on winter afternoons.

*Rothschild's Rock Wallaby

Petrogale rothschildi   (Pilbara)
Found in a wide range of habitats and sites in the Pilbara, including Burrup Peninsula and Dampier Archipelago (7.17), Karijini NP, and the Hamersley and Chichester Ranges. It is occasionally seen on railway embankments and mine slag heaps , but it has very restricted movements during the day in this torrid environment, sheltering in caves and among boulder piles. One of the best ways to see it is to take a cruise to the Dampier Archipelago, where it can be seen on several islands, including Enderby, West and East Lewis Is.

Other names: Roebourne Rock Wallaby

*Sharman's Rock Wallaby

Petrogale sharmani   (southern Wet Tropics)

The most restricted of the 'cryptic' rock wallabies. Known from only the Seaview and Coane Ranges west of Ingham, where it can be seen on a few outcrops on cattle stations. Mt Claro (1.09) is the best known and probably most accessible site; it also occurs at Hidden Valley and in Mt Zero-Taravale AWC Sanctuary (1.11).

Other names: Mount Claro Rock Wallaby

*Yellow-footed Rock Wallaby

Petrogale xanthopus   (inland Qld, NSW and SA)

A striking species, arguably Australia's most attractive macropod and unmistakable if seen well (although it is so well camouflaged among fractured boulders that it is easily overlooked until it moves). The Flinders Ranges NP (6.10) is the stronghold of the darker subspecies *P. x. xanthopus*; other populations occur in the Gawler Ranges (6.14) and near Broken Hill, NSW (where fewer than 100 survive). *P. x. celeris* occurs in south-west Qld at Idalia NP (1.31). During the day this species lies up under shady trees and bushes, often some distance from feeding sites.

Other names: Ring-tailed Rock Wallaby

*The **Quokka** is endemic to south-western Australia and taxonomically anomalous, having a naked tail, among other features. It is something of an icon of Rottnest Island near Fremantle and 'Rotto' is by far the best place to see it.*

*Quokka

Setonix brachyurus   (south-west WA)

This rabbit-sized macropod is almost impossible to miss at Rottnest I. (7.02), where the population numbers 8–12 000. Quokkas also occur on the mainland at, for example, Two Peoples Bay (7.09), but they are timid and much harder to see. It is the only macropod on Rottnest I., but at Two Peoples Bay it could be mistaken for the ultra-rare Gilbert's Potoroo, with which it shares the dense heath. Quokkas are larger and more robust than potoroos, with ginger to rufous ears and shoulders. You could also try looking in suitable habitat – thickly vegetated swamps and Jarrah forests – at Dwellingup, Jarrahdale, Harvey, Collie and in the Stirling Range NP (7.06).

Other names: Ban-gup

*The three species of **pademelon** are compact, short-tailed wallabies that shelter in forest understorey during the day and emerge to graze in clearings at dusk. Pademelons typically move on all fours, dragging their tails, and use their forepaws to manipulate food; they rarely move more than 100 m from cover and when startled retreat quickly using well-worn runways. All three species are common, although the Rufous-bellied (Tasmanian) Pademelon is extinct on the mainland.*

*Rufous-bellied (Tasmanian) Pademelon

Thylogale billardierii   (Tasmania)

This pademelon formerly occurred in Vic and SA, but as it is now extinct on the mainland it is generally by default known as the Tasmanian Pademelon. It is common to abundant and can readily be seen at, for example, Cradle Mountain-Lake St Clair NP (5.09), Narawntapu NP (5.10) and basically in any suitable habitat throughout the state.

Other names: Tasmanian Pademelon, Red-bellied Pademelon, Rufous Wallaby, 'Rufus'

Red-legged Pademelon

Thylogale stigmatica   (eastern Australia; New Guinea)

In the southern part of its range this species co-occurs with Red-necked Pademelon, with which it could be confused. The two are sympatric between north-east NSW and about Rockhampton, Qld; where they co-occur, the Red-legged Pademelon is almost never seen outside of rainforest; its pale leg stripe is diagnostic. It is more common (or more commonly seen) in the northern part of its range, where it is partly diurnal, for example near Julatten (1.03) and at Iron Range NP (1.17). In the south it can be seen at Lamington NP (1.37).

*Red-necked Pademelon

Thylogale thetis   (subtropical eastern Australia)

The commonest pademelon in subtropical rainforest and wet forest between the central Qld coast and north-east NSW. Very common at Lamington NP (1.37), it also occurs at Barrington Tops NP (2.22a).

Other names: Pademelon Wallaby

*Like the Quokka, the **Swamp** or **Black Wallaby** has been placed in its own genus owing to its likely affinities with an early lineage of browsing macropods. In most other respects, however, it looks like a typical wallaby and because it is abundant over much of the eastern seaboard it is one of the macropods you are most likely to see.*

Swamp (Black) Wallaby

Wallabia bicolor   (eastern mainland)

Probably the most abundant medium-sized macropod in south-east Australia. This species is commonly seen haring across forest roads, mainly in the evening and early morning, and consequently is a frequent road kill victim. Note that the name 'Swamp' Wallaby is in general usage even though Black Wallaby is probably more descriptive. 'Swampies' are generally darker than other species of similar size and sometimes have a white-tipped tail, and have distinctive locomotion, with the body held almost horizontally. The Swamp Wallaby ventures from dense vegetation near waterways at dusk, but is also found in open forest, on ridges and hilltops, and often far from water. It is approachable and usually solitary. Swamp Wallabies are often encountered in denser habitat than Red-necked Wallabies, though their ranges overlap extensively and the preceding species is found on forest edges. Good sites include hills near Canberra (3.06), the NSW south coast, The

Grampians NP (4.21) and parts of Brisbane Forest Park. These animals on North and South Stradbroke Is. are about 20 per cent smaller than on the mainland.

Other names: Black-tailed Wallaby, Fern Wallaby, Black Pademelon, Stinker, Black Stinker

*Despite its common name, the **Banded Hare-wallaby** is of uncertain affinity and is usually placed in its own subfamily. Genetic and morphological evidence suggests it may be the last survivor of a now-extinct family of giant macropods, the sthenurines.*

*Banded Hare-wallaby

Lagostrophus fasciatus   (islands of Shark Bay, WA)

Unfortunately extinct in the wild on the mainland and now restricted to Bernier and Dorre Is. (7.15c), where it has been reintroduced and is not uncommon; and to Faure Island AWC Sanctuary (7.15b), where a small population has become established. On Bernier and Dorre Is. it often frequents dense *Acaica–Ficus* thickets, where several individuals may shelter together during the day. There is a captive population at Dryandra (7.05). This is a distinctive, boldly marked species whose 'zebra stripes' are diagnostic if seen well.

Other names: Munning

■ EUTHERIAN MAMMALS – SUBCLASS EUTHERIA

The third subclass of Australian mammals – the most modern in evolutionary terms – is the eutherians, often called 'placental' mammals but some marsupials also have a placenta. Native species are represented by one species of shrew, plus numerous rodents, marine mammals and bats, which together make up a large percentage of Australia's mammals. Australian waters are rich in sea life and the cetaceans (whales, dolphins and porpoises) are well represented; other marine species include the seals and sea lions, and the Dugong. Native terrestrial eutherians are thought to have arrived in several waves after the Australian tectonic plate collided with the South-East Asian plate. There are some fascinating examples of the great rodent family, as well as several introduced species. The third large group of placentals is the bats, which include flying foxes and related fruit bats, and the insect-eating microbats; again, many unique and fascinating forms have evolved. Humans arrived here some 40 000–60 000 years ago, but it wasn't until about 4000 years ago that the Dingo was introduced to Australia by Asian seafarers and caused further changes to the existing mammal fauna, both as a hunting tool of Aboriginal people and as a free-ranging wild animal. For example, the Thylacine is known to have coexisted on the mainland with the Dingo, which undoubtedly caused its extinction there. A second wave of destructive placental mammals arrived with white settlers, including for the first time hoofed animals and the Rabbit, which collectively caused massive destruction of Australia's fragile topsoil and paved the way for further mammalian extinctions.

Insectivorous mammals – Order Insectivora

This great order is made up of hedgehogs, shrews, tenrecs, moles etc., and represented in Australian territory by only one species.

Shrews – Family Soricidae (world 376; Australia 1 (endemic))

These hyperactive insectivores comprise the largest mammalian family on Earth, as well as the smallest living placental mammals (Savi's Pygmy Shrew weighs as little as 2 g). Only the Christmas Island Shrew has been recorded in Australian territory, presumably becoming established after hitching a ride on vegetation drifting from nearby Java, Indonesia.

*Christmas Island Shrew

Crocidura attenuata   (Christmas Island)

Almost certainly extinct. This endemic formerly occurred only on Christmas I. (9.03). It was apparently common in 1900, but its decline was so speedy after Black Rats and Cats got ashore that it was already deemed extinct by 1908. However, two specimens were encountered in 1958 near South Point and another two in 1985 on the western side of the island. Despite extensive searches, intensive trapping effort and unconfirmed sightings, it has not been seen since. It may hang on in small numbers because the eroded limestone terrain is difficult to survey and offers plenty of shelter for these small animals; unfortunately, it also offers shelter for introduced predators such as snakes.

Bats – Order Chiroptera

Both flying foxes (also known as fruit bats) and insect-eating bats (microbats) are well represented in Australia. More than 70 species of Australian bat, a high percentage of which are endemic, are currently recognised and new species of microbat are still being described. 'Watching' flying foxes is relatively easy at their daytime roosts (camps), some of which occur even in large cities. Microbats are another matter, being small, nocturnal and almost indistinguishable in flight. Some microbat species can be recognised by sound or sight, especially at daytime roosts, and places where this is possible have been described in the text. But there is no substitute for seeing microbats up close; indeed, positive identification for many species is possible only in the hand. This normally involves live-trapping for study, and those interested in learning more about these fascinating animals are urged to join the Australasian Bat Society (www.ausbats.org.au), which holds regular meetings, campouts and surveys in which members can participate.

There are several cave complexes around the country with spectacular bat concentrations; some of these have become important tourist attractions, but many microbats, especially breeding females, are sensitive to disturbance, and access may be restricted at certain times of year. Each state or territory chapter has a section on watching bats in that region, with tips on where at least some bat species might be seen.

Be aware that the potentially fatal lyssavirus (often called 'Hendra' virus in the media) occurs in Australia and being bitten by a bat could put you at risk of contracting the disease. If you find a sick or injured bat, do not handle it with your bare hands unless you have been inoculated against lyssavirus. Use gloves and contact a bat specialist as soon as possible.

Megabats – Suborder Megachiroptera

Traditionally bats have been separated into two suborders: the megabats and microbats. Recent research has shown that this approach is possibly too simplistic, and some families formerly considered to be microbats appear to be more closely related to the megabats. However, the traditional classification makes convenient distinctions and most wildlife-watchers needn't worry about the intricacies of bat taxonomy.

Flying foxes and fruit bats – Family Pteropodidae (world 177; Australia 11 (3 endemic))

Flying foxes are the largest of all bats and reach their highest diversity in the south-west Pacific region. They are common in northern and eastern Australia, forming sometimes huge camps that can number tens, or even hundreds, of thousands of individuals. These camps form the largest wild mammal aggregations in the country and for sheer spectacle it's hard to beat the sight of thousands taking to the air at dusk during their nightly fly-outs. At least one species can be seen in major coastal towns and cities between Broome and Melbourne (they are absent from the south-west) and in recent years have become established in SA. Most Australian flying foxes are easy to see and identify during the day at camps. At night they can be detected by their noisy squabbling at food sources; they can be readily spotlighted at feeding trees such as figs, and have bright red or yellow eyeshine. Because of rampant coastal development flying foxes are increasingly coming into conflict with humans, who complain of noise, smell and disease from camps. It's a charged issue, with calls for removal or extermination hitting the news frequently. Legally or illegally, many flying foxes are killed annually by farmers.

Blossom bats and tube-nosed bats are small nectar- and fruit-eating bats of the tropics and subtropics. Identification is probably easiest in the hand, but by staking out their preferred food trees they can sometimes be identified by spotlighting.

Bare-backed Fruit Bat

Dobsonia moluccensis   (Cape York Peninsula, Torres Strait)

Uniquely among Australian flying foxes the wing membranes of this species join in the middle of its back, forming pockets between the leathery wings and the back proper. This adaptation allows it to manoeuvre among foliage and even fly backwards when feeding. It is a rainforest species that feeds at flowering eucalypts and fruiting trees. It is relatively common at Iron Range NP (1.17), but difficult to distinguish from other flying fox species at night. The loud popping noise caused by air trapped in its wing pockets is a useful indicator of its presence. It roosts in small colonies of less than 100 individuals, in hollow trees, among large boulders, in dense vegetation under rock overhangs and in fissures covered with vegetation. It forages alone, and is usually wary and silent at night. Favoured food plants include flowering Northern Bloodwood *Corymbia polycarpa*, Paw-paws and flowering Banana trees.

Other names: Spinal-winged Fruit Bat

Least Blossom Bat

Macroglossus minimus   (tropical eastern and northern Australia; South-East Asia)
Microbat-sized; this species looks like a miniature flying fox. Not uncommon, look for it at prolific nectar sources such as flowering *Melaleuca* trees, which it accesses with its extraordinarily long tongue. It is noisy and pugnacious when feeding, making a distinctive metallic call. It is common in the Top End, where good places to look include the Darwin Botanic Gardens (8.01) and trees lining the entrance to Fogg Dam (8.02) – be extremely careful of crocodiles here. Positive identification is probably assured where it occurs in the Kimberley and Top End; it co-occurs with Eastern Blossom Bat in tropical eastern Australia and the two can probably be separated only in the hand. In the Kimberley it pollinates Boab trees.

Other names: Northern Blossom Bat

Eastern Tube-nosed Bat

Nyctimene robinsoni   (tropical and subtropical eastern mainland; New Guinea)
One of the most distinctive Australian bats; as their name suggests, tube-nosed bats have extraordinary protruding tubular nostrils, the function of which is not clear. Their wings, nostrils and ears are boldly patterned with yellow blotches (each individual with a unique pattern), which give them excellent camouflage at roost in dappled light among rainforest foliage. Apart from coloration, field characteristics that could help with identification include bright red eyeshine and a distinctive whistling note emitted in flight. Regrettably this species is often caught on barbed-wire fences, where it rapidly dehydrates after sunrise. It is more common in the northern part of its range; roosts alone or in small groups in the rainforest canopy; and forages in rainforest and adjacent woodlands and heath.

Other names: Robinson's Tube-nosed Bat

Eastern Blossom Bat

Syconycteris australis   (eastern Australia; New Guinea, South-East Asia)
Superficially similar to the Least Blossom Bat and probably indistinguishable in the field where their ranges overlap (north of about Mackay, Qld); only the Least Blossom Bat occurs in the Top End and Kimberley. Both are very similar in size and appearance, but the Least Blossom Bat has a stubby tail and skin flap inside the legs (the Eastern Blossom Bat lacks the stubby tail and a fringe of hairs replaces the skin flap). This is more or less a

heathland specialist, commuting to heaths from rainforest roosts and feeding predominantly on *Melaleuca* and *Banksia* blossom. It is noisy and pugnacious when feeding (and in the hand), vocalising and wing-clapping at intruders.

Other names: Queensland Blossom Bat, Common Blossom Bat

Black Flying Fox

Pteropus alecto   (northern and eastern Australia; Indonesia, PNG)
Common around the northern half of Australia from about Shark Bay to northern NSW; it is spreading south down the east coast and some are seen every year in the Sydney area and beyond. This species forms permanent camps in mangroves, paperbarks and rainforest; large numbers occur at Woodend (1.33) and in Kakadu NP (8.03). It typically roosts high in the canopy, often in association with Little Red and Grey-headed Flying Foxes; where other species are present, Black Flying Foxes usually roost near the edge of camps. It occasionally roosts in cave mouths, such as at Chillagoe (1.06) and Tunnel Creek (7.21).

Other names: Gould's Fruit Bat

Percy Island Flying Fox

Pteropus brunneus
Some references list this as an extinct endemic species. It is known from only a single specimen, collected off the Qld coast in 1854, currently held by the British Museum of Natural History. No live specimen has been seen since its collection and there is no hard evidence to support its specific status. It could be an aberrant Little Red Flying Fox, another species altogether or a specimen of mislabelled provenance.

Other names: Dusky Flying Fox

Spectacled Flying Fox

Pteropus conspicillatus   (Wet Tropics and Cape York Peninsula; PNG)
In Australia this species is restricted to north Qld from about Tully to Torres Strait, where it is rarely found far from rainforest. It roosts in tall rainforest, paperbarks, gallery forest and mangroves, usually in single-species camps, but sometimes also in association with Black Flying Foxes; readily identified (even when spotlighted) by its 'spectacled' face and pale nape. It is generally easy to see in the Wet Tropics: there's a camp in Cairns (1.01) and individuals feed along the Esplanade at night. On the Atherton Tableland it is common at, for example, Kingfisher Park (1.03).

Other names: Spectacled Fruit Bat

Large-eared Flying Fox

Pteropus macrotis   (islands of Torres Strait; New Guinea)
A small flying fox that in Australia is known only from mangroves on Boigu (1.18) and has also been recorded on Saibai, although it is not clear if there is a permanent roost there. It roosts in mangroves with Little Red and Black Flying Foxes, decamping to the nearby New Guinea mainland at dusk. It is known to feed at Coconut flowers and Jackfruit.

Other names: Epauletted Flying Fox, Sappur, Kalong Makro

*Christmas Island Flying Fox

Pteropus natalis   (Christmas I.)

Endemic to Christmas Island (9.03), where it is the only species of flying fox recorded. Its population is apparently declining but roosts are difficult to locate, and may be in camps of several hundred individuals or in small groups, and either permanent or opportunistic. It is partly diurnal, active around dawn and dusk, and feeds at a wide variety of sources, especially Native Apple *Syzigium nervosum* and the exotic Jamaica Cherry.

*Grey-headed Flying Fox

Pteropus poliocephalus   (south-east Australia)

Australia's largest flying fox. Endemic to eastern Australia. Common at many coastal and subcoastal sites between Maryborough in south-east Qld and Melbourne; occasionally strays to Bass Strait islands and recently it has become established in SA. Highly mobile, making long-distance movements in search of food (mainly flowering eucalypts) and ranging up to about 200 km inland in good seasons. This species generally camps near water in gullies, rainforest, paperbarks, casuarinas or exotic plantations. There are permanent camps at many coastal and subcoastal towns, such as Singleton (with Little Red Flying Foxes), Maclean and Bellingen (2.20) in NSW; and in major cities including Melbourne (4.01), Sydney (2.01) and Brisbane (1.33).

Little Red Flying Fox

Pteropus scapulatus   (eastern and northern Australian mainland; New Guinea)

The smallest and most widespread Australian flying fox. Highly nomadic in response to nectar supplies, but movements are irregular and unpredictable: it usually occupies camps for only a few weeks or months before moving on. Occurs a great distance inland in suitable conditions, following the flowering of River Red Gums along major watercourses. Most common in northern Australia and it appears to be sedentary in parts of the NT. This species sometimes flies and feeds during the day in overcast, wet conditions. Often occurs in mixed camps, chiefly with Black Flying Foxes, as well as in single-species camps which may number a million or more. This is the only Australian flying fox that roosts in tight clusters. There's an enormous camp at Mary Valley on Cape York Peninsula (1.15), several at Kakadu NP (8.03) and near Katherine. It roosts in riparian trees such as paperbarks – check along river crossings, especially in the Top End and Kimberley, but exercise extreme caution in crocodile country! Its wings appear semi-transparent in flight.

Other names: Collared Flying Fox or Fruit Bat, Little Red or Reddish Fruit Bat

Microbats – Suborder Microchiroptera

The microbats are among the most abundant and diverse of all mammals. More than 60 species have been recorded in Australia and new ones are being described as their taxonomy becomes better understood. Traditionally they have been distinguished from megabats by size (microbats rarely exceed 170 g in weight and a wingspan of 30 cm – most are much smaller) and diet (most feed on flying insects); unlike megabats, all use echolocation to navigate in the dark. Nearly all are nocturnal and indistinguishable in flight; exceptions are indicated in the following sections. It is highly recommended that you join the Australasian Bat Society for opportunities to examine microbats in the hand and learn more about these amazing animals.

False vampire bats – Family Megadermatidae (world 5; Australia 1 (endemic))

A small family of large, cave-roosting microbats. False vampire bats have a fearsome appearance and indeed are bat super-predators, feeding on large insects, small mammals and birds. Only one species occurs in Australia: the amazing Ghost Bat.

*Ghost Bat

Macroderma gigas   (northern Australia)

This spectacular microbat is almost as big as some flying foxes and one of the largest microbats in the world. It is a cave-roosting predator that emerges at dusk to prey on insects, frogs, reptiles, rodents, other bats and birds (Budgerigars in particular seem to be a common prey item – staking out a budgie roost at dusk could pay dividends when looking for Ghost Bats). Currently the largest known roost is at Kohinoor adit near Pine Creek (8.05), and Mt Etna NP (1.23) has a seasonal population. This species occurs in a variety of habitats from the arid zone to rainforests. There are many small roosts at scattered locations across northern Australia, for example Victoria River, Tunnel Creek NP (7.21), Camooweal Caves NP (1.30) and Cape York Peninsula. Please note that its range appears to be contracting – on no account should you disturb a Ghost Bat roost. Ghost Bats take their prey to middens – feeding sites under rock overhangs or in a small cave, where piles of bones and other remains accumulate; such sites are useful indications of their presence. Typical roost sites are caves or mines with multiple entrances, boulder piles and occasionally deserted buildings. They utter a cricket-like chirping and a loud twittering call (like that of the Fairy Martin) before leaving roosts at dusk. Ghost Bats hunt by flying just above vegetation or from perches from which they scan or listen for prey.

Other names: Australian False Vampire Bat

Horseshoe bats – Family Rhinolophidae (world 145; Australia 2 (1 endemic))

Horseshoe bats are so-named because of their complex nose-leafs, part of which look like a horseshoe. They feed at all heights in forests, with a typically slow, fluttering and highly manoeuvrable flight while gleaning prey from foliage. Their ears are large and simple, and pointed rather than rounded as in long-eared bats. All Australian horseshoe bats roost in colonies in caves and mines. Genetic analysis has shown that there may be more than the two species currently recognised in Australia. This family formerly included the leaf-nosed bats, which are now generally included in a separate family, the Hipposideridae (p. 317).

Eastern Horseshoe Bat

Rhinolophus megaphyllus   (eastern Australian seaboard; South-East Asia)

The common horseshoe bat of eastern Australia; occurs east of the Great Dividing Range from the tip of Cape York Peninsula to south-east Vic. It roosts in small colonies in warm, humid caves, mines or old buildings, usually in complete darkness; roosts generally number less than 50 individuals although up to 2000 have been recorded (a recently discovered maternity colony numbering 10 000 individuals was probably exceptional). Dendetheda Cave (2.10) supports a large colony; most other roost caves are inaccessible, but this species is commonly found in culverts and other artificial structures. Eastern Horseshoe Bats hang from cave ceilings and individuals are usually spaced 15–20 cm apart, rather than clustered tightly. In the southern part of its range it becomes torpid during the colder months. It always hunts and commutes among or near forest and never crosses large open expanses, although tracks and waterways are used. Colonies in Qld often contain individuals with yellow or orange fur. Recent genetic work has shown that the northern and southern subspecies, *R. m. ignifer* and *R. m. megaphyllus* respectively, may actually be separate species.

*Large-eared Horseshoe Bat

Rhinolophus robertsi   (north-east Qld)

In Australia this species is restricted to coastal north Qld between about Townsville and Iron Range (1.17), and inland to cave systems at Chillagoe (1.06), Undara (1.05) and Broken River, Qld. It inhabits rainforest as well as eucalypt forest and melaleucas. At roosts its enormous pointed ears are a distinctive identification feature. It usually roosts as scattered individuals in caves and mines, often in association with Eastern Horseshoe Bats.

Other names: Greater Large-eared Horseshoe Bat

*Intermediate Horseshoe Bat

Rhinolophus sp.   (Cape York Peninsula)

A horseshoe bat intermediate in size between the preceding two species occurs on Cape York Peninsula between Iron Range and the McIlwraith Range. It has not been formally described and little is known of its ecology, behaviour or distribution. It differs significantly from Large-eared and Eastern Horseshoe Bats in body size, nose-leaf, ear length and echolocation pattern.

Leaf-nosed bats – Family Hipposideridae (world 91; Australia 7 (3 endemic))

The leaf-nosed bats are similar to horseshoe bats and considered by some taxonomists to belong in the same family. They differ in details of nose-leaf structure, skeleton and dentition, and are treated here as a separate family. All Australian leaf-nosed bats are restricted to the tropics (although some southern outliers occur), where they typically roost in colonies in caves, disused mines and, occasionally, old buildings. Each has a distinctive nose-leaf which is a diagnostic feature in the hand.

Dusky Leaf-nosed Bat

Hipposideros ater (northern Australia; south and South-East Asia)
Widely distributed and relatively common in limestone and sandstone caves, old mines and tree hollows. The colony at Bramston Beach (1.07) is well known and accessible. This species has slow, mothlike flight that enables it to hover, and is highly manoeuvrable as it hunts insects among dense rainforest and mangrove vegetation. It hunts below the canopy, over tall grass and even around people. Variable in colour; where this species roosts alongside Orange Leaf-nosed Bats it takes on the latter's fur colour and can vary from orange to white. It often shares caves or mines with Eastern Horseshoe Bats, Bentwing Bats and, at Kohinoor adit (8.05), with Ghost Bats, which prey on it. Two subspecies are recognised: *H. a. aurensis* from north-east Qld and *H. a. gilberti* from the Top End and Kimberley.

Other names: Dusky Horseshoe Bat

Fawn Leaf-nosed Bat

Hipposideros cervinus (Cape York Peninsula and Torres Strait; South-East Asia, south-west Pacific)
In Australia this species is restricted to rainforests of eastern Cape York Peninsula between Coen and Torres Strait. Larger than the Dusky Leaf-nosed Bat but otherwise very similar; identifiable in the hand by its diagnostic nose-leaf. Colonies inhabit deserted mine sites at Iron Range (1.17), sometimes in association with Eastern Horseshoe and Diadem Leaf-nosed Bats. The subspecies in Australia is *H. c. cervinus*.

Other names: Fawn Horseshoe Bat

Diadem Leaf-nosed Bat

Hipposideros diadema (north-east Qld and Top End; South-East Asia, south-west Pacific)
This is Australia's largest leaf-nosed bat, a distinctive and attractively marked species that generally eats large insects but also takes vertebrate prey, such as birds. Most individuals are piebald, varying from pale grey to rusty, orange- or even burgundy-coloured, and always with white patches on their upperparts. They occur at Iron Range (1.17) and Chillagoe (1.06), and are sometimes seen hanging from a hunting perch above a track or creek through forest, when they are identifiable by spotlighting if seen well. They sometimes hunt for up to an hour after dawn. This species usually roosts by hanging from the ceiling of large caves with multiple entrances, often with the Eastern Horseshoe Bats, but also uses old mines, sheds and large culverts; individuals are usually spaced 20–25 cm apart. The subspecies *H. d. reginae* occurs in coastal north Qld south to about Townsville, while another form endemic to the Top End, *H. inornatus*, is now regarded as a separate species.

Other names: Large Horseshoe Bat, Diadem Bat, Diadem Horseshoe Bat

*Arnhem Leaf-nosed Bat

Hipposideros inornatus (Top End)

First discovered in 1969, formerly regarded as a subspecies of the Diadem Leaf-nosed Bat and recently recognised as a species endemic to the Arnhem Land escarpment. The two are not likely to be confused as their respective ranges are separated by hundreds of kilometres. The Arnhem Leaf-nosed Bat is smaller, paler and lacks white patches on its upperparts. This species roosts in sandstone caves with multiple entrances near water. Known from several sites in Kakadu NP (8.03) and at Tolmer Falls in Litchfield NP (8.10), although it has not been recorded at the latter for many years. Hunts in forest, woodland and heath with fast and agile flight.

Other names: Diadem Leaf-nosed Bat

Semon's Leaf-nosed Bat

Hipposideros semoni (north-east Qld; New Guinea)

A rather uncommon species found in a variety of forest types from rainforest to tropical woodland. Mainly recorded north of Townsville, although there have been records much further south. Differs from the similar Northern Leaf-nosed Bat in having a longer central 'wart' on its nose-leaf. It has seldom been seen foraging more than 2 m above the ground and apparently utilises more open woodland during the drier months. This species has also been recorded roosting with Eastern Horseshoe Bats.

Other names: Wart-nosed Horseshoe Bat, Semon's Bat, Greater Wart-nosed Horseshoe Bat

*Northern Leaf-nosed Bat

Hipposideros stenotis (Kimberley, Top End, south-west Gulf Country)

Similar to the preceding species in appearance, although their ranges don't overlap. Little known and secretive. Roosts in sandstone caves, boulder piles, culverts and disused mines, and apparently associates with steep hills and escarpments. This species has a slow, fluttering flight and tends to feed close to the ground.

Other names: Dahl's Horseshoe Bat, Lesser Wart-nosed Horseshoe Bat

*Orange Leaf-nosed Bat

Rhinonicteris aurantia (northern Australia, Pilbara)

A brightly coloured bat with a distinctive rounded nose-leaf; most individuals have a bright orange body and brown, yellow and white forms have also been recorded. Roosts in hot, humid caves and mines in colonies numbering from five to 20 000. Relatively common in suitable caves in the Top End, such as Cutta Cutta (8.07), although this site is not open to the public when the bats are present. A small colony lives at Tolmer Falls in Litchfield NP (8.10), and it occurs at Camooweal Caves NP (1.30) and at Tunnel Creek (7.21). Its flight is rapid, zig-zagging, and often close to the ground or over waterholes in gorges. It is sometimes seen in vehicle headlights and can be identified by spotlighting if seen well. The isolated Pilbara population may be a separate species.

Other names: Orange Horseshoe Bat, Golden Horseshoe Bat

Sheath-tailed bats – Family Emballonuridae (world 51; Australia 8 (4 endemic))

The tails of sheath-tailed (spelt 'sheathtail' in some references) bats are only partly enclosed by the tail membrane, and protrude from its upper surface. All species are large (for microbats), with handsome, rather doglike faces and long, narrow wings. At roost they typically hang from a vertical or near vertical surface, such as a cave wall, and scuttle crablike into narrow crevices when disturbed. When alert they prop themselves up on their forelimbs before taking flight. The exposed tail gives them extra leverage and sheath-tailed bats can also move about rapidly on the ground. Sheath-tailed bats have fast, direct flight and usually forage above the canopy (closer to the ground in open country); they are rarely caught in traps and, with one or two exceptions, sightings are probably best at roost sites. The echolocation clicks of some species are audible (to some ears). Some bask at the mouth of caves in cold weather.

Yellow-bellied Sheath-tailed Bat

Saccolaimus flaviventris   (northern and eastern Australia; New Guinea)
A large, handsome microbat that can be readily identified in flight by its pale-yellow or whitish underparts and glossy black upper body. It can be confused only with Papuan Sheath-tailed Bat, which does not occur outside of Cape York Peninsula. Most common in northern Australia, with a partial migration to south-east Australia in summer-autumn (January–April). Its echolocation call is audible to some people. It roosts alone or in small groups in tree hollows, and has been recorded in the abandoned nests of Sugar Gliders. Exhausted individuals are sometimes found clinging to the side of buildings.

Other names: White-bellied Sheath-tailed Bat, Yellow-bellied Freetail Bat

Papuan Sheath-tailed Bat

Saccolaimus mixtus   (Cape York Peninsula; PNG)
Similar to the preceding species but smaller, with grey upperparts. In Australia this species is known only from open forest on Cape York Peninsula. It and the Yellow-bellied Sheath-tailed Bat can be spotlighted together near Weipa, where they could be told apart by the former's smaller size and faster, more agile flight and the latter's audible call.

Other names: New Guinea Sheath-tailed Bat, Wing-pouched Saccolaimus, Troughton's Sheath-tailed Bat, Allied Freetail Bat, Cape York Sheath-tailed Bat

Bare-rumped Sheath-tailed Bat

Saccolaimus saccolaimus (Top End and north-east Qld; south and South-East Asia)
An attractively marked but high-flying species, rarely seen in the hand. It roosts in small groups in hollow limbs and trunks; most records are from Poplar Gums and Darwin Stringybarks in tropical woodland. The subspecies *S. s. nudicluniatus* occurs in coastal woodland between Bowen and Cape York in north-east Qld, and has recently been

discovered roosting in Cairns Botanic Gardens (1.01), among other sites. *S. s. saccolaimus* occurs in the Top End and has been recorded in *Pandanus* woodland near the South Alligator River. Their high-pitched calls can be heard by some human ears.

Other names: Naked-rumped Freetail Bat or Saccolaimus, Tomb Bat

Coastal Sheath-tailed Bat

Taphozous australis   (coastal north Qld; New Guinea)

Found between Rockhampton and Torres Strait, rarely more than a few kilometres from the coast. Roosts in crevices, sea caves, boulder piles and abandoned concrete military bunkers. Usually feeds within a kilometre of the sea over dune vegetation and *Melaleuca* swamps. Similar to Common and Hill's Sheath-tailed Bats but paler. Wangetti Beach near Cairns (1.01) has a small colony; others occur at Cape Hillsborough and it is apparently common among the Whitsunday islands. Utters an audible chirp when leaving the roost.

Other names: Neck-pouched Taphozous, Little Sheath-tailed bat, North-eastern Sheath-tailed Bat

*Common Sheath-tailed Bat

Taphozous georgianus   (northern Australia)

Widespread in rocky parts of northern Australia, where it roosts in the twilight zone of caves, mines and crevices. Forages over many vegetation types, water and, in hilly country, along gullies and the tops of escarpments. Similar to Hill's Sheath-tailed Bat, with which its range overlaps in the Pilbara, although the two do not apparently share caves and this species shares with Troughton's Sheath-tailed Bat where the two overlap in Qld. Often chirps loudly before leaving the roost. Roosts in cracks in caves at Cania Gorge, Qld.

Other names: Unpouched Freetail Bat, Sharp-nosed Bat

*Hill's Sheath-tailed Bat

Taphozous hilli   (central Australia)

A sheath-tailed bat of the inland, including the driest deserts, where it requires rocky habitat and abandoned mines for roost sites. Similar to Common Sheath-tailed Bat, with which it often shares roosts. Roosts in rocky ranges, breakaways and cliffs near waterholes, hunting over woodland, scrub and grassland.

Other names: Slender-toothed Sheath-tailed Bat

*Arnhem Sheath-tailed Bat

Taphozous kapalgensis   (Top End)

Distinctively marked, with whitish flank stripes contrasting with pale brown upperparts. This feature may be seen in flight and is diagnostic, although this species is rarely observed. Widespread over the western Top End, where it feeds over waterways, mangroves, woodlands and *Melaleuca* swamps. Roosts in tree hollows and possibly at the base of *Pandanus* leaves; a colony was recently discovered roosting in a sea cave with Ghost Bats.

Other names: White-striped Sheath-tailed Bat

*Troughton's Sheath-tailed Bat

Taphozous troughtoni (central Qld)

Once thought to be rare and known only from near Mt Isa and Cloncurry, Qld this species has recently been shown to be widespread in Qld. In the arid zone it occurs in hilly country with River Red Gum–lined creeks; and roosts in abandoned mines, caves and fissures, usually not far from daylight, and sometimes with Common Sheath-tailed Bats, which are noticeably smaller. This species also frequents pipes under rocky overhangs. In other areas it hunts over a variety of forest types. A large sheath-tailed bat that lacks a throat pouch.

Freetail bats – Family Molossidae (world 100; Australia 10 (8 endemic))

Members of this family have a narrow tail membrane from which their short, thick rather ratlike tail protrudes freely. Other characteristics include thick, heavy ears, and they are sometimes called mastiff bats because of their large, doglike heads, broad muzzle and massive gape for catching large beetles in flight. They roost in tight spaces, often in buildings and roof cavities. The taxonomy of Australian molossids has long been unstable; some texts use Tadarida *instead of* Austronomus; *some species formerly regarded as* Mormopterus *have recently been reclassified in the genus* Micronomus. *Likewise, common names have probably not been finalised for some newly described species. Several of these are indistinguishable externally but have distinct echolocation calls and most are allopatric, so area of occurrence may be a good guide to identification. The* Micronomus *molossids are commonly caught in harp traps and nights spent in the company of bat experts will not be wasted.*

*White-striped Freetail Bat

Austronomus australis (southern Australian mainland)

A large, stocky microbat with diagnostic white flank stripes contrasting with its black belly (variants with additional white patches on the throat and chest occur). This is one of the few microbats in Australia that can be located by the unaided human ear – its echolocation call is a metallic *ting-ting-ting* at a frequency of 1–2 per second. It is found in a wide variety of habitats, including urban areas: it is common in Adelaide, Melbourne (where it uses bat boxes) and Brisbane (commonly associated with Forest Red Gums), and in King's Park, Perth. White-striped Freetails roost in small groups (rarely up to 100 individuals and usually far fewer) in tree hollows, sometimes alongside Common Brushtail Possums, but they are not usually recorded sharing with other bat species. It makes loud chirping call from late afternoon until leaving the roost 30–40 minutes after sunset. This species is a seasonal migrant found mainly south of 30°S in summer (November–February) and mainly north of 30°S in the cooler months (April–September). It flies high and fast (up to 40 kph) above the canopy or through clearings, and also moves quickly along the ground.

(Greater) Northern Freetail Bat

Chaerophon jobensis   (northern Australia; Indonesia, PNG)
A large, robust bat with strongly wrinkled lips. Mainly tropical and found in a wide variety of habitats, including forests, woodlands, mangroves (for example, at Charles Darwin NP, NT) and deserts. It roosts in tree hollows, caves and abandoned buildings, but also under bridges (for example, at Finniss River (8.10) and the jetty at Derby, WA). Its loud social calls are a good way of locating roosts; its echolocation calls are within the range of human hearing and this species can be heard feeding around streetlights at night. Known to roost with Northern Bentwing Bats and Yellow-bellied Sheath-tailed Bats.

*East-coast Freetail Bat

Micronomus norfolkensis   (subtropical east coast)
Endemic to eastern Australia, where it is found in a coastal strip between southern NSW and Brisbane. It occurs in a variety of wooded habitats, including dry forest, farmland and woodland. It is not uncommon in urban areas and forages near powerful lights at car parks and sports stadiums. It roosts in tree hollows, including mangroves, and is occasionally found in buildings with other species.

*Bristle-faced Freetail Bat

Mormopterus (Setirostris) eleryi   (inland eastern Australia)
The smallest Australian freetail bat, known from only a few sites west of the Great Dividing Range in central Qld and adjacent parts of SA, NSW and NT. Roosts in tree hollows, squeezing into tiny cracks and fissures. Recognisable in the hand by its long muzzle and facial bristles. Its flight pattern is distinctive, foraging closer to vegetation and the ground with a slow, fluttering pattern. It has been observed feeding mainly along creek channels in mulga country.

Other names: Hairy-nosed Freetail Bat (*Mormopterus* species 6)

*Mangrove Freetail Bat

Mormopterus (Ozimops) cobourgianus   (north-west WA, Top End)
Known only from mangroves and adjacent vegetation between Exmouth Gulf and the Roper River at the south-west Gulf of Carpentaria. Roosts in Grey Mangrove *Avicennia marina*, emerging early and gathering in groups of up to 100 above the canopy shortly after sunset before dispersing to feed.

Other names: North-western Freetail Bat, Northern Coastal Freetail Bat

*Cape York Freetail Bat

Mormopterus (Ozimops) halli   (central Cape York Peninsula, south-east Gulf
Country)
Little known but most often encountered in tropical woodlands, especially near fresh water. Roosts unknown.

Other names: Little Northern Freetail Bat, Cape York Free-tailed Bat

*South-western Freetail Bat

Mormopterus (Ozimops) kitcheneri (south-western Australia)

Found in semi-arid woodlands of the south-west, where its range partly overlaps with *M. petersi*. Roosts in tree hollows.

Northern Freetail Bat

Mormopterus (Ozimops) lumsdenae (northern Australia; Indonesia, PNG)

Widespread, from semi-desert to woodland and rainforest in northern Australia; common along watercourses. Roosts in tree hollows, roof cavities and under flaking bark. A fast-flying species, with narrow, pointed wings and rapid wingbeats, that feeds in rather open areas; flight is straight with gentle curves rather than tight turns.

Other names: Beccari's Freetail Bat

*Inland Freetail Bat

Mormopterus (Ozimops) petersi (southern inland Australia)

Occurs across much of arid and semi-arid southern Australia, typically in woodland and along River Red Gum–lined watercourses. This species roosts in cracks in trees and also in artificial structures such as fence posts, roofs and pipes; often roosts in association with the Inland Broad-nosed Bat. It shows considerable size variation across its range – the largest specimens occur in central Australia. Sometimes aggressive towards other species when foraging and will crawl on the ground or tree trunks in pursuit of prey.

Other names: *Mormopterus planiceps* (small penis form), *Mormopterus* species 3

*Eastern Freetail Bat

Mormopterus ridei (eastern mainland)

Occurs in a wide variety of forest types along the entire eastern seaboard between Torres Strait and Geelong, Vic. Roosts in tree hollows, under bark, in buildings and cracks in fence posts, sometimes sharing with Gould's Wattled and Eastern Broad-nosed Bats.

Bentwing Bats – Family Miniopteridae (world 11; Australia 4 (3 endemic[1]))

Members of this small family have characteristic wing morphology, with an extended third digit and narrow wingtips that fold back when the bats are at rest. Formerly placed

---

[1]The three subspecies of *M. schreibersii* are treated here as endemic in anticipation of their elevation to full specific status.

in the large evening bat family Vespertilionidae, the subfamily Miniopertinae has recently been elevated to full family status. All bentwing bats are cave-roosting and require domed ceilings to form their large, sometimes spectacular maternity colonies. There are currently two recognised species in Australia, but the Miniopteris orianae *complex could be split into three full species in light of recent genetic work. All are rather similar in appearance. Maternity sites are vulnerable to disturbance and should not be entered during the breeding season (summer). At other times of year the bats disperse to smaller, winter roosts, animals in the south going into torpor during cold weather. Established roosts are known for all taxa, the three subspecies of* M. orianae *forming separate maternity colonies. Note that the spelling of common names varies, with some authors preferring 'bentwing bat' over 'bent-winged bat'.*

Little Bentwing Bat

Miniopterus australis   (eastern seaboard; South-East Asia, south-west Pacific)
Found on the tropical and subtropical east coast, from about Sydney to Cape York; forages in a variety of wooded habitats, including rainforest, wet and dry forest and *Melaleuca* swamps. It roosts in caves, tunnels, mines and drains. This species forms the largest known maternity roost of any Australian cave-dwelling bat: up to 200 000 are present annually from October to February at the Mt Etna complex (1.23), making a spectacular sight when they emerge at dusk (a small number of Ghost Bats and Eastern Bent-winged Bats share the Mt Etna Bat Cleft with this species). Where they co-occur, this species tends to be found more coastally than Eastern Bent-winged Bat.

Other names: Little Bent-winged Bat, Tomes' Bat

*Southern Bentwing Bat

Miniopterus schreibersii bassanii   (south-east SA, western Vic)
This subspecies is restricted to a relatively small area between Robe, SA and Colac, Vic where it roosts in caves and lava tubes, sometimes alongside Eastern Bent-winged Bats. Only two nursery caves are known: at Naracoorte Caves NP (6.06), where they may be seen emerging in spring and summer; and at Starlight Cave near Warrnambool, Vic, which is on private property. The Southern Bent-winged Bat is regarded as critically endangered.

Other names: Common Bentwing Bat

*Eastern Bentwing Bat

Miniopterus schreibersii oceanensis   (eastern Australia)
The commonest and most widespread subspecies of *M. schreibersii*, forming maternity colonies of up to 100 000 bats in caves, lava tubes, deserted mines and disused military bunkers; it is found between Castlemaine, Vic and Cape York. About 2000 share the Mt Etna Bat Cleft (1.23) with Little Bent-winged Bats; there are major maternity caves in Bungonia

Gorge (2.26) and Church and Dip Caves at Wee Jasper (2.27). Other major maternity sites include Riverton Cave in southern Qld, which hosts 30 000 bats; Willi Willi in northern NSW; and Nargun in eastern Vic. In Sydney they occur in the old North Sydney railway tunnels and WWII bunkers at Malabar. This species passes through Canberra (3.01) in autumn en route to wintering caves at Marble Arch, near Braidwood, NSW and on the coast. It forages in a variety of timbered country, especially forested valleys, where it generally feeds above the canopy and also around street lights. A reddish colour form occurs in Qld.

Other names: Schreibers' Long-tailed Bat, Schreibers' Bat, Common or Large Bentwing Bat

*Northern Bentwing Bat

Miniopterus schreibersii orianae (Top End, Kimberley)

Smaller than and not nearly as well known as other Australian subspecies of *M. schreibersii*. It forages in tropical woodlands and at the edges of monsoon forest and riparian vegetation, and roosts in caves, concrete military bunkers, drains, tunnels and artificial structures. There is a dry-season roost at Tolmer Falls in Litchfield NP (8.10); others are known around Darwin and this species inhabits storm-water drains under the city; Tunnel Creek (7.21) also has a colony.

Other names: Common or Large Bentwing Bat

Evening bats – Family Vespertilionidae (world 300 (approx); Australia 39 (33 endemic))

Separating microbats into their various families is relatively straightforward in the hand: most can be identified by structural features such as nose-leafs and tails. In general, anything that doesn't fit easily into the smaller families belongs with the 'evening' bats, also known as verspertilionids. The Vespertilionidae comprise almost half of Australia's microbat species and make up a high percentage of the bats seen at dusk. It is difficult to generalise about this large family: most lack nose-leafs (long-eared bats being the exception); they usually land on vertical surfaces, rather than suspending themselves freely; when alighting they land with the head up, then turn round and cling with their toes, head down. They can be distinguished from other bat families in Australia by a relatively long tail and a tail membrane extending more or less from the tail-tip to each foot. And because many go into torpor or hibernate during cold weather, they have been able to colonise the most southerly parts of the continent and Tas.

However, identifying individual species in this large family can be difficult: most are small, some are tiny; positive ID may rely on dentition, penis morphology and accurate measurements of features such as forearm length. Even separating genera can be difficult for beginners. One or two could feasibly be identified in flight, but all produce echolocation calls with a frequency too high for human ears. There are few sites where vesper bats can be seen at a regular roost as they utilise a huge range of microhabitats.

Natural sites include under bark, in tree hollows and logs, in caves and overhangs, and among boulders. Many take advantage of artificial structures, such as empty buildings, concrete military bunkers, disused railway tunnels, roof cavities and eaves, fence posts, streetlight fittings, expansion gaps in culverts, the spaces between planks in old wooden bridges and piers, even old clothes hanging up in buildings. Several use abandoned birds' nests, such as the bottle-shaped mud nests of Fairy Martins. They may change roosts frequently or seasonally; they may roost in small or large groups, with other species and in single-species groups. In short, your chances of encountering evening bats are very high, but getting to know them better will require specialised equipment and knowledge. Consequently, few sites are listed here for seeing them.

Some bats readily use bat boxes and joining a survey group is a great way to see some vesper bats in the hand. Otherwise, you are urged to join the Australasian Bat Society or accompany experts as a volunteer on field surveys to get the most out of this diverse, abundant and fascinating family.

Several widespread species in the Vespertilionidae are now recognised as being made up of a number of separate species with, in some cases, unresolved taxonomy – keep abreast of scientific literature for the latest changes. Note also that some taxonomists separate the Bentwing bats into a separate family, Miniopteridae, a treatment which has been followed here (see the previous section).

Woolly or painted bats – Subfamily Kerivoulinae

In Australia this subfamily is represented by only one species, the extraordinary **Golden-tipped Bat***. Many texts place it in the widespread genus* Kerivoula.

Golden-tipped Bat

Phoniscus papuensis   (eastern seaboard; New Guinea)
A spider-hunting specialist of wet forest edges, particularly near creeklines and at the ecotone with dry forest, where it gleans prey from webs among dense vegetation. Its flight is slow and fluttering, with long glides and hovering (often for several minutes at a time). This species roosts most commonly in disused, suspended birds' nests, particularly those of Yellow-throated Scrubwrens and Brown Gerygones, and also in tree hollows and dense vegetation. It is easy to recognise in the hand by its golden-tipped fur.

Other names: Dome-headed Bat

Tube-nosed microbats – Subfamily Murininae

A primarily South-East Asian group with one representative in Australia. Its sideways-oriented tubular nostrils are unique among Australian microbats and make it unmistakable in the hand.

Flute-nosed Bat

Murina florium (coastal north-east Qld; Indonesia, PNG)

This extraordinary species is restricted to rainforests and nearby wet forest between Paluma and Shipton's Flat, Qld to about 1000 m above sea level; a specimen collected at Iron Range may belong to a separate species. It is vocal while foraging, uttering a loud, high-pitched whistle in flight. It has a slow, fluttering flight and hovers as it gleans prey from foliage in the mid- to upper canopy, generally avoiding open areas. It roosts in the understorey beneath hanging bunches of leaves, wrapping its wings around its body to form an 'umbrella', and in suspended nests of small birds, such as Yellow-throated Scrubwrens and Fernwrens.

Other names: Tube-nosed Insectivorous Bat

Long-eared bats – Subfamily Nyctophilinae

Long-eared bats, as their name suggests, have broad, elongated ears, and differ from other evening bats in having a rudimentary nose-leaf and a truncated snout. The Greater Long-eared Bat Nyctophilus timoriensis *is now generally regarded as several distinct species and is currently under taxonomic review. Superficially, long-eared bats resemble horseshoe bats, but their ears are larger than the height of their heads, with heavy ribbing on the upper half; other distinctive features include a short muzzle and typical evening bat tail morphology.*

*Arnhem Long-eared Bat

Nyctophilus arnhemensis (Top End, Kimberley)

Found in a wide range of vegetation, including mangroves, *Pandanus*-lined waterways, monsoon forest and woodland. Roosts in dense vegetation, under peeling *Melaleuca* bark, among *Pandanus* fronds or (rarely) in buildings. Slow, fluttering flight; forages below the canopy. Recorded in Prince Regent NR, Drysdale River NP and Coulomb Point NR, WA and from Kakadu (8.03) and Keep River (8.15) NPs.

Other names: Northern Long-eared Bat

Eastern Long-eared Bat

Nyctophilus bifax (eastern Australia; New Guinea)

Associated mainly with wet forest, such as rainforest and riparian forest, between northern NSW and Cape York; sometimes in adjacent dry forest or woodland. This species is most often seen foraging at forest edge; its flight is more direct and rapid than other long-eared bats, but it also hovers, gleaning insects from foliage, and may take prey from the ground and perches. It roosts under peeling *Melaleuca* bark, in tree hollows and among dense vegetation. Chillagoe Caves NP (1.06) is one site where it occurs.

Other names: Northern Long-eared Bat, North Queensland Long-eared Bat

*Northern Long-eared Bat

Nyctophilus daedalus   (Top End, Kimberley, Pilbara)
Formerly regarded as a subspecies of Eastern Long-eared Bat, with similar habits. It is
distributed from the south-west Gulf Country to the western edge of the Kimberley, with
an isolated Pilbara population. *N. daedalus* inhabits wetter forest than *N. bifax*, including
monsoon forest (for example, at Holmes Jungle Nature Park near Darwin) and riparian
vegetation, roosting in hollows in melaleucas, at the base of *Pandanus* leaves and in
foliage. It is known to hunt from perches.

*Lesser Long-eared Bat

Nyctophilus geoffroyi   (Australia inc. Tas)
The most widely distributed long-eared bat, absent only from the tropical Qld coast and
Cape York Peninsula. Common, abundant and found in nearly all habitats from deserts to
rainforests, including urban areas. Small colonies roost in tree hollows, under bark, in
Fairy Martin nests and in a wide variety of artificial structures. Forages among low
vegetation, gleaning prey from foliage or the ground with fluttering, highly manoeuvrable
flight. Three subspecies are recognised: *N. g. geoffroyi* in WA, *N. g. pallescens* in northern
SA and *N. g. pacificus* on the eastern mainland and in Tas.

*Gould's Long-eared Bat

Nyctophilus gouldi   (east coast, south-west WA)
On the east coast this species is found from south of Cairns to south-east SA; west of
the Great Great Dividing Range it occurs along River Red Gum–lined watercourses and
in woodland; in south-west Australia it inhabits wetter forests. It roosts under bark or in
tree hollows, often along creeklines, and forages below the canopy in dense vegetation,
such as shrubs and regrowth, with slow, manoeuvrable flight on broad wings.

Other names: Greater Long-eared Bat

*Lord Howe Long-eared Bat

Nyctophilus howensis   (Lord Howe I.)
Extinct. Known only from a single skull discovered in a cave on Lord Howe I. (9.01).
Thought to have been exterminated by rats accidentally introduced to the island after a
shipwreck in 1918, or by owls deliberately introduced to control the rats.

*Western Long-eared Bat

Nyctophilus major   (south-west WA)
A large long-eared bat of south-western forests and woodlands, including Karri, Jarrah,
Tuart and Marri, as well as stands of *Banksia*, *Casuarina* and *Melaleuca*, particularly
where there is a well-developed shrub layer. It roosts in tree hollows, under bark (especially
of Flooded Gum and Swamp Paperbark) and among foliage, and forages on the ground as
well as in flight. There is an isolated population near Eyre Bird Observatory (7.24).

*Tasmanian Long-eared Bat

Nyctophilus sherrini (Tas)

Endemic to Tas, where it is most common in wet forest, particularly along tracks, in Blackwood and *Melaleuca* swamps, and *Acacia melanoxylon* forests in the north and east. The slowest-flying Tas bat and highly manoeuvrable among dense foliage; it also hunts on the ground. Roosts in tree hollows and under bark.

Other names: Greater Long-eared Bat

*Central Long-eared Bat

Nyctophilus sp. undescribed (southern semi-arid Australia)

A distinct form of long-eared bat that occurs in the semi-arid zone between the Eyre Peninsula and the Goldfields region of WA, in woodlands, mallee, shrublands and spinifex grasslands. Similar to other species of the *N. timoriensis* complex, with manoeuvrable, fluttering flight; also hunts from perches and takes prey from the ground. Roosts in tree hollows, under bark and in foliage. Populations are known from Jilbadji, Mt Manning, Dundas and Nuytsland NRs in WA, and in the Nullarbor NP in SA.

*South-eastern Long-eared Bat

Nyctophilus sp. undescribed (semi-arid south-east Australia)

A little-known form of the *N. timoriensis* complex. Uncommon in a variety of wooded habitats in the Murray–Darling Basin, including mallee and woodland and especially where there is a well-defined canopy and understorey; most common in the Pilliga Scrub of NSW. Roosts in tree hollows.

Other names: Greater Long-eared Bat

*Pygmy Long-eared Bat

Nyctophilus walkeri (Top End, Kimberley)

Australia's smallest long-eared bat; usually encountered among riparian vegetation, such as melaleucas and *Pandanus*, in rocky gorges and valleys, but also in adjacent monsoon forest and savannah woodland. It roosts in dense vegetation, for example, among dead palm fronds, and in tree hollows, and forages low to the ground among dense foliage or over water with a slow, fluttery flight. Common on the Mitchell Plateau (7.21) and Drysdale River NP, WA; and Lawn Hill NP (1.29), where it roosts noisily in dead *Livistona* palm fronds.

Other names: Territory Long-eared Bat, Little Northern Territory Bat

'Typical' evening bats – Subfamily Vespertilioninae

*The remainder of Australia's evening bats belong to this large subfamily, membership of which defies generalisation. The five species of **wattled bat** in the genus Chalinolobus are so named because they have lobes of skin on their face and mouths (visible only in the hand). **Pipistrelles**, familiar to people from the Northern Hemisphere, are represented in Australia* *by only three species (including the recently extinct Christmas Island Pipistrelle), reflecting perhaps the genus's comparatively late colonisation of Australia. The **Large-footed Myotis** fills the fishing bat niche occupied by many species elsewhere in the world and is Australia's only representative of this widely distributed genus. **Broad-nosed bats** are robust bats comprised of two genera: the widespread* Scotorepens *(also under taxonomic revision) and monotypic* Scoteanax*, a powerful, predatory species thought to take other bats in flight.* **False pipistrelles** *are rather large, pipistrelle-like microbats.*

*Large-eared Pied Bat

Chalinolobus dwyeri   (subtropical Qld, NSW)

An uncommon inhabitant of wet and dry forest between the Blackdown Tableland, Qld and Ulladulla, NSW especially near cliffs and caves. Most records are from sandstone escarpments in the Sydney (especially near the Blue Mountains) and Hunter Valley regions. Small groups roost in the twilight zone of caves, overhangs, deserted mines and in abandoned Fairy Martin nests. It sometimes roosts alongside Eastern Cave Bats and probably forages below the canopy.

Other names: Large Pied Bat

*Gould's Wattled Bat

Chalinolobus gouldii   (Australia inc. Tas)

The largest Australian lobe-lipped bat and the most widespread, absent only from Cape York Peninsula, the Nullarbor Plain and some islands (formerly including Norfolk I.). It is found in most habitats, including forest, woodland and mallee, farmland and urban areas. This species roosts in tree hollows, especially in large live trees (for example, River Red Gums and *Callitris* pines), buildings and a variety of artificial sites, and in abandoned Fairy Martin nests. It leaves roosts early, 20–30 minutes after sunset and 'buzzes' constantly when handled. Previously attributed subspecific differences are now regarded as a distinct geographic size gradient.

*Chocolate Wattled Bat

Chalinolobus morio   (central and southern Australia inc. Tas)

Common in a wide variety of habitats, including wet and dry forests, woodland, mallee and shrublands. Its inland distribution is allied to large, tree-lined watercourses. Roosts in tree hollows, caves (including large caves on the Nullarbor Plain), artificial structures such as roof cavities and Fairy Martin nests. Isolated populations occur in central Australia and the Pilbara. This is one of the last species to go into hibernation in winter and among the first to emerge in spring.

Other names: Chocolate Bat, Chocolate Lobe-lipped Bat

Hoary Wattled Bat

Chalinolobus nigrogriseus   (northern Australia; New Guinea)

Found in northern Australia from Derby, WA to the Clarence River Valley in northern NSW; more common in the tropics. Hoary Wattled Bats utilise a range of habitats such as woodland, forest and scrub, often foraging around swamps and watercourses, and roosting in tree hollows, occasionally in crevices and buildings; they are common in urban areas. White-tipped fur gives this species a 'frosted' appearance, specimens from the Kimberley being more frosted and smaller, while those from Qld can be almost black. Two subspecies are recognised: *C. n. nigrogriseus* from the east coast including Cape York Peninsula; and *C. n. rogersi* from western Qld, NT and WA.

Other names: Eastern Wattled Bat, Pied Bat, Blackish-grey Bat, Hoary Bat, Frosted Bat

*Little Pied Bat

Chalinolobus picatus   (inland eastern Australia)

Uncommon and poorly known, this small but distinctive, glossy black bat has a white 'V' on its flanks and vent. Its flight is fast and darting, so its markings probably aren't visible in the field without exceptional views. A microbat of dry forest, woodland, mallee and scrub that often forages along watercourses and above ephemeral pools. It is apparently most common in the Willandra Lakes area of NSW and riverine forests of central-west Qld. It roosts in tree hollows (especially dead limbs of large, mature trees and hollow stumps), caves, mines and old buildings.

Other names: Pied Bat

*Western False Pipistrelle

Falsistrellus mackenziei   (south-west Australia)

The largest evening bat in WA, confined to subcoastal wet forests south of Perth and west of the wheatbelt. Recorded mainly from Karri forest, but also in wetter stands of Jarrah, Tuart and mixed woodlands. Roosts in tree hollows and flies fast and directly while foraging between the canopy and shrub layer; otherwise poorly known. Recorded from D'Entrecasteaux NP.

Other names: Western Falsistrelle, Mackenzie's False Pipistrelle

*Eastern False Pipistrelle

Falsistrellus tasmaniensis   (south-east Australia inc. Tas)

A large, uncommon bat of tall, wet forest and adjacent areas, particularly at higher elevations and where there is a dense understorey. Its flight is swift and direct in a horizontal plane, with sudden changes of course; it forages among or under the canopy. This species roosts in hollows of living eucalypts, sometimes in caves and buildings.

Other names: Tasmanian Pipistrelle, Eastern Falsistrelle

Large-footed Myotis

Myotis macropus   (eastern and northern Australian mainland; New Guinea)

Australia's only fishing bat: it feeds by raking its large feet through the water, snatching small aquatic animals, including fish, from the surface; it also takes insects on the wing. Several may follow each other on a similar flight path while feeding. It is always seen close to water, for example over creeks, dams, lakes and estuaries (including large urban waterways in Sydney and Melbourne); and usually roosts near water also, in a variety of sites such as caves (including exposed caves overhanging pools), mines, culverts (including storm water drains in Darwin), under bridges, in tree hollows (mainly in the south) and in Fairy Martin nests. The southern population may be a separate species. In the hand, its large, rake-like feet are an unmistakable diagnostic feature.

Other names: Large-footed Mouse-eared Bat, Southern Myotis

*Forest Pipistrelle

Pipistrellus adamsi   (Cape York, Top End)

A generally common but little-studied inhabitant of monsoon forest, *Melaleuca* swamps, mangroves and watercourses in savannah woodland. This species is not generally abroad until the late evening and apparently most active after midnight. Its roosts have never been recorded, but probably include tree hollows.

Other names: Cape York Pipistrelle, Northern Pipistrelle

*Christmas Island Pipistrelle

Pipistrellus murrayi   (Christmas I.)

Almost certainly extinct. Despite a well-documented decline and warnings from scientists, by the time a captive-breeding program was finally instigated, no specimens of this endemic pipistrelle could be found. It was the only microbat recorded on Christmas I. and was last seen in the western part of the island in 2009. This was an agile species that foraged above and below the canopy, along roads and forest edges, and was sometimes abroad well before sunset. It typically roosted in hollows of tall dead trees 5–20 m above the ground, under bark and among dead palm and *Pandanus* fronds. if you see any microbat on Christmas I. please report it immediately to the Australasian Bat Society (www.ausbats.org.au).

Other names: Christmas Island Bat, Murray's Pipistrelle Bat

*Northern Pipistrelle

Pipistrellus westralis   (northern Australia)

Australia's smallest bat. This is a coastal pipistrelle, found from Cape Bossut near Broome, WA along the north coast east to Karumba, Qld. It hunts along waterways in mangroves (and in WA is known only from mangrove habitats), *Melaleuca* swamps and *Pandanus* thickets; also in adjoining subcoastal habitat including savannah woodland in the eastern part of its range, although its roosts are unknown. It has highly manoeuvrable flight, with rapid, shallow wing beats. It occurs in Prince Regent NR, WA and Kakadu (8.03) and Keep River (8.15) NPs.

Other names: Mangrove Pipistrelle, Western Pipistrelle, North-western Pipistrelle

*Greater Broad-nosed Bat

Scoteanax rueppellii   (eastern seaboard)

A powerful microbat (much bigger than other broad-nosed bats) that feeds on large insects, may also take smaller bats on the wing, and is known to perch-hunt. It is uncommon, but typically encountered in wet forests, along tree-lined waterways and around remnant trees in agricultural land. Its distribution appears to be correlated with high rainfall and mild winters, between southern NSW and the Carbine Tableland, north Qld, usually below 500 m in the south but restricted to upland forest in the north. It has relatively slow, direct flight. This species roosts in tree trunks and hollows, under bark and under roofs, sometimes sharing with Chocolate Wattled Bats; it occurs in mangroves in the Hunter Estuary, NSW.

Other names: Rüppell's Broad-nosed Bat

*Inland Broad-nosed Bat

Scotorepens balstoni   (inland Australia)
A common and widely distributed species in a variety of arid and semi-arid habitats, including woodland, mallee, shrubland and tree-lined watercourses. It roosts in tree hollows and abandoned buildings, sometimes with South-eastern Freetail Bats; and often emerges before dusk. Fast in flight, with flickering wingbeats; forages among and below the canopy, also taking prey from the ground.

Other names: Western Broad-nosed Bat

*Little Broad-nosed Bat

Scotorepens greyii   (inland and northern Australia)
Similar to the preceding species, with which its range overlaps inland. It is abundant in northern Australia but not well known. It occurs in varied habitats including deserts, grasslands, savannah woodland and monsoon forest; common along watercourses and at waterholes, and in coastal urban areas, for example Brisbane. It roosts in tree hollows and artificial sites such as buildings, fence posts and under the metal caps of telegraph poles. Its flight includes abrupt horizontal turns with near vertical banking.

Other names: Grey's Broad-nosed Bat

*Eastern Broad-nosed Bat

Scotorepens orion   (south-east Australia, Wet Tropics)
An inhabitant of tall, wet forest of the Great Dividing Range between about Brisbane and Melbourne, and drier forest on the western slopes with outlying records from the Atherton Tableland. Uncommon and poorly known; roosts in tree hollows and buildings.

Northern Broad-nosed Bat

Scotorepens sanborni   (north-east Qld, Top End, Kimberley; Indonesia, PNG)
Found in two separate populations. The eastern form occurs from Cape York to about Rockhampton, Qld and inhabits monsoon forest, woodland and heath. The western form occurs from near Broome, WA to the western Top End and occupies more varied habitat, such as riparian forest including mangroves. This species roosts in tree hollows and buildings, emerging early in the evening. It typically feeds along watercourses with swift flight and frequent changes of direction; it feeds around streetlights (for example, in Darwin). Almost impossible to separate in the field from the Little Broad-nosed Bat.

Other names: Little Northern Broad-nosed Bat

*Central-eastern Broad-nosed Bat

Scotorepens sp. undescribed   (northern NSW, south-east Qld)

An undescribed broad-nosed bat, intermediate in size between Little, Eastern and Inland Broad-nosed Bats. It occurs from south-east Qld south to the Hunter Valley, NSW in dry forest, woodland and heath in coastal and subcoastal areas. A fast-flying species that roosts in tree hollows and buildings.

*Inland Forest Bat

Vespadelus baverstocki   (inland Australia)

Widespread in arid and semi-arid woodlands, mallee and shrublands. Roosts in groups in tree hollows and old buildings; in arid and semi-arid areas it will use surprisingly small trees as roosts, sometimes close to the ground. Fast-flying, with rapid wingbeats; often seen drinking at farm dams and waterholes.

*Northern Cave Bat

Vespadelus caurinus   (Kimberley, Top End)

An inhabitant of rocky escarpments, where it roosts in crevices near cave entrances; also among boulders, in abandoned mines, buildings, and WWII bunkers (for example, at Casuarina Coastal Reserve, Darwin), in culverts and abandoned Fairy Martin nests. Forages in nearby monsoon forest and savannah woodland, particularly along watercourses. Often shares roosts with Dusky Leaf-nosed and Common Sheath-tailed Bats. Highly agile flight.

Other names: Northern or Little Brown Bat, Little Northern or Western Cave Bat

*Large Forest Bat

Vespadelus darlingtoni   (south-east Australia inc. Tas)

Common in many wooded habitats between south-east Qld and Adelaide, in Tas and on major islands including Lord Howe I. (9.01). Found above 300 m in the northern part of its range. Roosts in tree hollows (in Banyan Figs on Lord Howe I.), forages among and below the canopy at all heights, particularly along trails and waterways. With experience, it can be told from Little and Southern Forest Bats by its less agile, more direct, flight pattern.

Other names: Large Forest Eptesicus, Large Forest Vespadelus

*Yellow-lipped Cave Bat

Vespadelus douglasorum   (Kimberley)

Restricted to the West Kimberley in a region bounded by the 800 mm rainfall isohyet. It typically forages along *Pandanus*- and *Melaleuca*-lined streams through tropical woodland. Small colonies roost in limestone and sandstone caves, typically near water, and sometimes in association with other species (for example, the Northern Cave Bat); also known to roost in abandoned buildings. Several aberrant specimens may represent an as-yet undescribed subspecies or species.

Other names: Kimberley Cave Bat, Large Cave Eptesicus

*Finlayson's Cave Bat

Vespadelus finlaysoni   (inland Australia)

The most widespread cave bat; common near rocky hills and breakaways in many habitats over much of arid and semi-arid Australia. Forages with fast, fluttering flight with frequent zigzags, often over waterholes. Roosts colonially in the twilight zone of caves, crevices and abandoned mines; also in old Fairy Martin nests, sometimes in association with sheath-tailed bats and Ghost Bats, which prey on it. Colonies occur near Tennant Creek, NT.

Other names: Inland Cave Bat, Little Cave Eptesicus, Little Brown Bat

*Eastern Forest Bat

Vespadelus pumilus   (eastern seaboard)

A bat generally of wet forests with a disjointed distribution along the eastern seaboard between the Atherton Tableland and Newcastle, NSW; it also occurs on Lord Howe I. (9.01). Roosts in tree hollows in mature forest; and forages among trees and between the canopy and the shrub layer, rather than along tracks.

*Southern Forest Bat

Vespadelus regulus   (southern Australia inc. Tas)

Found in a wide variety of habitats including wet and dry forests, woodlands and mallee, where it forages at all forest heights; active along tracks. Found at higher elevations in the northern part of its range; eastern populations co-occur with other *Vespadelus* species, such as Little, Eastern and Large Forest Bats. Roosts in tree hollows and buildings, sometimes in association with Chocolate Wattled, Lesser Long-eared and South-eastern Freetail Bats. This species is very agile, flying with spirals and long, gliding arcs, and often approaching close to vegetation but avoiding fragmented blocks of forest and open areas.

Other names: King River Pipistrelle, King River Little Bat, Little Bat

*Eastern Cave Bat

Vespadelus troughtoni   (tropical and subtropical eastern Australia)

An uncommon and little-known species most often recorded near sandstone or volcanic escarpments between Iron Range, Qld and about Sydney, NSW. A microbat of rainforest edge, wet and dry forest, and woodlands. Roosts in well-lit parts of caves and overhangs, among boulders, in mine shafts and culverts, and commonly in Fairy Martin nests. There is a well-known maternity roost at Undara Lava Tubes NP (1.05).

Other names: Troughton's Vespadelus

*Little Forest Bat

Vespadelus vulturnus   (south-east Australia inc. Tas)

One of Australia's smallest microbats, this species is common in a wide variety of habitats from coastal wet forest to woodland and mallee in the semi-arid zone. It forages mostly below the canopy with agile, fluttering flight, and may take prey to feeding roosts. It roosts in hollows of dead, often rather isolated trees, as well as in artificial structures.

This species co-occurs with other *Vespadelus* species, such as Southern, Large and Inland Forest Bats and the Eastern Cave Bat.

Other names: Small Forest Eptesicus, Little or Little Brown Bat, Vulturine Little Bat

Rodents – Order Rodentia

Native rodents – mice and rats – make up nearly 25 per cent of Australia's mammal fauna. Worldwide, they are one of the most successful of all animal groups, occupying hundreds of niches in virtually every terrestrial habitat. All are eutherian or placental mammals, including the Australian species: they lack a pouch and give birth to comparatively well-developed young; indeed, the great reproductive rate of many rodents explains their abundance and, when conditions are favourable, plagues that have been the scourge of humans for centuries. All rodents are characterised by gnawing teeth, and (usually) a long, narrow tail. They are not the easiest group to watch in the wild, and in Australia specialised knowledge or traps are needed to locate and positively identify most species. However, with thorough research and careful observation, sightings and positive identifications of several species are possible in the field.

Mice and rats – Family Muridae (world 710; Australia 68 (58 endemic))

All Australian rodents belong to the Muridae, the largest mammalian family. Rodents evolved outside Australia and in biogeographical terms arrived quite recently, when the Australian and South-East Asian tectonic plates collided. With the two land masses in close proximity rodents invaded Australia in several waves, resulting in distinct patterns of distribution. There are some fascinating endemics, such as the pebble-mice, and specialised forms, such as the Water Rat and hopping-mice. However, nearly all are nocturnal or primarily so and, like some marsupial groups, Australian rodents have been hit hard by extinctions: 11 species have disappeared since white settlement. Taxonomists split the Australian murids into two broad subgroups – Australo-Papuan Old Endemics and New Endemics, reflecting their affiliations and likely arrivals on the continent; these groups are further subdivided as described below. A basic understanding of these subgroupings will help with sorting and identifying some of the bewildering variety. Rodent taxonomy appears to be relatively stable in Australia, although genetic work may yet lead to some new species being recognised.

*The **Australo-Papuan Old Endemics** group includes the majority of Australia's native rodents (50 species, according to the most recent taxonomy) and is further divided into four subgroups: the Australasian Old Endemics, the mosaic-tailed rats (Uromys and Melomys), water rats (Hydromys and Xeromys) and New Guinea Old Endemics, represented by a single species of Pogonomys.*

Rabbit-rats are an endemic genus of large, semi-arboreal rats. Only one species survives and it is getting scarce in parts of its range.

*White-footed Rabbit-rat

Conilurus albipes   (south-east mainland)
Extinct. Last recorded in about 1862. It was a nocturnal, semi-arboreal species that was apparently once common in south-east woodlands. The cause of its demise is unknown.

Other names: White-footed Tree-rat

Brush-tailed Rabbit-rat

Conilurus penicillatus   (Kimberley, Top End; New Guinea)
Patchily distributed in the Kimberley and Top End, where it is becoming rare. A mainly arboreal species that also forages on the ground, where it bounds rapidly with tail held high, flicking from side to side. Optimum habitat appears to be stands of coastal she-oak, tropical woodlands, dry forest and *Pandanus* thickets with a grassy understorey. It was formerly seen in Kakadu NP (8.03), but is apparently now almost extinct there; it is still recorded from the Cobourg Peninsula (8.04) and Kimberley (7.21). Two subspecies occur in Australia: *C. p. penicillatus* from the mainland and islands in the Gulf of Carpentaria, and *C. p. melibius* from Melville and Bathurst Is. (8.11).

Other names: Brush-tailed Tree-rat, Rabbit-eared Tree-rat

Short-tailed mice make up a small endemic genus of inland and tropical mice. In the hand (and sometimes in the field) they can be distinguished by their short tails, which are slightly over half head-body length. Their ranges apparently don't overlap.

*Forrest's Mouse

Leggadina forresti   (central Australia)
Sparsely distributed over a wide area in the arid zone. Frequents a variety of habitats, including tree-lined creeks, tussock grassland, stony plains with saltbush and spinifex hillsides. Occasionally recorded at Arid Recovery (6.11). This species does not appear to undergo dramatic population fluctuations and may be nomadic.

Other names: Central Short-tailed Mouse, Desert Short-tailed Mouse, Waite's Mouse, Berney's Queensland Mouse, Short-tailed Mouse, Southern Short-tailed Mouse, Forrest's Territory Mouse

*Northern Short-tailed Mouse

Leggadina lakedownensis   (northern Australia)
Found in several discrete areas across northern Australia including the Pilbara, Kimberley and subcoastal Top End, and north-east Qld from Cape York Peninsula to about Paluma in the Wet Tropics. A large form occurs naturally on Thevenard I. off the north-west coast and has been introduced to Serrurier I. nearby, which is free of the introduced House Mouse. This is a little-known species that inhabits tropical woodlands, monsoon forest,

Acacia shrublands, moist tussock grassland and, in the Pilbara, stony hummock grassland. Seasonally inundated red or white sandy-clay soils seems to be an important indicator of its preferred habitat.

Other names: Lakeland Downs Mouse, Tropical Short-tailed Mouse

Stick-nest rats are among Australia's largest rodents, although only one species survived white settlement. They construct large nests of interwoven sticks at the base of shrubs, under rock overhangs or in small caves. Both species once occurred over a large part of the arid zone, coexisting in the south with only the Lesser Stick-nest Rat occurring in the north. Their nests were glued together with a mixture of faeces and urine, called ratamber, which was extremely durable and lasted thousands of years; ancient, abandoned stick nests can still be found in remote rocky ranges.

*Lesser Stick-nest Rat

Leporillus apicalis   (arid and semi-arid Australia)
Extinct. The last specimen was collected in 1933, although it could have persisted until about 1950 in remote areas. It was nocturnal, much smaller than the Greater Stick-nest Rat and apparently gregarious.

Other names: White-tipped Hapalotis, White-tipped House-building or Stick-nest Rat, Tjuwalpi

*Greater Stick-nest Rat

Leporillus conditor   (islands of southern SA)
Like its smaller relative, this species was wiped out on the mainland. Luckily a population survived on Franklin I. (6.17) and after a successful captive-breeding program, specimens were introduced to Reevesby I. in the Sir Joseph Banks Group CP, SA and Salutation I. in Shark Bay, WA; followed by releases on St Peter I. in the Nuyts Archipelago CP; and on the mainland at Venus Bay CP, SA, Arid Recovery (6.11), Faure I. (7.15b) and Heirisson Prong (7.15d). This species builds impressive nests up to 1 m high and 1.5 m across, centred on and incorporating a bush, in which a dozen or more animals may shelter. It sometimes also nests under buildings and in abandoned vehicles.

Other names: House-building Rat, Large Stick-nest Rat, Stick-nest Rat, Franklin Island Stick-nest or House-building Rat, Wopilkara

*The **Broad-toothed Rat** is the sole member of an endemic genus. It is almost exclusively herbivorous and in appearance and ecology resembles the voles of the northern hemisphere.*

*Broad-toothed Rat

Mastacomys fuscus   (south-east Australia inc. Tas)
A docile and rather guinea pig-like species. The subspecies *M. f. mordicus* occurs on the mainland in alpine and subalpine heaths in Barrington Tops, Kosciuszko NP (2.16) and

the Victorian Alps, and in densely vegetated clearings in wet forests in the Dandenong and Otway Ranges. *M. f. fuscus* inhabits buttongrass plains, sedgelands and heathlands in northern and western Tas. It is uncommon and found from sea level to 2200 m, mainly at higher elevations on the mainland, where it creates tunnels through dense vegetation that enable it to remain active through winter even under snow; the remains of these tunnels can be seen with the spring thaw. It is mainly nocturnal but partly diurnal in summer.

Other names: Tooarrana

*The two species of **tree-rat** inhabit tropical savannah woodlands and are the largest of the Australasian Old Endemics. They are spectacular, rabbit-sized, tree-climbing rodents with very long, brush-tipped tails.*

*Black-footed Tree-rat

Mesembriomys gouldi   (northern Australia)
A large tree-rat that occurs in discrete populations in the Kimberley and Top End (*M. g. gouldii*), on Cape York Peninsula and coastal north-east Qld south to Townsville (*M. g. rattoides*) and on Melville I. (*M. g. melvillensis*). It favours damp areas in tropical woodlands with a well-developed shrub layer, especially sites protected from fire. It was formerly common around campsites in Kakadu NP (8.03), from where it has now all but disappeared for reasons unknown; elsewhere it is localised and becoming rare, though still locally common in Arnhem Land and on Melville I. (8.11). This species is mainly arboreal but also forages on the ground; it is difficult to spotlight as it turns away from lights and is hard to see among foliage despite its large size. It feeds on ripe *Pandanus* fruits in the cooler months. It can become a nuisance in Macadamia nut plantations in the Mareeba area (1.04c).

Other names: Long-haired Rabbit-rat, Shaggy Rabbit-rat, Djintamoonga

*Golden-backed Tree-rat

Mesembriomys macrurus   (Kimberley)
Formerly more widespread, this attractive species is now restricted to the north-west Kimberley, where it occurs in a variety of habitats including tropical woodlands, adjacent vine thickets and monsoon forest in valleys. It is mainly arboreal, but also looks for food on the ground and has been seen foraging on the tideline after sunrise.

Other names: Golden-backed Rabbit-rat, Western Rabbit-rat

The genus Notomys *is comprised of five extant species of **hopping-mouse** (five others have become extinct since white settlement). All except the Northern Hopping-mouse inhabit inland sand country (diversity is highest in the Lake Eyre Basin, where Spinifex, Dusky and Fawn Hopping-mice all occur); most are common though identification is normally possible only in the hand. Their adaptations for life in the arid zone include elongated hind feet, large ears and large eyes; all inhabit burrows, usually in sandy substrate, and are strictly nocturnal. Hopping-mice should not be confused with the*

Kultarr, a predatory dasyurid which also has elongated hind feet. (The so-called 'kangaroo mice' of North Africa are named after their preferred mode of locomotion and are not marsupials.) Some hopping-mice went extinct without a live specimen ever being seen by scientists; several are known only from skeletal remains and reasons why they died out while others survived is a mystery.

*Spinifex Hopping-mouse

Notomys alexis   (arid Australia)

Most widespread of the extant hopping-mice, this species is found across a wide area of central Australia, where it is common in places. It is an inhabitant of sandy deserts, found both on dunes and swales among hummock grass; also in mulga and *Melaleuca* on loamy soils. It is easily seen around the campground at Uluru-Kata Tjuta NP (8.18) and abundant at Arid Recovery (6.11). Three subspecies are recognised: *N. a. alexis* from WA and the NT, *N. a. reginae* from Qld, and *N. a. everardensis* from north-west SA. This species overlaps with Fawn and Dusky Hopping-mice at the eastern end of its distribution.

Other names: Brown Hopping-mouse, Northern Hopping-mouse, Tarrkawarra

*Short-tailed Hopping-mouse

Notomys amplus   (arid Australia)

Extinct. Huge by hopping-mouse standards – twice as large as any surviving species. Known from only two specimens taken from south-east NT in 1895, although remains have been found in owl pellets in SA.

Other names: Brazenor's Hopping-mouse, Yoontoo

*Northern Hopping-mouse

Notomys aquilo   (Top End)

Abundant among dunes with *Acacia* scrub, heath and grassland in north-east Arnhem Land. Common on Groote Eylandt but notoriously trap-shy. Watch for signs of its presence such as tracks in the sand and spoil heaps near burrows, which are up to 2 m away from the centre of the spoil heap.

Other names: Woorrentinta

*Fawn Hopping-mouse

Notomys cervinus   (central Australia)

More or less confined to sparsely vegetated gibber plains and clay pans of the Lake Eyre Basin and Channel Country of south-west Qld. Digs shallow burrows in gibber.

Other names: Ooarri

*Dusky Hopping-mouse

Notomys fuscus   (central Australia)

Smallest of the hopping-mice and known only from the Strzelecki Desert of north-east SA and south-west Qld, where it inhabits sparsely vegetated sand dunes with cane grass. It co-occurs with the Fawn Hopping-mouse in south-west Qld, where the Dusky Hopping-mouse occurs on sandy substrates and the Fawn on dune swales and gibber plains. It is apparently common near Montecollina Bore on the Strzelecki Track (6.12), although positive identification without trapping would be difficult.

Other names: Birdsville Hopping-mouse, Wood Jones' Hopping-mouse, Wilkiniti

*Long-tailed Hopping-mouse

Notomys longicaudatus   (arid Australia)
Extinct. Last seen in 1901; formerly ranged across a wide part of central Australia from western NSW to the Pilbara coast. Apparently it was most often associated with clay soils.

Other names: Koolawa

*Big-eared Hopping-mouse

Notomys macrotis   (south-west Australia)
Extinct. Known only from two specimens collected north of Perth before 1844.

Other names: Noompa

*Mitchell's Hopping-mouse

Notomys mitchelli   (arid and semi-arid southern Australia)
A large hopping-mouse of southern semi-arid Australia between south-west WA and western Vic. Common in mallee and heath growing in deep sand at sites such as the Big Desert (4.22).

Other names: Pankot

*Darling Downs Hopping-mouse

Notomys mordax   (south-east Qld)
Extinct. Known only from a skull, collected in the 1840s in the Darling Downs of south-east Qld.

*Broad-cheeked Hopping-mouse

Notomys sp. undescribed   (Flinders Ranges, SA)
Extinct. Known only from skulls collected from old owl roosts in caves in the Davenport and Flinders Ranges, SA.

Other names: Great Hopping-mouse

The 23 species of Pseudomys *make up the largest genus of Australian 'mice' (and the largest genus of any Australian mammal). Taxonomists further subdivide* Pseudomys *into up to seven subgroups although many mammal texts list the species in alphabetical order, a counter-intuitive convention (they certainly didn't evolve alphabetically) as there are some clear evolutionary affiliations within the genus, for example pebble-mice. Following one system (see Breed W, Ford F (2007)* Native Mice and Rats. *CSIRO Publishing, Melbourne), the* Pseudomys *can be subdivided into:*

- *four species of 'false' mouse (**Plains**, **Shark Bay**, **Long-tailed** and **Long-eared** (extinct)), found mainly in the southern half of the continent; some are large enough to have formerly been called rats;*

- *four species of 'velvet' mouse (**Ash-grey**, **Silky**, **Smoky** and **Blue-grey** (extinct)) with a coastal and subcoastal distribution in southern Australia; all have silky grey fur;*

- *five species of 'delicate' mouse (**Bolam's**, **Delicate**, **Sandy Inland** and **New Holland** (Delicate Mouse));*

- *two species of 'chestnut' mouse (**Eastern** and **Western**), with which the Broad-toothed Rat is affiliated;*

- *four species of 'pebble' mouse (**Kakadu**, **Western**, **Central** and **Eastern**) that have a disjunct tropical distribution; all construct complex burrow systems and dump piles of stones at the mouth of one entrance, and mounds may stay in use for centuries;*

- *two species of 'grizzled' mouse (**Desert** and **Heath**), one an inhabitant of the arid zone, the other of southern heaths;*

- *three anomalous species (**Western**, **Hastings River** and **Gould's** (extinct)) that don't appear to be closely related.*

In general, it is rare to find more than one representative of each subgroup in any part of Australia, although more than one subgroup can occur in the same area.

*Ash-grey Mouse

Pseudomys albocinereus   (south-west Australia)

Found in a wide band of heath and shrubland with tussock grass understorey between Shark Bay and Israelite Bay, WA (*P. a. albocinereus*); another subspecies (*P. a. squalorum*) occurs on Dirk Hartog, Bernier and Dorre Is. (7.15c). An uncommon mouse that shelters in deep burrows or in nests on the surface among leaf litter or hollow logs.

Other names: Ashy-grey Mouse, Noodji

*Silky Mouse

Pseudomys apodemoides   (south-east SA, western Vic)

A distinctive species in the hand, with soft, dense fur. Locally common but restricted to semi-arid heath and mallee in north-west Vic and south-east SA, especially patches 3–10 years after fire. It shelters in deep burrows under dense vegetation (and builds large spoil heaps near burrow systems), especially Desert Banksias which provide an important food source during winter.

Other names: Silky-grey Mouse, Silky Desert Mouse, Silky-grey Southern Mouse, Finlayson's Mouse, Nalpo

*Long-eared Mouse

Pseudomys auritus (south-east SA, south-west Vic)

Extinct. Recently identified from specimens and subfossils as a separate species, previously regarded as the Plains Mouse. It formerly occurred in woodland, heath and mallee and probably died out around the 1850s.

Other names: Long-eared Pseudo-Mouse, Basalt Plains Mouse

*Plains Mouse

Pseudomys australis (central Australia)

The largest arid-zone *Pseudomys* species and often referred to as the Plains Rat. It is found mainly west of the Lake Eyre Basin, with an outlying population west of Lake Torrens; most common on gibber plains and clay-based soils, as well as adjacent dune systems during good seasons. It is abundant and regularly trapped at Arid Recovery (6.11). This species shelters in deep cracks or in burrows, and may be partly diurnal.

Other names: Plains Rat, Eastern Mouse, Eastern Rat, Palyoora

*Bolam's Mouse

Pseudomys bolami (semi-arid southern Australia)

A species generally found among chenopod and mallee shrublands, especially in areas that flood, from Woolgangie and Norseman, WA to western SA and NSW. It is regularly trapped at Arid Recovery (6.11) during fauna surveys. Easily confused with Sandy Inland Mouse, which shares the northern part of its distribution.

Other names: Poonta

*Calaby's Pebble-mouse

Pseudomys calabyi (Top End)

Known from only a few locations, including Litchfield NP (8.10) and the southern part of Kakadu NP (8.03), this species inhabits gravelly slopes in open woodland with a tall grass understorey. Like all pebble-mice, it shelters in burrows disguised with a small mound of pebbles, often built around the base of a tree.

Other names: Kakadu Pebble-mouse, Calaby's Mouse, Pinti

*Pilbara Pebble-mouse

Pseudomys chapmani (Pilbara)

Restricted to stony hillsides among hummock grassland, often among shrubs and woodland, in the central and eastern Pilbara, including Karajini NP, and the adjacent Little Sandy Desert. Mounds are often constructed near drainage lines with *Acacia* scrub. Active mounds have crater-like cones.

Other names: Western Pebble-mouse, Western Pebble-mouse, Ngadji

*Delicate Mouse

Pseudomys delicatulus   (northern Australia)

As its name suggests, this is a small, delicately built mouse, although it is widespread and locally abundant across northern Australia from the Pilbara to northern NSW. It is nocturnal and terrestrial, an inhabitant of open, sparsely vegetated grassy habitat, such as dunes and spinifex country; sheltering in a burrow or hollow log. It seems to be most common shortly after fires. Where it overlaps with Kakadu Pebble-mouse, this species prefers sandy soils lacking in stones and rocks. Recent studies have indicated that the population from the NT's Victoria River District, the Kimberley, Great Sandy Desert and Pilbara are in fact an undescribed species. The so-called Pilbara Mouse (formerly *P. pilligaensis*), a little-known endemic of the Pilliga scrub between Barradine and Narrabri, NSW now appears to be a southerly population of Delicate Mouse.

Other names: Molinipi

*Desert Mouse

Pseudomys desertor   (central Australia)

Widespread in the arid zone in a variety of habitats with dense ground cover, including hummock grassland on sandplains, woodlands, samphire, Nitre Bush, sedgelands and canegrass on dunes. Numbers fluctuate after rainfall. Present at Uluru-Kata Tjuta NP (8.18) and there are relict populations on Bernier I. (7.15c) and at Telowie Gorge (6.09); it is sometimes trapped during fauna surveys at Arid Recovery (6.11). This species constructs shallow burrows and nests in dense tussocks from which obvious runways and trails radiate.

Other names: Brown Desert Mouse, Wildjin

*Djoongari (Shark Bay Mouse)

Pseudomys fieldi   (islands of north-west WA)

A large, shaggy-coated mouse now confined to predator-free islands off the north-west coast. Formerly found over a large part of the arid zone, it survived only on Bernier I. (7.15c), where it is most abundant among spinifex-covered dunes; and has been introduced to Doole I. in Exmouth Gulf, Trimouille I. north of Barrow I. and Faure I. in Shark Bay (7.15b). It nests in shallow burrows and among surface vegetation, including piles of beach-cast seagrass. Note that the Aboriginal name Djoongari is gaining popularity.

Other names: Shaggy Mouse, Shaggy-haired Mouse, Alice Springs Mouse

*Smoky Mouse

Pseudomys fumeus   (south-east Australia)

Little known and seldom seen. This rare mouse has a fragmented population that stretches from The Grampians (4.21) in western Vic, through isolated patches of the Great Dividing Range in Vic, NSW and the ACT, to coastal East Gippsland and adjacent forested hills of extreme south-east NSW. It seems to prefer forested ridges with a highly diverse understorey of heath and tussock grass; it also occurs in coastal and alpine heath, and seems most common in vegetation communities that develop at least 10 years after fire.

Other names: Konoom

*Blue-grey Mouse

Pseudomys glaucus   (southern Qld, northern NSW)
Extinct. Known from only three specimens collected in the central NSW–Qld border region, there have been no records since the 19th century and nothing is known of its ecology or behaviour.

*Gould's Mouse

Pseudomys gouldi   (central NSW, south-west WA)
Extinct. Last recorded in 1857. Formerly occurred in the central-western NSW, in the Upper Hunter Valley, Liverpool Plains and lower Darling River; and in the Moore River region north of Perth.

*Eastern Chestnut Mouse

Pseudomys gracilicaudatus   (eastern seaboard)
Patchily distributed in coastal and subcoastal habitats from about Cooktown, Qld to Jervis Bay, NSW. In the northern part of its range it is found in open wet and dry forests with a grassy or heathy understorey; in the south it inhabits coastal heath (especially two years after fire) and swampy grasslands (where it often co-occurs with Swamp Rat). Mainly nocturnal, using runways through dense grasses and sedges, although it is also partly diurnal or crepuscular.

Other names: Karrooka

*Sandy Inland Mouse

Pseudomys hermannsburgensis   (inland Australia)
Common in arid Australia from the Pilbara coast to western Qld and NSW. It inhabits open vegetation, such as hummock and tussock grasslands on dunes, dune swales and loamy flats, and constructs shallow burrows but also uses holes made by lizards. Populations fluctuate according to rain. This species is similar to the House Mouse in appearance.

Other names: Hermannsburg Mouse

*Long-tailed Mouse

Pseudomys higginsi   (Tas)
The largest *Pseudomys* species is endemic to Tas, although subfossil deposits on the mainland indicate that it was once more widespread. It is most abundant in western and central Tas in alpine boulder fields and scree slopes at elevations up to about 1600 m, but also in wet forest, rainforest and alpine heath and it occurs on Bruny I. (5.04). Mainly nocturnal and terrestrial, during winter this species is sometimes seen during the day and visits bushwalkers' huts at Melaleuca and on the Overland Track.

Other names: Long-tailed Rat, Looringa

*Central Pebble-mouse

Pseudomys johnsoni   (northern Australia)

Now recognised as the same species as the Kimberley Pebble-mouse (formerly *P. laborifex*); their combined distributions therefore cover the Kimberley, central NT and south-west Gulf Country. It inhabits stony ridges, rises and gravelly hillsides among woodland, hummock grasslands and grevilleas. The mounds of this species vary in size from small cones to carpets covering several square metres.

Other names: Central Pebble Mouse, Kimberley Pebble-mouse, Kimberley Mouse, Ilyema

*Western Chestnut Mouse

Pseudomys nanus   (Top End, Kimberley)

A wide-ranging species from Port Hedland, WA to the Barkly Tableland, NT; found in woodland with an understorey of shrubs and dense tussock grass, especially along watercourses but not necessarily so. It is confiding and readily observed, and gives a high-pitched whistling call. Mainland animals belong to the subspecies *P. n. nanus*; the subspecies *P. n. ferculinus* occurs on Barrow I. (7.18). This species builds a nest of grass and it is not known whether it burrows.

Other names: Little Mouse, Barrow Island Mouse, Moolpoo

*New Holland Mouse

Pseudomys novaehollandiae   (south-east Australia inc. Tas)

This species has a strangely disjointed distribution from south-east Qld to southern Vic and north-east Tas; it is known from Ku-ring-gai Chase NP, NSW, Anglesea, Vic and Mt William NP (5.11). Rare in the south, but relatively common in the northern part of its range and also found at higher elevations up to 600 m. It is typically found in dry coastal heath or in woodland with a heathy understorey, where it shelters in long burrow systems. The south-east Qld population is found in dry forest with little or no ground cover and may represent a separate species.

Other names: Pookila

*Western Mouse

Pseudomys occidentalis   (south-west Australia)

The Western Mouse formerly occurred in a band of semi-arid south-west WA from Shark Bay to the Nullarbor Plain; it is now restricted to the Ravensthorpe Range, Fitzgerald River NP and a few small reserves in the wheatbelt. It apparently prefers long unburnt shrublands and woodlands on gravelly soil. It is timid and nocturnal, sheltering by day in burrows; where they are available it feeds on Quandong nuts, which it hoards under dense vegetation near mature trees.

Other names: Walyadji

*Hastings River Mouse

Pseudomys oralis (subtropical eastern Australia)

A rather rare species with a disjunct distribution in open forest between Lamington NP (1.37) and Barrington Tops, NSW. Occurs mostly between 300 and 1200 m, and especially above 500–600 m. Generally found along drainage lies in dense fern or sedge understorey, but also in drier habitats with heathy or grassy understorey. It shelters in hollow logs, old burrows and under tree roots.

Other names: Hastings River Rat, Koontoo

*Eastern Pebble-mouse

Pseudomys patrius (eastern Qld)

Another little-known species, with a patchy distribution in central Qld, inland of the Great Dividing Range, between Paluma (where it is reputed to occur near Hidden Valley), through Charters Towers south to about Gympie. It occurs in woodland with a grassy understory on rolling ridges where pebbles are sufficiently abundant for the construction of mounds. Mounds are typically conical with their entrances at the base of trees or among larger rocks.

Other names: Eastern Pebble Mouse, Queensland Pebble-mouse

*Heath Mouse

Pseudomys shortridgei (south-east and south-west Australia)

A large, docile species with a disjunct range: it is found in western Vic in The Grampians (4.21) and a small area bounded by Nelson, Dergholm and Mt Clay; on Kangaroo I. (6.13); and in south-west WA in Ravensthorpe Range, Fitzgerald River NP and Dragon Rocks. It is a mouse of species-rich heath, particularly where it has been burnt within the last 5–15 years or even longer; it also occurs in open forest with a heath understorey and scrubby mallee. It can be partly diurnal, and shelters in a shallow burrow or a surface nest.

Other names: Heath Rat, Blunt-faced Rat, Shortridge's Native Mouse, Dayang (WA)

*The five species of **rock-rat** form an endemic genus found in major sandstone complexes in tropical Australia, with an outlying species in the arid zone. Three are common within their range but two are very rare indeed. All may have a fattened base to their tails and their tails readily break off, probably as a defence mechanism. Rock-rats may venture some distance from rocky habitat into surrounding vegetation; they leave piles of half-eaten seeds to accumulate on safe ledges and under boulders, which can be a good indication of their presence.*

*Common Rock-rat

Zyzomys argurus (northern Australia)

The smallest, commonest and most widespread rock-rat, with disjunct populations in north Qld, and the Mt Isa region, Top End, Kimberley and Pilbara; it is most common in the Top End and Kimberley, common and readily spotlighted at Kakadu NP (8.03). It frequents rocky outcrops, especially sandstone, but also scree slopes of igneous or limestone origin. It inhabits a greater range of habitat than other *Zyzomys* species, typically tropical woodland with a grassy understory, monsoon and open forest and dry vine thickets. Its range overlaps with Kimberley, Arnhem and Carpentarian Rock-rats, all of which are less abundant; the Common Rock-rat is smaller with a longer tail. There is an isolated population at Bladensburg NP, Qld.

Other names: White-tailed Rat, White-tailed Rock-rat, Dory

*Arnhem Land Rock-rat

Zyzomys main   (Top End)
This species occupies boulder scree and boulder-strewn gorges with a cover of deciduous vine-thicket and monsoon forest at the western edge of the Arnhem Escarpment. Kakadu NP (8.03) is the most feasible place to see it and it occurs at Little Nourlangie Rock and Gunlom, among other sites. The Common Rock-rat is more common at many sites, but much smaller and less densely furred; where the two co-occur, this species occupies wetter, more densely vegetated areas. Piles of chewed seeds on sheltered ledges are an indication of its presence.

Other names: Large Rock-rat, Kodjperr

*Carpentarian Rock-rat

Zyzomys palatalis   (south-west Gulf Country)
Endemic to the NT but restricted to a series of gorges and escarpments on Wollogorang Station (8.13), where it frequents isolated patches of rainforest and vine thickets. The only feasible way of seeing this species would be to join a survey.

Other names: Aywalirroomoo

*Central Rock-rat

Zyzomys pedunculatus   (central Australia)
An enigmatic species thought to be extinct until 1996, when a specimen was discovered in the West Macdonnell Range near Alice Springs. It was subsequently found at a few other sites within a 70-km radius, including Ormiston Gorge (8.17), all but vanished from the landscape after fires in 2002, then trapped again in small numbers after a series of good years in 2011–12. Its preferred habitat seems to be boulder fields and scree slopes and eroded sandstone cliffs, among hummock and tussock grasslands with a sparse shrub layer. If seen at all, it is unlikely to be confused with other species within its range.

Other names: Antina

*Kimberley Rock-rat

Zyzomys woodwardi   (Kimberley)
Confined to the northern Kimberley, particularly the north-west, and several islands offshore. It is found in rugged boulder habitat, including scree and stacks, among monsoon

forest, woodland, *Pandanus* thickets and hummock grasses. This species occurs on the Mitchell Plateau (7.21) and in Prince Regent NR, where its range overlaps with that of the Common Rock-rat (the Kimberley Rock-rat is almost twice its size).

Other names: Large Rock-rat, Woodward's Thick-tailed Rat, Djookooropa

The Hydromys *group of Papuan Old Endemics includes the* **Water Rat** *and* **Water Mouse**, *two primarily carnivorous rodents adapted to aquatic habitats and the mangrove littoral zone, respectively. The Water Mouse belongs to a monotypic genus unique to mangroves and associated habitats in subtropical Qld and the coasts of northern Australia. The Water Rat is one of Australia's largest rodents and has evolved to fill a niche occupied by otters and diving shrews on other continents. It has broad, partially webbed hind feet, among other adaptations, and is most often found in or near a large variety of fresh, brackish and saline waterways, including mangroves.*

Water Rat

Hydromys chrysogaster (Australia except arid zone; New Guinea)

A large, spectacular rat with a powerful, white-tipped tail and often yellowish underparts. It is common in a wide variety of waterways, including slow-moving rivers, lakes, dams and mangroves in eastern states (including Tas) and coastal northern Australia, and is also found in the south-west and on many large islands. It is readily seen at a number of sites in or near large cities: Canberra (3.01) and Melbourne (4.01) are particularly good, as is Fogg Dam (8.02). It is mainly nocturnal or crepuscular, but readily seen in quiet areas in the early morning or even later. It is large enough to be confused with a Platypus (see boxed text on p. 243) and the two often co-occur. Water Rats habitually use feeding platforms on which accumulate middens of inedible bones and crayfish exoskeletons.

Other names: Beaver Rat, Rakali

Water Mouse

Xeromys myoides (south-east Qld, Top End; PNG)

Another amazing aquatic rodent, though much smaller than the Water Rat with which it often co-occurs. The Water Mouse's favoured habitats are mangroves, saltmarsh and coastal wetlands, where it burrows in the littoral zone in earth banks on the tideline, piles of spoil and root systems of felled trees; it also rests in hollow logs and uses artificial structures such as sea walls. It is best known for elaborate mounds with a nest chamber inside near the top and access tunnels near the bottom, much like a beaver's lodge. It is uncommon in the NT but relatively common in mangroves of southern Qld; however, the best chance of seeing it would be to join a survey team. It is nocturnal and follows the receding tide over mangrove mud as it forages. Middens accumulate at favoured feeding sites, where it leaves a distinctive, pungent scent. Mounds can be seen at North Stradbroke I. (1.35). *Do not* go looking for this species in mangroves of the NT because of the serious risk from crocodiles.

Other names: Thomas's Rat, False Water Rat, Yirrkoo

The Uromys *group of Papuan Old Endemics comprise the six species of so-called* **mosaic-tailed rats**, *including the genera* Melomys *and* Uromys. *All have nearly naked tails with criss-crossed indentations, and are confined to wet areas of northern and north-eastern Australia, with the highest diversity occurring in north Qld rainforests. 'Melomys' is now commonly used as the common name for five species of small native rat;* Uromys *includes one of Australia's largest rodents, the Giant White-tailed Rat, and a little-known endemic found only in the Wet Tropics. All are good climbers, feeding mainly on fruits and leaves, and probably arrived on the Australian land mass from the Papuan region comparatively recently.*

*Grassland Melomys

Melomys burtoni   (eastern and northern Australia)

Locally abundant in grasslands, sedges, canefields, rainforest edge, forest and woodlands with a grassy understorey. There are two discrete populations: one extending from Cape York to about Gosford, NSW, and the other in the Top End and Kimberley. Those in the north inhabit grassland, monsoon forest, riparian vegetation and mangroves. This species is nocturnal and mostly terrestrial, but a capable climber with a partly prehensile tail; it constructs a nest of grass and leaves up to 1 m up in vegetation or on the ground in suitable cover. The Grassland Melomys is variable in size – animals from the Kimberley are largest, those from Cape York Peninsula smaller with a longer tail.

Other names: Banana Rat, Cape York Scale-tailed Rat, Groote Eylandt Melomys, Hayman Island Melomys, Khaki Rat, Little Cape York Melomys, Little Melomys, Long-tailed Melomys, Lonnberg's Scale-tailed Rat, Small Khaki Rat, Small Mosaic-tailed Rat, Tree-rat, Western Melomys, Burton's Melomys, Looloong

*Cape York Melomys

Melomys capensis   (Cape York Peninsula)

A small, semi-arboreal melomys, found only at the north-east corner of Cape York Peninsula, including Iron Range (1.17) and the McIlwraith Range, where it occurs in rainforest, monsoon forest and adjacent woodland. It is nocturnal and both arboreal and terrestrial, nesting in a tree hollow or artificial cavity; it is sometimes seen around habitation and entering buildings. This species is confiding, easily spotlighted and recognisable by its long, almost naked tail. It climbs branches and vines at night.

Other names: Kala

*Fawn-footed Melomys

Melomys cervinipes   (eastern Australia)

Found on the east coast between northern NSW and about Cooktown, Qld. Common in rainforest, especially among vine thickets; in the southern part of its range it also occurs in wet forest, coastal woodlands and mangroves. It is nocturnal, both arboreal and terrestrial (although it nests in the canopy) and most common at forest edges and along roads. This species visits feeders at Kingfisher Park (1.03).

Other names: Large Khaki Rat, Fawn-footed Scale-tailed Rat, Korril

*Bramble Cay Melomys

Melomys rubicola   (Bramble Cay)
Possibly extinct. A large, distinctive melomys restricted to Bramble Cay (1.19) at the northern tip of the Great Barrier Reef. It is the only terrestrial mammal on the cay, but its population has apparently collapsed for reasons unknown and it has become extremely scarce, if not already extinct (an expedition in 2014 failed to find any specimens). It foraged among beach vegetation and herbfields, and nested in burrows.

Giant White-tailed Rat

Uromys caudimaculatus   (north-east Qld; New Guinea)
Common from about Townsville to Cape York. In Wet Tropics rainforests it is sometimes seen crossing roads at night and is recognisable by its great size and white-tipped tail. This species visits the feeders at Kingfisher Park (1.03) most nights, proffering close-up views, and is easily spotlighted in the park itself. It makes loud honking calls when alarmed and, when approached, a high-pitched sound that can be felt rather than heard. It is mainly terrestrial (but climbs well) and shelters in burrows or tree hollows during the day; scratch marks on trees may indicate their location. This species accumulates middens of chewed seeds and also hunts crabs in mangroves.

Other names: White-tailed Rat, Giant Rat, Giant Naked-tailed Rat, Giant Mosaic-tailed Rat, Cape York Uromys, Atherton Uromys, Hinchinbrook Island Uromys, Mati

Masked White-tailed Rat

Uromys hadrourus   (Wet Tropics; New Guinea)
A little known, difficult-to-see species of upland rainforests. It is apparently restricted to a few discrete areas in the Wet Tropics: above 550 m on the Thornton massif and the McDowall Range north of Daintree; above 890 m on the Carbine Tableland west of Mossman; at 740–780 m in the Lammin's Hill area on the Atherton Tableland; and on Mt Bartle Frere. It is mainly terrestrial, rarely enters traps and appears to frequent dense undergrowth where there is an abundance of large logs. It makes a rasping honk and a high-pitched call when alarmed.

Other names: Pygmy White-tailed Rat, Thornton Peak Rat, Thornton Peak Melomys, Kookoo

The Pogonomys *group makes up the third group of Old Papuan Endemics, and is represented in Australia by only one species, the **Prehensile-tailed Rat**.*

*Prehensile-tailed Rat

Pogonomys sp. undescribed   (north-east Qld)

An agile, mainly arboreal rainforest rodent known from two discrete areas: monsoon forest at Gordon Creek in Iron Range NP (1.17), and in rainforest between Shipton's Flat and Millaa Millaa on the Atherton Tableland (1.04). It has previously been described as *P. mollipilosus* and *P. loriae*, both of which are also found in New Guinea, and is currently regarded as an unnamed endemic species. It can be spotlighted (although it feeds high in the canopy) and recognised by its long tail, which it curls around branches for support, white underparts and black eye-ring. It has been seen at Kingfisher Park (1.03), Lake Barrine and in the Kuranda area. It is mainly nocturnal but has also been observed at dawn and dusk. When spotlighted it runs up and down trunks, showing its white underparts (in contrast, the Fawn-footed Melomys runs to the ground to escape and the Long-tailed Pygmy Possum jumps to the ground).

Other names: Tree Mouse, Soft-haired Tree-mouse, Djidiparra

*The **Australo-Papuan New Endemics** are comprised of the* Rattus *group – the genus most commonly associated with **rats** – which reach their greatest diversity in Asia and are thought to be the most recent arrivals in Australia. Here they are represented by eight native and three introduced species (listed in Appendix A). Interestingly, introduced* Rattus *species have so far not made great inroads inland, perhaps because native species exclude them from natural niches; however, they are definitely responsible for extinctions on numerous offshore islands.*

*Dusky Rat

Rattus colletti   (Top End)

A rat of floodplains and dense grass in treeless, swampy plains of the subcoastal Top End, inland to the Daly River. During the Dry it shelters in cracks in the soil, moving to higher ground during wet season flooding. At this time it is commonly seen in Kakadu NP (8.03), clinging to floating vegetation and sheltering on high ground, sometimes in large numbers. Visits to Kakadu during the Wet are often difficult because of flooding, but during the Dry these rats are not nearly as active. When wet seasons are mild and the Dry season is wetter than usual, breeding extends and the population increases, leading to increased daytime activity and vocalisations.

Other names: Collett's Rat, Territory Dusky Rat, Mulbu, Marrawata

*Bush Rat

Rattus fuscipes   (eastern and south-west Australia)

Common but nocturnal and retiring. This species frequents moist, dense undergrowth, such as heath and fern brakes, from sea level to the treeline, often but not always near water; southern subspecies also occur in drier habitat and it occurs among boulder scree in alpine areas (where it remains active during winter). *R. f. assimilis* is found from Rockhampton, Qld to western Vic; *R. f. greyii* occurs from Portland (4.18) west to Kangaroo I. (6.13) and Eyre Peninsula (6.15); *R. f. fuscipes* of the south-west occurs between Israelite Bay and Jurien Bay; and *R. f. coracius* inhabits rainforest between Townsville and Cooktown, Qld. It is difficult to separate in the field from some other *Rattus* species.

Other names: Western Swamp Rat, Allied Rat, Southern Bush Rat, Mootit

Cape York Rat

Rattus leucopus (Cape York Peninsula; New Guinea)

This species is not restricted to Cape York Peninsula: the subspecies *R. l. leucopus* occurs between the McIlwraith Range and Cape York, including Iron Range NP (1.17), and often has white mottling on its tail; *R. l. cooktownensis* occurs in rainforest between Cooktown and the Paluma Range, at the southern end of the Wet Tropics. It is the only rainforest-dwelling rat found north of Cooktown, but southern specimens are similar in appearance to the Bush Rat, with which they co-occur. The Bush Rat seems to require wetter forest habitat while the Cape York Rat may also occur in smaller, dry rainforest fragments. It is largely terrestrial, burrowing under leaf litter, in hollow logs or at the base of trees.

Other names: Mottle-tailed Rat, Mottle-tailed Cape York Rat, Spiny-furred Rat, Rarrayn

*Swamp Rat

Rattus lutreolus (south-east Australia inc. Tas, north-east Qld)

An inhabitant of dense wet areas, including heath, fern brakes, sedges, grassland and fallow pasture, between Fraser I. (1.41) and south-east SA including Kangaroo I. An isolated subspecies *R. l. latus* that occurs in montane rainforest between Paluma and the Atherton Tableland may be a separate species. *R. l. velutinus* occurs in Tas in forests up to about 1600 m. Partly diurnal, the Swamp Rat is sometimes seen in enclosures at Healesville Sanctuary (4.06). It forms runways through dense vegetation and is active day and night though rarely seen.

Other names: Velvet-furred Rat (Tas), Eastern Swamp-rat, Tawny Rat, Tawny Long-haired Rat, Dusky-footed Rat, Water Rat, Koota

*Maclear's Rat

Rattus macleari (Christmas I.)

Extinct. A semi-arboreal species endemic to Christmas I. (9.03), where it was formerly abundant. It probably went extinct between 1902 and 1904 following the accidental introduction of the Black Rat, which may have transmitted trypanosome blood infections.

*Bulldog Rat

Rattus nativitatus   (Christmas I.)

Extinct. Larger and shorter-tailed than Maclear's Rat, it was probably less abundant but now no less extinct. It also probably succumbed to disease spread by the Black Rat; no specimens were obtained after about 1900.

*Canefield Rat

Rattus sordidus   (eastern Qld)

Found in open, grassy areas, among sedges and in canefields, sometimes in great numbers, on the Qld coast between about Mackay and Cape York, with isolated populations in the Darling Downs, the Sir Edward Pellew Is. in the Gulf and on North Stradbroke (1.35) and Moreton Is. It is entirely terrestrial, digging burrows that may be in large colonies.

Other names: Field-rat, Field Ground Rat, Dusky Field Rat, Sordid Rat, Annam River Rat, Sombre Downs Rat, Minkala

*Pale Field-rat

Rattus tunneyi   (northern and eastern Australia)

Found in a variety of habitats, including grasslands, woodlands and monsoon forest with a dense grassy or sedge understorey, also pasture and canefields in eastern Qld. The subspecies *R. t. culmorum* occurs from Coen on Cape York Peninsula to about Brisbane; *R. t. tunneyi* is found from the Kimberley to the south-west Gulf Country. This species is common in Kakadu NP (8.03) and may be seen around campgrounds and on rocky slopes; it also occurs around campgrounds on Fraser I. (1.41). It digs shallow burrows in loose sandy soil.

Other names: Tunney's Rat, Paler Field Rat, Chiiny Chiiny, Djini

*Long-haired Rat

Rattus villosissimus   (central Australia)

An enigmatic species of the inland, with the Channel Country (1.32) and the Barkly Tableland (8.13) its strongholds. After significant rainfall it irrupts into plagues, which have spread across the inland as far as Uluru, Hall's Creek, Mt Isa and Woomera, SA; in 2010 they reached at least as far as Alice Springs (8.16). An outlier from such expansions has become established around the Ord River scheme in the East Kimberley (7.23). During plagues it occupies most habitats, retreating to damp areas such as drainage lines and bores as the country dries out. At other times it apparently vanishes from the landscape and can be very difficult to locate. During plagues it should be easy to spot, even during the day, and can be a nuisance around campsites. It utters high-pitched vocalisations.

Other names: Plague Rat, Mayaroo

Dugongs and Sirenids – Order Sirenia

These gentle marine herbivores occur in shallow tropical and subtropical waters, where their habit of grazing on seagrass has earned them names like 'sea cow'. Only one species, the Dugong, occurs in Australian waters; it is related to the three species of manatee found in Central America and West Africa.

Dugongs – Family Dugongidae (world 1; Australia 1)

Fortunately Australia still has a healthy population of Dugongs, although threats include injuries inflicted by boat propellers, drowning in fishing nets and hunting by Indigenous people in north Qld and Torres Strait.

Dugong

Dugong dugon   (tropical and subtropical Australia; Indo-Pacific)
Herds of Dugong graze on seagrass beds in sheltered estuaries and channels. They are most abundant along the north coast between Moreton Bay in south-east Qld and Shark Bay, WA, although individuals are sometimes seen further south. Numbers fluctuate according to season, with greater concentrations at major sites in summer. Moreton Bay (1.34) has a fairly large, year-round population; other Qld sites with more or less permanent populations include Pumicestone Passage, Hervey Bay and Gladstone; they could also be encountered on cruises among Great Barrier Reef islands, as they have been recorded more than 50 km from the coast inside the Reef. The largest population is in Torres Striat and some are present year-round in Darwin Harbour (8.01). However, the standout site is Shark Bay (7.15), where some 11 000 have been recorded and tour operators are switched on to Dugong watching. Otherwise this species occurs rather sporadically and unpredictably throughout its range. With good views, it should be unmistakable and the lack of a dorsal fin is an excellent identification feature.

Carnivorous eutherians – Order Carnivora

Another large order, this one includes eutherians as diverse as dogs, cats, bears and weasels, none of which occurred naturally in Australia. The only ones that did were the pinnipeds – the seals, fur seals and sea lions – although the Dingo has been established so long here that it is regarded as a natural part of the lansdcape.

Seals, sea lions and fur seals – Suborder Caniformia

Seals and sea lions are divided into several families, two of which occur in Australia. The 'eared' seals – more commonly known as sea lions and fur seals – have external ears and can move their rear flippers independently of the body, allowing relatively high manoeuvrability on land. All are rather similar in appearance but have the characteristic pointed snout, upright resting posture and familiar barking vocalisations. The 'true' seals are highly varied, lack external ears and have backward-pointing rear flippers which cannot be moved independently (their movements on land are consequently rather limited). Posture and locomotion are good indicators of family: true seals can only lie flat on their belly and 'hump' along like a caterpillar; eared seals have a rather upright posture and 'walk' on solid surfaces. Only members of the eared seal family are resident in continental Australia and Tas; 'true' seals are all sporadic visitors to southern shores from Antarctic and subantarctic waters. Although stragglers haul up on southern beaches and headlands quite frequently, there is no hotline for sightings. The seals often don't stay long and many are reported only after the animal has departed (usually in local media). Check birding chatlines, as many birdwatchers are interested in other areas of natural history and use online forums to share sightings (often listed as 'off topic').

Sea lions and fur seals – Family Otariidae (world 14; Australia 3 (1 endemic + 2 vagrant)

The three common species (the Australian Fur Seal, New Zealand Fur Seal and Australian Sea Lion) can be seen at well-known colonies along the southern coast; two subantarctic species occasionally haul up on southern coasts as well, albeit unpredictably. The various species are difficult to tell apart; identification is safest at known breeding sites and haul-outs. Sea lions and fur seals look very similar and are best told apart where they co-occur, the former preferring open beaches and rock platforms, and the latter more sheltered coves and broken rocky areas.

Antarctic Fur Seal

Arctocephalus gazella   (subantarctic islands)

This species has two breeding colonies at Macquarie I. (9.05), several on Heard I. (9.06) and at least one at nearby McDonald I. It interbreeds with the Subantarctic Fur Seal at Macquarie I. The major world concentration is on islands of the Scotia Arc (South Georgia, South Orkneys, etc). To date there have been no confirmed records from Australia proper, although there is one unconfirmed record from Kangaroo I. (6.13).

Other names: Kerguelen Fur Seal

New Zealand Fur Seal

Arctocephalus forsteri   (southern Australia; New Zealand)

Despite its name, in Australia this species is most abundant on the south coasts of WA and SA. It also breeds on Maatsuyker I., Tas; stragglers have occurred as far north as southern Qld. The highest concentration is in SA, especially on Kangaroo I. (6.13) where there are several major breeding sites, and islands off the southern Eyre Peninsula, such as South and North Neptune Is. The largest colony in WA is at Salisbury I., a rather remote location with no ready access; in NSW it occurs in low numbers at Montague I. (2.11) among

Australian Fur Seals. New Zealand Fur Seals prefer jumbled rocky terrain and occupy colonies year-round, although most animals are present during summer.

Other names: South Australian Fur Seal, Long-nosed Fur Seal

Australian Fur Seal

Arctocephalus pusillus (south-east Australia)

Islands of Vic, Bass Strait and Tas are the stronghold of this species, although it ranges from SA to NSW and there are several haul-outs in these states. The largest colonies are at Lady Julia Percy I. and Seal Rocks (4.09) in Vic; it is also easily seen at Cape Bridgewater (4.18) and a few hang around Pope's Eye (4.04) in Port Phillip Bay. In Tas it can be seen at Hippolyte Rocks (5.05) and boat operators visit sites around the Tasman Peninsula (5.05) and Tenth I. (5.15) off the north coast. Montague I. (2.11) is the best site in NSW. Colonies are active year-round, with a peak in summer. Note that the Australian Fur Seal is regarded as a subspecies *A. p. doriferus* of the South African (Cape) Fur Seal. It often shares haul-outs with New Zealand Fur Seals, which in the field are probably best distinguished by their longer snouts.

Other names: Tasmanian, Giant, South African or Cape Fur Seal

Subantarctic Fur Seal

Arctocephalus tropicalis (subantarctic islands)

The only Subantarctic Fur Seal breeding colony in Australian territory is at Macquarie I. (9.05), where there are about 100 animals (which interbreed with Antarctic Fur Seals); it also hauls out at Heard I. (9.06). Elsewhere, the largest colonies are at Gough and Amsterdam Is., and it also occurs at Prince Edward I. and Îles Crozet. There have been more than 50 records in southern Australia from WA to NSW.

Other names: Amsterdam Fur Seal

*Australian Sea Lion

Neophoca cinerea (southern Australia)

The only eared seal endemic to Australia, this species is restricted to the western half of the continent. Approximately 85 per cent of its population is in SA, where the most accessible site is at Seal Bay on Kangaroo I. (6.13); other major colonies in SA are at Dangerous Reef and The Pages Is. (both rather inaccessible) with smaller but accessible sites at Point Labatt (6.16) and Jones I. at Baird Bay. In WA this species occurs as far north as the Houtman Abrolhos (7.12), with mainland colonies at Baxter Cliffs west of Twilight Cove (also known as Thundulda) and at the base of the Bunda Cliffs in the WA-SA border area of the Nullarbor Plain. The Australian Sea Lion is placed in a monotypic genus because of its atypically long breeding cycle: 18 months, with no synchronisation between colonies. This species prefers the sheltered side of islands and avoids the rocky headlands preferred by New Zealand Fur Seals. Stragglers have been recorded in NSW, Vic and Tas.

Other names: Hair Seal

'True' seals – Family Phocidae (world 19; Australia 5)

In the Southern Hemisphere the stronghold of the so-called 'true' seals is Antarctica, and the five species resident there visit Australian shores with varying frequency. These seals lack external ears and can't move their rear flippers independently; many have bold markings, unlike the rather homogeneous eared seals. Elephant and Leopard Seals haul up on southern shores reasonably often (they may even become more common as populations recover from the depredations of 19th-century seal hunters). If you find a beached seal report it to wildlife carers or a relevant authority; although they have limited locomotion on land do not approach too closely as all seals can bite.

Leopard Seal

Hydrurga leptonyx   (Antarctica and subantarctic islands)

This impressive carnivore is common on the pack ice of Antarctica and the Southern Ocean, where its population is estimated at 300 000. It regularly hauls out on subantarctic islands such as Heard (9.06) and Macquarie (9.05). Stragglers to Australia are relatively frequent (most reports are of juveniles, between July and November): most records are from Tas, but Leopard Seals have been recorded from southern Qld to WA, and on Lord Howe I. They usually don't stay more than a few days (local media can be a good source for news of sightings). Beached Leopard Seals should never be approached closely (even if they look dead or sick) – they are dangerous predators that will readily take dogs and have caused one human fatality in Antarctica. Bizarrely, a Leopard Seal was once recorded taking a Platypus after entering a river mouth!

Weddell Seal

Leptonychotes weddellii   (Antarctica)

An attractive seal that rarely strays far from the fast ice adjacent to the Antarctic mainland and nearby islands. It is abundant, with a world population estimated at 800 000, and sightings are more or less guaranteed in AAT (9.07). There has been one record from SA, and several from Macquarie (9.05) and Heard Is. (9.06).

Crab-eater Seal

Lobodon carcinophagus   (Antarctica)

Although it is thought to number some 10 million animals, making it one of the most abundant large mammals on earth, the Crab-eater normally lives among the ice floes of the Southern Ocean, where its movements are associated with the seasonal expansion and contraction of pack ice. It is readily seen close to the Antarctic land mass in AAT (9.07). There have been at least 20 mainland records, all from the southern states, and several from Macquarie (9.05) and Heard (9.06) Is.

Other names: White Seal

Southern Elephant Seal

Mirounga leonina (Antarctica, subantarctic islands; southern continents)
There are major colonies of this behemoth at Macquarie I. (9.05), where there are about 85 000 individuals, Heard I. (13 000), and also at Kerguelen Is. and South Georgia. On islands it favours beaches, tussock grass and inland mud wallows; it is also sometimes seen on ice floes and there is a small number at Casey Station in AAT (9.07). Elephant Seals formerly bred at King and Maatsuyker Is. in Tas, and still turn up occasionally from WA to NSW; indeed, several births have been recorded in Tas, Vic and SA. There are no real patterns of occurrence for this species in Australia and luck plays a big role in seeing one outside its normal range.

Other names: Sea Elephant

Ross's Seal

Omnatophoca rossii (Antarctica)
This is a little-known species that rarely leaves Antarctic waters and generally occurs singly among the thickest pack ice. Although it occurs in the AAT, it is not often encountered and sightings appear to be a matter of luck. Ross's Seal has been recorded once in SA and once at Heard I. (9.06).

Other names: Big-eyed Seal, Singing Seal

Dogs – Family Canidae (world 35; Australia 1)

No true canids (dogs and doglike animals) – or any other placental carnivores – ever reached Australia by natural means. Instead, their niche was filled by the incredible Thylacine, a marsupial carnivore which is often cited as a textbook case of convergent evolution: in size and general appearance it so resembled a dog that it earned the alternative epithet 'Tasmanian Wolf'. Although it is a comparatively recent arrival, the Dingo is now part of the Australian landscape and is here treated as a native mammal.

Dingo

Canis lupus dingo (mainland Australia, except densely settled areas)
Loved and loathed in equal measure, Australia's famed wild dog was introduced to the mainland by seafarers from South-East Asia about 4000 years ago. Since then it has played a commensal role in Aboriginal hunting, as well as existing as a wild pack animal in its own right. Dingoes have been implicated in the extinction of the Thylacine and other large predators on the mainland; Aboriginal rock art at many mainland sites clearly shows that the Thylacine once existed over much of the continent and the Dingo never made it to Tas, the last stronghold of the Thylacine. Dingoes are regarded as vermin by many pastoralists and a 'dog fence' measuring more than 5500 km in length has effectively capped Dingo numbers in south-east Australia. Even north of the fence 'true' Dingoes are getting scarce in some parts of their range; those on Fraser I. (1.41) are regarded as pure and are readily

seen; they are common in Kakadu NP (8.03), the Kimberley and throughout the arid zone. Pure Dingoes are handsome animals and quite variable in colour; unfortunately, you are more likely to see 'wild dogs' in various stages of hybridisation over much of Australia.

Whales and Dolphins – Order Cetacea

The last great mammalian order that occurs in Australia is the Cetacea, which gives its name to the collective term for whales and dolphins: cetaceans. These animals should need no introduction: all are marine carnivores (even if they sometimes enter fresh or brackish waters) and many are large to gigantic. This order is subdivided into the two suborders Mysticeti and Odonticeti.

Baleen whales – Suborder Mysticeti

Members of this suborder are characterised by rows of baleen – curtainlike bony plates through which they filter small fish, krill and plankton while feeding. The mysticetids include the largest animals on Earth.

Right whales – Family Balaenidae (world 3; Australia 1)

So-called because they were considered the 'right' whales to hunt, both Southern and Northern Right Whales were once close to extinction. Happily, the Southern Right Whale has started to recover and as many as 2000 visit Australian waters annually. Right whales differ from other baleen whales (rorquals) in lacking a dorsal fin and throat pleats.

Southern Right Whale

Eubalaena australis   (southern oceans)

After the Humpback Whale, the Southern Right is the commonest large whale in Australian waters. A distinctive species with obvious white callosities on the head; each animal has a unique pattern, which can aid in identifying and tracking individuals. It summers in Antarctica and migrates to southern Australia, where females give birth in shallow bays. From April to September it could be encountered virtually anywhere between Sydney and Perth. Most aggregations are between western Vic and the south-west, with exceptional records as far north as Exmouth, WA and Hervey Bay, Qld. Regular calving sites include Warrnambool (4.17) and Head of the Bight (6.19). It may also be encountered inshore sporadically on migration.

Pygmy Right Whale – Family Neobalaenidae (world 1; Australia 1)

At up to 6 m in length, this is the smallest baleen whale. It is restricted to southern waters between about 30° and 50°S, and distinguished by its high-arched jaw and exposed baleen plates (like a miniature Southern Right Whale).

Pygmy Right Whale

Caperea marginata   (southern oceans)

Little known and rarely encountered in Australian waters: the few records are mainly of strandings in the southern states, especially Tas. It is inconspicuous and usually solitary or in small loose groups, although it has been sighted associating with other cetacean species.

Rorquals – Family Balaenopteridae (world 8; Australia 8)

The term 'rorqual' is derived from the Norwegian røyrkval ('furrow whale'), which refers to the muscular longitudinal throat pleats that expand to allow these whales to swallow tonnes of water, which are then forced through bony plates (baleen) to filter out krill and baitfish. Rorquals are also known as baleen whales, although non-rorqual mysticetids also have baleen. This family includes the largest animals on Earth although some species are difficult to separate in the field; their flat head profile and presence of a dorsal fin help to identify them from right whales. Those inveterate whalers the Norwegians also gave us the words 'minke' and 'sei', and even Bryde (pronounced bru-de) was a Norwegian.

Dwarf Minke Whale

Balaenoptera acutorostrata   (southern oceans and subtropical waters)

This striking species summers and calves in subantarctic waters, migrating as far north as north Qld from December to March. In Australia it is more often seen in continental waters than Antarctic Minke Whales. A small industry centres on dive encounters with groups of these boldly marked whales at Ribbon Reefs, north of Cairns (1.01), in June and July.

Antarctic Minke Whale

Balaenoptera bonaerensis   (southern oceans)

Larger than the Dwarf Minke Whale and rarely seen as far north. Summers in Antarctica and migrates north to about 35°S in winter. It is more oceanic than the preceding species, usually remaining offshore, and in Australia it is more commonly encountered in the mid- to low latitudes, alone or in small groups.

Sei Whale

Balaenoptera borealis   (circumglobal)

A shy and fast-moving species that apparently never approaches ships, which may explain the paucity of sightings in Australian waters. Usually seen in small groups of fewer than five, this is the third-largest whale species – a very slender animal that reaches a length of 21 m. There have been records from WA, Qld, the Great Australian Bight, Bass Strait and southern Tas. It is occasionally seen in the Bonney Upwelling between November and April; and associated with oceanic fronts south of Tas.

Bryde's Whale

Balaenoptera edeni   (circumglobal)

One of the more commonly encountered rorquals (except in NT), with concentrations occurring off central WA, for example near Shark Bay, and the Great Barrier Reef. It tends to occur in waters warmer than 17°C and occasionally enters estuaries. Note that this taxon may in fact make up two species, although at present there are no distinguishing characteristics to separate them in the field. It may be attracted to baitfish concentrations.

Blue Whale

Balaenoptera musculus   (circumglobal)

This giant rorqual – the largest living mammal – reaches a length of 30 m and occurs in deep waters off south-west Vic, south-east SA and south-west WA, where most individuals are thought to be 'Pygmy' Blue Whales *B. m. brevicauda*. There are no regular cruises aimed specifically at seeing this species, but pelagic birding trips from Portland (4.16) and Port Macdonnell (6.07) occasionally encounter them at sea. The Blue Whale is most often seen in the Bonney Upwelling between November and May, but also in the Perth Canyon. A fast-moving rorqual that migrates between summer and winter breeding areas.

Omura's Whale

Balaenoptera omurai   (tropical and subtropical Asian waters)

A little known species reaching 10–12 m. Recently described and separated in the field from Bryde's Whale by a single median strip along the top of its head (Bryde's has three such strips). Chiefly known from the tropics and subtropics, there is one record of a stranded animal in SA.

Fin Whale

Balaenoptera physalus   (circumglobal)

The second largest whale species, this is a deep water whale recorded in all states except the NT. It is fast and usually seen alone or in small groups; its large dorsal fin is a useful identification feature. Also recorded in the Bonney Upwelling and Perth Canyon.

Humpback Whale

Megaptera novaeangliae   (circumglobal)

The commonest large whale in Australian waters, visiting west coastal waters north to The Kimberley and the east coast at least north to Cairns. They migrate annually from Antarctica to spend winter (May-Oct) in Australian waters; some 17 000 follow the eastern seaboard and as many as 29 000 the west coast. A large (and growing) whale-watching industry has developed around this species; sightings are now well documented just about everywhere it occurs. Females calve in warm, sheltered areas such as Hervey Bay, inshore of the Reef proper and at Camden Sound in the Kimberley. Dozens of whale-watching cruises operate out of centres such as Eden (2.12), Byron Bay (2.21), Southport

(1.36), Hervey Bay (1.40) on the eastern seaboard and Albany (7.09), Perth (7.01) and Geraldton on the western. There are many others and all virtually guarantee close up views at peak migration season. Best results are during the migration proper, when Humpbacks can be very active crowd pleasers, breaching, fin-slapping and approaching boats for stellar photo opportunities. In truth it is hard to miss them at the right time of year: a sea watch from any major headland in WA, NSW or sthn Qld will almost guarantee sightings. Good places to start looking include Point Lookout (1.35), Green Cape in southern NSW and Cape Byron (2.21). Humpbacks are readily identified in the field by their dorsal fin and long flippers; close up, you may be able to discern barnacle infestations on the head and fins in patterns that help identify individual animals.

Toothed whales – Suborder Odontoceti

All members of this suborder are characterised by having teeth in their lower jaw, asymmetrical skulls adapted for echolocation and a fatty melon. Many eat fish and squid, and the Killer Whale is famous for hunting other cetaceans and pinnipeds.

Sperm Whale – Family Physeteridae (world 1; Australia 1)

The sole member of its family, the Sperm Whale is the largest of the toothed whales: males can reach 18 m in length and females 2–3 m less than that. This species preys on deep-dwelling cephalopods, including the fabled giant squid.

Sperm Whale

Physeter macrocephalus (circumglobal)

A distinctive species when seen well, with a large, square head, forward-angled blow, small dorsal fin and distinctive dive pattern. It occurs in all Australian and subantarctic waters and herds seem to concentrate where the seabed rises steeply from great depths. Such conditions occur in the Perth Canyon, south-west of Kangaroo I., along the south and west coasts of Tas, Eden (2.12) and off North Stradbroke I. (1.35). Although it is rarely seen from shore, this is the second most frequently stranded cetacean in Tas.

Pygmy sperm whales – Family Kogiidae (world 2; Australia 2)

The two species of pygmy sperm whale are among the smallest of the true whales. Encounters are uncommon although they may escape detection in all but the smallest seas owing to their size, often solitary nature and habit of diving without a splash or roll. Both species 'log' in the water with only the back of their heads exposed, tail hanging down, and defecate when alarmed, leaving a dark cloud in the water that may act as a 'smokescreen' while they dive. Both are very similar in appearance and even stranded specimens can be misidentified.

Pygmy Sperm Whale

Kogia breviceps   (tropical and temperate seas)

Uncommon and usually seen offshore, close to the continental slope. Most Australian records have been of individuals or small groups in south-eastern waters. Strandings have occurred in all states. A slow-moving species that dives to great depths and feeds on crustaceans.

Dwarf Sperm Whale

Kogia sima   (tropical and temperate seas)

Occurs mostly in deep subtropical and temperate waters; strandings have occurred in the NT, WA, SA, Tas and NSW. It is rarely encountered, difficult to observe and is usually solitary, although mother–calf pairs and small groups have been recorded. The prominent dorsal fin of this species helps to identify it from the Pygmy Sperm Whale.

Beaked whales – Family Ziphiidae (world 21; Australia 12)

In Australia nearly all members of this family are rare or uncommon, though strandings indicate that some may be relatively abundant in places. Encounters are infrequent and unpredictable. There is much to be learned about their behaviour and movements in Australian waters. Most are deep water species thought to feed mainly on squid. They tend to avoid boats and can dive for long periods, spending little time at the surface. Most encounters at sea are beyond the continental shelf, well away from the coast, but even these are rare. Several species are known mainly from strandings and tooth shape is an important identification feature. Some genera have only one pair of teeth (females lack teeth altogether), which are thought to be used by males in fighting; many stranded animals show heavy scarring.

Arnoux's Beaked Whale

Berardius arnouxii   (temperate and subpolar southern oceans)

The largest beaked whale, reaching a length of 9.8 m. This is an animal of deep, cold waters, typically seen in herds of 6–10. It is shy and there have been few observations of live animals in Australia; it has possibly been seen off SA and southern NSW. Strandings usually occur in summer and have been recorded in southern WA, SA and Tas.

Southern Bottlenose Whale

Hyperoodon planifrons   (temperate and polar southern waters)

Occurs mostly below 30°S in deep oceanic waters as far south as the pack ice, typically in small herds; breaches. Strandings have been recorded in southern states.

Tropical Bottlenose Whale

Indopacetus pacificus   (tropical Pacific and Indian oceans)

Similar to the preceding species and in Australia known from only one stranding. A pelagic species that travels in tight pods, usually of 5–20 individuals, in deep waters beyond the continental shelf.

Other names: Longman's Beaked Whale

Andrews' Beaked Whale

Mesoplodon bowdoini   (southern temperate waters)

At less than 5 m in length, this is one of the smallest beaked whales. It is rarely seen at sea and approaches the coast only where the continental shelf narrows or in the vicinity of underwater canyons. There have been more than a dozen strandings in Australia, with records from southern WA, SA, Vic and NSW. It is presumed to be a deep water species that avoids boats.

Blainville's Beaked Whale

Mesoplodon densirostris   (tropical and temperate seas)

A deep water species, usually seen in small groups, thought to reach higher latitudes with warm currents. It is inconspicuous and wary, although it has been sighted off Point Lookout (1.35). Strandings have occurred in all Australian states except SA and the NT, with no apparent pattern.

Gingko-toothed Beaked Whale

Mesoplodon gingkodens   (cool temperate to tropical waters)

No confirmed sightings of live animals at sea. Known in Australia only from four strandings: three in NSW and one in western Vic. Males have teeth that resemble leaves of the gingko tree of China, which are thought to be used for fighting.

Gray's Beaked Whale

Mesoplodon grayi   (mid- to high latitudes of southern oceans)

After the Strap-toothed Beaked Whale, this species gets stranded more often than any other beaked whale in Australia. It is rarely seen at sea, but strandings have occurred in all southern states, usually between December and April, and often in groups – one event included 28 specimens. Gray's is a gregarious species that seems to spend more time at the surface than other beaked whales. It has been known to breach and even to porpoise when travelling at speed.

Hector's Beaked Whale

Mesoplodon hectori   (cool temperate southern waters)

One of the smallest beaked whales and in Australia known only from strandings in WA, SA and Tas. Males have a single, flattened tooth.

Strap-toothed Beaked Whale

Mesoplodon layardii   (mid-latitudes of the Southern Hemisphere)

This is the most commonly stranded beaked whale in Australia, with strandings in all states except NT. Most events have occurred December–March along east and southern coasts. Shy of boats, it rolls on its side and shows a flipper before diving. Look for its distinctive markings and beak as it surfaces.

True's Beaked Whale

Mesoplodon mirus   (cool temperate waters)

Shy; difficult to approach and positively identify at sea. In Australia known only from strandings, which have occurred in WA, Vic and Tas.

Shepherd's Beaked Whale

Tasmacetus shepherdi   (mid- to low latitudes of the Southern Hemisphere)

A little-known species that hit the media in 2012 when a herd was filmed in Bass Strait; it was subsequently seen in Vic also. Otherwise known from only a few strandings in WA and SA.

Cuvier's Beaked Whale

Ziphius cavirostris   (temperate to tropical seas)

Mostly occurs in waters greater than 100 m in depth. Strandings have been recorded from all maritime states including the NT. Generally inconspicuous but approaches boats at times, alone or in groups of up to 15. If seen well can generally be identified by stubby beak (giving it its alternative name), pale head and exposed teeth (of males).

Other names: Goose-beaked Whale

Dolphins, blackfish and Killer Whale – Family Delphinidae (world 36; Australia 21)

This family includes the familiar dolphins, as well as the Killer Whale (Orca) – the world's largest dolphin – and the so-called 'blackfish': small, toothed whales that are mainly black in coloration and tricky to identify in the field. There are few real 'sites' for seeing these animals, yet several species could be encountered on ferry crossings, in large bays, feeding outside breakers at surf beaches and on pelagic birdwatching trips.

Short-beaked Common Dolphin

Delphinus delphis   (tropical to temperate waters)

Very common, sometimes in large schools, both inshore and offshore. An active, appealing species that often rides bow waves and leaps alongside vessels. Its 'hourglass' pattern on the flanks, coloured cream, yellow or pale orange in front of the dorsal fin, is diagnostic (although it is most obvious in good light). Common Dolphins could be seen on any sea voyage around the entire coast, for example on ferry crossings and pelagic birding trips. Groups of 20–30 are common, but aggregations of thousands are not unknown. This species is frequently stranded.

Pygmy Killer Whale

Feresa attenuata   (tropical and subtropical oceans)

A small (less than 3 m in length) inhabitant of deep water south to about 35°S. Slow moving, rarely seen and probably difficult to spot in big seas. Exposes its entire head when breaching, showing white lips. Travels in groups of 12–50; frequently spy-hops, leaps, tail slaps and logs.

Short-flippered Pilot Whale

Globicephala macrorhynchus (tropical and subtropical oceans)

The two species of pilot whale are relatively common. The Short-flippered is mostly seen north of 30°S (rarely to 40°S), both coastally and offshore. It overlaps in range with the Long-flippered Pilot Whale in the southern part of its distribution and the two are hard to separate at sea. Typically seen in pods of 20–40 and subject to strandings.

Other names: Short-flippered Pilot Whale

Long-flippered Pilot Whale

Globicephala melas (subtropical and temperate seas)

The pilot whale most likely to be seen in temperate and cooler, especially deep, waters. A gregarious species with a bulbous melon; some animals have a whitish saddle and line behind the eye. Common near the shelf edge in southern Australia and at the subantarctic convergence in summer. Travels in pods of 10–50, sometimes in thousands, and one of the most frequently stranded whales in Australia, particularly in Tas.

Other names: Long-flippered Pilot Whale

Risso's Dolphin

Grampus griseus (tropical and temperate oceans)

An active species that often associates with other cetaceans. Usually seen in pods of 4–25, although hundreds may aggregate, at the outer shelf and near sea mounts, chiefly in warmer waters. Encountered relatively frequently off Sydney (Chapter 10) on pelagic birding trips; reputedly common inshore near Fraser I. (1.41) and known from seas near Wollongong and Eden NSW in waters 120 to more than 1000 m deep.

Fraser's Dolphin

Lagenodelphis hosei (tropical and subtropical oceans)

A fast, high-leaping species of warm seas, usually seen in deep water or where there is a steeply sloping shelf near islands. Often encountered in large pods (hundreds or even thousands) and occasionally rides bow waves. Recorded with other cetaceans, such as Melon-headed, Sperm and False Killer Whales.

Dusky Dolphin

Lagenodelphis obscurus (southern oceans)

Usually encountered south of 26°S and rarely recorded in Australia, with sporadic records from Bass Strait, southern Tas and Kangaroo I., all in summer.

Hourglass Dolphin

Lagenorhynchus cruciger   (Antarctic and subantarctic waters)
A small, beautifully marked dolphin of cool southern oceans. Usually seen far from land in pods of 8–10. Easily identified by its black-and-white hourglass pattern, this is an active species that leaps frequently and often associates with Long-flippered Pilot Whales, Southern Right Whales and Fin Whales.

Southern Rightwhale Dolphin

Lissodelphis peroni   (colder southern oceans)
Another southern cold water species, so-called because it lacks a dorsal fin, like a right whale. Usually seen between 30 and 65°S in deep seas. Fast and highly gregarious, often seen in large groups, actively leaping and lob-tailing (occasionally rides bow waves). Associates with pilot whales, Common Bottlenose and Dusky Dolphins. Few Australian records, mainly in Tas, WA and the Great Australian Bight.

*Australian Snubfin Dolphin

Orcaella heinsohni   (tropical and subtropical waters)
An inshore specialist, found in shallow coastal waters, mangrove-lined estuaries and large river mouths. Found in similar habitat to Indo-Pacific Humpback Dolphin. Slow moving, often in pods of 5–21 animals. Occurs in the Brisbane River (1.33) and in Roebuck Bay near Broome (7.20).

Killer Whale

Orcinus orca   (pan-oceanic)
Most common outside of the tropics, especially in cold waters; recorded off all maritime states except NT but not well known in Australia. Unmistakable if seen well. Unpredictable in occurrence, but most common near areas with high whale densities and near seal colonies. Most records are from the continental shelf in south-east Australia, Macquarie I. (9.05) and AAT (9.07). Not uncommonly seen near Eden (2.12), where Killer Whales once cooperated with whalers by herding Humpback Whales to slaughter. Most often seen in small groups, but may also be solitary or in aggregations of up to 100.

Other names: Orca

Melon-headed Whale

Peponocephala electra   (tropical and subtropical seas)
Another small, highly gregarious blackfish, typically encountered in warm, deep open sea. Distinguished from Pygmy Killer Whale by its bulbous melon and taller dorsal fin. A fast swimmer that makes short, low jumps and may aggregate in herds of hundreds or even thousands. Known to associate with Spotted, Spinner and Fraser's Dolphins.

False Killer Whale

Pseudorca crassidens (tropical and temperate waters)

A large, fast blackfish ((up to 6 m) with a cigar-shaped body and distinctive flipper shape. Gregarious, travelling in herds of 20–50, rarely in hundreds; most herds are seen May–September. Strandings have occurred in all states and in all months. Swims with mouth open showing large, conical teeth. Associates with Bottlenose Dolphins; bow rides and makes spectacular leaps.

Indo-Pacific Humpback Dolphin

Sousa sahulensis (tropical and subtropical waters)

An inshore species usually seen in small groups in coastal waters of less than 20 m depth, such as estuaries and shallow reefs. Disjunct populations occur along the northern coastline between south-east Qld and north-west Australia. It is shy but has a distinctive diving profile; Australian animals have a less well-developed hump and have recently been recognised as a distinct species. Generally fairly easy to see at North Stradbroke I. (1.35), in Darwin Harbour (8.01) and near Broome (7.20).

Pantropical Spotted Dolphin

Stenella attenuata (tropical and subtropical oceans)

Colour and dorsal fin shape are diagnostic in this species, although Australian specimens tend not to be heavily spotted until they age. Pantropical Spotted Dolphins are acrobatic, leaping and bow-riding, and may occur in huge herds of hundreds or even thousands. Most often seen at the outer shelf in waters of 25°C or more.

Striped Dolphin

Stenella coeruleoalba (tropical and subtropical oceans)

A short-beaked, distinctively marked species with a tall dorsal fin, pronounced forehead and striped markings. Little known in Australia, it is oceanic, most often seen near the shelf slope and possibly feeds at night.

Spinner Dolphin

Stenella longirostris (tropical and subtropical oceans)

A small, graceful species that makes spectacular leaps during which it spins longitudinally. Its long beak, spinning behaviour and striped pattern should be diagnostic. Frequently bow rides and occurs in large herds, mainly in deep water near the shelf slope, remote atolls and sea mounts. Both the 'Dwarf Spinner Dolphin' and long-beaked forms occur in north-western waters off the Kimberley.

Rough-toothed Dolphin

Steno bredanensis (tropical and subtropical oceans)

Known from only a few records in northern Australia, typically in deep water beyond the continental shelf where the surface temperature exceeds 25°C. Occurs in herds of 20–50, often associated with floating debris, dolphin fish (on which it feeds), and pilot whales and other dolphin species.

Long-beaked Bottlenose Dolphin

Tursiops aduncus   (tropical and subtropical Indian and Pacific Oceans)
The most common inshore dolphin species, encountered year-round off beaches, in estuaries and near reefs. There are resident populations at Shark Bay (7.15) and Port Stephens (2.19), where dolphin-watching activities are well developed and you should have no trouble seeing them. Note that it is similar in appearance to the Offshore Bottlenose Dolphin, which may also visit inshore waters (though rarely); the Long-beaked is smaller but they are difficult to separate at sea.

Other names: Indo-Pacific Bottlenose Dolphin

Offshore Bottlenose Dolphin

Tursiops truncatus   (tropical and temperate oceans)
Another common species, especially around southern shores, although it occurs in every state. Usually found in deeper water than the preceding species, as far as the shelf. Feeds around rocky reefs, larger than than Long-beaked Bottlenose Dolphin and more likely to bow-ride than it. Groups usually number up to 30 but may be as large as 100. Note that a localised population in Port Phillip Bay and nearby Vic waters has been proposed as a new species, the Burrunan Dolphin *Tursiops australis*. However, this classification has not been universally accepted.

Porpoises – Family Phocoenidae (world 6; Australia 1)

Although 'porpoise' and 'dolphin' are sometimes used interchangeably, 'porpoise' technically refers to small, stocky toothed cetaceans that lack a beak. Most species are found in the northern hemisphere and only one, the Spectacled Porpoise, has been recorded in Australian waters.

Spectacled Porpoise

Phocoena dioptrica   (subantarctic waters)
This small species is usually restricted to subantarctic and Antarctic waters. In Australia it is known from only two strandings, one in SA and one in Tas, possibly associated with unusually cold currents at the time. If seen well it should be unmistakable, with black lips, blunt snout, small rounded flippers and a tall, more or less triangular dorsal fin.

Appendix A: Introduced mammals

Since white settlement 23 species of exotic mammal have become established in the wild in Australia. Some were deliberate introductions: Foxes and deer were released for sport, Rabbits for food. Some were unwanted anywhere, such as rats and the House Mouse; another wave of exotics, descended from domestic stock, has more recently become established in the Outback and northern Australia. The effects of introduced species in Australia have rarely been beneficial to native wildlife or vegetation; in some cases they have been disastrous and the combination of exotic predators and introduced herbivorous competitors, such as Rabbits and Sheep, spelt extinction for many Australian mammals after white settlement in 1789.

The Dingo is treated as a native animal in the Mammal-finding Guide (see p. 360), but all other established exotic species are listed here. Unlike birdwatching, there are no rules for whether or not you should count introduced mammals as part of your Australian mammal list – they certainly won't be going away. According to birdwatchers, if a population has been self-sustaining in the wild for at least 10 years it can be 'counted'. All 23 exotic mammal species fall into the 10-year category, but to many Australians 'ticking' introduced mammals would be anathema on account of the great damage most cause to the natural environment. Some species are undoubtedly attractive, even difficult to see in their natural environment (e.g. Bali Banteng), but it would be hard to get enthusiastic about a feral moggie. Nearly all the introduced species are easy to see, even during the day; indeed, some may be the only mammals you'll see in certain areas. Ironically, the domestic Sheep, source of much of Australia's wealth and cause of incalculable environmental damage, probably could not survive in the wild without human care.

House Mouse *Mus musculus* **(accidental introduction)** Common near human habitation throughout the continent, sometimes reaching plague proportions in rural areas.

Polynesian Rat *Rattus exulans* **(possible deliberate introduction)** Recorded from Adele I. in the Kimberley and Murray Is. in Torres Strait, where it was possibly left behind by seafarers.

Brown Rat *Rattus norvegicus* **(accidental introduction)** Established near coastal towns and cities.

Black Rat *Rattus rattus* **(accidental introduction)** Established on the eastern seaboard, in the south-west, Tas and near tropical settlements. More widespread than the Brown Rat.

Five-lined Palm Squirrel *Funambulus pennanti* **(deliberate introduction)** Feral at Perth Zoo, where it was introduced 'to add colour', and nearby suburbs.

Feral Dog *Canis familiaris* **(descended from domestic animals)** Domestic and farm dogs have run wild in the High Country, deserts and mallee, among other areas, where they often hybridise with Dingoes. Packs have become a nuisance to livestock, native animals such as Koalas and people in some areas.

Red Fox *Vulpes vulpes* **(deliberate introduction)** Common throughout the continent outside the tropics, irrupting into arid areas in good years. This species has recently been discovered in Tas, where it was possibly introduced deliberately.

Feral Cat *Felis catus* **(descended from domestic animals)** Common to abundant throughout the continent.

Feral Donkey *Equus asinus* **(descended from domestic stock)** Herds survive in parts of the inland and tropics.

Feral Horse *Equus caballus* **(descended from domestic stock)** Feral herds survive in parts of the inland, tropics and High Country; often known as the Brumby.

Swamp Buffalo *Bubalus bubalus* **(descended from domestic stock)** Floodplains of the Top End; some can usually be seen in Kakadu NP (8.03) and the Mary River regions. Buffaloes have blue eyeshine when spotlighted.

Feral Goat *Capra hircus* **(descended from domestic stock)** A common pest in some areas but absent from large parts of the continent. Feral Goats are being controlled in some reserves where herds cause widespread damage, such as Flinders Ranges NP.

Banteng *Bos javanicus* **(descended from domestic stock)** These handsome wild cattle were introduced to the Top End in 1849, but persist only on the Cobourg Peninsula, where they are protected and form the largest extant herd in the world.

One-humped Camel *Camelus dromedarius* **(descended from domestic stock)** Herds roam the arid inland and have become abundant in some areas, such as the Great Victoria Desert.

Chital *Cervus axis* **(deliberate introduction)** These handsome cervids (also known as Axis Deer) are resident at Maryvale Creek, 170 km west of Townsville, Qld.

Common Fallow Deer *Cervus dama* **(deliberate introduction)** Wild herds are established in scattered areas between south-east SA and SE Qld; common in central Tas and near Canberra, ACT.

Western Red Deer *Cervus elaphus* **(deliberate introduction)** Probably most easily seen at Cumberland Dam near Toowoomba (1.38) – this deer appears on Qld's coat of arms – and there are herds in the Grampians (Gariwerd) NP (4.21).

Hog Deer *Cervus porcinus* **(deliberate introduction)** Easily seen around the campground at Wilson's Promontory NP (4.24) and in the Gippsland Lakes area (4.28) of eastern Vic, for example at Rotamah I.

Javan Deer (Rusa) *Cervus timorensis* **(deliberate introduction)** The subspecies *C. t. russa* is established in Royal NP (2.02) near Sydney and something of a menace to traffic near Wollongong (2.05). The subspecies *C. t. moluccensis* has become self-established on Saibai I. (1.18).

Sambar *Cervus unicolor* **(deliberate introduction)** Becoming a pest in parts of the NSW High Country and in north-eastern Vic.

Feral Pig *Sus scrofa* **(descended from domestic stock)** Unfortunately common over eastern and northern Australia; these destructive omnivores cause much damage to vegetation and wildlife alike.

Brown Hare *Lepus capensis* **(deliberate introduction)** Common in the south-east, though nowhere as common as European Rabbit.

European Rabbit *Oryctolagus cuniculus* **(deliberate introduction)** Common over the southern half of the continent, depending on season. Introduced for sport and food, the Rabbit has proliferated and spread until it has become one of Australia's greatest environmental disasters, overgrazing vegetation and causing widespread erosion.

Appendix B: Directory

PLANNING YOUR TRIP

High on any wildlife enthusiast's list would be to see several of the groups that make Australia's mammal fauna so distinctive, such as the Platypus, Koala, various kangaroos and Common Wombat (boxed texts list good sites for these sought-after species in each state or territory). Most of these iconic species are readily seen in the appropriate habitat in south-eastern Australia a short distance from, or even within, large cities such as Brisbane, Sydney and Melbourne. Most international travellers will end up in these major centres at some point and all have good sites for watching mammals (and other wildlife) only a few hours' drive away.

Seeing more than a few common species will require a bit of planning because the vast majority of Australian mammals are nocturnal or crepuscular. If your goal is to see as many mammals as possible, the main areas to concentrate on are north Qld (especially the Wet Tropics and Iron Range area of Cape York Peninsula), the island state of Tas, south-western Australia and the Top End of the NT; if time and money are no object, then north-western Australia could be added to this list. Concentrating on these sites will ensure you the greatest number and variety of species. If you have time to visit only one or two sites, then make sure you take in either the Wet Tropics or Tas – ideally both. They are a long way apart, but by driving the eastern seaboard you can also visit many other good sites where particular species can be seen (this would be feasible over, say, 3–4 weeks, and even more so if you fly Cairns–Brisbane–Sydney or Melbourne–Tas and hire a vehicle at each centre to visit local sites).

Travel further afield from these main concentrations of mammals is expensive, time-consuming and will yield proportionally fewer results (however, if you also wish to see other wildlife, such as birds, or visit scenic sites, many other areas are *definitely* worth visiting). Many of the most common species have a wide distribution and travelling to remote corners, such as the Pilbara, will need a lot of extra time and money with no guarantee of seeing extra species unless you are part of a survey or scientific expedition.

A plethora of cruise operators on the east and west coasts gear up for the annual Humpback Whale migration (June–October), and numerous dolphin-watching trips operate from various ports; several are listed later in this chapter. Otherwise, pelagic birding trips are a good way to watch cetaceans in Australian waters; Chapter 10 describes the various options, most of which run monthly more or less year-round, subject to weather conditions.

Those with more specialised requirements, such as bat enthusiasts, will have to team up with local experts to take part in trapping nights or surveys (members of the Australasian Bat Society in particular welcome interested amateurs; visit www. ausbats.org.au for contact details). Volunteering as part of a university team is another good way to get up close and personal with hard-to-see species; check university websites to see who's researching what or join the Australian Mammal Society (www.australianmammals.org.au) to establish some local contacts. Be aware though that researchers are usually looking for a commitment of a week or even several weeks from volunteers; field conditions can be basic but the rewards potentially immense.

TIMING

With some exceptions, there is no real mammal-watching season, other than that dictated by prevailing weather conditions. For example, the wet season in northern Australia can curtail travel and wildlife-watching; deserts are best avoided in summer; and southern winters can be cold and wet. Most mammals that can be easily seen, such as kangaroos, will be seen in all seasons (although unusually hot, dry or cold conditions may limit viewing); others will be difficult to see regardless of weather conditions. The main exception is migratory whales, which visit Australian waters between April and October. Some dasyurids (marsupial carnivores) may be easier to see during the breeding season, when males are hyperactive and may be active during the day; and some microbats migrate between maternity roosts and non-breeding sites. As with just about anywhere in the world, the lead-up to breeding and the breeding season itself are the best times to be looking for most wildlife.

AIR TRAVEL

Australia is well served by international air routes from all continents. The main international hubs are Sydney, Melbourne, Brisbane, Cairns, Darwin and Perth; the only international connections from Hobart (Tas) are to New Zealand. If your visit is mammal-specific and/or time-limited, consider entering Australia through Cairns or Darwin; Melbourne is the closest hub to Hobart (capital of Tas), but there are also direct flights there from Sydney. Check if your international ticket allows stopovers in more than one capital (for example, arriving in Perth and departing from Sydney), as flying is the preferred mode of travel between state capitals if time is limited. Otherwise, by travelling outside of school holidays and during the week, you could pick up some good-value airfares online between major centres. The key ones to look out for are between Perth and the east coast, between southern cities and Cairns, and to Tas. Qantas is the national carrier but rarely offers bargain fares. Better value is often to be had with Virgin, its main competitor on major routes, JetStar, which is Qantas's budget arm, and Tiger Airways, which periodically offers great bargains. Qantas is the main carrier to many rural and Outback centres; travel by air to these places is usually expensive.

GETTING AROUND

On the ground, a vehicle will be essential for visiting all but inner urban locations in large cities. A regular (2WD) car will be fine for travel over most of the eastern seaboard, south-east corner, Tas and the south-west. A four-wheel drive (4WD) is desirable for Kakadu NP, and essential for visiting Cape York Peninsula, Fraser I., the Kimberley, Pilbara and the central deserts (with the exception of Uluru-Kata Tjuta NP (Ayers Rock), for which 2WD is fine). SUVs are popular city vehicles in Australia and are fine for most Outback driving; however, they are *not* suitable for travelling in the Kimberley or on Cape York Peninsula, where a long wheel base vehicle, such as a LandCruiser, is essential. In any remote area, it is essential that you are properly equipped, with adequate water (allow at least 2 L per person per day just for drinking), spare tyres (at least two), a working radio, distress beacon (EPIRB or similar) and GPS at the least. Even in the 21st century, people get lost and die in remote areas through inadequate preparation.

Vehicle hire is available in all capital cities and the main rental agencies usually have offices in major rural centres as well. Two-wheel drives can be very cheap to hire and usually come with unlimited kilometres if hired on the east coast or in Tas. Vehicle hire in the south-west, Kimberley and Top End usually comes loaded with a charge per kilometre, exorbitant insurance and a raft of regulations. Pay attention to the fine print, because if anything goes wrong and you are liable, you could end up paying a lot of money. For long stays and overland exploration, a feasible option may be to buy a second-hand vehicle in (say) Darwin, drive it to Perth, taking in the sites en route, then selling it at your destination. Given the high cost of hiring a 4WD for an extended trip to the Kimberley, this could be an option worth investigating.

Campervans are also a good way to get around, and give you the freedom of self-driving without the need to stop at a town or motel every night. The major centres for campervan hire are in northern Australia (for example, Darwin, Broome and Cairns) and Alice Springs. They come in many shapes and sizes, from Winnebago-style to 4WD versions suitable for travel in the Kimberley and Cape York Peninsula. These are an excellent way to explore remote areas; no special licence is necessary, but be aware of road and weather conditions, take out adequate insurance and read the fine print on your rental contract – an accident would be inconvenient at the very least and tourists often come to grief on unsurfaced roads. If travelling to a remote area, such as the central deserts, always advise someone in a position of authority (such as the police station at the last town before you strike out into the wilderness) where you are going and when you intend to return.

Australia has numerous road hazards that won't be encountered in other countries. First, there's a long list of large animals with which a collision is possible, including kangaroos, feral and domestic stock, wild Camels, and Emus and Cassowaries (large, flightless birds). Driving after dark is not advisable if you have a long way to travel, as kangaroos in particular can be abundant; collisions can cause a lot of damage and serious injury to drivers or passengers. If you are stranded in a remote area it could be a while before help arrives. There's also a risk of collision with smaller animals, such as wombats, wallabies, Koalas and possums, with usually fatal consequences for the animal.

Driver fatigue is another killer. Travel away from the densely populated south-east can mean long drives on straight roads through often featureless landscapes. Stop for regular breaks (carry a hot drink in a thermos as it can be a long way between roadhouses) or pull over for a power nap. Standards vary, but in the south-east there are many driver rest areas with toilets and picnic shelters; these are rarer in the Outback but in general it's safe to pull over on any suitable stretch of road. Roadhouses in remote areas usually have 24-hour diners, showers and basic accommodation.

On major outback routes watch out for road trains – large trucks towing an extra trailer or two; they build up considerable speed and require plenty of time to slow down. Most road train drivers are skilled and considerate, but allow plenty of space when overtaking as they are longer than they look. Highways can vary from new dual carriageways in the south-east to barely serviceable, crumbling blacktop in remote areas, to rutted tracks in south-west Qld, the Kimberley and much of the Outback. Some major outback routes, often covering hundreds of kilometres, may be impassable after rain. These include the Kimberley's Gibb River Road (do *not* attempt this after rain), and the Tanami, Strzelecki, Birdsville and Oodnadatta Tracks (4WD only). Others, such as the Canning Stock Route, require a properly equipped 4WD expedition, preferably in convoy, to tackle rolling desert dunes in some of the remotest country on Earth.

ACCOMMODATION

Every type of accommodation is available for travellers. Camping is the cheapest option and often preferred by independent travellers. Many national parks allow bush camping at basic 'carry-in, carry-out' sites; others, such as Kakadu and Wilson's Promontory, have first-class facilities, with barbecues, flush toilets and hot showers. Bookings for popular campgrounds are essential in peak holiday season but prices are very reasonable.

Cheap non-camping options include backpackers' lodges, which often offer single or double rooms as well as dorms, and older-style country hotels (usually with a public bar downstairs), where rooms can be as little as $50 a night including breakfast; self-contained cabins at caravan parks or holiday parks can also be excellent value.

Roadhouses on long-haul outback routes usually offer cheap rooms (in prefabricated structures called demountables or 'dongers') with communal showers and toilets. There are various 'ecolodges' around the country, although 'eco' could mean anything from recycled water to a genuine wildlife experience. Some recommended ones are listed later in this section. Several high-end wilderness camps try to replicate the African safari experience; these can be pleasant places to stay but they don't necessarily guarantee better wildlife-watching than cheaper, more accessible locations. Don't hesitate to contact them and ask what wildlife can be seen – some probably won't know, while others may have a competent guide stationed there permanently.

CLIMATE

Sun and heat have played a huge role in shaping Australia's natural environment. As a general rule, it is hot all over in summer (December–March) – hot and wet in the north, very hot in the centre and hot with periodic cool changes in the south. It is generally inadvisable to travel in the central deserts during summer owing to excessive temperatures. While the thought of constant sunshine might be appealing, Australians have an off-the-scale rate of skin cancer: make sure you cover up with a wide-brimmed hat and wear sunscreen – it is possible to get sunburnt even on cold winter days if the sun is out. Take particular care in exposed situations such as beaches, on boats, in snowfields and deserts. And drink plenty of water – 2 L a day is the recommended intake under normal conditions, not including tea and coffee.

Northern Australia is tropical and subject to a prolonged wet season (often called simply 'the Wet') that may last from December to April (although its duration varies from year to year). The Wet features high humidity, heavy rain, flooding that can cut off towns and roads for days on end, and, in most years, violent cyclones that cause high seas, widespread damage and sometimes loss of life. Trying to watch anything during a cyclone is pointless, but more seriously travel can be impeded by swollen rivers, muddy roads and washed-out bridges. Northern Australia is generally best avoided during these times. The dry season in northern Australia (usually June–October) and in the Centre features very pleasant temperatures and is the best time to travel in these parts of the country (although it can get surprisingly cool at night). These months correspond to winter in southern Australia, when it can get very cold and wet; large, common mammals remain active (hibernation is almost unknown in Australian mammals), but conditions may impede mammal-watching in general. As in most countries, 'spring' (September–November) is probably the optimal time for watching mammals in the south. Perth, Adelaide and Melbourne have a pleasant Mediterranean climate, with cool, wet winters and hot summers. Sydney and Brisbane are subtropical, with higher humidity and rainfall. Canberra is the only capital that experiences truly cold winters, with subzero temperatures at night, freezing fogs and sleet. The New England Tableland in northern NSW has a similar climate, and the so-called High Country is blanketed in snow for a few months every year.

NATURAL HAZARDS

Australia's much-vaunted dangerous wildlife is not as bad as it sounds. The main exception is the Saltwater Crocodile *Crocodylus porosus*, which occurs around the entire northern coastline from about the Mary River, Qld to the Kimberley in WA, and hundreds of kilometres inland on major rivers and wetlands. These animals are extremely dangerous and people often get killed by them, usually when they are standing in or near the water's edge. Always heed croc warning signs and in the tropics it's best to assume crocs are present even where there are no signs. Australia's other crocodile species, the Freshwater or Johnstone's Crocodile *C. johnstonei* is shy and regarded as harmless, but it's probably not a good idea to swim near large specimens. Shark attacks also occur most years – this won't be of concern to most mammal-watchers, unless you plan to dive near seal colonies, and it doesn't stop thousands of Aussies hitting the waves every day. You should also be aware of several forms of venomous marine life, some of which can deliver a lethal dose. They include the Box Jellyfish *Chironex fleckeri* of inshore tropical waters and present during the wet season; do not enter coastal waters between Rockhampton, Qld and Broome, WA during the wet season without adequate protective gear (though it is safe to swim in waters surrounding the Great Barrier Reef and other offshore reef systems). When walking over exposed reefs at low tide always wear appropriate footwear, as there are several well-camouflaged sea creatures that can inflict a potentially lethal bite or sting; coral itself can cause serious cuts and abrasions.

There are numerous dangerous snake species, some of which are quite common, but they are generally unobtrusive and retiring. If you come across any snake of whose identity you are uncertain, back away and it will most likely also beat a retreat. The various species of death adder are exceptions – they tend to remain motionless on the ground, relying on camouflage to ambush prey and if stepped on accidentally can deliver a serious bite. It goes without saying that you should always wear sensible footwear when walking in the bush, especially at night. Funnel-web spiders are aggressive spiders, fortunately restricted to sandstone country near Sydney and the subtropical coasts of NSW and south-east Qld; they are usually sedentary, but males wander in search of females and this is when most people get bitten by them. The other dangerous spider, the Red-backed Spider, is very common around old buildings and rubbish, especially among rusted metal sheets and barrels; however, it is extremely retiring and it is difficult to get bitten by one. Antivenenes are available for all dangerous snake species as well as the two dangerous spiders.

You will almost certainly come in contact with nuisance species, such as ticks and mosquitoes, some of which have the potential to spread debilitating disease. Ticks are common along the eastern seaboard and parts of tropical Australia. Bites can transmit scrub typhus and Lyme disease; one species may cause paralysis in children, domestic pets and livestock. Always check for ticks after walking in long grass; they can be removed with tweezers. Mosquitoes occur year-round everywhere except in the very coldest and driest locations; they are most abundant in the tropics. Several mosquito-borne viruses occur in Australia, including Ross River fever, dengue fever and encephalitis. With mozzies prevention is better than cure – make sure you cover up, wear long trousers and a long-sleeved shirt, especially at night, in areas where they are common. Cover any exposed skin with insect repellent; DEET-based creams seem to work best. Leeches are the other common nuisance animals; fortunately they occur only on the east coast and don't spread any disease. They are most common in tropical and subtropical rainforests, especially in wet conditions. Their bite is painless and they can be removed by applying a lighted match, by rubbing salt on them or by giving them a powerful flick of the finger (they are extremely difficult to dislodge if you try to pull them off). If you can keep it dry, carry a shaker of salt with you when walking through wet forests where leeches may be common.

Of particular note to mammal enthusiasts is the small but potentially serious risk from bat-borne viruses. Some Australian bat species (especially flying foxes) are natural carriers of lyssavirus – the group of viruses that includes rabies, with the same potentially serious consequences if you are bitten. To date very few people have died, but domestic animals have also been affected, and bats have recently attracted widespread community concern and media hysteria. Unfortunately this has resulted in persecution of bat camps near towns and cities, at worst involving culls, more often relocation of colonies. If you encounter an injured bat, do not handle it unless you have been inoculated and are wearing stout gloves; contact an experienced wildlife carer as quickly as possible. Some microbats also carry the disease, and should be handled only by experienced people taking the correct precautions.

Another major natural hazard that you need to be aware of is bushfire. Fires occur annually all over the country, varying from limited, relatively 'cool' burns caused by lightning strikes in savannah grasslands to raging infernos that destroy people, livestock, wildlife, towns and entire forests. Bushfires are at their most dangerous in southern Australia during summer, when high temperatures and strong winds can quickly turn a spark into a holocaust; nearly 200 people died in Vic's bushfires in 2009. Always obey bushfire warnings, which are broadcast regularly over media at critical times. Some national parks may be closed at these times and every year authorities declare total fire ban days when it is illegal to light a fire or even to use a barbecue in the open (penalties apply for infringements).

BOOKS ON AUSTRALIAN MAMMALS

The Field Guide to Australian Mammals by P. Menkhorst and F. Knight is a good general identification book and is the only one that covers every species, including cetaceans, microbats and rodents, in the conventional field guide format. *The*

Handbook of Australian Mammals by R. Strahan (edited by S. van Dyck) is a weighty tome that goes into considerable detail on every species and has some excellent photos, although it is too unwieldy to carry around in the field. *The Field Companion to the Mammals of Australia* by S. van Dyck, I. Gynther and A. Baker is designed to accompany it and includes identification keys. *Tracks, Scats and Other Traces* by B. Triggs is the classic guide to reading signs of mammals' presence.

As most of Australia's cetaceans are also found in other parts of the world, a number of guides are suitable for identification in Australian seas. Good ones include *Whales, Dolphins and Porpoises* by M. Carwardine, *Sea Mammals of the World* by R. Reeves *et al.* and *A Complete Guide to Antarctic Wildlife* by H. Shirihai (although it covers only those species that occur in the Southern Ocean and Antarctic waters). *Whale Watching in Australian and New Zealand Waters* by P. Gill and C. Burke is also a useful book.

Two of the best books on bats are *Australian Bats* by S. Churchill and *Bats: Working the Night Shift* by G. Richards and L. Hall. The former covers every species and has lots of excellent identification and ecological information; the latter is a more general treatment with excellent photos. Both are recommended for bat enthusiasts.

In general Australia is poorly served with regional natural history guides and mammals tend to get very general treatment. Exceptions include *Where to See Wildlife in Tasmania* by D. Watts, which has excellent photos as well as intimate information on finding many species; and the *Natural History Guide to Kakadu National Park* by I. Morris. CSIRO Publishing has a series of monographs on Australian mammals which make excellent background reading (visit www.publish.csiro.au).

Recordings of vocalisations won't be necessary for watching mammals in Australia. Few native mammals have loud vocalisations (exceptions being some of the gliders) and those that do won't necessarily be attracted to playback.

WEBSITES

Australian Mammal Society AMS is the peak mammal study organisation (visit www.australianmammals.org.au). Membership includes the peer-reviewed *Australian Mammalogy* journal and there are annual scientific congresses that rotate around the states, usually with post-conference tours.

Australasian Bat Society The ABS (visit www.ausbats.org.au) is comprised of bat researchers, amateur enthusiasts and carers of injured, sick and orphaned bats. It has a biennial meeting and campout, held in a different state each time, and an informative interactive website.

Jon Hall's excellent **Mammal Watching** website (www.mammalwatching.com) is a fund of information on Australian and other mammals.

The Kangaroo Trail (www.rootourism.com) is a helpful website with information about all of Australia's macropods and where to find them.

The **Atlas of Living Australia** (www.ala.org.au) is an interactive site with up-to-date information on distribution of Australian wildlife, including mammals.

Some state and territory government websites have good information on common and threatened species; others barely repay the effort of searching. In general, national parks information leaflets contain little of value to wildlife-watchers, except where animals are the main draw, such as at Mt Etna Caves and Naracoorte. As government conservation agencies' names change regularly there's no point in listing their websites – just Google national parks in each state or territory.

CETACEANS (WHALES AND DOLPHINS)

Several centres for whale tourism have set up museums and visitors' centres.

Bunbury Dolphin Discovery Centre www.dolphindiscovery.com.au

Byron Visitor Centre www.byron-bay.com/bvc

Eden Killer Whale Museum www.killerwhalemuseum.com.au

Monkey Mia Dolphin Visitor Centre www.sharkbay.org/monkeymia

South Australian Whale Centre (Victor Harbor) www.sawhalecentre.com

Warrnambool Visitor Information Centre www.warrnamboolinfo.com.au

Whale World Albany www.discoverybay.com.au/historic-whaling-station

Some also run whale festivals:

Eden Whale Festival www.edenwhalefestival.com

Hervey Bay Whale Festival www.visitfrasercoast.com/whalefestival

TOUR OPERATORS

There are any number of nature tour companies based in Australia and elsewhere, although most have a birding focus.

Alan's Wildlife Tours (www.alanswildlifetours.com.au) Nocturnal spotlighting tours on the Atherton Tableland, with a good success rate with Lumholtz's Tree Kangaroos.

Birding Tours Australia (www.birdingtours.com.au) Runs good-value trips to Christmas I., Torres Strait and even Heard Island.

Heritage Expeditions (http://heritage-expeditions.com) Cruise ship company operating from New Zealand that runs regular trips to subantarctic islands including Macquarie Island.

Inala Nature Tours (www.inalabruny.com.au) Based on Bruny I., Tas, offering tailored expert tours with a mammal focus.

Kimberley Bird Watching (www.kimberleybirdwatching.com.au) Runs the annual Ashmore Reef birding trips, on which many cetaceans have been seen.

Nature Trek (www.naturetrek.co.uk) UK-based company that runs an Australian mammal tour.

Wait-a-While Tours (www.waitawhile.com.au) Runs rainforest spotlighting tours in Wet Tropics rainforests, starting from Cairns.

WILDLIFE-FRIENDLY ACCOMMODATION

The following are wildlife watcher–friendly accommodations that have been tried and tested by many enthusiasts. Most cater mainly to birders, although guides and proprietors usually have a good working knowledge of the local mammal fauna and may also arrange feeding and/or spotlighting excursions; some provide mammal lists.

Anderson Lake (www.lakeandersoncaravanpark.com.au) Camping and self-contained cabins in Chiltern, Vic, close to Chiltern-Mt Pilot NP.

Binna Burra (www.binnaburralodge.com.au) In Lamington NP, Qld; a pleasant rainforest lodge close to subtropical rainforest wildlife.

Broken River Mountain Resort (www.brokenrivermr.com.au) Comfortable self-contained cabins near stellar Platypus-viewing site; mammal spotlighting walks.

Broome Bird Observatory (www.broomebirdobservatory.com) On the shores of Roebuck Bay, WA; cabins and self-contained chalets near Crab Creek mangroves.

Cassowary House (www.cassowary-house.com.au) Tropical rainforest lodge in the heart of the Wet Tropics; Musky Rat-kangaroos in the grounds.

Chambers' Wildlife Lodge (www.rainforest-australia.com) Near Lake Eacham on the Atherton Tableland; Sugar Gliders a nightly feature.

El Questro (www.elquestro.com.au) Luxury Lodge in the East Kimberley, WA; Northern Quoll and Scaly-tailed Possum a possibility.

Eyre Bird Observatory (www.birdlife.org.au/visit-us/observatories/eyre) Remote mallee location south of the Nullarbor Plain; Western Pygmy Possums common in the area.

Hidden Valley (www.hiddenvalleycabins.com.au) Eco-friendly lodge on western edge of Wet Tropics rainforest; Mount Claro Rock Wallaby in the grounds!

Jabiru Safari Lodge (www.jabirusafarilodge.com.au) Luxury accommodation at Mareeba Wetlands in the Wet Tropics; skilled guides and a good mammal list.

Kingfisher Bay (www.kingfisherbay.com.au) Modern resort on Fraser Island, Qld overlooking Hervey Bay; great whale-watching.

Kingfisher Park (www.birdwatchers.com.au) A perennial birdwatchers' favourite at the foot of Mt Lewis, Qld with an excellent mammal list.

Little Desert Nature Lodge (www.littledesertlodge.com.au) Comfortable birdwatchers' lodge in the Victorian mallee, with native mammals in the grounds.

Lotusbird Lodge (www.lotusbird.com.au) Birdwatchers' lodge in Lakefield NP on Cape York Peninsula; advice on where to see mammals freely given.

Montague Island Lighthouse (www.montagueisland.com.au) Great lighthouse accommodation off the southern NSW coast, surrounded by Australian and New Zealand Fur Seals.

Mountain Valley Wilderness Lodge (www.mountainvalley.com.au) Self-catering cabins at Loongana, Tas with Tasmanian Devils outside your window.

Mungumby Lodge (www.mungumby.com) Luxury rainforest lodge near Cooktown, an ideal base to look for Bennett's Tree-kangaroo.

O'Reilly's Rainforest Retreat (www.oreillys.com.au) Luxury rainforest lodge in Lamington NP with adjoining campground; a stellar mammal list and annual Wildlife Week.

Tangalooma (www.tangalooma.com) Bottlenose Dolphins are fed daily at this lodge on Moreton I., Qld overlooking Moreton Bay.

Appendix C: Glossary

Following is a list of specialised terms that will be encountered in this book. See also the separate Botanical Glossary (Appendix D) for some botanical terms that are useful for wildlife-watchers but perhaps unfamiliar to non-Australian readers.

abdomen – the lower part of a mammal's torso; the belly.

adit – mine entrance.

allopatric – an organism whose natural range is separate from that of another.

alpine – the area above the treeline with a continuous cover of snow for several months each year.

Anabat™ – electronic detector that decodes bats' ultrasonic calls.

arboreal – living in trees.

arthropod – an animal with a segmented body, jointed legs and a hard exoskeleton, such as insects, crustaceans, spiders, millipedes and centipedes.

Australasia – the region that includes Australia, New Zealand, the island of New Guinea and its satellites.

baleen – comb-like plates that hang from the upper jaw of baleen whales and are used to filter prey, such as plankton, krill and small fish, from the water.

beak – in some dolphins and toothed whales, the elongated forward part of the skull that corresponds to the mouth.

billabong – a meander of a river that has been cut off and survives as a wetland; ox-bow lake.

bipedal – moving on two legs (that is, the hind legs).

blackfish – whalers' term for small, largely black, toothed whales such as pilot whales, Melon-headed Whale, etc.

blow – in cetaceans, a spout of exhaled water vapour, usually characteristic according to species and a useful identification feature or means of locating cetaceans on the surface.

blowhole – the aperture through which a cetacean exhales (*see* blow).

boulder scree – piles or fields of boulders on a hill or mountainside, used for shelter by rock wallabies and other species.

bow-riding – swimming alongside the prow of a boat; behaviour shown by some species of dolphin and small whale.

breach – (cetaceans) to leap bodily from the sea as a display; this spectacular behaviour is often exhibited by Humpback Whales on migration.

brindled – brown and tan coloration.

browse – to eat leaves.

brush – fur at the tip of a mammal's tail, especially when it is enlarged or of a contrasting colour.

calcar – in bats, a small bone that supports the tail membrane; its absence or presence is a useful identification feature.

callosities – external growths caused by barnacle encrustations on cetaceans; particularly prominent on Southern Right Whales and a useful identification feature.

canine – large, prominent teeth ('eye teeth').

canopy – the upper layer of trees.

cape – in cetaceans, a marking across the back that contrasts with the general body coloration.

carnivore – an animal that eats meat.

carrion – dead flesh.

cephalopod – a large, free-swimming marine mollusc characterised by tentacles, and lacking a shell, for example octopus, squid and cuttlefish.

cetacean – the class of marine mammals that includes whales, dolphins and porpoises.

chevron – V-shaped marking.

circumglobal – occurring around the world.

circumpolar – occurring in all polar regions (both Antarctica and the Arctic).

class – the taxonomic division that contains one or more orders, for example Mammalia (mammals).

commensal – living with an organism of a different species in an apparently mutually beneficial arrangement.

congener – species in the same genus as another and therefore similar or closely related.

confiding – approachable, tame.

continental shelf – the area of shallow water fringing continental land masses, usually to a depth of 1000 m.

crepuscular – active at dawn and dusk.

crustacean – an invertebrate characterised by a hard exoskeleton, jointed legs and more or less dependent on water to survive, for example crabs, lobsters, shrimps and yabbies.

cryptic – remaining hidden.

dasyurid – a carnivorous marsupial, such as Tasmanian Devil, quoll, and antechinus; unique to Australasia.

diagnostic – a defining characteristic that helps with identification.

digit – a finger or toe.

diprotodont – a marsupial order, characterised by one functional pair of lower incisors, for example, possums, macropods, wombats and Koalas.

distal – furthest from a point of attachment, for example the tail-tip (*opposite to* proximal).

diurnal – active by day.

dorsal – upper surface.

drey – a globular nest of leaves, twigs etc used as a daytime rest by possums (and squirrels in other countries); constructed among leaves and branches, not in a hollow.

echolocation – high-frequency sound, usually inaudible to humans, emitted by bats and cetaceans to locate prey and obstacles in dark conditions.

ecotone – the transition zone between one habitat and another.

endemic – unique to a geographical region (e.g. an island) or political entity (e.g. state or country).

erectile – able to be raised, especially for defence or display, such as spines or a crest of hairs.

eutherian – a mammal that is gestated in its mother's body, rather than as an egg or in a pouch; most mammals belong to this classification.

extant – an organism that is still alive in its natural state.

extinct – a taxon that has died out and no longer exists as a living organism.

extralimital – occurring outside normal distribution.

facial stripe – contrasting facial marking, useful for identification in some macropods and gliders.

falcate – backswept, as in the dorsal fin of some cetaceans.

family – a taxonomic grouping containing one or more genera; one or more families make up a taxonomic order.

fast ice – the region of permanent polar ice adjoining the Antarctic land mass; a favoured haul-out of some seal species.

feral – free-living but descended from domestic or released stock.

fin – narrow, upright dorsal protruberence or paddle-like limb of cetaceans and the Dugong.

flanks – the sides of the body.

flippers – the flexible, paddle-like limbs of pinnipeds and cetaceans.

fluke – the tail fin of a cetacean.

flying fox – a large, fruit- and blossom-eating bat; unlike microbats, flying foxes have well-developed eyesight and do not use echolocation.

forearm – the part of the front limbs between the wrist and elbow.

form – a variation in colour, size etc. from normal appearance, for example the white form of Lemuroid Ringtail Possum.

fossorial – burrowing or living in burrows.

fruit bat – a small fruit-eating bat in the same family as flying foxes; sometimes used as an alternative name for flying fox, although some researchers eschew its usage because of pest connotations.

gape – width of an animal's open mouth.

genera – the plural of genus.

genus – the taxonomic grouping containing one or more species; generic names are always capitalised and italicised, for example *Macropus*.

gestation – the period for which an animal is nourished internally by its mother.

gibber – (pronounced with hard 'g') stony desert.

glean – to feed by picking prey off foliage or other surfaces.

graze – to eat grass.

Great Dividing Range – Australia's largest mountain range, forming a ridge and watershed of varying height that stretches from north Qld to western Vic, and reaching its highest point in southern NSW. Also known as 'the Great Divide' or just 'the Divide'.

gregarious – occurring in groups.

grizzled – having grey or greyish hair.

guard hair – thick bristle that grows outside normal fur; sometimes a diagnostic feature, for instance for the Fawn Hopping-mouse.

habitat – the area in which an animal lives, with characteristic associations of plants, such as rainforest or mallee.

herbivore – an animal that eats plant matter.

herd – a group of hoofed animals, cetaceans (whales and dolphins) or Dugongs.

hibernation – the strategy used by some mammals to survive harsh winters by shutting down all but essential body functions and remaining in deep sleep until better conditions arrive.

home range – the area used by an animal or group of animals where all food and shelter requirements are met.

incisor – front cutting tooth.

insectivore – an animal that eats insects and other invertebrates.

in situ – literally 'on site', used to describe a procedure, such as conservation breeding, that occurs where an organism occurs naturally.

invertebrate – animal without a backbone, such as an insect, spider, crustacean, worm or mollusc.

irruptive – occurring in large numbers in response to favourable conditions, with an ensuing population crash when conditions change, for example the Long-haired Rat.

joey – a young marsupial, especially a kangaroo or wallaby, but also possums, etc.

keel – in cetaceans, an obvious ridge on the top or bottom (or both) of the tailstock.

Kimberley – region in the far north of Western Australia, characterised by rugged sandstone massifs and a wet-dry monsoonal climate.

krill – shrimp-like crustaceans of the Southern Ocean, occurring in sufficient numbers to be a staple food for many whale species.

larva – young of many invertebrates and some vertebrates, such as fish (plural: larvae).

lobe – fleshy projection, usually in the facial region.

lob-tailing – in cetaceans, behaviour where the tail flukes are slapped against the surface.

logging – in cetaceans, behaviour where the animal lies still in the water, often just below the surface.

macropod – the general term for any kangaroo, wallaby or closely related animal, for example potoroo.

mane – the region of long hair around the neck and shoulders.

mantle – the area between the shoulder blades (that is, the upper back).

marine – in or of the sea.

marsupial – a mammal that gives birth to under-developed young that are then raised in an external pouch.

Mediterranean – a climate characterised by hot summers and mild winters; or habitat comprised of hardy shrubs on poor soils.

melon – in cetaceans, the bulbous region of the head, often a diagnostic identification feature.

microbat – any small bat of the order Microchiroptera, characterised by echolocation, among other features.

microhabitat – a habitat favoured by small animals, for example under logs.

midline – a line along the middle of the nape and/or back of contrasting colour, for example in the Black-striped Wallaby.

molar – large crushing or chewing tooth at the back of a mammal's mouth.

monotreme – one of five species of egg-laying mammal, for example the Platypus, unique to Australia and New Guinea.

monsoon – a weather pattern in northern Australia characterised by a distinct wet season, with flooding and tropical cyclones.

montane – living in mountains.

moult – the process of shedding hair (in mammals), usually alternating between a light summer coat and a thick winter coat.

muzzle – the jaws, mouth and nose of a mammal.

nomadic – moving from place to place in search of food, or other resources, often in response to climatic conditions.

noseleaf – the characteristic fleshy area around nostrils of some bats, thought to assist with echolocation.

oceanic – associated with oceans.

omnivore – an animal that eats a mixed diet, for example meat and plant matter.

opportunist – an animal that feeds or breeds when conditions allow.

order – the taxonomic division that includes one or more families, for example Pinnipeda (seals, sea lions, etc.).

pack ice – a region of temporary ice that diminishes in summer and expands in winter.

pelage – a mammal's coat.

pelagic – pertaining to the open ocean.

pendulous – suspended or hanging.

Pilbara – rocky, arid area of north-western Australia characterised by endemic plants and animals.

pinniped – a member of the taxonomic order that includes seals, sea lions, fur seals, etc.

pod – a small group of cetaceans.

porpoise – in cetaceans, the act of leaping from the water while moving forward quickly.

pouch – a flap of loose skin or deep external pouch on a marsupial, protecting the teats and sheltering young until they are old enough to fend for themselves.

prehensile – flexible; for example the tail of some possums, which can be wrapped around a branch strongly enough to hold the animal's weight suspended.

proboscis – the nose.

puggle – a young Echidna.

quadrupedal – having four legs capable of supporting an animal's weight.

ratamber – substance used by stick-nest rats, comprised of a mixture of faeces and urine that forms a resin-like material when it dries, to bind their nests together.

relict – surviving after the extinction of related species, for example the Musky Rat-kangaroo.

rhinarium – the bare fleshy area of a mammal's muzzle surrounding the nostrils; diagnostic feature for separating wombats and some kangaroos.

riparian – occurring alongside rivers, streams and other waterways.

riverine – occurring in or next to rivers.

roan – chestnut colour.

rodent – a mammal belonging to the order Rodentia, which includes rats and mice.

rorqual – a cetacean characterised by throat pleats, baleen plates and usually great size.

rostrum – in rorquals, the top of the head in front of the blowhole.

rump – the lowest part of an animal's back.

scat – mammal excrement, usually in the shape of a pellet, which in many cases can be an aid to identification.

scavenger – an animal that feeds on dead flesh or discarded remains, rather than hunting its own prey.

scree – a field of loose stones or boulders on a hillside or mountain.

sirenid – a mammal belonging to the order Sirenia, which includes the Dugong.

spatulate – broad, rounded at one end and compressed from top to bottom (e.g. a Dugong's tail).

species – the primary taxonomic division; each species has a binomial, usually derived from Latin or Greek and comprised of a unique combination of genus and species, for example *Macropus rufus* (Red Kangaroo).

spy-hopping – in cetaceans, floating upright with head protruding above the surface.

squat – a den of leaves and other vegetation, usually in the shelter of a fallen log, buttress root or large rock, used by bettongs and small macropods (for example, the Mala) as a daytime retreat.

sthenurine – a member of an ancient order of kangaroo-like animals, the only modern survivor of which is the Banded Hare-wallaby.

striated – striped lengthways, for example along the breast.

subantarctic – the region of the Southern Ocean that lies between approximately 46°S and 60°S.

subniveal – beneath snow.

subspecies – the taxonomic division below species, usually referring to a distinct or isolated form of a species; written as a trinomial, for example *Antechinus swainsonii insularis*.

succulent – a fleshy or water-holding plant, for example a cactus.

swale – flat or gently sloping space between sand dunes.

sympatric – occurring in the same area as another species (*opposite of* allopatric).

tailstock – the thick hind part of a cetacean's body just before the tail flukes.

taxon – a taxonomic category, e.g. species, genus.

taxonomy – the study and classification of evolutionary relationships between organisms.

teat – the point where milk is exuded from a female's body for young mammals to suckle; nipple.

temperate – an area characterised by mild climatic conditions year-round; generally regarded as occurring south of the tropics and subtropics.

terrestrial – occurring on the ground.

throat pleat – in baleen whales, longitudinal creases that allow for the expansion of the throat to engulf water and prey.

throat pouch – a pouch formed by loose skin on the throat.

Top End – the most northerly point of the Northern Territory, subject to monsoonal wet–dry conditions, with many unique species and high concentrations of others.

torpor – a condition similar to hibernation, whereby an animal goes into slowed metabolism in order to survive harsh conditions.

tropics – the region between 23°26'S (Tropic of Capricorn) and 23°26'N (Tropic of Cancer), generally with high year-round temperatures, often high rainfall and high biodiversity.

upwelling – an area of nutrient-rich oceanic water, caused by undersea features forcing detritus and small animals to the surface, attracting cetaceans and seabirds.

vegetarian – an animal that eats only plant matter.

vent – the anus or cloaca.

ventral – underside.

vertebrate – an animal with a backbone.

vestigial – a rudimentary relic of an ancient lineage, for example the appendix in humans.

volplane – a controlled downward glide, such as performed by gliders.

warren – a network of underground burrows, often with multiple entrances.

wean – the transition of a young mammal from survival on its mother's milk to adult foods.

Wet Tropics – World Heritage–listed area of north Qld between Townsville and Cooktown, featuring ancient rainforests, and many unique and relict species.

woodland – an open forest, typically of the semi-arid zone and tropics, often with a grassy understorey.

Appendix D: Botanical and habitat glossary

Most Australian plants and habitats are unique to the continent and in many cases do not resemble plants found elsewhere. Owing to high diversity, comparatively few have a common name. Consequently, many common names were derived from Aboriginal words, coined by early settlers or borrowed from similar (but unrelated) species with which early European botanists were familiar. Generic names are often used as common names (for example, banksias) and common names may also be used to describe habitats (for example, mulga). Knowing a few plant names will help with finding mammals and enrich your Australian wildlife-watching in general. For other terms see the Glossary (Appendix C).

Acacia – genus of woody shrubs and trees, in Australia numbering approximately 600 species, including the so-called 'wattles', which are characterised by globular yellow flowers; seed pods of some species are a food source for small mammals.

Banksia – genus of woody shrubs and low trees, typically growing in sandy soils and forming dense 'banksia heath', especially in coastal dune swales; their distinctive flowering spikes attract small possums.

belar – a native conifer (*Callitris*); also spelt belah.

bluebush – an arid-zone shrub (for example, *Chenopodium*) with leathery leaves and blue-green coloration.

Boab – a large, spreading tree *Adansonia gregorii* of the tropical north-west, related to African baobabs and characterised by a thickened, bottle-like trunk.

bottlebrush – nectar-rich flowering shrubs of the genus *Melaleuca* (formerly *Callistemon*); the flowers look like colourful bottlebrushes and are favoured by small possums, fruit bats and birds.

box – the common name for several species of eucalypt with characteristically tough bark and dense wood, for example box ironbark and white box.

brigalow – semi-arid woodland, dominated by Brigalow *Acacia harpophylla*, that formerly stretched from central Qld to northern NSW but is now largely cleared and fragmented.

Buffel Grass – an introduced grass *Cenchrus ciliaris* that forms a dense ground cover and out-competes native vegetation.

buloke – a species of *Allocasuarina luehmannii* (closely related to *Casuarina*) that grows in the semi-arid zone; also spelt bull-oak.

Callitris – a genus of native pine trees, typically occurring in arid and semi-arid regions.

cane grass – a slender grass growing on top of dunes in the arid zone.

Casuarina – a genus of evergreen trees (also used as a common name) with drooping, pine-like 'needles' that are actually branchlets with tiny leaves; often found in groves, especially in sandy soil.

cauliferous – an outgrowth of flowers or fruits growing from the trunk of a tree.

chenopod – a woody shrub found in the arid and semi-arid zone, often forming large swathes.

chenopod steppe – an association of arid-zone shrubs, such as bluebush and saltbush, often growing on stony soil and broken ground.

cumbungi – reeds of the genus *Phragmites*; common at the edges of ponds, dams, lakes and slow rivers.

epiphyte – a plant growing on another for support or to reach moisture sources, for example many orchids.

Eremophila – a genus of inland shrubs with distinctive tubular flowers, usually red with a yellow base.

eucalypt – the generic name for trees of the genera *Eucalyptus*, *Corymbia*, *Angophora*, etc., also known as gum trees, which dominate many Australian landscapes and ecosystems; their flowers are a rich source of nectar and mature trees provide hollows sheltering possums, gliders and bats.

fig – plants of the genus *Ficus*, ranging from vines and pioneer shrubs to massive trees; many species are attractive to mammals and birds when in fruit; for example the Rock Fig *F. platypoda* attracts Rock Ringtails in the Kimberley.

forb – a flowering plant that is not a grass, rush or sedge.

gallery forest – a tall forest lining rivers, often creating dense, moist habitat that can extend a long way into surrounding dry habitat.

Gastrolobium – a genus of flowering shrub with toxic properties; its ingestion by native animals makes their flesh toxic to feral predators.

grass tree – an endemic plant of the genus *Xanthorrhoea* with a bare, woody stem, 'skirt' of grasslike leaves and a tall flowering spike; also known as 'blackboys', they are rich in nectar and attract small possums.

Grevillea – a genus of shrub or tree with nectar-rich, often red, flowers attractive to small possums and gliders.

Hakea – a genus of shrub or tree with nectar-rich flowers attractive to small possums and gliders; some species are known as corkwood.

heath – habitat comprised of dense, low shrubs, usually in windswept coastal or subcoastal areas with poor soils; often rich in plant species and providing shelter for cryptic mammals and birds.

hummock grass – a spiky grass, usually *Triodia* (also known as spinifex) that grows in dense clumps accessible only to small animals, such as rodents, reptiles and insects.

ironbark – a group of eucalypts with tough, fire-resistant bark, formerly widespread west of the Great Dividing Range and a popular source of building materials during the 19th century; now decimated in places; flowering ironbarks provide a valuable winter food resource for gliders.

Jarrah – a tall, long-lived eucalypt (*Eucalyptus marginata*) unique to south-western Australia.

Karri – a very tall eucalypt (*Eucalyptus diversicolor*), unique to south-western Australia, that grows in dense stands in wetter areas and is equivalent to Mountain Ash in south-eastern forests.

lantana – an introduced tropical herb that forms dense thickets and is used by many animals for cover.

lignum – a thick, flexible cane-like plant that grows near inland waterways.

mallee – any of several species of low, multi-stemmed eucalypt trees growing from an underground tuber; also used to describe the distinct habitat zone in semi-arid southern Australia dominated by these species (some other eucalypts also grow in the mallee form, for example Snow Gums, although they rarely dominate).

mangrove – a tree specialised for growing at the edge of the sea, characteristically in estuaries and other sheltered sites, and with specialised air-breathing roots for use at low tide. Flowers of the Apple Mangrove *Sonneratia alba* burst open at dusk and have a sour-milk smell attractive to Least Blossom Bats.

Marri – a species of eucalypt *Corymbia calophylla* unique to south-western Australia.

Melaleuca – genus of shrubs and trees with characteristically short, spiny leaves and thin, flaking whitish bark, hence the alternative name paperbark.

Mitchell Grass – thin, clumped grass (under 1 m high) of the genus *Astrebla* that grows in arid northern Australia.

Mountain Ash – giant eucalypt species *Eucalyptus regnans* that forms wet montane forests in south-eastern Australia; habitat for Leadbeater's Possum, gliders, etc.

mulga – habitat dominated by Mulga *Acacia aneura*, a tree that dominates huge areas of the Outback.

Pandanus – a genus of palm-like tropical plants with characteristic bare trunks and a crown of spiky leaves. Also called screw pines; accumulations of the dead leaves below the crown are used for shelter by bats and native rats.

paperbark – *see Melaleuca*.

quandong – a native tree of the sandalwood family that grows in the semi-arid and arid zones, and bears edible fruit attractive to mammals and birds.

rainforest – habitat characterised by tall forest with interlocking canopy in high rainfall areas; in Australia, restricted to the east coast and Tas.

River Red Gum – a large, spreading eucalypt *Eucalyptus camaldulensis* that grows on floodplains and riparian habitat, sometimes for hundreds of kilometres along inland waterways.

saltbush – salt-tolerant shrubs, for example *Atriplex*, that may cover vast arid and semi-arid plains.

Sandstone Cocky Apple – a low tree, *Planchonia careya*, that attracts the Wyulda (Scaly-tailed Possum).

satinash – a tropical tree, for example Bumpy Satinash, with cauliflorous growths attractive to fruit bats and small possums, such as Long-tailed Pygmy Possum.

savannah – grassland with widely spaced tree cover; in Australia this habitat occurs mainly in the tropics; also spelt 'savanna'.

sclerophyll – literally 'hard-leaved', a general term for many species of Australian plant characterised by tough leaves, for example eucalypts, banksias, etc.; sclerophyllous forests (usually designated 'wet' or 'dry' sclerophyll) dominate much of the landscape and many rely on periodic fires to trigger seed germination (true rainforests are not dominated by sclerophyllous species and do not rely on fire for regeneration).

she-oak – see 'sheoke'.

sheoke – common name (also spelt 'she-oak') for several species of *Casuarina* or *Allocasuarina*, for example Rock She-oak *A. huegeliana*, favoured by Red-tailed Phascogales.

spinifex – prickly arid-zone grasses of the genus *Triodia* that grow in dense clumps accessible only to small animals, such as rodents, reptiles and insects (to confuse matters, the genus *Spinifex* is comprised of soft grasses that grow on coastal sand dunes and do not form hummocks).

wandoo – a species of eucalypt *Eucalyptus wandoo* unique to south-western Australia.

wallum – coastal heath habitat of south-east Qld; threatened by urban developments.

wattle – see *Acacia*.

woodland – low (under 30 m), open forest, typically in tropical Australia but also in parts of the south-west (for example, Dryandra SF).

Common name index

Scientific name index

Site index

www.ingramcontent.com/pod-product-compliance
Lightning Source LLC
Chambersburg PA
CBHW042133280526
45792CB00019B/2352